THE ROSES MATCHES 1919 – 1939

THE ROSES MATCHES
1919 – 1939

Neville Cardus

*With a Foreword
by John Arlott*

SOUVENIR PRESS

483001672

Printed in Great Britain by
Ebenezer Baylis and Son Ltd
The Trinity Press, Worcester, and London

ACKNOWLEDGMENT

The publishers are grateful to the editor of *The Guardian* newspaper for his co-operation in the assembly of articles in THE ROSES MATCHES 1919 – 1939 and to Mr John Arlott for kindly agreeing to contribute a foreword to the book.

PHOTOGRAPH ACKNOWLEDGMENTS

For permission to use the photographs in this book, the publishers are most grateful to the following:
MCC
Central Press Photos Limited
PA-Reuter Photos Ltd.
Sport & General Press Agency Limited

FOREWORD

ANYONE with a liking for cricket writing must feel honoured to share, however unimportantly—the covers of a book with Sir Neville Cardus. Thus I am grateful to Margaret Hughes, who has handled the posthumous publication of his work so sympathetically, for her invitation to contribute a foreword. It is not a matter of performing a service to the memory of a colleague who was also the revered writer and stimulus of my youth, and who became a friend, but a privilege.

The salient fact is that Neville Cardus was not merely a cricket writer. One recalls C. B. Fry's comment while talking, over a good dinner, of W. G. Grace: 'W. G.,' he said, 'was not just the greatest batsman, he created modern batting; so no one can ever be greater than he was without remaking the entire game.' So it was with Sir Neville; he created modern cricket writing. Until his day it was a matter of dutiful reporting: so many minutes for the hundred; so many for two hundred; the detailed analysis—which bowlers and which batsmen had performed well; how each wicket fell; solid but without a spark.

'Cricketer' of *The Manchester Guardian* changed all that. In 1919 he was a junior reporter and aspiring understudy to the paper's drama and music critics when he had a breakdown. While he was convalescing, the News Editor, W. P. Crozier, despatched him to Old Trafford to report the start of post-war cricket. True, his first effort was literate enough, but conventional. He continued and, with amazing rapidity by the normal standards of literary development, he assumed a romantic style which captured the imagination not only of readers, players, spectators and his professional rivals, but, going beyond that, of people not normally interested in cricket.

What he did was, in effect, to create—in that elegant, flowing hand of his—a mythology of the game, so that his characters, both as men and cricketers, assumed more than life size. Indeed he once wrote in as characteristic a passage as could be wished, 'As I look back on my twenty years of days in the sun (sometimes it rained, I admit) I can scarcely believe that all the juicy characters I came to know on cricket fields have actually existed. I get them confused with the creations of the nation's comic writers. Emmott Robinson of Yorkshire; Rhodes and Hirst; Maurice Leyland and Parkin—they all come back to my mind endowed with the gusto of humorous genius.'

They were of the north country like himself; his knowledge of them was matched by a deep sympathy; and sometimes—when he was, at heart, a boy again watching them wide-eyed from the cheap seats—he used to paint them as they—or he—would have wished them to be: ideal in an ideal situation.

However that may be, he implanted them in the minds of many readers who never met them, more distinctly and impressively than others whom they knew well.

The five players he mentioned above all played, of course for Lancashire or Yorkshire; and they were his kind. Indeed it may well be that this is the richest collection ever made of Neville Cardus' work. So much of his most memorable writing came from Roses matches: especially at Old Trafford where he watched the cricket of his most impressionable days.

He drew readers to his newspaper, *The Manchester Guardian* (now *The Guardian*), as few journalists have ever done. The circulation department used to send reams of extra copies to grounds where Lancashire were playing away matches to sell them on the name 'Cricketer', which was Cardus' by-line for many years.

There has been no cricket writer of any stature since the middle twenties who did not owe much to Sir Neville Cardus. He created a style of reporting the game; and then virtually re-created it in the years of his maturity.

FOREWORD

Here, he is at his splendid best, when he conjures up Archie MacLaren, Harry Makepeace, Wilfred Rhodes, 'Cec' Parkin, the 'young' Herbert Sutcliffe, Ted Macdonald, Bill Bowes, the fiery George Macaulay, that ripe character, Bill Worsley—but then, so are they all, all his Yorkshire and Lancashire cricketers, ripe characters—plucked at their best. In a way, too, this is both a period piece and a social study.

Now for the first time exhumed from the files of *The Manchester Guardian,* this will be completely fresh to virtually all its readers; and that is the word—fresh—for it is as live, as true, as relished, and as relishable now as when it was set down by the master hand.

John Arlott
March, 1982.

Contents

CONTENTS

LANCASHIRE AND YORKSHIRE

INTRODUCTION

ON Saturday next I shall go to Leeds to watch the forty-second match since the war between Lancashire and Yorkshire; the occasion will complete my twenty-first year as a commentator in this paper on the greatest of all tussles between county rivals. In most matches the critic endeavours to be impartial; he sits aloft in the press-box, like an impersonal god, seeing all things moving, towards their predestined end. The Lancashire and Yorkshire match is an exception; I step down from the pedestal of impartiality. I become for a few days as prone as anybody else in the crowd to the passions of the partisan. If two Yorkshire batsmen make a long stand (and if one of them happens to be Arthur Mitchell by name and by nature) I do my best to exert an influence of will over the field of play—some current of hate and malice calculated to cause mishap, if not death and destruction, to take place at the wicket for the benefit of my native county. I have found that a partnership can often be broken by leaving the press-box and retiring for a moment (usefully) behind the scene. I have this way taken a hundred wickets for Lancashire in twenty-one successive seasons.

The mind holds events in these games vividly; they remain coloured by imagination in a frieze of memory, set against a grim and humorous background of North of England life. No other match expresses so much character. The crowd is part of the whole; it exults and it suffers—especially does it suffer. A year or two ago Lancashire defeated Yorkshire somehow at Sheffield. When the winning hit was about to be made, when the fact became clear that no power on earth could save Yorkshire, a man wearing a cloth cap was sitting miserably amongst the litter on the great and forbidding

15

mound which stands on one side of the ground. And his wife said to him: 'Well, tha would come, wouldn't thi?' Many years ago another Lancashire victory happened at Leeds in surprising circumstances. On August Bank Holiday Lancashire, according to long custom, collapsed. I wrote severely about the weak play exhibited by our batsmen. Next morning Yorkshire needed only a few runs to win, and everybody thought they would get them without the loss of a wicket. We turned up at Headingley merely as a matter of form. I believe that Emmott Robinson resented having to go through the ritual of changing into flannels. 'Waste o' time and money,' he probably said. Yorkshire collapsed incredibly, and Lancashire won by some twenty runs. That evening I received an anonymous postcard from a patriot who had read my diatribe on Lancashire's batting; it was brief and to the point, but not entirely fit for publication: 'You ——— fool,' it said; simply that and nothing more.

I shall remember all my life the finish of this match. After Yorkshire's last wicket fell I rushed from the Headingley ground and got on a tram, eager to carry the good news, hot from the burning, to Manchester. The tram guard came jauntily to me for my fare; he was whistling. 'What ha' they won by?' he asked. I said, 'They haven't won; they've lost.' He replied, 'Ah mean t' cricket match—did they lose any wickets?' When I assured him I had referred to t' cricket match, and that Yorkshire really had been defeated he suspended business on the spot; he did not give me a ticket, but turned his back on me and walked to the front of the tram, where he opened the door and told the driver. Then the tram proceeded a mile or so into Leeds by its own volition. In Leeds the dreadful news had travelled before me; you could see the effect on most faces. I went to the railway station, and as my train would not come for half an hour I entered the refreshment room. Shortly a few of the crowd dribbled in, sadly returning home. A Yorkshireman sat down at my table. He looked at me and said, 'Hey, this is a reight do. Fancy Yorkshire put out for fifty. Ah thowt better of them.' There was no anger in his voice, only sorrow. Then he looked at me again, harder. 'Tha doesn't seem to be takin' it to 'eart very much,' he said, I told him that, as I was from Lancashire, I naturally could not see the disaster from his point of view. He inspected me now from a different angle. 'Oh,' he said, 'so tha comes from Lancashire?' Once more I admitted that I did. 'And tha come specially to see t' finish this mornin'?' I answered in the affirmative. 'Ah suppose tha's feelin' pleased with thisen?' I did not deny it. 'And tha's goin' back to Manchester by this two-twenty train?' Yes, I said, I was. 'Goin' back reight now?' Yes, I reiterated. 'Well,' he said, slowly and in measured terms, 'Ah 'opes tha drops down de-ad before thi gets theer.'

There is no crowd in the world to equal the Lancashire and Yorkshire cricket crowd. Sutcliffe once stonewalled at Old Trafford for half an hour, almost without scoring. The afternoon was warm, and a huge multitude sat in silence. The game seemed to become suspended out of time and space. Nothing disturbed the illusion of eternity. Suddenly a voice addressed Sutcliffe, not critically, but with simple, honest inquiry: 'Erbert,' the voice solicited, ' 'Erbert, coom on; what dost tha think thi are, a —— war memorial?'

In August, 1919, the first season after the war, two-day county matches were played, and at Sheffield on the Tuesday after Bank Holiday Hallows batted from noon till evening and saved the match for Lancashire. The crowd worked hard to get him out. Twenty thousand of them emitted a staccato noise as soon as each ball bowled at Hallows left the bowler's hand. 'Hoo!' they said (I cannot find an onomatopœic sign eloquent enough). At six o'clock the crowd gave up the bad job and began to leave the trying scene. Rhodes vainly sought to tempt Hallows, but Hallows continued to push the ball away with his own stately ease and insolence. A solitary man remained on the mound. He was black in the face. All the afternoon he had done his utmost with his 'Hoo!' Rhodes bowled the last over of the day. The lonely man on the mound let out six desperate 'Hoos!' The final one exploded in the darkening air. Hallows patted the last ball of the last over, and the players began to leave the field. The man on the mound surveyed Hallows, gathered together all his remaining energy and passion, and howled forth, 'Oh, —— you!' and went home.

Twenty-one years of rare sport! The Lancashire and

Yorkshire match is not understood in the South of England. They think there that slow scoring in Lancashire and Yorkshire matches always means dull play. A few seasons ago when Lancashire and Yorkshire cricket was as rich in character as it has ever been, Makepeace and Hallows scored slowly not because they could not have scored faster had they tried. They scored slowly on principle. What a sight for the comic gods!—Rhodes pitching the ball cannily wide of the off stump, not risking a boundary against Makepeace, who would not have taken a boundary in the circumstances if you had offered one to him on a plate. Makepeace was usually a great cricketer in these games; down on his bat he went, clever and shrewd as Rhodes himself, quick to glance 'round the corner' or cut late. And as good with his pads as Emmott Robinson. I count Makepeace amongst the immortals of Lancashire and Yorkshire cricket.

The frieze stretches away to the distance as I write these lines: Sutcliffe hooking Macdonald, Ernest Tyldesley crashing boundaries one Saturday evening at Sheffield, Richard Tyldesley leaning sideways and peering mathematically down the pitch, preparing in advance for an appeal for lbw. He would shake his head as though saying, 'Noa—that weren't out, noa.' He implied that he would not have accepted a decision in his favour even if the umpire had proffered one. Then, after several other calculating leans to the right side, with accompanying gestures of refusals by the hand, he would suddenly declaim his 'How was it?' Nothing could have been fairer or more tolerant.

These last twenty-one years have seen the Lancashire and Yorkshire match enriched by Sutcliffe, Holmes, Kilner, Robinson, Macaulay, Leyland, Hutton, Waddington (most lovely of bowling actions), Dolphin, Wood, Mitchell, Bowes, Verity, Hallows, Parkin, Cook, Macdonald, Richard Tyldesley, Iddon, Hopwood—to name only a few names. From the legendary pre war years Rhodes and Makepeace and Ernest Tyldesley came striding into a new epoch. We are at another period of transition; old faces are giving way to new. Soon it will be Oldfield and Hutton, Place and Smurthwaite (!) And at Rydal School another Sutcliffe is in the making; they say he will beat all his father's records. But

18

he will not, nor will anybody else, bring to Lancashire and Yorkshire cricket more than the incomparable Herbert's sang-froid and haloed sense of mastery by natural right.

YORKSHIRE V LANCASHIRE 1919

June 9/10   Old Trafford

THE old cricket feud between Lancashire and Yorkshire broke out again at Old Trafford yesterday, in a contest that went on through the long day with unfailing keenness. There was a vast holiday crowd—11,818 alone paid at the turnstiles—which gave us all the old intentness and knowledge of the game. If Lancashire can be said to have finished the day in a comfortable position—but what team is really comfortable with Yorkshire until it has actually won?—it was only after play which must have left the eleven in a pretty state of collapse at the close. The determination of Lancashire, indeed, was admirable and went a long way to make one willing to forget certain ignominies of the latter years against the 'Tykes'.

Lancashire had luck—that much may be said without detracting from their day's work. They batted first on a good wicket, and, in putting up a respectable 319, one or two batsmen had reason to be devoutly thankful. Then in the Yorkshire innings Denton was badly injured just as he was beginning to see the ball, and had to retire. It was a bumping fast one from J. Tyldesley that injured Denton. But while commiserating with Yorkshire in this misfortune, it ought to be said in fairness to the Lancashire bowlers that Denton needed to take an ample share of his traditional leaven of luck against Lancashire to stay as long as he did. He was not actually missed in the field, but a series of bad pulls off Dean only just dropped out of harm's way.

When the Denton and Kilner partnership was broken by the injured player's retirement, the Lancashire bowling was beginning to get itself into all sorts of knots. At one time the score was 149 for two, Rhodes and Holmes having given the side a capital send off with 79 for the first wicket. After Denton left, the Lancashire bowlers recovered somewhat. Parkin bowled Hirst with his slow ball, the great old veteran

21

attempting a prodigious drive. This inspired Parkin to gigantic labours. He was brought back to the Old Trafford end, and after getting Burton caught—a catch at the third attempt—he bowled Claughton in the last over of the day. This last spell showed Parkin at his best. He was most resourceful, varying his length and pace skilfully, seeking out the weak points in the batsman's defence audaciously—it was a stroke of genius to send that slow one to Hirst just when he did—and through all bowling with immense concentration of purpose. And as Marriott clean bowled Kilner for 45 at a time when his bat seemed hopelessly wide and straight from the ring, the closing phase of the day was a great one for Lancashire. Yorkshire's fine beginning dwindled into a doubtful 193 for six. The tail will doubtless save the follow on—it would be just like Yorkshire for it to add a 100 or so!—but today Lancashire stand a fair chance of forcing a win, and the cricket will be keen indeed.

The cricket before lunch was dour in the extreme. The Yorkshiremen were on their toes, and runs had to be sought patiently. And the crowd played its part in the old eruptive way, going off into slight hysterics at a mishit or a near shave of the wicket. The beginning of the Lancashire innings, too, was sufficiently characteristic of the occasion, for the first man was out at 3—Hollins caught and bowled by Blackburne. The amateur gave the impression of getting himself out, as indeed he has done so in too many innings this season. Yesterday he tried to drive a fast ball in front of the wicket, and one cannot reasonably expect to do anything of the sort during the fast bowler's first few overs in a big match. The Tyldesley and Makepeace partnership did not begin quite majestically either. Tyldesley would most certainly have been caught at short square leg when only 2 had Hirst been the active man of a few years ago. One run later he made a bad shot through the slips off Blackburne, was beaten by the same bowler at 4, while his first boundary hit was a lucky snick. Blackburne was again the bowler.

Blackburne with a bit of luck might easily have started a 'rot' just at this critical stage. Makepeace got a dangerous boundary from him through the slips with his score at 17. A fast bowler is very much at the mercy of his slip fielders, and

Yorkshire has no Tunnicliffe this year.

Stage by stage Tyldesley and Makepeace took the edge off the Yorkshire attack and added 80 for the second wicket. Tyldesley never really settled down. Yet, while he was always unsteady, and Makepeace safety itself, it was always Tyldesley who obviously got the more relish out of the cricket. Only a player who has felt the sense of complete mastery over all sorts of bowling would have ventured so far as he did with Blackburne's rising ball. And if he demanded rather too much from an eye that can hardly be as quick today as it was, he had the satisfaction of bringing off one or two of the old flicks past point, and a daring pull. Sharp stayed with Makepeace till the score was 161, thus helping to add 78. He, too, had immense luck, and never took anything like the measure of the bowling. With Sharp out there was a slight collapse, just after lunch and five were out for 189. The tail wagged though. Young Hallows played exquisite cricket on the off-side—he is his famous brother all over again with the drive past cover, so strong is it in combined arm and shoulder action with the body beautifully poised. Then J. Tyldesley and Parkin gave us the happiest cricket of the day. Parkin attacked Rhodes with a zest that set the crowd simmering, and two terrific drives in one over sent it boiling over uproariously. J. Tyldesley scored 59 not out, and played lusty cricket, not polished, maybe, but tremendously plucky. It was a great thing to see Lancashire without a tail in a Yorkshire match.

Makepeace's innings must be discussed all by itself. He alone mastered the bowling when it had its dangerous moments. Fifth out at 189, he scored 105 of them and had to work hard for the bulk. It was never a brilliant innings, but it could hardly have been improved for correctness and all round workmanship.

The great feature of Makepeace's innings was his watchfulness. Rarely, indeed, are modern batsmen so vigilant. Even in his forward strokes he seemed to watch the ball right onto the bat—no matter what C. B. Fry may say of the certain element of speculative blindness in every forward stroke. One has not witnessed such consistent wariness since Clement Hill was in the country. Makepeace's judgement, too, was admirable. He gave a chance in the slips at 70, but only then did he select the wrong ball. He watched Blackburne's fast deliveries on the off side go by with incredible patience, but never missed the ball that wanted hitting. The way he got on to his toes to a bumping ball and played it down with a straight bat was an object lesson for every schoolboy on the ground—and for that matter one, or two of his colleagues in the Lancashire team. How certain he was in picking out the loose ball may be seen from the fact that, though his innings included thirteen boundaries, there were only two threes. When he did decide to hit it was the right ball. Among his strokes one noticed the late cut now and then, beautifully done. This stroke is not often seen nowadays but yesterday Makepeace brought it off at least twice in a way worthy of J. T. Brown himself.

Yorkshire bowled and fielded in patches of excellence and mediocrity. The fielding was not reliable. One is not referring to dropped catches—they will happen in the best fielding elevens. But there was not much of the old Yorkshire dash or the ability to anticipate strokes and so get into position for them before they are made. The picking up, too, was slovenly at times. Yorkshire's bowling, this year, will probably be pretty deadly on a soft wicket. Smith, who worked well and very hard yesterday without luck, has all the tricks of a really first-class 'sticky' wicket man. Blackburne is a great tryer, but he is not above fast medium and does not seem to vary his pace when he varies his direction. One without the other is not much use. Rhodes bowled with judgment and well deserved his capital figures. Hirst was tried for only a brief spell, and apparently he considers his old swerving days over. Yesterday he sent down some quite good medium-paced ones, though he no longer bowls his fast swerves.

Hirst is looking very fit and even younger, for he has discarded his moustache. Is it that he is really only just about 'to begin' and has given us notice by assuming this youthful air, a sort of taking off his coat, like Mr. Snodgrass, as a charitable warning of the fact?

SECOND DAY

There was a day of great cricket yesterday at Old Trafford.

Play see-sawed thrillingly hour by hour, and there was an exciting finish five minutes from time, with a Lancashire victory over Yorkshire. At seven o'clock most people had given the match up for a draw.

Yorkshire had gone in at four o'clock to play the clock out, and after losing five wickets for 65 and finding Parkin almost unplayable, they took advantage of a drizzle of rain which put the bowlers at a disadvantage. Sutcliffe and Claughton stayed together an hour and five minutes, adding 69. Then Parkin, whose finger-spin it has been impossible to exploit with a wet ball, returned to find the wicket drying. Immediately he set to work. At 6.40 with fifty minutes to go, Sutcliffe was caught off his bowling. After that the batsmen could hardly look at him. He captured the seventh wicket at 7.5 and the eighth at 7.12 and the ninth at 7.16.

With less than a quarter of an hour of play, Denton was in last, and Smith was his partner. Denton's thumb was badly crushed from Monday's accident, and the crowd gave him a big-hearted cheer for his pluck in batting at all. At the same time there were agitated shouts to Parkin to 'settle' him. Denton shaped only too well from Lancashire's point of view, while Smith kept his end up with any amount of the old Yorkshire grit. The minutes ticked away—things were getting oppressive. Parkin, though, was not to be denied after that afternoon of heroic work of his, and five minutes from the close of play he clean bowled Denton. Thus in fifty minutes Parkin dismissed no fewer than five Yorkshiremen. And altogether they could scrape but 19 runs. The fall of Claughton, who batted for over an hour and a half, added immense excitement to a moment quite crowded enough with palpitations. The young stonewaller just played defensively at a good ball and cocked it up. Boddington flung himself at it desperately, got one hand to the ball, and held it though he rolled over. A great catch and a great moment! The crowd was ecstatic.

Yorkshire's innings began in a way that never for a moment suggested a finish to the match. Declaring their second innings closed at 206 for nine, Lancashire left their rivals with 294 to get for victory. Rhodes and Holmes began sedately but seemed to see the ball well. The wicket was wearing a little, and the Yorkshiremen themselves did not think too highly of it. Holmes was first out at 22 trying—and a first class cricketer ought to know better—to force a bumping ball to the on. Kilner and Rhodes defended stubbornly for twenty-five minutes and then both left in quick succession.

It was now that Parkin began to give some hint of the mood that had taken hold of him. At the opening of the innings the Yorkshiremen found a few loose balls in his attack, and two fours were hit off his first two overs. Finding his length, Parkin proceeded to send down, before the rain came and left him temporarily helpless, 17 overs, of which no fewer than 10 were maidens. He even had Hirst tied up, though one must say at once that Hirst was not quite sound in the knee. No batsman played him with confidence until the rain came, and it would be safe to say that had the ground kept dry neither Caughton nor Sutcliffe would have survived as long as they did. The gift of the wet ball must be accounted as compensation to Yorkshire for Denton's injury. That, with Sharp's unfitness thrown in, makes the misfortunes of both sides fairly even. The sides were on the whole well matched, and Parkin turned the scale. He was the one great bowler in the game, and Lancashire would have got into a pickle without him. No other bowler troubled the Yorkshiremen much, though J. Tyldesley had bad luck yesterday afternoon, while Marriott was always steady. Parkin took 14 wickets in the two innings, and not once was he taken in hand firmly by any batsman.

The secret of Parkin's success is not due to any particular delivery or even to a specific characteristic of spin. All of his deliveries, taken singly, might be seen sent down in a first-class match any afternoon with only normal effectiveness. It is the manner in which Parkin manages his deliveries that tells, the consummate alternating of one with the other according to the special needs of the moment, as discovered by a watchful study of a batsman's play. To a man, for instance, with a tendency to drive on the off he will begin by tossing them well up at a good speed just short of hitting distance and gradually slacken pace, yet driving the ball a wider curve, so that at last the batsman is deceived into 'having a go'. Again with a player who indulges the 'pull',

Parkin will actually feed it until his man is on his toes, and then send up a delivery that hangs as though he had pulled it back with a string. Not since Albert Trott played, in fact, has one seen the 'hanging' slow ball managed so skilfully.

On present form Parkin is probably the finest bowler in the game. A little more experience of big occasions and he must surely pass into the very front rank. He is at present just a little inclined to get his nerves on edge—when he beats a man without hitting the wicket his gesture is one of sheer agony—and perhaps he is not economical enough with his stamina. Above all else he is a player of tremendous determination; so much so that when he is matched with a batsman of equal skill it is concentration of purpose that wins through. If Parkin should ever come upon Hobbs on a good wicket there will be a great struggle.

The cricket in the earlier part of yesterday was a fine prelude to the superb end. Yorkshire's tail in the first innings did not wag, and Lancashire had a lead of 87. Lancashire's second innings was started, no doubt, in a forcing mood with the idea of piling up a winning score in good time to get Yorkshire out. Hollins, for the second time in the match, tried an impetuous shot at a fast, bumping ball from Blackburne and was caught. J. T. Tyldesley was missed after he had scored a single, made a bad stroke off a rising ball, and from the next, a delivery just as difficult to get well over, gave a catch which Smith held magnificently. Hallows and E. Tyldesley failing, the responsibility was on Makepeace's shoulders for the second time in the match. He did not fail. The extraordinary soundness of his cricket made the general weakness of his colleagues inexplicable. Only occasionally was he in trouble during the two hours and a quarter he was at the wicket. Again it was vigilance that gave his batting its main characteristics; that and wonderfully correct foot-work and strong wrist play. On his showing in this match, Makepeace must go in with the safest and best-schooled professional batsmen of the day. J. Tyldesley played another enormously plucky game and helped Makepeace to add 102 for the fifth wicket in a period of urgent need for his side. His driving on both sides of the wicket was capital, shoulder work rather than arms, with the feet placed perfectly. The rest of the Lancashire batting is better not discussed, though Parkin again hit for a while.

Yorkshire lost because they had no match-winning bowler like Parkin. No doubt their batting is better than Lancashire's; it would be difficult to match from our present eleven Holmes, Sutcliffe, Rhodes, Hirst and Kilner to say nothing of Denton. The Yorkshire bowling is good, but mainly of the kind that needs assistance from the ground. The fielding of both sides is uneven, with uncertain slip-catching. No doubt some of the missed catches yesterday were the result of over-keenness rather than any inherent lack of agility or grip. A brilliant feature of the game was Dolphin's wicket-keeping.

The crowd deserved a good word. Keen though it was, in bulk, for a Lancashire victory, it never failed to give due homage to the merit of the Yorkshiremen. It was, throughout the match, a crowd typical of these old tussles, intent, jealous of the county's good name, but always sportsmanlike and quick to appreciate the foeman's steel.

SCORES

LANCASHIRE

First Innings		Second Innings	
J. C. H. Hollins, c & b Blackburne	0	c Kilner, b Blackburne	3
Makepeace, c Blackburne, b Smith	105	c Blackburne, b Rhodes	78
Tyldesley (J.T.), c Hirst, b Rhodes	38	c Smith, b Blackburne	10
J. Sharp, c Kilner, b Blackburne	29	not out	16
Tyldesley (E.), c & b Blackburne	6	b Smith	1
Hallows, b Rhodes	24	c Holmes, b Hirst	10
Tyldesley (J.), not out	59	st Dolphin, b Rhodes	49
R. A. Boddington, b Blackburne	11	c Holmes, b Rhodes	2
Dean, c Hirst, by Rhodes	7	c Rhodes, b Smith	7
Parkin, c Hirst, b Rhodes	20	st Dolphin, b Rhodes	19
C. S. Marriott, c Kilner, b Rhodes	4		
Extras	16	Extras	11
Total	319	Total (for 9)	*206

*Innings declared

28

YORKSHIRE V LANCASHIRE 1919
YORKSHIRE

First Innings		Second Innings	
Rhodes, c Parkin, b Dean	36	c Hollins, b Parkin	7
Holmes, c Tyldesley (E.), b Dean	44	c Tyldesley (E.), b Tyldesley (J.)	20
Denton, retired hurt	24	b Parkin	4
Kilner, b Marriott	44	lbw, b Marriott	19
Hirst, b Parkin	3	lbw, b Parkin	5
D. C. F. Burton, c sub, b Parkin	12	b Parkin	0
Sutcliffe, b Parkin	26	c Tyldesley (J.T.), b Parkin	53
H. M. Claughton, b Parkin	3	c Boddington, b Parkin	15
Dolphin, lbw, b Parkin	11	b Parkin	2
Smith, b Parkin	7	not out	6
W. E. Blackburne, not out	5	c Hollins, b Parkin	0
Extras	17	Extras	22
Total	232	Total	153

BOWLING ANALYSIS

Lancashire—First Innings

	O.	M.	R.	W.		O.	M.	R.	W.
Blackburne	28	1	95	4	Claughton	13	1	39	0
Smith	32	7	82	1	Hirst	5	0	13	0
Rhodes	24·3	4	74	5	Kilner	1	1	0	0

Second Innings

	O.	M.	R.	W.		O.	M.	R.	W.
Blackburne	17	0	74	2	Rhodes	23·5	8	49	4
Smith	24	7	58	2	Kilner	1	0	2	0
Hirst	8	2	12	1					

Yorkshire—First Innings

	O.	M.	R.	W.		O.	M.	R.	W.
Tyldesley (J.)	7	1	35	0	Marriott	26	5	56	1
Parkin	32·3	8	88	6	Dean	7	0	36	2

Second Innings

	O.	M.	R.	W.		O.	M.	R.	W.
Parkin	28·4	13	52	8	Tyldesley (J.)	28	6	35	1
Marriott	9	4	17	1	Dean	9	1	27	0

YORKSHIRE V LANCASHIRE 1919

August 4/5   Bramall Lane

TO the man with a sense of the scene, Bramall Lane on yesterday's dull morning was a fit stage for a Lancashire and Yorkshire match. The squat chimneys outside the ground loomed black against a lowering sky, and Bank Holiday or no Bank Holiday, there was a suggestion of smoke about and steel smelters. All these things told eloquently of the stiff energy of North-country life, making the proper dramatic accompaniment to a battle between ancient hosts whose informing spirit is the dour combativeness of hardy northmen. Lancashire had the good luck to win the toss and bat first on a quite satisfactory wicket. A crowd that was swelling visibly sent up a good imitation of the Sheffield roar as the Yorkshire eleven took the field. In these big games the cricket at the outset is always a wily sparring for positions, the bowlers seeking out weak points in the batsmen's defence, the batsmen striving determinedly to blunt the edge of the attack.

The start yesterday was not a good one for Lancashire. Makepeace began well, scoring eight runs off two overs in the most confident and capable way. Then he was brilliantly caught at the wicket. A few minutes later J. T. Tyldesley was also out, and there was no mistaking the Yorkshire roar then. It was authentic. The bowlers were definitely on top when Ernest Tyldesley came in. Waddington had gone on after a single over by Hirst, and with Williams maintained a beautiful attack for thirty minutes. Anything might have happened to Lancashire in this period. But Ernest Tyldesley is a most masterful bat, and he began as though his side were well placed instead of in a moment of incipient crisis. Again and yet again he produced that exquisite stroke in front of forward short leg which is rapidly becoming his very own. He went back to the wicket with the dainty toes of a dancing master and forced William's swinging ball to the on with all

30

conceivable neatness and nonchalance.

Hallows assisted him most big heartedly. The crowd was inclined to wax derisive at his calculated Fabianism. He played the Barlow game after the manner born, and it was the right game for the situation. In forty minutes these two young cricketers pulled the match round a little, taking the score to 56 without a mishap. Rain then drove everybody indoors. There had been an hour's cricket, and nothing further was done until after the luncheon interval. Then we had a Lancashire catastrophe, one dolefully reminiscent of a certain morning at Old Trafford some eighteen years ago, when George Hirst started a panic amongst MacLaren's men and got them all out for 44. In the first over after lunch yesterday Hallows put an end to a promising partnership by trying to hit a rising ball from Waddington beyond point. It was making an upward trajectory even as it passed the wicket and ought to have been left alone.

The young left-hander's mistake had dire consequences. He at least had played the Yorkshire bowling skilfully, but after his downfall nobody else, Ernest Tyldesley excepted, could produce any ability at all. For some twenty minutes Tyldesley was compelled to look on helplessly while Waddington and Rhodes spread ruin. James Tyldesley, Heap and Hollins were all out in less than twenty-five minutes for no more than 11 additional runs. It was a case of rank bad batting. The bowlers were handicapped by a wet ball and Waddington, who at this point did most of the damage, sent down many short ones that went by unpunished. Ernest Tyldesley set the proper light on the debacle by playing as usefully as ever. With the 'tail' in, however, he was under the necessity of hitting at everything. He completed a superb 50 before he gave a chance, or indeed made a faulty stroke and was only dismissed in the end in an attempt to get the bowling. He has rarely played a more valuable game. Seen in perspective, the Lancashire innings suggested a failure of nerve somewhere after the speedy dismissal of Makepeace and J. T. Tyldesley. Waddington had a capital analysis but it was flattering. He has a free, swinging action and the left hander's conventional going away ball, varied with the break-back. Yesterday though, his length was not at all skilfully

31

managed.

Rhodes was easily the best of the Yorkshire bowlers. In his 42nd year Rhodes has recaptured a characteristic which made his bowling unique twenty years ago. There were slow bowlers before Rhodes who had his enormous finger spin, but they could only get it to operate on the average wicket by tossing the ball well into the air, which had the defect of giving quick footed batsmen time to jump in and drive. Rhodes seemingly set a scientific principle at defiance by spinning at a tantalisingly slow pace, yet with the low flight of the medium paced man. The result is a twisting ball that defies the offensive tactics best calculated to cope with it, and one has perforce to wait for the ball and allow the spin to come off, which of course, is the very thing one wants to prevent. This combination of a characteristic of the slow bowler with one belonging definitely to the medium paced bowler got Rhodes his wickets yesterday, three of them significantly enough lbw. He is a delightful bowler to watch even when he is working destruction against Lancashire. The Yorkshire fielding was brilliant throughout the morning. How pitifully the Lancashire batting broke down is best understood from the following sequence: 1/10 2/19 3/56 4/57 5/60 6/67 7/88 8/92 9/110 10/124.

Lancashire's one hope when Yorkshire went in was that Parkin would find a mood of inspiration, but Lancashire's luck was out this sorry day. Parkin's length was deficient: his slow ball went up too wide and obvious a flight, and the other bowlers looked simple enough after a few minutes of Holmes and Sutcliffe. These batsmen played a high spirited game, which made the Lancashire display seem more and more ignominious. They sent up 50 in as many minutes and in another half hour passed the hundred. There were 14,000 spectators on the ground at this point, and with every boundary hit by the young Yorkshiremen, and they came fast and furious—the cheering was fit to split the skies. A few Tykes with memories so short that Whit-week was forgotten were scornful at Parkin's slow ball. There is surely no crowd in the world as vocal and as partisan as the Sheffield crowd.

When rain came on the Lancashire side no doubt were glad to be so early rid of a parlous day. They played consistently poor cricket but in justice to them it must be said that nothing 'came off' for them. As there is a possibility of the wicket developing into a thoroughly sticky one tomorrow Lancashire have got a great deal for which to hope.

SECOND DAY

Lancashire made a fine eleventh-hour rally at Bramall Lane yesterday and pulled the game with Yorkshire out of the fire. At three o'clock everything seemed lost. Yorkshire sent their rivals in to bat again after the luncheon interval with 193 to save an innings defeat and four and a half hours through which to struggle. The beginning was as catastrophic as Monday's. Makepeace and J. T. Tyldesley were both dismissed in twenty minutes with only 13 up. A crowd of 14,000 waved gleefully in anticipatory triumph, and even staunch Lancastrians hinted at an hereditary streak amongst their men. Then Ernest Tyldesley and young Hallows for the second time showed fight. The two defended for two hours, and carried the score from 13 to 134. Ernest Tyldesley was then bowled by a yorker at 5.20 and Lancashire still needed 59 to send Yorkshire in again. This was Ernest Tyldesley's sixth successive 50 in successive innings and it was a little masterpiece.

There remained two hours and ten minutes in which the Yorkshire bowlers might yet show their match winning mettle, and everybody advertised the presence of a long Lancashire tail. With James Tyldesley in, Rhodes, Waddington, Williams and Kilner all bowled grimly, sparing themselves nothing. But the batting was just as dour, just as skilful. Hallows continued to play with the patience and the coolness of a veteran and Tyldesley maintained a resolutely straight bat. The crowd, or rather a section of it on the popular side, lost its temper. There was a systematic jeering at Hallow's stubbornness. It availed nothing. At six o'clock, it is true, the young left-hander was missed by Williams from a lofty hit to forward square leg. He was then 53 and the total Lancashire score 169. After this James Tyldesley hit so finely that he completed 50 in 75 minutes. Heap and Hollins failed and excitement was whipped up again, but only a hat trick could serve Yorkshire's purpose now and that was not forthcoming. Rhodes made a magnificent effort to catch R. Tyldesley at five past seven, but the main interest at this stage was whether Hallows could find time to get his century. This he accomplished at 7.15 and stumps were then drawn. Hallows batted for just over four hours—a superb achievement in a match of such an order for a player in his first season. His innings was really beyond praise. He rarely looked like getting out, and was never daunted by the painful trend of events in the beginning. He has not yet a command over a large number of scoring strokes, but this is developing day by day. Not many left-handers possess his straight bat.

Again the day began badly for Lancashire. In the first over from Parkin, Holmes hit hopelessly across a capital leg break well pitched on the wicket and skied the ball. It offered a reasonably easy catch, but Ernest Tyldesley seemed to lose the ball and it dropped yards away from him. Holmes was 51 at this point. The wicket did not assist the bowlers despite Monday's rain and there was no sun to bake the ground. Sutcliffe and Holmes made the Lancashire attack look quite plain by totally contrasted methods. During the first thirty minutes, runs came at the rate of 90 an hour, and there was an astonishingly small number of singles. Sutcliffe is more forward in style than the average modern professional. He takes his left leg over freely to the off ball, while yet maintaining for the most part the approved full faced stance to the bowler, which in these latter years batsmen have cultivated as a defence against leg breaks. Sutcliffe was a promising man at Old Trafford in Whit-week but he has improved vastly since then. He has widened his range of strokes considerably. If he could produce anything like a consistent mastery over the cut it would be permissible to write him down amongst the complete batsmen as far as they go nowadays. A stroke which he gave us early on yesterday morning will linger in one's memory. Heap sent up a short delivery that broke hugely from the off. Sutcliffe made one swift movement to the wicket, then he pivoted into the authentic grand position and swept the ball to the square leg boundary at a most dramatic velocity.

Holmes despite a wrist action quite lacking in Sutcliffe, was not so attractive to watch. He is inclined to overdo the

George Gunn trick of showing his chest to the bowler and pushing a straight ball away with his arms, instead of giving a free swing through. He has more than Sutcliffe's resource behind the wicket, but yesterday he suggested the sheer workman, while his colleague made of his cricket something of an art. Even the little flourish with which Sutcliffe completes an everyday forward push is hardly irritating, since it tells of an aesthetic delight in his batting and a happy desire to polish it consummately.

These two batsmen sent up the 200 after three hours' work. Sutcliffe reached his century in two hours and fifty-five minutes and Holmes succeeded thirty minutes later. Holmes lost a lot of time in the nineties after offering another chance, this time at the wicket when 82. A little mishap like this, however, seemed accidental, for so completely was the Lancashire bowling mastered that the batsmen never got into really serious trouble. The first wicket fell at five minutes past one with the score 253. This magnificent first wicket partnership lasted three hours and a half. It sets up a new record for Lancashire and Yorkshire matches. No other opening batsmen have rounded the 200 mark in these games. The ball that bowled Sutcliffe was something of a curiosity. It broke almost two feet, struck the batsman's pad, and trickled thence into the wicket. Sutcliffe hit fifteen fours and eight threes. His only mistake was a return to Cook on Monday afternoon when he was 42.

Holmes left a few runs after Sutcliffe, caught in the slips. His boundaries were sixteen. There was some joyful hitting by Hirst just before lunch, and then Yorkshire declared the innings closed.

The Lancashire bowling analysis makes sorry reading; Parkin was a big disappointment. He rarely had a batsman in trouble. His bowling lacked spin and even length. It was difficult to believe that this bowler was the genius who defeated Yorkshire at Old Trafford in Whit-week. Heap worked steadily through it all, but the fielding was indifferent. Only occasionally did one notice the ball picked up cleanly and there were too many feeble returns from the outfield.

SCORES

LANCASHIRE

First Innings		Second Innings	
Makepeace, c Dolphin, b Williams	8	b Waddington	0
Hallows, c Dolphin, b Waddington	16	not out	102
Tyldesley (J. T.), c Dolphin, b Waddington	2	c Kilner, b Williams	10
Tyldesley (E.), run out	65	b Williams	82
Heap, b Waddington	2	b Williams	1
Tyldesley (J.), lbw, b Rhodes	1	b Williams	52
J. C. H. Hollins, c Burton, b Waddington	6	b Williams	4
		not out	7
Tyldesley (R.), lbw, b Rhodes	11		
R. A. Boddington, b Rhodes	1		
Parkin, lbw, b Rhodes	2		
Cook not out	0		
Extras	10	Extras	13
Total	124	Total (for 6)	271

YORKSHIRE

First Innings

Holmes, c Cook, b Tyldesley (J.)	123
Sutcliffe, b Heap	132
Denton, c Hallows, b Heap	16
Kilner, c Heap, b Tyldesley (J.)	0
Rhodes not out	16
Hirst, c Hallows, b Heap	19
Extras	11
Total for five (declared)	317

BOWLING ANALYSIS

LANCASHIRE—First Innings

	O.	M.	R.	W.		O.	M.	R.	W.
Williams	7	0	31	1	Waddington	23	10	49	4
Hirst	1	0	3	0	Rhodes	17·2	7	31	4

Second Innings

	O.	M.	R.	W.		O.	M.	R.	W.
Waddington	31	11	91	1	Kilner	18	5	33	0
Williams	22	4	67	5	Hirst	5	2	20	0
Rhodes	23	8	47	0					

YORKSHIRE—First Innings

	O.	M.	R.	W.		O.	M.	R.	W.
Parkin	30	6	97	0	Tyldesley (J.)	15	3	47	2
Heap	32·3	9	87	3	Tyldesley (R.)	6	1	20	0
Cook	17	2	55	0					

YORKSHIRE V LANCASHIRE 1920

May 22/24/25 Bradford

FIRST DAY

THIS has been a day of spineless cricket. Five hours and a quarter's play—an innings of 208 by Yorkshire, with a half hearted response of 77 for five from Lancashire. In all that time we have had not more than ten minutes of batting worth walking a hundred yards to see, while not more than an hour of the bowling has touched first class quality. On top of all this a pitifully small crowd for a match with such a tradition behind it. Moreover an apathetic crowd that went to sleep now and again. Shades of Hornby and Hirst, is it true this has been a Battle of the Roses?

The batsmen blame the state of the turf. In fact they apologised for their failures well in advance of the match, even before the morning's practice. There had been unsettled weather during the preceding 24 hours and a mere drop of rain is enough to lower the spirits of your average modern professional. It rarely occurs to him, seemingly, that a bad wicket of itself is not enough to get a batsman of quality out; good bowling is necessary also. On a veritable 'gluepot' a half-volley remains a half-volley. Today's wicket never suggested the Oval or Sam Apted, true. The ball could spin. But for the most part its work was slowly done. Rarely came the 'bite' that upsets even the skilful cricketer. And even had the ground been difficult today, runs would have rattled from the bat of a J. T. Brown or a Tyldesley, so feeble was the bulk of the bowling.

Towards the afternoon's end Waddington sent down as curious a species of bowling as one can recollect ever having seen in a first class match before. One over contained probably more long hops than Alfred Shaw bowled in his life. Yet this same Waddington's analysis remained at the close of play quite respectable. The Lancashire batsmen treated his worst ball with infinite politeness. It is conceivable that his almost half-volleys were suspect because of the possibility

37

that they might break back. But nine out of every ten of Waddington's deliveries swing in the air, or even swerve, away from the bat; it is not likely then, that many of them will break on pitching. A ball will swing or swerve only if the seam keeps more or less in the perpendicular during flight, whereas, of course, the turning ball needs to rotate either from left to right or right to left.

The eighth ball of the match this morning bowled by Cook, saw Sutcliffe caught off a tame stroke. This was a heartening start for Lancashire—especially after the strong dose of Sutcliffe and Holmes at Sheffield last August. But this good work was not continued for another hour and a quarter. Holmes and Denton added 96 for the second wicket—easily the longest partnership of the day. The next best, however, was Hallows' and Makepeace's 35 for Lancashire's first wicket. Neither Holmes, nor Denton, played well. Denton hit but a couple of fours, although one must admit the outfield was very slow and dead. He had his usual supply of luck. Holmes defended as though Trumble and J. T. Hearne were after him. One could not help admiring his watchfulness.

But where is that 'two-eyed stance' going to land modern batting in the end? Most of today's batsmen have used it—and quite unnecessarily, considering the wicket and the loose bowling. The 'two-eyed stance' which means that you stand with your left shoulder pointing towards mid-on instead of down the wicket was a position adopted by batsmen who wished to defeat the off theory bowlers by pulling the ball round to the on. The full front to the bowler, of course, favours the on drive; also it enables a batsman to see a fast leg break well and encourages the modern method of pad play to turning balls. But it is a game for especially trying conditions—conditions which cannot be coped with by the free, straight swinging bat. For, of course, the straight bat demands the 'left shoulder forward' stance—unless one has the wrists of an R. E. Foster. The conditions at Park Avenue were most decidedly not of a sort to tie up the straight hitting batsman. Yet he was missing—excepting for a brief spell from Rhodes. Owing to this 'two-eyed stance' balls which simply asked to be hit on the half-volley past mid-off were either left alone or clumsily pulled for a mere single. Short

YORKSHIRE V LANCASHIRE 1920

balls were allowed to pass well outside the off stump at a lovely cutting altitude. 'Thou thrice majestic cut' as the old cricketers sang of it—where was it today? How can one cut if the 'two-eyed stance' drags the left shoulder and left away leg from the ball?

Yorkshire would have totalled rather less than 208 had the Lancashire fieldsmen taken all their chances. Holmes was missed at 29 and at 63; Rhodes should have had marching orders in the mere twenties. Dean and Cook worked hard, but neither had much spin or resource. R. Tyldesley bowled skilfully for periods. He used his customary leg break accurately, but this time I noticed that now and then he sent up an off break as a contrast. I had never seen him bowl this ball so well before. It adds enormously to his power. He now needs to try and conceal it. At present it announces itself by a flight much lower than that of his leg break.

The Lancashire batting, so far, has been unadventuresome. Hallows played neatly and was out to a ball that swung viciously in the very last yard of the flight. Makepeace and Ernest Tyldesley were both cunningly led by Rhodes to play too soon. Rhodes, with R. Tyldesley sent up the only really high grade bowling of the day. I liked the promise for James Tyldesley's innings at the close. He was hitting manfully. While he is in there is still hope for Lancashire.

SECOND DAY

Cricketers are very salamanders for sun. The hotter it is the more they show us their own selves. This morning was like mid-June and straightaway the cricket took on the light and radiance of the day. Saturday, which saw the great match travestied both by dull cricketers and a dull crowd, we speedily forgot. Here was something like the old event in the old setting—keen play, a fine and animated crowd.

The wigs were on the green right at the outset. James and Richard Tyldesley went to the wicket with the air of men for whom Lancashire's reputation for long tails carried no conviction, while the Yorkshire bowlers spared no nerve or muscle to keep the ancient foe under.

The first round at any rate went to the batsmen. In just half an hour they lifted the score from 77 to 112 and then James

Tyldesley was caught deep on the off side by Denton. He played a most resolute game. Day by day this big-hearted cricketer is developing as a batsman. I like his straight, swinging drive, with its full-blooded follow through. His defect at present is fast-footedness. Were he only to use his left leg freely and correctly, many of his hits worth only two at present would find the boundary. Today he drove quite a lot of overtossed balls on the off side past cover with his left foot pointing more or less down the wicket. This meant of course that his weight was not all in the shot. He was playing, as cricketers say 'with his arms', and you cannot hit safely on the off side with your arms alone. The rest of the Lancashire innings was just a tale of Richard Tyldesley, and a lusty tale too. This young player's innings was a pretty scathing commentary on the bulk of the batting seen so far in the match. He showed everybody there what might be done even with a Yorkshire attack on Whit-Monday by means of resolution and a bat that swings through strongly. He actually smote 63 out of 92 in something like an hour and a half. His scoring strokes amounted to no more than 24 and this was their sequence: 1 1 4 2 4 2 1 2 4 1 4 4 2 2 1 1 2 2 2 4 1 4 6 6. The last three shots came from one over by Rhodes, who before Tyldesley got at him had bowled five maiden overs in succession. Every one of these hits was the sheerest clout to the on, either square or past mid on—not exactly 'Spoonerish', maybe, but ever so virile, ever so manful, all the better for the flavour of the village green. The Yorkshire bowling was variable. Rhodes is still a master of flight variation, but Waddington sends down almost as many bad ones as good. The worst of these swinging men is that to get any curve at all they must needs overpitch.

Leading by 43, Yorkshire lost this little advantage by lunch. R. Tyldesley bowled Sutcliffe with an off break which the batsman thought would turn the other way, and Dean completely defeated Denton by a glorious break-back. It was a battle royal after the interval—tense batsmen, tense bowlers and fielders, and a tense crowd.

This was the authentic note of dour rivalry. This, at last was a fight between the Roses such as A. N. Hornby would have recognised. The wicket was yards faster than on Saturday, but both Dean and Tyldesley could spin the ball. When Dean bowled Holmes neck and crop at 36 Lancashire's grip on the game was tightening. The ball pitched on the leg, kept low and came back like lightning to hit the off stump. Whatever happens eventually, some of us said at this stage of the game, that nothing would alter the fact of Dean's bowling just after lunch. In forty-five minutes he delivered seventeen overs for 17 runs and two wickets and he was an All-England bowler once again. His length was perfect, his break-back just vicious.

But Yorkshiremen take some getting rid of when they are fighting backs to the wall. Rhodes joined Kilner at 36 for three, and played sterling cricket against this beautiful attack, which, by the way, was helped along superbly in the field, Bardsley in particular working magnificently. Slowly the Yorkshire score was lifted to 70. Then came one of those episodes dear to cricket, and especially dear to Lancashire and Yorkshire cricket which set the crowd a-palpitating. Cook went on for R. Tyldesley and got Kilner lbw first ball. His next but one similarly settled Burton and with the total still 70 Dean bowled Rhodes with yet another gorgeous break-back. Again Lancashire were on top, and never since the pre-war epoch did Lancashire's bowling look so deadly. But, despite it all, the Yorkshire tail was stiff enough. Yorkshire cricketers, who are bowlers first and batsmen only by an afterthought, have from time immemorial possessed the knack of sticking in. Moreover, some little cherub sitting up aloft has invariably assisted them. It was so today. Norman Kilner alone of Yorkshire's tail played flawless cricket. Robinson was immensely plucky but at 18 he hit an easy catch to Hallows and the sun blinded the fieldsman. Anyhow, by good and bad batsmanship weirdly mixed, Yorkshire's total touched 144 leaving Lancashire 188 to win.

Dean's bowling was beyond praise. He was on unchanged throughout the innings and worked most nobly. I could not detect in all his thirty-six overs more than four bad balls. His pace superbly varied, went with the best break-back I have seen this season. How accurate his length was may be understood from the fact that only once was he forced to the boundary, and he hit the wicket every time he secured a

41

victim, presumably on the old fashioned principle that a job well done is best done oneself. Dean takes his benefit soon and surely Lancashire cricket lovers will not forget this sterling work at Park Avenue when the right time comes. The wicket gave him little assistance. It was quite good. So the Lancashire players thought at any rate. They entered on their task of getting the runs feeling hopeful, and ready to blame only themselves in the event of failure. Hallows and Makepeace have given their side the nicest of send-offs, and 144 more runs will give Lancashire the victory.

THIRD DAY

This afternoon Lancashire went under to Yorkshire by 22 runs after some three hours of grim fighting. It was cricket almost too painful to watch for those of us who cannot be brought to value the traditions of Lancashire and Yorkshire cricket lightly. From beginning almost to the end the day's play was swaying now in Lancashire's favour now in Yorkshire's, and this dramatic changefulness struck out all the old antagonistic fire between the rivals. The tale of the Red Rose's downfall is best told in this sequence of the fall of the wickets: 1/56 2/63 3/68 4/70 5/141 6/149 7/153 8/161 9/162 10/165.

In broiling sun the Lancashire batsmen went through the very labours of Sisyphus rolling a stone up the steepest slope again and again only to find it down at the bottom after all. First Makepeace and Hallows gave their side the most confident send-off imaginable. They lifted the overnight score to 56 by very neat cricket. Not a cloud, not one even the size of a man's hand, cast a shadow over the radiance of our prospects as these men so competently took the measure of Robinson and Waddington. And then Makepeace got himself out. That is the only way to put it. The ball he was caught from swung almost a yard away from the off-wicket towards slip. Makepeace 'went to fetch it' as they say, and compelled to reach at the ball with his arms well on the full stretch, he had no power over his stroke. A thousand pities this mistake, for Makepeace was batting so hopefully.

This was the beginning of Lancashire's tribulation—but only the beginning. Then evil genius had a finger in the over throw of Hallows' second out at 63. He was given out lbw in rather distressing circumstances. A ball from Robinson swung across the wicket and hit the batsman's pad. Nobody appealed, not even bowler or wicket-keeper, both of them of course the very men who usually appeal for 'leg before'. But, despite the absence of a challenge—as soon indeed as the ball hit Hallows' pad, the umpire half raised his hand and then withdrew it hastily, seemingly to scratch his neck. Of course this action was seen all over the field and interpreted as a decision given in advance of an appeal. Whereat somebody in the Yorkshire slips murmured a belated "How's that?" and Hallows had to go.

The Lancashire players considered this episode questionable and with some justice. Hallows played capital cricket. He is using his feet more like a high-grade batsman every day. The faster the wicket, though, and the less the bowler sees of his chest the better—when he pushes a ball defensively forward.

Ernest Tyldesley was brilliantly caught in the slips and Bardsley again failed, so that an hour of that golden morning had added just 26 to Lancashire's overnight total for the loss of four wickets. Lancashire were on the mat once more.

Now Sharp and James Tyldesley had to tackle the Sisyphus job. And nobly did they roll their burden up the heart-breaking ascent. I cannot imagine that Sharp has ever, in all his long cricketing life, needed to strive so bitterly for runs. He was baffled by the eighth ball Robinson sent down to him. At 15 he fluked one 'down the gully' where Waddington nearly made a catch by flinging himself desperately at the flying ball. Also he was in trouble with Roy Kilner. What a game it was just now! The setting of yellow sunshine and Park Avenue seemed quite tame for the occasion. Better far, to quicken the dramatic flavour of it all, would have been Sheffield's murky air and a gloomy Valkyrian sky.

James Tyldesley kept his bat in the perpendicular and checked his passion for a clout. From 12.20 till 1.45, the lunch interval—these two batsmen held the breach, and to such admirable ends that the Lancashire XI could take their sustenance with light hearts. The score was now actually 136 for four, Sharp 39 and Tyldesley 31.

After lunch Yorkshire took the field with that sinister aspect which we know of old. There was determination written in every player's face; they all moved to their places in the field without scarcely a word from Denton, who was captain in Burton's absence. Robinson bowled again—he had been rested during the stand before lunch. Sharp immediately hit him rather finely to square leg and there, to the vast surprise and delight of the crowd, Norman Kilner made a magical catch right off his toes. Great fielding of course, and beyond praise, but surely rough luck for Sharp and Lancashire. The fifth wicket added 71 precious runs in the hour and 50 minutes. Sharp's bat throughout came down as straight as ever, and if his feet did not find position for driving with the old agility, that lusty square cut was on view more than once. And how skilfully he selected the ball for cutting, and how infallibly he swung the bat down on the ball from above.

The passing of Sharp was followed in quick time by the downfall of R. Tyldesley who after a fine leg hit to the boundary off Robinson tried to repeat the stroke with a shorter and straight ball, and stopped it with his pads. Lancashire now wanted 39 for victory with four wickets to fall. On paper the chances appeared quite pretty, and there was excitement in the crowd. But some of us looked only to James Tyldesley now, for verily the 'rabbits' were in. Lancashire's tail end is made up of plucky men, gifted in their own departments but not exactly batsmen for a Yorkshire attack like yesterday's at such a moment of crisis. James Tyldesley started to use his fine shoulders as soon as Richard left. It was not Lancashire's day though. A ball from Robinson 'kicked' abominably just as Tyldesley was bringing down his bat quite correctly. The ball hit the side of the blade and some safe hands in the slips scooped it gleefully. Of the rest of the Lancashire innings let there be silence. The present writer, at any rate, has little appetite for the harrowing details concerning the finish. He is a Lancastrian and makes no pretence, in these matches at least, to the calm detachment of one on high Olympus. Let it merely be recorded that Yorkshire won, and well they deserved their spoils.

The result perhaps was a nice valuation of the merits of the two teams. Lancashire's batting is hardly up to Yorkshire's level. I doubt very much indeed whether Lancashire could have reached Yorkshire's second innings score against Dean's superb bowling on Monday. Dean was far and away the best bowler of them all—and I do not of course forget Robinson's excellent work yesterday. But Dean hit the wickets of all his men—better men on the whole than Robinson's victims, only one of whom was clean bowled. One or two of them, as we have seen, got out to him unluckily. Robinson made the ball swerve violently away from the wicket to the direction of short slip at a good pace. He kept a length just short of the half-volley, a very tantalising length in the circumstances the Lancashire batsmen found themselves. They were repeatedly tempted to hit, since their goal seemed such a graspable one, and yet they dare not.

Robinson, in the cant phrase, turned the psychological moment to good use. None the less, it must be pointed out that a bowler who swerves away from the wicket usually gets a lot of his victim's co-operation from the batsman himself. One or two of the Lancashire men—notably Ernest Tyldesley and Makepeace—gave Robinson all the assistance in the world by 'going after them'. With a bowler like Hirst one needs must play nearly every swerve, simply because they swing in, not away. Robinson was not afraid to try this trick time after time. A fine offside hitter, with an agile left leg and some judgment, might have found him easy going. He bagged the first nine wickets and it was bad luck alone that denied him the whole ten of them. As fine as anything else in his work was his immense grit and determination.

Perhaps it was Yorkshire's fielding that gave them the whiphand. Yesterday they snapped up all possible catches and, to use an Irishism, one impossible. And, as Lord Hawke said on an occasion, "good catches win matches".

45

THE ROSES MATCHES 1919-1939
SCORES

YORKSHIRE

First Innings		Second Innings	
Holmes, c Blomley, b Dean	68	b Dean	12
Sutcliffe, c Hallows, b Cook	1	b Tyldesley (R.)	11
Denton, b Tyldesley (R.)	54	b Dean	2
R. Kilner, b Tyldesley (R.)	13	c Blomley, b Cook	25
Rhodes, b Dean	49	b Dean	12
Robinson, lbw, b Dean	4	b Dean	37
D. C. F. Burton, b Dean	2	lbw, b Cook	0
N. Kilner, lbw, b Tyldesley (R.)	0	b Dean	15
Macaulay, st Blomley,			
b Tyldesley (R.)	0	b Dean	2
Dolphin, not out	4	b Dean	8
Waddington, c Hallows,			
b Tyldesley (R.)	3	b Dean	11
Extras	10	Extras	9
Total	208	Total	144

LANCASHIRE

First Innings		Second Innings	
Makepeace, c & b Rhodes	14	c Rhodes, b Robinson	26
Hallows, c Kilner (N.),			
b Kilner (R.)	23	lbw, b Robinson	28
Tyldesley (E.), lbw, b Rhodes	0	c Rhodes, b Robinson	3
R. V. Bardsley, c Kilner (N.),			
b Rhodes	4	st Dolphin, b Robinson	1
J. Sharpe, lbw, b Rhodes	12	c Kilner (N.), b Robinson	41
Tyldesley (J.), c Denton,			
b Macaulay	25	c Kilner (R.), b Robinson	43
Tyldesley (R.), b Rhodes	63	lbw, b Robinson	4
Cook, b Waddington	1	b Robinson	3
M. N. Kenyon, b Waddington	10	c Kilner (R.), b Robinson	1
Blomley not out	0	st Dolphin, b Kilner (R.)	0
Dean, b Waddington	2	not out	4
Extras	11	Extras	11
Total	165	Total	165

YORKSHIRE V LANCASHIRE 1920
BOWLING ANALYSIS

Yorkshire—First Innings

	O.	M.	R.	W.		O.	M.	R.	W.
Cook	23	2	55	1	Hallows	5	0	19	0
Dean	30	9	62	4	Tyldesley (R.)	32	4	62	5

Second Innings

	O.	M.	R.	W.		O.	M.	R.	W.
Tyldesley (J.)	4	1	11	0	Tyldesley (R.)	17	4	43	1
Dean	36	11	51	7	Cook	15	5	30	2

Lancashire—First Innings

	O.	M.	R.	W.		O.	M.	R.	W.
Waddington	28	8	59	4	Kilner (R.)	7	2	10	1
Robinson	6	0	13	0	Macaulay	8	2	25	1
Rhodes	22	11	47	4					

Second Innings

	O.	M.	R.	W.		O.	M.	R.	W.
Waddington	25	9	54	0	Rhodes	17	5	27	0
Robinson	31	15	36	9	Macaulay	7	0	18	0
Kilner (R.)	20	8	19	1					

YORKSHIRE V LANCASHIRE   1920

July 31/August 2/3   Old Trafford

FIRST DAY

LANCASTRIANS had to face cruel news at Old Trafford on Saturday morning. Makepeace and Hallows were out of the game with Yorkshire, the one down with lumbago, the other with a strained tendon in the left arm. Thus in the match of the season Lancashire went into the field on crutches, so to speak. And if this slight from fortune were not ample, Yorkshire must needs to win the toss on a soft comfortable wicket. The turf might have developed a slight 'stickiness' in the late afternoon but—one more dig in the ribs for Lancashire from the fates—rain came at twenty-five minutes past four and left Parkin and his helpmates with a slippery ball. What little progress Lancashire made, then, was got by the sweat of the brow; Lady Fortune sent no Rose Cavalier waiting on the team.

There was play for four and a half hours and Yorkshire turned all their happy chances to admirable account by scoring 201 for six wickets—a formidable total in view of the likelihood of a deteriorating wicket today. But how the batsmen had to work for the runs. It was indeed a dour tournament, worthy of the lowering skies overhead. Sutcliffe and Holmes gave Yorkshire a good send off scoring 67 in the ninety minutes before lunch for the first wicket. Slow cricket this, you may say. On paper maybe, but actually most fascinating to behold. The Lancashire bowlers worked hard and determinedly. They gave nothing away. Dean perhaps bowled loosely in the first ten minutes. At the other end though, Cook was a latter day Alfred Shaw, pitching the ball to a hair's breadth. His opening nine overs contained four successive maidens. The ball could be made to turn, but ever so sluggishly. Sutcliffe and Holmes were watchful enough.

It was difficult to believe that Sutcliffe is at present on what cricketers call a 'bad patch'. His manner was all confidence, his method all conceivable grace. Frankly, while

48

Sutcliffe was on view we forgot Holmes. For the moment Holmes struck us as just 'the other batsman', he impinged on the consciousness no more than a conventional figure—like the brown tree in the old fashioned landscape paintings, like the hackneyed bass accompaniment to a delightful Viennese waltz. Sutcliffe filled the picture; it was he who made the melody. The writer cares not a jot that Sutcliffe this year is not doing too well; he will none the less chance the prophecy that Sutcliffe is an All England batsman of tomorrow. How effortless his cricket on Saturday. For him batsmanship is seemingly too precious an art for mere brute strength to enter. He persuades the ball to the off side, deflects it to leg with the daintiest wrist play. And at the end of each stroke his bat performs an artistic flick in the air. One is reminded of the proud flourish with which our grandfathers used to round off their signatures, one thought of how Charles Dickens, with the artist's variety, wrote his name. Sutcliffe is a most delightful artist and had the match been any other than a Lancashire and Yorkshire match there was at least one onlooker on Saturday that would have been sorry to see him neatly caught at the wicket by Musson in the last over before lunch.

After luncheon Lancashire had a period of success. Denton was clean bowled third ball by Parkin's slow one. The batsman shaped as the ball was in the air, for a drive. Then he found he had picked a 'wrong un'. Denton's behaviour when the ball pitched was indeed remarkable. If he had been put by Parkin into a state of considerable hypnosis he could hardly have stood there more helplessly than he did while the ball broke or rather curled into his wicket. Denton, apparently, knew not where he was until the rattle of the broken wicket awoke him to the painful job of the lonely trail back to the pavilion. Kilner, who came next found Parkin a problem too. True, he hit out strongly. But it was the hitting of a man desperate with anxiety, as if to say 'I must do something with the bowling but heaven knows what. A fellow can't stop here poking at the air with umpteen thousand people looking on, so here goes!' Kilner was third out at 73 from a wild slash at a break-back. James Tyldesley caught him at slip beautifully with the right hand high above his head. Such a catch was it

49

that public school boys dream they will make some day when the other side want one run to win and the last ball of the match has been bowled.

Yorkshire lost Rhodes at 107, and now four Yorkshire wickets were down. Hirst came next, welcomed back to Old Trafford joyously by a crowd some 25,000 strong. The great Yorkshireman gave us a taste of his old grit and helped to hold the breach for an hour and a quarter, while the score was hoisted to 168. But he was lucky. Had only Sharp caught him—and the chance was not difficult—when he was but five, Lancashire's day's work might have had quite a happy ending. Let nobody rub in Sharp's misfortune though. The man who misses a catch at cricket feels it more than anybody else. Sharp's face as the ball dropped from his hands was for a moment a terrible study in tribulation. El Greco might have painted the hollow cheeks and the drawn lines at the mouth. In the middle of Hirst's innings, the weather, which had all the forenoon been admirably self-restrained, gave way. A rainstorm swept over the field and stopped cricket for 75 minutes. Then there was less than an hour to go and in that time Yorkshire scored another 43 runs for the loss of two more wickets.

More than half of the runs scored from the bat by the Yorkshiremen went to the credit of Holmes. He has been batting four hours and a half for 103. Today he most likely will add to this number. On Saturday, at any rate, he never looked like getting out save at 13, when Cook beat him and just missed the wicket with a fine break-back. His bat was always quite straight, and never did he play at the pitch of the ball. With the turf so easy he could depend wholly on his superb back play and retreat before the turning ball until he was right on the wicket and the spin had worked away. All the time Holmes watched the ball, and at the right moment brought his bat down, always getting the middle of it. His defensive back-stroke was invariably made off the right foot with the left quite high in the air at the moment of impact. So much right wrist action went into the stroke that in the 'follow through' the left hand relaxed its grip altogether. His scoring strokes were all round the wicket, but he rarely drove a ball hard. His hits to the off were wristy pushes, wonder-

fully placed, rather than drives. On the leg side his timing
never went wrong. One stroke through the slips he brought
off again and again—a delicious late cut made at the last
second as the ball passed the wicket. J. T. Brown was a
master at this late cut and Holmes managed it neatly enough
on Saturday to bring back Brown's rare art most gratefully to
the memory. How skilfully Holmes picked out the right ball
for hitting may be realised when it is known that in his score
so far there are only 18 singles.

Parkin was again the life and soul of the Lancashire
bowling. He was skilfully nursed by Sharp yet had a lot of
work to do, and never did he spare himself in the slightest.
All that he had in him of energy and gusto went into his every
ball. He bowled like a man who is in love with bowling—who
would rather be doing that than anything else in the world.
And how tenaciously he stuck to the batsmen. He declined to
run away from any proposition—and Holmes presented a
few tough ones. Not for Parkin the safety methods of a
length bowler who is content to toss them down on the off
side in the hope that sooner or later the batsman will make a
mistake and get himself out. Not for Parkin the discreet
nibbling tactics of a Joffre! Parkin is always ready to take on
the onus of getting a batsman out; always employing the
attack direct. How astonishingly accurate, too, is his bowling, considering the amount of finger spin he uses and the
experiments he is perpetually trying. There is certainly no
bowler playing the game today half so interesting as Parkin to
watch, and it is highly doubtful where there is one as skilful.
Cook bowled finely on Saturday also and Heap's steadiness
deserved a wicket or two. Richard Tyldesley was not asked to
bowl until the score was 140 for four. This was surely a
mistake, for he was obviously in form and managed his leg
break accurately. Lancashire fielded smartly all the time.

SECOND DAY

There was no mistaking the occasion at Old Trafford
yesterday. Here once more we have a Lancashire and
Yorkshire match of the authentic breed. Play keen to the
point of bitterness, a vast crowd that sprawled itself even on
the sacrosanct green and—true especially to type—

Lancashire getting the worst of it. 'Tell me the old, old story,' sang a disgruntled Lancastrian, as at the close of play he vanished homewards through the dust of Warwick Road. He had cause for irony. At half past three yesterday afternoon Lancashire, batting against Yorkshire's first innings' score of 253 were 104 for two wickets. And the tenth wicket fell at half past five for a paltry total of 179. Possibly the wicket got a little nasty as the day passed. Certain it is that Waddington just before tea now and again caused the ball to rear even after pitching a good length. But one is getting to the end of one's stock of excuses for the Lancashire 'tail'.

Only Musson of Lancashire's later batsmen yesterday could blame the turf for his downfall. The others—James Tyldesley excepted, who fell to a great catch—failed either through lack of skill or lack of resolution. Parkin threw his wicket away absurdly; he walked out to Rhodes almost before that cunning old soldier had delivered the ball. Cook's wicket was also thrown away after the manner of boys in a house match. Thus Lancashire lost on the first innings by 74 runs and Yorkshire, going in a second time, increased this lead to 112 without losing another wicket. Holmes again batted capitally and assumed the aspect of a double centurion.

The Lancashire innings, with all its disappointments, had one purple patch on which the mind will linger for many a long day to come. Spooner made 62. Think of it and thank the fates that once again we have seen it all—Spooner at Old Trafford against Yorkshire, and the crowd welcoming his fifty with roars of delight and affection. Who in the dark days of the war could have hoped for such a glimpse into the golden past as this! Where were MacLaren and Johnny Tyldesley? Why were they not there to make the picture complete?

This innings of Spooner's yesterday has had no peer at Old Trafford in grace and proud masterfulness these last half dozen years. He went in first with Heap and a magnificent catch on the deep leg boundary from a fine hit got him out after nearly two hours' batting. Waddington gave him some trouble before he found the pace of the turf but even then there was nothing awkward in his cricket. The manner was

52

perfect; only the eye faltered. His first boundary made before lunch was a glorious off drive. We all hailed it as a sure indication that the master was now in tune with himself. And first thing after lunch he drove twice to the off boundary from successive balls by Rhodes. From that moment until the end Spooner gave us the poetry of the game—an ineffably charming 'L'Allegro' in batsmanship. 'Wrist work, wrist work' is the usual comment on Spooner's driving. And it really does seem that he makes the stroke even as an artistic housemaid uses a feather duster. But no man could force a ball in front of the wicket, with Spooner's strength, by wrist work alone. There must be some latent body energy in the hit; the muscular mechanism works so smoothly that it deceives us. A fountain is a thing of fairy spray to the eye, but underground some violent pressure goes on. It may be in some such wise with Spooner's batsmanship. Yesterday the average cricketer of our time would have felt justified in using the two eyed stance so that he might meet the turning ball with his pads if it beat the bat. Most certainly he would have been content with pushes to the on side. Spooner gave us nothing so prosy as this. On that wicket, against spin bowlers like Rhodes, Kilner and Wilson, against a left-arm inswinger, indeed, like Waddington, he actually drove to the off-side with his left shoulder pointing towards the direction of the stroke. And he played straight ones so that you could see his three wickets after the bat had hit the ball. Wonderful to behold, this classic style! And great tidings for all cricketing England that Spooner is Spooner still.

When Kilner caught Spooner yesterday taking the ball from his toes on the boundary, it was as though he had put out the sun. 'L'Allegro' while Spooner was at the wicket, and Martin Tupper afterwards. Musson played a plucky game with Pewtress for fifty minutes, and this partnership added 35 precious runs. Musson now and then made a lovely drive, but the cricket on the whole was dull and stodgy after Spooner departed. A word of praise must be given Ernest Tyldesley for his steady innings of 23. He helped Spooner to put on 57 for the second wicket in seventy minutes. The Lancashire innings lasted some three hours and a half. Yorkshire bowled and fielded admirably, and Burton managed his men with tact. He had a fine team of slow wicket bowlers at hand and he so used them that they were always fresh. Wilson, who bowled better than anybody else, got no wickets. This often happens at cricket. Wilson is slow to medium and as fine a length bowler as we have in the game today. Yesterday the ground was so congested that one could not take one's customary observations from behind the wicket, but from the way the batsmen shaped at him Wilson was always turning the ball. He varied his flight craftily, dropping a foot shorter without altering the upward trajectory. After lunch, in one spell of work, he sent down eight overs for three runs only. Rhodes, too, bowled slow stuff cunningly. One ball early in Spooner's innings was a beauty. It pitched outside the batsman's legs and whipped across at a tantalising length. Spooner tried to play it and luckily missed the ball. The astonishing thing about Rhodes's bowling is the way he can combine a low flight with a very slow pace.

Waddington put in a lot of clever work. After lunch they thought he was going to run through the rabbits in quick time, but luckily for Lancashire things did not 'come off' for him. He has a gloriously rhythmic action, and he bowls the swinger 'with the arm' in a way promising big things in Australia. A big cheer went up from the crowd when Hirst was asked to bowl. Hirst is not fast nowadays, but he manages the conventional medium-paced bowler's tricks skilfully. Dean batted so neatly that it would be as well next innings if he went in a little earlier.

In the first hour of the day the interest lay in Holmes's innings. He just failed to carry his bat through. Musson finely caught him and he was ninth out. His 126 was made out of 247 in five hours and a half. Musson's wicket-keeping in this match has so far been, on the whole, quick and sure—almost as good as Dolphin's.

THIRD DAY

Rain put an end to the Lancashire and Yorkshire match just before six o'clock yesterday afternoon. Lancashire then had six wickets in hand and an hour left through which to struggle against an impossible deficit. The match thus leaves a nice problem whether Lancashire's tail could have played out time against Rhodes at his best. And we may be sure that Lancashiremen and Yorkshiremen will argue themselves into dizzy circles over this problem for many a day to come.

Both teams came out of the encounter with a diminished championship percentage and, truth to tell, both teams got their deserts—Lancashire because of shocking fielding yesterday morning. Yorkshire because they had not the spirit to go boldly for a win even when they were in an impregnable position. Burton was compelled by sluggardly batsmen to delay his declaration until three o'clock. Before lunch, in two hours, the Yorkshire batsmen could muster only 121, with all the advantage they had over Lancashire, and assisted as they were by sleepy Lancashire fielding. Rhodes and Holmes, coming together when their side was 161 to the good with seven wickets in keeping, dawdled seventy minutes for 80. Holmes again scored a hundred. He was labouring 65 minutes at the outset of the day for 23. There was, of course, no getting away from his skill. The bowlers were impotent before his defence. Only once did he make a serious mistake. At 73 he tried to place Cook to leg and hit the ball not very high behind the wicket. It was a perfect 'dolly' catch for either Musson or James Tyldesley. Tyldesley went for it, but he can do nothing right just now and he dropped the ball. This was the one technical flaw in Holmes's second century. Still, it was hardly a match winning effort.

Lancashire's second innings was again shot through and through with the imperial purple of Spooner's art. Despite a hopeless outlook and the loss of Heap's wicket at 13, Spooner batted with such freedom that Lancashire had 50 up in fifty minutes. After the tea interval the downfall of Ernest Tyldesley and Sharp in ten minutes made the responsibility on Spooner's shoulders overpowering, and then even he had to go at a wary pace. The Lancashire score was now 79 for three and two hours and ten minutes remained. But Spooner is a joy for eyes tired by dullards even when he is not scoring. After all, the interest which comes from runs scored is rather adventitious to the consideration of batsmanship purely as a spectacle. A great artist-batsman is delightful to watch even in the nets. Yesterday Rhodes bowled so cleverly that even Spooner had to play a strictly defensive game after the first forty-five minutes, but how sweetly did he flick those spinning balls away to the offside. He was all exquisite curves; there was nothing that seemed ponderable about him. For the second time in the match we cheered his 50 home. How the hundreds of little boys on the ground chortled. They squatted on the grass, and they sought to bring to the boundary every hit of Spooner's into the outfield by waving their hands in the direction they wanted the ball to go—for all the world as though they were passing some 'influence', as the hypnotists say, on the ball. Spooner batted for one hour and fifty minutes, and made his 63 out of 98. He forced the bowlers six times to the boundary, gave no chance and was in trouble only at 43, at 51 and at 54.

Spooner was most brilliantly stumped at 5.30, the score then reaching 98 for four. Ninety minutes to play yet. The passing of Spooner seemed to herald the end for most Lancastrians present, but Musson and Pewtress were stubborn for nearly half an hour, and then the rain came. Pewtress batted on Barlow lines for an hour: a plucky innings indeed.

Had Lancashire been soundly thrashed it is hard to believe the side as a whole would have been surprised. They went on to the field in the morning plainly carrying themselves like a beaten side. The fielding was incredibly bad. There was no gusto in it, too few men were on their toes. So low-spirited was the demeanour of the eleven that it was commented on all over the ground.

The blunder which gave Holmes another innings came simply as the climax of a dreadful morning's work. The out-fielding had no speed, the returns to the wicket were ex-asperatingly inaccurate. The outlook for Lancashire at the day's beginning was, of course, bad. But cricket teams there have been in the past which have won through from an even more hopeless dawn—Yorkshire for instance and against Lancashire too! What has happened indeed to Lancashire these last two weeks?

YORKSHIRE V LANCASHIRE 1920
SCORES

YORKSHIRE

First Innings		Second Innings	
Holmes, c Musson, b Heap	126	not out	111
Sutcliffe, c Musson, b Parkin	26	lbw, b Parkin	8
Denton, b Parkin	0	b Heap	21
Kilner (R.), c Tyldesley (J.), b Parkin	3	c Spooner, b Cook	6
Rhodes, lbw, b Cook	15	b Parkin	35
Hirst, lbw, b Tyldesley (R.)	31	b Parkin	2
Robinson, b Parkin	8	not out	15
D. C. F. Burton, b Dean	10		
E. R. Wilson, b Parkin	4		
Dolphin, st Musson, b Cook	16		
Waddington, not out	3		
Extras	11	Extras	18
Total	253	Total (for 5)	*216

*Innings declared

LANCASHIRE

First Innings		Second Innings	
R. H. Spooner, c Kilner, b Waddington	62	st Dolphin, b Rhodes	63
Heap, b Waddington	5	b Waddington	2
Tyldesley (E.), c Dolphin, b Kilner	23	c Sutcliffe, b Rhodes	22
J. Sharp, b Waddington	15	st Dolphin, b Rhodes	0
A. W. Pewtress, lbw, b Rhodes	10	not out	8
F. W. Musson, c & b Rhodes	26	not out	13
Tyldesley (J.), c Robinson, b Rhodes	6		
Tyldesley (R,), b Waddington	3		
Parkin, st Dolphin, b Rhodes	6		
Dean not out	11		
Cook run out	2		
Extras	10	Extras	8
Total	179	Total (4 wkts)	116

THE ROSES MATCHES 1919-1939
BOWLING ANALYSIS

YORKSHIRE—First Innings

	O.	M.	R.	W.		O.	M.	R.	W.
Dean	28	8	43	1	Parkin	45	10	86	5
Cook	35	11	54	2	Tyldesley (R.)	17	4	29	1
Heap	26	13	30	1					

Second Innings

	O.	M.	R.	W.		O.	M.	R.	W.
Parkin	29	8	65	3	Tyldesley (R.)	4	0	20	0
Heap	13	0	49	1	Dean	6	0	20	0
Cook	24	9	44	1					

LANCASHIRE—First Innings

	O.	M.	R.	W.		O.	M.	R.	W.
Waddington	27	8	64	4	Wilson	16	6	16	0
Robinson	2	0	5	0	Kilner	9	4	17	1
Rhodes	22·2	3	60	4	Hirst	6	2	7	0

Second Innings

	O.	M.	R.	W.		O.	M.	R.	W.
Waddington	11	5	22	1	Rhodes	24	7	49	3
Robinson	4	0	12	0	Kilner	11	5	8	0
Wilson	9	2	17	0					

YORKSHIRE V LANCASHIRE 1921

May 14/16/17   Old Trafford

FIRST DAY

EVERYTHING was ready on Saturday for another tussle between Lancashire and Yorkshire—everything that is, but the weather. The Old Trafford cricket field gave us an artist's arrangement in red, white and green, and the proud pavilion looked down on us with the air of a living but venerable presence, mellow with age and majestic because it remembered a mighty past. And the right crowd was ready for the game too—a real Red and White Roses crowd which buzzed its anticipation of a dramatic day as the cricketers moved into action. But spoil-sport weather came, and not only cut holes into the actual play; even during the dry periods it lingered on in a leaden sky. And since cricketers are as responsive to light and colour as chameleons, the game itself assumed a dull grey.

With rain in the air, Lancashire had vast luck to win the toss and bat first, for the turf was hard. The rain did little harm to the wicket—it merely left the Yorkshire attack with a greasy ball. And how your bowler does loathe a wet ball. It is like soap in his hands; he cannot spin it—nay he is sorely tried to pitch the slippery thing straight. How on earth Hugh Trumble managed to bowl his immaculate length with a wet ball must remain one of the larger mysteries of cricket. On Saturday only Rhodes, among the Yorkshire bowlers, could keep a consistent length. The Lancashire batsmen, then, had a rare chance for furious driving. That they turned the occasion to the tune of 140 for one wicket looks so handsome on paper that to complain might seem churlish. But that score of 140 came only by nearly 3 hours and a half's work on a pitch divinely after a batsman's heart. What would MacLaren, J. T. Tyldesley, or Harold Garnett have given us of flashing boundaries in like circumstances?

On Saturday we had some eight or nine boundaries bleakly isolated in time. The first two hours of the day saw a mere 80 runs crawl round the scoring board. Hallows for two hours and a half was phenomenally wary for one with youth nipping sharp in him. Will it sound credible to those who know Makepeace, when it is said that one hour and a half after Makepeace had departed for 32, Hallows' score reached 37? Makepeace played excellent cricket but not until Ernest Tyldesley had been on view for some time—and then it was late in the day—did we get the right game for the conditions. Had that game been played all the time Lancashire could have looked forward to the sticky wicket which Saturday's weather promised for today with some serenity.

For the best part of the day the Lancashire batting seemed so impolitic that one had reason to suspect the bowlers of all sorts of arts. On the pavilion indeed—which being at right angles to the wicket is not the best position from which to study an attack—I heard opinions to the point that the ball was turning. It was excusable to think so, in view of the Lancashire batsmen's tremendous caution. As a fact, though, the Yorkshire bowlers could not spin the ball to any purpose all day; until 4.15 I did not observe from behind the bowler's arm one really marked break. By that time Rhodes was beginning to turn them, but only at a slow pace from the pitch. Kilner managed to get a little spin on all the time, but not enough to trouble a first-class cricketer. Macaulay bowled fast medium and tried to bump the ball. Still his attack was hardly above good club level. Robinson and Waddington too were for the best part of their work fairly 'penny plain' bowlers, though towards the afternoon's close Waddington accelerated his nip from the wicket.

Yet against this definitely mediocre attack the Lancashire batsmen behaved in this Fabian way: Hallows scored two from the first 38 balls sent up to him; Ernest Tyldesley did not make a run until 21 balls had been bowled at his wicket. At 3.25 the score was 51; at 4.30 it was 88. Rhodes's first six overs cost some five runs. Waddington's first six overs cost some twelve runs. Macaulay's first seven overs cost some six runs, all this on an easy turf with a ball more often than not greasy. What would Lancashire have produced in the way of caution on a sticky wicket?

These following points must be made in extenuation of

Makepeace, Hallows and Tyldesley. Their responsibilities were heavy—with that tail waiting to wag. And the light was never good. Still, I believe more runs could have been made by Lancashire, because the batsmen invariably found the ball with the middle of the bat. They gave us the cricket of men who were 'seeing' the ball. The trouble was they would not hit it, after having got into the position to hit. The occasion plainly lay heavily on their minds. A score of 140 for one after all, is no common achievement in a Lancashire and Yorkshire match. But supposing we have a sticky wicket at Old Trafford today, and Lancashire are all out for 200: will that be ample to force a victory? or will it give us only a nominal advantage at the half-way stage with Rhodes to tackle on a 'gluepot'? How we should sigh then for the runs wasted on Saturday through our batsmen's timidity with innumerable long hops and half-volleys. Even if events at Old Trafford today and tomorrow justify, in the end, Lancashire's batting policy on Saturday it will be justified only from the match winning point of view. And cricket is not merely a contest—another form of tug of war. It is the loveliest game in the world, the most poetic as well. Cricketers should never forget for a moment that it is white flannels they are wearing, not blue overalls, and that they are assisting at a game, not at real industry under trade union regulations.

Yet, with all its greyness, Saturday struck the right note for a Lancashire and Yorkshire match. One felt of course a longing for the old masters, and it is too true that nowadays the sad melody of Andrew Lang's song might on these occasions go to other words—

> Ah, where be Jackson, and where be Hirst,
> MacLaren and Hornby, where be they?

But a Lancashire and Yorkshire game simply cannot fall into littleness. The match has a mighty tradition, and the reflected glory of other days will transfigure mediocrity into something fine for the while. Dull of soul a cricketer would need to be not to find himself thrilling with inspiration as he went into a match so majestic with history as a Lancashire and Yorkshire match. It is one of those occasions that take

61

men for a brief day rather out of themselves—into a tenser air. Such days come at least once in a life-time to all of us—even Blanco White had his moments of high poetry. And so on Saturday, despite the lack of the old masters, there were cricketers on view who, though of the common world most days in the week, were moved by the grandeur of a match murmurous with tradition to the authentic heights. They had their moments of high poetry, too, and the Battle of the Roses was itself again.

At any rate, as the crowd walked home in the rain the ancient spirit was among the people, and satisfaction in a good day for Lancashire was there, too, not expressed audibly maybe, but implicit, and warm enough to change the temperature rain or no rain. The Yorkshire fieldsmen had a need of praise too. They deserved it, although Hallows was badly missed at 35.

SECOND DAY

Not until the closing hour of yesterday's play did the authentic spirit of Lancashire and Yorkshire cricket descend upon us all. From the morning onwards for long hours it was a pedestrian occasion with no drama about. The game went on pleasantly enough in the sunshine, but as jejune as an old play after Robertson. Until six o'clock, indeed, it was a match which was living, like too many institutions in these days, quite definitely on its past. The Lancashire innings proceeded just as we might have expected it to proceed—after the fall of the third wicket. There was no rear-guard action fought and the innings petered out for 239, the last eight wickets falling for 78.

At the outset of the Yorkshire innings the game turned uneasily in its sleep for a while. Holmes, the cricketer who exhibited himself to us last August on a quite comprehensive scale, was run out amid the rejoicing of the multitude. He played a ball to the leg side from Dean. It was Sutcliffe's 'call' and the batsmen had one of those brief mid-wicket conversations which all of us that play cricket know well enough, the while Spooner neatly whipped in the ball to Blomley, who had time to remove the bails which a flourish before Holmes could get home again. Then Tyson came in, the man who has had us wondering for nearly nine days. In the morning practice Tyson revealed immense skill. But in the middle yesterday we might have exclaimed 'God bless thee Tyson, how thou art translated!' Cook seemed to set him problems the like of which we had never considered before. And Cook got him out lbw, for none, by sheer brainwork. He bowled a slower ball than those which went immediately before; Tyson was much too soon at it, tried to force it to the onside, and finished his stroke a fraction of a second before the ball hit his pads.

At twenty minutes past three Rhodes came in, and with Sutcliffe stopped the rot by cricket that had in it a rhythm so monotonous that it put the game in a nice condition of catalepsy once again. This continued until ten minutes to six and precisely then it was, with Yorkshire's score reading 123 for four, that James Tyldesley, bowling for the first time in the match, kindled the real fire. Your fast bowler always makes for high drama; there is in his sheer pace, and the fact of the nerve called for in the batsman to stand up to it, thrilling conflict. Last evening as the light was mellowing to softness James Tyldesley bowled faster than he has yet bowled this summer, with determination written grimly on his face. In six overs he overthrew two batsmen and had the slips tense with anticipation. Lightning snicks flashed by the wicket from the bowling he hurled down with all the strength of his shoulders. The game was transfigured; you could feel something electric in the air running through the crowd. Lancashire, by this mighty last minute effort, got on top of the ancient foe. Today the match may be drawn, but a first innings victory for Lancashire will be better than no blood at all.

The day's play happened on a seemingly tiny island of green in a vast black sea of a crowd. Never has a bigger crowd been packed into Old Trafford. It overflowed on to the once sacrosanct green. Now and again the game had to be held up while the waves of it were stemmed just as it threatened to engulf the outfielders. It attained a fine high tide on the summit of grandstands, and occasionally made an eddying backwash in the ladies' pavilion. There must have been well over 30,000 people there, hanging on to every movement of the cricketers, for all the world as though cricket was thrilling. Those with an eye to nice points were fascinated by the bowling of Rhodes in the morning. This bowling, indeed, kept the first hours of the day from a descent into the commonplace. It was of such excellence that the mystery of Douglas's neglect of Rhodes as a bowler in Australia must now be written down as incomprehensible.

The turf was not perfect; an amount of moisture on the top layer of a hard wicket allowed Rhodes to cause a ball to 'pop up' at times. He could spin the ball, too. But it was not his break, nor was it his periodical rise to an awkward angle after pitching a good length that got his wickets. It was flight, beautifully controlled. No doubt that the batsmen gave him every opportunity to exploit his variations through the air; no doubt that quick-footed cricketers would have jumped to the pitch of them. But yesterday the Lancashiremen permitted Rhodes to draw them out on a right foot rooted at home—in distrust of Dolphin—in which positon of elongation they met the ball with the bat just at that danger point in front of the left leg which spells disaster. Or if they did try to drive Rhodes they did it so straddle-legged and fast-footed that they could not meet the ball at the effective point in the bat's swing. Rhodes has still that old amazing knack of sending down a slow ball with a flight of a slow medium ball—that is, a narrower flight than his pace leads one to expect.

Ernest Tyldesley played Rhodes cleverly yesterday, and made from one of his few short deliveries a superb pull to the on boundary. Tyldesley was shaping for a fine century when Rhodes deceived him into a stroke timed just too soon. Sharp promised a happy innings too. He stayed long enough to drive Rhodes to the off side most brilliantly; it was a stroke of the pre-war period, made with the left leg flung at the ball's pitch and a resolute swing of the bat. Sharp too fell to a shorter ball than he had reason to expect from its flight.

Spooner was not himself. He could not 'see' the ball. The strokes he made were beautiful, but they met nothing but air. The innings had its grace—for the sculptor. What was lacking from the scorer's point of view was accurate timing. The mechanism of the strokes seemed as beautiful as ever: the eye only failed to do its work. It will be the biggest mistake in the world to assume from this innings that Spooner's work is done. A cricketer with the style he showed us yesterday needs but a season of practice to get the necessary vision to direct it.

The turf rolled out well for Yorkshire and most of us expected an amount of bright cricket. Instead we had the stodgiest batting imaginable. Yorkshire laboured for one hour and 35 minutes before tea and scored 54. They reached 100 after two hours and a half of dawdling. One of the umpires motioned a policeman near the sight screen to remove himself away from the line of the batsman's vision. The policeman misunderstood the umpire's gesture and came forward a few steps as if in response to a summons for his presence. It is possible the policeman thought the umpire had the idea of handing over the Yorkshire batsmen to the law for loitering in a public place.

Sutcliffe batted one hour and twenty-five minutes for 30. But if he was slow he was not prosaic. One does not object to cautious cricket so long as it is not undistinguished. Sutcliffe has style in all his strokes, the bloom of wrist work is there. He made few runs yesterday, and his batsmanship could therefore be admired purely as batsmanship, without any adventitious claims on our attention. It was, as the musician would say 'absolute' batting: the interest of it did not rest in effects—that is in runs—but in means. In other words, its interest was technical. He plays a nice straight bat, so much so that often at the finish of a defensive forward stroke his left grip is relaxed, the right arm alone supplying the leverage at the finish. His play to the offside must have won the heart of Spooner himself. Rhodes batted stubbornly and neatly. But on that wicket, in sunshine and blue sky, surely we might have witnessed at least some cricket that was not bleak and wintry.

The Yorkshire batsmen conceivably might extenuate their sluggard ways by reference to the Lancashire bowling. This, at any rate, was on a first class level. Cook had a capital spell, turned a ball from the off now and then, and his pace and flight had a shrewd changefulness. Heap, until he went tired, gave us a classic length and a nice admixture of spin. The ball that defeated Sutcliffe came into the batsman 'with the bowler's arm' and Sutcliffe played on. Dean worked hard, and James Tyldesley, as we have seen, had a galvanic moment. It was plain yesterday that Lancashire have a clever bowling team. The fielding was smart, despite at least one catch—and that an easy one—dropped. Ernest Tyldesley's catch was brilliant. Blomley's wicket-keeping had vigilance and, ignoring a lapse at the day's end, reliability and speed.

THIRD DAY

The Lancashire and Yorkshire match expired peacefully last evening in its sleep. There can have been few tears for it was a dull game from beginning to end. At lunch yesterday we had just a promise of a lusty finish. Lancashire then led by 146 over Yorkshire with eight wickets in hand. The crowd now expressed a hope of some brave hitting, so that Lancashire might declare with such time left as would give Cook, James Tyldesley and the other bowlers a fair chance of ridding themselves of Yorkshire.

As a fact, the pace of the Lancashire innings in the psychological period after lunch was this: 46 runs were scored in three quarters of an hour. After thirty overs had been bowled, not many more than 68 runs had come the way of Lancashire. After lunch Ernest Tyldesley made 32 runs in one hour and a quarter; Spooner after lunch had 21 balls bowled at him and he scored ten runs from them. James Tyldesley was batting for rather less than half an hour and his score of 10 was got by ten singles from 33 balls. Richard Tyldesley came in at 3.15 and straightway exploited the right game for the occasion. He hit—or rather clouted—the bowling to his heart's content, awoke the crowd to rapture and showed his colleagues that, after all, the Yorkshire bowlers were quite human and fallible. Richard Tyldesley's innings of 38 richly smacking of the village green, lasted only forty minutes. This honest energy came an hour too late, though; Spooner would not allow his bowlers to get at Yorkshire until a quarter past four, in which time Yorkshire needed to score 264 at the rate of just under 90 an hour to get a victory.

The time left at the Lancashire bowler's disposal was not ample on a fair wicket. Holmes and Sutcliffe played a slow safety game, for an hour or so, putting Yorkshire well out of danger. Still, even with a draw a foregone conclusion the

Yorkshire batsmen declined to take the slightest risk. One might have expected, with the game secure for them, that they would proceed to entertain the crowd. But they didn't. Holmes missed at 14 in the slips from a fine ball off Cook, gave us an eternity of dullness.

Whatever of impatience Lancashire's indolent batsmanship may have provoked after lunch, its caution from the outset of the second innings at twelve o'clock until the interval was thoroughly justifiable. Lancashire's second innings began ruinously with Makepeace and Hallows out for 6, and at this point the advantage over Yorkshire was not as good in fact as it was on paper. For the turf until 2.30 gave the Yorkshire bowling plenty of scope for spin. When Sharp and Ernest Tyldesley defended stubbornly the third Lancashire wicket, they could not trust the pitch for a minute. Immediately Sharp came in to bat he had a ball from Waddington that pitched on the leg stump and would have hit the top of the off stump but for a resolute and beautifully straight bat. Tyldesley and Sharp played a superb game in this moment of crisis.

Sharp's little innings of 20 was compact of skill, pluck and despite the strain of circumstances, even of brilliance. He was out trying nobly to knock Rhodes off his length and to quicken Lancashire's pulse. The total was 45 for three when Dolphin stumped him, and had Spooner and Tyldesley failed now—well we know what Yorkshire can do at the table turning game, granted a real opportunity. But Spooner was, like Tyldesley, soundness itself. One has nothing but praise for the work of these batsmen before lunch—after that it could be argued that by freer methods they would have served Lancashire's purpose the better. Spooner improved vastly on his Monday's form. 'He saw the ball and timed it accurately. His defensive forward play was in his sweetest vein. He flicked the ball to the offside time and time with the familiar supple wrists, and by doing so he restored cover point for a while to its position of dignity.

Ernest Tyldesley gave us an innings in a vein of gracious tranquillity, a lovely slow movement in batsmanship which as batsmanship—that is leaving out the question whether he might not have put on speed in the afternoon to Lancashire's advantage—could hardly have been matched by more than a half dozen cricketers in the land. Plainly this little masterpiece was addressed to the Selection Committee. He could not well have sent them an example of his cricket better calculated to convince them that he is a Test Match man in the making.

Towards the end of the day Sutcliffe batted immaculately against a first-class attack. Cook bowled his very best and with luck might have forced Yorkshire into the corner again. Tyson again shaped indifferently. He walked about too much, as cricketers say, as he made his back strokes.

SCORES

LANCASHIRE

First Innings		Second Innings	
Makepeace, c Dolphin, b Rhodes	32	c Holmes, b Macaulay	1
Hallows, c Oldroyd, b Rhodes	62	c Oldroyd, b Waddington	3
Tyldesley (E.), c sub, b Rhodes	60	not out	62
J. Sharp, c Kilner, b Rhodes	14	st Dolphin, b Rhodes	20
R. H. Spooner, c & b Kilner	8	b Macaulay	20
Tyldesley (J.), c Oldroyd, b Rhodes	22	b Macaulay	10
Heap, c Macaulay, b Rhodes	0	b Rhodes	8
Tyldesley (R.), c Waddington, b Rhodes	14	c Oldroyd, b Kilner	38
Dean, b Macaulay	4		
Cook not out	5		
Blomley, st Dolphin, b Macaulay	4		
Extras	14	Extras	16
Total	239	Total (for 7)	*178

*Innings declared

68

YORKSHIRE V LANCASHIRE 1921
YORKSHIRE

First Innings		Second Innings	
Sutcliffe, b Heap	30	c Tyldesley (R.), b Cook	31
Holmes run out	4	not out	52
Tyson, lbw, b Cook	0	lbw, b Tyldesley (R.)	23
Rhodes, c Blomley, b Heap	41	not out	0
Kilner, c Tyldesley (E.), b Tyldesley (J.)	50		
Oldroyd, b Tyldesley (J.)	11		
D. C. F. Burton, b Tyldesley (J.)	8		
Dolphin, b Cook	1		
Waddington, b Tyldesley (J.)	0		
Robinson, c Blomley, b Cook	2		
Macaulay not out	0		
Extras	7	Extras	10
Total	154	Total (for 2)	116

BOWLING ANALYSIS

LANCASHIRE—First Innings

	O.	M.	R.	W.		O.	M.	R.	W.
Waddington	24	6	58	0	Kilner	32	17	34	1
Robinson	9	3	19	0	Macaulay	17	6	34	2
Rhodes	51	14	80	7					

Second Innings

	O.	M.	R.	W.		O.	M.	R.	W.
Macaulay	20	1	53	3	Rhodes	25	11	36	2
Waddington	12	2	39	1	Kilner	16	5	34	1

YORKSHIRE—First Innings

	O.	M.	R.	W.		O.	M.	R.	W.
Cook	27	11	35	3	Tyldesley (R.)	13	6	23	0
Dean	11	2	18	0	Heap	22	7	52	2
Tyldesley (J.)	8·4	4	19	4					

Second Innings

	O.	M.	R.	W.		O.	M.	R.	W.
Dean	9	3	16	0	Tyldesley (R.)	9	1	21	1
Tyldesley (J.)	13	2	26	0	Heap	7	0	26	0
Cook	12	5	17	1					

YORKSHIRE V LANCASHIRE   1921

July 30 August 1/2   Leeds

FIRST DAY

IT was a season of feebleness at Leeds on Saturday. Lancashire were not tough enough to strike sparks of true antagonism out of Yorkshire steel, and Yorkshire are never quite happy against a wavering foe. They thrive on hard usage. The day's cricket, then, was dreary. At times, indeed, it was not easy to believe that we were all actually at a Lancashire and Yorkshire match. Even the crowd—despite that Yorkshire were winning—had no character, no responsive humanity. Time was when the fall of a Lancashire wicket happened to an exultation that split the skies. But on Saturday boredom was incarnate in the multitude; the crowd was often enough just one considerable yawn. This occasion came as close to the Lancashire and Yorkshire match of tradition as a second rate engraving of 'The Fighting Temeraire' to the original, and no closer. The outlines were more or less reproduced, but the power, the colour, lacking. At the end of the afternoon a disgruntled cricketer on his journey home to Manchester suggested to the writer as a text for this article "What came you out for to see?" The monotonous day had invited irony indeed.

Lancashire batted first on a perfect batsman's wicket. The turf had little life in it to assist the bowler. Its pace was consistently easy. Yet Lancashire gave us an invertebrate innings—a paltry 153 all out, after three hours and a half of struggling batsmanship. It might be said, even, that there was not really a decent struggle in the batsmanship. Lancashire seemed always at the Yorkshire bowler's mercy. No wonder the crowd was not moved to high emotion; there is no thrill to be extracted from the spectacle of the overthrow of irresolution. And it was irresolution and little else that led to Lancashire's downfall. The Yorkshire bowling had a consistent respectability—now and again it was admirable—but on that wicket of easefulness it is conceivable that better

70

bowling than Yorkshire's on Saturday would have been impotent against swashbuckling batsmen. This year-by-year inability of Lancashire to work up a dare-devil aspect against Yorkshire is possibly a matter less to be explained in terms of cricket technique than in terms of psycho-analysis. Lancashire in these matches look to be suffering from an inferiority complex. That, at any rate, is one good-mannered way of putting it.

The trouble came to Lancashire on Saturday by the sudden dismissal of Hallows and Ernest Tyldesley. Both of these batsmen fell to simple catches in the region of forward mid-on or leg. Hallows had shaped well enough—he made two beautiful boundary strokes to the leg side of Waddington—and one could only gasp in astonishment to see him place an ordinary length ball 'straight down the throat' of Sutcliffe. He certainly indulged a gasp of astonishment himself. Ernest Tyldesley's innings consisted of fourteen balls—six from Robinson, from which he scored a single to leg, an off-side boundary, and another single—and eight from Waddington, seven of which he could not score from, and the eighth of which he hit, most politely into Macaulay's hands—another victim of the so called leg trap, very fashionable in these days. Had Ernest Tyldesley come upon the ball that got him out on Saturday later in the afternoon with, say, his score well beyond 50—he would surely have treated it with a stroke that swung strongly through and clumped it to the boundary. As it was, some suggestion of 'half-cock' could be discerned in the stroke that he actually used.

Hallows and Tyldesley out at 34, Makepeace and Sharp had no choice but to play warily. Yet with all their obvious distrust of the bowlers—and of themselves—they managed to assume the air of men about to settle down. The Yorkshire bowling had to be rearranged. Wilson exploited old fashioned leg bias (not break)—circa 1802 or thereabouts—and with the Lancashire total 53 for two Rhodes was called up, to put his old spell on the batsmen. And they promptly gave themselves up to his mesmerism. His first three overs were maidens, yet not one ball in them spun in a dangerous way. With the Lancashire score 79, Rhodes had his customary luck in getting Makepeace caught very cleverly at extra mid-off, by Robinson. Astonishing how batsmen when they do at last, after long periods of dubiety, decide to hit Rhodes, manage to hit him straight to a fieldsman. No further misfortune came Lancashire's way before lunch; the score at the interval—90 for three—might easily have reassured the batsmen still to go in that even Rhodes is compact of flesh and blood just like the rest of his fallible species.

It was after lunch, none the less, that the Lancashire batting fell into a palsy. Macaulay and Waddington bowled unchanged for an hour and ten minutes, and Lancashire in this period lost three wickets for not more than 29 runs. And 'Mr. Extras' contributed a few of these.

In all 19 overs, 10 maidens, 20 runs from the bat, for three wickets—all in one hour and ten minutes, on a perfect wicket. 'What came you out for to see?' indeed. In one hour and three quarters after lunch on Saturday Lancashire scored 37 runs, including one boundary hit. Even Kenyon, nowadays one of the team's most courageous batsmen, could hit no more than two singles in forty minutes. The Lancashire batsmen even allowed no-balls to pass by without a fine fling at them. Three no-balls were patted to fieldsmen. Thus did Lancashire ignobly pass along the way to defeat. Seven wickets tumbled down in two hours after lunch for 64.

Kenyon, at the inning's very end, awoke to his true game and drove powerfully in front of the wicket. He fell to a fine catch in the deep field from a capital hit. Barnes, after the lunch interval batted for 90 minutes for 16. Often he was trying his best to make runs, but he had to suffer a well-placed field for his cover drives. Moreover, Barnes has in his method still a fault that takes the power from his offensive play. He frequently drives off the right (that is, the wrong) foot, his body tending to fall back towards the wicket-keeper as the stroke meets the ball. Consequently not all of his body energy goes into the drive. Sharp played as well as anybody else, after Makepeace. Boddington had, one fancies, rather bad luck to discover himself given out lbw.

Macaulay, I thought, was the cleverest of Yorkshire's bowlers. From a position beautifully behind and above the bowler—one was thankful indeed to be so favourably placed for the game—Macaulay's length had a dangerous look about it. He is medium to fast medium, and he can break the ball back with a nasty nip from the pitch. He gets a full and free body action into his bowling—as happens with all good bowlers—and his work is nicely varied. Macaulay is certainly amongst the country's most promising bowlers. Waddington, the cricketer who is ever raising hopes that real greatness will come from him, only to disappoint again and again, had excellent moments on Saturday. His action is so lovely that one simply cannnot deny that he is a good bowler. His best ball is plainly dangerous. He runs from the on side of the wicket, passes behind the umpire and delivers left-handed, often from the corner of the bowling crease, round the wicket of course. Thence the ball goes with the arm at a fine angle, cutting diagonally an imaginary straight line between wicket and wicket, just short of a perfect length. The ball is a nasty swinger, and on Saturday Waddington bowled it to a leg trap.

Yorkshire's innings began at twenty minutes to five. Holmes and Sutcliffe played good utilitarian cricket and scored 53 for the first wicket. Sutcliffe was bowled then by a beautiful off-break from Cook. Oldroyd, who came next, did not begin comfortably, but it was not Marriott's lucky hour. There is promise of another opportunity today for a study of these batsmen. Lancashire fielded neatly, but only Cook bowled with sting. Marriott, though he always managed his work intelligently, needed a slightly faster wicket. Yorkshire's 121 for one was scored in on hour and fifty minutes.

And so the day ended as it started: it was given over to cricket whose only note was sullen combat. And a little more of sullenness than combat—from Lancashire at any rate.

SECOND DAY

The game between Lancashire and Yorkshire today has again been so one-sided that the cricket had keen interest only for the sheer partisan. And along with the absence of combative appeal had been missing a sufficient amount of spectacular charm to compensate. There was plenty of strong competent batsmanship from Yorkshire, but a personal touch such as Hirst's was needed to give fascination to a match whose issue has been steadily and painfully obvious. The Yorkshire innings persisted until well on five o'clock, and in the end amounted to 489. Lancashire thus found themselves at the wicket again in the last hour and a quarter of the day, with the light not too bright and the future before them definitely gloomy. Makepeace assisted the prevailing pessimism by playing a simple offside ball into his wicket by means of a rather indecisive stroke. There was a lack of things favourable to Lancashire now save a sound turf. The Yorkshire bowlers and fieldsmen were, of course, on tiptoe. Hallows and Ernest Tyldesley needed agile wits about them to shake the ancient foe away. This much at any rate the cricket possessed at last—antagonistic fire. Ernest Tyldesley played a strong, dignified game, though at 21 he came perilously near to getting stumped from a lovely ball by Wilson. Yorkshire until the day's end fought to the battle cry of 'No quarter,' and short of rain or a landslide or some epic batsmanship a vile overthrow is in store for Lancashire.

The cricket before lunch prompted a question of relativity. Had the innings of Holmes an absolute quality, or needed we to some extent to see in it the measure of Lancashire's poor bowling? There's nought in batting good or bad, but bowling makes it so. A far less admirable cricketer than Holmes might well have scored a century against Lancashire today and yet not have convinced us that he was of the class that tells.

James Tyldesley opened the Lancashire attack at the day's outset with a full toss on the leg stump—a reliable enough harbinger this of the character of the bulk of the bowling to follow. Even Cook was not steady, despite that his third ball of the morning bowled Oldroyd. The first twelve overs sent down—six from Tyldesley and six from Cook—cost Lancashire 49 runs and eight boundaries were amongst them, three from Tyldesley and five from Cook. It is conceivable that Tyldesley's full tosses and long hops would have provided a few more big hits than actually happened had the bowler not taken now and then the precaution of pitching conveniently wide of the wicket out of the batsmen's reach. Marriott was again disappointing. His bowling had little life from the pitch and little enough break considering his definitely medium pace. One is inclined to think that the

Selection Committee took time by the forelock vigorously last week in naming Marriott an All-England bowler.

A mediocre attack then did not give an adequate test of Holmes's mettle. This much, however, can safely be said of his innings; though it did thrive on poor bowling there was nothing bandy about it. Simple the problems may have been that the Lancashire bowlers set him, still he solved them like any Senior Wrangler. Holmes scored his 132 out of 232 in three hours and ten minutes. This morning he made 55 in twenty-two strokes, including nine boundaries. In all he hit eighteen fours. Thrice only in his innings did he make a mistake—at 39, when he was nearly stumped, at 116, when he was beaten by a fast length ball from Cook, snicking it through the slips and when he got out from a poor stroke to mid-off. It was not an artistic innings in the sense that an innings by his colleague Sutcliffe cannot fail to be. That is to say, there was no sting of the player's personality in it. It was batsmanship that told us nothing of the man himself except of such of his physical attributes as keen eyesight and quick feet. There was no warm temperament in the innings, none of the animal spirits. Shelley's mechanical automaton might easily have batted like this had it taken to cricket. It is not that Holmes was slow; as a fact he was unusually bustling for Holmes. Besides, slow batsmanship does not always mean batsmanship of no individuality. Quaife even in his most passive mood is an artist, solving his problems in his own way, applying a technique which is as native and as unselfconscious as his respiratory system itself.

Holmes is invariably the manufactured batsman, working definitely to rule. He bats as he does, it seems, because he has been well drilled to it. This, of course, is not to deprecate his play: one is merely seeking to classify him. He is a utilitarian through and through—and by no means a dull fellow. Jeremy Bentham himself must have had his skittish Bank Holidays. Holmes showed to all of us the uses of watchfulness and swift footplay. His on drives were cleverly timed with the body over the ball. They had no free body swing in them; rather was there a touch of the short-armed pull in the strokes. Holmes puts a large amount of forearm action into all his hits; even his defensive forward push is made with his body more or less erect and the bat far away from it at arm's length. He has a late cut which is most dexterously placed. This was his fourth century against Lancashire in six games played during the post-war period.

Before the Lancashire attack was collared, Kilner flashed an adventuresome bat at all balls to a gay purpose. He hit Cook's bowling five times to the boundary in a bright but valuable innings. His cavalier ways must have done much to reassure his colleagues in the pavilion that Oldroyd's over-throw in the second over of the morning had been a mishap and that the Lancashire bowlers had few terrors. At lunch the Yorkshire score was 285 for five wickets. Thenceforward the crowd of some 29,000 had occasion for joyful noisiness as Burton, Robinson, Macaulay, Wilson and Allen cut and drove the faltering attack to their hearts' content. Even the last wicket made 52 in 25 minutes. Of two characteristics only had Lancashire reason consistently to be proud. The fielding was always keen and sure—Boddington behind the wicket had most skilful moments—while through all the gruelling hurly-burly the bowlers showed a brave and sportsmanlike spirit. One was thankful indeed to note this latter grace, for on too many occasions this summer Lancashire bowlers have been known to accept ill-fortune with ugly faces. Cook again endured to the point of sheer martyrdom and such is the diverting nature of cricket that during Cook's best bowling spell of the day—in his first seven overs in fact—six fours were hit.

The Yorkshire innings lasted six hours and twenty minutes and 466 runs came by the bat from 140 overs and two balls. Lancashire's score of 153 on Saturday took three hours and a half, and the Yorkshire bowlers sent down 77 overs and two balls. These figures will perhaps point eloquently enough the difference in spirit between Lancashire's and Yorkshire's batsmanship in the first act of the game.

THIRD DAY

There was but an hour and three-quarters play in the Lancashire and Yorkshire game today. Rain came to Lancashire's rescue and just before five o'clock Yorkshire gave up the struggle against the weather which they had been engaged in all through the day.

When the game went on at half-past eleven the wicket was slow and easy. At the end of three-quarters of an hour's cricket Rhodes and Kilner started to spin the ball rather abruptly. Then, just as Lancashire folk in the crowd were getting definitely anxious, the first rain of the day came and drove the cricketers to the pavilion for forty minutes, and more important still for Lancashire, placed the turf again in a state of innocence. Before lunch there was an hour and thirty-five minutes' cricket, and Lancashire lifted the Monday evening's score of 63 for one wicket to 139 for two wickets.

Ernest Tyldesley was brilliantly caught from a drive off the thirty-eighth ball of the day. This was sent by Waddington. It pitched a short length and Tyldesley hit it strongly towards mid on. It looked a good boundary until Oldroyd jumped up from nowhere, snatched the ball and, though he slipped on the wet grass and fell on his back heavily, kept a tight and triumphant grip. Tyldesley had batted like a man impossible to get out. Though circumstances pressed heavily on him there was nothing unhappy in his play. It was magnificent to see a cricketer facing an inimical hour so strongly with such dignity. He did not allow the imminence of defeat for Lancashire to cast a blight on his play; he was true to himself all the time. His strokes had the ring of decision, his forward drives were resolute. His old half-cock bane was not on him. His innings had sound and most polished technique, and his eye for a poor ball never failed. He hit ten fours and batted one hour and a quarter, scoring his 51 out of a total of 74.

With Tyldesley out Hallows and Sharp had to go cautiously. Backed up by the weather they held the third Lancashire wicket till twenty minutes to five. Neither batsman worried about boundary hits. In the pre-lunch period the Yorkshire bowlers sent down 174 balls and thirty scoring strokes only were made. Hallows was caught at slip from the fifth ball bowled when the game was allowed to go on at half-past four. Then, with Barnes in, the rain put an end to the game. Hallows was batting two hours and three-quarters. Yorkshire bowled and fielded determinedly, but only Kilner gave the batsmen any large amount of trouble.

Kilner is a most attractive left-handed bowler and the Yorkshire authorities, so it has always seemed to the writer, tend to underrate his ability to get men out. On a turf that in the slightest degree favours the spinning ball Kilner can be very dangerous. In such circumstances his break is most disconcertingly pitched on the middle and leg stumps—the place where the good left-hander is ever striving to pitch—and the ball whips across just as the bat comes down. His length is good and he has a nicely varied flight.

Sharp's batsmanship today has been exceedingly skilful. The Yorkshire bowlers used all their wits for some ninety minutes to rid themselves of his obstruction, but he hardly ever gave them the faintest hope. He played the good length breaking ball with a forward lunge, keeping the bat close to the left leg and the left foot close to the line of the ball. Not often, nowadays, does one see the forward method used as a specific to the turning ball. The wicket today, of course, has been so slow that it permitted this so-called old-fashioned method. On a really sticky wicket maybe back play is the safer way. Sharp, whether his game be offensive or defensive definitely hits the ball; rarely does he merely hang out his bat passively. Even in doubt—when a ball has baffled him—he makes a recognisable stroke. 'Always make some sort of a stroke' was the advice of a great Yorkshire cricketer to the boys of a public school a season or two ago—'even if it's the wrong stroke. Anything is better than a dead bat.'

YORKSHIRE V LANCASHIRE 1921
SCORES
LANCASHIRE

First Innings		Second Innings	
Makepeace, c Robinson, b Rhodes	39	b Robinson	0
Hallows, c Sutcliffe, b Robinson	10	c Holmes, b Macaulay	43
Tyldesley (E.), c Macaulay, b Waddington	6	c Oldroyd, b Waddington	51
J. Sharp, lbw, b Macaulay	28		
J. R. Barnes, b Rhodes	19	not out	37
Tyldesley (J.), b Waddington	2	not out	1
Tyldesley (R.), c Macaulay, b Waddington	6		
M. N. Kenyon, c Holmes, b Rhodes	19		
R. A. Boddington, lbw, b Wilson	5		
Cook, c Sutcliffe, b Wilson	4		
C. S. Marriott not out	0		
Extras	15	Extras	12
Total	153	Total (for 3)	144

YORKSHIRE

First Innings	
Holmes, c Kenyon, b Cook	132
Sutcliffe, b Cook	10
Oldroyd, b Cook	21
Kilner, c Boddington, bTyldesley (J.)	39
Rhodes, b Cook	9
Robinson, c & b Tyldesley (R.)	59
D. C. F. Burton, c Marriott, b Cook	52
Macaulay, lbw, b Marriott	72
Waddington, c Boddington, b Cook	6
E. R. Wilson not out	33
Allen, c Hallows, b Marriott	33
Extras	23
Total	489

THE ROSES MATCHES 1919-1939
BOWLING ANALYSIS

Lancashire—First Innings

	O.	M.	R.	W.		O.	M.	R.	W.
Robinson	7	2	21	1	Rhodes	21·3	12	22	3
Waddington	17	5	38	3	Macaulay	17	10	20	1
Wilson	15	3	35	2					

Second Innings

	O.	M.	R.	W.		O.	M.	R.	W.
Robinson	10	2	29	1	Rhodes	14	2	36	0
Waddington	14	3	23	1	Macaulay	11	3	22	1
Wilson	11·3	5	17	0	Kilner	6	4	5	0

Yorkshire—First Innings

	O.	M.	R.	W.		O.	M.	R.	W.
Tyldesley (J.)	33	4	140	1	Marriott	36·2	5	109	2
Cook	53	12	145	6	Tyldesley (R.)	18	2	72	1

YORKSHIRE V LANCASHIRE 1922

June 3/5/6 Bramall Lane

FIRST DAY

ONCE again comes the ancient feud and the scene this time is the bleak wastes of Bramall Lane, Sheffield, a place where the sun seems to shine only as it shines on a withered heath putting all things in an inimical light. A proper setting for cricket so grimly antagonistic as the cricket we get in Lancashire and Yorkshire matches. Lancashire had first innings on Saturday, and it lasted from noon till close on six o'clock, and at the finish was worth 307 runs. There were, of course, the customary intervals for the taking of sustenance, and urgently the cricketers must have needed it, for the action was rather harrowing. All day long Fortune was wayward, wooing the Red Rose now, wooing the White Rose next. To the end she was a coquette; the game is still anybody's.

The wicket was good and fast. Occasionally it seemed to the writer to have a lively kick; such wickets have been known to crumble on the third day. In excellent spirits the Lancashire innings started, thanks to Makepeace who played a sweet game. Three handsome boundary hits did honour to his new white bat almost before one had settled down in one's seat. (The term is merely conventional—one cannot really settle down at Bramall Lane.) A little over half an hour's play put Lancashire on a prosperous track. Then Makepeace was seized with madness. He played a ball crisply to the off side and dashed down the wicket. 'No' shouted Hallows in high panic. Makepeace turned and his face showing an apprehension of the worst kind, he struggled to get back, but was run out comfortably. The desperate convulsions of the batsman to regain his crease and the easeful deportment of the wicket keeper as he broke the stumps made a sight for the ironic gods. Makepeace departed in sorrow; he said afterwards he was feeling perfectly set when the accident happened. The run ought never to have been attempted—there was no need to steal runs on a fast wicket, with the batsmen going along so confidently. The crowd roared out its rapture a little cruelly, one thought, at this dashing to earth of the dainty piece of porcelain in batsmanship Makepeace had fashioned.

But the crowd had little enough to shout about for a long time after. Ernest Tyldesley and Hallows with responsibility plainly sitting on the shoulders of both—hopping from one batsman to the other—put solid bats to the Yorkshire bowlers, who made frantic efforts to take advantage of the good luck sent to Yorkshire in Makepeace's downfall. But Tyldesley and Hallows prevailed, and at lunch the Lancashire score was 111 for one wicket.

The hurly-burly went on in the afternoon, the stunted field taking on the shadow cast by the great multitude that sat around—18,000 frankly partisan Yorkshire folk. And as soon as it became evident Tyldesley and Hallows were to go their ways further, waiting their chances, keeping straight bats for good balls, cracking loose ones here and there, now it was that the crowd got restive for a while. As Tyldesley and Hallows' partnership grew formidable minute by minute a strange quiet fell on the ground. 'They don't like this,' said a Lancashire man. 'If it goes on much longer they'll all go home.' 'Put Wilfred Rhodes on,' howled a voice from the multitude's interior. And Rhodes was put on. Cunningly he set his field; cunningly he dangled the bait before the batsmen—luscious half-volleys now and then went up to the wicket. There is a quite ingenuous simplicity about Rhodes's bowling today; his old-time spin looks to have gone and even his length falters. He seems frankly to exploit the power of his reputation when he bowls nowadays. 'They'll get out to me because I'm Rhodes,' he appears to say. And one can also imagine him saying, like La Pucelle in 'Henry VI': 'For I have loaden me with many spoils. Using no other but my name.' But Rhodes the spell-binder did not work on Saturday.

There was, for a good hour after the lunch interval, perfect peace in the Lancashire ranks. One looked on Hallows' and Tyldesley's cricket and saw in it a baffling problem for the perspiring bowlers.

At three o'clock Lancashire's score was 150 for one wicket.

The bats of Hallows and Tyldesley were wide and solid. 'Shall we get 400 up today?' asked a Lancastrian affably. 'For four or five wickets?'

Once Robinson, who plays the part of Yorkshire's fast bowler, seemed to get a horrid vision before him of the whole afternoon spent in the field in vain against these two obstructing men, Tyldesley and Hallows. For Robinson having once in a way missed the broad bat of Ernest Tyldesley and hit the pad of him instead, shrieked to the umpire an appeal for lbw. And the umpire answering 'not out', Robinson stood in the middle of the wicket, head down, but eyes glaring daggers left and right. He was so discommoded he walked to his wrong position when the field crossed over.

It was a brief space of time after this that Fortune decided to play the coquette.

Perhaps there was not enough of the adventurous spirit about Lancashire batsmen to keep her true to them. At 3.15 Hallows attempted a leg-glance from a fast ball sent by Macaulay. He missed it, and it grazed his leg and went to the boundary. Macaulay appealed, and the umpire pointed his finger to the heavens. Lancashire 165 for two. Hallows' innings was great in spirit if not in technique. He gave us, once again, a hint of his 'big match' temperament, but his cricket had hardly the range of scoring strokes demanded of the high-class batsman. He achieved four beautiful straight drives, and these caused one to feel more than ever that his true game is not the game of passive resistance. Hallows' innings lasted nearly two hours and he hit eight boundaries: his partnership with Tyldesley produced 127 runs. The Sheffield crowd roared appreciation at Hallows as he walked back to the pavilion: they admire a good Lancashire innings in Yorkshire—when the batsman is out.

The crowd now indeed had reason to wake up. Sharp obviously short of practice, shaped indifferently and was soon out. Barnes showed a touch of quality in one or two wristy strokes to the off side, but he, too, got out lbw. James Tyldesley tried to hit a ball out of the county; Parkin batted like a man blindfolded; and Richard Tyldesley was caught from the most wretched full toss on the leg side one could imagine. The game turned right over in one sudden movement. Lancashire 163 for two—and Lancashire 216 for seven. The crowd was alive and kicking at this. Out of the heart of it came the passionate greeting 'Good owd Yorkshire'. And on the pavilion a man said 'it's a very funny game is cricket' and said it with the air of one to whom the thought had just at that second come as quite a new and beautiful thought. The Yorkshire bowlers discovered fresh energy all at once; the fieldsmen stood on the toe points. Even Robinson forgot his trials and disappointments.

At the tea interval Tyldesley was 101 not out. Immediately the game was taken up Kenyon was caught. Cook, the last hope of his side, came in, the total 232 for eight wickets—a sad state of affairs after so heartening a prelude. Cook straightaway played a stonewall game. His bat went tap-tap-tap, making the noise of a woodpecker on a quiet day. And Tyldesley announced his new policy over the field by the swinging blows of his bat. Skilfully the two batsmen arranged for the bulk of the bowling to go to Tyldesley's end. Tyldesley's temper was challenging; he played like a man forgetful of the wickets behind him. Only the ball and the boundary existed for him now. And Cook went on with his careful tap-tap-tapping. ''It 'em' the crowd roared in derision. Yet when Ernest Tyldesley did hit them—and what is more hit them out of the field—the crowd did not appear perfectly satisfied. One of Tyldesley's on-drives crashed to the top of the pavilion, just missing the window, but causing flight and some palpitation among committee men watching the game inside.

Tyldesley's batting after tea was as valiant as his batting in the Test Match at Old Trafford last summer. And in this mood he is as brilliant as Hobbs, and perhaps even more powerful. His on-driving had grandeur because of the fury of the blows and the proud poise of the body. He jumped down the wicket, turning good length balls into bad. But though he batted in a gloriously wanton way, there was nothing cheap or thoughtless in his innings. All but a few of his strokes were correctly made. His technique was just as sound as ever, only a new spirit informed it, a 'death or glory' spirit. For 35 minutes Tyldesley kept his bat straight. The ninth Lancashire wicket added 53 priceless runs, four of them made by Cook, whose innings was admirable. This last minute rally by Lancashire plainly tasted bitterly in the crowd and in the Yorkshire side. Lancashire had been down on the carpet surely at tea time. And with Blomley the last man in, Lancashire needed but 15 for the highly respectable score of 300.

'Well,' said Rhodes, Robinson, Macaulay, Kilner and Waddington in vehement unison, 'they won't get 'em.' At least so they appeared to be saying, as into action they went for a last shaking onslaught. Frustration for them again. Tyldesley's fury increased immediately Blomley revealed great gaps in his armour. A giant heave of the bat sent a ball from Robinson to the on-side, and Lancashire, after all, reached the third hundred. 'Who'd a'thought it?' asked a Yorkshire man, and then went in search of a drink.

Tyldesley was last out, caught in the quest of more glory. His innings lasted four hours and twenty minutes. After the tea interval he scored 77 runs in an hour out of 87. He gave no chance, unless one calls a chance a terrific return to Macaulay with his score 78. The hit was a superb straight drive and the bowler was lucky not to get badly hurt. Hardly ever did he cut. Yet with all the predominance of on-side play Tyldesley's innings was always good to watch, for the reason that he never allowed the on-drive to degenerate into a mere pull. Tyldesley's on-drive is made, indeed, with a bat swung down straight from above the head, the left leg going to the ball's pitch and pointing in the direction of the stroke. When he does hit square it is a beautiful turn over the wrist and not a crude mow of the bat to get the ball round. His glances to the leg-side were crisp and safe. Young cricketers on the field must have learned excellent lessons from his treatment of the ball bowled well up to the batsman on or just outside his legs. The left foot was kept close to the line of flight and the stroke made with a straight bat in front of the left leg, a quick turnover of the right wrist controlling the hit's direction at the last second.

The Lancashire total was just good enough, but the making of it told too eloquently of the team's batting weaknesses. Only three batsmen are really to be trusted yet. The Yorkshire bowling looked excellent when it was getting wickets, but commonplace when it wasn't. Macaulay is a good but by no means great bowler. He has the exceptional merit of 'nip' from the pitch and a length a little too short for hitting. But one did not get the impression of resource from his work.

SECOND DAY

Life no less than art achieves now and again an expressive picture. In the scene at Bramall Lane this morning, we had a complete representation of Lancashire and Yorkshire cricket: the stern spirit of it was given significant form by the crowd's mountainous bulk, the hard antagonism of the play, the ugliness of the setting of chimneys and huddled tenements, all of them telling of the utter competitive life that is led in this part of England. Almost the only note in the cricket that went on to a ceaseless roar from the multitude was the note of conflict, harsh indeed. Almost, one says, but not wholly. Scourging though the fight, one cricketer there was to remind us of the grace which is the game's very soul. Sutcliffe's bat made sweet curves, and like the true artist, he was aware of the beauty he was fashioning. The contrast his batting made with the dominant unloveliness of the morning's action moved one romantically, and provoked the thought of the jewel in the toad's head.

The Lancashire bowlers got their first taste of blood after half an hour's work, Holmes attempting to cut Cook's fast ball and sending it into slip's hands. And from then for some gruelling ninety minutes onwards no other satisfaction came to Lancashire. In a stand for Yorkshire's second wicket Oldroyd and Sutcliffe added 92 runs, playing with a confidence that put the crowd into a state of blessedness. Yet it cannot be said that the batsmen, any more than the bowlers, were ever masters: the issue was dramatically even—one got the sense from the play now of a violent tug-of-war, the rope taut, with no man giving ground at this end or that end.

Only a solitary boundary hit came in the first hour. Cook's bowling had matchless length: in 65 minutes he bowled 13 overs, five maidens, for 20 runs and one wicket. The authentic Sheffield roar went into the sky as Yorkshire reached the first hundred, after some hundred minutes' toil. Lunch time was nigh, and vast appetites eager for it, when a disaster fell on Yorkshire, turning to vanity the thought of meat and drink. Oldroyd pushed a ball to the off side, and to the crowd's dismay Sutcliffe dashed down the pitch. Stung to madness he was by the very imp of mischief that pricked Makepeace to ruin on Saturday. Oldroyd did not budge an inch, and Sutcliffe saw his wicket broken far away behind him—in sad perspective indeed must his wicket have looked to him for he was in Oldroyd's crease when the stumps were broken. A Lancashire man witnessed Sutcliffe's unhappy downfall with mixed feelings—gladness it provided because a dangerous Yorkshire stand had been ended, but sorrow also at the sight of sheer grace trapped in a snare.

Sutcliffe batted for two hours and a half. He is surely the most artistic professional batsman in the country. Forward play is his main game, and he manages it with an elegant thrust of the left leg, the most easeful swing of the bat, with the wrists putting polish on the stroke at the penultimate second. There is indeed a pretty little flick of his bat at every stroke's end: it is the artist's way of expressing delight in work well done—one sees it and thinks of Dickens' flourish of a signature. Whistler's vain but charming butterfly. Sutcliffe perhaps is wanting the power necessary to handle an attack drastically and so win a match. But amongst defensive batsmen he stands apart: he gives to utility coloured feathers to preen. The score at lunch was Yorkshire 188 for two. In the two hours and a quarter's play of the morning, the Lancashire bowlers sent 57 overs down, including 17 maidens, for 110 runs. In this time only nine boundaries were hit.

From the first ball after lunch Roy Kilner was lbw to Richard Tyldesley. Rhodes and Oldroyd added 44 and then Rhodes was caught, fourth out at 182. Seven runs later Oldroyd fell to a cunning ball by Richard Tyldesley and with Yorkshire's total unchanged, Robinson was leg before wicket. Thus in quick time the game suffered yet again one of those convulsions which strike fire out of a lover of cricket. We had all imagined the play in the morning to be strenuous but soon it was apparent we have been living in a place becalmed. For the match waxed fit for the fighting gods. The two sides set teeth grimly in the struggle for the first innings lead—for points that might well have a critical value. As Norman Kilner and Wilson bent low on their bats the pot started a-boiling. One seemed to feel the heat of the antagonistic fires that were setting it in motion. The batsmen were plucky and attacked the bowling. Runs came from cracking bats and the roars of the crowd were like the winds in the woods on a wild day. It was war to the knife now; art and method were not heeded by the batsmen or the bowlers. Nothing but naked conflict mattered in this hour; grit and brute strength were pitted openly against grit and brute strength. Surely cricket has never been played more fiercely than these rivals played it at this period: surely it has never had its airs and graces so ruffled.

For three quarters of an hour the pace of the game was too giddy for the eyes to follow. One got only an impressionistic picture of it—bowlers scowling and heaving themselves to the wickets; bats handled drastically; fieldsmen agitated and awry; snicks through consternated slips, taking your breath away; heavy thuds to the boundary. And all the time a packed mass of 26,000 Yorkshire folk turning the sunny afternoon into Bedlam. Madder and madder went the speed of the match. The batsmen were getting on top by sheer desperation and quick eyes. And suddenly the Lancashire fielding went to pieces. With Yorkshire's score 237 there happened one of the craziest kettle of fish surely ever witnessed in the cricket field. Kilner and Wilson got into a muddle over a run and discovered themselves in the same crease. Blomley had the ball in his hand and needed but to throw it to the other end to run Kilner out by half the length of the pitch. But as Kilner dashed down the wicket confusion fell upon Blomley, who, instead of sending the ball through the air after Kilner, rolled it along the grass, like some old gentleman on a bowling green. Kilner stumbled, but none the less he got home in time.

The howls of the crowd as Kilner fled to his crease, the ball following him, were the howls of the Furies that Orestes heard. Never, indeed, has one known a crowd so explosive as this one; never has one known on a cricket ground such noise as this one made at every ball bowled. The passions of the mob passed like hot fluid through the ranks; it was a

Shakespearian crowd in the sudden changefulness of its emotions. Cheers greeted a good hit; mockery fell on the fieldsman that bungled. In the Wilson-Kilner stand Parkin's bowling was punished severely and the crowd taunted him. And when at last Parkin gave way to Cook and the batting went into comparative quiet again, the crowd shouted 'Put Parkin on; put Parkin on.'

The seventh Yorkshire wicket fell at 244, Kilner falling to a magnificent catch by Hallows. At tea Yorkshire's score was 263 for seven. Forty-five were needed by Yorkshire for a first innings victory when the game went on. Macaulay and Wilson played capitally, tackling the bowling with true Yorkshire pugnacity. The total reached 283 before Macaulay was caught on the leg side. Dolphin, next man in, hit a lusty on-side boundary; Wilson, still playing a resolute game, cut a ball from Richard Tyldesley through the slips for four. At 296 Dolphin fell into Richard Tyldesley's lbw trap. One Yorkshire wicket to fall now and a dozen runs wanted. Waddington came in as calm as a master batsman. 'Put Parkin on' again moaned the crowd. Kenyon arranged and rearranged his field, and trusted his length bowlers.

Cook went at it with all his heart; Richard Tyldesley controlled his leg break with amazing steadiness. Still, the batsmen persisted; seven overs they withstood, and at the finish of them Yorkshire were 306, one run behind; Tyldesley now got himself ready to bowl at Waddington; the Lancashire field crept close to the wicket. And the crowd got itself ready to roar out Yorkshire's victory to the world. The ball which Tyldesley at length bowled was slow, well pitched in the air, and so spun as to break away as it hit the turf. And how did the man Waddington play it—Waddington, who had so far been all composure, all confidence? He jumped recklessly out of his crease, missed the break, and was stumped. The match so far was Lancashire's. At the vision of this lunacy of Waddington's the crowd did not believe its myriad eyes. It had been ready to move Sheffield with a shout of triumph; its pent up breath passed out of its ranks like air from a pricked bladder. A silence fell over the field more sensational even than the loudest of the afternoon's thousand ear-splitting noises; it was the silence of men and women sick at heart through hope outraged.

Much of the anxiety Lancashire passed through during the afternoon was of the team's own making. Good fielding would have put an end to Yorkshire's innings long before the race became neck and neck. After the fall of Yorkshire's sixth wicket the fielding fell into slovenliness. An easy chance of stumping given by Oldroyd when he was 34 went begging. Wilson was missed in the slips with his score 21. The frenzy of the crowd seemed to upset the Lancashire men badly. Before lunch the bowling had all round excellence; in the crisis during the afternoon Richard Tyldesley alone and perhaps Cook, kept a cool head. Parkin was a big disappointment, and it seems that the Sheffield ground—and crowd—will be the death of him. Three years ago he bowled against Yorkshire at Bramall Lane and had no wickets for 99. This afternoon 74 runs were hit from his bowling, and again his wickets were none. Thus his record at Bramall Lane is none for 173. Yet before lunch today he bowled really well, and at least one catch was missed from him. James Tyldesley on the whole possessed little length or direction. Cook was mainly his own steady self. But had Richard Tyldesley not been present Yorkshire might really have left Lancashire a hundred behind. He bowled all day with the coolest art, using his leg break with the nicest judgment and keeping a length astonishingly accurate for a bowler of his spin.

Oldroyd's innings was the work of a sound craftsman, but Wilson's cricket had a keener sting in it. There was the flavour of the public school in his batting; he was the Captain of the House fighting odds. His driving often had both style and power.

The stormy day—the stormiest the writer has ever known at cricket—proceeded to a calm end with Hallows and Makepeace putting confident bats to the Yorkshire bowling. As the crowd beat up the dust on the homeward journey one felt a touch of disillusionment somewhere. And if one has written of the crowd in this account almost as much as one has written of the cricket itself, one's excuse must be that the crowd acted a considerable part in the day's play. It was, indeed, the villain of the piece.

THIRD DAY

The Lancashire eleven was afflicted by its annual attack of Yorkshiritis this afternoon and lost to their old rivals once again. The Lancashire innings which began so promisingly on Monday evening petered out for 144 and Yorkshire at the expense of only four wickets were the conquerors.

The crowd, though not half the size of Monday's, found itself equal to all the joyful noise the occasion demanded from true men of Sheffield. It was a finish that brought to the mind of a Lancashire man recollections of many an old unhappy battle long ago—battles between Lancashire and Yorkshire in which greater cricketers fought than those of today's fight, and yet in which even Lancashire's greatest men were unable to hold on to an advantage, even when they had all but pressed the enemy down to the mat. Why has Yorkshire the toughness of mind in these games never to lose hope and determination to win till the day is lost, and why has Lancashire not got it? The students in the psychology of 'county' might find interesting uses for research here.

The Lancashire innings was only too plainly activated by the skinflint philosophy of 'What we have we'll hold.' Seemingly the two points won yesterday on the first innings contented the Lancashire batsmen, who from the outset this morning played as though for a drawn match. They did not even exploit their natural game, but remained passive at the sight of half-volleys. The Yorkshire bowling had excellent length, but little else out of the common. Yet no attempt did Lancashire make to disturb this excellent length by a brave flourish of the bat. And so it happened that though the innings persisted till after three o'clock not more than 114 runs were added to Lancashire's score of Monday evening. And the whole of the side's ten wickets toppled down miserably in this time.

The downfall of Makepeace just after noon apparently shocked his companions, especially as soon afterwards Ernest Tyldesley was out rather unfortunately to a ball that kicked suddenly up to his bat's shoulder and thence went daintily into the slips. At this point Lancashire's dire need was for a bold, punishing batsman to go in and keep company with Hallows, who played the right game for the side by defending one end of the crease with a resolute bat. But at the other end it certainly should have been somebody's business to try to take the Yorkshire bowling by the scruff of the neck. And not a batsman of ample skill and courage showed himself.

Even a long stand by Hallows and Barnes for the fourth wicket hardly served Lancashire's purpose fully, for though it lasted 65 minutes it produced but 54 runs. This feeble pace on a reasonably good wicket against bowling of length but bowling definitely lacking real venom! Of course the Yorkshire attack thrived on the jejune batsmanship. The bowlers found themselves tall men in contrast to the diminished fry from Old Trafford. It was the old, old story—Yorkshire on Lancashire nerves, Lancashire irresolution and Yorkshire grit. Hallows batted in fine, defensive style, but a policy of caution may be perfectly consistent with a determination to smite half-volleys. The Yorkshire fielding was brilliant —Robinson on the off-side a very Australian in agility and swiftness. Barnes's innings promised excellent work in due time in the best cricket.

When Yorkshire went in to make the 146 needed for victory it seemed for a while that there was going to be a fight. For Cook bowled magnificently, and the Yorkshiremen batted for all the world as though they had been contaminated by the Lancashire palsy. In some eighty minutes they could score only 47 for two wickets. In this time Cook bowled eleven overs for six maidens, seven runs and one wicket. Then came Roy Kilner to show how far a cavalier heart will take a man. In less than half an hour afterwards, the doom was spoken, as they sing in Verdi, of Lancashire.

Kilner and Sutcliffe added 58 runs, mainly by dashing boundary blows from Kilner's defiant bat. And so Lancashire went to dust, and moreover went there unmourned, even by men in the crowd from their own county. For Lancashire had all too obviously lost the match through cricket having in it little fineness of spirit. When Yorkshire needed but six to win a ball was driven to the outfield, and one saw a Lancashire fieldsman running leisurely after it, as if to say, 'Why should I put myself to hard labour now? The game is Yorkshire's.' It is not easy to be sympathetic with a side that will not to a man fight an issue till the last second of the last minute. Makepeace, at any rate, played the game to the bitter end, sternly chasing the swiftest hit to the edge of the field, no matter how close to victory Yorkshire were moving.

The match was over just before six o'clock, and the better men won. It was a match, indeed, that ruthlessly exposed the Lancashire side's weaknesses. Lancashire at present possess three reliable batsmen, three good bowlers, and a number of nondescripts who could scarcely have found a place in county cricket ten years ago.

Sutcliffe again conducted himself like an England batsman. His innings, if not chanceless, was good enough. He had stronger claims than any other Yorkshire batsman to a share of the good fortune thrust at his eleven from the 'butter-fingers' of the Lancashire fieldsmen. One could not count the catches dropped by Lancashire in this game; there were enough of them to lose a match against the next team of rustic policemen.

SCORES

LANCASHIRE

First Innings		Second Innings	
Makepeace, run out	19	lbw, b Robinson	20
Hallows, lbw, b Macaulay	66	lbw, b Kilner (R.)	47
Tyldesley (E.), c Kilner, b Robinson	178	c Robinson, b Macaulay	4
J. Sharp, c Dolphin, b Robinson	1	b Robinson	1
J. R. Barnes, lbw, b Robinson	3	b Rhodes	43
Tyldesley (J.), st Dolphin, b Macaulay	4	c Robinson, b Rhodes	12
Parkin, b Robinson	1	c Robinson, b Kilner	5
Tyldesley (R.), c Kilner, b Waddington	6	b Rhodes	0
M. N. Kenyon, c Kilner, b Macaulay	4	c Macaulay, b Kilner	3
Cook, lbw, b Rhodes	4	c Macaulay, b Kilner	3
Blomley not out	0	lbw, b Rhodes	0
Extras	21	Extras	9
Total	307	Total	144

THE ROSES MATCHES 1919-1939
YORKSHIRE

First Innings		Second Innings	
Holmes, c Tyldesley (R.), b Cook	19	b Cook	5
Sutcliffe run out	65	not out	73
Oldroyd, c Hallows, b Tyldesley (R.)	77	c Blomley, b Tyldesley (R.)	8
Kilner (R.), lbw, b Tyldesley (R.)	1	st Bromley, b Parkin	47
Rhodes, c Tyldesley (R.), b Cook	13	not out	8
Kilner (N.), c Hallows, b Tyldesley (R.)	36	lbw, b Parkin	0
Robinson, lbw, b Tyldesley (R.)	0		
Wilson not out	49		
Macaulay, c Barnes, b Cook	15		
Dolphin, lbw, b Tyldesley (R.)	5		
Waddington, st Blomley, b Tyldesley (R.)	3		
Extras	23	Extras	7
Total	306	Total (for 4)	148

BOWLING ANALYSIS

LANCASHIRE—First Innings

	O.	M.	R.	W.		O.	M.	R.	W.
Robinson	25·1	7	68	4	Macaulay	28	5	79	3
Waddington	22	4	54	1	Rhodes	21	2	48	1
Kilner	19	7	37	0					

Second Innings

	O.	M.	R.	W.		O.	M.	R.	W.
Robinson	22	12	32	2	Kilner (R.)	22·5	10	25	3
Waddington	5	0	21	0	Rhodes	20	8	28	4
Macaulay	22	9	29	1					

YORKSHIRE—First Innings

	O.	M.	R.	W.		O.	M.	R.	W.
Parkin	23	6	74	0	Tyldesley (J.)	14	0	59	0
Cook	46	16	80	3	Tyldesley (R.)	36·1	11	70	6

Second Innings

	O.	M.	R.	W.		O.	M.	R.	W.
Parkin	15	4	41	2	Tyldesley (J.)	1	0	7	0
Cook	19	7	41	1	Tyldesley (E.)	0·4	0	6	0
Tyldesley (R.)	16	5	46	1					

YORKSHIRE V LANCASHIRE 1922

August 5/7/8 Old Trafford

FIRST DAY

THE old occasion comes again—Lancashire and Yorkshire at Old Trafford, the game spiky with antagonism, the crowd now shouting joy to the sky and now tasting bitter ashes in the mouth. The old familiar occasion, as it always was and always will be. A multitude of some 20,000 watched the cricket, a multitude that as the day passed grew to immensity from the handful of tiny boys who were at the gates very early in the morning, their eyes still full of sleep. These little boys had the usual packages of sustenance wrapped in paper, which sustenance, again as usual, they ate long before the legal luncheon hour. Throughout the afternoon came the piping applause of these youngsters, in whose eyes every cricketer on the field is a hero with a halo. The crowd overflowed on to Old Trafford's sacrosanct turf—the greenest and the most beautiful turf in England—and there was the customary restlessness of the sea in the ladies' pavilion. Members of the club had come from all parts of the county; there were old men who talked wistfully of Hornby and Barlow—just as in a few generations hence old men will mumble, on this same Old Trafford pavilion, 'Ay, but we've no Hallows, now, no Tyldesley, no Parkin—heigh he were a rum 'un!' Saturday, at Old Trafford was a Lancashire and Yorkshire match set on its ideal stage; perhaps a touch of Sheffield's frenzy in the crowd was needed for perfection—there's nothing untrue to the spirit of a battle of the Roses in Bramall Lane's honest temper.

Well, the folk that walked down the Warwick Road on Saturday evening and beat up the dust had the stuff for hot conversation; they also might well have suffered from a sort of indigestion of mind, for the Lancashire cricketers had served out to them a dish of cricket most drastically mixed. The crowd—compact mainly of Lancastrians—had seen Lancashire bat so badly that shame might well have passed

95

like a warm wind into every corner of the county where cricket is played; yet also had the crowd seen Lancashire bowl with the hero's skill and determination in circumstances that easily might have put hope out of their hearts for a long time. After the superb attack of Lancashire at the fall of the day—oh that one could forget the mean-spirited batsmanship that had gone before! Perhaps it will be said Yorkshire made runs on Saturday not much more handsomely than Lancashire; someone is sure to ask: Is there such a difference between Lancashire's 118 and Yorkshire's 108 for six? The truth is Yorkshire's batsmanship was set a stiffer task than Lancashire's. On the dubious but by no means bad wicket, Yorkshire's bowling had not a tithe of the spin and nip of Lancashire's. Wilson and Kilner turned the ball slowly. Cook and Norbury caused it to break and 'pop' from the turf in a way that disconcerted a spectator's, let alone a batsman's eye. The Yorkshire bowling was good, but not uncommonly good; the Lancashire bowling was so excellent that less resolute batsmen than the Yorkshiremen would have found it a scourging labour even to reach a hundred all out. In a word, Yorkshire batted moderately well against a capital attack, and Lancashire batted with weakness against an attack of not uncommon quality. Moreover Yorkshire scored at the respectable rate of 50 an hour, and Lancashire tottered about the crease for three hours and forty minutes for their 118. In ninety minutes before lunch Lancashire made only 49, and 30 of these came in the first half-hour. Makepeace and Hallows, indeed, began to score in a normal way. That 19 runs only came in an hour after Makepeace and Hallows were out—surely this looks as though early disasters set panic stalking through the Lancashire ranks. Barnes in an hour could discover three solitary runs; in seventy minutes he compiled (compiled surely is good!) eight. Ernest Tyldesley, at the end of his first hour and a quarter at the wicket was 15. No wonder the indulgence of the Old Trafford crowd found itself moved at last to derision; no wonder the voice of mockery let out a noise simulating apprehension when once Barnes had an authentic fling at a ball.

Ernest Tyldesley and Barnes added 25 runs for Lancashire's third wicket in seventy minutes. In that time

Barnes had some 100 balls bowled at him and Tyldesley some 70. While these two cricketers were together—two forlorn lambs at the mercy of a pack of wild Yorkshire beasts!— eighteen maidens were bowled, six of them by that most menacing cricketer—of the demoniac aspect, rolling eye, with brimstone from the nostrils—E. R. Wilson. Had Saturday's wicket been fashioned out of glue, had Wilson been Wainwright and Kilner been Peel—why even than such irresolute batsmanship as Lancashire's would have been hard to justify.

As one has suggested, the day began with some promise of a fair innings by Lancashire. Hallows played an excellent game despite risky stroke to Holmes in the fifteenth over of the day. Hallows was the first Lancashire batsman out, with the total at 33. One run more, and Ernest Tyldesley went after a short run—Makepeace was not quick at backing up, and he saw himself well run out as he struggled with every muscle and nerve to get in. Makepeace was a study in dejection as he left the field, seemingly having little enough spirit in him to move his legs over the long homeward track. And so, one supposes, out of these mishaps to Lancashire at the outset, came the policy (heaven save the mark) cultivated by the others. In other words, the Yorkshire bowling was not treated on its merits, but in the light of what happened to Hallows and Makepeace, neither of whose downfalls was an evidence of a deadly attack. Of course, Wilson, Kilner and Macaulay bowled a steady length. But as Mr. Robey would observe, 'what of it?' Once upon a time it was a rule among cricketers that if a bowler was getting on top through a nasty length—why, then it was somebody's business to go in at once with a hefty bat and knock the fellow off—or perish in the attempt. There was no attempt—or little—to knock the Yorkshire bowlers off their lengths; there was merely plenty of perishing. Norbury was caught in the deep field endeavouring to play the game that it was at least the duty of one Lancashire batsman to play at the moment. Richard Tyldesley also looked like using his bat forcibly just as he got out. One does not suggest that after the unfortunate beginning of Lancashire's innings on Saturday, everybody should have run at the bowling trusting to luck and a quick eye; in a crisis there must always be one end of the wicket stubbornly defended. At the other end, though, an offensive needs to be going on. 'Get at the bowler,' said 'W. G.' a long time ago, 'before he gets at you.'

At the close of the Lancashire innings a gloom was upon the piled-up thousands. The match seemed as good as over already. Even the Yorkshire cricketers who love a fight could scarcely have looked on in contentment while palsy descended on their ancient foe. A Lancashire and Yorkshire match must surely provide a fight—not a walkover. When Yorkshire went in to bat they had only too good reason for saying, like the Constable in 'Henry V', 'Do but behold yon poor and starved band, and your fair show shall suck away their souls, leaving them but the shales and husks of men. There is not work enough for all our hordes.' If Yorkshire did nurture such sentiments, however, they were forgetting a notable fact; Lancashire, timid in batsmanship, can roar at you like any lion when it comes to attacking the wicket.

Holmes, the old thorn in Lancashire's flesh, was brilliantly caught by Richard Tyldesley from James Tyldesley's bowling—the second ball of Yorkshire's innings—and rapture came at last to Old Trafford. And when James Tyldesley caught and bowled Oldroyd in his fifth over, and Cook clean bowled Kilner in the over succeeding, the crowd had more than rapture to express; one got the hint, in the loud noise that went to the heavens, of exultant vengeance. The ball which upset Kilner's wicket deserved to be preserved somehow in a museum for cricketers—that future ages might understand that even in our time, supposed to possess little beautiful bowling, there happened on a day a break-back by Cook fit to do honour to any cricketer that ever lived—let his name be Lohmann, or J. T. Hearne, or Noakes or Stoakes, or Stiles or Brown or Thompson.

Yorkshire 13 for three—here was consolation for the afflicted crowd! Did a vision of a Yorkshire debacle come before its eyes? You could feel in the air the tense action of the will-power of thousands, all of them wishing their hearts to aching-point that another and yet another Yorkshire wicket might fall. Rhodes had reason to go down on the fresh green grass and thank his stars that he did not die the death right away. The Lancashire field gave him two innings; Cook broke through his defence and missed his stump 'the Lord knows how'—as the sailors in Mr. Kipling's verses sing. And Rhodes survived; with all his ugly two-eyed stance he survived, keeping guard in company with Sutcliffe until 60 runs were scored in three quarters of an hour. Each run made in this partnership, coming as it did after the tide seemed to have turned in Lancashire's favour, was as a hot iron plunged into the body of the crowd. 'They're in for the afternoon,' moaned a Lancashire man with a garden of red roses in his coat; ' 'Eaven 'elp us.'

When Yorkshire's score was 62 for three wickets Kenyon asked Norbury to bowl. It was a shrewd move. Sutcliffe made a snick from Norbury through the slips for four—his first bad stroke. The next ball swung and, pitching a perfect length, clean bowled Sutcliffe. In his next over Norbury had Rhodes lbw to a ball that whipped quickly from the pitch, and at 79 G. Wilson was lbw to Richard Tyldesley. The game was in the balance now; after all the hurly-burly, after all Lancashire's humiliation at the wicket, the game was now as much theirs as Yorkshire's. Here, as one waited for Macaulay to come in to join Robinson, one had a notion of the two antagonists taking breath face to face—flushed with the action, both belaboured, both scowling defiance at one another, and waiting the chance of a spring in and a decisive blow.

Macaulay and Robinson put an end to Lancashire's movement onward on Saturday. Oh, these Yorkshire rearguard actions—who does not remember them of old? Count no Yorkshire batsman out till you see the pavilion door close on his back and hear his bat flung into a corner. Robinson and Macaulay clung on till 6.30, and what is more, discovered 29 precious runs for Yorkshire. They are still to be got out, and from the excellent way they batted on Saturday we must consider them a dire menace to Lancashire this morning. Robinson was hewn out of the same rich lump of Yorkshire stuff—is it pudding?—that the gods used for the making of Hirst. The shape of his body, the roll of his movements about the field, the hang of his eye—all these are as a strident announcement of Yorkshire's character. On Saturday Robinson accomplished one or two glorious late cuts, and as he contemplated them there was a glint of satisfaction on his face. But Robinson does not expand as Hirst did, like the genial sun: there is something tart in his humours, moist though they can be. One did not like the look of his quick bat on Saturday—would that he were out, alongside Rhodes and the others.

Norbury bowled with rare life from the pitch, and dropped his off-break just at the length that draws a batsman forward, only to get him unpleasantly into two minds at the crucial moment. One has already suggested how well Cook bowled. James Tyldesley put every ounce of his strength into his attack at the beginning of the innings and Richard Tyldesley's leg-breaks were as accurate as leg-breaks well can be. But the day's play contained nothing happier than Sutcliffe's innings. It was the very sweet of batsmanship—batsmanship with a bouquet. His off-side pushes came from a light flexible bat; his body fell gently forward, telling of supreme confidence and the artist's enjoyment of his own work. Even his purely defensive strokes are free and curving in swing and pretty to see. That Sutcliffe is an England batsman must be obvious to any cricketer that knows a hawk from a handsaw. Why is he not recognised as such by Lord's? Parkin had a poor day. His bowling yet again lacked sting, and he threw his wicket away in the Lancashire innings after the manner of one for whom motley and the cap and bells are easier put on than taken off.

SECOND DAY

After rain, conditions were so bad that play was abandoned for the day.

THIRD DAY

The finish of the Lancashire and Yorkshire game at Old Trafford flung us all into high agony. The issue of it was unresolved—Lancashire frustrated, Yorkshire frustrated, the multitude frustrated. When Parkin girded up his loins to unloose the last shots of the encounter, and when the old war horse Rhodes got himself and his bat ready for the onslaught, Yorkshire needed but five runs for victory and Lancashire needed but one wicket for her greatest triumph since 1919. The crowd sat in dumb futility all aching eyes but helpless. The tension seemed to have a low throbbing sound; one would not have been astonished had a poor hysterical wight jumped out of the thousands huddled there and shouting 'Misery!' died as mad as the wild waves be.

Parkin in that last over aimed at Rhodes's defence four times, and the cricketer who is growing grey in Yorkshire's service stopped every ball. At the fifth ball the umpire let out 'No ball'. One more to Yorkshire. Yorkshire may win now in one lusty boundary hit. Bless us, Parkin, why did you not look at the crease; heaven forbid that Yorkshire should be given a shadow of a run now. So did we mumble to our distracted selves when Parkin walked on his way back to his attacking ground. Two balls to bowl and a four made anyhow—a Ranji glide or a monstrous snick—will turn the Yorkshiremen into exultant conquerors. And one little mistake by Rhodes, a quick catch or a tumbling wicket, will be as a lightning flash announcing the advent of such a clap of thunder from the crowd as will go resounding even over Yorkshire's own moors.

Did Rhodes go for glory; did he think of whiteheaded old Robson, of Somerset, who last week smote a mammoth six from the last over of the day and won immortal laurels for Somerset? Rhodes did not; he played the two last balls cannily, and scored a single from the one and only shaft left for Parkin to shoot. A drawn game, after all the hurly-burly—it was rank anti-climax. Let no one taunt Rhodes because he was more of a realist than a romantic. Yorkshire had won on the first innings; she was in possession of points immensely valuable for her championship enterprise. A sheer jump into the unknown by Rhodes—a wild speculative swipe at a good ball—and the spoils from the match in Yorkshire's keeping at this last second of the last minute are gone to an inveterate foe—and perhaps gone also is the tourney's prize. Rhodes saw no gifts from the gods in Parkin's last over—in a phrase, he did not clout his way to victory simply because Parkin was on his way there too. They jammed at the gate and then it closed.

Yorkshire did not suffer the keener prostration. At half-past six it was Lancashire's game. For a minute before then Makepeace most dazzlingly ran out Waddington, and with Geoffrey Wilson away, Waddington was the last Yorkshireman but one to keep guard with Rhodes. Waddington was out at 6.30, Yorkshire 24 to the bad, half an hour to play and only one wicket for Lancashire to send flying—of course it was Lancashire's game! Waddington plainly thought so in the moment of his anguish that afflicted him when he saw his wicket put down as he raced down the pitch. 'Out?' he very obviously demanded of Justice, and demanded in consternation 'Out?' He remained at the wicket despite the umpire's upward-pointing finger. But he could not stand long against the laws, he had to depart. And realising at last that the law is not such an ass that it can be argued out of all sense, he made his way to the pavilion, running all the way, as though temper and mortification were driving him along.

Wilson walked calmly into the cockpit at twenty-five to seven (the extra half-hour of course was claimed), Yorkshire's score 108 for eight wickets. Rhodes looked a Gibraltar of certitude. Responsibility, therefore, sat himself impishly and heavily on Wilson's shoulders. But the shoulders of this Yorkshire gentleman were broad enough. In the great last wicket stand with Rhodes, Wilson had to tackle six or seven overs. Once Parkin hurled a yorker at his middle stump and then came towards the base of his wicket a red-hot shooter. Wilson stopped them and could even smile at the devilry of them. The gallant rearguard action of these two Yorkshire ancients—Rhodes and Wilson—was rather moving in bravery and in the way it hinted at both men's affection and pride for Yorkshire cricket.

The antagonists first got the strangle-hold on one another at five minutes past three. Lancashire were then batting a second innings which had started only four runs in arrears, and were 105 for five wickets. This innings had begun in dubiety. Hallows, Ernest Tyldesley, Norbury, and Makepeace all more or less failed, while a paltry 42 runs were scraped. Barnes and James Tyldesley swung the battle round in a notable stand for the fifth wicket, which lasted sixty-five minutes and was worth 63 to Lancashire. Barnes used a

straight bat in defence while James Tyldesley drove powerfully.

The wicket all day had been heavy with moisture; the
question now, as Tyldesley and Barnes batted, was whether
the pitch would get difficult for Yorkshire. The collapse of
Lancashire's last five wickets caused the crowd to imagine the
fragile sun really was getting to work making glue out of the
mud. But Lancashire's later batsmen do not of necessity re-
quire a bad turf for a tottering procession. As a fact, the pitch
never got really sticky all day; what of venom ever came to it
came in the last hour. Lancashire's tail simply collapsed in
the familiar way; it collapsed before steady bowling, and
probably habit had something to do with it. James Tyldesley
did not find the attack unplayable. He put forth his finest
abilities. He defended shrewdly, and though he has only one
stroke—a drive in front of the wicket—he found it ample for
many punitive expeditions against Rhodes's bowling. The last
five Lancashire wickets fell for 35, and so Yorkshire had time
enough wherewith to get the 132 necessary to win.

It was at four o'clock that the scuffle got noisy and acute.
Yorkshire went in then, and straightaway Barnes beautifully
caught Sutcliffe on the deep on boundary from Parkin's first
ball of the innings. Oldroyd, at 30, was another victim of
superb fielding; Makepeace ran him out just as brilliantly as
later he ran out Waddington. Kilner hit wildly at a well
pitched ball from Norbury at 36 and heard the horrible rattle
in his wicket. And at this sultry moment of affairs there was
an adjournment for tea. It was as though the curtain were
rung down as the knocking at the door in 'Macbeth' made its
bodeful noise in the theatre.

In the third over after tea Holmes was caught at the wicket.
Here it was that Lancashire found a footing near the hilltop
and caught a glimpse of the victorious sun. Holmes batted
beautifully, his blade as straight as the Guadanarian spindle
Cervantes talks about. With sixteen runs more somehow
stolen from the Lancashire bowlers and fielders, Robinson
was given out lbw. He did not like it—he never does—but he
bowed to the law with more philosophy than Waddington.
Macaulay and Rhodes stood fast, for an eternity it seemed,
and made 20 in partnership. When at six o'clock Rhodes hit

two boundaries in one over from Parkin and contrived to get a leg bye for 4, sending the Yorkshire total soaring to 88, what was the price of Lancashire stock with those shrewd men in the pavilion who know what's what about futures?

At 89 there happened a miracle. Why did the heavens grant it for Lancashire if it was not that Lancashire should be conquerors? Macaulay made a fine hit to the on boundary. Barnes saw it coming with an eye sure and eager; he faced forward and took a catch fit for the Elysian playing fields. He gripped it in front of his toes. The grace of his motion, the lovely poise of his body falling forward, might have driven a sculptor into ecstasy—and yet an ecstasy spoiled with chagrin that marble is not animate enough for such swift curves as Barnes made now. Dolphin lingered till 106; then came the Waddington episode and the closing scene.

It was a day that turns an effort at quick narration into vanity. Only in tranquillity could one hope to put one's recollections into some order of art. Honours were even—though the championship way of reckoning a cricket match will put no value on Lancashire's quality. Lancashire have never since the war bowled and fielded with the magnificence of yesterday. Everybody was lifted by the occasion to greatness. In the throes of the crisis Norbury and Parkin let us see an attack good enough for the purple past. Blomley at the wicket, Makepeace, Barnes, Richard Tyldesley—all of them were most admirable scouts. But so were the others—why name names? The innings of Rhodes was a Test match cricketer's, cool, skilful—Yorkshire through and through.

For those who love to make dizzy circles of argumentation out of tussles such as this here are one or two provocative points. Yorkshire scored only three runs from the last five overs of the match. Lancashire had nearly half an hour for the taking of the last Yorkshire wicket. Did not Yorkshire bat at the finish on a wicket definitely bad? Had Kenyon ever displayed finer captaincy for Lancashire? Could any cricketer have led a team in a crisis with finer judgment? Would Yorkshire have won with the aid of Geoffrey Wilson? Who would be an umpire in a Lancashire and Yorkshire match?

YORKSHIRE V LANCASHIRE 1922
SCORES

LANCASHIRE

First Innings		Second Innings	
Makepeace, run out	11	b Robinson	8
Hallows, c & b Macaulay	18	b Waddington	1
Tyldesley (E.), c Waddington, b Macaulay	45	lbw, b Robinson	14
J. R. Barnes, b E. Wilson	8	c Dolphin, b Macaulay	28
Norbury, c Holmes, b Kilner	1	b Robinson	9
Tyldesley (J.), lbw, b Kilner	1	not out	55
Tyldesley (R.), c Macaulay, b E. Wilson	14	b Rhodes	0
Parkin, run out	0	b Macaulay	6
M. N. Kenyon, lbw, b E. Wilson	5	run out	0
Cook, c Rhodes, b Macaulay	2	lbw, b Macaulay	5
Blomley, not out	5	c Dolphin, b Macaulay	0
Extras	8	Extras	9
Total	118	Total	135

YORKSHIRE

First Innings		Second Innings	
Holmes, c Tyldesley (R.), b Tyldesley (J.)	0	c Blomley, b Norbury	21
Sutcliffe, b Norbury	38	c Barnes, b Parkin	1
Oldroyd, c & b Tyldesley (J.)	5	run out	9
Kilner (R.), b Cook	4	b Norbury	1
Rhodes, lbw, b Norbury	26	not out	48
Robinson, b Parkin	19	lbw, b Parkin	20
G. Wilson, lbw, b Tyldesley (R.)	2	absent ill	0
Macaulay, c Blomley, b Cook	22	c Barnes, b Parkin	1
Dolphin, lbw, b Parkin	0	c Tyldesley (R.), b Norbury	8
E. R. Wilson, b Cook	1	not out	2
Waddington, not out	4	run out	1
Extras	1	Extras	17
Total	122	Total (for 8)	129

THE ROSES MATCHES 1919-1939
BOWLING ANALYSIS

Lancashire—First Innings

	O.	M.	R.	W.		O.	M.	R.	W.
Robinson	10	3	14	0	Macaulay	15·3	5	25	3
Waddington	5	1	16	0	E. Wilson	23	9	28	3
Kilner	24	13	27	2					

Second Innings

	O.	M.	R.	W.		O.	M.	R.	W.
Robinson	18	10	25	3	Kilner	8	3	16	0
Waddington	5	0	11	1	Rhodes	11	1	37	1
E. Wilson	7	1	21	0	Macaulay	10	3	16	4

Yorkshire—First Innings

	O.	M.	R.	W.		O.	M.	R.	W.
Tyldesley (J.)	7	0	20	2	Tyldesley (R.)	10	3	21	1
Cook	17	3	40	3	Norbury	9	2	25	2
Parkin	11	3	15	2					

Second Innings

	O.	M.	R.	W.		O.	M.	R.	W.
Cook	18	4	25	0	Tyldesley (R.)	10	2	23	0
Parkin	20	11	28	3	Norbury	15	5	36	3

YORKSHIRE V LANCASHIRE   1923

May 19/21/22   Old Trafford

FIRST DAY

THE weather gods were doubtful sportsmen at Old Trafford, for they ordained that rain should prevent the bowling of a single ball. It was nearly five o'clock before the match was postponed till this morning, and throughout the dreary afternoon a little crowd waited outside the gates, hoping against hope, their patience eloquent of great devotion to the game of games.

In the pavilion members watched the rain and looked at the sky from time to time, some of them even convincing themselves it was clearing up. One saw old familiar faces—men who can talk to you of Barlow and Crossland. How the years fall from a man as soon as he sets foot in a cricket pavilion. Despite the weather, there were men on Saturday at Old Trafford for whom the first of the season's visits to a place with happy memories meant a sudden release from all the winter's bondage to the things of this world, to the daily getting and spending. Just one sight of Old Trafford's sweep of fresh grass charmed definitely economic Manchester men out of acute mental preoccupation with, say the latest income-tax iniquities. Conversation in the pavilion went on about bygone days in the open air watching splendid cricket. One heard again the thrilling tale of how Briggs ensnared Ulyett in a Lancashire and Yorkshire match thirty years ago; of how Albert Ward stood on the edge of the field, waited for the ball to drop like a stone, and made a catch which won the game for Lancashire by five runs. 'I can see it all as though it happened only yesterday,' boasted these old men in the pavilion 'I was as near to him when he caught it as I am to you.' Good times, indeed.

And times equally good, we may be sure have been filched from the history of cricket by many a wet day in summer. Had the sun shone on Saturday, what might not have been achieved of derring-deeds for Lancashire and Yorkshire cricketers to talk about for years to come? Perhaps some marvellous batsmanship, some incredible scattering of wickets; perhaps Parkin would have hit a century. Who knows? The age of miracles is not yet over. Magnificence is, indeed, lost to the game on a blank day at Lancashire and Yorkshire matches. There seemed to be a dim realisation of this in the mind of a little boy who stopped the writer at the gates on Saturday, after the match had been abandoned for the afternoon, and in plaintive tones asked 'Won't there really be any cricket today?' It was hard to tell him the truth; his clothes were wet from hours of faithful waiting. One could only assure him it was certain to be gloriously fine on Monday. 'Curse the weather,' said one at the sight of the disconsolate lad turning on his heel and trudging a weary way home down the Warwick Road.

The match now falls under the declaration of innings law which operates in a two-day match. A lead of 100 runs will be sufficient to force a follow on.

SECOND DAY

A vast crowd sat round the field yesterday, and well might the lot of them have sung that pathetic ballad 'Tell me the old, old story.' For once again Old Trafford on Bank Holiday witnessed Lancashire cricketers humbled, not to say humiliated, by Yorkshire cricketers—saw the county's picked sons bent low over their bats, like infirm ancients over crutches.

Lancashire had the advantage of first innings on a pitch that was easy for the opening two hours at least. To what ends did they turn this advantage? Before lunch Lancashire's best batsmen could scrape together no more than a beggarly 57 runs from 48 overs. After lunch when it was again as plain as a pikestaff that the turf was getting more and more difficult every minute, the Lancashire batsmanship—wave the mark—persisted in a policy of little faith, of distrust not only of the Yorkshire ability but of its own ability. In one hour and a half after lunch—will it be credited?—Lancashire scored 47. Moreover Lancashire, in that time, did not palpably try to score more than 47. And all the while, as one has said, the wicket was developing steadily in the bowler's favour. Not until the Yorkshire attack had definitely got on top and obviously was airing a fine opinion of itself, did a Lancashire cricketer take courage in his hands and strive to meet aggression with aggression. And—would you believe again?—this Lancashire cricketer was none other than J. T. Tyldesley. But of this more anon, as they used to say in the novels of our grandfathers.

As one watched palsy come over the accredited batsmen of Lancashire before lunch, on the fairly comfortable pitch, a solitary question hammered in one's head: 'If we cannot get runs now, heaven forbid what the afternoon will bring of travail to Lancashire.' The afternoon, in fact, saw the mightiest Lancashire landslide of modern times, as may be understood from a glance at this harrowing sequence of the fall of the county's wickets: 1/25 2/31 3/68 4/86 5/104 6/104 7/108 8/108 9/108 10/108. Most tolerable and not to be endured, as your Dogberry might have declaimed had he been present at this station by the sight-screen keeping young malefactors off the grass. Yet some extenuation (let us be merciful) is to be put forward for the rout of the Lancashire tail. They got to the crease as the turf was behaving abominably, and one or two of them, notably Hickmott, fell to brilliant fieldsmanship. The writer blames the front rank of Lancashire's batsmen wholly for yesterday's ignominy. Why had they not the heart—ay and the sense—to take the offensive in the morning while Yorkshire's bowling was merely respectable and while the pitch had no particular venom?

Is tactics in batsmanship not studied in these days? Once on a time it was the recognised plan for a team batting first on a slow pitch to try to force the runs before the sun and wind did bowlers a service. Is it a fact that nowadays batsmen are so much the bondslaves of routine that they have power to play only one game? Must we say Lancashire batsmanship has legs capable of but a solitary pace—like the horse of Oliver Wendell Holmes? Or must we decide that yesterday the trouble with Lancashire was a subject less for the cricket specialist than for the psycho-analyst—that in these great games Lancashire suffers from an inferiority complex: in less

109

elegant language, from a feeling of down-troddenness wherever Yorkshiremen walk? The writer watched the Yorkshire attack before lunch most closely from behind the bowler's arm; he will agree it was a good attack. But he will swear before the high gods of cricket that it was not deadly, and that many loose balls passed by a Lancashire bat unpunished. When is a half-volley not a half-volley? Why, when a Yorkshireman bowls it at Old Trafford on Bank Holiday. But stay! We must not make ribald mirth out of the half-volley; is it not the deadliest ball in modern cricket?

Yet cold statistics themselves arraign the earlier Lancashire batsmen yesterday. From the first sixteen overs of the game came 20 runs; in the first hour came 28. From 174 balls came 33 runs, including five extras. The first boundary hit of the match happened after one hour and three-quarters' cricket. In Lancashire's innings which lasted three hours and ten minutes, the writer could keep count of only three boundary hits. So widely separated in time were these mighty blows that memory could not, so to speak, achieve a synthesis of them without hard thinking. Before lunch there were 23 maidens out of 48 overs. Before lunch no single over added more than five to Lancashire's total. Hallows was on view 50 minutes for seven; Makepeace was on view 70 minutes for 19; Ernest Tyldesley was on view one hour and 35 minutes for 24. The evidence of mistaken tactics by Lancashire's earlier batsmen seems good enough; the jury need not leave the box. Yet one would not be unfair: Lancashire even in this game must depend heavily for runs on Hallows, Ernest Tyldesley and Makepeace. But has not long and painful experience taught us that merely negative batsmanship is exactly the stuff that Yorkshire's length bowlers thrive on?

Barnes, after lunch, showed us that, even though Kilner and Rhodes were able to spin the ball nastily, the bowling could be hit. He was playing the politic game for his side when he most unfortunately got out to a ball that kicked suddenly. But the Lancashire cricketer with the hardest blow in his bat yesterday was clearly J. T. Tyldesley. He reached the crease at the wicket's most sticky period; he remained there for half an hour. His score was merely nine, yet with what energy and courage he let himself go at the few loose balls he found. To see him jump at the overtossed length and punch it to long-on, this was a sight that did tired eyes good. Tyldesley, true, was frequently in trouble with quick-turning balls from Kilner. But never did he give us the sense that trouble was making for distress in his soul. He plainly kept his mind alert and antagonistic; plainly he was always seeking for the counter-stroke wherewith the opposition might be for a time thrown back. Even at times that saw him beaten you could get a hint of the mastership which was the glory of Lancashire cricket. The crowd gave him a magnificent welcome when once more they saw him walking to the wicket. Then we saw him face to face again with his old foeman Rhodes—and imagination made a picture known well enough in the years gone by, a picture of Tyldesley at bay, with Hirst, Rhodes and Haigh at him, his bat a sword of fire. Yesterday Tyldesley died fighting; he was brilliantly caught by Macaulay from a hit with the right temper in it.

Green was 85 minutes making 12 runs; he defended skilfully, but when the rabbits were in it was his game to fight desperation's fight. Parkin threw his wicket away in search of high jinks. It was not the right moment for the cap and bells, maybe. Still, we must take the oddities in our Parkin as we find them, and not be too censorious about a little misplaced waggishness from him now and then. Say that he suffers from the defects of his qualities—and of course high energy and spirit are qualities rare enough in first class cricket today. Say that, like Yorick, in Sterne, he has an invincible dislike and opposition in his nature to gravity, and let this latest lapse in a most solemn hour—too solemn perhaps we permitted it to become—to pass with a caution.

After lunch Kilner exploited beautiful left-hand spin bowling. He looked to find a spot on the pitch at the Manchester end. At any rate he caused the ball to kick unpleasantly, and of course, he caused it to break away from the bat. His length was just short enough, after a widish flight through the air, to prevent the batsmen—at least the Lancashire batsmen—from jumping to the pitch of it, and yet it was so short that one could go back and play it at leisure. Rhodes let us see all his old length, and also let us see he has not quite lost his spin yet. His field was set cunningly and a Rhodes field is the most tactfully set field for slow bowling that one could wish to look on.

When Yorkshire batted the game seemed suddenly to be put into a brighter light. Not that Sutcliffe and Holmes scored at all dashingly. They found twice Lancashire's pace, and well they might have done and not died of heart failure. The point about the batsmanship of Sutcliffe and Holmes which achieved a nice contrast to Lancashire's was its perfectly calculated touch. Both of them played like men who were keenly aware of what they were at and, moreover, of what the bowlers were at. Sutcliffe, true, was nearly caught and bowled by Cook with his score 11—Cook threw his vast and likeable bulk with a marvellous agility at an impossible chance. True, also that Sutcliffe sent a difficult catch deep to the leg side, where Hallows just failed to hold the ball, hurting his hand in the attempt. These mischances, though, were faint flaws on the fine art of Sutcliffe. All manner of perfection in this world, said one of the old saints, hath a manner of imperfection annexed thereto. Sutcliffe certainly gave us perfection in his offside play—cricket bloom with delicate wrist-play. Two strokes he accomplished—thrilling sweeps to the leg boundary, shot through and through with MacLaren's old grandeur—strokes, maybe, that do not belong properly to the strictly classical style of his play. But style is the man after all and Sutcliffe being human, must have his moods of superb rebellion against too much of purity in this world.

The Lancashire bowlers stuck grimly to their work and towards the day's fall Parkin had his consolation. Hickmott's pace was slower than the writer has seen it before, and in consequence he looked much more like a capital left-hand bowler. The crowd, more than 20,000 strong, went home disgruntled. But we must be loyal to our lads; nine days out of a season's ten they are good enough. Then comes Yorkshire across their path and something goes awry in the ranks—against Yorkshire a performance of Lancashire's like yesterday seems nowadays in the course of nature—to some such situation they must come as Mrs. Bardell would observe. Did Yorkshire discover an improved wicket for their innings? It certainly seemed to have rolled out easefully.

THIRD DAY
There was less than an hour's cricket at Old Trafford yesterday, and it did not begin till four o'clock. In that time Yorkshire scored 29 runs for the loss of two wickets and then rain fell again, putting an end to the match. The cricket yesterday is not to be seriously considered—the pitch was never really fit for an exhibition of first-class ability.

There was a notable scene during the afternoon. The crowd had been sitting patiently in the sunshine for an hour and a half, waiting for some sign that the cricketers had not gone home to bed (oh, the reluctance of your county men to get into flannels). At half past three a portion of the crowd invaded the playing pitch, roundly demanding something for their money. Happily it was not necessary for the Riot Act to be read; the players were on the field half an hour after the demonstration. This slight disturbance caused a deal of hot discussion in which hard things were said about (1) the Committee of the Lancashire County Cricket Club (2) the umpires, (3) the current method of reckoning the championship and (4) the noble game itself. It was the opinion of many experienced cricketers present that the wicket was never in a condition amenable to decent cricket; that at no time of the day was it probable the turf would recover sufficiently for the needs of county men. The argument against the Committee was that the gates should never have been opened to the public. But the Committee claimed that the gates were opened out of sheer kindness of heart; would it not have been cruel to deny the multitude clamouring outside a sight of Old Trafford's green—a sight in itself worth the price of admission. The writer was assured by Lancashire and Yorkshire cricketers engaged in the match that at four o'clock the pitch was not far removed from a quagmire. Sutcliffe was temporarily blinded by mud splashed from a ball of Parkin's. Parkin and Cook found it difficult to get a foothold, and both bowled at some slight risk of a strain. No doubt the turf was always good enough for club cricketers to play on, but the public surely do not journey all the way to Old Trafford and part with their money simply to watch club cricket. The umpires, presumably, were in sole charge of the decision as to whether or not the ground was fit. Apparently they were of opinion it was not. That cricket came so quickly after the great voice of the public made itself heard must be regarded as beautiful testimony to the umpires' breadth of mind.

SCORES
LANCASHIRE
First Innings

Makepeace, b Macaulay	19
Hallows, c Sutcliffe, b Macaulay	7
Tyldesley (E.), c Waddington, b Kilner	24
J. R. Barnes, c Holmes, b Kilner	28
L. Green, not out	12
J. T. Tyldesley, c Macaulay, b Kilner	9
Tyldesley (R.), c Leyland, b Kilner	0
Parkin, run out	2
Hickmott, c Sutcliffe, b Kilner	0
Cook, c Leyland, b Rhodes	0
Whewell, c Kilner, b Rhodes	0
Extras	7
Total	108

YORKSHIRE
First Innings

Holmes, b Parkin	33
Sutcliffe, b Parkin	48
Oldroyd, b Parkin	4
Robinson, c Whewell, b Cook	9
Kilner, b Cook	7
Rhodes, not out	10
Leyland, not out	2
Extras	13
Total (for 5)	126

BOWLING ANALYSIS
LANCASHIRE—First Innings

	O.	M.	R.	W.		O.	M.	R.	W.
Waddington	7	2	11	0	Kilner	40	20	33	5
Robinson	8	4	8	0	Rhodes	17·4	7	22	2
Macaulay	25	12	27	2					

YORKSHIRE—First Innings

	O.	M.	R.	W.		O.	M.	R.	W.
Parkin	21	8	32	3	Tyldesley (R.)	11	7	10	0
Cook	25	5	51	2	Hickmott	6	0	20	0

YORKSHIRE V LANCASHIRE   1923

August 4/6/7   Bradford

FIRST DAY

IN one of the Baroness Orczy's novels the Spaniards wail 'The enemy is on us. Sauve qui peut.' Do Lancashire cricketers, when they see a Yorkshire XI advancing on them, make moan likewise? For on Saturday at Bradford Lancashire yet again faltered against Yorkshire; yet again did we seem to see the very souls of our batsmen shrivel in the presence of the ancient enemy. On a wicket which the Lancashire captain described as one of the easiest paced conceivable Lancashire were all out for 188—and these scant runs came only after four hours and a quarter's agony.

This is the sixth time, at least, since the war that a Lancashire innings has crumpled spinelessly against Yorkshire bowling on a good wicket. 'Is it luck that trips us; is it scare?' as the old cricket song asks. My own view is that on Saturday, at any rate, Lancashire were irresolute and unlucky: and if this is a true reading of the Lancashire innings we have here, maybe, a case of cause and effect. Fortune woos the courageous, especially at cricket. (Remember David Denton's and J. T. Tyldesley's happy adventures in the slips at an inning's beginning.) Two Lancashire batsmen—Hallows and Richard Tyldesley—fell to wonderful catches: they were of the kind of catch which somehow sticks in a fieldsman's hand—every cricketer brings off such a catch in a lifetime, to his delight and bewilderment. In charity, then, let us admit that these two disasters to Lancashire were the churlish work of the gods—who, of course, are always on the side of the big battalions. But even with this admission made, Lancastrians have still to explain away the failures of the rest of their batsmen.

It was argued by the Lancashire cricketers themselves that Makepeace and Sharp also were out unluckily. Makepeace tried to glance a ball to leg and was finely caught at the wicket; and Sharp, trying for a boundary from a loose ball,

115

missed it and was bowled off his foot. But to my thinking, if these two batsmen may fairly be said to have been unlucky then all batsmen are unlucky when they get out from anything but an unplayable ball. What indeed is 'luck' at cricket? 'Well hit,' says the crowd as a batsman drives a good ball nobly into the horizon—and the batsman murmurs: 'How clever I am.' But the bowler murmurs to his heart: 'Lucky cuss—he'd a' been bowled if he'd a' missed it.'

Luck or unluck, here are one or two ugly facts Lancashire cannot readily get away from. On Saturday the innings lasted more than four hours—on a capital pitch, mark you—and only 188 runs were scored, from 582 balls. Kilner, a slow left hand bowler—on a most excellent pitch, mark you again—bowled 27 overs and four balls, 18 maidens for 21 runs and three wickets. By these simple facts we are forced to one of these two conclusions—either that the Yorkshire bowling on Saturday was always a miracle of accuracy and 'unhittableness,' or that Lancashire batsmen had not the heart to play the game natural to them. In the old days, when Yorkshire had Hirst, Rhodes (at his finest), Haigh and Jackson, how many times did it occur that on a good wicket Lancashire batted for four hours and a quarter and scored but 188? Was even Attwell or Shaw frequently permitted to surpass Kilner's bowling figures on Saturday? Are the Yorkshire bowlers today better than Yorkshire bowlers ever have been in the history of cricket. In two matches against Lancashire this summer Kilner's bowling analysis works: 67 overs, 33 maidens, 54 runs and 8 wickets.

Now Kilner is a clever bowler—the writer indeed claims to have discerned his skill as a bowler even before Yorkshire themselves fully realised it. But consider those figures above and ask: Since the mud blossomed and the world was made has any bowler ever bowled well enough, on good wickets, to deserve such respectful treatment as this by any batsman brave enough to play every ball that he gets on its merits? On Saturday after lunch, Kilner was allowed to deliver eight consecutive maidens. In those 48 balls are we to believe there was not one that could have been scored from? Or were the Lancashire batsmen trying to tire Kilner out? (This last as Artemus Ward used to say, is 'writ sarkastic'.) Close observations of the cricket on Saturday convinced me that though Kilner was hard to drive he ought not to have been unusually difficult to stay in to or to get singles from, and that a really decent amount of runs could have been made by confident batsmen from Wilson, Rhodes, Macaulay and Robinson. Macaulay and Robinson bowled well, true, but not incredibly well.

The Lancashire batsmen, as we have seen, put down one or two of their disasters to ill-fortune. But they had arguments more rational than this in an attempt to extenuate the total of 188. The Yorkshire attack, it was argued, aims at 'keeping the batsmen pegged to the crease'; it cultivates the length 'that can't be hit.' Not a bit of use trying to hit these Yorkshiremen, the story goes, 'if you do you get out.' 'And if you don't you get out just the same' is an obvious retort to this tremendous logic. As proof of the Lancashire men's argument, it was pointed out that when Ernest Tyldesley, Sharp and Parkin attempted to drive on Saturday they got caught. Well; well! Ever since cricket was cricket batsmen have been getting out to catches—more catches, of course, are made than wickets bowled down—and yet batsmen have somehow gone on with the delectable game of hitting boundaries; or at least they do go on with it till recently. The defence put forward by some of the Lancashire batsmen for this latest obeisance of theirs to the Yorkshire hosts would make engaging reading—wouldn't it?—if it were paraphrased, as without injustice it might be in some such burlesque as this, written in the manner of the police-court reports: 'A number of Lancashire batsmen were arrested for loitering at Park Avenue, Bradford, on Saturday. They pleaded not guilty and said they had gone to Park Avenue with the purpose of making runs but were prevented from doing so, owing to a conspiracy to stop them on the part of certain Yorkshiremen named Wilson, Robinson, Macaulay, Kilner and Rhodes. The defendants not being able to claim the protection of the First Offender's Act, were remanded till August Bank Holiday.'

There was a great crowd sitting in the luscious sun all day, and most of them being Yorkshire to the bones' marrow, they enjoyed themselves. In the first hour or so the crowd possibly

117

suffered a little discomfort of mind; for then it was not dead certain Lancashire were going to collapse as a Lancashire side is expected to do at festive gatherings in Yorkshire. Hallows and Makepeace scored 26 for the first wicket, and though Makepeace was beaten by the third ball of Robinson's third over, the bowling did not look at all deadly while these batsmen were in. Hallows played excellent cricket, and let us see one glorious straight drive. Just now, at any rate, the sun shone on Lancashire. Then out of the blue, came the bolt that destroyed Hallow's innings just as it was beginning to spread brave wings. He hit a ball hard and low—the stroke was worth four of the best as cricketers say. Rhodes, at short leg, caught it magnificently. It was one of the most dazzling catches I have seen this year; but Rhodes accomplished it without emotion, without fuss. He simply took the ball as it sped to him, not more than mere inches from the green grass. We all blinked eyes at the sight of this swift happening; next we saw Hallows leaving the wicket sadly, and a little group of Yorkshire fieldsmen gathered round the wonderful Rhodes, who tossed the ball from hand to hand as though to say 'It's all in the day's work.'

This was first blood to Yorkshire and from now onwards Lancashire were definitely the underdog. The Yorkshiremen attacked Ernest Tyldesley and Makepeace passionately; Robinson hurled himself to the crease as though only these two thoughts in all the world moved him to action: 'There's three wickets yon, me lad, and nobbut a Lancashire bat to cover them.' Yet Tyldesley and Makepeace stayed in till the score board announced Lancashire 51 for one which was good to read. At the sight of this glad score a Lancashire man in the crowd got up and said, 'I'm off to mi lunch while mi appetite's good.' Was he an optimist or a pessimist?' He went in time, and only just in time. If he had a morsel in his mouth before Tyldesley was bowled he got served far quicker than most of us at lunch on Saturday. As a fact, few Lancashire men can have felt like lunch after they had seen Ernest Tyldesley fall into ruin. He made a ghastly mistake, hitting across a ball of doubtful quality. Seven runs after this Makepeace and Barnes were dismissed in quick succession. Makepeace defended for eighty minutes and made 35 out of

58. He was not at his best; the fourth ball of Waddington's fourth over was overtossed and Makepeace missed it, and he rarely misses a ball once he decides to hit it. Makepeace, at this mishap, stood still at the wicket like a man pondering the problem of existence.

With the four best batsmen gone and the total a miserly 58, Lancashire were neck-deep in the slough. After lunch Sharp, following a quiet look at the bowling, hit five great hearted boundaries. Here did we get the old time bigness of style; here did Sharp himself show that Yorkshire bowling could be hit. True, he got out in attempting an ambitious drive; but that unhappy event did not alter the fact that he had powerfully and confidently hit bowling just as good as that which has hypnotised so many cricketers this season.

When Lancashire had lost seven wickets for 128 and Lancashire heads were bent in shame, Watson and Duckworth achieved a most plucky stand for the eighth wicket, which lasted fifty-five minutes and was worth 40 precious runs. Duckworth faced these redoubtable Yorkshire bowlers with a 'don't care tuppence a bunch for the lot of you' air. Immediately he arrived at the wicket he took an upward look at Kilner, beginning at his boots and ending at the crown of his head, and then he took a downward look at him, beginning at the crown of his head and finishing at his boots—which two looks, as Dickens has informed us, are expressive of defiance. Duckworth scored 25, mainly by 'cheeky' little chops through the slips: his innings had a gamin sort of insolence. And there was great merit in Watson's three hours and a half's defiance of the Yorkshire attack; here was a youth forced by circumstances into responsible old age. Watson had the veteran's patience and composure on Saturday; if also he had the veteran's grey hairs at the end of his innings one could hardly have been surprised. The last three Lancashire wickets added 65 runs—Parkin, Cook and Duckworth all were eager for runs while Watson kept one end of the wicket intact. Against length bowling like Yorkshire's there should always be one batsman attacking it, if at the other end of the wicket there stands a safe defensive batsman. Richard Tyldesley, as I have hinted, was unfortunate; he drove a ball powerfully only to see Kilner take a catch.

The Yorkshire fielding was superb all day—it might even be said the Yorkshire fielding was more deadly than the Yorkshire bowling. E. R. Wilson was playing in his first county match this summer: again he exhibited his famous collection of slow bowling of the 'leg curl' period—a collection of rare quality and antiquity. Wilson is a delightful cricketer—one who brings a little sweetness and light into the grim infallibility of Yorkshire cricket. When Kilner or Macaulay takes a wicket he takes it rather as a Mohawk Indian might have taken a scalp; that is with a gesture of merciless conquest. But when Wilson gets your wicket he almost smiles apologetically, as though to say 'Awfully sorry; but one is expected to do these things now and then, I suppose.'

> He kicks you downstairs with such infinite grace
> You might think he was handing you up.

Sutcliffe and Holmes began Yorkshire's innings with all possible assurance. The change that came over the game as soon as these two batsmen set to work was beyond belief. The ball had been the bat's master all day, and now the ball was the slave of the bat. In half an hour came 38 sparkling runs. And yet Parkin bowled just as well, for the most part, as any Yorkshireman had done. Faint heart ne'er hit good bowling and here we had confidence personified by Holmes and Sutcliffe. Parkin's reputation did not appal these two batsmen—and yet Parkin's reputation is just as notable as Kilner's or Macaulay's. A bad day for us, goodness knows; will victory over Yorkshire come no more to Lancashire 'till Birnham Wood remove to Dunsinane'?

SECOND DAY

Lancashire cricket lovers have passed through a bitter hour or two at the close of this iniquitous day. They have seen the batsmen of their county humbled as Lancashire cricketers can rarely have been humbled before—even by Yorkshire. One really has no heart to discuss this latest bowing of the knee by our XI before the old enemy. Some of the most mournful pages in Lancashire cricket history would be written if the county's second innings today were considered at length.

Lancashire all out for 73! The Yorkshire bowling was good, of course, but had Spofforth and Lockwood been attacking Lancashire this afternoon could a worse fate have befallen the county than actually happened? Hallows was bowled with a single scored; Makepeace was rather unluckily caught at the wicket three runs afterwards. When Ernest Tyldesley was given out leg before wicket—a decision which he obviously did not like—the Lancashire ship foundered with all hands, riven fore and aft. The only excuse I can put forward on Lancashire's behalf is that the wicket at one end was worn—but all the wickets did not fall at this end. Besides, one is getting a little tired of making excuses for Lancashire in matches against Yorkshire—indeed, one's stock of excuses, is, like the Yankee's cigar in 'Chuzzlewit,' 'considerably used up.'

'Cricket in hell,' said a South of England man today as he saw the Bradford field for the first time in his life. Strong language, maybe, but language picturesque and rich with imaginative truth. From noon till evening the place has been like some vast underworld, discordant, ugly, uncomfortable. Even before noon the ground was full and the gates locked. Some 26,000 souls were inside making writhing congested ranks, and surely torment was their lot, what with the sun and the heavy air. Outside the unlovely field gloomy chimneys sent out smoke that curled into the summer sky sulkily. From the height of a mound black with sweaty humans one could look down on the grass—and upwards came the sense of the crowd's stress of body and spirit. One thought of the description in 'The Dynasts' of the scene in the Victory's cockpit. The crowd had little of the fluid humour of a Sheffield crowd: it was dull and seemingly a little stupid from its own bulk and unwieldiness. As the day passed on, the crowd broke bounds and overflowed on to the playing piece. Mounted police were called in to drive the derelicts back, and then we saw the green edge of the field littered with rubbish—it was as though a dank tide had gone out, leaving behind its scum.

Yet the unhappy scene had its uses: it provided a dramatic setting to the match, giving it a sort of reflected grimness and inimical life. In a more tranquil place, maybe, the cricket before lunch would have been dull. For the Yorkshiremen in the day's first hour or so were dour and unadventuresome. Sutcliffe was bowled by a perfect length ball just as noon came, and with his passing grace went from the Yorkshire innings for a long while. Now we had Holmes and Oldroyd to gaze on—Cromwell's 'rude mechanic men' for a certainty. The lissom art of Sutcliffe always strikes me as something ironically presented on these blasted heaths of Yorkshire; He makes one think of the butterfly lost in a noisome street. Sutcliffe in the Yorkshire team is as the jewel in the toad's head. The first Yorkshire wicket fell at 72, and Oldroyd, in next, apparently hung to the crease only by a thread. When his score was three he gave a chance to Parkin, who had to run to a stroke that was going away from him. He got his capacious hands to the ball and dropped it. At the spectacle of Parkin's blunder, the howls of the multitude were 'organs' as Mrs. Gamp would have observed. Oldroyd scraped about for thirty-five minutes for three runs the while Holmes in his own yard, metallic fashion made runs of excellent value to Yorkshire.

Just now Parkin bowled splendidly; his first spell of work during the morning resulted in twelve overs, seven maidens and fourteen runs. That he got no wickets in these overs can be accounted for only by saying that the batsmen would take not the slightest risk against his attack. Once he sent seven overs down for a solitary run. Hereabouts I have the notion that Parkin might have been at his best, a more successful bowler against batsmen of the MacLaren and Trumper stamp than he is today, for surely those masters would have met the challenge of Parkin by a challenge of their own just as finely tempered, and so given Parkin a sporting chance. But, as I have said, Parkin could make little advance today on the ancient foe. It was R. Tyldesley who put an end to the Oldroyd-Holmes partnership, which lasted one hour and thirty-five minutes and was worth 59. Just before lunch Leyland was caught from a ball by Parkin—his only wicket in the innings. At lunch Yorkshire's total was 132 for three wickets.

Immediately after the interval Lancashire, for once in a

way, took on the manner of a winning side in a Yorkshire match. This phenomenal occurrence came about because of some remarkably good bowling by Richard Tyldesley. His fifth ball after lunch got Holmes capitally caught by Hickmott: sixteen balls after this Tyldesley had Rhodes stumped: three overs later he dismissed Robinson, and in the succeeding over Macaulay fell to him. These four Yorkshire wickets did Tyldesley capture in eight overs for fifteen runs—beautiful work to which I will refer later. The game by now was anybody's—Lancashire had played up nobly. Yorkshire with but three wickets in keeping, were fifteen runs behind Lancashire. Had only Richard Tyldesley been aided by a strong Lancashire bowler at the other end Lancashire might have won on the first innings. And the moral stimulation that would have come to our men from such a blessed happening would surely have sent them to the wicket in their second innings loftier in stature than the Lilliputians we were fated before the day's end to behold.

Unhappily Parkin's bowling went to pieces after lunch; he lost length and liveliness of heart. One fancies he permitted a decision against a leg-before-wicket appeal to upset him. At any rate, from that moment he was his own shadow—a mere husk of the Parkin we had watched and admired in the morning. After the interval this afternoon Parkin bowled nine overs for 32 runs: at the crisis of Yorkshire's innings his attack got so loose that four boundaries were struck from it in sixteen balls. And so Yorkshire won on the first innings after all, and Lancashire definitely were bottom dogs.

And to be under dog to Yorkshire is to be amongst the 'demnition bow-wows' to whose kennels Mr. Mantalini vowed he was always drifting. Another disastrous mishap befell Lancashire when Makepeace, safest of fieldsmen in the county, missed a catch Kilner sent with his score none—as an Irish cricketer might observe. Kilner survived to play the finest innings of the match, to give us batsmanship full of cavalier courage and colour. He batted fifty-five minutes for his 44, and flashed nine boundaries through the stygian gloom of the scene. He was, beside Sutcliffe, the only batsman that has been on view in the match to put the power of his forward shoulder into his strokes. Yorkshire were all out at a quarter to four, happy in the advantage of twenty-five. 'Not as wide as a church door,' the Yorkshire captain might have said of the advantage, 'but 'twill serve.'

Richard Tyldesley has never bowled better than he did today; his length was admirable and his spin keen throughout. The Lancashire fielding was not consistently reliable, though now and again good work was done. Duckworth again kept wicket handsomely, and if he missed stumping Holmes towards the end of that magnificent utilitarian's innings the chance could not be called easy. Holmes batted three hours, skilfully and unemotionally, and he hit nine boundaries. The Yorkshire rate of scoring was not much better than Lancashire's on Saturday, but Holmes, Sutcliffe, and Kilner gave their side's innings a backbone quite lacking in Lancashire's. It may be argued also that in Tyldesley Yorkshire had to grapple with the best bowler of the match.

THIRD DAY

Play was delayed for an hour this morning at Park Avenue because of a wet wicket, and when Yorkshire began their comfortable task of making 49 runs for victory the ball turned but not quickly. Still, Parkin and Richard Tyldesley bowled so finely that Yorkshire had to toil for an hour before the match was won at the expense of the wickets of Holmes and Oldroyd.

With the weather having broken, Yorkshire were probably thankful Lancashire did not set them on Monday a heavier task; 150 runs might well have been beyond them. Certain it is that had Lancashire only stayed at the wicket on Bank Holiday evening and for another hour today—say three hours in all—then Yorkshire would have been compelled to bat a fourth innings on a really bad pitch, for when the match finished at half-past one today the turf was getting sticky every minute.

Lancashire's superb work in the field before and immediately after lunch on Monday gave them a rare chance of a first-innings advantage. And had Parkin kept up the accuracy of his attack while the Yorkshire tail were in, surely

124

that first innings victory would have come to Lancashire. The moral effect even of a half-way advantage over Yorkshire must have sent our batsmen in a second time feeling a new born confidence in themselves. The Yorkshire spell would, for the moment at any rate, have been broken. Parkin's dwindling attack at the critical point of Yorkshire's first innings, therefore, may be said to have cost his side dearly. Parkin seemingly allowed a decision of one of the umpires to upset him, from that point onwards his bowling was a travesty of the magnificent work he had shown us before and for a period after lunch. My own view is that whatever disappointment Parkin suffered from the umpire's decisions, he ought to have been kept in good heart simply by the spectacle of Richard Tyldesley bowling like a hero at the opposite crease.

Parkin would be wise to cultivate some philosophy—even a great bowler needs to take the changing fortunes of cricket with an easy heart. On several occasions this summer Parkin, when bowling against the better-class counties on good wickets, has apparently permitted his art to fall away in quality simply because success has not immediately crowned his efforts. It seems he is a bowler who on perfect wickets and against good batsmen must always be doing well and must begin well straightway. He is as they say 'temperamental'. This can frequently develop into an expensive luxury for a bowler—as may be understood from these figures which tell what Parkin has done recently for Lancashire on good wickets against the three counties that matter: 2 for 100 against Notts, 2 for 131 and 2 for 48 against Surrey, 1 for 82 and 1 for 23 against Yorkshire. Parkin, as we know, is a great bowler; Peel, the old Yorkshire cricketer, gave me the other day a fervent assurance that Parkin would have been great in cricket's best days. Parkin, then, owes it to himself to get used to the umpires. They certainly have to adapt themselves to him.

Yesterday Parkin, as one has suggested, was a master bowler again and his part in Lancashire's losing fight was performed gamely to the bitter end. But well though he bowled, he bowled no better than Richard Tyldesley, who throughout this match has once again proved himself to be Lancashire's most dependable bowler whenever our county has to climb a stiff hill.

Lancashire's poor batting in the match has of course caused sorrow all over the county, but nobody has felt it more acutely than the players themselves. And though we all could have hoped for bolder bats than Lancashire displayed on Saturday and Monday against the old enemy, none the less must we remember that it is no disgrace to be defeated by a grand side like the present Yorkshire XI. Yorkshire are easily the best county side in the land—a team almost perfectly balanced, and every man thriving on success. Bad as Lancashire's batsmanship was on Monday evening, nobody could deny the excellence of the Yorkshire attack. The faith and fierce spirit with which Macaulay and Robinson set about the Lancashire second innings might well have moved mountains.

The form of Lancashire's batsmen since Saturday noon has not, of course, been true. Why our county cannot play a natural game against Yorkshire is still a mystery. The men who collapsed on Monday evening were anyhow not the sterling cricketers who brilliantly vanquished Middlesex at Lord's and at Manchester, and who fought through that heroic day at the Oval last month. Let us try to forget the disaster to Lancashire at Bradford; or, if we think of it at all, let us regard it as an aberration on Lancashire's part. After all, Lancashire has lost only two matches, and it is now August: a side that can steer clear of defeat as cleverly as this must possess cricketers somehow worthy of our pride and applause.

SCORES

LANCASHIRE

First Innings		Second Innings	
Makepeace, c Dolphin, b Macaulay	35	c Dolphin, b Robinson	3
Hallows, c Rhodes, b Robinson	12	b Macaulay	0
Tyldesley (E.), b Macaulay	6	lbw, b Macaulay	6
Watson not out	33	b Macaulay	10
J. H. Barnes, c Waddington, b Macaulay	0	c Rhodes, b Kilner	16
J. Sharp, b Wilson	26	c Macaulay, b Wilson	4
Tyldesley (R.), c Kilner, b Wilson	8	c Rhodes, b Wilson	4
Parkin, c Oldroyd, b Wilson	12	b Macaulay	13
Duckworth, c Robinson, b Kilner	25	c Waddington, b Kilner	6
Cook, c Dolphin, b Kilner	21	not out	4
Hickmott, lbw, b Kilner	0	c&b Kilner	0
Extras	10	Extras	7
Total	188	Total	73

YORKSHIRE

First Innings		Second Innings	
Holmes, c Hickmott, b Tyldesley (R.)	80	c Cook, b Tyldesley (R.)	17
Sutcliffe, b Tyldesley (R.)	30	not out	19
Oldroyd, lbw, b Tyldesley (R.)	22	c Sharp, b Parkin	7
Leyland, c Tyldesley (R.), b Parkin	0	not out	8
Rhodes, st Duckworth, b Tyldesley (R.)	5		
Kilner (R.), c Tyldesley (E.), b Tyldesley (R.)	44		
Robinson, c Cook, b Tyldesley (R.)	4		
Macaulay, c Cook, b Tyldesley (R.)	4		
Waddington, b Cook	14		
Dolphin not out	6		
E. R. Wilson, c Sharp, b Cook	0		
Extras	4	Extras	10
Total	213	Total (for 2)	61

BOWLING ANALYSIS

LANCASHIRE—First Innings

	O.	M.	R.	W.		O.	M.	R.	W.
Waddington	6	0	20	0	Kilner	27·4	18	21	3
Robinson	14	6	17	1	Wilson	18	7	46	3
Macaulay	25	2	68	3	Rhodes	7	4	6	0

Second Innings

Robinson	11	8	5	1	Kilner	11	3	17	3
Macaulay	17	3	32	4	Wilson	4	2	12	2

YORKSHIRE—First Innings

	O.	M.	R.	W.		O.	M.	R.	W.
Parkin	37	15	82	1	Tyldesley (R.)	33	10	71	7
Cook	20·4	4	38	2	Hickmott	12	6	18	0

Second Innings

Parkin	13	5	23	1	Tyldesley (R.)	9·4	2	21	1
Cook	3	1	7	0					

YORKSHIRE V LANCASHIRE 1924

June 7/9/10 Leeds

FIRST DAY

LANCASHIRE against Yorkshire—and the ancient bone of contention and the ancient dogs still worrying it! A vast crowd looked at the game on Saturday at Leeds; some 20,000 mostly Yorkshire folk, all of them proud and jealous of their county's cricket. Before play began, I stood in the multitude in front of the pavilion; nothing of moment was happening on the field, which stood vacant—a waiting stage. But a Yorkshireman in the crowd, at this period of preludial inactivity and peace suddenly and without warning, hooted to the sky, 'Good owd Yorksheer'. There was, as I say, no action on visibly about him to provoke the outburst; I can only conclude that, while sitting there, waiting for the battle to begin, our Yorkshireman had suddenly vouchsafed an overwhelming vision of his county's greatness in the past. For his 'Good owd Yorksheer' was not uttered with the tone of mere term of encouragement; it was given the emphasis of positive statement, and once he let it out triumphantly on the air, we did not hear it again, even though a Lancashire man gave a counter-call: 'Good owd Lancasheer!' Our Yorkshireman heeded not the challenge; he was deep in meditation again, seeing his visions, dreaming his dreams. It was as well, though, that the Lancashire man grasped this opportunity for a passionate 'Good owd Lancasheer'; after play began, no further occasion for such sentiments presented itself.

The day, in truth, told us the old, old story—these Lancashire affairs with Yorkshire have a most damnable iteration. If the reader will turn to the files of this paper and glance through my accounts in 1920, 1921, 1922 and 1923, of Lancashire's batting against Rhodes, Kilner and the rest, he will find much the same language as the language I hope moderately to use now. Since 1920 Lancashire have, season after season, trusted to purely defensive batsmanship against

129

Yorkshire, and not once has it achieved success, though all sorts of wickets, fast, slow and moderately fast, have been available in the period for the experiment. The only instance since 1920 of a Lancashire advance in the face of a Yorkshire attack happened at Sheffield, the day Ernest Tyldesley let all his energy go in a bold, finger snapping foray. That afternoon the far-famed Yorkshire length vanished for a blissful while—it was exposed to the world as a length like unto the lengths of other and quite mortal bowlers from, say, Surrey or Notts—a length relative to a batsman's use of his feet.

On Saturday the lesson taught by Ernest Tyldesley at Sheffield, was forgotten by Makepeace and Hallows, who had the good fortune to bat first on a slow pitch, one not yet difficult by any means. Makepeace permitted Robinson to begin the morning with three successive maidens; Hallows just as lacking in virility as Makepeace played two maiden overs out of three from Macaulay. In thirty-five minutes eleven overs were bowled for seven runs; after seventeen overs had been aimed at decrepit bats, we had yawned through eleven maidens, and had observed, but only just observed, the making of eleven runs, for the loss of a wicket. At lunch, after 105 minutes, all of them glimpses into eternity, Lancashire's total, if that is not too strong a term, was 39 for two!

But why labour the narrative? it is a familiar one; every Lancashire man not at Leeds on Saturday, but who has witnessed our county's batsmanship against Yorkshire in the last three or four years, such Lancashire men will be able to see with their own eyes the way most of our batsmen comported themselves. Hallows and Makepeace never inspired confidence: they were from the first ball bowled seemingly men with a world of concern weighing them down. From the outset the Yorkshire attack was given opportunity to get on top, given cause to think highly of itself. I watched the opening overs of Robinson and Macaulay in a position excellently placed—high above the wicket and straight behind the bowler's arm. And I will swear an oath over a red, red rose that neither Robinson nor Macaulay at the beginning were unplayable. Robinson in fact was guilty of many over-pitched balls that invited castigation. But the root of the batsmen's troubles was in themselves, in their methods. Even had the Yorkshire attack been actually bad, Makepeace and Hallows could not have hit it, simply because they rarely were in a position in which a free swing of the bat was at all possible. To every ball, and BEFORE it pitched, they put the right foot over towards the off wicket and faced square to the bowler. Every cricketer knows how that stance ties up a batsman's strokes; it is a stance which enables you to make no action with the bat other than a feeble push. Moreover it is a stance that makes it easy for any bowler of ability to get a length.

Time after time in the first hour on Saturday, the dead bat was on view in the Lancashire innings. This technical term denotes a bat held out to let the ball find it and hit it. The other day I discussed the use of the dead bat with one of the greatest professional cricketers of all time. The dead bat, he said, was permissible only at those times when a batsman, after having found himself deceived into making a forward stroke, wished to change to a back-stroke but had no time for the re-adjustment. 'He makes a compromise and trusts to half-cock.' But it was a stroke which definitely indicated that a batsman had been caught in two minds, not a stroke to be cultivated as one of the approved strokes. I informed my old professional that the dead bat had come to be regarded by many cricketers in these days as a stroke worth while using regularly, as an authentic stroke. His reply was beautiful: I commend it to nearly all present-day Lancashire cricketers. 'Why,' he said, 'even supposing the dead bat pays and is worth while, which I don't for a moment believe, look at the dignity a cricketer loses by it!' That is the thought which afflicted some of us as we watched Hallows and Makepeace on Saturday; had they scored centuries in that unbeautiful style we should still have been weary at heart. Better far the majestic 'duck' by MacLaren's living, gloriously-moving bat.

Hallows was out leg before at seven; he walked over his wicket to a straight ball and deserved his doom. Makepeace, at 33, could not counter a length ball from Rhodes and had his wicket broken. Makepeace batted for eighty minutes, and possibly he accumulated for himself as many grey hairs as runs. The one substantial partnership of the Lancashire innings was for the third wicket, and Watson and Ernest Tyldesley made it. Both played admirably, even though the turf by now was getting unpleasant at one end—and how stern a criticism this batsmanship provided for the tentativeness of Hallows and Makepeace. Watson had confidence; he did not score heavily, but he was always hitting the ball. Tyldesley nearly attained to his finest form; his strokes told you of a mind at ease, of a heart confident. He played Rhodes superbly, jumping to the ball's pitch.

After lunch these two batsmen raised the score to 64, and now since only two wickets were down, the day was not looking at all downcast for Lancashire. Alas, our County's luck was out: with Tyldesley and Watson nicely set, rain came and stopped play for thirty-five minutes. Immediately the game went on again Watson was caught from a mis-hit, and in the following over Ernest Tyldesley was given out leg-before-wicket, a decision which, I take it, he relished no more than I did myself. Another stand that gave a hint of promise was interrupted by rain; this was between Sharp and Pewtress for the fifth wicket. Sharp was bowled almost as soon as the cricketers took the field once more. But though Lancashire are at liberty to say that twice on Saturday rain disturbed a batsman's innings when apparently he was set, there is also the bowler's case to be put. Bowlers as a rule do not find their arts thriving on a wet ball.

The last five Lancashire wickets fell for 31. Pewtress gave us more than a taste of the only sort of batsmanship that counts on wickets like Saturday's, strong, vehement batsmanship, accomplished by a cricketer not only with skill but with a good opinion of himself. One of his hits, a veritable cut, sent an old player by my side into a delirium of joy. As this cut sped over the field his eyes were the eyes of a man who sees suddenly an oasis in a desert. 'A cut' he babbled. 'A cut! Would you believe it—a cut.'

The boy Iddon batted some fifty minutes, and his little defensive innings possessed unmistakable talent; it also contained proof that a few of his colleagues fell to troubles of their own making. Surely the fact that Iddon with his lack of experience and frail shoulders, could keep the Yorkshiremen at bay for so long, is evidence that the pitch could not have been wicked—it was merely naughty—or the bowling irresistible. Kilner was the best bowler of the day according to the testimony of one's eyes and not that of the score card. His length was accurate and his break keen. If only he would learn to flight the ball what a beautiful art his would be. Rhodes now and again unloosed a rasping break back—Sharp got one of them and it made him wince. But Rhodes was guilty, from time to time, of a half-volley—perhaps in his ripe age he is learning how to bowl half-volleys for the discomfiture of modern batsmen. Macaulay's attack had unwavering keenness; his length after lunch improved, and he exploited a neat off-break. But many times he bowled a short ball, once an over I should say, all of them balls J. T. Tyldesley would have given 2s.6d. each for. The Yorkshire fielding did not impart to the side the aspect of champions.

In the last quarter of an hour of the day Parkin got Sutcliffe out—a great trimph and some consolation for a barren day. Though if it is decreed that some Yorkshireman has to make a good score in this match I would that Sutcliffe had survived. During his brief life on Saturday evening his bat was lovely to watch, for its confident graceful curves. Parkin and Richard Tyldesley bowled with superb spirit—oh it Lancashire would only bat in these games with the hearts of her bowlers!

SECOND DAY

The first ball bowled by Parkin this morning was as a harbinger of doom to batsmen. It pitched outside the off stump, broke back a foot, and spat viciously at Holmes. Parkin contemplated his handiwork with glee: his smile was a gloat over rich spoils to come. The wicket was full of guile and going to the bad every minute. In Parkin's second over of the day Holmes played for a break that wasn't specially there, and discovered himself woefully bowled. This, we thought, was the beginning of a season of tribulation for all the Yorkshire batsmen. As I looked on the spinning venom of Parkin I mentally gave Yorkshire some eighty runs all out. But

Yorkshiremen are tough and how magnificently realistic they are.

That Parkin began the morning like a Spofforth incarnate did not blind Oldroyd and Leyland to the fact of Richard Tyldesley's indifferent length at the other end or to the fact that even Parkin could now and again send along a bad ball. In a word, Oldroyd and Leyland played every ball strictly on its merit; they did not distrust a bad one merely because its predecessor had been very good indeed. Oldroyd and Leyland gave us courageous batsmanship and scored 58 for the third Yorkshire wicket in an hour. A pregnant contest this lion-hearted cricket made to Lancashire's tentative batting on Saturday, when the pitch was easy. Here we had a turf inimical to batsmen and Parkin not far below his best. Yet runs were hit almost at the pace of sixty an hour—on Saturday's comfortable pitch before lunch Lancashire could score but 39 in one hour and three quarters.

Both Leyland and Oldroyd had large smiles from Lady Fortune, but that is the way of the world; luck favours audacity, as a certain Latin poet assured us years and years ago. Sharp was unfortunate in having but two first-class bowlers at his service, and one of these, Richard Tyldesley, not particularly suited by the wicket. I presume he did not give Iddon a chance through a quite reasonable doubt about this young bowler's ability on an occasion so severe. The Oldroyd-Leyland resistance was broken by a misunderstanding between the batsmen which ran Leyland out. Here at any rate was one slice of good luck for Lancashire. Leyland's cricket was tasteful and brave. His wicket was the third to fall with the Yorkshire total 68. Nineteen runs afterwards Oldroyd was clean bowled by Richard Tyldesley, and hereafter Lancashire's attack was no longer to be denied.

Sharp judiciously ordered Parkin and Tyldesley to change ends—tactics which put new life and subtlety into Tyldesley's work. The last six Yorkshire wickets fell for 43; the procession would have gladdened Old Trafford's heart. 'Lo,' Old Trafford might have said in the accents of the hostess in Henry IV, 'these Yorkshiremen do it like any Lancashire cricketers as ever you see.' Tyldesley took the last three Yorkshire wickets for seven runs. Parkin's break-back had rare spitefulness, save for a dubious period during the Oldroyd-Leyland partnership when his faith seemed to dwindle ever so slightly.

Yorkshire conceivably would not have passed Lancashire's first-innings total had a luscious opportunity been grasped of running out Kilner with his score only 11. Kilner dashed down the pitch after Robinson had been completely beaten by one of Parkin's breaks, which went far beyond the wicket for potential byes. But Robinson did not run. He had perplexity in his face as he stood there pondering the mystery of the ball that had just passed down his way. Thus Kilner found himself in Robinson's crease, engaged in involved conversation with the immobile Robinson, himself far, far away from his own safe crease. He ought to have been leisurely and artistically run out but the ball was returned to the wrong end, and the agony of the crowd changed suddenly to devout thanks-giving. Kilner then drove brilliantly for a period, making priceless runs for his county. His off drives were deliciously clean and impudent. Yorkshire's first innings was finished at ten minutes to three, and their score of 130, excellent for the uneasy turf, was hit in an hour less than Lancashire required to amass 113 on a pitch comfortable in the opening two hours.

A crowd of some 30,000 souls sat round the field when the Lancashire second innings was born into a world of trouble. The spectacle of the heaped up masses, most of them magnificently Yorkshire to the marrow, was impressive and beautiful. And the roars of delight which went into the sky as Lancashire batsman after batsman bit the dust caused one to think of the savagery that must have been in the noise of the multitudes in the days of old as innocents were driven to slaughter. The turf was now treacherous: the best batsman going might well have been childlike on it. Sharp made a gallant gesture by sending Pewtress in first with Makepeace, but a glorious break-back from Macaulay upset the enterprise. Ernest Tyldesley was the next victim caught in the slips from a speculative stroke at a ball that whipped away sharply. A typical Robinson catch somewhere near silly point got Makepeace's wicket—Robinson might stand square to the whole world as a sufficient image of dour honest Yorkshire.

He is one of the great characters in modern cricket, with his shambling walk, his keen North Country face, and those honourable grey hairs of his. Makepeace batted three-quarters of an hour this afternoon, playing a resolute game all the time. Some loose bowling by Rhodes, after all he is fallible, gave Watson scope to hit four fours from three overs. Watson again conducted himself like a cricketer of excellent temper and skill; he seemed nicely set when he was given out leg-before-wicket. Hallows once more was guilty of obstruction; I did not agree with the decision, but Hallows deserved his fate because he hardly attempted to put the bat to the ball.

The remainder of Lancashire's innings was composed of shreds and patches—though Sharp's sturdy blade prevailed for 80 minutes. There was excuse this time for our county's frailty; the turf might have been fashioned by Yorkshire's superb spin bowlers themselves. Had Rhodes not taken so large a share in the attack and trusted to Macaulay in larger measure Lancashire's innings might have had a Falstaffian alacrity in sinking. On sticky wickets Kilner is without equal amongst the left-handed bowlers of England. His flight is so low that a batsman cannot jump to the ball's pitch and smother the break before its devilry begins. On a hard turf, though, the lack of ample flight in his bowling might well be a grave defect.

Yorkshire were left with an easy enough task even on this wicket. Our bowlers will work nobly to the end, of course, but spineless batting on Saturday before lunch all but lost the match for Lancashire.

THIRD DAY

This morning at Headingley we have been led out of the wilderness; we have entered the promised land. A great Lancashire victory over the ancient enemy has happened again, at last, and Old Trafford's jubilee year is crowned and garlanded. Not even the annals of Lancashire cricket contain a page more thrilling, more splendid, than the one written to-day, for this triumph over Yorkshire was snatched by the lion-hearted Richard Tyldesley and Parkin out of a pit dug on Saturday by batsmanship of no great faith. Last evening, when all seemed lost, I wrote that though our bowlers would strive nobly to the end of the match, it was all but thrown away on the opening morning. Much resided in that same 'all but' and how shamed and chided we men of little faith have been this day by the superb skill and courage of Lancashire's two great bowlers.

When the struggle began Yorkshire needed merely 57 for victory, with all their batsmen ready and confident. By twenty minutes to one they had been overthrown for 33, the fourth smallest Yorkshire score on record and the tiniest they have ever scraped against Lancashire. Let it be stated straightway, in honour of the fine arts of Richard Tyldesley and Parkin, that Yorkshire, or at least the earlier batsmen, did not contribute to their undoing by want of resolution. Many a determined effort to knock Lancashire's beautiful attack off its length was made by Kilner, Rhodes, Oldroyd and Macaulay. The truth is that these Yorkshire batsmen discovered for once in a while bowling far beyond their powers.

The pitch was still bad, but no worse—perhaps a little slower—than on Monday. Holmes and Sutcliffe went to the wicket with the aspect of men for whom life had little that was not pleasant and prosperous. Quite a considerable crowd turned up, plainly that they might offer yet one more laurel wreath to the champions. It was an affable crowd—how it laughed as a small dog followed at the heels of the cricketers while they walked into the middle. And then came the thunderbolts, out of the blue sky of everybody's complacence. The third ball of Parkin's second over, directed from round the wicket, broke back, beat Sutcliffe's pads and he was lbw. To the fifth ball of the next over, bowled by Richard Tyldesley, Holmes also was clearly out in the same way. Tyldesley deceived him artfully; four balls he sent Holmes which pitched on the stumps and broke away. The fifth 'cut through' straight—the notorious top-spinner. It sped from the turf sinfully. And in Tyldesley's following over he caught and bowled Leyland; three wickets for three runs. It was here that the crowd had its first dreadful glimpse of the writing on the wall. There was something combustible in the air now; the Lancashire men were on their toes. Rhodes, the next Yorkshireman in, began straightway to hit desperately; his recklessness told a poignant tale to the incredulous onlookers. But with Yorkshire's score but three Oldroyd was missed, if the stroke could fairly be called a chance at all. He made the sheerest reflex action at a lightning break-back from Parkin; the ball shot from his bat into the leg trap where Iddon flung himself with all his young heart and muscle at the hit, only to fall full length on the grass with empty hands. Rhodes let his bat go vehemently at the deadly attack, and as he did so he was an unforgettable picture of the old war-horse at bay. Ten precious runs were added by the fourth wicket; then Rhodes was utterly confounded by a leg-break to which he could only respond with a 'Heaven help me' sort of stroke. The second ball of the next over—a stinging off-break from Parkin—clean bowled Oldroyd. Five for thirteen read the score-board as Oldroyd departed, whereat a man in the crowd said, with the air of one discovering a profound and new truth, 'It's a funny game is cricket.' Funny, indeed—why our hearts were beginning to beat unpleasantly; our stomach took on a hollow feeling. Not the least of the general lacerations was caused by a sudden shower of rain; had it lasted ten minutes the Lancashire bowlers would have been left helpless with a greasy ball. The shower passed as quickly as it came, and we mopped moist apprehension from our brows.

Kilner was Yorkshire's great hope at this convulsive point. He marched defiantly into action, got down on his bat with a 'Death or glory' look on his face. Robinson was brilliantly run out at 16, the sixth wicket to fall, but Kilner's bat became all the more militant in the face of this fresh disaster to his county. The writer freely confesses that he suffered excruciating torment all the time that Kilner faced the bowling; for Kilner's every brave slash was a boundary potential. Moreover, to a left-handed batsman Tyldesley's attack loses half of its power; Kilner, indeed, smote a passionate four from Tyldesley's eighth over, and the Yorkshire total moved to 23 with an alacrity painful to all Lancashire men sitting there storm-tossed in hope and doubt. Kilner's bat also made menacing action at Parkin's bowling. 'If only somebody can stay with Roy,' babbled a Yorkshireman, 'we'll win.'

The Lancashire men had an acute sense of this possibility, and like shrewd campaigners they saw to it Kilner was manoeuvred into an inactivity that must have chafed his very soul. At 23 Turner was as dramatically bowled as a batsman can be. Macaulay, his successor, emulated Kilner's pugnacity for a few gruelling minutes; Parkin's best ball accounted for him, but not until he had assisted Kilner in a mountainous partnership of nine. When his wicket fell, the man from Laisterdyke sitting next to me got up and in a voice admirably controlled said: 'That's done it. I'm off! Who'd a' thowt it?' His was prophetic vision indeed; Tyldesley bowled Waddington and got Dolphin stumped (was he caught at the wicket into the bargain?)—both great deeds accomplished in the over after Macaulay's and the man from Laisterdyke's departure. Kilner, though unbeaten was foiled; down into the abyss he had to go with the rest.

As the last Yorkshire wicket fell the Lancashire cricketers leaped on the grass for joy. And not only did the light of their own happiness shine in the faces of all but surely a glow that was thrown from the posterity awaiting them. Old Trafford will talk about this famous day till the end of cricket's history; men of ripe age will sigh, in the presence of tomorrow's children, for the good old times when a Richard Tyldesley and a Parkin walked the earth! Of course the crowd yesterday had at the finish mouths that were full of ashes; still they gave the conquerors a generous reception. Let Old Trafford assemble in its thousands tomorrow, fine weather or foul, and do homage to its team. And at the same time make appropriate reward for the sterling service of Ernest Tyldesley.

The Yorkshire innings lost its wickets in this sequence: 1/3 2/3 3/3 4/13 5/13 6/16 7/23 8/32 9/33 10/33. Parkin took the first, fifth, and eighth wickets; Tyldesley the second, third, fourth, seventh, ninth and tenth. Both bowled like men possessed, like men who were for the while vessels of plenary inspiration. Tyldesley's accuracy was beyond praise; have we ever known before a leg-break bowler with his certainty of pitch? Armstrong was accurate, but he did not possess the spin of Tyldesley, not at least when his length was good. I saw only three bad balls leave Tyldesley's clever fingers: the rest were dropped on the proverbial sixpence. But even more impressive than his technical excellence was his calm, masterful manner. He did not permit the crisis to hinder his confidence; he might well, and with good excuse, have pitched short to Kilner, but he didn't. Parkin wavered for one over in the face of Kilner's long handle, but Tyldesley never for a moment.

How can we measure Tyldesley's skill and brave spirit in that trying hour? It was only cricket, you might insist, only a game. But the testing times of this life are just what a man makes of them; if he feels a responsibility at cricket as keenly as another man feels a responsibility in mortal battle, who shall say he does not come just as close to the heroic? The faith and composure of Tyldesley was noble enough to shift mountains; I have rarely been moved so much to a sort of adoration for cricket and cricketers as when today Tyldesley went on with his duty, running up to the wicket with all his own true magnificent doggedness. Parkin, through getting the wickets of Oldroyd, Sutcliffe, and Macaulay, did his county rare service too, it shall not be forgotten.

Nor will the fine fieldsmanship of the side. Pewtress ran Robinson out with only one stump to aim at; Duckworth kept guard like an England wicket-keeper of tomorrow; Watson saved a certain boundary at a time when boundaries were worth guinea gold to Yorkshire. And from start to finish of the hurly-burly Sharp was a captain worthy of the occasion; he possessed equanimity and shrewdness, and spread a heartening sense over the field that he had his hand on his side's helm in the stormiest passages. Thus time has brought its revenge and consolation; the jubilee year of Lancashire cricket is already assured success.

YORKSHIRE V LANCASHIRE 1924

SCORES

LANCASHIRE

First Innings		Second Innings	
Makepeace, b Rhodes	17	c Robinson, b Kilner	9
Hallows, lbw, b Macaulay	5	lbw, b Rhodes	0
Tyldesley (E.), lbw, b Macaulay	29	c Waddington, b Kilner	2
Watson, c Waddington, b Rhodes	13	lbw, b Kilner	21
A. W. Pewtress, b Macaulay	20	b Macaulay	5
J. Sharp, b Kilner	12	c & b Kilner	14
Iddon, b Macaulay	6	b Rhodes	4
A. Rhodes, c Oldroyd, b Macaulay	1	b Macaulay	6
Tyldesley (R.), c Holmes, b Kilner	3	b Macaulay	0
Parkin, lbw, b Macaulay	0	not out	2
Duckworth, not out	0	c Robinson, b Macaulay	0
Extras	7	Extras	11
Total	113	Total	74

YORKSHIRE

First Innings		Second Innings	
Holmes, b Parkin	10	lbw, b Tyldesley (R.)	0
Sutcliffe, c Tyldesley (R.), b Parkin	0	lbw, b Parkin	3
Oldroyd, b Tyldesley (R.)	37	b Parkin	3
Leyland, run out	21	c & b Tyldesley (R.)	0
Rhodes, lbw, b Parkin	18	c Makepeace, b Tyldesley (R.)	7
Kilner, b Parkin	35	not out	13
Robinson, c & b Parkin	1	run out	2
Turner, lbw, b Tyldesley (R.)	2	b Tyldesley (R.)	1
Macaulay, c & b Tyldesley (R.)	0	b Parkin	4
Waddington, b Tyldelsey (R.)	0	b Tyldesley (R.)	0
Dolphin, not out	0	st Duckworth, b Tyldesley (R.)	0
Extras	6		
Total	130	Total	33

141

THE ROSES MATCHES 1919-1939
BOWLING ANALYSIS

Lancashire—First Innings

	O.	M.	R.	W.		O.	M.	R.	W.
Robinson	11	7	10	0	Rhodes	20	7	28	2
Macaulay	33	14	40	6	Kilner	26·3	12	28	2

Second Innings

	O.	M.	R.	W.		O.	M.	R.	W.
Macaulay	16·2	7	19	4	Kilner	23	16	13	4
Robinson	2	1	3	0	Rhodes	15	5	28	2

Yorkshire—First Innings

	O.	M.	R.	W.		O.	M.	R.	W.
Parkin	27·2	9	46	5	Watson	7	2	9	0
Tyldesley (R.)	27	9	69	4					

Second Innings

	O.	M.	R.	W.		O.	M.	R.	W.
Parkin	12	7	15	3	Tyldesley (R.)	11·5	6	18	6

YORKSHIRE V LANCASHIRE 1924

August 2/4/5   Old Trafford

FIRST DAY

A SODDEN pitch prevented cricket at Old Trafford on Saturday until twenty minutes past three, but the occasion's keenness brought a splendid crowd, and the game began with the air humming expectantly. Turnstiles clicked in agitation; the multitude minute by minute got bigger, and as it did so made those dramatic noises, those dramatic alarums, which seem to give a Lancashire and Yorkshire match a thousand tongues whereby to express superb temper and fighting spirit.

The game had a suitably grand beginning. Yorkshire won the toss, and Sutcliffe and Holmes found themselves confronted by Macdonald. Here was additional spice to a dish calculated always to warm the palate. For it is no secret that Yorkshire cricketers hold strong, stormy views about Lancashire's use of an Australian in these ancient feuds. 'Play up Yorkshire,' howled a man (possibly from Sowerby Bridge) as Macdonald got himself ready to attack on Saturday. And I imagined I heard an accent of pride in his pronunciation of 'shire'. But the most radical Yorkshireman would, one feels certain, gladly admit that Macdonald in action is a spectacle that does honour to the greatest of all county cricket matches. His long sinuous movements to the wicket, a glide rather than a run, and that beautiful flexion of the wrist, just before he lets the ball go, which has a snake-like poise and hint of venom. And on Saturday the grandeur of Macdonald's action was confronted by a young Yorkshireman whose movements were just as deeply steeped in grandeur. These two cricketers went through a swift period of conflict that will not quickly be forgotten because of its mingled antagonism and grace.

The match during its opening three-quarters of an hour was indeed nothing but a duel between Sutcliffe and Macdonald. The fast bowler got in his blow first, but

143

unfortunately for Lancashire it was not fatal. The last ball of his fifth over beat Sutcliffe's bat completely. And the second ball of his next over morally bowled Yorkshire's Adonis. Sutcliffe also fluked an off-ball from Macdonald in front of Hopwood, while an over or two afterwards he sliced another dangerously above the slips' heads. But by now Sutcliffe was conquering his man. The fourth and fifth balls of Macdonald's sixth over were proudly and powerfully pulled to the leg boundary. A few minutes later Sutcliffe hit four boundaries in one over from the fast bowler, three to leg and the other the dangerous slip stroke just mentioned. Rarely has one in recent summers seen batsmanship ride a more magnificent foray against fast bowling than this of Sutcliffe. He reached 52 out of a total of 63 in just under the hour. When he had scored 36 he had hit Macdonald for six boundaries. There were eleven fours in his innings when it had reached 56 and also a five, a single of which came from an overthrow.

Sutcliffe's strokes to leg from the fast bowler possessed the authentic grand manner; they were, in truth, MacLarenesque. They were, in bulk, accomplished from short rising balls. Despite the slow turf Macdonald made the ball get up splendidly. Sutcliffe hit them round by pivoting on his back foot, his body upright and confident. As Sutcliffe's bat swerved across the line of the ball with the loveliest and most thrilling curve, one had a sudden feeling of rapture at the breast and in the throat. Extravagant language, do you think? Very well, let us describe Sutcliffe's masterpiece in the circumspect way: 'he got Macdonald to leg repeatedly, his strokes being admirably timed.' The old tag simply will not do. One might as well write circumspectly of a great fiddler making glorious music for us: 'Kreisler played his Caprice Viennois with admirable tone, his phrasing being especially good.' We shall be wise to think of Sutcliffe's cricket on Saturday as something full of heroic poetry. And the more extravagantly we remember its beauty the better for our souls.

Sutcliffe probably routed Macdonald with our fast bowler in a destroying vein. For Macdonald began to bowl with four successive maidens in which there were many unmistakably great deliveries. As I have hinted Macdonald rose superior for a while to the dead turf; he made the ball rear and his pace was killing enough. Holmes—one has already forgotten that there were other batsmen in with Sutcliffe—scored 10 to Sutcliffe's 50, and he like Sutcliffe, was lucky to survive the Australian's first few overs. Considering the sluggish turf, Macdonald's attack was wonderfully alive. It is not to his discredit that 28 runs were hit from him in five overs; that fact is testimony of Sutcliffe's merit.

Holmes was out leg-before-wicket at 64 to Richard Tyldesley, who bowled in place of Parkin after Parkin had struggled for three overs against a strong wind, obviously not happy in the ordeal. Tyldesley's attack was even less suited to the turf, and because of its slow pace, less suited to exploitation against a wind than Parkin's. Yet Richard contrived to bowl well and deserved his wicket, though Holmes really got himself out by a shocking stroke. Oldroyd also threw his wicket away; he impetuously dashed for a run from a hit to mid-off and Parkin smartly threw in and hit the stumps.

Immediately after the tea interval—was it really necessary after so late a start?—it was plain that the turf was drying. Both Tyldesley and Parkin turned the ball, and Sutcliffe found himself preoccupied with a spot in the wicket which he smote hard with his bat almost after every ball bowled. The crowd obviously expected another Yorkshire wicket or two hereabouts, and disappointment came over the field like a cloud as Leyland managed to dig himself in following a tentative beginning. Parkin was unlucky, without quite finding his best form, though now he had the advantage of the wind. It might have been a wise move to have given Macdonald the wind again immediately the interval was over, for the ground was then a little drier; moreover, it is always policy to slip your fast bowler at batsmen just in after a break. Macdonald did not bowl, after his first spell, until the Yorkshire score reached 104, and then he worked against the wind and exploited his not very impressive medium off-breaks. At 132 he crossed over and took the wind again, in place of the unsuccessful and on the whole unlucky Parkin. But it was Watson who broke the too prosperous stand for Yorkshire's third wicket, which added 72 runs at a time when the bowlers were getting some assistance from the pitch. Watson had Sutcliffe caught at the wicket in his second over; he bowled excellently, once again proving that his attack ought to be used more than it is.

After tea Sutcliffe's innings lost its first lustre. He continued to play gracefully—his defensive strokes are freer than most batsmen's major strokes—but he could not score quickly from the spinning ball. In 40 minutes from tea he made only ten. In all, his innings lasted two hours and 35 minutes: his last 40 runs took him an hour and a half to get. Yet throughout he was the England batsman all over. The crowd were aware of this; they seemed to look at his play with a delighted sense that they were watching a young cricketer in the blossoming time of his art. Sutcliffe has his fingers on the hem of Hobbs's imperial purple; there are, of course, still things in batsmanship for him to learn. But happily he knows it, and at this stage of his development self-criticism will be his best coach.

At 56 Sutcliffe mishit a ball from Parkin behind the wicket, but nobody could get to it. Sutcliffe deserved his luck; it may be said, in fact, that he provoked it—for Fortune is glad to smile at the dauntless. And in his duel with Macdonald Sutcliffe was the embodiment of brave and skilful youth; he lived up to the pictures of the hero in the school stories of our boyhood. Without him on Saturday Yorkshire would have seemed more grim than ever. How did this young Cavalier come into the Roundhead army?

SECOND DAY

There was an enormous crowd at Old Trafford yesterday, amounting to some 36,000. This concourse began to gather early in the morning, possibly before the cricketers were successfully through their shaving. (Not one player in this game, by the way, is at liberty not to use a razor; other times, other manners! Lancashire and Yorkshire matches in the past have been fought by cricketers bearded like the pard, big hairy giants!). The advance guard of yesterday's mighty crowd was small boys, with sustenance wrapped up in brown paper. By half past eleven the multitude had spread everywhere, even to the roof of the pavilion. It was a nicely behaved crowd, though not, one imagined, as humorous as the crowds of pre-war years. In the old times, whenever cricket got as dull as it invariably was yesterday, the packed thousands quickly discovered means of their own to make amusement. Yesterday a policeman was allowed to walk in silence round the ring, even during a tedious stretch of play. A period has been known at Old Trafford when the majestic patrol of the law went on to the rhythmical command of 20,000 voices—'Left, right, left right.' And at the end of the constable's march 20,000 voices would cheer at its own waggishness. There was no such jollity yesterday from the crowd, which possessed the most excellent manners. There is much to be said after all on behalf of a crowd of spirit, though nowadays there are to be found folk who expect the summer game to be watched with a well-bred reserve that would suit croquet better than cricket.

Possibly a dull day, with the help of dull play, was responsible for Old Trafford's sedate Bank Holiday. Yorkshire batted till ten minutes past four on an easy wicket and in 200 minutes they scored 212 runs, lifting their Saturday's score to 359 all out. Then, at 25 minutes to five Lancashire went in with the turf still comfortable enough, and in just under two hours made 78 for two. The day's cricket had one spirited period in which Kilner gave us just a hint why in the course of the evolution of the cricket bat from its primitive shape it has come to possess a hump in the blade's middle. But Kilner's innings lasted only half an hour; he was but one Mercutio in a company of workers by the book of arithmetic. There was plenty of honest craftsmanship on view all day, but the writer would have as soon watched skilled bricklayers putting up a wall as these cricketers putting up their various totals. At any rate, one could have looked at the work of bricklaying without experiencing any unfulfilled expectations. Cricket presumably is a game; where in yesterday's play was that speculation, that adventure, which is as breath of life in sport?

Yorkshire, with a good start accomplished on Saturday, surely might have tried to get runs quickly yesterday with a view to an early declaration and a bold bid for victory in the time available. Yorkshire did not—save while Kilner batted—force the pace; runs came slower, in fact, in the middle of the innings than at the beginning. Play could not begin till 12 o'clock because of a wet wicket, which left the pitch lifeless. In ninety minutes before lunch Yorkshire added 83 and these runs included the brilliant innings of Kilner, which was worth 37. And from a quarter past two till ten minutes past four, excluding five minutes for a stoppage by rain, Yorkshire scored merely another 129. Had the sun been shining no doubt Wilson would have closed Yorkshire's innings with the 300 up. But the fact that the pitch kept easy all day gives the batsmen little excuse for their dilatoriness.

The Lancashire bowling did not explain the slow pace of scoring. Macdonald and Richard Tyldesley are both rather at a discount on slow grounds. Parkin was far below his form, and Watson, though he usually bowled satisfactorily in his short spells, never got a sustained chance. After lunch Parkin bowled without rest for an hour and 25 minutes, a rather inexplicably long trial seeing that he rarely found a good length and was hit for 43 runs in 14 overs, which included only two maidens. His attack lacked those variations of pace which made him a delightful bowler a year or two ago; once only did I see him exploit his slow ball, and not at all until the Yorkshire tail was in. Macdonald had atrocious luck; two slip catches were missed from him, one when Leyland was 92. Richard Tyldesley gave us one or two interesting stretches of bowling. To Leyland he usually trusted to off-breaks, presumably on the principle that left-handers as a rule relish a right-hander's leg break. Unfortunately Tyldesley seems unable to give a tempting flight to his off-break, and on yesterday's dead wicket it was not good enough to beat the bat.

Leyland scored his first century, and was undefeated at the close of the Yorkshire innings. He batted four hours and three-quarters. It was an innings full of technical points interesting and admirable to cricketers. He watched the ball closely and seemed to judge its length quickly. His back play was straight—no common virtue in left-handed batsmen—and his feet were on the whole neatly and correctly placed. It was good to see him counter the turning ball mainly with his bat; he exploited his pads legitimately—that is, as a safeguard in case a stroke failed of its purpose. Too many batsmen nowadays trust first of all to their legs when confronted with a bowler capable of spin. Leyland is still stiff in his bat's swing; he is modern enough in his use of the restricted 'lift-up' of the bat. On slow wickets perhaps there is something to be said in favour of this kind of 'lift-up,' for it goes well with the back play that is necessary on slow grounds. Yet one recollects MacLaren's free swing of the bat when he played back; one recollects how Spooner would hit a boundary from a back position. Leyland of course is not to be judged by these exacting standards; he is still in the 'promising' stage, though very far advanced in it. But the restricted 'lift up' is so popular even with leading batsmen today that one might usefully refer now and again to an older, more beautiful, and not less efficacious method. Kilner's innings was true to his cheerful and confident nature—what's bred in the bone will come out in the shortest innings. Dolphin also played well and assisted in a ninth-wicket partnership of 75 made in fifty minutes, a giddy speed in comparison with the day's general loitering.

Makepeace and Hallows in seventy minutes scored 57 for Lancashire's first wicket. Hallows made two beautiful straight drives; he does not however seem to extend his range of strokes. Ernest Tyldesley could not settle down, and a typical Robinson catch got him out at 64. Robinson fielded at 'silly' mid-off, a position which he obviously revels in. He gives one the impression that he expects a hot catch from every ball bowled. I have known games go their entire course, without opportunity coming once to Robinson for a solitary catch; and I have thought that in these games Robinson has been a man not only frustrated but bitterly disappointed. He is, as the crowd says, a 'character'; made of good Yorkshire stuff, a man who seems all shambling feet and slouching body—until a ball comes his way. Then energy concentrates in him and he moves with superb alacrity. He has a keen Yorkshire face, and there is an honourable iron grey in his hair.

THIRD DAY

The condition of the pitch at Old Trafford was so bad on the third day that the Lancashire and Yorkshire match was abandoned.

SCORES

YORKSHIRE

First Innings

Holmes, lbw, b Tyldesley (R.)	10
Sutcliffe, c Duckworth, b Wilson	90
Oldroyd, run out	1
Leyland, not out	133
Rhodes, b Macdonald	12
Kilner, b Watson	37
Robinson, c Pewtress, b Tyldesley (R.)	1
Macaulay, b Macdonald	18
G. Wilson, b Parkin	1
Dolphin, c Tyldesley (E.), b Tyldesley (R.)	33
Waddington, b Watson	7
Extras	16
	—
Total	359

LANCASHIRE

First Innings

Makepeace, not out	35
Hallows, c Oldroyd, b Macaulay	33
Tyldesley (E.), c Robinson, b Kilner	2
Watson, not out	3
Extras	5
	—
Total (for 2)	78

BOWLING ANALYSIS

Yorkshire—First Innings

	O.	M.	R.	W.		O.	M.	R.	W.
Parkin	48	11	125	1	Tyldesley (R.)	37	12	97	3
Macdonald	35	11	88	2	Watson	18·5	9	33	3

Lancashire—First Innings

	O.	M.	R.	W.		O.	M.	R.	W.
Robinson	8	3	14	0	Macaulay	10	5	20	1
Waddington	12	4	18	0	Rhodes	3	2	4	0
Kilner	14	6	17	1					

YORKSHIRE V LANCASHIRE 1925

May 30 June 1/2   Old Trafford

FIRST DAY

LANCASHIRE did very well on Saturday to get Yorkshire all out for 232 on a wicket that in the main was of comfortable pace. Despite a confident prelude to the innings by Sutcliffe and Holmes, the innings of the ancient enemy could but intermittently work up to the conqueror's pace and amplitude, and when the end came at half-past six we had witnessed some five hours of rather gruelling cricket.

Now and again the scoring was so slow that noises came out of the crowd of a few souls in some torment, but, on the whole, the onlookers were as patient as the batsmen. Usually the Old Trafford crowd is quick to get ironic at the expense of somnambulism at the wicket; on Saturday the instincts of most spectators were sound—it was understood that here we had a case where slow batsmanship was justified by the responsible occasion and by an attack of uncommon excellence. Slow cricket does not necessarily mean poor-spirited cricket; one attacks dull batting when the hour and the bowling call out for livelier measures. There are few batsmen in the game today with the ability to hit freely against an attack as good as that of Lancashire on Saturday afternoon after lunch.

The principal limitation of Yorkshire's batting was one common enough in modern cricket—an inability to deal drastically with the off-side ball. Granted a bowler of Macdonald's pace and general direction at hand, cricketers of a dozen years ago might have ravished our senses with an amount of cutting—especially of late cutting (shades of J. T. Brown!). Of Yorkshire's total of 223 from the bat, only 32 came from strokes behind the nowadays obsolete position of point. No fewer than 138 were scored to the on and to leg. The best off-side cricket of the day was Robinson's, whose drives and cuts in that direction were as clean as they were gallant in temper.

151

The cricketers took the field at noon in a gusty, searching wind that never held its peace all day. There was much applause for Sutcliffe—now a handsomely bronzed man. (Even the gale of Saturday could not disturb the smooth gloss of his black hair—a gloss that J. W. H. T. Douglas might well envy.) The game was about to begin when there was a cloudburst that drenched the field with 'torrents of summer,' whereat the cricketers fled the spot. Even the umpires were to be seen in quick, agitated motion, a departure from time-honoured dignity which no doubt will be brought to the notice of the great Panjandrum of Umpires, whoever and wherever he may be. This rainstorm held back activities till twenty-five minutes past twelve, and possibly it was worth a few valuable runs to Yorkshire; it certainly left the bowlers grappling with a greasy ball for some time after the match's outset. Holmes and Sutcliffe were undefeated at lunch, the Yorkshire score then being 50. So long as the bowling 'cut through,' Sutcliffe was at his most graceful. From Macdonald he quickly made a hit that transcended the graceful and achieved the dramatic. This was a leg hit, accomplished by means of a thrilling swing of the body on the right foot. The stroke at its finish saw the young batsman in beautiful poise, the bat held on high masterfully. Here was a proper sight for a sculptor. And why do our sculptors (assuming, as the sentry in 'Iolanthe' might sing, that we have got any)— why do they not turn to the games of a nation for inspiration, as the Greeks did, and fix for us in marble the glory of life when it is young? Sutcliffe was at ease with the Lancashire attack until the ball began to turn. Parkin defeated his bat with a fine break-back when he was 20; after lunch Richard Tyldesley's spin caused ripples of unease to come over the cool surface of his art. But it was Macdonald, and not a slower bowler, who eventually over-threw Sutcliffe when Yorkshire's total was 66 and the time of day half-past two. Sutcliffe played out confidently at a well-pitched-up ball of less than Macdonald's customary pace; how he missed it he did not know and never will. The ball broke back after pitching—if that information will throw any light on his problem.

Oldroyd, who took Sutcliffe's place at the wicket, ran into some very fast bowling from Macdonald and into Richard

Tyldesley at his steadiest. He could score only two runs in half an hour. For fifty minutes after lunch the Lancashire attack was on top; the pitch hereabouts gave a hint of susceptibility to spin. During this fifty minutes Yorkshire made 34, thanks largely to Holmes, who played well. His wicket was the second to fall at 84. He had just reached his half-century when, seemingly flushed with pleasure, he hit too soon at a good 'bad' ball from Tyldesley. It was the sort of ball that looks 'certain for four' from the ring, but which, in fact, is not so silly as it seems. It was tossed slow and high, but dropped quite short. Holmes half hit it, and Barnes at mid-on brought off the catch. Holmes was on view for two hours; his innings was full of cricket in his own smart, dapper style. When he was thirteen he survived an appeal by Richard Tyldesley which was 'werry fierce'; and Parkin broke through his keen-eyed defence with the last ball of his first over at the beginning of the match.

Four runs following the downfall of Holmes, Parkin bowled Oldroyd, and now the pot was on the boil, for since lunch Yorkshire had lost three good batsmen for 38. The old war-horse Rhodes, with Leyland, staved the collapse that might easily have happened. It was perhaps not wise policy that Watson should have been put on to bowl hereabouts, with two 'fresh' batsmen in. No doubt the Lancashire captain exploited Watson at this point because Parkin was now at his best with the wind behind him—and because Watson is usually thought to be better at keeping a length in the face of a gale than other Lancashire bowlers. The truth is that Richard Tyldesley was a better bowler on Saturday against the wind than he was with it behind him.

Watson tackled the icy blast with great courage and praiseworthy steadiness of technique from a quarter past three till the tea interval and for twenty-five minutes afterwards. Rhodes and Leyland, who added 47 for the fourth Yorkshire wicket, were both well 'off the mark' before Macdonald attacked them. (This is not intended as a criticism of Barnes' captaincy; rather do I draw attention to the fact that Saturday's gale made unenviable the task of deploying the Lancashire attack in full strength at both ends.) Leyland and Rhodes batted cleverly; it was a delight to see how

Rhodes once countered Parkin's slow ball. It came to him with a high flight, but instead of attempting to drive—as a less experienced batsman would have done—he allowed it to pitch, went back on his wicket, and cut it powerfully for four; a stroke from the fore-arms and wrists. Rhodes plainly did not relish Macdonald's fastest bowling—which is why some of us wished it could have been possible to slip Macdonald at him immediately he came to the wicket. Leyland's cricket mingled sound defence with watchfulness and aggression for the loose ball.

Half the Yorkshire wickets were accounted for at 143. The sixth wicket, held by Rhodes and Robinson, lifted the score to 208, and now for the one and only time in the afternoon the batting had a dash of sweetness and light. Robinson, good old Yorkshire in the flesh, cracked the ball between point and cover with no little stylishness. The contrast between his clear-cut cricket on the off side and his clumsiness to leg was engaging. On the whole, though, his innings provoked a sense of brilliance—so sullen had been most of the cricket since lunch; in wintry gloom your good candle can shine a welcome light. Rhodes's innings lasted two hours—cricket that always told of shrewdness, the horse-sense of the game. After he departed the last four wickets collapsed with a suddenness not at all like the Yorkshire of old. Robinson was unbeaten, but when he was 41 some of the Lancashire cricketers thought he was out. He hit a ball to the on side, where Pewtress dashed forward, held the ball with both hands for a second or two, but lost grip as he rolled over on the earth. The umpire, as I thought, rightly gave the batsman not out: in making a catch 'falling down' it is necessary for a fieldsman to hold the ball all the time, not merely part of the time.

The Yorkshire innings probably disappointed the Champions; its course, through the afternoon, may be said to have resembled those Arabian torrents which, instead of growing larger as they progress, steadily diminish. Lancashire's out-cricket was better than any we have had from the side so far this season. There were complaints in the crowd about uncertain fielding, but whoever made them did not take into account the chill of the day. Macdonald occasionally let us witness his most destructive speed; now and again he seemed to falter. Parkin for a period after lunch was at his best; his spin was excellent and also his length. As I have already suggested, Richard Tyldesley himself exploded the notion that he cannot attack with a high wind against him; his length was not often seen to waver.

The threat of bad weather at noon kept the crowd on the small side, though it reached some 15,000 before the day was out. In the afternoon, play of sunshine and shadow over the grass was pretty to see; now would the gloom of a great cloud come over us and then a sudden light that seemed to put the field and the cricket into a glass. The cold wind probably was the cause of the multitude's stillness—there was little of the old humour and pomp and circumstance. After lunch a voice was heard to raise itself many times from the depths in mournful supplication of 'Good old Wilfred.' But what boon the voice craved after in its sorrow no man could tell; for the voice uttered it not; it had no words to the end but (always supplicatory) 'Good old Wildred.'

SECOND DAY

There was scourging cricket yesterday at Old Trafford from morning till the fall of the afternoon. Hour by hour the match smouldered like a dull fire; then, at the very finish, came a great wind of contention that blew hot antagonism over the field. At a quarter past six, Lancashire, with only two wickets in hand, still needed thirteen to beat Yorkshire on the first innings. One wicket was defended by Hallows, who the day long had been playing the greatest game of his career so far; he was as a rock against which wave after wave of the enemy's attack broke in vain. Macdonald came to the crease at this moment of crisis; it was on his defence the Yorkshiremen concentrated a last desperate onslaught.

Old Trafford hereabouts experienced severe beatings of the heart; could Macdonald be trusted? We all knew him to be an impetuous hitter; a trafficker in fortune with bat and ball. Would the wily Kilner ensnare him? Would the old Adam come out of him? But Macdonald is an Australian and they are as canny as any of your Tykes. Macdonald was not to be tempted; he did not flick his bat at the air; he played with caution, steady in mind if not always steady in technique. At 6.20 Hallows drove a ball from Robinson to the off-boundary and completed his century. Then, at 226, seven short of the advantage, Macaulay was asked to bowl—a shrewd move.

He put all his heart and energy into six bolts aimed at the bat of our Australian; one was a no-ball—another single to Lancashire. Two more overs brought in two runs; Macdonald was applauded for masterful self-denial. One of his defensive strokes was actually stylish; we laughed as we cheered. But the excitement grew; we quite forgot there was another batsman to come should Macdonald fail. Another injustice to Parkin! Hallows settled the issue, for the time being (remember Bramall Lane a year or two ago!), with a lion-hearted drive; and the crowd sang like the morning stars in their joy—the whole 30,000 of them, including a man from (I take it) Sowerby Bridge who afterwards, when the tumult and the shouting was done went sadly away from the scene saying 'Eh Emmott, ah thowt better of thi, mi lad, than this!'

Old Trafford looked a brave, multitudinous place so early in the morning as eleven o'clock. The crowd that sat round the field was splendidly English in its easefulness and spaciousness of spirit. Hum and buzz of expectation were in the air even before the action began, and when the Yorkshire team took the field some 20,000 souls settled down to a day of anxiety, grief and pain and ecstacy. Duckworth and Hopwood, sent in on Saturday evening as stop-gaps, were quickly accounted for by the inveterate Macaulay. Yet brief life though their portion was both Duckworth and Hopwood played pluckily; one looked on with some emotion at the sight of the bravery of these innocents, thrown quickly into sacrificial fires.

At a quarter to twelve Hallows and Makepeace stood on guard; the hurly-burly was 'set-agate', as the children used to say in the old game. Rain in the early morning had eased the turf, but Macaulay and Robinson attacked with some venom. It was a nasty break-back that upset the stump of Hopwood, a ball that plainly inspired Macaulay and gave him to think that his arm now possessed a strength capable of moving the mountain named Makepeace. Makepeace in a Yorkshire match, with the hour not propitious for Lancashire, is a grand sight to see. As he bends down over his bat he is the image of responsibility and resistance. His eyes are pin-points of suspicion; his tense aspect at the wicket reminds us of the words of the poet, 'Obstinacy takes its sturdy stand to disconcert what Policy has planned.'

Yorkshire's obvious policy, after the quick fall of two Lancashire wickets yesterday morning, was writ large on the face of every man in the field. Robinson was an almost comical picture of vehemence—he is in repose (as the painters say) a man of shambling, loose-limbed appearance. But when he bowls, determination renders every muscle in him taut and deliberate. He lives an excited life all day long; he seemingly expects a wicket every ball when he is bowling and a catch every ball when he is fielding. With such an appetite for glory (in the behalf of 'good owd Yorkshire') a man is bound now and again to suffer frustration and disappointment. At the end of each unsuccessful over Robinson goes slowly to his place in the field communing with himself, apparently upon the wickedness of the world, that a Yorkshireman should put forth the labour of a lion all to no immediate purpose!

Makepeace stayed in with Hallows, till the last over before lunch, and these two cricketers raised their county's score to 94. Makepeace was stumped from one of the only balls of the morning that 'whipped away' after pitching. Rhodes bowled it, and a moment or two before he did so he had pitched Makepeace a loose one to leg and seen it hit with a proud sweeping action to the boundary. Rhodes is never so dangerous a bowler as he is just after he has been driven for four; he is quick to take advantage of the wine of success that goes to the batsmen's head. Makepeace played severe cricket for two hours; the batting throughout his partnership with Hallows can but seldom have raised hopes in the Yorkshire breast. Robinson's relief when Dolphin brilliantly stumped Lancashire's Stonewall Jackson must have been tremendous.

There was another fine Lancashire stand after the interval, which was prolonged by a rainstorm. This time the helpmate of Hallows was Ernest Tyldesley. Slowly but certainly the edge was ground away from the attack of the ancient host: the batting even looked to be moving in a confident way.

Tyldesley occasionally flashed the dramatic spark of his hook over the grass. And all the time Hallows persisted, his bat a safe shield. Lancashire passed the 150 mark with only three wickets down; the bowling hereabouts took on a baffled air. So well did Hallows and Tyldesley play that rarely did we see the ball beat the bat. Only once did Hallows falter; this was with Lancashire's total 107. He mishit an almost full toss from Macaulay, who allowed a possible chance of caught and bowled to go through hands stretched up over his head. A heavy reckoning for Yorkshire did Macaulay's blunder bring in its train—O, the unspeakable torment in the soul of Robinson!

At ten minutes to four a bolt shot out of the blue and struck the Lancashire ship fore and aft; calm sea and prosperous voyage were over for a while. Ernest Tyldesley, when obviously firmly set to the earth as a tree, hit a ball from Kilner stylishly to leg and Waddington caught it superbly. Bad luck, indeed, for a cricketer to get out from so worthy a stroke. A quarter of an hour afterwards Watson was out leg-before-wicket and Pewtress ran himself out, Lancashire six for 176; Yorkshire in grip of the game again; life worth living for Robinson. Barnes had some lines of care on his face as he joined the imperturbable Hallows; none the less he gave us a captain's innings. Not only did he defend his wicket, but also contrived to get on to some of his strokes the bloom of wrist play. It seemed to the writer that he gave a chance at the wicket when he was six and the Lancashire score 186. He served his county well while 29 priceless runs were made. His innings was interrupted by yet another rainstorm, which possibly unsettled him almost as much as it unsettled the Yorkshire bowlers. His wicket fell to a trap on the legside set by Kilner—215 for seven. Richard Tyldesley was utterly bowled five runs later, and now came Macdonald and the day's crisis and consummation which I have already attempted to describe.

Hallows began his innings at a quarter to twelve, with Lancashire two wickets to the bad with only a dozen runs in hand. He was unbeaten at the close, after some five hours and a half of sterling batsmanship. I can make no better description of his innings than to say it was 'serene'—the word denotes mastery and ease and Hallows' cricket yesterday was both. He rarely got himself into difficulties; physical hurt, caused by a blow on the knee from a fast ball, was apparently the only trouble the Yorkshire attack caused him. His defence was constantly sound, but with it went a quick forcefulness for the loose ball. His runs, as is his custom, were mainly hit to leg or by swinging drives. Not once did he cut substantially. There was, indeed, nothing finer in this very fine display than Hallows' palpable understanding of exactly which are and which are not his strong points. Those hits over which he has command he let us see time after time in a splendid light. No cricketer will complain that his batting was slow; all the time he was sustaining a stern burden of responsibility. All in all, it was the best innings he has yet achieved. The writer praises it with the greater heartiness because recently he has had cause not to be satisfied with some of Hallows' batting. Those of us who know the pure gold of this cricketer's craft will not be fobbed off with counterfeit. Hallows' cricket had the guinea stamp, and the great crowd recognised it.

THIRD DAY

The cricket at Old Trafford yesterday was futile and hardly worth discussion. Yorkshire's second innings began just before noon; there remained then only some four and a half hours for play, and including the extra time that may be claimed in a crisis, Yorkshire obviously thought they had nothing to aim at but a draw. Lancashire, on the easy wicket, could scarcely hope to force a victory against batsmen determined to risk nothing.

Yorkshire obtained their objective and rarely seemed likely to miss it; but the crowd had ample justification for asking whether county batsmen could not have played for a draw with a little more spirit and grace than was shown by Yorkshire throughout the sunny afternoon. The Yorkshiremen declined to take risks; that was their policy—a policy in proper keeping with the game's best traditions. If a team is unable to win a match it is not unsportsmanlike for it to strive to stave off defeat. But yesterday the Yorkshiremen would not put freedom into their batsmanship even after they

159

had placed defeat out of question. At a quarter to five Yorkshire were more than a hundred runs ahead with half their wickets in hand and less than an hour left for play. Yet the batting remained intolerably ca'canny. It was not until Barnes placed the proceedings beyond serious consideration by asking Hallows and Makepeace to bowl that one saw a bat swing vigorously at the ball. Hopwood was given another chance to show his promise as a bowler and he did.

The day's play was not of a kind likely to do good to the reputation of championship cricket. But teams of the North of England are not wholly to blame for playing the game in the rather inglorious way they frequently do play it. So long as the public in this part of the world continues to hold the view that championship laurels are 'worth while' at any price the price will occasionally be stiff indeed.

P.S. A happy thought? How to brighten cricket. Let us forthwith make Yorkshire Honorary Champions For Ever, so that they will not have to slave after the honours in future. The rest of us could then get on with the game undisturbed.

SCORES

YORKSHIRE

First Innings		Second Innings	
Holmes, c Barnes, b Tyldesley (R.)	51	lbw, b Tyldesley (R.)	20
Sutcliffe, b Macdonald	27	c Parkin, b Macdonald	40
Oldroyd, b Parkin	6	run out	4
Leyland, lbw, b Macdonald	27	b Hopwood	29
Rhodes, lbw, b Parkin	59	not out	54
Kilner, lbw, b Macdonald	3	c Tyldesley (E.), b Hopwood	14
Robinson, not out	45	c Watson, b Pewtress	14
Macaulay, b Parkin	1		
A. W. Lupton, b Tyldesley (R.)	3		
Waddington, lbw, b Tyldesley (R.)	1	not out	5
Dolphin, b Parkin	0		
Extras	9	Extras	6
Total	232	Total (for 6)	186

YORKSHIRE V LANCASHIRE 1925
LANCASHIRE

First Innings

Hopwood, b Macaulay	8
Duckworth, c Oldroyd, b Macaulay	1
Makepeace, st Dolphin, b Rhodes	42
Hallows, not out	111
Tyldesley (E.), c Waddington, b Kilner	35
Watson, lbw, b Kilner	7
Pewtress, run out	0
J. R. Barnes, c Robinson, b Kilner	17
Tyldesley (R.), b Robinson	3
Macdonald, b Kilner	16
Parkin, c Robinson, b Macaulay	12
Extras	13
	—
Total	265

BOWLING ANALYSIS

YORKSHIRE—First Innings

	O.	M.	R.	W.		O.	M.	R.	W.
Parkin	27·2	8	63	4	Tyldesley (R.)	29	9	47	3
Macdonald	32	8	75	3	Watson	23	6	38	0

Second Innings

	O.	M.	R.	W.		O.	M.	R.	W.
Parkin	25	11	35	0	Hallows	3	0	13	0
Macdonald	18	6	30	1	Makepeace	3	0	8	0
Tyldesley (R.)	21	10	24	1	Pewtress	2	0	10	1
Watson	19	8	34	0	Barnes	3	3	0	0
Hopwood	11	1	26	2	Tyldesley (E.)	1	1	0	0

LANCASHIRE—First Innings

	O.	M.	R.	W.		O.	M.	R.	W.
Macaulay	38·4	9	86	3	Waddington	10	2	29	0
Robinson	30	11	45	1	Rhodes	15	7	25	1
Kilner	39	12	67	4					

YORKSHIRE V LANCASHIRE 1925

August 1/3/4   Bramall Lane

FIRST DAY

THE ancient feud broke out again on Saturday, this time in the cockpit of Bramall Lane. Low clouds and dim light suited the play; the smoke that hung here and there over the field might well have come out of the slow, smouldering fires of the match.

A crowd of 25,000 watched the cricket—a crowd which, true to Sheffield, was full of character. It was an honest multitude, unashamedly partisan and yet not blind to merit in the enemy's ranks. Makepeace was cursed by thousands between noon and evening on Saturday, cursed for his stubbornness in the teeth of Yorkshire's attack: but even while passionate men from Sheffield wished him in the bottomless pit they vowed in the next breath that ' 'e's a reight plucky little owd ———, is Makepeace.' The Sheffield crowd is constantly getting into the bad books of the game; none the less, I confess I would not have it lose its own true heart, temper and vocabulary. It is better that we should have authentic character in this world of the North, rather than those good manners which make for dullness of spirit.

Many things, besides the crowd, were at Bramall Lane for us to admire—the Yorkshire bowling, the obstinacy of Makepeace and Hallows, and not least, the hardihood and courage of the grass to keep growing in so discouraging a place. At such times, when the field is vacant of cricketers in a big match at Sheffield, the crowd ought to stand by and cheer the grass upwards and on in its gallant if silent and unobtrusive struggle against heavy odds.

Barnes did Lancashire good service by winning the toss, for the wicket was excellent and the weather unsettled. Sharp at the last moment stood down from the Lancashire side; with good sense and sportsmanship he did not wish to displace either Iddon or Sibbles. Macaulay and Robinson began the Yorkshire assault—Robinson suddenly losing his shambling

162

walk and making his energy concentrate by gigantic will power into a bowling action clean and determined; while Macaulay at the other end, was lithe and tense, the image of lean antagonism. So finely did Macaulay bowl that he deserved at least thrice to get Makepeace's wicket in the first quarter of an hour. His fourth ball to Makepeace broke back, beat the bat, and just missed the wicket; later another quite bad tempered off-break might have uprooted a stump if Makepeace had not got his legs there just in time. A violent appeal split the air, but Makepeace survived. It was a near thing indeed.

The morning's first half-hour brought to Lancashire only 18 runs; six maiden overs were bowled one after another by Macaulay and Robinson. Hallows, though unable to get the ball away profitably, played cool and polished cricket; he rarely missed making a stroke that he set his mind on. His bat seemed all 'middle' from the match's outset. Slow scoring provoked irony in the multitude, and as time passed and no success fell to Yorkshire, irony gave way to a silence which I thought possessed no little eloquence. Lunch and not a single wicket down against Yorkshire! Why, Emmott, owd lad, what was t'thinkin' abowt! The truth is that Robinson, Macaulay, Milner, and Waddington each bowled finely; most other counties in England would have been satisfied not to have lost three batsmen before lunch. That Makepeace held the wicket is a tribute to his tenacity, for clearly he was out of form in the technical sense, and won through by sheer determination to endure. Makepeace, one imagines, discovers a dour sort of satisfaction in a Lancashire and Yorkshire match; Ironsides here is amongst ironsides; he is free to put on his heaviest armour now and move at his most dogged pace. In an hour on Saturday he made 9; in an hour and a half he made 13. 'For Gawd's sake,' moaned some soul in distress, out of the crowd's depths, ' 'it 'em.' Makepeace merely smiled a little, bent down, knit his brow, and carried his cross again. Before lunch Yorkshire bowled fourteen maidens out of thirty-nine overs; in 105 minutes Lancashire scored 77, Hallows 44 and Makepeace 19. The partnership was all but broken at 59. Makepeace played one from Kilner to the off side, and a quick spurt for a run happened. The ball was returned smartly, and Hallows was not in his ground when Dolphin broke the wicket with his hand—but without gathering the ball. At the sight of Hallows' danger and his escape the howls of the multitude 'were organs' as Mrs. Gamp would have observed; I fancied that strong men beat their breasts.

Rain fell during the luncheon interval; good Yorkshire heavens weeping that superb Yorkshire bowling had suffered injustice! On went the battle at 2.40. Hallows accomplished a few strokes that were like fitful lightning over the heavy sky of the cricket. In an over from Kilner, Makepeace again was beaten completely, but somehow managed to struggle through. It was all struggle, struggle, struggle,—in fact cricket at its starkest and unloveliest. From 54 balls by Kilner three scoring strokes were achieved. Hallows arrived at his 50 after two hours of skilful effort; the 100 was reached in 150 minutes—the first century first-wicket partnership against the Champions this season. Hallows got his 50 out of a total of 94; then Makepeace—'the Yorkshire-born batsman,' as he was tactfully described by one of the Yorkshire newspapers on Saturday—did most of the run-making for a while and made his 50 out of 121 in two hours and a half. The Gradgrindian nature of the play is the excuse I make for this prosaic catalogue of facts. At a quarter to four, rain put an end to the travail for one hour and fifty minutes. And throughout the whole of that long period of waiting, the score board displayed the incredible news: 'Lancashire 129 for 0.' Did Emmott Robinson look at it and put his hands to his eyes as though to blot out a dreadful apparition?

Lancashire's first wicket fell at half-past six with the score 171. It was left to Rhodes to make an end of a partnership that threatened to become the scandal of Yorkshire cricket. Hallows batted three hours and fifty minutes for 79, and he hit three boundaries, no more and no less. He was slow but not dull. He gave us an essay in strongly tempered resistance; he fought a match-saving rather than a match-winning game but he fought it handsomely. His bat is always alive; his defensive strokes were positive, not negative. Despite the skilful Yorkshire attack after lunch, he never for a moment looked to be in trouble. So complete seemed his mastery that

I expected he would drive the bowling to some tune after the rain had made the ball greasy for the bowlers. He gave no chance and was beaten seldom. A few minutes before Hallows was out lbw, Makepeace, his score 72, hit a ball back to Kilner. Many onlookers, the writer included, decided the stroke was 'trapped'. My reasons for thinking it was not a catch were: (1) Kilner casually put out one hand to the ball; (2) there was no sign of dismay in the Yorkshire team when he missed it; and (3) Robinson did not fall down in a fit at the sight of a Lancashire batsman missed, with the score 168 for none. But I was assured after the game that it was a true catch and a true miss. Kilner put one hand to it because he had hurt the other earlier on. I can only congratulate the Yorkshire eleven, especially the great-hearted Emmott, on their stoic philosophy at the escape of Makepeace.

Lancashire cricketers were highly satisfied with the afternoon's work, as well they might have been in view of the team's recent form. Hallows and Makepeace played a stubborn game and played it well. I thought that offensive measures might have been taken safely and politically in the closing stages, with the foundation of a good score laid and the bowlers under the handicap of a wet ball. But in a match of this dagger keenness, and in the face of a champion county, perhaps Hallows and Makepeace were wise to play to the end the game that is best suited to the technique and temperament of Lancashire cricket at the present time. The Yorkshire fielding saved many runs; Kilner on the off side had the nimbleness and ubiquity of a Johnny Briggs. Lancashire's chances now hang largely on the bowlers; let us trust that Macdonald, Parkin, Richard Tyldesley and Sibbles will be in good vein.

SECOND DAY

Rain fell in Sheffield this morning and the Lancashire and Yorkshire match was held back till noon. The wicket was not spoiled; now and again during the Lancashire innings Macaulay made a ball rise at an awkward angle even after pitching a fair length, but, all in all, the turf remained respectable. Again we had a vast crowd, and the squat mound along the side of the field was thick with tough humanity, expectant and vociferous.

The Sheffield roar broke out straight away, for in Kilner's second over Duckworth discovered himself bowled off his pads, obviously to his astonishment. It is amusing to see, as one frequently does, batsmen of extreme fallibility overcome by perplexity in those recurring moments which prove that they are extremely vulnerable. Pewtress went to the wicket with Lancashire's score 183 for two, and after 14 had been added Makepeace fell to a catch by the stumper—batsmen are usually in form when they are able to find any point of contact with the quick rising ball of Macaulay. Makepeace batted well this morning, judged the length speedily and accurately, and unlike the Makepeace of Saturday, he put his bat to the ball more times than he put his pads. Not that pad play is to be belittled in a defence, and Makepeace understands it well. No indiscriminate pushing of the legs in front of the stumps will avail a man for long against Yorkshire, and Makepeace's bat alone could not have saved him in the face of Macaulay's superb attack on Saturday morning.

Pewtress forced the game with good sense and plenty of pluck; he swung his bat at any ball in the slightest overtossed, and accomplished three drives off Macaulay that were, as the man in Pickwick would say 'werry fierce.' But the other Lancashire batsmen proceeded to regard discretion as the better part of valour. Watson stirred the multitude to comments that lacked charity and aspirates alike. Watson time after time permitted himself to be drawn out on the full stretch by Kilner—surely an error of style to a bowler not at all likely to give the ball too much air, as cricketers say. It is curious that Watson, who can drive hard at times from a correct stance, does not develop the all-round technique of footwork that makes for sound back play. He batted fifty minutes this morning for eight singles. At lunch Lancashire's score was 243 for four; in 100 minutes 66 runs had been added to Saturday's comfortable foundation. Of these, 39 came from the bat of Pewtress—an old fashioned bat cricketers of today might call it since Pewtress lifts it high and makes use of that hump in the blade which modern batsmen reserve for the job of flattening out the pitch. The Yorkshire bowlers quickly found out Pewtress's love of the half-volley—that deadly ball for most of us at the moment—and they pitched a canny short length. Thus despite an innings of splendid spirit, Lancashire had not got into a match-winning speed when Pewtress was out leg before wicket to Rhodes.

The play before lunch, though not profitable enough in runs for Lancashire's purpose, was not as slow as the scoreboard might have led us to think. There was stern conflict in the match all the time; bowlers and fieldsmen goaded themselves into scalding energy, and the batsmen set their teeth and passed through moments of anguish and joy—joy in the knowledge that the Yorkshire attack, at last, was compelled to sweat hard for an inch's advance. After the interval Lancashire had no choice but to get runs or get out; the hour was opportune for the quick foot and free bat. In the field we could see a slightly chastened Yorkshire—gone now the familiar air of easy, confident mastery. Macaulay plugged away in bitter but splendid antagonism. Kilner alone gave us a hint of a buoyant heart—his smile might have been likened to the brass plate on the coffin of Yorkshire's hopes of complete victory. But one can never trust Yorkshire for long—at least not to go on losing championship points.

Barnes attempted to force the pace, and at 277 he was caught on the off-side. He drove the ball from the back foot, which, of course was the wrong foot. Lancashire's last six wickets fell for 79; it was not exactly a collapse, for the batsmen were taking risks now. Lancashire are not a good side at making quick runs: you cannot hit well and powerfully from the back foot. But acquaintance day by day with doubtful wickets these last few summers has tended to force most Lancashire batsmen almost to live on the back foot. Iddon played another promising innings, unripe maybe, but full of the sap that proves growth.

The prosaic afternoon was touched with glory by a wonderful catch. Richard Tyldesley drove a ball in massive fashion towards the on boundary. The ball soared high and heavily far into the deep field. Sutcliffe ran from long on, covered some twenty yards and with his right hand held the ball. It must have dropped into his grip like a ponderous stone yet he caught it with a grace lovely to see. Here was the catch of the season—the thrilling kind of catch one reads about in school stories and sees on the book's cover painted in gaudy colours. Bramall Lane stood up as a man and roared out wild applause at the hero, who, one must agree, looked the part—happy, youthful and proud.

Parkin revived his old harlequinade at the end of Lancashire's innings, and his antics even provoked laughter in the Yorkshire ranks, for all except, I imagine, Emmott Robinson, who as he saw Lancashire's last wicket making 21 runs was apparently saying to himself, 'A joke's a joke, but this is a match with Lankysheer and let's 'ave no larkin'.' Lancashire's innings lasted the eternity of seven hours, and Yorkshire went through their gruelling with little or no dwindling in energy. This morning before lunch Kilner bowled ten maidens in thirteen overs.

The Yorkshire innings began in rather warlike mood. Sutcliffe and Holmes plainly were not letting the Lancashire attack get on top if they could help it; their bats were as ready for offensive as defensive strokes. Macdonald opened with three admirable maiden overs then, for no reason obvious to rational minds, began to exploit the short bumping ball. Good batsmen thrive on this wild and whirring stuff and Sutcliffe and Holmes thumped it heartily. Consequently Yorkshire reached 50 in fifty minutes. Sibbles was the bowler who, with Macdonald, started the Lancashire attack; he was clever enough with the new ball to justify the confidence placed in him. His length had a cool accuracy excellent to look at in a colt, and occasionally he caused the ball to swing away. Holmes batted in his own clean, dapper fashion until Macdonald bowled him at 86. The rate of scoring slackened then, and the day finished as it began—in quietude with the bowlers given cause to think they were fine fellows.

THIRD DAY

For the second time in this summer of Yorkshire's content, Lancashire have taken three points out of the old enemy. Out of this achievement Old Trafford will get consolation for one or two of our fickle county's lapses of late. One cannot understand the feebleness of Lancashire against Middlesex and Surrey the other week in the light of the determined cricket shown by the side here at Bramall Lane since Saturday. We have at last seen Lancashire playing like a team with every man in his place working his hardest. Lancashire, in brief, have proved that they can do it—granted an amount of collective effort.

The canny batting tactics on Saturday by Makepeace and Hallows no doubt were open to criticism from a certain point of view—a point of view which Rhodes and Emmott Robinson would surely be quick to denounce as impossibly romantic. Lancashire went into action as Yorkshire did at Old Trafford in Whit-week, intent first on saving themselves and on forcing the match into a position calculated to damage the other side's percentage. It has come to this in these great contests, the team that bats first on a good wicket plays from the outset not so much to win as to prevent the other side from winning. Here is a 'negative' policy that might seem inglorious to a cricketer old enough to cherish in these days the ideal philosophy which has been well expressed in these words: 'Get at the other fellows before they get at you.' But other times, other manners. Cricketers of today in the North of England at any rate are what county championship circumstances of the moment compel them to be. Lancashire went into this match not with rapiers but with weapons of a lethal sort made for the occasion by Yorkshire last Whitsuntide. One should always bear in mind that Lancashire must have begun the match feeling themselves to be very much the poorer side; it is not bad tactics, after all, for the weaker vessel to assume the defensive. Possibly Lancashire laid themselves open to criticism on Monday, when, after Saturday's solid foundation score, there was little all-round attempt to force the pace until lunch. Even on this point it is hard to be emphatic. For one thing, the Lancashire team is well aware of its weakness at the quick-scoring game; for another the Yorkshire attack notoriously thrives on impatient batsmen. A few years ago maybe, Lancashire cricketers could have been found clever enough to hit Kilner, Macaulay, and the rest hard and often; nowadays the safe forcing technique is missing not only from Lancashire but from most other counties. Middlesex, richer than any other eleven in dashing batsmen, fell easy victims to Yorkshire bowlers the other week. The sense of 'stalemate' that comes into Lancashire and Yorkshire matches in these times is to be deplored, of course; these are contests with a courageous tradition. Until cricketers have learned again the art of hitting bowling off its length we must hope for sticky wickets whenever Red Rose meets White Rose.

From the first over by Sibbles this morning the Lancashire bowling seemed to tighten; this young man is not only clever and thorough in himself, but the cause of thoroughness in other Lancashire bowlers. The success of Sibbles today seemed to put the recognised Lancashire attack on its mettle; an old hand at the game does not feel he is of less account than a colt. It was Sibbles who placed Lancashire definitely on top this morning in the opening half-hour; he bowled a splendid out-swinger to Sutcliffe, one that the batsman could not safely refrain from playing— it kept too close to the off-stump for that—and Sutcliffe was neatly caught in the slips by Richard Tyldesley who took the ball in elegant style. One of the comicalities of modern Lancashire cricket happens at these moments in which a sudden and quick movement somehow brings a hint of grace into the mountainous bulk of Richard. Three runs after the downfall of Sutcliffe, Sibbles clean bowled Oldroyd with a nicely flighted swinger. Yorkshire now were 117 for three, and the crowd on Spion Kop chewed the cud of reflection.

Sutcliffe batted two hours and twenty minutes for his 62; his innings was an example of how to be a delight to the eye though essentially a North country batsman. Sutcliffe's cricket was dogged enough to suit Yorkshire's purpose in this game, and yet it was touched with that bloom of style which possesses no utility value; a boundary by Sutcliffe counts for no more on the score sheet than one by Oldroyd. Sutcliffe now and again made daring and dazzling hook strokes from Macdonald. They were 'like the lightning which doth cease to be, Ere one can say it lightens.' Rhodes did not enjoy Macdonald's pace when he came in to bat with Leyland; one spiteful break-back just missed his stumps, and Rhodes attended to the turf with the hump of his bat. He was out leg-before-wicket to Macdonald at 132, and Yorkshire now had lost four men. A stand by Leyland and Kilner for the fifth wicket promised to pull the game round to even points again; Kilner swung his bat at the over-tossed off-side ball—sometimes without taking his front leg across—and with Leyland almost in his best form runs came at a pace that seemed frivolous on such an occasion. The match was moving in Yorkshire's favour, and the inhabitants on Spion Kop appeared less husky than they had been earlier on, when Parkin broke through the hole that is always to be found somewhere in Kilner's sprightly bat. It was not a good ball; Emmott Robinson would have perished on the spot rather than have got out to a ball as easy to see as this. Parkin settled Yorkshire's chances of three points with this fortunate ball; he had bowled steadily from the moment he went on, but did not seem likely to discover a wicket. A man, no doubt, is able sometimes to find a needle in a haystack at one thrust of the hand.

Robinson struggled for a while with Leyland and might have settled down to sound cricket but for a shrewd move by Barnes. Robinson does not love the spinning ball; his feet are not as nimble as his wit. Tyldesley bowled Robinson with a capital break which pitched on the leg stump and hit the off.

The crowd now resigned itself to the worst; there was no touch of chagrin in their sorrow—no wish to break their idols. A Yorkshire crowd is loyal; the truth, maybe, is that deep down in their hearts Yorkshire folk can never believe that cricketers of Yorkshire are really being beaten, skill for skill. When a Lancashire batsman fails at Old Trafford the crowd there thinks the bowler has well and truly beaten his man and sometimes indulges in sceptical views about the Lancashire players' ability. The Yorkshire crowd is incredulous when it sees a Yorkshire batsman overthrown, and says, in effect, 'It must 'a been a good 'un else 'e'd 'a hit it for fower reight enough!' All Yorkshire is behind the county to a man. Yorkshire battled to the innings' end—after lunch Dolphin and Leyland scored 41 for the last wicket, and again Spion Kop sent out its roars to the world.

At the finish of every over that he contrived pluckily and skilfully to live through, Dolphin was given cheers that were tokens not only of praise but of affection. When at last Tyldesley bowled him and the first innings points fell to

Lancashire, the crowd did not seem to feel the sting of adversity; it saw the decisive wicket topple, made the most of Dolphin's gallant rally, and shouted, 'Good owd Yorkshire.' Later in the afternoon this devoted crowd had the bliss of watching Lancashire stumps skittled in the good old-fashioned way. Not a man on the ground gave signs that he was feeling the taste of ashes in the mouth. There was none to ask Kilner with a sour accent, 'Why didn't t'a do this on Saturday?' No! Spion Kop looked on the Lancashire collapse in mighty pride and joy. 'Theer's boughlin' for thi!' so Spion Kop seemed to say. And boughlin it was. Possibly Emmott Robinson, at the finish, held up to ridicule the current method of reckoning the championship value of an un-finished match; possibly he has been a bitter Yorkshireman this evening. But everybody else at Bramall Lane went home seemingly as proud of Yorkshire cricket as ever—points or no points. 'We'd 'a' had thi whacked before Bre'kfast in t' mornin' ' was the comment confidently thrown at Lancastrians. Leyland, 80 not out, gave another proof of ability which in time will make an All-England cricketer of him. He is quick and clever on his feet and is coming to some command over a wide range of strokes. His leg-glancing is pretty and safe; he drives strongly too. But his defence is not yet solid enough for good bowling; he plays at many balls close to the wicket and misses them, and the finished batsman does not do that. Tyldesley and Sibbles were Lancashire's best bowlers throughout; while the fielding was good—for Lancashire.

YORKSHIRE V LANCASHIRE 1925
SCORES

LANCASHIRE

First Innings		Second Innings	
Makepeace, c Dolphin, b Macaulay	90	c Holmes, b Kilner	14
Hallows, lbw, b Rhodes	79	c Holmes, b Kilner	23
Duckworth, b Kilner	5		
A. W. Pewtress, lbw, b Rhodes	44	c & b Kilner	0
Watson, c Dolphin, b Waddington	8	lbw, b Kilner	1
J. R. Barnes, c Oldroyd, b Macaulay	10	not out	12
Iddon, c Oldroyd, b Macaulay	21	c Dolphin, b Rhodes	9
Sibbles, not out	6	b Kilner	1
Tyldesley (R.), c Sutcliffe, b Kilner	3	not out	13
Macdonald, b Macaulay	15		
Parkin, b Kilner	11		
Extras b17, lb9, nb2	28	Extras wl	1
Total	320	Total (for 6)	74

YORKSHIRE

First Innings	
Holmes, b Macdonald	41
Sutcliffe, c Tyldesley, b Sibbles	62
Oldroyd, b Sibbles	5
Leyland, not out	80
Rhodes, lbw, b Macdonald	7
Kilner, b Parkin	22
Robinson, b Tyldesley	6
Macaulay, c Watson, b Sibbles	19
Waddington, c & b Sibbles	0
A. W. Lupton, b Macdonald	1
Dolphin, b Tyldesley	14
Extras b15, lb3, nb2	20
Total	277

THE ROSES MATCHES 1919-1939
BOWLING ANALYSIS
LANCASHIRE—First Innings

	O.	M.	R.	W.		O.	M.	R.	W.
Robinson	22	6	35	0	Kilner	45	23	61	3
Macaulay	50	10	121	4	Rhodes	22	11	20	2
Waddington	32	11	55	1					

Second Innings

	O.	M.	R.	W.		O.	M.	R.	W.
Robinson	6	3	13	0	Waddington	7	3	13	0
Macaulay	7	3	12	0	Rhodes	5	0	21	1
Kilner	14	8	14	5					

YORKSHIRE—First Innings

	O.	M.	R.	W.		O.	M.	R.	W.
Macdonald	31	12	94	3	Tyldesley	30	11	59	2
Sibbles	29	8	60	4	Watson	9	4	10	0
Parkin	21	11	34	1					

YORKSHIRE V LANCASHIRE 1926

May 22/24/25 Bradford

FIRST DAY

THE year's wheel has gone round again, and here is the old feud with its slow fires ready to break into flames at the first breath of antagonism. On Saturday, at Bradford, the crowd, though big, was not unwieldy; it had the proper Yorkshire pride in the cricketers of its county but enthusiasm remained tolerant the day long; never was the game's action dramatic enough to stir the multitude to the fine clannish vehemence which makes a Yorkshire crowd the most loyal and the most vociferous in the land.

Today, maybe, we shall hear the authentic Yorkshire roar splitting the skies; these dour conflicts usually begin in a calm that hints bodefully of the brewing storm; the first day's play is given mainly to a suspicious searching for position; then the hurly-burly bubbles and passion spins the plot. This morning we shall see Macaulay running his intense run to the wicket, moving bitterly along as though a battleaxe and not a cricket ball were in his grip—Macaulay the image of lean enmity ('Let me have men about me that are fat.') Macaulay bowling like a Fury crowned with snakes—Lancashire batsmen must 'circumwent' him (as Sam Weller would say) on this Whit-Monday or the Yorkshire roar will send us mad.

I would rather watch Yorkshire in attack than Yorkshire making runs. Saturday's play sometimes compelled a watcher here and there to emulate the Frenchmen at the Court of Frederick the Great and conjugate the verb *s'ennuyer*. Not that the cricket had quite the lethal dullness of other Lancashire and Yorkshire matches of recent times; some event was usually taking place, and now and again Kilner and Holmes scored runs at a speed almost vulgar for an occasion so heavy and solemn. My complaint against Saturday's cricket is that (like this account of it) it was a long time coming to the point. The style of the play was loose and the action drifted rather aimlessly.

175

A missed catch in the morning's first quarter of an hour obviously upset for a while the confidence of Lancashire; another Lancashire fielding blunder proved that the stars were shining for Yorkshire and yet Yorkshire apparently could not decide whether to meet good luck half-way, and take the offensive, or whether to regard as warnings the fortunate escapes of one or two of her best batsmen, and draw in horns and go warily. Thus the day and the policy of the match lacked much of the traditional sense of stern steel crossing stern steel.

Sutcliffe gave an easy slip catch when his score was two and Yorkshire's total was nine; the mistake happened in Macdonald's third over. A ball swung away rather late and Sutcliffe edged it straight to Watson at second slip; an easier catch it would be hard to imagine. Watson somehow contrived to drop it, whereat everybody that has ever played cricket sent out his heart to the unhappy Watson; the erring fieldsman always suffers for a blunder of this sort sorrows of humiliation far more painful than the bitter frustration felt in the partisan crowd. Yet Watson's dropped catch was calculated to make one laugh as well as cry. The simplicity of it! Once, long ago, the present writer missed such a catch, and at the over's end the irate bowler declared: 'I suppose you prefer a catch handed to you on a plate with parsley round the ball.'

Macdonald palpably accepted his bad luck on Saturday with the utmost philosophy; he proceeded to bowl a half-dozen fastish overs, some very good and some not good at all, and then, as the saying goes, surrendered the ball to Richard Tyldesley. Sutcliffe gave another chance when the Yorkshire score was 45 and his own 21; this time he cut a ball from Watson hard and low to Makepeace at backward point; Makepeace gripped the catch after a desperate fling forward of the whole of his being, but dropped it. And as he did so lines of care marked his face.

Lancashire's fielding, keen enough on the ground, could not be trusted in the air. The costliest mishap was Ernest Tyldesley's. Kilner flashed his bat at a short rising ball from Macdonald; the hit was quick and Tyldesley had to jump a little to reach the catch; he stopped the ball but could not hold it. When this happened Kilner was 0—he made 85. Iddon gave him yet another innings at 70, missing a dainty caught and bowled opportunity.

These dropped catches, of course, did Lancashire damage; yet I do not grumble at them now half so much as I grumble at the lack of consistent length in the Lancashire attack. The best fieldsman in the world cannot safeguard himself, try as he may, against missing a catch; a good bowler, by concentrating his mind, can avoid bowling a long-hop. On Saturday I saw a dozen rank long-hops bowled by one Lancashire bowler in half an hour.

Apart from Holmes, Yorkshire did not too clearly possess more than one batsman in true form; had the Lancashire bowlers pegged away at the good length all the time; had they acted on the Rhodes doctrine (which we shall witness in force today)—'Length, length! Mak' 'em fetch 'em. Length, length!'—Yorkshire could scarcely have made 298. The Lancashire attack was good whenever things were coming off, as cricketers say, for Lancashire; it wavered in technique and spirit at the first sign of an unfavourable wind. The grim efficiency of Yorkshire bowling may be relied upon never to throw runs away in the face of the most conquering batsmen; today Lancashire will have to fight for every run, even if not a single wicket should fall to Yorkshire for hours. A third of Yorkshire's 298, I imagine, was given—a present from Lancashire, Whitsuntide, 1926.

Richard Tyldesley bowled accurately for a while; at the afternoon's fall it seemed he would go through the Yorkshire tail (and there is one nowadays) in quick time; but he was taken off, and Macdonald put on instead; I could understand Green's move; he probably thought, like MacLaren of old, that fast bowling in a fading light is the specific at an inning's finish. Taking the day in the lump Watson provided Lancashire's most reliable attack; Parkin was steady at times but the easy pitch deprived his spin of sting.

Macdonald bowled with a perplexing changefulness. In one over his speed and length would be good; the next it would dwindle to medium pace; then, suddenly, the man's energy would shoot out in a violent bumping ball, terribly short, which would fly at a batsman's head like a deadly bolt. As a fact, a great batsman would more often than not have hit this fast bumper out of the field. MacLaren's way with crude violence of this kind was to assume a position which placed him not full-fronted to the ball, but rather across its flight, so that if he missed his stroke the ball would pass safely by the left side of his head and not hit him. MacLaren's stroke for the bumper was not the blind short-armed sweep frequently attempted on Saturday; it was a calm, deliberate stroke to the on, rather to leg, made by moving over the wicket and hitting the ball, with a turn of the wrist as it passed by, with little or no chance of doing him physical hurt. How magnificently he would achieve this stroke; he would lift himself up to his proudest height; the sweep of his bat was like a disdainful gesture at the sight of bowling that was merely so much brute strength. MacLaren did not hit the bumping ball; he dismissed it from his presence.

Holmes countered Macdonald's shock tactics like the Test-match cricketer he is; he hit the short ball to leg, not across the flight but from the side of it; sometimes he even got behind it! Holmes never seemed likely to lose his wicket; his batting was the best of the day by far. His footwork is as quick as it is scientific and pretty; few other cricketers possess Holmes's elegance and versatility on the leg side. In contrast to Holmes, whose feet are always in nimble motion, Sutcliffe is an almost static (or shall we say statuesque!) batsman. On Saturday Sutcliffe was not in a good vein; his bat had more than its customary edge. But his style was as polished as ever; it was his timing, not his strokes, that was wrong. Fast, hard grounds will find Sutcliffe an England batsman still.

Oldroyd's innings of 64 lasted beyond two hours and a half— sturdy work, more body than bouquet, to reverse Mr. Asquith's description of Dr. Jowett's conversation. Kilner's cricket, as I have suggested, possessed a liveliness that was even flippant, considering the day and the occasion. He did not go into the safe shell of circumspection, as most batsmen would have been glad to, after his lucky escape from Tyldesley's fingers. His bat made many a merry impudent fling in the face of Fortune—her humorous ladyship. Some of his cover-hits were dazzling; some were off the edge as the old pro used to say at Shrewsbury. Good or bad hits were all the same to Kilner, who is a happy cavalier in a company of Ironsides. I often wonder what Emmott Robinson thinks of Kilner's riskily-flung bat; he must regard it as a vain pagan thing. Kilner hit two sixes and 10 fours, batted one hour and fifty minutes for 85.

Rhodes fell to a lovely diving catch by Macdonald, who also caught Holmes cleverly after getting himself into a position totally unscientific. Yorkshire's fifth wicket did not fall till the score was 273, and the long day closed with the stirring sight of Waddington and Major Lupton holding back the advancing Lancashire bowlers.

SECOND DAY

The air was stirring with the proper Yorkshire temper when the match went on this morning. A great crowd sat in the sunshine and expectantly stood on tip toe. Major Lupton astonished and delighted the multitude (and possibly himself) by achieving a superb off-drive from Macdonald, also a savage blow to the on—both boundary hits.

Yorkshire scored 326; then at high noon, with summer opening graciously all around us, the game got to grips fiercely; Lancashire's innings began in the teeth of an attack far more determined than any I have seen this year. Robinson and Macaulay bowled—the familiar Emmott Robinson, with the same old grizzled face, the same lumbering yet antagonistic run to the wicket, the same old Yorkshire faith in rough honest muscle—and with the same old boots, though today I thought they looked to be suspiciously clean. Makepeace passed through an over of tribulation straightway; Macaulay broke down his defence with balls that swung away very late and at a rare speed from the ground. In Robinson's fourth over Makepeace again was beaten, but he got his pads there in time. Robinson's appeal might easily have stunned the umpire into deafness, and as he heard judgment given against him he stood in the middle of the wicket and seemed to arraign justice eternal. How magnificent is the fighting passion of these ancient Yorkshiremen—the younger cricketers of the county, clever though they be, possess a manner that is mildness itself in contrast to the vehemence of the old clan.

Hallows, though compelled to play a defensive game, was pleasant to watch. His cricket made one think of young Samson in chains. Time after time, he accomplished a strong blow for freedom with a defiant bat, only to find his strokes and his runs checked by the tight prison made by Yorkshire's close and watchful field. Forty minutes passed before Hallows drove the first Lancashire boundary—a lovely hit straight by the bowler, which was Emmott, now rather more outraged than ever. 'There ought to be no fours allowed by high heaven against Yorkshire in a match like this,' he was apparently saying.

From the outset the Yorkshire bowlers were on top; despite the easeful movement of Hallows' bat Lancashire had the aspect of a struggling team. The field was set with a silly mid-off and a silly mid-on while Makepeace batted to Kilner, whose first five overs were maidens. Oh, the royal agony of these Lancashire and Yorkshire matches! Some of us are growing grey in the service of them. In fifty minutes this morning Lancashire scored 27; then Hallows was caught at slip off a ball from Macaulay that made spiteful pace from the turf and swung a little at the last second away from the bat. Thus was the promise of Hallows suddenly and sadly ended.

Immediately before getting this wicket, Macaulay's attack was wavering, and he seemingly asked his captain to give him a rest. At any rate, he was seen to be taking his sweater back from the umpire. But as he did so Rhodes had a word with Lupton—and Macaulay returned to work and ensnared Hallows without loss of time. Whereat the crowd wagged a sage admiring head and said, 'Good owd Wilfred; he knows a thing or two' which, of course, he does.

Makepeace fell to a ball like that which baffled Hallows; the stroke was much the same, and Sutcliffe again was the fieldsman. Lancashire's honourable old 'Stonewall' Jackson had batted seventy minutes, suffering devotedly in the cause of his county. Watson did not do justice to his talents—his bat was without sight, and Kilner quickly had him confused and confounded. And now Yorkshire were definitely winning, for the Lancashire score read 49 for three.

The crowd roared out delight as these wickets were taken,

and the occasion assumed a fine irony—we saw the aspect of tragedy come over the Lancashire batsmen as each understood that he was ruined, and shouts of savage joy must have been in the ears of the victims as they passed out of our sight. In this trying situation Barnes came into Lancashire cricket for the first time this summer. And no sooner had he got to the intense middle than he saw Ernest Tyldesley missed by Waddington from a hard hit to the leg side. Had this catch been held Lancashire's score would now have been 50 for four. Barnes entered the responsible air like a brave cricketer; true, he was nearly bowled immediately by a capital break from Kilner. This, though, was Barnes' only mistake in a stern innings; his ability to stop the advancing Yorkshiremen for a long period is proof, if proof were needed, that a sound method will serve well even a cricketer who is out of practice.

Ernest Tyldesley was disconcerted by his indiscreet stroke to Waddington; he quickly settled down to cool, manly cricket, subdued maybe, but deliberate. Tyldesley and Barnes slowly, very slowly, heaved the match round a little in Lancashire's way. The cautious play hereabouts was no longer that of batsmen overwhelmed by circumstances and severe bowling. We were watching at this point the stubbornness of batsmen who themselves chose to be stubborn; defensive measures were not any longer being forced on Lancashire—Lancashire was of purpose cultivating obstinacy. The crowd in a while sniffed the change in the air and did not like it. The voice of the barracker was heard in the land: ' 'It 'em,' mourned a man in deep travail. 'For the Lord's sake, 'it 'em.' It was frustration's own voice.

Barnes and Tyldesley went their dour Fabian way for ninety minutes and made 65. Then temptation lured Tyldesley to self-destruction. Rhodes tossed him a slow hanging ball, and Tyldesley, visited by the vision of the distant boundary—an oasis in the afternoon's desert—swung his bat at the ball and sent it high but not far enough into the deep. Sutcliffe ran in from long-off and held a charming catch. A few balls after this disaster for Lancashire Iddon walked across his stumps unscientifically and his off stump was knocked out of the ground. Lancashire 114 for five, 63 wanted yet to save the follow-on—thus in a trice the match had turned round again. Ernest Tyldesley must have watched the tide change with unhappy feelings; if only he had resisted Rhodes' simple old trick he might have—I am certain he would have—stayed at the wicket for as long and just as untroubled as Barnes himself. But herein is the fascination that cricket has for us; how it does play on the weaknesses of men!

Between half-past two and four o'clock Lancashire scored a mere 47; in ten overs a solitary run was hit from the historic—nay—legendary Rhodes. Ernest Tyldesley batted one hundred and ten minutes for his fifty; in one hour and a half Barnes stoically refused to make more than 22; Green, too played patience coolly and cleverly for forty minutes. And, in the end all of this scourging of self, all the eating of this bitter dust, all of this more or less noble renunciation by Lancashire of the gaudy vanities that hang on the boundary's edge—all came to nothing. Green was defeated at 136; then the Lancashire rearguard collapsed and the follow-on, with its indignity, had to be suffered.

Could Lancashire have fared less prosperously had the batsmen exploited a normal game? For the persistent policy of not hitting the ball, witnessed today, has been abnormal even for Lancashire. It is a vain ambition to try to wear out Yorkshire's patience. Ernest Tyldesley got himself out, it is true, by chancing a big drive. But must a cricketer never venture a bold hit simply because other cricketers have been known to get caught near the boundary? These questions I ask in good faith. I am seeking to discover whether the canny risk-equals-nothing method of batsmanship is the wisest in the world to exploit against Yorkshire throughout a warm day. Obviously, a cricketer needs to have his eyes about him and go warily at the outset of an innings against Yorkshire. Today, though, Lancashire did not hit the ball hard even when the Yorkshire attack was palpably failing, and even though the batsmen were frequently in position for ripe strokes. The problem is difficult. Most counties in the country have asked these many seasons, 'Can the Yorkshire attack possibly be hit?' Apparently it cannot—at least by batsmen of a definitely modern technique.

The Bradford wicket today was not, I thought, quite so docile as on Saturday. At any rate, Kilner was able to spin the ball sharply at times. I am afraid, however, that this argument does not help to explain Lancashire's failings against Rhodes, who, truth to tell, seldom turned the ball quickly. His was the conquest of what may be called artful dodgery. Rhodes was at liberty this evening to leave the field saying, like somebody in one of Shakespeare's chronicle plays: 'I have gathered many spoils, using no other weapon but my name.'

Macaulay's bowling had a deadly pace from the pitch and a disconcertingly late swing, but only for so long as the ball remained new and glossy. He was a good, hard-working length bowler with the old ball and little more than that. The secret of Yorkshire's persistent conquest is an attack that never give runs away.

The Lancashire second innings ran into further trouble; I have not the heart to tell the sorry tale further. But this much I would like to ask: Why at the critical moment, with the follow-on almost saved, did Lancashire's later batsmen throw wickets to the winds by careless hitting? Bold cricket surely does not mean indiscriminate hitting. The high-class batsman mingles defence and offence in proportion. The Yorkshire fielding was excellent, and Dolphin on North-country grounds is our best wicket-keeper.

THIRD DAY

Lancashire lost this match easily at a quarter past four this afternoon after letting Bradford witness an exhibition of cricket which, taken in the whole since Saturday, must rank as one of the very worst ever known to have happened in the long history of these games.

The trouble is not that Lancashire have proved themselves not as clever at cricket as Yorkshire; most of us have known this much for a long time and more or less philosophically accepted the truth. The charge against our county in this game is that several of our men played apparently with lack of thought and responsibility, and also that, through seeming not to concentrate overmuch during the crisis, did less than justice to their proper talents. Why did some of the later batsmen in the first Lancashire innings throw wickets away wantonly, just at a point where a little patience would have saved a fatal follow-on? Does every member of our eleven always bear in mind, as he takes part in these great contests, that lovers of the county's cricket everywhere are anxiously watiting for news about the event, taking to heart all that has happened, is happening, and likely to happen—and all the time sending forth their good wishes to Lancashire cricket? We have traditions in our county as superb as Yorkshire's, which ought always to be an inspiration to every Lancashire cricketer whenever he faces the old enemy, good days or bad.

This morning a wet wicket prevented activity; not until three o'clock could Yorkshire get at their prey again. How the weary waiting must have chafed the soul of Robinson! The wicket helped the bowlers to spin the ball, but it was not too difficult. Barnes and Green again let us admire cool and intelligent defensive batsmanship. Between them Green and Barnes batted for nearly two hours of the Lancashire second inning's brief life; the more one sees of Barnes the more one is convinced that if he could play the game regularly he would quickly be known as one of our most reliable amateur batsmen. Even when he is not scoring, Barnes is attractive to watch; with him, slow cricket does not mean dullness. He is always thinking upon the problems of the game as they are presented to him by all sorts of bowling. And he is always seeking to solve them by means of a cultured batsman's strokes. His main defect is one to which I have referred before; sometimes his drives to the off side are made from the back foot, and as a consequence, his full weight does not go forward into the hit. All in all, though, Barnes makes his runs in a style which rarely fails to please the student of the game.

Green is certain to play a fruitful innings before long. Perhaps he exploits his gifts too diffidently. He possesses far more strokes than ever he has shown us in county cricket. Obviously, he has much command over a real technique; let him trust it freely some fine day. Duckworth also gave a useful account of his batting parts today; the probability is that if hc had gone to the wicket on Monday evening, after Green was out, Lancashire would have saved the follow-on. Duckworth can at least play a straight bat—which is more than we can say of some of Lancashire's later batsmen. How is it that any county cricketer, with seasons of experience behind him, is unable to find a little acquaintance with the very rudiments of batting?

Kilner bowled cleverly today, and Major Lupton achieved a good catch. From the evidence of this game, Macaulay is not a Test-match winner on a hard wicket.

SCORES

YORKSHIRE

First Innings

Holmes, c Macdonald, b Watson	33
Sutcliffe, lbw, b Macdonald	36
Oldroyd, c Iddon, b Watson	64
Leyland, c Tyldesley (E.), b Macdonald	29
Kilner, b Iddon	85
Rhodes, c Macdonald, b Tyldesley (R.)	21
Macaulay, b Tyldesley (R.)	1
Robinson, c Tyldesley (R.), b Macdonald	3
Waddington, b Macdonald	15
A. W. Lupton, st Duckworth, b Tyldesley (R.)	28
Dolphin, not out	6
Extras	5
Total	326

LANCASHIRE

First Innings		Second Innings	
Makepeace, c Sutcliffe, b Macaulay	18	c Dolphin, b Robinson	0
Hallows, c Sutcliffe, b Macaulay	18	c Leyland, b Waddington	4
Tyldesley (E.), c Sutcliffe, b Rhodes	52	c Kilner, b Macaulay	13
Watson, lbw, b Kilner	3	c Holmes, b Waddington	9
J. R. Barnes, c Sutcliffe, b Rhodes	37	c Kilner, b Macaulay	13
Iddon, b Waddington	0	c Holmes, b Kilner	7
L. Green, b Kilner	12	c Lupton, b Kilner	14
Macdonald, c Holmes, b Rhodes	10	c Holmes, b Kilner	0
Tyldesley (R.), c Macaulay, b Kilner	4	c Holmes, b Kilner	0
Parkin, b Rhodes	0	not out	0
Duckworth, not out	2	c Lupton, b Waddington	7
Extras	3	Extras	6
Total	159	Total	73

BOWLING ANALYSIS

YORKSHIRE—First Innings

	O.	M.	R.	W.		O.	M.	R.	W.
Macdonald	41	8	110	4	Watson	27	4	60	2
Parkin	23	6	56	0	Iddon	16	7	35	1
Tyldesley (R.)	30·2	13	60	3					

LANCASHIRE—First Innings

	O.	M.	R.	W.		O.	M.	R.	W.
Robinson	10	4	21	0	Waddington	9	5	11	1
Macaulay	27	4	64	2	Rhodes	20·1	12	20	4
Kilner	35	16	40	3					

Second Innings

	O.	M.	R.	W.		O.	M.	R.	W.
Robinson	7	5	7	1	Kilner	15·5	5	19	4
Macaulay	12	2	24	2	Waddington	11	4	17	3

LANCASHIRE V YORKSHIRE 1926

July 31/August 2/3   Old Trafford

FIRST DAY

TWENTY-FIVE years from today, I imagine that some old gentleman from Ramsbottom will sit on the pavilion at Old Trafford, during a Lancashire and Yorkshire match, and speak to his son in these words: 'Tha does well to clap thi hands at yon fellers, but tak' it fro' me, mi lad, tha's nivver seen t' game played as it ought to be played. Now when Ah were a youngster, Old Trafford were worth comin' to. Ah remembers, as tho' it were yisterday, Lankysheer stayin' in all t' afternoon agenst Yorksheer, and scorin' nigh on three hundred, and on'y two wickits down. Aye, tha might well gape, but Ah'm tellin' thee t' gospel truth. It were twenty-five years ago, and Hallers and Mekpeace started t' fun. By gum, 'ow they laid into that theer Yorksheer bowlin'—tha nivver sees such 'ittin nowadays. Then there were Ernest Ty'd'sley—'e couldn't be got out for less than a nunderd. But Mekpeace were t' feller to watch; it were a bobby-dazzler and no mistake. Boundaries every blessed ball. Personally, Ah allus thowt 'im a bit on t' rash side; 'e played a bit for t' gallery. Watson were more in my line; there were some dignity abowt 'is battin'. But this soart of cricket that tha's a cheerin' now—why, mi lad , it's not t' same game as they played in my time. They does nowt but push and poke all t' day long; they used to 'it 'em hard twenty year ago. No, son; cricket's not whot it were—and Ah'm allus tellin' thi mother so.'

And indeed, Saturday at Old Trafford might easily be remembered gratefully all over the county for many days to come. The lovely afternoon was in itself enough to win memory affectionately. Summer fires burned out all the while, and a great crowd sat happily in the heat. Laughter of friends and an English cricket field—the lover of the game often lets his mind dwell on such a happy time when he is deep in mid-winter, and sees it far behind him, far away, and wishes it back again for him to live through once more.

On this delicious afternoon, Lancashire scored 297 for two—here was a performance calculated to warm the cockles of Lancastrian hearts even in a season of chill winds. Winning the toss was good luck for Lancashire. The pitch lay there smooth and polished—at the very first sight of it Emmott Robinson might well have broken down and cried like a child. But he did no such weak thing. On the contrary, he straightaway set about himself and bowled one of the most finely tempered attacks that Old Trafford has witnessed for a long time. Given a fair turf—an average pre-war good pitch—Robinson would have come quickly into wickets on Saturday. His length was admirable from his first ball, his pace and late 'out-swing' potential of danger. But immediately the ball fell on the absurdly easy turf all of its skilfully contrived venom dwindled to nothingness. Robinson worked hard in his efforts to rise superior to that heartbreaking cushion of green earth; for an hour he let us see his old hop on the right foot and then his loose, shambling, yet determined action to the crease.

Macaulay bowled with Robinson at the game's beginning. The wicket also frustrated his technique, and he had little of Emmott's noble passion. Makepeace and Hallows chanced not the shadow of a risk. Each batsman let himself take root in the comfortable soil, and his innings grew like a plant.

The serenity of the opening half-hour was twice disturbed by good Yorkshire appeals. One of them was against Makepeace for a catch at the wicket when he had scored only two. The bowler, I fancy, did not join in the appeal, and his name was Robinson. Whenever in these matches an appeal is made from Robinson's bowling and Robinson himself refrains from taking the tenor part, clearly the batsman must be given the benefit of the doubt. The other appeal to disturb our morning slumber was by Waddington, for lbw, also against Makepeace. Waddington let out a high quick howl as he saw the ball hit Makepeace's pad and he twisted his body round to the umpire's sight like a man afflicted by terrible whips and scorpions. Later in the day, as the Lancashire batsmen became more and more set, the Yorkshire appeals gathered in number and vehemence. Some parts of the crowd protested against this, but not those of us who relish the fun of the clannish temper of these superb games. I think it was the most genial of the present Yorkshire eleven who, with delicious humour, once summed up a Lancashire and Yorkshire match in this language: 'Ay, they are grand tussles and no mistake. T' two teams meets in t' pavilion before t' match and says "Good mornin' " to one another, and then none of us ever speaks agen for three days, exceptin' to say "How's that?" '.

In ninety minutes before lunch Lancashire made 74 for no wicket. Holmes was struck on the knee by a cut from Hallows, and had to leave the field for the day. Mitchell was his substitute—a very good one, too. The play of Hallows and Makepeace was mainly interesting for the number of runs scored through the slips by late cuts (or rather 'dabs'—they don't cut nowadays). Many of these little strokes were done from the late 'swing' of Robinson's bowling.

Hallows was leg-before-wicket at 84; he batted some hundred minutes and seemed in good form. Ernest Tyldesley walked into the gleaming middle with applause in his ears all the way. And there he stayed till the long day's close. It was three hours and five minutes, following the passing of Hallows, before Yorkshire could upset another Lancashire wicket. Tyldesley was as canny as Makepeace—even more so. Makepeace got his runs faster than Tyldesley; or, in the interests of truth, perhaps I ought to say he got them less slowly.

The Makepeace-Tyldesley stand, worth 169, fell three short of the highest partnership against the Yorkshire attack this year. Makepeace was bowled by Rhodes, attempting, most unnaturally, a huge drive. Lancashire's honourable 'old man' had obviously been tiring for some time. He batted four hours and fifty minutes and hit nine boundaries. A more characteristic Makepeace innings one could not wish to see; with all its slowness the student of cricket could scarcely complain that it was dull. Makepeace has a good range of strokes—all of the strokes, in fact, which a cricketer may accomplish without a high lift-up of the bat and without a full follow-through. Makepeace's cricket is, as the engraver would say, done on a small surface; his batsmanship is etched —just as MacLaren's was splashed about in spendthrift colour over a wide canvas. Only by looking at Makepeace closely may you appreciate the neat craftsmanship of his work; sometimes you will need the watchmaker's eye of George Meredith. But there it is, going on all the time in his least spectacular innings—clean, discreet footwork and a thoroughly scientific bat, yet one that is quick and sensitive.

Makepeace never gives us the stone-walling of the dullard. His mind is always active, solving problems ball by ball. Moreover, we can feel in his cricket the man's pride in honest craftsmanship; for that reason, if for no other, we must watch our Makepeace patiently and admiringly. He accumulated his runs by stealth on Saturday afternoon, and at the end of his innings he might have said, in the accents of Autolycus: 'In this time of lethargy I picked and cut most of their festival purses, and had not the old man (Rhodes) come in with his half-volley I had not left a purse alive in the whole army.'

Until the tea interval Lancashire's cricket was excellently devised to circumvent the Yorkshire strategy, which is based on the 'make 'em fetch 'em' philosophy. All the Yorkshire bowlers, save Rhodes, pitched a length just too short for a safe hit. Here was the familiar wearing-down process at work. The Lancashire batsmen responded by methods as canny. Medicine for medicine! Few teams in the land could have turned blind eyes for as long as Lancashire to the temptation which hangs on the boundary (especially when Rhodes is bowling) like ripe fruit. Tyldesley once succumbed to this temptation. With his score 79, he drove a ball from Rhodes high and beautifully to long-off, and Leyland, on the edge of the field, missed the catch. Possibly he was bothered by the crowd sitting on the grass behind him. I have no doubt that Tyldesley, immediately he saw his catch soaring in the air, cursed his rashness: 'See what happens if you let go heartily in a Lancashire and Yorkshire match.' Perhaps Lancashire were wise to play to the day's end the cautious risk-nothing game; experience has frequently taught us what can happen to modern batsmen whenever they risk a blow at the Yorkshire length. Only a week or two ago I saw

Middlesex collapse against Yorkshire after having reached 200 for three; the later batsmen tried to force the pace. Yet after tea on Saturday surely Lancashire discovered too few runs; with 200 up and only one wicket down, the rate of scoring could have been quickened a little without the slightest risk. In the concluding two hours only 100 runs were made. This was the speed of the day's first two hours. It is hard to believe the Yorkshire attack did not lose something of its edge as the hot day passed by. Ernest Tyldesley played stylish cricket always: but none of us will believe that Tyldesley is at his best and truest when he plays, on a perfect wicket, an innings at Makepeace's pace.

Evidently Lancashire and Yorkshire elevens no longer go into battle with the old chivalrous cry of 'War to the death.' The policy nowadays of each side is not so much to strive after victory outright as to prevent the others from winning. First innings points and a consequent hurt to 'percentage' is the aim of the more or less happy warrior who wears the red or white rose in these spacious times.

The Yorkshire attack connived to keep runs down rather than get wickets. Kilner exploited a species of Rootism, bowling over the wicket and swinging the ball to a place well outside the batsman's legs, with his field containing six men on the on-side and no slip. I wonder what Colin Blythe would have thought to see a gifted left-handed bowler trusting to this negative device. Rhodes bowled with more than Kilner's flight through the air; moreover, he bowled the seductive length, on the wicket, which is likely to get batsmen out of patience even on a heavenly turf. But until Robinson was fit to drop he was the edge of the Yorkshire attack. The fielding rarely faltered; usually it went beyond accuracy and achieved brilliance. A quick stop and throw-in by Macaulay, on the offside, was as fierce as it was handsome to see in its low, diving grace. Major Lupton will bat to-day at least '25 up': let young cricketers watch the Yorkshire captain and observe how a man is able to get vast pleasure out of cricket by sheer keenness in the field, despite some smack of age in him, some relish of the saltness of time.

At one part of afternoon I noticed that Robinson was fielding on the boundary; never before have I seen him so much as this out of conversational touch with the wicket. He seemed a little Low (as Mrs. Micawber used to say of her Wilkins), a little out of sorts. Perhaps it was the Lancashire total, perhaps merely the native austerity of this rare old cricketer. Great men, as Aristotle tells us, are naturally melancholy. And, of course, Emmott Robinson is the greatest man in Yorkshire county always excepting Wilfred.

SECOND DAY

Lancashire might have forced the pace in the way demanded by the position of the game before lunch yesterday had it not been for Watson. Ernest Tyldesley played for Lancashire and got out through trying to drive a ball from Rhodes out of the field. But Watson, after batting excellently for a while, discovered his score was in the eighties, and then, seemingly, he must needs look covetously towards his hundred. When Tyldesley was bowled at twenty-five past twelve Watson's score stood at 56. At 12.30 Lancashire reached 400 for three. In the next hour Watson got 20 runs, mainly behind the wicket. At lunch with Lancashire 451 for four and everybody waiting for a declaration, Watson condescended to make three runs in just under half an hour. Out for 92 runs he failed to get a hundred after all. Plainly the gods who are sportsmen, I hope, thought he didn't deserve the honour. Watson's cricket hung like the Old Man of the Sea on Lancashire's movement onwards before lunch: Iddon, too, so far forgot his true heart that in half an hour he scored only nine—and he came to the wicket when Lancashire's grand total was safely poised at 385 for three.

At lunch, as I say, Lancashire were 451 for four. Most of us imagined the county would now close the innings and go for a win outright. Such was our innocent chivalry. Lancashire went on batting, and, though a few wickets fell, the game at last assumed the aspect of cricket. Green played in the right spirit and hit a mighty six. Duckworth also smote a ball into the crowd. This hitting by Lancashire rearguard let us have a most eloquent commentary on the innings of Watson in its later part, which was after the school of Samuel Smiles, self-help so to speak.

To many of us the Lancashire captain's diffidence about

192

declaring at lunch was surprising. But, as the philosopher told us, there is reason in all things. Lancashire's innings was prolonged on some such strategy as this. The longer Yorkshire fielded in the hot sun the more weary the batsmen might be when they went to the wicket. A lunch interval would give them some amount of rest. Moreover, if Lancashire did not begin bowling till three o'clock or so the Yorkshire batsmen might be denied the opportunity of getting easy runs from a Lancashire attack tired in the day's last hour, after sustained activity, excepting the tea interval, from lunch to close of play. Finally it was thought that the longer the Lancashire innings lasted the better the chance of the wicket losing some of its bloom. I give the outline of Lancashire's policy for what it is worth.

In the light of the great stand by Sutcliffe and Holmes it is no doubt just as well Lancashire helped themselves to as many runs as were there for the picking on the absurdly easy turf. A declaration at lunch would have left Yorkshire wanting 452 to win the only points the game seemed likely to offer now. Yorkshire already are nearly halfway towards this total, and today it is not impossible that they will outrage Old Trafford by a victory on the first innings. But what a farcical pass the game has come to—a captain may not safely close his innings at lunch on the second day even though his side has scored 450 runs!

Yet there were many good things for us to revel in at Old Trafford yesterday—the game is more than the players of the game. There was the beneficent sunshine too—good to see and feel as it burned on our faces. And the crowd—the biggest ever seen on a county ground. Who could be dull with all its splendid humanity about him? Never has Old Trafford made a handsomer sight than yesterday; 45,000 sat (or stood) there rank on rank, happy as sandboys, happy in their applause happy in their grumblings. May not an Englishman have his grievance, let it be, the Government, the income tax, Mr. Cook, or Frank Watson. It is the sign, as Meredith puts it, of our affection for a thing that we can complain at it occasionally without loving it the less.

At three o'clock there was no place I would rather have been than at Old Trafford. Torrents of sunshine fell on the ancient field; the multitudes were drenched in them. The superb pavilion stood in the summer light, and during the silences that came over the game from time to time it seemed to cummune with itself—perhaps upon the mighty past it has known in those days when a Johnny Briggs would risk a match against Yorkshire by tossing up a slow ball audaciously, and when George Ulyett was brave enough to accept the challenge and make a lion-hearted bid for victory. White clouds sailed in yesterday's blue sky; a gentle wind sent the Lancashire colours rippling in the air. Shadows fell black and tiny in front of the cricketers like soft pools. And the crowd indulged the old familiar humours—they never grow weary of them. ' 'It 'em! Get a shovel.' Grand cheers hailed a flashing bit of fielding, roars fit to split the heavens went out when Lancashire's score touched 500, the highest ever against Yorkshire by Lancashire, for it went well beyond the 471 achieved in 1892 against the old beloved enemy. A golden day, a noble crowd, the greenest grass in all England. Many a Lancashire and Yorkshireman, exiled from this blessed country, now imprisoned across the seven seas, was thinking yesterday of Old Trafford and saying in his heart, 'O to be there—whoever's batting!'

There was another sight well worth our while at Old Trafford—Rhodes bowling his beautifully curved flight. The man's action is just as always it has been these many years, easy and masterful. History hangs all about him—the legendary Rhodes. Men who are playing with him in this match were not born when first he came to us, the greatest of our slow bowlers—and only a youth with an innocent, unrazored face. He was England's last man in then, and he won a match for his country, with Hirst, by one wicket. Whereupon he sighed for new worlds to conquer; with every batsman, even Victor Trumper in his thrall, he turned from bowling and took up batsmanship. He went in first for England, with Hobbs, and over the seas on the scorched earth of Australia, he was the helpmate of Hobbs in the greatest first wicket stand ever accomplished for England. Rhodes and Hobbs in partnership on the world's other side, cutting and driving the day long, and letting the crowd see, time after time 'the run-stealers flicker to and fro.' And here is this same Rhodes with us yet, top of the English bowling averages. His performance in this game, on a flawless wicket, in torrid heat, out of a total of 509 for nine—seven wickets for 116 in 42 overs—why the man has surely taken hold of Time and thrust him, scythe and all, behind him. This Rhodes who saw Grace and Shrewsbury plain, is without end. His face is dyed with the stain of a thousand days in the sun; he is the image of the 'Old Soldier' as he waits to bowl, tossing the ball from hand to hand, fingering it with the intimacy of one of whom the touch of round leather is nature's own touch. If he does not play again for England at the Oval next week, then our Selection Committee is lacking the sense that knows greatness.

Ernest Tyldesley's innings lasted five hours and five minutes; he gave chances at 72 and 99. The snick through the slips by which he got his hundred was certainly not a 'business' stroke. Watson, until the temptation of a century dangled in his eyes, was at his best; many of his strokes were clean and forceful. It is a pity he apparently cannot look the score-board boldly in the face whenever his innings is in the eighties and nineties.

The Yorkshiremen stuck to a gruelling job with unfailing spirit; the imperturbability of Rhodes, the way he persisted in 'tossing them up' was delightful to see. Rhodes, who passed through the ordeal of Jessop's fires, is not the bowler who is likely to be intimidated by an occasional six from him in a Lancashire innings in 1926.

The Sutcliffe-Holmes partnership entered on its processional course at twenty-five minutes to four. So far it has lasted some 165 minutes and has made 183 runs—prodigiously fast scoring for this engagement. Holmes reached his 50 in ninety minutes—easily the quickest 50 of the game so far. With Yorkshire's score 137 and Holmes's 77, he ought to have been run out, but Richard Tyldesley did not gather quickly enough a not very accurate return. Holmes and Sutcliffe both played effortless cricket, and though no stupid risks were taken by either I did not get the impression that the boundary resided somewhere on the horizon from the batsman's point of view. Many of Sutcliffe's strokes were elegant; he was pretty to watch and this time his gentle way

195

with a ball that he might have hit hard did not cause annoyance. He brings a pleasant flavour into these grim games, for about him is the air of confident and handsome manhood. A few years ago it seemed he would develop into a batsman both stylish and brilliant; the responsible atmosphere of Test cricket has perhaps taken the sting from some of the strokes he once let us see—that flashing hook for instance. But if he is rather a utilitarian today he puts a bloom on conscientious labours. He is the craftsman, not the artisan. Holmes played a versatile game for a man in a side facing 509 runs. Once or twice he hit quite recklessly at Macdonald's bumpers and I expected to see Robinson appear on the players' balcony and utter a stern call to strict reason. From one of these bumpers Holmes hit a six—a sort of Derbyshire cut over the long-leg boundary. Lancashire's attack seemed too short for the occasion. With vast runs to play with the bowlers might to advantage have tried a few tricks. Anything to get a batsman nodding. Routine length is not the stuff for Yorkshire batsmen fighting with backs to the wall. Somebody in the crowd shouted, 'Bowl 'em underhands'; it was the voice of imagination. Lobs have been known to produce strange effects on perfect grounds against batsmen a little inclined to stand on their dignity. The fast full-toss, too, not infrequently makes a sad mess of glass of fashion and mould of form.

THIRD DAY

Ten minutes from time Lancashire won the first-innings points of this game. So this, as any American visitor might have said, is county cricket between Lancashire and Yorkshire—the half-way stage reached at the end of the third day and in all the hours of it less than 900 runs made on a beautiful wicket. 'Only a first-class batsman is capable of cricket as dull and slow as this,' was the witty comment of one of the country's best judges of the game. There was humour too in Roy Kilner's remark to me: 'Tha doesn't want to alter anything in county cricket; it's all reight enough. Tha simply need to educate t' crowd up to it.'

The play yesterday was no doubt interesting always to the cricketers. But until the crisis, watching was a penance. Hour after hour it was a case of 'Block, block, block at the foot of thy wicket, O batsmen.' The occasional boundaries which we saw were probably hit under protest. The quick overthrow of Sutcliffe no doubt gave the enemy reason for drawing in horns. On Monday evening he and Holmes had scored faster, in the face of a total of 509, than Lancashire. Sutcliffe was leg before wicket at 199; his innings had almost as much bouquet as it had body.

And now happened a distressing incident—which must have further taken the wind out of any sails set by Yorkshire likely to lead them to prosperity. Oldroyd, after shaping dubiously at Macdonald, was hit on the back of the head by a rising short ball. He seemed prepared to attempt a half-hook; then, at the last second, he wavered as he saw Macdonald's bumper rising. He fell like a stone and was carried from the field unconscious. Leyland came in next and when a few more balls had been bowled the umpires held a consultation and signalled to the scorers that Oldroyd was out. Apparently he had, in the opinion of the umpire, hit his wicket with his bat in the act of playing the ball. The dramatic episode and everybody's concern for poor Oldroyd produced confusion. I take it that Oldroyd was adjudged 'out' in the approved way before the next batsman arrived at the wicket and that somehow the decision was not declared officially until the scorers made an inquiry. It would not, of course, be in order for an umpire to deliver a decision at the prompting of the scoring box. The intimation of the scorers yesterday must be regarded not as a decision formed there and then but rather as an official announcement to the scorers of a decision given on appeal from the proper quarter at the right time. It was cruel luck on Oldroyd and we must all wish him a quick recovery from his accident. The point is worth discussion whether a ball ought not to become definitely 'out of play' the moment it strikes a batsman and, in the sternest sense of the term, puts him out of play.

The unhappy accident did not prevent Leyland and Holmes from defending most obstinately. Macdonald was rested immediately after Oldroyd was knocked out of action, and here it might be argued that Macdonald could rightly claim that he, too, suffered his share of bad luck. It is hard

197

lines on a fast bowler that he should innocently be the cause of an accident while legitimately using his arts towards circumventing a perfect turf. For after he has hurt a batsman seriously 'moral' pressure is bound to embarrass his attack.

Holmes and Leyland held the third Yorkshire wicket from ten minutes past twelve till half-past two with a defence so easy and solid that Lancashire could indulge no hopes of points at all while they were on view. Even when Holmes skied a ball to mid-on and was caught, the odds were all in favour of a 'no decision' match. Holmes's innings lasted some five hours and a half; yesterday, at one period, he made 31 in 95 minutes. None the less, it was a cricketer's innings in the circumstances. He was never uninteresting to the student of the game, and he hit two sixes and 16 fours.

Kilner was fourth out at 3.10 but the turning point of the afternoon was when Leyland, after playing with a grim yet stylish obstinacy for two hours and a half, scoring only 31, suddenly became seized by demons of folly and hit wildly across and over a well-pitched length from Sibbles and was clean bowled. I cannot imagine what he was thinking about. But, later, we were to witness an even more astonishing act of indiscretion—committed by none other than Rhodes, the Wise Man of the Yorkshire clan. He stonewalled with all his heart and soul for 40 minutes and then—tell it not in Luddendenfoot or Laisterdyke—he tried to cut a ball from Watson which was spinning well away from the wicket. O, Wilfred, Wilfred, how could you so far forget yourself as to take a fancy to the cut in such a heavy moment for Yorkshire? Did the good man momentarily fall into the delusion that this was a cricket match? Watson must be praised for exploiting his leg break in this responsible hour; with this trick, which he too rarely plays, he got Rhodes and Macaulay with consecutive balls, and so opened, by the tea interval, a way to the first inning spoils.

After tea the struggle was tense—a tug-of-war, both sides at an intolerable strain, the rope taut, with no man giving ground at this end or that. The agony called for all the fine passion of Robinson. His was stonewalling of positively spiteful resistance. Richard Tyldesley tossed him 'dolly' balls, but Emmott got down on his broad bat to them. 'Dost think ah'm a fooil—like young Leyland?' he seemed to say to Lancashire. Waddington and Emmott, standing for the eighth wicket, slowly heaved the situation round in Yorkshire's favour. They put canny blades to every sort of ball for nearly three-quarters of an hour. When only 25 minutes were left, Yorkshire had three wickets in hand. Green changed his attack frequently, but, so it looked now, all to no purpose. Iddon was asked to bowl and the crowd demanded Macdonald. It was Iddon, though, who at the pinch got a clutch on the day's booty. In one over he rid us of Robinson and Major Lupton. Robinson, though he lost his wicket at a time when no doubt he would have given pounds sterling to hold it, passed from the action without a stain on his character. No silly hitting or cutting for this ancient warrior. He perished in high Roman fashion—as good men and true ought to perish for Yorkshire whenever the old county has its back to the wall—he was out leg-before-wicket! And I calculated that he wasted not a hair's breadth of his two battle-scarred pads.

Of course Yorkshire fought bitterly to the last man. Waddington and Dolphin bit their teeth into the last wicket and clung there for ten minutes—every second to blow on our patience. Waddington seemed to give a quick slip catch to Macdonald. Green was compelled to change his bowling once again. I congratulate him for wisely thrusting in Watson once more, who, granted he would exploit leg-spinners further, was the very man for Waddington or Dolphin. I congratulate Watson too for chancing his hand at leg-spinners in this difficult position. Leg spinners are exceedingly difficult to bowl—expecially if you are not, as Watson isn't, accustomed to bowling them. Watson pitched one well up to Waddington, and a catch to the on side, which Iddon held in excellent glee, gave Old Trafford its heart's desire.

Even half a victory over Yorkshire may be taken as wine good enough to wash down a certain pill that has been sticking in Lancashire's craw since Whitsuntide.

SCORES

LANCASHIRE

First Innings

Makepeace, b Rhodes	126
Hallows, lbw, b Robinson	41
Tyldesley (E.), st Dolphin, b Rhodes	139
Watson, c Dolphin, b Kilner	92
Iddon, c Dolphin, b Rhodes	15
Macdonald, c Leyland, b Rhodes	19
Tyldesley (R.), c Oldroyd, b Rhodes	2
Taylor, c & b Rhodes	3
Sibbles, b Rhodes	6
L. Green, not out	30
Duckworth, not out	9
Extras b8, lb14, w1, nb4	27

Total (for 9)   *509

*Innings declared

YORKSHIRE

First Innings

Holmes, c Hallows, b Macdonald	143
Sutcliffe, lbw, b Tyldesley (R.)	89
Oldroyd (hit wkt), b Macdonald	12
Leyland, b Sibbles	31
Kilner, c Iddon, b Macdonald	17
Rhodes, c Duckworth, b Watson	12
Robinson, lbw, b Iddon	12
Macaulay, c Iddon, b Watson	0
Waddington, c Iddon, b Watson	17
Major Lupton, b Iddon	0
Dolphin, not out	4
Extras b11, lb3, w1	15

Total   352

BOWLING ANALYSIS

LANCASHIRE—First Innings

	O.	M.	R.	W.		O.	M.	R.	W.
Rhodes	42	7	116	7	Macaulay	34	4	94	0
Kilner	47	15	90	1	Oldroyd	4	0	16	0
Waddington	28	2	86	0	Robinson	41	10	80	1

YORKSHIRE—First Innings

	O.	M.	R.	W.		O.	M.	R.	W.
Macdonald	49	11	154	3	Watson	17	9	16	3
Sibbles	47	18	72	1	Iddon	21	10	35	2
Tyldesley (R.)	45	22	60	1					

YORKSHIRE V LANCASHIRE 1927

June 4/6/7   Old Trafford

FIRST DAY

A LANCASHIRE and Yorkshire match often is sullen for hours like a dull fire, waiting for some chance wind of antagonism to blow its combustible stuff into flame. But on Saturday at Old Trafford the match sent out sparks and lightning before the crowd, especially those from Laisterdyke, quite knew where they were. A shower just before noon threatened to spoil cricket altogether; a wind blew the rain away and Macdonald began his silent run over the grass. His first over, pitched short, sent ball after ball flying about the skulls of Leyland and Sutcliffe; the air quickly became thrilling with a sense of danger. Macdonald's ninth ball did not drop short, did not bump and bounce at all savagely; it was pitched well up to Sutcliffe's bat, and somehow he missed his stroke. 'Zat!' shrieked Duckworth and the slips—also a small, frantic little boy near the sight screen behind Macdonald's arm. The umpires finger went up; Sutcliffe was lbw for none and Yorkshire 5 for one wicket. The crowd shouted with sudden unexpected joy—a shout that might have been heard a mile away. Along Warwick Road people who were late said 'O Lord!' and began to run in a panic, for fear of missing something.

Macdonald had a sinister aspect as he hurled down his first devastating overs. When, after every ball, he walked to his bowling place, his face was drawn with lines of determination. His fourteenth ball kicked as though evil were in it; Leyland could not get out of harm's way in time. 'S'elp me,' said his bat, and just edged a swift catch to Watson at second slip. Yorkshire 10 for two in a quarter of an hour, and the crowd pitiless in its exultation. Let it now be said that though many of us thought that the pitch contained at the outset some moisture harmful to batsmen, one of the Yorkshire cricketers told me, after his team's first innings was over, that the wicket could not be grumbled at on the whole. 'It were

201

good enough at one end!' he said. Probably no bowler other than Macdonald in all England would have made a ball rear head high on the turf; he put the whole of his energy into his attack, and the old ease and rhythm were rather missing. The new glossy ball seemed to help his grim plan—which obviously was to get the Yorkshiremen caught behind the wicket from bats moved by reflex action.

Yorkshire sadly missed Holmes, who was resting a strained muscle. But this loss was almost equalled on the Lancashire side by the absence from the eleven of Makepeace, who is a great cricketer in these mighty matches. The Lancashire team without Makepeace in a Yorkshire match is 'Hamlet' without—let us say, Polonius. Yorkshire also had, at the last minute, to find somebody to take the place of Major Lupton, also injured. Thus a cricketer named Kennie was flung into the furnace for baptism. Our hearts went out to the lad in his visibly mingled emotions of apprehension and pluck.

Oldroyd and Mitchell held Yorkshire's third wicket for half an hour. Mitchell stood up to Macdonald's fury like a stout batsman, playing the ball with his body erect and bold. Oldroyd made one or two steps sideways, towards the square-leg umpire, yet contrived to slash the ball several times through the slips for useful if not dignified runs. I did not get the impression that Oldroyd was going to play a long innings; none the less he remained at or contiguous to the wicket until ten minutes to one. Mitchell's was the third Yorkshire wicket to fall; he flicked his bat at another of Macdonald's rising balls, and Richard Tyldesley held the second slip catch of the battle. Mitchell proved himself a batsman of ability; I shall not be surprised if he gets a good score next innings. Oldroyd did not, after all, get out to Macdonald; facing Sibbles, he made a bold vigorous hit to square-leg, worth four in any match. We all looked towards the boundary, but Taylor jumped forward from his place at the side of the umpire and held a glorious catch, while the multitude stood up and made its many-tongued tribute to beautiful fieldsmanship. Kennie was quickly leg before wicket to Richard Tyldesley, who bowled after Macdonald had for seventy minutes played havoc with Yorkshire wickets and Yorkshire confidence. But before Macdonald put on his sweater he sent a terrible bumper right at Kilner's head: Kilner ducked just in time, and so great was his concern that for a moment he lost his customary broad grin. Kilner also gave a sharp chance to Sibbles at first slip from another streak of Macdonald's abruptly forked lightning. The fact must here be mentioned that Oldroyd's innings lasted 55 minutes—every moment of it a crisis.

Ten minutes before lunch Rhodes walked into the field, acclaimed all the way to the wicket by a crowd sensible enough to know that they were looking upon one of the country's most notable men. The legendary Rhodes!—why, to some of us, though we have played and watched cricket all our years, and though we are not young any longer,—to us this same Rhodes has always been part of our never-dying love and enthusiasm for the game, part of cricket's seasonal pageantry summer after summer, part of the cricket scores in the newspapers, ever since we were old and big enough to open and read them for ourselves on warm afternoons after we had come home from school. Away in the remote past a small boy in a Manchester street once saw a dreadful newspaper placard. From the distance it seemed to cry out:—

DEATH OF
RHODES

The small boy ran in an agony over the street; to his unspeakable joy he then saw that the poster really stated:—

DEATH OF
CECIL
RHODES

And here on Saturday, in the year 1927, Rhodes was still to be seen on Old Trafford's field, with history hanging about his head cloud on cloud. A quarter of a century ago he stood in the same place, at one end of the wicket, while at the other end Tate suffered on the rack of the most tragic of all Test matches. 'We'll win if Wilfred can get another ball,' the watching crowd told itself, hoping, fearing. But Wilfred never did get another ball..... This most famous of living cricketers played a cool skilful game against Lancashire on Saturday. After lunch he and Kilner lifted, by the sweat of their brow, the Yorkshire score to 93. Watson then made a very pretty slip catch, and Kilner was out. Robinson tried bitterly to dig himself into the earth, but he too was caught by Watson, who all the time fielded admirably.

Macaulay and Rhodes scored 37 for Yorkshire's eighth wicket, and Macaulay hit three boundaries full of the fighting temper. Richard Tyldesley got him out leg before wicket. Waddington was obstinate for twenty minutes; then he 'let fly' at one of Tyldesley's slows and drove powerfully towards mid-off, whereat Macdonald jumped upwards, all grace and nonchalance, and held with two hands an astonishing catch as the ball went away from him while both of his feet were off the grass. He seemed to draw the ball down out of the air by some magnetism in his fingers. Rhodes and Dolphin, resisting like proper men of their county to the very end, put strong bats to the ball for twenty minutes. Macdonald had to bowl again to get Yorkshire's last wicket, which he did with his first ball. It pitched short and soared over the head of Rhodes, who so far forgot his authentic circumspect philosophy that he flashed up his bat and gave his innings away—caught by Duckworth, who always was as vigilant for chances behind or above the stumps as a cat for the taste of cream. This stroke by Rhodes was certainly not a 'business' stroke.

The Yorkshire innings lasted three and a quarter hours; Rhodes alone made it vertebrate. He batted as though there were little or nothing in the bowling or the wicket. Many of his on-side hits were handsome and cleverly placed. His shrewd, unruffled innings lasted two hours. The Lancashire fielding was beyond praise; activity in the slips while Macdonald bowled must have been a severe trial for nerves and eyes alike. Here let it be said that there is no pleasanter fact about the Lancashire XI today than the fresh, healthy flavour brought to the team by the younger cricketers. Each of them gave a winning bloom to Lancashire's energy on Saturday. It was, of course, Macdonald's attack that shattered the Yorkshire innings, but Sibbles and Richard Tyldesley were willing and clever helpers. Sibbles made a charming picture of eager and determined youth; over after over he bowled with all his heart, and the rosy flush on his cheeks was good to see.

Yorkshire's wickets fell in this sequence:—

1	2	3	4	5	6	7	8	9	10
5	10	38	54	57	93	102	139	153	166

It was an innings full of frail batting—not so much an innings, indeed, as an outline of one, 'a dem'd outline,' as M. Mantalini might have said.

The Lancashire innings was not much better than Yorkshire's for a while. Watson was bowled off his legs, not attempting a cricketer's stroke. Lancashire had then made only 11. Ernest Tyldesley and Hallows put our misgivings to quiet. Both batted with ample coolness, ease, and skill. Runs came slowly, but none of us objected to that. The fifty was reached in an hour, and Emmott Robinson bowled very hard—without his cap. There are now honourable grey hairs in his fine Yorkshire head, yet not more I think, than there were when I saw him a few weeks ago—before Yorkshire were beaten by Warwickshire.

At six o'clock Lancashire's fortunate wind suddenly veered round. Hallows attempted an off-drive from Macaulay; perhaps the ball 'lifted' after pitching. Whatever the cause, Hallows made a bad stroke and was caught by Kennie. Hallows looked to be thoroughly comfortable when he lost his wicket at an hour crucial to Lancashire. Green was third out ten minutes after. Thus, with twenty-five minutes left for play, and the Yorkshiremen sniffing somewhere a chance to mend a dubious day—at this testing time Eckersley had to come forth and face the music of a Lancashire v Yorkshire match for the first time. As he bent down on his bat, pale and tense, his face was twitching with plucky endeavour. If he makes not another run this morning he will return to the pavilion with a gallant innings behind him. His defence in Saturday's closing period was most valuable; had he failed, possibly Yorkshire would now be in a position to win with some ease on the first innings. As it is, Lancashire's chances seem to rest heavily on Ernest Tyldesley. So far he has batted like a great cricketer, moving with certainty towards a big score.

SECOND DAY

Yesterday at Old Trafford was a triumph for Lancashire's young men. When Ernest Tyldesley fell to a dubious stroke in the third over of the morning, Lancashire were 72 runs to the bad with four wickets down, and Rhodes and Kilner, the old falconers, had only to catch a few gawky nestlings who have yet to beat a strong flight in the severe air of Lancashire and Yorkshire cricket. What a sight the day gave to the vast crowd—Rhodes spreading his snares, his birdlime in vain! Hour after hour the Yorkshire bowlers tossed up spinning guile, and hour after hour there was, as they say, nothing doing.

It was little use our complaining that the batting was tedious, that on a slow easy wicket the boundary seemed always on some distant horizon. It was little use (and it was unfair) for us to expect Eckersley, Taylor, Sibbles and Duckworth to tackle Rhodes and Kilner as MacLaren, Spooner, and Tyldesley most certainly would have done.

'Ah, my friends,' says Mr. Chadband, 'consider the birds of the air and how they soar. Why can we not soar?' And Mr. Jellaby tentatively suggests, 'No wings.' The point about Lancashire's batting yesterday is not that runs were got very slowly by young cricketers, but that wickets were got more slowly still by old bowlers of international rank. Not for years will Old Trafford forget the afternoon's humorous spectacle—Sibbles giving grandmother Wilfred admirable instructions concerning the delicate art of sucking an egg.

The week-end rains had left the turf heavy; the ball would spin, but so slowly that it could be watched in ease. Ernest Tyldesley attempted a cut and was caught at short slip by Sutcliffe. And here the agony set in, the intolerable strain of watching ball by ball plucky but unschooled bats doing their best in the cause of Lancashire. Iddon, I thought, might have played a stronger game; he drove twice to the boundary from successive balls sent by Macaulay and then never again trusted his ability to hit. For an hour after Ernest Tyldesley's downfall the game seemed without motion; in this time Eckersley made 9 and Iddon 13. The stand for Lancashire's fifth wicket lasted 70 minutes for 33, each run a notable event in time and space. Rhodes then confounded Iddon with a ball that spun away from the bat after finding contact with the edge.

At 11.35 Lancashire reached 100; an hour afterwards the grand total was 127. In this long, scourging hour Eckersley made 9. He crouched over his bat in an attitude of tremendous watchfulness; Makepeace by comparison would have seemed negligent. He never took his eye from the ball for a second. His white blade was thrust to the earth, a door bolted against evil. He was caught at square leg just before the lunch interval. For two hours and thirty-five minutes had he circumvented Yorkshire, incidentally scoring 28. His innings was a clear case of determination and discipline overcoming the limitations of immature technique. He has given proof that he has nerve enough; let him now play the game that he can play. Not all cricket matches are of the Lancashire v Yorkshire sort. From morning to lunch two hours and twenty-five minutes crawled by and Lancashire's score arrived at 146 for six.

After lunch the crowd made a stirring sight; rank on rank it was heaped round the field's green circle. As Sibbles and Taylor dragged the Lancashire score closer and closer to Yorkshire's the noise of excitement began to hum in the air. 'Come on Yarksheer!' cried a voice from somewhere; it was a little hoarse. Whereat there was a shrill response from a throng of defiant schoolboys 'Come on Lankyshire!'

Little lads, the game belongs to them, after all, and we older cricketers must envy their infinite hero-worship, their fresh eyes that see only things to wonder at on a county cricket field. For them every pro is a god who can do no wrong. Do they, as we used to do when we were young, get out of bed very early on Bank Holiday mornings and go apprehensively to the window to see if it is raining; then let their hearts beat with delight as they see through the curtains the streets dry and clean and silent in the dawn?

At twenty minutes to three Taylor drove beautifully to the off-side; Kennie misfielded the hit, and a mighty roar announced that at last Lancashire had won the first innings prize. As I looked down from the high press-box at the cheering multitude, the oldest man a boy again, I thought that, in spite of all the pains and penalties of this our modern county

207

cricket, it was indeed good to be at Old Trafford at Whitsuntide, of all the spots on the earth. I thought also of the many Lancashire men, separated by the seven seas from their own land and county—how at this very moment they would be thinking of Old Trafford, sending their thoughts to the place and to the match, wondering what was going on now, envying us who were present and asking in their hearts, 'Does the old pavilion stand where it did and are Lancashire winning?'

At ten past three a shower stopped play for ten minutes, just after Richard Tyldesley had shown us his Westhoughton cut. While the cricketers were absent from the field a Yorkshireman in the crowd kept up his spirits by singing (with commendable energy of tone, in the circumstances) a merry ditty to these words:—

> Yorkshire lads are happy and gay
> Always win at home, never lose away.

The burden of the song was not quite true to history, but it was, I fancy intended less as a statement of fact than as an affirmation of everlasting faith. True belief is a priori and rises beyond the circumstances of the transient, material world.

Taylor hit four superb fours—there were not more than seven boundaries in three hours and three-quarter's play. At 150 Taylor missed a ball from Rhodes and it hit his pads; he was lbw before the ball bounded into the wickets from his leg. Taylor gave us real batsmanship; he played the good bowling with as much care as anybody else, but he had the strokes needed by the bad balls. His cricket shone like a warm fire in a cold, dark habitation. The quick overthrow of Richard Tyldesley and Macdonald emphasised the value of the staunch opposition of the younger Lancashire batsmen. When Macdonald was caught indeed, Lancashire were merely 26 ahead; had all the dreary grind been worth the feeble advantage, we asked.

None of us for a moment expected the diverting scene which followed the fall of the ninth wicket. For Duckworth and Sibbles outraged the dignity of Rhodes and Kilner for an hour and a quarter before tea. Only by aid of rest and sustenance got in the interval did Yorkshire capture the wicket of Sibbles, and even then a new ball and a new bowler—name of Robinson—had to be called into action. Rhodes and Kilner probably spun their fingers into a paralytic condition in their attempts to get Duckworth or Sibbles out. Dignity could not well be served by crying out 'Ah'm done—give me mi sweater.' Rhodes sent three fielders to the boundary's edge for Duckworth's antagonistic bat. A funnier sight has not been witnessed at Old Trafford for years. What Emmott Robinson was saying all the time it is not easy to guess. Yesterday's broadcasting arrangements ought to have seen to it that a microphone was placed at the wicket.

Sibbles' innings, from a quarter-past two until ten minutes past five, with slight interruptions by the rain and tea, must have tried very hard the patience of all proper Yorkshiremen. It was an innings of immense coolness and not a little defensive skill. He might have been run out, and Lancashire's innings finished, at 196. And he looked so modest and quiet all the time as though butter wouldn't melt in his mouth! Does he not know, on the authority of the learned Bacon, that age will not be defied? The Lancashire innings lasted six hours and a half; Yorkshire bowled 151 overs and five balls, 64 maidens, from which 220 runs were made by the bat. This last stand of Duckworth and Sibbles was worth 42.

Yorkshire went in again, 68 in arrears, at half-past five. The pitch rolled out comfortably. In Macdonald's first over Leyland flung a bat aloft at a bumper of great velocity. He struck the ball deep to leg, where Taylor held a clever and thrilling catch. Yorkshire none for one. Oldroyd, unhappy again in front of Macdonald, edged a ball to Richard Tyldesley in the slips at 29. The noise of the crowd seemed to fill the whole sky. Sutcliffe played like the great cricketer he is in a crisis; thrice he hooked Macdonald bravely and dramatically to the boundary. Mitchell defended for twenty minutes and it seemed now that the long day was at an end. Macdonald put on his sweater. Iddon bowled instead of Sibbles, and straightway spun a ball so quickly from the turf that Mitchell mishit to E. Tyldesley on the off-side. Another nail in the Yorkshire coffin. Folk came hurrying back to the ground from the railway station. 'Train be blowed!' said an

209

elderly man with an umbrella and a good face. With Kilner in, Green had an inspiration; he recalled Macdonald and in the afternoon's very last over Sutcliffe made a mistake and Richard Tyldesley caught him out, his face a rising sun of joy as he did so. Sutcliffe's innings was the best of the match so far. It was batsmanship of noble style and temper.

Down the Warwick Road streamed the crowd at close of play, every Lancashire man and woman and boy and girl glad to be alive and exultant at the sight of a victory for Lancashire just round the corner.

THIRD DAY

At twenty minutes to six last evening Lancashire defeated Yorkshire for the first time at Old Trafford since Parkin's whirlwind victory over the old enemy in 1919.

The day was often a rack of torture on which we were stretched hour by hour, while circumstances goaded us. Heavy rain in the night left the wicket soft, and not until a quarter past twelve could Lancashire go on with the job of forcing home Monday's advantage. And as we waited for cricket to begin apprehension stalked visibly over Old Trafford. Would the pitch be easy at first for Yorkshire, help them to get a good score, and then, later in the day, would it turn into an ally of Rhodes and Kilner?

It was plain from the day's outset that the moist earth had, so to say, drawn the teeth of Macdonald. His first over was directed from round the wicket, to a leg trap—a certain sign that he did not fancy his chances at fast, bumping stuff, but instead was giving preference to his off-spin. But after eleven balls he decided to experiment with his speed after all and straightway he bowled young Kennie. And he contrived to send a short length soaring over Kilner's head, no mean act of energy on that wicket. It was obvious, though, that Macdonald could only circumvent the sluggish ground by putting an intolerable strain on his back and shoulders. He went out of action, and Richard Tyldesley hauled himself from the great extent of his sweater—always a mighty spectacle this.

Rhodes and Kilner played well. Kilner plainly was determined to get runs quickly before the turf began to bite. Yorkshire saved the innings defeat, with five wickets in

210

reserve, at half-past twelve. Then the day hurled at us its first shock. Kilner, with his score 21, struck boldly against the spin of Iddon; the ball went up high like a straight tower and came down with a circling motion. Richard Tyldesley at forward square leg utterly 'lost' the catch and the ball fell in front of him. He could not even get his hands to it. The crowd's heart moaned, and Richard swallowed emotion in one vast gulp. A few minutes afterwards he retrieved his blunder. Kilner drove hard just a little to Tyldesley's left. Richard stuck out a hand of immense capaciousness and stuck to the ball, accomplishing a magnificent caught and bowled with all the coolness in the world. His attitude, as he gripped his prize, seemed to say: 'That's that! Ah'm none such a butterfingers as tha thinks. Pavilion, Roy, mi lad.'

Yorkshire were 94 for six when Emmott Robinson shambled to the field's middle with his widest pads on. And here followed another sting of agony. Rhodes smote a ball hard back to the bowler, who was Iddon. The catch went to grass—and a man near the Stretford sight screen committed a grave blasphemy upon all things in heaven and earth and the waters under the earth. Had Rhodes been got rid of now, Yorkshire's score, 94 for seven, would have been a sure herald of a Lancashire victory. As it was we had to take lunch with Robinson and Rhodes still undefeated, and Yorkshire four wickets still to go, 42 ahead. Moreover, tidings from the action informed us that the pitch was very nasty. Considering this indeterminate situation, we all did very well to eat as much as we did.

From one o'clock to lunch Yorkshire were fortunate not to collapse. That they avoided disaster hereabouts was the consequence of the sound straight bats of Rhodes and Robinson, the insecure Lancashire catching, and the variable length of Iddon. Iddon caused the ball to spin a great deal but his pitch was short. Richard Tyldesley also exploited a pretty break, without good luck. Twice he completely beat Robinson's bat, to miss the stumps by an inch. Whereat Tyldesley seemed to make a comment to Robinson, and likely enough he received a prompt answer.

For three-quarters of an hour after lunch the match was being snatched, over by over, out of Lancashire's grasp.

Iddon, who ought to have bowled well on the turf, repeatedly dropped a short length and Tyldesley lost his 'bite'. The truth is that the wicket became drier and easier after half-past one. Another dish of trouble stuck in our craws when Iddon, attempting to stop a throw-in, fell on the grass and strained his neck. He had to leave the field. Whereupon Rhodes and Robinson went on with their circumspect batting.

Macdonald bowled again, over the wicket, round the wicket, fast and slow. But virtue apparently was leaving the Lancashire attack. 'If Yorkshire get 200 by four o'clock,' said a faithless person in the pavilion, 'they'll declare and bundle us out for 30—confound them.' Christian fortitude and charity depart from all of us in struggles between Lancashire and Yorkshire.

At five minutes past three the field was full of sunlight, and Lancashire's energies were palpably about to slacken. I got a sense that deep down in the battle's sullen waters the tide was turning, and about to carry the Lancashire ship away from her goal.

The afternoon's turning-point was like a gift to Lancashire from the gods gathered together aloft over Old Trafford (they are, of course, Lancashire gods, sitting as they do above this ancient ground. Every field is presided over by its own deities). Robinson cut a ball from Tyldesley to Eckersley at backward point and Rhodes dashed from the other end for a run. Robinson stood still—perhaps in admiration of a neat Yorkshire cut all of his own making. When he returned from the world of aesthetic contemplation to the world of things as they are he found Rhodes almost on his doorstep.

Rhodes swung round desperately and sought to get back to his own crease, but far, far away it must have seemed to the old war-horse. The ball was thrown to the bowler, who was Tyldesley, and Tyldesley removed a bail with a leisurely touch that was terribly ironical. So ended a great fighting innings. Rhodes walked from the field with his head bent downwards. Old and hardened as he is, he has yet the capacity to feel bitterness in the face of dire misfortune to Yorkshire.

The running-out of Rhodes was crucial; had it not happened I believe Yorkshire would have escaped. Rhodes is his county's prop and stay. His downfall was most certainly the beginning of the end; the bottom fell out of Yorkshire's innings the moment his wicket was thrown to the winds. Rhodes was stolid defiance in the flesh for one hour and fifty minutes; he and Robinson made 53 runs for the seventh wicket in just over an hour. 'Oh Emmott, Emmott,' I imagine that all Yorkshire is crying today. 'What were t'a thinkin' about, at thy time of life?'

Macaulay was cleaned bowled by a fizzing length ball from Macdonald. Yorkshire 147 for 8. With only another single hit, Robinson himself lost his wicket; he cracked a short ball triumphantly to square-leg and Metcalfe, a young Lancashire lad fielding in the place of Iddon, held a brilliant catch and set Old Trafford on fire. As Robinson left the scene he made with his grey head certain symbolical nods. He did his damnedest for Yorkshire for 75 minutes. But I can hear, with my mind's ear, Horatio, another cry from Yorkshire's distressful county: 'Oh Emmott! what were t'a thinkin' of agean? Why didn't tha get out leg before t'wicket? Thee and thy fancy stroakes!'

Waddington, the last Yorkshire batsman to be vanquished, tried to hit Macdonald into Stretford and had his stumps shattered enormously. Yorkshire's last three wickets fell in ten minutes for six runs; shades of Lord Hawke and David Hunter, who fought many a bitter rear-guard action against a conquering Lancashire! Macdonald was again Yorkshire's bane; without his fierce bowling Lancashire could scarcely have got Yorkshire out on yesterday's turf, which, as I have suggested, turned comfortable after lunch-time. No other bowler in England could have drawn so much spite from the heavy ground; he is Yorkshire's evil genius indeed. ('And,' so I hear a voice, very like Robinson's, 'he comes fra' Tasmania.')

Lancashire needed to make 89 for victory and two hours and a half remained for cricket. Watson quickly presented his wicket to Rhodes and his men. He reached to an outswinger from Robinson, and with no body control over a hit made at arms' length, he sent a catch to cover-point.

The subsequent movement of Lancashire to the match's prize was slow and trying. Hallows and Ernest Tyldesley ventured not a hair's breadth beyond security for a long time.

Ball after ball hit a passive bat. In an hour only 37 runs were scored. When Hallows was six he sent a sharp chance to Leyland at forward square leg: Robinson was the bowler. What an afternoon he was having! I did not feel, however, that Hallows was likely to get out; he was composure itself. Tyldesley too played the Yorkshire attack with the utmost calm.

The crowd became restive; they wanted to taste the blood of Yorkshiremen. ' 'It 'em!' moaned some soul in the depths. The minutes went by and the runs did not seem to be coming. With only an hour left Lancashire wanted 39. The ironical truth is that the crowd, at this stage, was in part the maker of its own misery.

In its impatience the crowd could not see the grim significance of Lancashire's unhurried course to victory. There was ample time for the scoring of the runs, and Lancashire did not disdain to claim extra time; why need there have been haste in tightening the stanglehold? Yorkshire have burned captives enough in slow fires. Yet, there was, at one point, a suggestion that Lancashire were carrying the grisly humour dangerously far. Ernest Tyldesley lost his wicket in an obvious attempt to force the pace a little. He hit dramatically to square leg and Oldroyd achieved with one hand above his head not the least handsome of the game's many clever catches.

Green and Hallows were forty minutes going from 47 to 89, the goal. Hallows completed his thousand runs for the season. And all the while that he batted one could not doubt that Lancashire would win. It was his cool untroubled aspect which made me think that Lancashire's Fabianism was of their own calculating and not forced on them by Yorkshire bowlers. Rhodes, Kilner and Robinson let us see many arrangements in their field; their signs and gestures were intended to have a dark and subtle look. Hallows' cricket turned, by its confidence, all this show of strategy to the stuff of laughter. At least, that is how one saw it in the end. And a good end crowns and justifies everything.

The match was won mainly by Lancashire's flashing work in the field. Macdonald was for once backed up by catching which, on the whole, had certainty, anticipation and swiftness. The mistakes before lunch yesterday were lapses from a vast amount of uncommon grace in the eleven. Again, the batting of Lancashire's young men on Monday was staunch and of great utility, if not beautiful to look upon.

But victory by attrition is not, let us hope, to be Lancashire's policy in each and every game. Against Yorkshire discretion is probably the better part of valour. In games with other counties—Sussex, for example—what about a return to cricket according to the gospel of A. N. Hornby? There is an endless merit, so Carlyle says, in a man's knowing when to have done with a certain line of action. May we hope that the wine of a win over Yorkshire will quicken the blood of our batsmen henceforth, and that today our eleven, which we applaud and admire more than ever now, will celebrate this glorious triumph by bats that are gay and sportive—in, of course, reason?

SCORES

YORKSHIRE

	First Innings		Second Innings	
Sutcliffe, lbw, b Macdonald	0	c Tyldesley (R.), b Macdonald	38
Leyland, c Watson, b Macdonald	5	c Taylor, b Macdonald	0
Oldroyd, c Taylor, b Sibbles	34	c Tyldesley (R.), b Macdonald	11
Mitchell, c Tyldesley (R.), b Macdonald	9	c Tyldesley (E.), b Iddon	2
Kilner, c Watson, b Macdonald	27	c & b Tyldesley (R.)	22
Kennie, lbw, b Tyldesley (R.)	0	b Macdonald	6
Rhodes, c Duckworth, b Macdonald	44	run out	29
Robinson, c Watson, b Sibbles	6	c sub, b Tyldesley (R.)	31
Macaulay, lbw, b Tyldesley (R.)	20	b Macdonald	0
Waddington, c Macdonald, b Tyldesley (R.)	9	b Macdonald	4
Dolphin, not out	8	not out	0
Extras b2, lb1, w1	4	Extras b8, lb1, w1	10
Total	166	Total	153

LANCASHIRE

First Innings		Second Innings	
Hallows, c Kennie, b Macaulay	29	not out	43
Watson, b Robinson	4	c Kilner, b Robinson	4
Tyldesley (E.), c Sutcliffe, b Macaulay	42	c Oldroyd, b Kilner	20
L. Green, lbw, b Macaulay	3	not out	19
P. Eckersley, c Oldroyd, b Kilner	28		
Iddon, c Macaulay, b Rhodes	15		
Taylor, lbw, b Rhodes	36		
Sibbles, c Dolphin, b Robinson	40		
Tyldesley (R.), c Macaulay, b Kilner	4		
Macdonald, c Mitchell, b Kilner	0		
Duckworth, not out	19		
Extras b4, lb6, nb4	14	Extras b1, lb1, nb1	3
Total	234	Total (for 2)	89

BOWLING ANALYSIS

YORKSHIRE—First Innings

	O.	M.	R.	W.		O.	M.	R.	W.
Macdonald	21·1	2	68	5	Watson	9	0	28	0
Sibbles	22	5	41	2	Iddon	2	1	10	0
Tyldesley (R.)	12	5	15	3					

Second Innings

	O.	M.	R.	W.		O.	M.	R.	W.
Macdonald	21·3	6	67	6	Tyldesley (R.)	19	6	31	2
Sibbles	18	8	19	0	Iddon	11·3	4	26	1

LANCASHIRE—First Innings

	O.	M.	R.	W.		O.	M.	R.	W.
Waddington	16	3	33	0	Kilner	53	28	46	3
Robinson	13·5	5	29	2	Rhodes	33	15	45	2
Macaulay	36	13	67	3					

Second Innings

	O.	M.	R.	W.		O.	M.	R.	W.
Robinson	12	5	17	1	Macaulay	7	0	18	0
Waddington	3	0	15	0	Rhodes	4	3	4	0
Kilner	17·3	7	32	1					

YORKSHIRE V LANCASHIRE   1927

July 30/August 1/2   Leeds

FIRST DAY

LEEDS was a gloomy place on Saturday morning. Rain held play back until a quarter to one, and after fifteen minutes of action a heavy shower sent the cricketers running for shelter with the umpires following after in all their white dignity. The game began again at a quarter past one, and a quarter of an hour later another cloudburst happened. I thought now that we had come to the end of cricket for the day, but though the heavens sulked and threatened throughout the afternoon the rain was, by means of some wonderful powers, blown away. At half-past four sunshine was detected on high and the crowd applauded the sight.

When Yorkshire won the toss the Lancashire captain was disconsolate. For the turf had the easy sluggishness of a hearthrug; moreover the mid-summer showers threatened to (and did) burden and handicap the Lancashire bowlers with a greasy ball.

Yorkshire batted against a steady attack most feebly; the innings was saved from paltriness by Sutcliffe's superb batsmanship. Until the eighth wicket fell no Lancashire bowler was able to spin the ball with any venom. Macdonald, Sibbles and Richard Tyldesley each worked hard and cleverly to circumvent the lifeless turf. It is not to underrate the Lancashire attack that I declare that the Yorkshire batsmen were really upset by some strange weakness of their own. Yorkshire threw away the good fortune given by the gods to them in the shape of first innings on an unspoiled pitch. The questions for discussion amongst Lancashire cricketers this morning are: Will the Leeds turf remain fairly harmless as the top gets knocked away? Will not this notorious turf develop nastiness if no more rain should fall? Has the art of Nash, of Old Trafford, exorcised the devil from the Leeds pitch altogether? A few weeks ago the Surrey batsmen came to

217

Leeds and, no doubt, wept like anything to see such quantities of sand. May the Lancashire batsmen today be quite easy in mind (if and when the sun shines) that Rhodes, Kilner and Macaulay will not discover some helping substance in the grass as it is worn away hour by hour? Has all the sand actually gone?

> 'If seven maids with seven mops
> Swept it for half a year
> Do you suppose,' the Walrus said,
> That they could get it clear?'
> 'I doubt it' said the Carpenter
> And shed a bitter tear.

Lancashire have done very well so far but the game's destiny is still uncertain. Frankly I cannot bring myself to believe in any Yorkshire eleven which lacks the energy to kick back mightily. Man and boy I have been suffering under Yorkshire cricketers these many, many years, and I simply would not recognise a Bank Holiday on which my heart was not sent sooner or later into apprehensive beats by some Yorkshireman or other.

Macdonald opened the onslaught on Saturday against Sutcliffe. He ran his beautiful run along the grass, silent and sinister. We saw the old, thrilling cobra-droop of his right wrist. And then a bumper whizzed by Sutcliffe's head. But even Macdonald could not get a cricket ball to bounce on the spiritless earth, and Sutcliffe and Holmes scored seven from his first over. At lunch Yorkshire were 25 for none, and Yorkshire appetites were, I gathered, as usual. Just before the interval Sibbles missed an easy slip catch from Holmes. Macdonald was the bowler, and he regarded the fallen prize with stoical philosophy. It is fascinating to watch Macdonald as a match goes this way and that. What does he think and really feel? For his face tells you little; he wears always the guise of masterly indifference. His every movement is inscrutable and handsome. A ball merely thrown by Macdonald in the field to the bowler seems to go through the air with a lovelier curve than when it is thrown by anybody else. It was Macdonald who broke the back of Yorkshire on Saturday afternoon—broke it by quick stealthy blows. With

Yorkshire's total 35 Holmes tried to cut an off-side ball and Richard Tyldesley held a neat catch. Holmes never seemed to see the ball well. The first three Yorkshire wickets all fell to Macdonald at 35, in seven balls.

Oldroyd came to the middle dubiously. He has expressed recently in print a high opinion of Macdonald's bowling. Macdonald this time knocked his off stump out of the ground with a straight well-tossed ball at which Oldroyd played with a slanting bat. Possibly Oldroyd was unsighted by somebody moving in the crowd behind the bowler's arm. Which reminds me of the excuse made once to W. G. Grace by a young cricketer who got a 'duck' for Gloucester. 'A man walked across the pavilion, Doctor, just as the ball was in the air.' 'And what the hangment were you doing looking at the pavilion?' asked 'W.G.' 'Why didn't you keep your eye on the ball?' The thud of Oldroyd's stump as it fell back must have sounded very sickening in his ears. Leyland, too, made a lame stroke at Macdonald, and was miserably bowled off his pads. He walked too far across the wicket, and probably the ball came back. The first ball received by Kilner was popped gingerly into the air on the on side. Then Sutcliffe sliced an outswinger from Macdonald dangerously through the slips—his one indifferent stroke in a long and noble innings.

Richard Tyldesley attacked in the place of Macdonald at 54, and for a while his length was uneven. Sutcliffe drove him to leg with a commanding gesture. Then Tyldesley sent to Sutcliffe his slow ball—tossed high in the air, only to pitch absurdly short. Sutcliffe pulled it gigantically to the square-leg boundary. Kilner let us admire two most brilliant off-drives for fours from Sibbles. Kilner and Sutcliffe added 34, and promised to revive the hearts of the crowd—of which some 5,000 paid at the gates. But Kilner at this moment of the tide's turning threw his innings away by flashing his bat at a ball much too wide for a controlled hit. The sight of this impolitic stroke must have seemed incredible to the eyes of Wilfred Rhodes, watching from the pavilion. It was Rhodes who helped Sutcliffe to perform the biggest stand of the Yorkshire innings—59 for the fifth wicket in 43 minutes. Of these runs Rhodes scored only 18. The old warhorse has seen Yorkshire cricket pass through many spring and autumn days; history hangs about his bronzed face—the legendary Rhodes. Will he play long enough to see his county back again in the seats of the mighty? Let us hope so. I for one do not find the spectacle of a faltering Yorkshire eleven at all pleasant. And I certainly cannot imagine a cricket season without Rhodes and his shrewd and beautifully curving slow ball.

A pretty one-handed slip catch by Richard Tyldesley got the wicket of Rhodes. One of the most humorous of the many humorous things that happen in Lancashire cricket is the way that the great bulk of Tyldesley will at times suddenly achieve a miracle of superb poise and alacrity. Emmott Robinson came in to bat wearing pads that bore many eloquent scars from battles long ago. Another honourable mark was quickly added thereto, for he was out leg before wicket.

Robinson's was the sixth Yorkshire wicket to fall, at 131. Sutcliffe hereabout had made no fewer than 80. The end of Yorkshire's innings would have been pitiful to see, but the mantle of Sutcliffe covered it to the end. He lost his wicket in a brave bid for his hundred, and was the ninth out at 151. Iddon caught him from a high hit to square leg. Sutcliffe batted just under three hours for 95; he provided the Yorkshire innings with backbone and substance and heart and soul. It would be impossible to sit down and imagine a finer piece of cricket than this. His play against Macdonald's bumpers set the blood coursing through our body quickly, so brave and lovely was his upright stance as the ball flew upwards at him, so imperious and passionate was the sweeping blade that struck across the danger-point in the line of flight and accomplished the boundary hit. His hooking had a fine mingling of dignity and aggression; in his off-drives strength passed imperceptibly to graciousness. It was an innings of which it is possible to use a lofty phrase, for it gave us sweetness and strength, pleasure with surprise, an energy which seemed at every moment to break through all the conditions of comely form, recovering touch by touch a loveliness found usually only in the simplest natural things. Today Sutcliffe is a better batsman than ever he was; he is maturing perfectly and his cricket keeps the game in touch

220

with the great classical tradition of the straight elegant yet punishing bat.

Yorkshire's last five wickets fell for 26—shades of David Hunter and Schofield Haigh. Major Lupton batted No. 9 and was out to a glorious slip catch by Watson, who held a flying ball one-handed near the earth, his body falling sideways. The fall of the Yorkshire wickets had for Lancashire an invigorating regularity of rhythm: 1/35 2/35 3/35 4/69 5/128 6/131 7/145 8/146 9/151 10/157. Sibbles and Richard Tyldesley bowled, as I have suggested, with skill, but again Macdonald was Yorkshire's thorn.

Lancashire had less than an hour's batting at the day's fall. Watson drove the first ball of the innings from Emmott Robinson straight past him for three. Was Robinson astonished at this sudden offensive action by Lancashire in a Yorkshire match? Did he say 'what is the world coomin' to these days?' Watson played with style and spirit. He cut Robinson for four through the slips; he drove Robinson to leg for four—all in less than 40 minutes. Robinson has lived to see strange goings-on in a match between the ancient enemies. Degenerate times, old man; wild, reckless times indeed. Watson's cricket delighted my heart, for though hard words have appeared from time to time in these notes they have been prompted by the thought that (as George Robey used to sing, in a high falsetto) 'One has to be cruel to be kind.' Watson is a real batsman, and whenever he overlooks the fact he must be reminded of it. He was lucky once or twice with rising balls from Jacques. Hallows was lbw at 40, and then Ernest Tyldesley played out time with the mercurial Watson, who has already played one of his finest innings of the year.

The easy state of the turf for the day's best part will be realised from these evidences: Sutcliffe scored only a dozen runs through the slips; he was free to indulge his pull and hook strokes at ease; Macdonald, though unable to get his fastest pace from the pitch, never bowled off breaks from round the wicket. And Iddon's left-handed spin was not once called into action.

SECOND DAY

The authentic atmosphere of a Lancashire and Yorkshire match could be keenly felt at Leeds this morning. A great crowd sat round the field rank on rank, and hot humours moved the people to stirring, war-like noise. Behind the sight screen sat a man on a form; he could not find a seat which gave a view of the action. There he sat in solitary state, and though the play had not yet started, he let out on the air a great shout, 'Good owd Yorkshire!' Nothing so far had happened to prompt this passionate utterance, and I take it that this man was afflicted suddenly in his isolation by a wonderful vision of Yorkshire's historic greatness in cricket.

From the first overs bowled by Macaulay and Jacques it was clear that we were about to witness a bitter struggle. For the pitch has become faster and more helpful to bowlers than it was on Saturday. In a quarter of an hour several balls were seen to nip sharply from the earth, and it was an acceleration of pace after pitching that put an end to Watson's capital innings when Lancashire were 67. Watson flashed his bat rather indiscreetly at an off-side ball from Macaulay. On Saturday's slow pitch the stroke would have been safe enough. Watson's free play was refreshing to see, but let him beware of rashness.

Makepeace had to tackle two splendid break-backs of Macaulay during his first few minutes in the middle. Jacques exploited an admirable inswinger with a nasty pace and rise from the ground, and it was this inswinger which defeated Makepeace at ten minutes to twelve. The ball whipped across from the off-side, completely baffled Makepeace's bat, hit his pads and then rolled gently on the stumps and disturbed the bail. Makepeace was unlucky, yet Jacque's good ball deserved its prize, as Makepeace was fairly and squarely beaten. Another break-back by Macaulay which whipped away from Taylor's bat got rid of Lancashire's fourth wicket when the score was 99. Thus in an hour Lancashire had lost three good batsmen for 41 and the match was hanging dizzily in the balance.

The wicket was of a kind rather difficult to describe. It lent an amount of vitality to fastish spin, but did not possess the sting upon which slow left-handed bowling thrives. It certainly could not be called a difficult turf; rather let us say it challenged a good batsman's judgment and defence and yet did not put him definitely at a disadvantage. The Yorkshiremen very cleverly exploited the pitch for what it was worth to them in its varying paces. Kilner kept the runs down by attacking to a leg trap from over the wicket while Macaulay made a shrewd use of his offbreak and his straight ball. For an hour and forty minutes he bowled without a rest, and hardly ever faltered from accuracy of length and direction. More than once the batsmen had to depend on their pads to frustrate his keen break-back. He ran to the wicket head down—a bull-at-the-gate attitude. His left hand wore a bandage which somehow added to his customary aspect of lean, joyless antagonism. Jacques also bowled usefully; he takes a lumbering run and swings his arm over in a heavy wheel of energy. He tends to pitch too wide of the wicket, a defect that allows the batsmen to detect his inswinger rather easily. Still Jacques is a valuable man to Yorkshire just now, and his fast medium attack may well get him plenty of wickets on firm grounds in dry weather.

The stand by Green and Ernest Tyldesley was crucial. Had Green failed I imagine Macaulay would have gone mad—as George Formby used expressively to say. Green brought his bat stoutly if unbeautifully down on a break-back or two and relied on Tyldesley to play great cricket. Tyldesley was at his best; his defence, though watchful, never seemed overburdened. The note of mastery sounded in his every stroke—that healthy sound of good willow hitting ball in the blade's middle. Tyldesley hooked a short ball from Jacques dramatically to the boundary. The stroke flashed out swiftly, a sign that Tyldesley's general calm was but the mask of a cricketer of opportunist temper. In all of his strokes, offensive or defensive there was a bloom of wristwork and his glances to leg flickered prettily over the field. It is probable that had Tyldesley been able thoroughly to trust his colleagues not to get out he would have hit the Yorkshire bowlers harder and sooner than he did, for he played all the time with an ease which suggested power held in reserve. But no other Lancashire cricketer let Tyldesley see, for long, a confident bat. Possibly they exaggerated the difficulties in the wicket. Green pushed the ball cannily out of his way for 63 minutes, and in this period Tyldesley and he added 40 for the fifth wicket. The partnership's value is not to be estimated in the small number of runs it gave to Lancashire: Green and Tyldesley, as I have suggested, were called upon to look crisis in the face and stare her out of countenance.

The first innings victory was achieved after lunch by a stroke through the slips of Sibbles, who played a cool game and lifted up his bat like a cricketer of taste and confidence. The pity is he threw his innings away by means of a speculative slash at a widish fast ball. Dolphin was reliable and agile behind the stumps: he caught four out of the first six Lancashire wickets to fall—a certain sign this that the turf was faster than on Saturday. Between lunch and tea it dried almost to harmlessness and, frankly, the Yorkshire attack lost its edge with a sad alacrity. A stand by Tyldesley and Iddon reduced it to an impotence the like of which I have never before witnessed on a Yorkshire ground during an August Bank Holiday. Kilner persisted with his safety-first over-the-wicket tactics, rarely spinning the ball, rarely flighting it craftily. Macaulay did not keep his bowling bitter in the face of determined bats and an improving wicket, and though Robinson wrenched up all his shambling energy to vehement and concentrated aim his attack lacked the ancient fire. Age has laid a weighty hand on Yorkshire. Today it is taking away even as it has given much of its shrewdness in the past.

The partnership of Iddon and Tyldesley proved exceeding obstinate, and by degrees the crowd was moved to howls of impatience and of chagrin. The morning's promise of a Lancashire collapse had raised the hearts of thousands, and now the taste of ashes was in their mouths. ' 'It 'em,' groaned the multitude. And when Ernest Tyldesley did hit them very aggressively there were few shouts of satisfaction and ecstasy. Disappointment hung over the scene in clouds, and once or twice when Iddon made a dangerous stroke which sped through the slips the crowd gave ten thousand tongues to frustration. Iddon hit three boundaries in one over from Macaulay whereat somebody in the depths wailed out, 'Put Oldroyd on.' This, I take it, was the voice of irony; the hope of the morning had turned sour in the afternoon. By a quarter past four the Tyldesley-Iddon partnership put on 100 runs. 'Coom and 'ave a drink, 'Erbert,' said a man evidently from Laisterdyke, and he and Herbert departed entirely from view while the score board read Lancashire 274 for six.

Lancashire's recovery was done in championship fashion—by reliant cricket which dealt as severely with bad balls as it dealt judiciously with good ones. Tyldesley reached his 100 out of a total of 184 in four hours and ten minutes. Never did he give the faintest hope to the Yorkshire bowlers, the Yorkshire fieldsmen or the Yorkshire crowd. His bat must have looked to have a most unfair width in the eyes of Robinson and his fellow workers. Time's whirligig has brought us its changes. Often in the old days have Lancashire cricketers suffered under Yorkshire's power to throw back their old enemy and turn round the wheel of battle. It used to be Lancashire who were all out immediately after fifth wicket fell. Yorkshire this day have stomached well a medicine of their own brewing. Sceptre and crown must topple down and Amurath succeed unto Amurath.

At the tea interval Lancashire were 122 ahead with four wickets in reserve. The Yorkshire attack was mastered and the weather gave hints of rain. The moment was crying aloud for out and out offensive action by Tyldesley whose score now stood at 150. He scored 18 in half an hour following tea, and Iddon scored four. This pace, of course, was calculated to please Rhodes, and so Tyldesley began to use his feet quickly and hurl his bat on high. Iddon did his best to get runs, but his strokes are few nowadays, and the Yorkshiremen were able to keep him quiet enough to serve their purpose, which by this hour was to save themselves from defeat outright. The best allies of Yorkshire at this stage were the clock and slow scoring. Tyldesley worked hard to defeat this Fabian Yorkshire strategy; he repeatedly accepted the challenge of Rhodes to make a bid for the boundary, and at last Rhodes got him caught at long-off. Tyldesley batted beautifully for five hours and a half. It was an innings with scarcely a technical flaw.

Tyldesley and Iddon scored 164 for the seventh wicket in two hours and forty minutes—a trusty and decisive stand.

The only criticism that can be set against the sterling play of these two cricketers is that they could not, after they had left the Yorkshire total well behind, make their own scoring opportunities. The good-length ball was usually respected and not turned into a hittable length often enough by quick footwork. But perhaps this is to find fault unreasonably considering the occasion and the doubtful position of Lancashire when Tyldesley and Iddon came together. Lancashire's main task today has been to avoid having to play a second innings with many runs to get, for a Leeds wicket is not to be trusted at the end of a three-day match.

After Tyldesley was out, Iddon sought to force the runs and quickly lost his wicket. He batted nearly three hours for 77, and his defence came at a time that saw Yorkshire striving might and main to crash through Lancashire's rearguard. Iddon hit one six and seven fours, and Tyldesley hit eighteen fours. Neither batsman gave a perceptible chance to the field. Richard Tyldesley smote one enormous sixer from Rhodes and then fell to a clever catch by Major Lupton from a most humorous mishit. And then Green declared his innings closed 203 runs in advance—a move of commendable enterprise which made a challenging end to a Lancashire innings that pulled itself out of the morning's disagreeable situation by a combination of skill, patience and defiance which the Yorkshire cricketers themselves were surely the first to appreciate.

Rhodes set his field wisely, and bowled to it like the old soldier he is. He packed the off side, and the Lancashire batsmen could not hit him on the on side at all fruitfully. Jacques had little pace when the new ball was claimed at 200, and Kilner's attack was a shadow of its old spinning self.

At a quarter past six Sutcliffe and Holmes walked to the wicket to begin Yorkshire's uphill journey. The crowd gave them applause full of resounding hope and pride. Macdonald bowled fast in a bad light, and the crowd hummed excitedly. Sutcliffe hit a ball from Macdonald to square leg, and Duckworth, Sibbles and Green all chased after it. The day was closing in a stormy air. Duckworth tried to stump Sutcliffe, and the crowd waxed ironical at his quicksilver smartness. Lancashire attacked and fielded with all their hearts, and a priceless gain came to them at the long day's very end; Holmes failed to distinguish between Sibble's outswinger and his straight ball, and was out leg before wicket. Sutcliffe again played superb cricket; he hooked Macdonald's short bumpers magnificently. As he swung his bat bravely at the upward flying ball he fired the imagination with the image of some young god, thrown out from power on high, and now hurling defiance at the unfriendly heavens. But Macdonald's bumpers ought never to be bowled at Sutcliffe; he revels in them.

THIRD DAY

There has happened much bitter antagonism at Leeds today; Yorkshire face to face with almost certain defeat, having thrust adversity from their very doorstep by means of fighting spirit worthy of the country's greatest years. And Lancashire, betrayed by some dire weakness within themselves, have let slip a rare chance of thrashing twice in one summer the ancient enemy.

For a while this morning events went Lancashire's way most generously; Fortune smiled fulsomely on our cricketers. No wonder she spurned them later in the afternoon, when she saw her good influences falling in slack, thriftless places. The Lancashire attack had little sting at any time during the day, but between a quarter-past-eleven and half-past-twelve so feebly did Yorkshire bat, Sutcliffe always excepted, that three wickets fell in addition to that of Holmes, which was got on Monday evening. Leyland ran himself out absurdly when Yorkshire's score was 38; thirteen runs afterwards Kilner was bowled by a plain and not very energetic ball from Macdonald, whose bowling all day has lacked fire and accurate direction.

At 75 Yorkshire lost her fourth batsman—Oldroyd was out lbw, playing a stroke of immense dubiety at R. Tyldesley, who, like Macdonald has wheeled up much wan and faded stuff in the crisis of a memorable game. Only Sibbles was capable of keeping a consistently good length.

Rhodes joined partnership with Sutcliffe at half-past twelve; Yorkshire now needed 128 to save themselves from defeat in an innings and they had six wickets only in reserve.

Rhodes and Sutcliffe quickly placed an honest valuation on Lancashire's bowling; Sutcliffe gave us an innings radiant with style and yet hard as iron. the essential part of great batsmanship was to be discerned in his play—a quick and safe technique that answered the promptings of intelligence and experience.

The eye was pleased by his cricket's lovely motion, and the heart was made to swell because of the courage in it all. It was not only the innings of a gracious player but also that of a man who does not know what it means to bow before unfriendly circumstances. And with what a splendid patience did Rhodes defend his wicket while Sutcliffe got the runs. Poetry and sentiment ennobled the game as these two Yorkshiremen fought the good fight for their county—the young man with his career still spreading in front of him like a shining track of promise; the other the battle-scarred veteran, his great work behind him, his eye and flesh perhaps faltering a little now but his grit and spirit keen and reliant as in the legendary days when he would bat last in for England and help to snatch victory from Australia's grasp at the battle's dreadful crisis.

The cool patience of Rhodes's batting today has moved us to admiration hard to express in words; he stonewalled and Sutcliffe hit; the old man was armour-bearer to the young knight. Sutcliffe and Rhodes held the fifth Yorkshire wicket for two hours and twenty minutes and added 126 inestimable runs. Neither batsman faltered much. When he was 121 and Yorkshire 169 for four Sutcliffe was completely beaten by a fine ball from Sibbles; the wicket was missed by an inch, and Green, at mid-on, jumped in the air with a gesture of anguish as he saw the great prize escape Lancashire. Sutcliffe's bat had no edge; it was all solid middle, a bat with eyes, senses, instincts, a living bat.

Yet, grandly as Rhodes and Sutcliffe played, the end of their partnership came all too soon, for Yorkshire. Lancashire claimed the new ball, and Sibbles quickly put a fresh edge on his side's attack. He bowled with a determination fit to burst his young heart; his unwavering endeavour put to shame the poor work of one or two of the other Lancashire bowlers. Yorkshire were 201 when Sutcliffe tried to drive Sibbles's out-swinger; he slashed the ball to deep point, where Hallows held a glorious falling catch an inch above the grass. Nine runs later Sibbles got Rhodes out leg before wicket.

Thus at ten minutes to four Yorkshire were only seven runs in front with six wickets gone. Robinson and Macaulay alone stood between the Lancashire attack and Yorkshire's tail—Major Lupton, Jacques and Dolphin, three brave but very fallible batsmen. The game, of course, was now thrown right into Lancashire's lap—a gift. A new swinging ball was still in the service of Lancashire's bowlers and only Robinson, or Macaulay to settle. Will it be replied that the Lancashire bowlers were tired? Then the answer is that Sibbles wasn't; moreover, the new opportunity ought to have come to Lancashire like refreshing wine.

Frankly the end of the match saw Lancashire without a real challenge, without, apparently, the imagination to realise that the dismissal of Rhodes and Sutcliffe in sudden sequence was a sign that the wind was blowing mightily again in Lancashire's favour. Macaulay and Robinson ought to have found themselves up against a battle-axe ordeal; they ought to have had to struggle for existence in a tense, inimical air. The sorry truth is that Robinson and Macaulay not only were at liberty to hold up their stumps almost effortlessly; they were actually free to flog boundaries gaily and play like happy-go-lucky cricketers on a village green. At the very moment when Yorkshire's tail ought to have been relentlessly harried and made to sweat for runs Lancashire's bowlers fell into raggedness for want of concentration, ambition and persistent antagonism. Sibbles did his utmost to maintain steadiness, but his gallant work was hopelessly undone by his frail colleagues at the other end.

The very demeanour of Robinson was a sufficient commentary on the general weakness of effort in Lancashire's bowling. Emmott is a solemn man whenever he sniffs danger for Yorkshire in the breeze; at this hour which most of us imagined critical for Yorkshire, our eyes stared incredulously at a sprightly Emmott Robinson, a Robinson dancing the motley, mark you, scampering in and out of his crease—a second Parkin come to Leeds to amuse the crowd. Had the atmosphere been kept bodeful for Yorkshire; had Lancashire hurled vehement bolts at the wicket in this hour, would Emmott have indulged his quips and conceits?

When Robinson first went to the wicket this afternoon he was a very grave man; he had just seen Rhodes come back to the pavilion with a face that spoke eloquently of Yorkshire's distress. I can only conclude that as soon as Robinson reached the middle and saw for himself how puny Lancashire's energy and ambition had become he breathed with relief and set about enjoying an unexpected escape from responsibility.

Macaulay had no difficulty in scoring 50 in about an hour; that, I think, is ample proof of the state of Lancashire's attack in one of those periods of a match when cricketers must always be expected to scourge themselves into one last bid for glory. A steady length ball by ball would have not permitted Macaulay and Robinson to play high jinks—in a moment of trial.

The example of Sibbles ought to have braced every other bowler stupendously; he put the whole of his will power into his work. Not for a long time shall I forget the splendid picture he made of young manhood wearing itself out for the cause of the county. One half of Sibbles's steady labour at the other end of the wicket would have won the victory for Lancashire.

As it was, many followers of the county left Headingley at the close of play irritated at the thought that two days of championship form—days stirring to our pride—should have been spoiled by a poor challenge at the finish. It is not simply that Lancashire failed to win; Lancashire men as well as Yorkshire men would have come away from the match exalted by a closing scene in which every player had obviously goaded himself to his best powers. No! it was not the result that disappointed us—it was the fact that at the very pinch only one Lancashire bowler was letting us see, all the time, his very best.

Robinson and Macaulay added 104 at a great pace, and were unbeaten in the end. They thoroughly deserved the crowd's acclamation. Sutcliffe batted four hours and Rhodes two hours and a half. I cannot gild the lily of Sutcliffe's innings; when the summer is over, cricketers who saw it will find their minds dwelling on its excellence for many a long day to come.

The Headingley turf lasted admirably, although Sibbles proved that energetic work could get the ball to nip now and again. But on the whole Lancashire's task this afternoon has had to be performed on a batsman's wicket; Nash, of Old Trafford, must be congratulated on the skill with which he exorcised the devil from the pitch.

SCORES

YORKSHIRE

First Innings		Second Innings	
Holmes, c Tyldesley (R.), b Macdonald	12	lbw, b Sibbles	4
Sutcliffe, c Iddon, b Sibbles	95	c Hallows, b Sibbles	135
Oldroyd, b Macdonald	0	lbw, b Tyldesley (R.)	2
Leyland, b Macdonald	0	run out	0
Kilner, c Hallows, b Tyldesley (R.)	11	b Macdonald	5
Rhodes, c Tyldesley (R.), b Sibbles	18	lbw, b Sibbles	43
Robinson, lbw, b Tyldesley (R.)	2	not out	43
Macaulay, b Tyldesley (R.)	6	not out	61
A. W. Lupton, c Watson, b Sibbles	0		
Dolphin, b Sibbles	5		
T. A. Jacques, not out	1		
Extras b2, lb5	7	Extras	21
Total	157	Total (for 6)	314

LANCASHIRE

First Innings	
Watson, c Dolphin, b Macaulay	39
Hallows, lbw, b Jacques	11
Tyldesley (E.), c Oldroyd, b Rhodes	165
Makepeace, b Jacques	4
Taylor, c Dolphin, b Macaulay	4
L. Green, c Dolphin, b Robinson	17
Sibbles, c Dolphin, b Jacques	9
Iddon, c Robinson, b Rhodes	77
Duckworth, not out	12
Tyldesley (R.), c Lupton, b Rhodes	6
Extras b6, lb6, w1, nb3	16
Total (for 9)	*360

*Innings declared

BOWLING ANALYSIS

YORKSHIRE—First Innings

	O.	M.	R.	W.		O.	M.	R.	W.
Tyldesley (R.)	16	7	29	3	Macdonald	17	3	49	3
Watson	7	1	18	0	Sibbles	25·3	10	54	4

Second Innings

	O.	M.	R.	W.		O.	M.	R.	W.
Macdonald	29	7	84	1	Watson	20	4	49	0
Sibbles	32	10	58	3	Iddon	13	4	22	0
Tyldesley (R.)	20	6	65	1	Green	3	0	15	0

LANCASHIRE—First Innings

	O.	M.	R.	W.		O.	M.	R.	W.
Robinson	29	9	72	1	Macaulay	29	8	61	2
Jacques	26	2	83	3	Rhodes	28·4	8	66	3
Kilner	39	15	62	0					

YORKSHIRE V LANCASHIRE   1928

May 26/28/29   Bramall Lane

FIRST DAY

THE sun shone when the Lancashire and Yorkshire match began on Saturday; Bramall Lane looked quite sylvan. At half-past eleven the Yorkshire eleven walked into the field, and as they did so I stood in the crowd next to a very large Yorkshireman. He surveyed the scene and the occasion. Having realised that Lancashire were batting first, he said, to all and sundry around him: 'Wheer's this Hallows? Let mi see him: let mi have a look at him!' It was a tremendous utterance, made in a challenging tone of voice. I felt that Hallows was about to be put on trial, weighed in the balance, and—perhaps—found wanting.

Robinson bowled at Hallows very fiercely the moment he got hold of the ball. In his first over he let out his own noise of 'Hzatt' (you simply can't spell onomatopoeic sounds—my there's a word for you, Emmott!). Hallows was utterly beaten by a ball that swung in late; he played back instead of forward. The ball hit his pads rather high up and the umpire said 'Not out.' Hallows was sorely troubled by Robinson for several overs and I expected the large Yorkshireman by my side to get sardonic at the expense of Lancashire's most prolific scorer. But the large Yorkshireman was magnanimous. 'It's good bowlin',' he said 'Reight good bowlin' '. Not a single reflection against the skill of Hallows did he make.

Robinson is still the country's ablest bowler with the new ball. On Saturday he caused it to swing late at a fine speed and at a ticklish length. How he does goad himself into hot action. He shambles along to his bowling place, all loose and bandy, his trousers obviously coming down bit by bit. Then he turns on his heels and suddenly all the energy of the man is gathered together, concentrated into one vehement fling at the wicket. Here is a cricketer in whose very shape the spirit of Yorkshire cricket lives and finds expression. I believe that

233

once on a time the Lord leaned down from heaven, scooped in His hands a great heap of good Yorkshire earth, breathed into it, and said: 'Go forth, Emmott Robinson, and bowl for Yorkshire.'

Watson batted excellently from the outset. He made several clean swift strokes. Alas, it was a butterfly innings which flattered for too brief a while over Sheffield's stunted heath. Watson glanced a fast ball from Jacques to leg—a pretty stroke. Wood, the wicket-keeper, dashed to his left and held the catch, rolling over and over like a tumbler in a circus. Bramall Lane roared for joy and admiration. The large Yorkshireman still by my side announced his approval, of course. But, magnanimous yet, he added, 'Aye, a good catch, but Ah've seen owd Dolphin hold just as good, many a time.'

With Ernest Tyldesley in there was another appeal for leg-before-wicket against Hallows. It was such a near thing that involuntarily I cried out with a slight agonised accent 'Steady!' Then I saw the large Yorkshireman regarding me curiously, and I tried hard to look as though I had been born in Kirkheaton. The dismissal of Watson was unlucky for Lancashire; at the day's end I thought it meant all the difference between Lancashire's present score and the 400 which ought to have been made from the poorest Yorkshire attack I have ever seen in these ancient and honourable matches. Watson, clearly in form, would have set the pace for Hallows, who, though a most skilful batsman, rather lacks imagination. He needs an example; rarely does he go along at a match-winning speed unless somebody in with him pricks him into activity by sheer force of contrast.

Hallows is one of our cleverest cricketers, but he lacks the will and opportunism of a great player. On Saturday, though he was not long in settling down after a bad start, he did not turn his mastery to the best possible account. Many a loose ball, on the leg side especially, was allowed to pass the lethargic bat of Hallows scot-free. In the first ninety minutes of the match Hallows scored 15, on an easy pitch, even if it was a little moist.

Ernest Tyldesley, who is by far the best batsman in Lancashire county, made 32 courtly runs in just over an hour.

He was out caught neatly at mid-off by Worsley, through a half-hearted drive at a tempting ball from the old soldier Rhodes. A really courageous drive could not have brought Tyldesley to a worse end, and it might have been a boundary stroke. Tyldesley achieved his own dramatic hook once, from Jacques. This was the best stroke of the day; the three or four others were good, but not quite as stylish as Tyldesley's.

When Tyldesley's wicket fell Lancashire were 71 for two. After the luncheon interval (rather a fanciful term this at Sheffield; at least, that was my experience on Saturday) Hallows and Makepeace played very poor cricket. With no new ball available for Robinson there was no positive danger in the bowling. Rhodes alone needed a watchful eye. Macaulay, Jacques and Leyland served up workaday stuff; you could see long hops for yourself, unmistakably. There is no gainsaying what a half-volley looks like. Moreover Jacques and Leyland occasionally wheeled up a full toss. I counted half a dozen in fifteen minutes. Not one of them was hit to the boundary by Hallows and Makepeace. Rhodes at one period bowled twelve overs for nine runs; in one hour and a half not a scoring stroke worth more than a single was hit from Rhodes. Yet today Rhodes has lost that spin which in the past got him his wickets. If Lancashire batsmen today are unable to muster heart and skill in the presence of Rhodes what brief, pitiful lives would they have lived against the real Rhodes, the wonderful slow bowler of cricket's greatest period? At half past two on Saturday Rhodes aged 50, was bowling to Makepeace aged 45, while Robinson aged 43 fielded close in at 'silly' mid-off. Our National Sports!

Makepeace batted seventy minutes for nine; he bent low on his bat most suspiciously, looked out for all he was worth, and yet did not seem ever to see the ball clearly. Like Argus, he was all eyes and no sight. But I can speak no harsh word against Makepeace; no cricketer has served his county with more than Makepeace's skill and faithfulness.

Hallows arrived at his 50 with a noble straight drive from Macaulay. Shortly afterwards he was bowled by Rhodes, trying, I thought, a late cut or push from a ball that came in with the bowler's arm and just disturbed the off bail. Hallows was on view for three and a quarter hours. Up to a point his

235

defence was valuable indeed. But one sign of a great batsman is the ability to punish weak bowling after he has been at the wicket for an hour. Hallows did not play the Yorkshire attack on its merits. His care against Rhodes was excusable, for Rhodes set his field most cunningly for Hallows, and bowled to it like the superb old strategist we have all known him to be, man and boy, these thirty years.

At half past three Yorkshire were doing very well; the four most experienced of Lancashire's batsmen were out for 142. And in another hour there would be the new ball again. Taylor and Iddon tackled this dubious situation with a confidence that put to some discredit the faint hearted efforts of one or two of their supposed betters. For the first time in the match the Yorkshire bowling was played on its merits. The good ball was stubbornly opposed; runs, or efforts to get runs, were made whenever bad balls came along. This was proper cricket. Taylor let us admire charming strokes to leg, and he showed much intelligence in his avoidance of Rhodes' lbw trap, although in the end he fell into it, not before he had scored 66 precious runs in two hours and a quarter. He and Iddon put on 112 for the fifth wicket in two hours. Their cricket had not only skill but wit in it. We were made to feel at least that Lancashire were getting on with the game and not letting it drift anywhere, anyhow. Iddon's cricket was stronger than Taylor's. He played really well, watching the ball, judging the flight and length quickly and finding ample time for the making of an authentic stroke. I thought that both Iddon and Taylor might with safety have trusted more than they did to the drive. Still, they could not be blamed if they hesitated about bringing into force a stroke which none of their seniors apparently have the heart to exploit in these Lancashire and Yorkshire matches—vastly overrated nowadays. Iddon and Taylor, at any rate, did not permit the occasion to render their bats strokeless altogether.

Before the close of play Iddon hit a ball from Rhodes to leg for six. I hope that his seniors and his supposed betters were watching from the pavilion when this outrage upon Rhodes was committed. Well done, Iddon and Taylor! Perhaps, after much waiting, cricket is again going to breed men big enough to play in Lancashire and Yorkshire matches with spirit.

There is a mistaken notion in the air at the present time that batsmanship in Lancashire and Yorkshire matches has always been canny, dull, slow, unbeautiful. Well, I have not the time or the wish to go into the records. But I seem to remember an innings by Kenneth McLeod at this same Bramall Lane; he came in with Lancashire three-parts beaten, 48 runs on, and only five wickets in hand. He scored a hundred in two hours. Spooner once played an innings of 200 at Old Trafford all on one and the same day I fancy. And I seem to remember cricket by Tyldesley, MacLaren, Garnet, Jimmy Hallows and Jack Sharp that was not exactly careworn, lame and halt and blind. Today it is argued that in the old years Lancashire, with all the MacLarens, Spooners and Johnny Tyldesleys, were in the habit of collapsing against Yorkshire. True they sometimes did collapse, before a hurricane of bowling by Hirst. But though Lancashire batsmen often broke our hearts in those years, they never committed the worst sin a cricketer can commit—stupidity and dullness of mind on a good wicket with bad bowling about. Since the war only three examples of fearless and beautiful cricket have been given us by Lancashire batsmen—Ernest Tyldesley's great innings of 178 at Sheffield in 1922, and the two innings played by R. H. Spooner in his very last match against Yorkshire.

Yorkshire's fielding was not at all handsome; frequently it was shabby. I missed the old precision. Also I missed the old atmosphere and glamour, in both teams and in the crowd. Rhodes is the last of the personalities. He stood out on high on Saturday from a mass of merely worthy journeymen. His action is beautiful yet. He looks the old master all over, with his face bronzed by the heat of many a famous day in the sun. What does he think in his heart as he feels (as he must feel sometimes) his loneliness now? The eagles are gone; crows and daws, crows and daws! Rhodes had to get through some heavy work on Saturday; his reputation makes him Yorkshire's best bowler (against Lancashire), even in his fifty-first year. As he bowled by the hour at Hallows and Makepeace, did not his veteran's spirit protest just a little that there was no younger Yorkshireman capable of bearing the day's burden? Did he not say, like Falstaff, 'I would my name were not so terrible to the enemy as it is: I were better to be eaten to death with a rust than to be scoured to nothing with perpetual motion.'

SECOND DAY

Green and Iddon went on with Lancashire's innings against Yorkshire on a warm morning with Bramall Lane looking very squat and stuffy. The Yorkshire bowling again had a very commonplace look. Green picked out a slow ball from Robinson, driving it to the on in triumphant style. Then he pushed a fastish one from Jacques gracefully through the covers; three were run and four overthrows made the stroke worth seven. Just imagine—a boundary overthrow by Yorkshire, from a return from the opposite end of the field. It is sad to see signs of looseness in a Yorkshire eleven, and there have been many such signs so far in this game. As a Lancashire man I am keen and fond of Yorkshire cricket; the game can never be its true self in the absence of a great and characteristic Yorkshire side.

Iddon's worthy innings came to an end at noon. He was neatly caught at the wicket, and it was a brilliant one-handed catch by Macaulay that settled, as Mr. Micawber would say, a promising little knock by Booth. These clever catches put into contrast much uneven work in the ground fielding, though Barber, Sutcliffe and Mitchell were always safe and handsome to see. The Yorkshire bowling got worse and worse. Jacques and Macaulay sent along an odd sequence of long hops. From one of these Green almost played on just as the ball was about to bounce for the second time—or was it the third? Lancashire's batting was unable to take advantage to the full of a situation most happy for real batsmen. For though sixty runs were scored in the first hour, any decent Free Foresters' eleven would have hit at least 90 in the same period, given ordinary luck.

For 70 minutes Robinson worked hard to give Yorkshire's attack a semblence of class; he is indeed a tenacious and faithful cricketer. Green's innings reached 50, but his batting fell away after a capital beginning. Richard Tyldesley hurled his bat about him with an energy which at one and the same time was cosmic and comic. He made several fine strokes, also one or two that flew off his bat at angles difficult to

238

reconcile with any known system of geometry. Lancashire's innings finished at one o'clock for less than the total of 400 that most certainly ought to have been hit on Saturday from an attack which can only be called a thing of shreds and patches. The badness of the bowling of Jacques and Macaulay was beyond my powers of description. The sight of it all gave me no pleasure. Next to Lancashire cricket I love best the cricket of Yorkshire. It is sad to see the bowling of this great county so pitifully reduced in power and resource.

Yorkshire had a few minutes' batting before lunch. In Macdonald's first over a fast and most beautiful ball broke back a little and hit Holmes on the pad. There was no appeal—strange taciturnity of Duckworth. After the interval the scene caught fire for the first time in the match. Temper and style entered the batting, for Holmes and Sutcliffe conducted themselves like real cricketers. They played forward with the utmost confidence, and the true crack of a cricket bat was to be heard in the land. Sutcliffe was all charming attitudes; Holmes was upright, incisive, soldierlike. The bad ball was looked for and pounced upon 'like a cat on a mouse', especially by Holmes, who is a dynamic batsman with a swifter and more resourceful stroke technique than Sutcliffe's—though Sutcliffe's leaning push drive through the covers makes one of the prettiest sights ever seen on a cricket field.

So confidently did the two batsmen play at Lancashire's bowling—which was better by far than Yorkshire's had been—that I imagined them to be calling out as they made their strokes 'come one, come two,' or even 'come five.' Fifty delightful runs were made in 45 minutes—the greatest and loveliest game of all was having honour done to its heart and spirit at last. Let us give credit where credit is due; we of the champion county can afford to be magnanimous. And the cricket of Holmes and Sutcliffe, against a heavy score, was as skilful and handsome as batsmanship well could be.

Two lightning hooks by Holmes set the blood tingling; the strokes had the ring and clamour of defiance. The ball was crashed to the rails at a speed that left the fieldsmen standing. When some steady bowling by Watson and Richard Tyldesley temporarily quietened Holmes and Sutcliffe, the batting was still a gracious sight for eyes tired by the hours of colourless labour on Saturday. Holmes and Sutcliffe let us see proper strokes even against balls from which no scoring could be done. Always was the ball being forced well away from the wicket. The attitude of mind of Yorkshire's two great cricketers was as different from that of Lancashire's on Saturday as faith is different from doubt, pride from humility. Holmes arrived at his fifty out of eighty in seventy-five minutes—a gallant movement and uphill at that. Admirable length bowling by Watson put a check on the runs, but obviously the game's initiative, as they say, was now Yorkshire's. Accuracy of pitch exposed Sutcliffe's lack of swift, short-armed strokes that circle round the wrist ends. He is a batsman who depends mainly on a long swing forward of the bat, hence a ball just short of a length will keep him quiet. But he stonewalls nicely, elegantly. He lets us see obstinacy reflected in the glass of fashion; he lends mould of form to canniness.

From ten minutes to three till four o'clock Macdonald did not bowl, though the wicket was of the sort on which a fast bowler is usually expected to get through most of the work. When Macdonald was called back to the action he overthrew Holmes with a really fast ball—one of the best. Yorkshire's first wicket fell at 142, scored in two hours and a quarter. Holmes's 79 was got by quick-witted cricket; his bat was always vital and the style and mobility of his footwork deserved very high praise. He hit nine boundaries, and one or two of his hooks shot splendour over the field.

After the tea interval the new batsman was Mitchell, and, for some reason not clear to the ordinary intelligence, Macdonald bowled merely a medium pace at him. Here was one of those instances of want of generalship which are the despair of cricketers who remember the strategy of the pre-war captains like MacLaren, Jackson, and the Hornbys.

On what principle does a fast bowler slacken pace for a young batsman only just come to the crease—especially a fast bowler who has been resting for an hour and has also had the refreshment available during the tea interval! Now and again Macdonald did send along a fast or faster ball; from one of them Sutcliffe made a dangerous slice through the slips with his score 70. But when Holmes departed it was as though the sun went behind a cloud. Sutcliffe went on playing his sweet monotonous elegy on his single-stringed lyre, but for a long while the only event was the beating and bowling of Mitchell by another fast ball by Macdonald—unfortunately a no ball. Mitchell so obviously did not like fast bowling that one could only look on with amazement while Macdonald bowled medium-paced stuff at him.

Mitchell wears the dress of honest utility, homespun in the North; he is one of that company (numerous at the present time) of whose batsmanship the score-board is able to tell everything, or nearly everything. He is young yet and will develop. At the moment he commands only that defence which was once considered the ABC of batting, but which today frequently comprises ABC and XYZ as well.

At 83 Sutcliffe made another doubtful stroke through the slips—his stroke-play has been unusually restricted this afternoon; his hook stroke was missing altogether—Macdonald wisely did not feed it with short rising balls. But once he had passed his customary century against Lancashire he improved his rate of scoring. Yorkshire reached 200 in as many minutes, and then in the day's closing half-hour runs were hit with splendid opportunism from weary bowlers. Yorkshire facing Lancashire's 385, played cricket; that was the freely expressed opinion of every Lancashire man present. Sutcliffe remained cool and unbeaten to the end; his innings, despite limitations in stroke-play, was continually attractive—bloom on the orthodox. Lancashire sadly needed a bowler of persistent determination and pace.

The fielding was variable; occasionally the throwing-in to Duckworth would have stirred A. N. Hornby to terrific words. Richard Tyldesley on the off-side did good work. Iddon, too, was a willing scout, and Duckworth kept an agile wicket. Hallows comported himself with all his own lordly ease and restraint.

THIRD DAY

For a long time today the cricket has been played keenly and well. Lancashire's bowling was steady enough before lunch to keep the Yorkshire batsmen on the defensive. At noon Lancashire made a substantial advance; Booth, who bowled well at the outset, got Sutcliffe caught at the wicket from a ball that came from the ground at a capital pace; Sutcliffe's innings of 140 lasted four hours and twenty-five minutes. It did not show his technique at its best and most varied. None the less, Sutcliffe's own splendid temperament was always to be felt in his play—that cool faith in himself which is a rare asset for Test matches. With Leyland and Mitchell in, Lancashire tried hard to get another wicket at this most critical stage of the game. But Mitchell's defence was very strong, and Leyland not only kept at bay the good ball, but sometimes he hit hard the loose one. The third Yorkshire wicket persisted for eighty minutes and put on 73 runs. Then Leyland impatiently slashed at Watson's bowling and fell to a mishit to third man. At lunch Yorkshire needed only 39 for the first-innings victory, and they had seven wickets in hand.

After lunch Macdonald bowled finely, using a medium pace as a mask for an occasional swift and sudden break-back. With his first ball he clean bowled Mitchell, whose stroke was much too late. Mitchell was on view nearly four hours for 74. In the circumstances this was a valuable and meritorious piece of work by a young player who some day will make a name among the country's consistent run-getters. He may not add much to the joy of living—unless he considerably extends and refines his present system of stroke play. But already he gets well over the ball with a straight bat—too straight perhaps. The left elbow makes the inverted 'v' rather elaborately—and after all, not every stroke can be played with the straight bat, commonly so called.

Mitchell's downfall gave Lancashire's attack a last chance, for now vulnerable men like Macaulay, Barber, Worsley and Jacques were to be got at, granted a little luck. Macaulay promptly assisted the cause of Lancashire by running Barber out—a great pity and shame, because young Barber shaped like a spirited batsman. Shortly afterwards Macaulay threw his own wicket away by hitting wildly at a ball from Macdonald that rose too high for a long-armed forcing stroke in front of the wicket to the on side. Watson caught Macaulay's mishit cleverly, taking the ball on the run.

Yorkshire now were 371 for six. Rhodes was stumped at 374; no, bless you, he was not trying a big hit, he was merely reaching out and feeling for Tyldesley's spin.

With three wickets to go Yorkshire wanted 12 for the first-innings points. The crowd was excited now. The sudden rally by Lancashire's bowlers was good to see. This was a fighting Lancashire. But it was curious to find a Yorkshire crowd anxious about their team's ability to score a dozen with three wickets in keeping. A crisis for Bramall Lane in such a situation. Shades of Schofield Haigh and David Hunter and that old Yorkshire tail that used to turn the wheel of a game right round and win a match after it had been three-parts lost. Wood and Robinson were more than equal to 12 runs this afternoon; they carried the Yorkshire score far beyond 400, and added 68 in 50 minutes. Whereupon Captain Worsley hit 23 in one over from Iddon: a six, four fours and a single.

The eighth wicket stand for Yorkshire was aided and abetted by wretched bowling. At the very crisis, when Wood had just reached the wicket, Tyldesley bowled two slow (almost immobile) balls which Wood thumped to the boundary with ease and gusto. Four or five times in a few minutes Tyldesley sent down balls of doubtful length and lame pace, and usually the crack of a boundary hit went over the field. It was difficult to understand the Lancashire captain's faith in Tyldesley hereabout. Why should Yorkshire batsmen be served at any time of a match with runs gratis and for nothing? After Yorkshire had won the first innings spoils Robinson, Wood and Worsley were able to enjoy themselves and entertain the crowd by lusty hitting. Why was a single run given away by Lancashire? In these games, skill and temper should be kept taut to the end. Lancashire's fielding was good at times and slip-shod at others. Iddon alone maintained brilliance. Hallows really must pull himself together in the field—else there will be no Test match honours in Australia for him. A few years ago he was a very fine outfield.

243

THE ROSES MATCHES 1919-1939
SCORES

LANCASHIRE

First Innings		Second Innings	
Watson, c Wood, b Jacques	12	b Jacques	5
Hallows, b Rhodes	58	not out	34
Tyldesley (E.), c Worsley, b Rhodes	32	not out	35
Makepeace, c Holmes, b Macaulay	9		
Taylor, lbw, b Rhodes	66		
Iddon, c Wood, b Robinson	87		
Macdonald, c Barber, b Leyland	2		
L. Green, hit wkt, b Rhodes	52		
Booth, c Macaulay, b Robinson	6		
Tyldesley (R.), not out	39		
Duckworth, run out	1		
Extras b8, lb13	21	Extras b6	6
Total	385	Total (for 1)	80

YORKSHIRE

First Innings	
Holmes, b Macdonald	79
Sutcliffe, c Duckworth, b Booth	140
Mitchell, b Macdonald	74
Leyland, c Booth, b Watson	38
Barber, run out	12
Macaulay, c Watson, b Macdonald	6
Rhodes, st Duckworth, b Tyldesley (R.)	13
Robinson, not out	30
Wood, c Macdonald, b Iddon	39
W. A. Worsley, c Hallows, b Tyldesley (R.)	24
T. A. Jacques, run out	3
Extras b4, lb5, nb6	15
Total	473

YORKSHIRE V LANCASHIRE 1928
BOWLING ANALYSIS

LANCASHIRE—First Innings

	O.	M.	R.	W.		O.	M.	R.	W.
Robinson	50	17	98	2	Rhodes	43	20	56	4
Jacques	31	2	93	1	Leyland	11·1	3	22	1
Macaulay	38	6	95	1					

Second Innings

	O.	M.	R.	W.		O.	M.	R.	W.
Jacques	5	1	9	1	Sutcliffe	9	3	12	0
Robinson	4	1	11	0	Mitchell	2	0	16	0
Rhodes	5	0	10	0	Rhodes	2	1	4	0
Leyland	8	4	12	0					

YORKSHIRE—First Innings

	O.	M.	R.	W.		O.	M.	R.	W.
Macdonald	42	5	134	3	Watson	36	14	53	1
Booth	29	9	64	1	Iddon	28	6	94	1
Tyldesley (R.)	51·5	15	113	2					

YORKSHIRE V LANCASHIRE 1928

August 4/6/7   Old Trafford

FIRST DAY

THE Lancashire captain probably enjoyed a feeling of relief when on Saturday evening he returned to the shade of the pavilion knowing that after nearly six hours of play on a good wicket, in torrents of sunshine, Yorkshire had been able to score only 338 for eight. At lunch Lancashire had seemed certain to drop much vain sweat before the day was over, for then Yorkshire were 115 for none. And Lancashire could point to only one dangerous bowler—Macdonald. His helpmates were Sibbles and the two comparatively inexperienced young men Hopwood and Rushton.

The Yorkshire batsmen missed a splendid opportunity; they seldom required to worry about the protection of their wickets at both ends of the pitch, and Sutcliffe and Holmes gave to the innings a solid enough foundation. Macdonald tired in the warm sun, physically if not spiritually. We must not do the Yorkshire batsmen the injustice of supposing that on a true turf they are at all times unequal to the performance of quick-scoring strokes against aspiring young bowlers like Hopwood, Sibbles, and Rushton. The fact is known all over the country that Yorkshire happily possesses several resourceful makers of runs. It will be discreet therefore to suppose that the rather strokeless batting witnessed towards the end of Saturday afternoon was the consequence not so much of technical limitations as of a policy. By twenty minutes to four Yorkshire had made 201 for four wickets; in another two hours and a half an additional 137 runs imperceptibly accrued. The day's last hour saw Yorkshire mainly on the defensive—against the said Macdonald (now thoroughly weary) and the said Hopwood, Rushton, and Sibbles (still aspiring and now definitely perspiring). Yorkshire may have to wait many years before they run across another Lancashire attack that has to depend on the labours of one bowler of recognised ability. It is true that Lancashire at Whitsuntide batted six hours against Yorkshire for 286; to drag that dismal event out of the abyss of time will not serve as an extenuation of Yorkshire's methods on Saturday. Lancashire and Yorkshire elevens alike ought to play according to the brightest and not the shabbiest of their traditions. Lancashire's batting at Whitsuntide would certainly have displeased A. C. MacLaren and R. H. Spooner; Yorkshire's batting on Saturday would as certainly have displeased Hirst and David Denton. County cricketers belittle themselves and the game as well whenever they stay in on a perfect turf waiting for a ball which is so harmless that any club batsmen could hit it. For a while Hopwood, Sibbles, and Rushton bowled a steady enough length, and both Sutcliffe and Holmes had at first to watch well and guard well. But who is going to believe that Hopwood, Sibbles and Rushton at the fall of a warm day are not sending down at least two 'hittable' balls every over? I would, indeed, like some modern county batsman to give me his idea (with plans and specifications) of a really bad length ball.

The match had an interesting beginning, with alarums and excursions in the air. The Lancashire team took the field without Richard Tyldesley, who hurt a bowling finger on Friday in the cause of charity. A telegram was sent to Hodgson, but he, too, was not fit for action. The morning's first score-cards informed us that the vacancy in the champion county would be filled by that celebrated cricketer Mr. A. N. Other, who, as it is well known, sometimes bats for the Devonshire Dumplings, invariably making an enormous drive for six over the head of third man; while at other times he bowls fast long-hops for the Puddleton Pilgrims, and not infrequently runs himself out together with several other batsmen of his enthusiastic side. Unfortunately for the gaiety of this Lancashire and Yorkshire match, Rushton came forward instead of A. N. Other. What we lost in merriment we had returned in solid work, for Rushton is a persevering bowler who seems occasionally to try to give the ball a twist from leg, by turning over his hand 'at the moment of delivery.'

A further point of interest at the game's outset was the

batting of Holmes. In two overs he hit two fours, one to leg and one to the on, off Sibbles, after Sibbles had troubled him with a sequence of beautiful swinging balls all of them keeping close to the wicket. This, of course, was most indecorous behaviour in a Lancashire and Yorkshire match of these days; Holmes bethought himself in time, and between twenty minutes past twelve and ten minutes to one he succeeded in scoring not more than two runs. In Macdonald's third over a very fast ball broke through Sutcliffe's defences and just missed the stumps; Sutcliffe then hooked Macdonald for three and cut him for four. In fifty minutes Holmes and Sutcliffe made 52; then Hopwood and Rushton went on and kept the game quiet by the simple expedient of pitching a length just too short for the forward push. Hopwood caused one or two balls to turn, whereupon the batsmen smote the earth hard and solemnly with their bats. Rushton swung the ball across the wicket, and when Sutcliffe was 39 drew him out of his crease and nearly bowled him. Sutcliffe arrived at his 50 in eighty-five minutes; the 115 made for no wicket before lunch were got by very good cricket. It was after the interval that the Yorkshire batting dwindled in temper and skill alike.

At a quarter past two the ground was tolerably full, and gracious sunshine fell on us all. The pavilion sat back in its seats, the full picture of English ease and affability. The sight of Old Trafford's pavilion following a good luncheon always reminds me of a remark of Mr. Pecksniff after he, too, had enjoyed his lunch. 'The process of digestion, as I have been informed by anatomical friends, is one of the most wonderful works of nature. I do not know how it may be with others, but it is a great satisfaction to me to know, when regaling my humble fare, that I am putting into motion the most beautiful machinery with which we have any acquaintance. I really feel at such times as if I was doing a public service.' And Mr. Agar's fare is certainly not humble, nor does the Old Trafford pavilion humbly regale itself of the same.

The first Yorkshire wicket fell at half past two, with the score 134. Holmes, after 'feeling' dubiously at one or two out-swinging balls from Macdonald, hooked a short one vehemently and then snicked another out-swinger into

248

Duckworth's gloves. Macdonald made the ball run away, as I thought, by the device of lowering his arm a little; it came, nevertheless, from the pitch with splendid speed. Holmes scored 54 in two and a quarter hours. Another fast ball of Macdonald, judiciously mixed amongst several of fast medium velocity, likewise accounted for Mitchell, who snicked another catch to the vociferous Duckworth. Leyland was then run out—at 161. He played a ball through the slips; it was misfielded and travelled as far as Hopwood at third man on the boundary. Leyland and Sutcliffe ran two, and Leyland doubled for a third, but Hopwood threw the ball in before you could say 'Emmott Robinson!' and hit the sticks. Leyland was a victim of impetuosity. But in nearly all cases of run out it takes two batsmen to make a mistake.

Barber played highly promising cricket for 20 minutes; he drove Macdonald through the covers like a proper batsman, and also he hooked him for four, his bat quick as a sword. Rushton, with a delightful swinging-away ball, barely short of a full length, got Barber caught at the wicket. These performances by Duckworth obviously stimulated the crowd and Duckworth himself. He rhetorically attempted to stump Sutcliffe at 97; a beautiful push-drive to the off completed Sutcliffe's hundred in three hours and forty minutes. On this same afternoon of Saturday, August 4, 1928, W. G. Quaife, at the age of 56, scored a century in three hours and forty-five minutes against first-class bowling. When Quaife was in his prime he used to get his hundreds at an average scoring rate of three hours and a half. And lovers of cricket used to write passionate letters to the newspapers declaring Quaife's stone-walling was killing cricket. The letters in question very often contained many paragraphs beginning with, 'Now, sir . . .' Sutcliffe's innings was always pretty to look at; he is so cool and composed and his brown face and black hair go so handsomely with white flannels. His very inactivity is masterly. But his innings had this defect (from the point of view of great batsmanship): he could not dominate the attack and increase his pace of scoring after his innings had lasted two or three hours. When a cricketer has made 70 on a perfect wicket the bowlers ought to be dancing utterly to a tune of his calling. Sutcliffe's score was 70 at twenty minutes to three; he did not reach 100 until five minutes to four. He has developed into a defensive batsman of polish and unfailing good taste; in 1920 I thought he was about to take his place amongst the great match-winners of the game. When Sutcliffe's innings stood at 113 he hooked a ball from Macdonald to square leg; Iddon dived swiftly as a swallow after a fly, and clutched at the ball as it was about to hit the ground. Clearly he thought he had caught Sutcliffe; but the umpire gave Sutcliffe the benefit of the doubt. Shortly after this event—which woke everybody up most disconcertingly—Sutcliffe fell to a neat catch low down at first slip by Watson. In all, Sutcliffe was on view for four hours and ten minutes.

The rest of the day's play is a chronicle of small beer. Rhodes was given a royal greeting, the pavilion rising to its feet at the sight of his bronzed face and sturdy build. Rhodes came to the wicket at four o'clock; he suffered many blows on the pads, and many aggressive, wild noises, supposedly appeals for lbw, were directed at the umpire and, I fancy, at Rhodes himself. But Rhodes hung on to the wicket somehow. So far he has been batting an hour and forty minutes for 39—a 'business innings!' Wood played excellently, his bat moving energetically and with no little science. Robinson achieved one brilliant hook from Macdonald, and was clearly so pleased with himself that he lost no time trying the shot again, with fatal consequences, for Hopwood, running from mid-on to square leg, caught out the little and by no means unhappy warrior.

Today, August Bank Holiday, seems certain to witness the familiar fight for first-innings points between Lancashire and Yorkshire. The old newspaper placards will do: 'Dour struggle at Old Trafford.' 'Century by————'—but this is to anticipate.

SECOND DAY

There was a mighty crowd at Old Trafford yesterday—more than 30,000 hot, congested, but on the whole happy folk, mainly belonging to the counties of Lancashire and Yorkshire. The multitude flowed into the field, thousands sitting on the ground, and Old Trafford's turf seemed like a green island in a vast black sea that now was still and calm and now roaring to a tempest. When the game was resumed in the morning the atmosphere was hot and combustible; expectation stood visibly on tip-toe everywhere. The noise of the crowd was as a wind that fanned into flame again the ancient fires of the match; this was better than Saturday, when the crowd was so quiet and dull that the event sounded less like a Lancashire and Yorkshire engagement than a chess tournament.

Captain Worsley quickly provoked the Yorkshire roar by a superb off drive from Sibbles; a minute or two afterwards the Lancashire roar went up, not less triumphantly, to the sky, for Hopwood caught Worsley out near the long-on boundary. So excited was the crowd, indeed, that the game might have been thought to be in its crisis, with Yorkshire's last batsmen struggling to get a few runs for victory. Yorkshire were all out just before noon—Rhodes undefeated for 45, made in two hours and a half. Lancashire did very well to get Yorkshire out for 352: with Iddon and Watson unable to bowl Macdonald had to be depended upon to keep an edge on the attack. He worked hard and skilfully, and Hopwood, Sibbles, and Rushton attended to the 'donkey' work. Hopwood's analysis was 30 overs, 9 maidens, 49 runs, no wicket; his length was steady throughout, and he will live to see more wickets coming his way by means of bowling less skilful.

At ten minutes past twelve the Lancashire innings began—sensationally. After the customary opening maiden over, a proper observance of the match's traditions, Watson in one over from Robinson achieved a strong on drive and a pretty forward push past mid-off, both strokes reaching the boundary. Then Hallows' bat directed a ball from Macaulay square for four; the next ball, the second of Macaulay's second over, swung across Hallows' pads and bowled him. This mad sequence of boundaries and a Lancastrian disaster with the score only 15 left the multitude in a wild welter of emotion, confused as the colours of a plaid. Watson did not let the downfall of Hallows trouble his spirit, which was for a period dauntless. In half an hour he delighted us all with five capital drives in front of the wicket.

The advent of Rhodes and his curving slow ball had the

customary effect of putting the batsmen on the defensive. Ernest Tyldesley drove Dennis prettily to the off for four, but, on the whole, the cricket hereabouts was for the student in love with the Fine Shades. Rhodes let us have a swift but fleeting glimpse into his essential fallibility by bowling a short ball which Watson hit to the square-leg boundary. Generally, though, Rhodes's length was just about the best that can be seen in modern cricket: a tempting flight with the ball dropping just too short for a drive—unless the batsmen happen to be possessed by Johnny Tyldesley's swift feet and fearless heart. We must not complain if present-day batsmen are unable to hit Rhodes for a boundary in every six overs; they would if they could. But a young bowler of Dennis's ordinary parts ought certainly to be cut and driven on a perfect wicket. Dennis has a nice action, but it is less that of a fast than of a medium paced bowler; perhaps George Hirst will teach him, as he taught Macaulay, to find the right technique for his gifts.

By lunch Lancashire in eighty minutes had scored 75. After the interval Macaulay attacked from round the wicket and caused an odd ball to 'straighten'. With Rhodes swinging over his old arm in the easy and beautiful way we have known man and boy these thirty years, the match for a while assumed the aspect of one being played on a sticky wicket. Ernest Tyldesley's bat went to the ball 'half-cock'; he was the image of philosophic doubt. Even Watson began to use the half-hit, so detestable to see on a good pitch. In twenty-five minutes Lancashire scored five runs: Ernest Tyldesley then got himself caught by Robinson at first slip through playing at Rhodes with that speculative push-bat which he has acquired by watching the methods of cricketers not blessed with his own quick feet and decisive scoring technique. I could quote several instances where Ernest Tyldesley has got himself out against Yorkshire since 1919 by trusting to a 'half-cock' stroke. I could also quote an innings of 178 made by Tyldesley against the old enemy mainly by means of bold driving, cutting, and hooking. What a brilliant batsman—as distinguished from a heavy scorer of runs—Ernest Tyldesley would have been in the years before the Battle of the Roses went underground, into trenches, and left the open field on which cricketers of old would cut and thrust face to face, each good knight challenging his foe to do his bravest and freest. Were there ever such times, or does one only imagine them? Is it a fact that once Spooner and Hirst and Tyldesley and Denton played in a Lancashire and Yorkshire match not only with skill, but with a risk that caused the blood of the onlookers to tingle? Is it a dream that Reggie Spooner once scored a dazzling hundred on a Bank Holiday against Yorkshire, and that Lord Hawke once came in with seven Yorkshire wickets destroyed by Walter Brearley for 80, and straightway attacked Brearley and the other Lancashire bowlers and hit 80 runs in less time than it takes a contemporary batsman to play himself in? An hour's cricket after lunch yesterday saw the scoring at 36—on a beautiful turf, with no Hirsts or Brearleys, or anything like them, about. Lancashire, of course, were playing the game dictated by the championship conditions of these days; until we get rid of the 'first innings points' decision, a Lancashire and Yorkshire match on a true wicket will remain a test of patience, while Chivalry must continue to go her ways begging.

Rhodes bowled his first twenty-three overs for twelve maidens, twenty-two runs, and a wicket. The cynic might well say of him, using the language of some knightly person in Shakespeare. 'Oh, he hath gathered to himself many spoils, using no other weapon but his name.' It would be less than the truth to say this, for Rhodes has yet masterful arts of length and direction, though his old spin, as Ranjitsinhji recently said, has lost its old vitality. When Rhodes rested, Leyland bowled in his place. Now Leyland has little of Rhodes's command over the ball, still he was treated as though he were Rhodes's very shadow by Makepeace and Watson. We could all of us bowl maidens in a Lancashire and Yorkshire match. The crowd went very quiet as Lancashire made 16 runs between 3.15 and 3.35; a quick return that sent old Harry Makepeace's legs and heart stirring violently woke up several thousands. The wine of high noon had rather left our heads now; the dregs of disillusion were slightly to be tasted in the mouth. A dour struggle for five points—in other words, the historic August Bank Holiday cricket match in

253

this so-called twentieth-century! In none other but championship cricket would a crowd tolerate the scoring of 25 runs in forty-five minutes on a warm day, with one of the bowlers no cleverer than Leyland. At a quarter to four Lancashire's score stood at 129 for two, after two hours and thirty-five minutes play; refreshment was now brought on to the field to the toilers. I was sorry to see that this refreshment was not carried by Old Trafford's beautiful old retainer; I hope he is not unwell. He belongs to the dignified old school, and his white hair reminds me, whenever he walks over Old Trafford's sunny ground, of the retainer in the popular melodrama who says to the hero: 'I will never forsake you sir; I believe in your innocence. A lifetime's savings are at your disposal, Maister Harry.'

When Ernest Tyldesley lost his wicket, Lancashire's situation presumably looked serious to Watson; anyhow, he changed his game. Before lunch he played fine cricket, treating the bowling on its merits, and getting 39 in eighty minutes. After lunch he batted 105 minutes for another 33, thus falling into the modern cricketer's habit of scoring the slower the longer he stays. Watson's methods before lunch were quite safe, even if he did hit four or five boundaries. Is it not bad policy not to leave well alone?—sense only changes its tactics when they are proving fruitless and dangerous.

Between a quarter-past two and half-past four Lancashire scored 88; in two hours and a quarter Watson scored 43. The bowling was not deadly enough to deserve this respectful reception; but, as I say, Lancashire were playing the game demanded by the circumstances. That game had little or nothing to do with cricket; it was a new game evolved out of cricket—wonderful enough in its way as an exercise in the Christian virtues of patience and self-denial. The crowd was noble in its fortitude and tolerance; hour after hour thousands stood there, heaped together, ready to cheer the most modest stroke, ready to suffer weary waiting in the cause of Lancashire cricket. 'The cause, my soul: it is the cause.' The pity of it is that the meadow game with a beautiful name is shorn of its own true grace and adventure by that same cause—the championship's incitement to strong sides on a good wicket to struggle for a first-innings decision.

Lovers of cricket will do well to agitate for the abolition of a first-innings decision, with its inevitable effect on the will to outright victory.

After tea Makepeace reached an indomitable 50; he had been watching the ball for two hours and twenty minutes. The next over saw the making of Watson's hundred, built truly and honourably in four hours and a quarter, out of a total of 200 exactly. The crowd gave him the acclamation he deserved; it was a real Lancashire and Yorkshire innings, remarkable for its self-control, patience, and devotion to the policy imposed on his county by the game's character. The applause given to Watson came from 30,690 people. Only a cricketer with a fine technique and the mind to put that technique under severe discipline could have played this innings. Watson deserves extra pay for working so well and for so long on a Bank Holiday.

Following the tea interval the batting assumed some amount of animation. The curious thing about this comparatively free cricket is that it was done against the day's best bowling, for with a new ball at 200 Robinson and Macaulay attacked with spirit and a deal of technical excellence. Macaulay throughout the day was a good bowler. In an hour, from ten minutes to five to ten minutes to six, Lancashire added 70; the crowd again shook the heavens with its noise as Makepeace hit Robinson to the on for a most violent four and in the same over drove in the style of a great batsman through the covers. Next over Macaulay broke the partnership by bowling Watson with a good length ball that probably swung late in its flight. Watson and Makepeace held the third wicket for three hours and made 153 runs. Watson's innings lasted four hours and three-quarters, and he hit thirteen boundaries and gave the Yorkshire fieldsmen and bowlers little or no sign that he could be removed from the wicket by anything short of torrential rain. Makepeace's cricket, following on his innings last week at Trent Bridge, was proof that on these solemn occasions he is still indispensable to Lancashire.

When the crowd went home through the dust of Warwick Road the conversation suggested that not everybody had enjoyed themselves, excepting as supporters of the championship county. But how can you have a game if hardly a player in it will take the ghost of a chance now and again?

THIRD DAY

Rain prevented play at Old Trafford yesterday, and the points were divided. The question now is whether the Lancashire batsmen on Monday would not have been wise, after the score had reached, say, 150 for two, to make a reasonable effort to force the pace. At any rate, an offensive might politically have been attempted then; if it had cost Lancashire a quick wicket the side would have been free to fall back on the defensive again with several steady batsmen in reserve.

It has been suggested that in this match Lancashire triumphantly played Yorkshire 'at their own game.' Now the position of the two counties in cricket at the moment happens to be this. Yorkshire are generally admitted to be under a cloud; they lack the old keen edge to their bowling. But Lancashire are champion county in these days, and can boast the world's greatest fast bowler. Is it for Lancashire, then, to play anybody's game but their own? Is it for the champion county to play cricket to Yorkshire's dictation? When Yorkshire were champions they certainly never dreamt of meeting Lancashire on Lancashire's terms: it was Yorkshire who then set the pace, which they invariably did by knocking Lancashire clean out well within three days.

Lancashire batsmen at the present time ought surely to try to enjoy themselves against Yorkshire bowling while it is below the deadly form of the years in which Yorkshire won matches right and left at their own pleasure, without condescending to study any side's tactics but their very own. If it is denied that Yorkshire bowling this season is below the county's best standards, the reply is that Yorkshire for the first time in many years cannot provide an England eleven with a single bowler for the first line of the attack.

Lancashire on Saturday and Monday morning performed a splendid feat in getting Yorkshire all out on a perfect wicket for 352. But, as Lancashire scored only 244 in five hours and a quarter on Monday afternoon, the situation at close of play was that rain might come and rob Lancashire of the advantage which their excellent bowling had won for them. And come, the rain did—with a vengeance!

SCORES

YORKSHIRE

First Innings

Holmes, c Duckworth, b Macdonald	54
Sutcliffe, c Watson, b Sibbles	126
Mitchell, c Duckworth, b Macdonald	7
Leyland, run out	4
Barber, c Duckworth, b Rushton	19
Robinson, c Hopwood, b Macdonald	17
Rhodes, not out	45
Wood, c Iddon, b Macdonald	39
Macaulay, c Iddon, b Macdonald	6
W. A. Worsley, c Hopwood, b Sibbles	10
Dennis, c Sibbles, b Macdonald	2
Extra b15, lb7, w1	23
Total	352

LANCASHIRE

First Innings

Watson, b Macaulay	110
Hallows, b Macaulay	5
Tyldesley (E.), c Robinson, b Rhodes	29
Makepeace, not out	81
Iddon, not out	3
Extras b5, lb11	16
Total (for 3)	244

THE ROSES MATCHES 1919-1939
BOWLING ANALYSIS

Yorkshire—First Innings

	O.	M.	R.	W.		O.	M.	R.	W.
Macdonald	45·5	8	144	6	Hopwood	30	9	49	0
Sibbles	42	14	81	2	Rushton	25	4	55	1

Lancashire—First Innings

	O.	M.	R.	W.		O.	M.	R.	W.
Robinson	27	8	50	0	Dennis	10	0	28	0
Macaulay	40	10	92	2	Leyland	10	3	16	0
Rhodes	40	20	42	1					

G. G. Macaulay (Yorkshire).

P. Holmes (Yorkshire).

F. Watson (Lancashire).

Lancashire's 'Artful Dodger', C. H. Parkin.

C. Hallows (Lancashire).

J. T. Tyldesley (Lancashire).

Emmott Robinson (Yorkshire).

G. H. Hirst (Yorkshire).

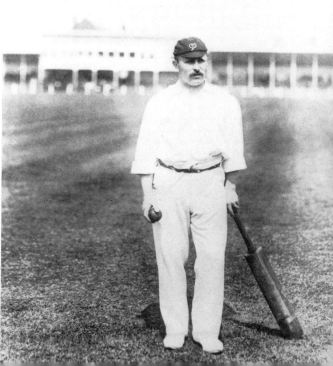

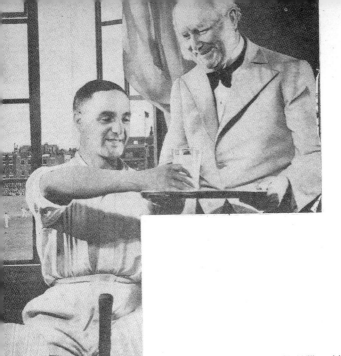

Herbert Sutcliffe, 'a sort of Sir Willoughby Patterne' (Yorkshire).

Lancashire's championship winning team, 1926. *Back row, l to r:* G. Duckworth, C. Hallows,
F. M. Sibbles, C. H. Parkin, J. Iddon, R. Tyldesley, F. Watson. *Front row, l to r:* E. Tyldesley,
J. R. Barnes, Major L. Green *(Capt.)*, H. Makepeace, E. A. Macdonald.

Wilfred Rhodes (Yorkshire).   H. Makepeace (Lancashire).

Eddie Paynter (Lancashire), in action against Australia at Brisbane in 1933.

Ted Macdonald (Lancashire).

Len Hutton (Yorkshire).

Cyril Washbrook (Lancashire).

A. Mitchell (Yorkshire).

A. B. Sellers (Yorkshire).

Lancashire CCC, 1934. *Standing, l to r:* C. Washbrook, J. L. Hopwood, J. Iddon, F. Booth, R. Pollard, L. Parkinson, N. Oldfield. *Seated, l to r:* E. Paynter, E. Tyldesley, P. T. Eckersley *(Capt.)*, W. H. L. Lister, G. Duckworth.

Yorkshire's army cricketers. *L to r:* Captain Verity, Sgt.-Major Smailes, Captain Sutcliffe, Sergeant Leyland and Sergeant-Instructor Hutton.

Patient crowds wait all day at Old Trafford for a few minutes' play.

Old Trafford before the Second World War – 'a batsman's dream of midsummer'.

'The packed crowd, rank on rank in the sunshine.'

Lancashire taking the field. *R to l:* Makepeace, E. Tyldesley, J. R. Barnes, Major Green, Duckworth, Sibbles, R. Tyldesley (stooping down), Iddon, Macdonald, Watson and Hallows.

Above: Major Green autographs one of the stumps used in the match that won Lancashire the County Championship.

Right: Ernest Tyldesley (Lancashire).

Left: Bill Bowes (Yorkshire).

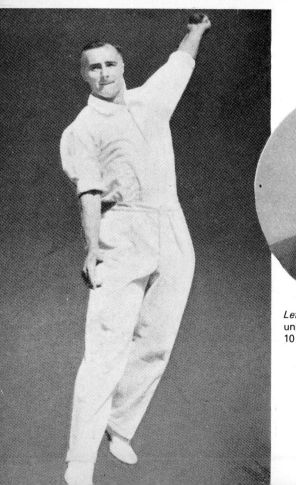

Left and above: Hedley Verity (Yorkshire) unplayable at Old Trafford where he took 5 for 10 on August 2nd, 1938.

Above and top left: George Duckworth, Lancashire and England wicketkeeper.

Below: Maurice Leyland, Yorkshire and England batsman.

Neville Cardus (right) leads out the Lancashire team with J. T. Tyldesley.

YORKSHIRE V LANCASHIRE 1929

May 18/20/21   Old Trafford

FIRST DAY

I OVERHEARD in the crowd at Old Trafford on Saturday much moaning and groaning. There was a cause for it, no doubt. Lancashire, in nearly six hours, made only 196 runs for seven wickets. But was anything more brilliant in batsmanship to be expected, seeing that Lancashire lost three wickets at the match's beginning for 14 runs? When Lancashire are doing well against Worcestershire they seldom get runs at a speed quicker than fifty an hour. It was hope and optimism gone mad, then, for the crowd on Saturday to look for vigorous runs from Lancashire following a collapse against Yorkshire.

To be frank, Lancashire do not possess a single batsman of known brilliance—one commanding forcing strokes all round the wicket. Ernest Tyldesley comes close to this category, but just now he is out of form. Hallows is a defensive player with a noble style. But his strokes are few; he has not the means whereby to take a situation by the scruff of the neck and drive danger violently away. Defensive batsmanship cannot alter a perilous day; it can only endure one. How long is it since Lancashire last scored runs at sixty an hour at the beginning of an important match? The reputation of Lancashire cricket up and down the country is fair and true-brilliant and versatile in bowling, but drab and commonplace in batting. All in all, the county did well not to lose the match outright after the disasters before lunch on Saturday.

The Old Trafford crowd, taking it in the lump, was sensible enough to understand that in the circumstances a stylish display of batsmanship was out of the question. They cheered every run, even the lucky snick. The crowd, indeed, reminded me of the little company which watches Worcestershire, expecting the worst, and always thankful for small mercies. The Yorkshire attack was capital in the first hour of the morning; towards three o'clock it bated and dwindled to

259

mere respectability. Turner and Leyland were obviously bowlers of Saturday afternoon class; Robinson and Macaulay were tired; Rhodes could not spin the ball with any amount of 'nip.' When Duckworth came to the wicket Lancashire's score was 124 for seven: he quickly hit a boundary and scored 20 while Hallows was scoring 12. Hallows had been batting for five hours when Duckworth came in. Hallows has every quality of a great batsman excepting imagination; that is why he is not famous now in England and Australia.

At the outset of the day the wicket was rather moist on the surface; one or two balls came from the earth at a good pace. I am assured, though on sound and impartial authority, that the wicket could hardly have been easier for good batsmen. The first ball of the match, from Robinson, was played to the on for a single by Hallows. The second ball swung outwards, and Watson tried to drive it to the off. He merely snicked it to the stumper's pads, and it bounced thence to the slips, where Macaulay held the ball, while Robinson, in mingled excitement, hope and apprehension shrieked, 'Catch it!' It is difficult to understand why Watson sought to hit to the boundary the second ball of a Lancashire and Yorkshire match. I can only suppose he had been reading pernicious literature by a certain writer on cricket whose incitements to licentious batsmanship are to be gravely condemned as harmful to championship morality. With Ernest Tyldesley in, Lancashire gave the 'initiative' entirely to Yorkshire—a mistake which, I am sure, was the cause of the day's sterility. Robinson bowled superbly, but Macaulay sent up occasional balls of loose length. The batsmen were never in a position to hit them hard. For invariably they moved their legs in front of the stumps even before the ball pitched. This was batsmanship which plainly confessed lack of confidence and spirit.

The fifty-seventh ball of the morning got Tyldesley out leg before wicket. Macaulay had just sent him a succession of in-swingers which Tyldesley pushed to the on, after getting his legs 'in front.' Macaulay moved Rhodes to the leg side. Tyldesley shaped for another in-swinger, shoved his pads over the wicket yet again, only to stop with them a faster straight ball. Hopwood also confused his bat with his pads; he stuck out his left leg to a straight half-volley. The play, in style and spirit alike, was unworthy of a first class county.

Iddon, from the moment he came into action, hit the ball with the middle of his bat, like a cricketer whose skill is the justification of a whole life-time devoted to a game. What a fine and joyous batsman Iddon would be if he played for Sussex and Surrey. He is chockful of the living energy of cricket, but alas, a soulless championship policy is laying hold of him. His defence on Saturday, in a crucial moment, was admirable. Hallows faced the evil menace with his own nonchalance, and never looked like getting out, though in Macaulay's third over a ball defeated his bat and hit his pads. There was no appeal, despite a wild look in the eyes of Macaulay. Gracious goodness, are we to have appeals in Lancashire and Yorkshire matches only when they are reasonable?

The stand by Iddon and Hallows before lunch was most praiseworthy; it is nothing to the discredit of either batsman that in two hours only 48 runs were made. The main job for them was to stay the Yorkshire advance; they achieved the purpose by skill and patience. Another Yorkshire success would hereabout have spelled ruin for Lancashire; when Iddon reached the wicket at 14 for 3, one needed much courage to look at the score-card and read the names of the county's batsmen to come. It was after the interval that the partnership of Hallows and Iddon invited criticism. The Yorkshire attack was considerably spent by this time. Robinson and Macaulay before lunch attacked for an hour and a half without a rest. Robinson, until the breath left his body, was a great bowler. He gathered his shambling energy to a point of passionate concentration as he leaped to the wicket. Over after over he worried the batsmen, and walked back to his place in the field with his flannels terrible loose and yellow. Robinson always seems to tighten up his trousers at the very last moment; you see his waistline getting lower and lower; you anticipate the worst—then, up the trousers go with a savage lurch and tug. Once Robinson's fires had burnt out, Yorkshire's bowling seemed as weak as Yorkshire bowling well could be. Could not Iddon and Hallows, after they had played themselves in for an hour, have attacked the very ordinary stuff wheeled up by Turner and Leyland? True, Iddon fell a victim to his first burst of freedom; he hit a ball from Rhodes hard to the off, where Turner held a clever catch. It is often the way with Lancashire batsmen—they lose their wickets the moment they begin to hit. Perhaps it is because they get so little practice at driving.

Iddon and Hallows held the fourth wicket for two and a half hours and scored 75. During the tedium of this stand I occasionally found relief by watching a cricket match on a field adjoining Old Trafford; you could see it from the press box—a match of perpetual motion to the wicket and back to the pavilion again! The umpire wore a bowler hat.

Halliday was out at 104—he also stuck his legs in front of the wicket, ball after ball. Is there no authority at Old Trafford to put an end to this defect of technique in Lancashire's young batsmen? It is neither stylish nor safe. Eckersley, after showing us one or two pretty hits in front of the wicket, sliced a ball low to the slips—not at all a bad stroke, good enough indeed to call from Leyland a dazzling catch. Yorkshire's fielding all day was a delight for tired eyes. Sibbles defended for a while in the clean composed way of a real batsman; he fell at 123, another error of lbw, and again because of Lancashire's mechanical trick of pad play.

At five o'clock Duckworth walked to the middle, to the acclamation of thousands. He walked quickly, with head cast downward, as though deploring as a moral vanity all of this tumultuous applause. He played excellent cricket and, as I have suggested, he, for a period, got runs quicker than Hallows. The edge of the Yorkshire bowling was now gone. Hallows reached his hundred after he had been on view for ten minutes less than six hours. Duckworth and Hallows did much to ease Lancashire's forlorn state and to put a surface touch of credit on to a day of cricket which on the whole, will not polish Lancashire's reputation in the land. Hallows' innings, by its coolness of mind and its shrewd defensive technique, was impressive; he gave the Yorkshiremen no hope, not a hint of human fallibility. It would have been a great innings had Hallows, towards the day's fall, shown us more frequently than he did his own powerful drive.

I was interested in the bowling of Leyland, for though the length lacked accuracy and ought to have moved county batsmen to aggression, there was a hint of possibilities of spin which, later, Leyland might be able to exploit to the full. He seemed at times to be trying his fingers at a 'googly'. Roy Kilner—may the earth rest on him lightly!—used to tell me that the next development in bowling was going to be left-handed 'googly' bowler. Poor Roy; he would have enjoyed Saturday's cricket, in his own sly, humorous way. I once protested to Kilner against the slow scoring in modern cricket. And I suggested that the rules of the game ought to be altered to the ends of compelling batsmen to get runs or get out. 'No,' said Roy,' ' 'T' game's all reight; only the public wants educatin' up to it. Listen. When I were a young lad I went to see a play by Shakespeare. I'd never seen one before. And I thought it were so dry that I came out and went home and told mi feyther that I'd had enough of Shakespeare. 'Never again,' said I. 'Now, Roy,' says feyther, 'that's where tha'rt wrong, my lad. T' fault is not Shakespeare, but thiself. Tha wants educatin' up to him. 'And,' so Roy concluded ' 'it's t' same with this cricket: t' crowd wants educatin' up to it.' I shall never forget the twinkle in Roy's eyes as he ended those remarks. Leyland has a great deal in common with Kilner; he shares the man's Yorkshire humour and relish of the game. His left-handed bowling may be ready by the time Rhodes retires. But at present it 'lacks the abilities that Rhodes is dressed in'—as the Senator says in Act 1 of 'Othello'.

The crowd was one of the quietest I have known at a Lancashire and Yorkshire match. Even the alarms and excursions before lunch did not provoke a jot of old clamour. There was a time when Old Trafford's crowd was Shakespearian in its large life and humour, its sudden wraths, revolts, and panics. Perhaps to-day's cricket will be worthy of the occasion and show us that the true crowd of a Lancashire and Yorkshire match is with us yet, even in an age when 'talkies' and other American tomfooleries are apparently stealing away the wits of men.

SECOND DAY

There was a finish to Lancashire's innings at Old Trafford

yesterday which had so much fight in it that we were almost (but not quite) compensated for the dish of humble pie forced down our throats on Saturday. The morning was pure green and gold—the sort of day a batsman sees in a dream. Duckworth from the beginning stuck out his chin and hunted for runs. He got four through the slips, and ran up and down the wicket with an alacrity which had about it a kind of gamin impudence. 'I'll show 'em,' he seemed to be saying. 'I'll show that "Cricketer" fellow whether Lancashire has a forcing batsman or not!' He made a dozen while Hallows, in his own lordly way, was, so to speak, savouring the May air.

Robinson strove might and main with the glossy new ball to put an end to this scandalous piece of resistance by Lancashire's tail end. Tradition lends no countenance to a tail-end rally by Lancashire against Yorkshire. Why, when I was a small boy, I never dared look at the match while Lancashire's five last batsmen were in. I used to rest my head on the iron rail which runs round the 'popular' side, close my eyes, and say 'Oh Lord, don't let George Hirst get any more wickets—not just yet, please, Lord; not this over anyhow.' In those days it was Yorkshire that did the tail-end batting— Lord Hawke and David Hunter. I remember Brearley bowling out eight Yorkshire men for 82; then Lord Hawke and Whitehead scored 100 together for the ninth wicket. Yesterday these hard memories were soothed at the sight of Duckworth and Hallows frustrating Yorkshire, pushing them off victory's very doorstep.

Amid roars of proud applause which might have been heard in Warrington, Duckworth reached a valiant fifty, after two hours and a half of very pertinacious cricket. When Rhodes got him out leg-before-wicket Duckworth had helped Hallows to hold the eighth Lancashire wicket for two hours and forty minutes and to lift the score from 123 to 251. The stand saved the champions from disaster, and Duckworth must be given the lion's share of the credit. We expect, as a matter of course, strong batsmanship from Hallows. When Duckworth came in on Saturday Yorkshire were a winning team; he got runs straightway at more than Hallows' pace even though Hallows had by then been thoroughly set for five hours. Yesterday Duckworth made 26 while Hallows made

29. Duckworth hit no fewer than six boundaries. One or two of them were through the slips and not in academic taste. But criticism must not play the purist about boundaries in a Lancashire and Yorkshire match.

Richard Tyldesley clouted a ball from Rhodes to the on for four—a crossbat blow born and bred in Westhoughton. Then he gave an easy slip catch to Robinson, who dropped the ball amidst great laughter, in which Robinson did not join, though Rhodes, the bowler, somehow contrived to do so.

It was almost lunch-time before Lancashire's innings came to an end—just after Macdonald had hit a beautiful six, a straight drive from Rhodes. The total 305 represented nearly eight hours of toil and trouble—a quite Herculean recovery. Hallows was unbeaten throughout; his innings had at the finish the aspect of a rocky permanence which even time would never corrode. By its sheer length and calmness it suggested greatness. The style was handsome in poise, sovereign in its display of the obvious criticism which its slowness was bound to provoke. Praise is commanded by any innings of which we can say that had it not been made a side would have been lost.

Hallows so dominated the Yorkshire attack that it was hard to believe he could not, had he chosen, have hit it harder. Time after time he got into position for a masterful drive, had the ball at his mercy. But he chose, more often than not, to make an assured defence doubly sure by remaining well within the great scope of his reserve power. All in all, the innings deserved that justification which cannot fairly be withheld from any exhibition of patient skill and self-control. The Yorkshire bowling yesterday was quite without sting. A bowler of pace from the pitch is sadly lacking in the county which once were champions as though by divine right.

Yorkshire's innings began at a quarter-past two with little for them to play for save a win on the first innings. In half an hour Yorkshire were definitely backs to the wall. Holmes stopped with his pads a straight ball from Macdonald when only six runs had been scored. At 20 Mitchell, whose form was promising—he achieved a thrilling leg-glance from Macdonald—was bowled. He seemed to be trying to push toward cover from a ball which suggested an out-swinger.

But it broke back, in Macdonald's own lovely way, on pitching; moreover, it was a shade slower than the bowler's customary pace. Leyland and Sutcliffe, of course, concentrated on defence; that was their clear policy. Between a quarter to three and four o'clock they scored 60, a slow tempo, but quicker than Saturday's. Yet it irked the soul of Old Trafford, where ideas of speed are relative to whichever team happens to be batting. As Sutcliffe played his elegant pendulum push stroke ball after ball somebody in the crowd was stirred to real irony. 'What d'you think you are,' the wag asked of Sutcliffe, 'a war memorial?' The cricket of both Leyland and Sutcliffe showed us that pure defence can be combined with graceful strokes. The ball was not merely smothered, but hit away to the field with active, sensitive bats. There was no ugly pad-play. Leyland's off side strokes were frequently handsome in the flash of his bat and the forward and gracefully falling movement of his body. An off drive from Macdonald saw the ball reaching the boundary quicker than it had left the bat—the first stroke of the match to deserve that high compliment—a compliment which implies perfect timing.

When Leyland was 30 and Yorkshire 89 for two, Leyland slashed a ball from Watson over the slips' heads, but this slight deviation from law and order was the only one committed by the batsmen in a stand which at the tea interval had lasted for an hour and a half and, by adding 77 runs, had eased Yorkshire's situation mightily.

Not until five o'clock did Lancashire take another wicket; it came when the bowling seemed thoroughly mastered. After tea, Sutcliffe and Leyland increased the rate of scoring: Macdonald's sting was drawn. At 136 he gave the ball to Richard Tyldesley and looked a worn-out man. Leyland off-drove Tyldesley's first ball brilliantly for four; the next he glanced for four to leg. The next bowled him: he played forward and over a length which drew him out of his crease seductively. Leyland batted for two hours, and in every stroke, or nearly every stroke, he was a delightful batsman, shrewd but opportunist, as watchful for bad as for good balls. He is perhaps the safest off-side player of any left-handed cricketer in the country: his body seems always over the ball as he hits it. Leyland and Sutcliffe for the third Yorkshire wicket added 124 in two hours and five minutes; the partnership was an example of how a very dangerous situation can be retrieved by play which, though involving no risks, does little or no abuse to the style which is the spirit of the game. Whatever the state of a cricket match it is the true batsman's duty to let us see resolute scoring strokes at every reasonable opportunity. In an hour after tea Yorkshire made 76 runs: yet nobody would have accused the batsmen of the slightest recklessness. Runs can be made safely enough on a good wicket, and with tolerable speed, given the will to get them—and the scoring technique.

At 173 Sutcliffe was beaten by the length rather than the pace of a ball from Macdonald. Again he proved himself, for three hours, a batsman for a big match. I find it hard to believe that England would have lost the fifth test match last winter had Sutcliffe been there to go in first with Hobbs. Robinson stayed with Oldroyd for twenty-five minutes while 24 runs were hit, mainly by Oldroyd, whose cricket was clean and confident. Robinson got out hitting protectively at a bumper from Macdonald: he sent a 'dolly' catch to Sibbles at mid-on.

At close of play the decision for first innings' points was hanging in the balance. Lancashire's bowling on the easy wicket was not much better than Yorkshire's. We had to look to Macdonald for quick wickets. On a sound turf, against real batsmen, Macdonald and nobody else is Lancashire's match-winner. But yesterday Macdonald's pace dwindled all too soon, and his arm seemed lower than one recollects having seen it before. Tyldesley bowled a clever length without spinning the ball with the 'nip' that kills. Hopwood is not dangerous on a hard pitch: he ought to try to lend to his flight some changefulness of curve. Given a dry season Lancashire's attack will be more dependent than ever on Macdonald.

THIRD DAY

The Lancashire and Yorkshire match, of course, resolved itself into a first-innings affair on Monday. Yesterday, in the first half-hour Yorkshire appeared certain to fall short of

267

Lancashire's 305; three wickets were lost for the addition of only 26 to Yorkshire's score of 216 for five of Bank Holiday evening. A swift catch at the wicket closed the innings of Oldroyd, and eight runs afterwards Sibbles got Wood lbw. Sibbles bowled at this stage with more than his customary vitality from the turf. Macaulay showed fight, while Turner batted with a cool judgment of technique remarkable in a young player. At 212 Macaulay was out leg before wicket to Macdonald, and now only Rhodes and Turner and Worsley stood between Lancashire and the precious five points for which nowadays all sorts of sins against cricket are committed in these games, once so chivalrous and grand in style and temper.

Rhodes did not time Macdonald at all well during his first moments at the wicket, but his vast experience came to his aid, teaching him which balls to leave alone. Turner proceeded with his safe yet not unattractive method, playing back from an upright position which left him free to make a scoring stroke if at the last second the length turned out to be not so difficult as seemed likely when the ball was coming through the air.

Rhodes and Turner naturally did not hurry themselves, but seldom missed a reasonable opportunity of a stroke. Turner frequently glanced Macdonald to leg handsomely, while Rhodes from time to time drove toward cover in the good old-fashioned manner. Incredible man!—the legendary Rhodes. Why, he was famous in this land when Queen Victoria was on the throne. And here he is still, playing cricket with the best and youngest of them.

Shortly after lunch Yorkshire won the first innings' points, and then Rhodes fell to a brilliant left-handed catch, taken near the ground at mid-off, by Eckersley. In two hours Rhodes and Turner scored 81 for the ninth Yorkshire wicket, a stand in which the young man was as calm and old-soldierly as the veteran himself.

Turner, after the game's interest was gone, helped himself to runs by strong pulls and drives off Richard Tyldesley's bowling. He played a decisive game in searching circumstances. Turner, an untried man, had to face the music on Monday evening in the day's closing period—always an

268

ordeal, especially against an advancing attack. His cricket was full of the common sense of batsmanship; his strokes, though not many at present, are based soundly on principles which have served cricketers well for years without number. He plays straight, watches the ball, keeps his body over the line of it, and never allows a preoccupation with the position of his pads to hinder his bat's movements.

He knows how to 'back up' to the turning ball, but knows also when the second line of defence is not wanted. Turner, given more physical strength, will do good work for Yorkshire.

With no responsibility to face, Lancashire batted again on a lovely afternoon. Yorkshire's main bowlers were rested, but, against Turner and Leyland, Lancashire quickly lost the wickets of Hallows and Watson. In an hour and a half only 80 runs were scored. When I left the ground, brilliant in sunshine. Ernest Tyldesley and Iddon were beginning to hit with power and style, and Holmes was bowling at one end.

It was good to be rid of the match which did little credit to the game. Cricket would never have taken a hold on the affections of people had it always been played in this graceless way. Lancashire's slow scoring on Saturday was thoroughly justifiable while Hallows and Iddon coped with a dangerous situation. It will be a bad day for cricket when every county decides to cut out for hours even a shadow of a forcing stroke merely because three wickets have fallen cheaply. This match did not come to a first-innings decision until after three o'clock on the third day. It is inconceivable that crowds will continue to be attracted to Lancashire and Yorkshire matches unless there is a sudden change of heart somewhere. There was a poor attendance yesterday; perhaps therein lies an argument which will count for more with the responsible parties than all the talk in the world about the spirit of cricket.

LANCASHIRE

First Innings		Second Innings	
Hallows, not out	152	c Rhodes, b Macaulay	6
Watson, c Macaulay, b Robinson	0	b Turner	18
Tyldesley (E.), lbw, b Macaulay	2	not out	54
Hopwood, lbw Macaulay	2	st Wood, b Turner	18
Iddon, c Turner, b Rhodes	33	not out	20
Halliday, lbw, b Turner	2		
P. T. Eckersley, c Leyland, b Turner	0		
Sibbles, lbw, Macaulay	5		
Duckworth, lbw, b Rhodes	55		
Tyldesley (R.), c Leyland, b Robinson	10		
Macdonald, b Rhodes	18		
Extras b14, lb12	26	Extras b8, lb2, nb1	11
Total	305	Total (for 3)	127

YORKSHIRE

First Innings

Holmes, lbw, b Macdonald	3
Sutcliffe, b Macdonald	69
Mitchell, b Macdonald	9
Leyland, b Tyldesley (R.)	65
Oldroyd, c Duckworth, b Sibbles	51
Robinson, c Sibbles, b Macdonald	8
Turner, not out	69
Wood, lbw, b Sibbles	7
Macaulay, lbw, b Macdonald	9
Rhodes, c Eckersley, b Tyldesley (R.)	42
A. W. Worsley, st Duckworth, b Tyldesley (R.)	5
Extras b6, lb3, nb1	10
Total	347

YORKSHIRE V LANCASHIRE 1929
BOWLING ANALYSIS
LANCASHIRE—First Innings

	O.	M.	R.	W.		O.	M.	R.	W.
Robinson	45	18	74	2	Turner	37	14	54	2
Macaulay	43	15	82	3	Leyland	15	3	25	0
Rhodes	44·3	27	44	3					

Second Innings

	O.	M.	R.	W.		O.	M.	R.	W.
Leyland	20	6	35	0	Oldroyd	10	2	29	0
Macaulay	6	1	12	1	Holmes	4	0	19	0
Turner	11	3	15	2	Mitchell	2	1	6	0

YORKSHIRE—First Innings

	O.	M.	R.	W.		O.	M.	R.	W.
Macdonald	44	10	119	5	Hopwood	10	3	17	0
Sibbles	44	12	81	2	Watson	21	9	35	0
Tyldesley (R.)	31·2	9	85	3					

YORKSHIRE V LANCASHIRE 1929

August 3/5/6 Bradford

FIRST DAY

AT half-past eleven on Saturday morning the Bradford cricket field was one of the most desolate places in the land; the others, I imagine, were Bramall Lane and any waiting-room in the Wolverhampton railway station. Heavy clouds hung over Park Avenue (in heaven's name, as Betsy Trotwood would have asked, why 'avenue'?), and no play was possible until ten minutes to one. The ground stood vacant in the wintry wind; the occasion might have been the beginning of football, save for the fact that only a handful of onlookers was present.

Lancashire had the good fortune to bat first on a sodden wicket before the top was knocked off it. To-day there will be innumerable spots on the pitch, and the Lancashire bowlers will merely need to keep a length. On Saturday Lancashire wasted some scoring chances while the turf remained easy, between one o'clock and half-past three. For an hour and three-quarters Lancashire played severely defensive cricket against bowling which, apart from an odd ball that 'lifted', possessed little vitality that the heavy earth did not kill at birth. Later in the day, when Makepeace reached the middle, the wicket was so sensitive to spin that Leyland was able to pitch on the leg stump and miss the off stump by six inches. Luckily for Lancashire, Rhodes was unable to play because of a strained leg muscle. This was the first Lancashire and Yorkshire match Rhodes has not taken part in since 1898, in which epoch Queen Victoria was on the throne, and the nation discussed Kruger and the Uitlanders, the launching of the *Oceanic,* and a wonderful new invention called the free wheel.

It did not look like a Lancashire and Yorkshire match with Rhodes not there. Never before had I seen this match and not seen Rhodes spinning the ball. Rhodes has always been a part of cricket since first I knew anything about the game. But if there was not the beautiful curving flight of Rhodes's bowling to delight me in this match on Saturday afternoon, there was the next best thing—the pleasure and privilege of watching the game with Rhodes sitting by my side and talking the wisdom of the serpent about the spin bowler's art. He thought that Lancashire's score was 'tidy'. And after the match Makepeace was satisfied on the whole with the total of 192. But it could easily have been larger by 50 if the batsmen had used their strokes before the turf took Leyland's spin and if the later batsmen had not thrown wickets away by thoroughly unscientific hits at the pitch of the spin. There seems no middle way in Lancashire batting just now between the negative push-stroke and a wild, full-lengthed swing at the ball just as it is turning.

Makepeace played a superb innings; it was Makepeace who showed the rest of the side how runs could be got at a decent speed. Watson batted two hours and forty minutes for 44, and he had the use of the pitch at its least harmful. Lancashire scored only 56 for three in two hours before Makepeace began his innings. And then, with the turf getting really awkward over by over, Makepeace scored 50 out of 74 in eighty minutes. Here we had a clinching manifestation of the difference between the pre-war and the post-war batsmen. Makepeace was able to get runs quickly and safely because his range of strokes was far wider and his footwork more flexible than that of his colleagues. You cannot play a match-winning game on a soft pitch if you are a slave to push-stroke made from a rigid right foot. And you most certainly cannot score quick and scientific runs when the ball is turning unless you can cut the left-handed bowler's spin after the ball has pitched and just as it is going across. Leyland bowled two short spinning balls every over, but only Makepeace had the wit or the technique to lie back and hit these short balls, with the spin, to the off side.

Hallows and Watson began Lancashire's innings dubiously. Watson flicked at rising balls from Bowes; from one of them he was missed at the wicket, an easy chance, when he had made three. At this escape you could see Watson drawing in all of his strokes for the day. Just before lunch Hallows tried to drive to the off from Robinson; the ball pitched too short for the stroke, and though Hallows had time to pull back his bat and play 'dead,' he went through with the swing, and then, as he realised his peril, he tried to flick the ball out of harm's way with his wrists. He was caught at mid-on.

Only 2,000 people watched the match after lunch. The day was, of course, all against cricket. Still, I have the feeling that the public are finding out that the Lancashire and Yorkshire match is getting rather short of personality and vision. Saturday's play, however, was uncommonly fascinating for the simple reason that on the wicket no batsman was at liberty to go to sleep. Ernest Tyldesley delighted us with a beautiful late cut. Leyland bowled instead of Robinson at 37, the time of day now being 2.40. Ten minutes later Tyldesley tried to drive Leyland to the off, but the ball turned away just as the bat struck it. Inevitably a catch toward cover was the consequence; A. T. Barber held the ball near to the earth. Leyland's spin had troubled Tyldesley from the moment he bowled at him. Watson moved backward to a short ball from Leyland and cut most brilliantly for four. To several other balls more or less identical in pace and pitch he merely pushed out a passive bat. Iddon concentrated on defence for half an hour; he allowed at least three half-volleys to escape punishment, sparing them, no doubt, 'on principle'—much as the man in Dickens demanded 'buttered crumpets.' At length Iddon's patience broke down, and, ironically enough, he picked out the very ball which Leyland wanted him to hit—a shortish spinning-away ball. Robinson, at extra cover, was the picture of diving grace as he achieved the catch. Handsome is as handsome does. Watson and Iddon, in 35 minutes, added 16 to Lancashire's score.

Makepeace had got only nine when he hooked a long-hop from Bowes into the hands of Wilfred Barber at short leg; the chance, no easy one, was missed. When he was 14 Makepeace nearly played a spinning ball from Leyland into his wicket. But Makepeace was the one batsman of the day to show us an all-round batting technique. He was as wary as ever at the sight of a good ball. But not once did I see him unready according to the true gospel. At one period Watson made nine in an hour, and then he cut Macaulay superbly for four.

Watson, in the first over after tea, hit at Leyland's short ball, and fell to a beautiful catch at silly mid-off by Yorkshire's latest captain, A. T. Barber, who is a fieldsman delightful to watch. Watson's innings had its dour value. He was too kind, though, with several balls which he could have punished safely enough. Hopwood was entirely in the dark about the spin of Leyland, and he was leg-before-wicket at 113, the fifth wicket of Lancashire to fall.

The finest cricket of the afternoon came now, just as Lancashire's position and the state of the pitch were decidedly unpleasant. Duckworth displayed a resolution which was a rather scathing commentary on the performances of every other batsman on his side, Makepeace, of course, excepted. He put a canny bat to the nasty bowling and a quick and quite spiteful bat to the easy ones. Meanwhile Makepeace was a great player; he took charge of the game, nursed Duckworth when Macaulay looked like getting him leg-before-wicket. Makepeace pulled Robinson's off break violently for four; Robinson hereabout bowled with no slip to a leg trap, and occasionally he caused the ball to come back two or three inches, though in the absence of the hot sun the turf never gave to the spin that nip which is unplayable save by the very greatest batsman. The fact that Watson, by strictly defensive measures, could stay in nearly three hours is proof that the wicket was not really sticky. On an 'unplayable' pitch, defensive batting is fatal. Saturday's pitch is best called one of a slow but varying pace up to 3.20, and afterwards, a rather awkward wicket sensitive to spin but not lending to spin the waspish angle of the 'gluepot.'

Makepeace and Duckworth held Lancashire's sixth wicket for 65 minutes, and they scored 67. It is possible that this partnership will in the long run stand out as one of the crucial periods of the match. Makepeace might have been stumped when he was 58: the ball, from Leyland, swung in astonishingly, missed the leg stump; possibly Makepeace's body unsighted the stumper. No other in-swinger did I see Leyland bowl all afternoon. At 183 Makepeace was caught by A. T. Barber; he was, I think, trying to 'push out' for a single to get to the other end. At 183, Duckworth's gallant innings came to a curious end; he drove a ball from Leyland to mid-off, where Macaulay missed the catch. A run was attempted, and Macaulay threw in the ball, not at all hopefully—obviously he was preoccupied with his own troubles. Duckworth was run out easily. Eckersley was bowled attempting a drive; Richard Tyldesley hit thoughtlessly at the ball when it was spinning out of his reach: and Macdonald was caught at long-on from a big drive. Lancashire's last four wickets were taken for only 12 runs. Yorkshire were thus able to get the roller on to the wicket before the holes and dents were rendered more or less permanent during the week-end's interval. Holmes batted one over from Preston, who bowled a no-ball; this brought us to the close of play.

Leyand's seven wickets for 52 were deserved; he bowled hard and, on the whole, well. His spirit could be seen from the boundary's edge. One ball an over was pitched on the leg stump, whipped across, and needed careful playing. But he lacks Rhodes' accuracy of pitch, and also he lacks Rhodes' flight. He bowls 'straight down' to the wicket, sometimes short enough for the spin to be cut as it goes across. The great left-handed spin bowler draws the batsmen forward by his flight; his spin then nips away just as the bat is groping for the ball. Against Rhodes the batsman is always tackling two problems; first of all he has to guess at the width of the curve through the air; then he has to tackle the break, and by that time he is usually drawn forward so far that he cannot watch the ball as it pitches. Spin is not difficult to counter if the batsman is free to watch it to the ground. The defect of Leyland's bowling at present is that his short and direct flight gives the batsman leisure to lie back and observe the spin pitch. And the glory of Rhodes' attack is that his curve through the air pulls the batsman out full strength, puts him on the rack, and deprives him of his strength and sight alike! Given fine weather to-day's play ought to be exciting.

SECOND DAY

The wet turf prevented cricket until one o'clock, and then Lancashire took the field without Macdonald, who was troubled by a cold in the back. But Lancashire did not expect to deplore his absence on the wicket; in the old days the

Lancashire captain, when rain had fallen, used to throw the ball as a matter of course to his slow bowlers while Mold kept his sweater on. Eckersley, with good sense, asked Hopwood to send down the first over of the day. Then Preston achieved an over which he is not likely to forget in a hurry. It contained three no-balls, two of which were hit drastically to long-leg for six by Sutcliffe. Each no-ball was a long-hop. I thought the over was never going to end; Preston probably suffered an age of perplexity as he went through it. In half an hour before lunch Yorkshire scored 29 for none. Holmes cut Hopwood late from a ball which popped significantly. Also Holmes pulled Preston square in handsome style. The batting was very militant, as though Holmes and Sutcliffe were determined to lay Lancashire's attack completely out before the pitch became really bad. Hopwood and Preston both pitched a length far too short for the pace of the moist unpleasant earth.

Before Holmes and Sutcliffe returned to the wicket after lunch I observed Hopwood spinning the ball a foot, and even Duckworth with gloves on could achieve a pretty break. But persistently did Lancashire pitch a short length, and Holmes pulled safely against Tyldesley's leg-break—a certain sign of bad bowling. Hopwood's pace through the air was too quick both for the use of flight or of spin. Sutcliffe and Holmes scored 50 in just under an hour, and then Holmes got himself out. Tyldesley pitched him a leg-break outside the off stump; it slightly popped, and Holmes followed the ball and touched it to Watson, who made a clever falling catch at slip. Holmes played like a great batsman; he lost his wicket through eagerness to score—a palpable characteristic of the great batsman. At five minutes to three Tyldesley bowled a superb ball to Sutcliffe, whose score was now 37. The ball drew the batsman forward and whipped away at a great speed. Curiously enough, Tyldesley did not apparently see the implications behind this ball, for he proceeded to drop his attack well in front of the bat, so that Sutcliffe and Oldroyd could watch the break with time to spare. Hardly ever was either Sutcliffe or Oldroyd compelled to play forward and fall for the spin; the bowling was phenomenally bad. Eckersley gave his men every chance. He rang the changes judiciously on Tyldesley, Hopwood, and Iddon, exploiting them in turn at different ends of the wicket, but not one bowler was able to find the length which makes a batsman lunge out speculatively.

The climax of an afternoon of a wretched waste of sensitive turf came when Hopwood let loose three consecutive full-tosses, from which 11 runs were hit. At the other end of the pitch Iddon sent a gorgeous long-hop, and of course it went for four. Next over Hopwood dropped a ball halfway down the pitch, and Oldroyd again smashed a boundary with obvious exultation. In the same over a ball of identical length—Mr. Croome would have called it a polyhop—was at the on boundary as quickly and powerfully as good willow could send it there.

If I ever see Puddleton-on-the-Water bowling as badly as Lancashire have bowled this afternoon I shall immediately conclude that Puddleton's best bowler is away on his holidays. After tea Iddon, by accident or design, pitched a length that drew Oldroyd forward; the consequence was a catch to second slip. From this one ball we could conclude safely that, had Lancashire's left-handed bowlers been to-day half as clever as Harry Dean, Yorkshire would not have scored a hundred all out.

Oldroyd and Sutcliffe added 79 for the second wicket in an hour and a half. Oldroyd strained his left groin trying to hit one of the afternoon's multitudinous long-hops out of the field. He played sound cricket in spite of the bowling's many temptations to play dissolutely. The student of cricket could draw enlightening conclusions from the fact that several times Tyldesley and Hopwood and Iddon were driven to the on by means of full-length drives. Strokes such as these, made against spin that was leaving the bat, would have been suicidal if the length had pitched just short of the half-volley. On a wicket at all moist the very worst kind of bowling is short bowling. Hopwood's full-tosses reminded me of Ted Wainwright's comment to the young bowler who excused a bad performance by saying that the wicket would not take spin: 'Thee and thy spin! I never saw thi hit t'floor.' It may be that to-day's wicket has not been definitely sticky: it was, however, convenient for turning the ball. Now and again a ball dropped well forward and then we invariably saw the batsman groping and playing with his bat's edge. These balls occurred according to that law of average that causes the worst bowler occasionally to find a nasty length. On to-day's turf Rhodes would have taken many wickets. If the ball did not spin waspishly it turned quite as awkwardly as it did on Saturday when Leyland bowled. Unfortunately Lancashire either could not hit the floor or they hit it too soon. Sutcliffe defended with much of his old charm of style and reached 50 in two hours.

Sutcliffe hit the third six of the day at a quarter-past five, a glorious straight drive off the unfortunate Hopwood. I submit that three sixes in one afternoon of a Yorkshire and Lancashire match is a desecration of a great tradition. With Leyland in we heard the fierce cracking of a cricket bat. He drove beautifully and savagely to the off, and the crowd roared the old Yorkshire roar. At twenty past five Sutcliffe smote another grotesque long-hop to leg for four, and now Lancashire's score was passed. In the next over Leyland was splendidly caught at deep long-off from a drive that nearly knocked Taylor, the fieldsman, over the rails. In 40 minutes Sutcliffe and Leyland scored 64, and Leyland's share was 42—a blasphemous innings for this ancient and most quiet engagement. Yorkshire were now 196 for three, and only one wicket had been taken by Lancashire by a worthy ball. When Sutcliffe was 92 Iddon completely beat his bat with a ball which whipped away after dropping well up the pitch. Here was yet another hint of the deadly way Rhodes would have bowled this afternoon. Apart from a sequence of good overs by Tyldesley just after lunch, Lancashire's attack utterly squandered a golden opportunity to confuse and confound the old enemy. Macdonald's inability to bowl turned out a misfortune for Lancashire after all, but to say that much is gravely to indict the team's slow bowlers, especially the left-handers. I doubt whether Macdonald could have made use of the wicket: it was not quick enough for the ball that turns into the bat.

Sutcliffe reached his hundred in four hours, an innings which was a triumph of temperament over a by-no-means perfect technique. As soon as he attained his heart's desire

Sutcliffe was badly missed by Hallows, and next ball he jumped out of his ground and was stumped—recklessness so out of keeping with Sutcliffe that I marvelled at it. In the day's closing hour Yorkshire went for the bowling and threw wickets away like a side fully satisfied that it was leading by enough runs to win in an innings. The game degenerated into the hit-or-miss jollity of the village green. It was all positively vulgar. Even Emmott Robinson scored 28 in 15 minutes. This innings must be regarded as the one blemish in an otherwise unimpeachable career.

Richard Tyldesley stuck to his work manfully, though the wicket was not of the kind a leg-break bowler enjoys. After tea Lancashire for the most part went deplorably to pieces; little attempt seemed to be made to stop the rate of Yorkshire's scoring.

THIRD DAY

Rain in the small hours of this morning made a morass of the Bradford wicket, and there was no play on the closing day of the Lancashire and Yorkshire match. It is possible that Lancashire escaped defeat by an innings, for had the weather kept fine the pitch this afternoon would have been well nigh unplayable.

Lancashire deserved to lose points; their bowling on Monday was so bad that only those who actually saw it can have any idea of its phenomenal looseness. Eckersley did all that captaincy possibly could do, but it was not in his power to compel his bowlers to keep a good length. He rightly trusted to his slow spin-bowlers, and though in the closing hour of Monday he might have kept the runs down by putting on Preston again—and this is by no means certain—a move so defensive on a bowler's wicket would have seemed a confession of weakness. Given a pitch sensitive to spin, one could scarcely wish for more than three bowlers who can turn the ball away from the bat, as Tyldesley, Iddon and Hopwood each can turn it. On Monday they all made the ball break away, but, unfortunately, they all pitched so short a length that the batsmen were free to lie back and watch the spin with time to spare. Hopwood rang the changes on his short stuff by bowling full tosses. Even Tyldesley, who knows well enough most days how to flight a ball, pitched short on Monday.

There seems nowadays a notion amongst bowlers to the effect that you must not toss the ball up on 'sticky' wickets, for fear the batsmen might be given easy runs. The fashionable plan is to bowl on the short side, with a man at 'silly point' to make catches from the occasional ball that jumps up. Rhodes has never exploited tactics so negative as this on a bowler's turf. He told me yesterday that the best ball a left-handed slow bowler can possibly send down on a sticky pitch is a spinning half-volley. No 'silly' point silliness is required when Rhodes is at work on a sensitive turf. You would imagine that every young left-handed slow bowler would be proud and satisfied to follow the example of Rhodes. When Rhodes has retired from cricket it is likely there will be nobody left to sustain the ancient art of left-handed bowling in which a full curving flight is as important a factor as the break itself. At the present time there is not one young bowler in the land who knows how to 'flight' a cricket ball.

SCORES
LANCASHIRE
First Innings

Hallows, c Bowes, b Robinson	5
Watson, c Barber (A.), b Leyland	44
Tyldesley (E.), c Barber (W.), b Leyland	12
Iddon, c Robinson, b Leyland	5
Makepeace, c Barber (A.), b Leyland	68
Hopwood, lbw, b Leyland	2
P. T. Eckersley, b Macaulay	4
Duckworth, run out	28
Tyldesley (R.), c Barber (W.), b Leyland	0
Macdonald, c Holmes, b Leyland	4
Preston, not out	1
Extras b13, lb2, nb4	19
	—
Total	192

YORKSHIRE
First Innings

Holmes, c Watson, b Tyldesley (R.)	22
Sutcliffe, st Duckworth, b Tyldesley (R.)	106
Oldroyd, c Hopwood, b Iddon	36
Leyland, c sub, b Watson	42
A. T. Barber, st Duckworth, b Tyldesley (R.)	14
Wood, lbw, b Iddon	6
Dennis, st Duckworth, b Tyldesley (R.)	5
Barber (W.), not out	15
Robinson, not out	28
Extras b8, lb1, nb2	11
	—
Total (for 7)	285

YORKSHIRE V LANCASHIRE 1929
BOWLING ANALYSIS

LANCASHIRE—First Innings

	O.	M.	R.	W.		O.	M.	R.	W.
Bowes	16	5	22	0	Leyland	36	14	52	7
Robinson	24	8	47	1	Dennis	7	1	18	0
Macaulay	20	6	34	1					

YORKSHIRE—First Innings

	O.	M.	R.	W.		O.	M.	R.	W.
Preston	4	2	17	0	Iddon	28	13	47	2
Hopwood	27	9	82	0	Watson	11	5	16	1
Tyldesley (R.)	34	7	112	4					

YORKSHIRE V LANCASHIRE 1930

June 7/9/10   Leeds

FIRST DAY

THERE were strange and outrageous doings at Leeds on Saturday. We came as near as anything to seeing 400 runs made on the very first day of a Lancashire and Yorkshire match. What is more, we actually did see two hits for six in one over. Leyland was the cricketer thus to abuse an austere tradition; Like Roy Kilner, Leyland has never seemed quite to realise that a game between Lancashire and Yorkshire is no laughing matter. Had it not been for an innings by Sutcliffe, Saturday would have been most reprehensibly indecorous. Sutcliffe saw to it that honour was done to the proper and ancient spirit of the occasion; he batted two hours and twenty minutes for 40. He made every ball sent to him look difficult; his cricket was like Mr. Tite Barnacle, 'buttoned up and weighty.' Sutcliffe did his best to keep in fashion the headlines which are always prepared by the newspapers for matches between Lancashire and Yorkshire. 'Dour Struggle at Headingley.' Yet even Sutcliffe cannot always convey to us the impression of a congenital severity. Now and again, on Saturday, he let us admire a pretty stroke, even a gracious one. He reminded me of Miss Barbary—if he had ever smiled he would have been an angel but he never really did smile.

There was another reason for our thinking we had mistaken the day and the occasion. Not more than 8,000 people paid for admission. As late in the afternoon as four o'clock it was possible for anybody to walk round the ground and pick and choose a pleasant seat. After the lunch interval I watched the game from a bench on the popular side; I was almost alone, my feet in long grass, the hot sun on my face. The scene was peaceful; only the crack of Leyland's busy bat disturbed the calm of an afternoon in June. Gone the old clamour and tumult of battles long ago! Today it will be Lancashire's duty to make a stand for traditional grimness.

284

On a Whitsun Bank Holiday surely there will be the authentic multitude, eager to suffer tormenting hours, willing to bear the heavy cross as of yore. Lancashire must get down on their bats and wipe out the memory of Saturday's lapse from historic gravity.

Until the luncheon interval the match promised well to pay respect to the unities, thanks, as I have written, to Sutcliffe. The engagement began in the appropriate funerary key. Holmes lost his wicket straightway, and came home to the pavilion in the silence which, on a Yorkshire cricket field, signifies much that is eloquent. Holmes' innings began and finished with dramatic sharpness; it was all over before you could say Jack or rather Emmott Robinson. He hit a short ball in Macdonald's first over for four to pull to square leg. Then with Yorkshire's score not more than 17, he was caught by Duckworth off a ball from Sibbles, which made surprising pace from the pitch. It was a very easy pitch, prepared under the most modern of anaesthetics. Macdonald did not for long try to bowl fast on it; he exploited off breaks at a pace which gave two of his four slips little to do but try to look impressive. For a while Macdonald was a very able medium paced bowler, but as the day passed by his attack seemed a mistaken waste of energy over a long period. Better for Lancashire surely had he concentrated his efforts into one or two bursts of real speed and temper. It was ironical to see Oldroyd, the moment he came in, playing Macdonald with leisure to spare. The whirligig of Time brings its revenges! Oldroyd cut and drove quite impertinently; a leg hit off Richard Tyldesley was actually contemptuous. In an hour and a half Oldroyd and Sutcliffe made 77 for Yorkshire's. second wicket. Then, just on lunch, Oldroyd hooked a long hop from Macdonald into Taylor's hands at forward square leg. He had, a few balls previously, achieved the same stroke rather recklessly. During twelve consecutive summers I have written many thousands of words about Lancashire and Yorkshire cricket, but never before have I, to my recollection, had occasion in these reports to use that blessed word 'recklessness'.

After the luncheon interval the match for a period went Lancashire's way, almost imperceptibly. Sutcliffe snicked an out-swinger and was caught by Duckworth at 121. Leyland from the first ball bowled in the afternoon looked like a cricketer at the top of his form. He drove handsomely to the off. And one of his first boundaries was a square cut aimed at a wide ball from Macdonald. Cutting in a Lancashire and Yorkshire match! Bless us, what are we coming to? Barber, by means of a stiff, straight bat, helped Leyland to put on 48 for Yorkshire's fourth wicket; he fell a victim to Tyldesley's leg-before-wicket dodge. Mitchell held on while Leyland scored 27; and then sent the simplest of catches to Macdonald at mid-on. Yorkshire had now lost five good batsmen for 197 on a flawless wicket; Leyland was 66. Lancashire's need hereabout was a fierce onslaught on Emmott Robinson's bat—and also on his pads—by a bowler unambiguously fast. Robinson plainly came forth determined to stay with Leyland or, in the attempt, to die the hero's death, which, of course, is called lbw in these encounters. He was perhaps fortunate to get the benefit of an appeal almost before he had scored. Then he not only settled down to obstinate defence; he found opportunity here and there for a really skittish cut through the slips.

Leyland proceeded to play great and beautiful cricket. His strokes always beat the Lancashire field; from the moment his bat hit the ball they went over the grass at a pace most lovely and thrilling to see. He was persistently taking a chance. I do not think he would for long have resisted the challenge of a clever bowler pitching a tempting length to a packed off-side field. But, frankly, the Lancashire attack did not seem ever to work according to a plan. Over after over was bowled piecemeal, so to say; when the good ball went along it seemed scarcely designed; there was no context to put before Leyland, not only a technical problem but a strategical problem as well. Leyland drove at a ball from Watson straight over the screen for six when his score stood at 44. In the same over he drove another six, again a straight hit, but this time a little to the off. One of Leyland's drives from Richard Tyldesley was apparently so beautiful it rendered Macdonald at long-off quite lost and immobile through aesthetic contemplation. Not for many years have I seen in a Lancashire and Yorkshire match any batsmanship so free and so clean in its power, so pretty in its sweep and curve, as this of Leyland. It was like a light thrown back from the golden age of Spooner, Garnett, Denton and Hirst. Before the war there were usually half a dozen Lancashire and Yorkshire cricketers, who when face to face, no matter how 'dour' the day, did not deny their hearts, their true skill, and the genius of cricket.

Leyland's innings, the first hundred runs of it especially, held the secret of our summer game; you could understand, while watching, how it came to pass in the old years, that cricket won the affection of the nation and put us all under a charm. Here was rare skill, but not a tyrannical skill that placed the spirit of delight into bondage. Leyland was always playing a game, always taking the risks without which there can be no sport whatsoever. The good balls found him as watchful as Emmott Robinson himself, but at the first sight of a long hop or half volley his bat was lifted up behind him. There was a boyish eagerness about Leyland's innings, which it did the eyes good to see and the heart good to feel. There was lustre and there was licence; artistry and adventure. Leyland's first instinctive move with his bat was to hit the ball, he played the strict defensive stroke only as a last resort. His drives to the off were at one and the same time sturdy and stylish. He swept the overtossed ball to leg in the happy old fashioned way. He did not, until he arrived at his hundred, allow the outline of a finished technique to become blunted by the too hurried breath of impulse. He batted only two hours and a quarter for his hundred, which he reached by a glorious drive to the on from Sibbles. At 118 he gave his first chance: a fairly easy catch to Hopwood at long on, from Richard Tyldesley's bowling.

Leyland and Robinson held Yorkshire's sixth wicket for an hour and a half and scored 115. The partnership was a most refreshing instance of how a cricket match can be pulled out of a dangerous situation by cricketers of skill and faith. Robinson ought to have been run out some forty runs before the stand was broken. Robinson clearly enjoyed his innings, not only his neat strokes, but his one or two narrow escapes from a leg-before-wicket decision. Leyland was unbeaten at the sunny afternoon's end; he lost something of control of stroke while he was proceeding from his 100 to his 150 in less than an hour. Macdonald might have caught him from the drive that made his score 150. But Macdonald is not an out-fielder, and in fairness to him he ought never to be sent into the deep which is not the most convenient place in which to rest the right arm of a bowler. So far, Leyland's innings has lasted three hours and fifty minutes and he has hit two sixes and 17 fours.

Yorkshire's 360 for eight wickets means a heavy task for Lancashire today, for despite the absence of Macaulay through injury, Yorkshire's attack will be keenly tempered. And it is not certain that the Headingley wicket will remain to the end of the match as smooth and as docile as it was throughout Saturday.

The quietness of the afternoon, the absence of the old multitudinous clamour, gave cause for reflection. Has this match since the war got on the people's nerves? Have patience and expectancy been worn out? A crowd of some 12,000 (including members) is a poor gathering for Lancashire and Yorkshire at Whitsuntide. Not only were the numbers few; more remarkable was the flat atmosphere. Leyland's innings galvanised dullness a little, but seldom if ever did the crowd give us the Yorkshire roar that once on a time would shake the air as George Hirst got down on his right knee and pulled a ball from Brearley to the on-boundary. Have we grown out of the heroic age or is it that there are nowadays no heroes left to stir us and fill our eyes with visions? Leyland was as fine a batsman on Saturday as any seen of old. But you cannot make an epic out of one man's fate and fortunes. In the pre-war years, every cricketer in these games seemed touched with greatness; even the scullions had genius. And the crowds were ready to collaborate, they believed in their heroes. On Saturday I actually saw two small boys reading their 'crook' stories while Leyland batted; they merely watched the match out of the corner of their eyes. Lord the way we used to go to Lancashire and Yorkshire matches when we were very young and on holiday at Whitsuntide! We got to the ground at nine o'clock in the morning, after a night disturbed by dreams either of wet weather or of Hirst and Rhodes. I remember one night before a Whit Monday when time after time I got out of bed to look at the sky. It was moonlit and calm, but I feared to go to sleep and leave it, lest clouds should steal up the heavens behind my back. I remember the joy that visited me at dawn, when once again I rushed to the bedroom window and saw the silent streets outside gleaming in sunshine. Cricket was safe now, Lancashire and Yorkshire, Reggie Spooner and MacLaren—and a crowded day of romance. Did we live in a simple credulous world then, too easy to please?

SECOND DAY

There was the proper crowd here today, very Yorkshire in aspect and accent, and most of them assembled early on a lovely June day to see whether Leyland would reach a score of 200. Rhodes was there as Leyland's helpmate, sturdy as ever and playing in this great game for the last time on Yorkshire soil. Rhodes as a No. 10 batsmen stirs the memory and also sets the imagination at work on some picture of the great wheel of the man's career coming a full circle. When Rhodes first played for Yorkshire 32 years ago his place in the order of going in was No. 10. Since those Victorian times Rhodes has opened the England innings magnificently, and now, in the summer of his passing from cricket, he is back to the place where as a batsman he began. He hit a boundary in Macdonald's first over this morning—a forward push of rare ease and ripeness. Macdonald's bowling suffered severe belabouring; fourteen runs came from twelve balls at the day's outset, but he compelled Rhodes to play a break-back on to his stumps when Yorkshire were 393 and Leyland was 194.

Yorkshire's last batsman, name of Bowes, thus had to face a responsible situation; he came to the middle knowing well that if he got out quickly a Yorkshire multitude would be mortified because Leyland was obviously about to share Reggie Spooner's honour of being the only cricketer to make 200 runs in a single innings in Lancashire and Yorkshire matches. Bowes, looking an inconsequential Mr. Toots, put his bat to the ball cool as a master. At high noon Leyland drove Macdonald straight for four and arrived at his heart's desire. His innings last in all only four hours and a half. An easy chance at 118 was an insignificant flaw in a splendid and happy exhibition of real cricket. It was good to think that Spooner's distinction had extended not to some covetous stonewaller but to a true son of the game. Leyland hit two sixes, 22 fours, and only one three. That solitary three speaks eloquently of Leyland's timing and placing, also of the speed of the Headingley outfield.

The bowling was merely moderate, and, without in the least attempting a disparagement of Leyland's cricket, I suggest that the Lancashire attack was at fault in not scheming consistently to get Leyland caught on the off side. He is a batsman always ready to take up the challenge of a ball pitched wide of the wicket. The Lancashire bowlers sent him too many balls which he was able to drive almost from where he stood—at any rate he had not often to 'go after' them with a cross bat.

At half-past twelve Lancashire began an innings which had little hope to live for but long labour uphill. I contemplated the crowd and wondered what they had come out for to see. My own way of spending a Bank Holiday would not be watching Lancashire batting against a Yorkshire score of more than 400. With the wicket easy and docile, immense faith in Yorkshire bowling was needed to envisage a Lancashire collapse.

Hallows and Watson from half past twelve until lunch gave the crowd no cause for optimism or for any other of human nature's more volatile emotions. Canny bats were thrust to every ball, good, bad or indifferent. The match was at last itself again and the faint noise of the barracker was heard in the land. Just before lunch Hallows might have been run out had the ball been thrown accurately down the wicket, but this was the only incident in an hour of cricket composed of the stuff of poppy and mandragora. At the end of this hour Lancashire were 42, Hallows 20 and Watson 10. Each batsman played the right game for Lancashire; for myself, I enjoyed the humour of it all, for humour certainly came in by reason of the contrast between what the crowd was hoping to see and what they were actually getting. The afternoon's charm and pleasantry were increased by a wind which caused dust and grit to get into the eyes and mouth.

At half past two precisely Hallows sent a very easy catch from Rhodes to Barber at forward short-leg. It was a ball of lovely flight and curve. Hallows played forward—and Barber reached out his hands and let the ball slip to the ground. The howls of the crowd were, as Mrs. Gamp might have said, 'organs': the crowd was indeed having a most delectable holiday. As Barber dropped his catch Emmott Robinson stood at mid-on still as a statue: his arms were folded like resignation's own wings. He seemed to be contemplating the vanity of all mortal doings. How many of his grey hairs have grown during Lancashire matches of his experience! When Hallows was given this second innings his score was 27 and Lancashire were 51 for none.

The batsmen took no risk against Rhodes' slow balls, and I thought of the days when David Denton waited eagerly in the deep field for big hits from Rhodes. He would wait in vain in this year of grace. Other times other manners!

I am writing this sentence at three o'clock and I am willing to risk nonsense being made of them by any subsequent event during the day. No batsman will be caught in the deep field: I am quite easy in my mind about that. Lancashire, as I say, were playing the proper political game—and if the crowd did not like it they were under no compulsion to stay. The situation of the match this morning promised a day of grim strokeless cricket. The crowd ought to have been grateful that they had a fine day for it. At three o'clock Rhodes' bowling analysis was—fifteen overs, ten maidens, seven runs, and no wickets.

I did not notice the seven runs scored from him; a man cannot hope to see everything on these historic occasions. Then three o'clock struck, and the crowd at last found momentary release from tedium and longing. Robinson began to bowl slow off-breaks from round the wicket. Hallows lashed out—yes—he actually lashed out wildly—at a ball well up to his bat. He was clean bowled. And from the very next ball Ernest Tyldesley was caught at forward short leg by Barber. The crowd definitely woke up now and roared itself hoarse. At the sudden downfall of Tyldesley, Emmott Robinson sat on the grass and laughed a laugh of enormous satisfaction, but not unmixed with incredulity.

At the end of nearly two hours of stern self-denial Lancashire were 68 for two. Perhaps before the day is over they will have cause to think that, whatever the state of a cricket match, there's nothing like a batsman who is sensible and skilful enough to play every ball on its merits. Even when your side is fighting against a high score and the clock as well, a bad ball remains a bad ball. Lancashire to-day seemed deliberately set upon stonewalling each ball that came along, stonewalling it on principle. Watson, after he had batted two hours for 20, apparently began to realise that runs might, after all, help substantially the cause of Lancashire. He hit two fours in consecutive overs from Robinson and Dennis. Also he pulled a long hop from Leyland to the boundary.

It frequently happens at cricket that a batsman defeats his own patient purpose. Watson actually lost his wicket by driving indiscreetly at a full-toss from Leyland. He got the ball too high up the bat and was cleverly caught at mid-off by Barber. Watson's innings of 36 lasted nearly two hours and a half. I firmly believe there is some law of reaction which lures the too wary batsman into some ultimate and fatal act of carelessness.

At 99 Lancashire were fortunate not to lose Hopwood caught at the wicket from Robinson; the snick went for two and Lancashire's total became 101 after two hours and forty minutes of severe and unsmiling effort. Lancashire's caution had become more than a little excessive. Hallows and Watson did well to pay respect to the bowling while it was fresh but later in the day it dwindled to mildness. Robinson was given full licence to pitch a slow off-break to three leg fieldsman almost on the batsman's premises. Ernest Tyldesley lost his wicket to one of these off-breaks through a misuse of the dead bat. He dabbed at the ball too hard. If he had chanced a true stroke he could not have fared worse than lose his wicket, while some Yorkshire men might have needed carrying out on a shutter. County batsmen ought to be capable of hitting half-volleys whatever a match's situation. MacLaren or John Tyldesley or Spooner or Leyland would have knocked the cover off the ball this afternoon, or have gladly perished in the attempt. To say this much is not to argue or to maintain but simply to make a plain obvious statement. Yorkshire's attack—mediocre in the absence of Macaulay—has this day been flattered out of all reason. In two hours and a quarter between lunch and tea Lancashire scored 78 runs.

For an hour Iddon and Hopwood defended Lancashire's fourth wicket; then at 127 Rhodes drew Iddon over his crease and Wood stumped the victim. Greater birds have fallen to this alluring snare of the old falconer Rhodes. At half-past five Rhodes had bowled 30 overs, 20 maidens, for 15 runs and one wicket. The issue was precariously poised when Taylor joined Hopwood in a stand for the fifth wicket. Hopwood's methods were those of common sense, for, though his bat was never free, he lost no opportunity to score useful runs by ones and twos to leg and through the slips. Taylor let us refresh our eyes at the sight of a gracefully swung bat. As soon as he came in I knew I had been venturesome in prophesying that no Lancashire batsman would to-day be caught in the deep field. I had indeed forgotten that Taylor was playing in this game when I risked my ironical forecast; he has not yet been broken in. His cricket to-day was delightful. Hopwood's score reached 50 after he had batted two hours and ten minutes. His innings was an admirable instance of the old head on young shoulders. The afternoon dragged drearily to its close, and when the end came the relief was considerable, but Lancashire's position still had a lugubrious look. There will be more hard labour tomorrow.

THIRD DAY

Cricketers at Leeds this morning were saddened by the news of the death of Sir Frederick Toone, Yorkshire's distinguished and most courteous secretary. I believe that in committee the question was discussed whether the match ought not to be forthwith abandoned. It was resumed at ten minutes to twelve after a short delay caused by a wicket slightly moist, following rain which had not been anything like as heavy as that which we had in Manchester on Monday night and early on Tuesday morning.

Hopwood and Sibbles proceeded with Lancashire's task of making 68 runs to save a follow-on with four wickets in hand.

Fifteen runs trickled over the field in half an hour, and then Sibbles played a ball from Bowes into his stumps. Duckworth was now Hopwood's helpmate; these two cricketers seemed very sure of themselves on the easy pitch. The Yorkshire bowling lacked sting; Rhodes in vain tossed up the most seductive balls. In fifty minutes Hopwood and Duckworth added 35 before Duckworth was caught at mid-off trying a very aggressive stroke. Richard Tyldesley straightway hit a catch to Sutcliffe at deep long-off, a piece of surprising recklessness seeing that Lancashire still needed 16 to save the follow-on. Macdonald, the last man in, placed Hopwood under no compulsion to scheme to keep the bowling; he pulled and drove Robinson for two quite contemptuous boundaries in a single over. Whereat Robinson's leg trap decided as one man to retire to a position discreetly at a distance from Macdonald's bat. Macdonald by a leg hit for two completely dispelled Yorkshire's faint prospect of victory by an innings. Then, just on lunch, Hopwood reached his hundred, an innings of sterling value. For four hours he was all patience and watchfulness; he watched the ball scientifically, seldom, if ever, committing an error of judgment, and generally conducting himself with the coolness and circumspection of a veteran. His stroke play, though never free, was almost always following to a nicety the intentions of a mind determined not to be disturbed from an obstinate policy for a single moment.

Lancashire's last wicket was not taken by Yorkshire until it had made fifty-three runs in just over half an hour; it was good to see Lancashire's tail end fighting hard against an enemy which in the old days was usually much too quick to knock a Lancashire innings clean out the moment the fifth wicket fell. Lancashire's innings lasted six hours and a half; Rhodes bowled forty-four overs, thirty-two maidens for 19 runs and 1 wicket.

Rain prevented Yorkshire's second innings from beginning until just on four o'clock. Macdonald then bowled one over from which six runs were scored. Here followed a scene of some mild comedy. The players came off the field, presumably because a drizzle was falling or about to fall. The crowd hooted disapproval, and the umpires declined to leave the middle. Whereupon, after having reached the pavilion and disappeared from sight, the players right-about-turned, and marched into action again to the mingled cheers and hoots of a small but very Yorkshire multitude. Straightway Sutcliffe was out, brilliantly and gracefully caught in the slips by Macdonald. Rain came again at this point, and this time heavily and decisively. Yorkshire thus won five points out of the match and Lancashire three. What an ado about next to nothing!

SCORES

YORKSHIRE

First Innings		Second Innings	
Holmes, c Duckworth, b Sibbles	9	not out	4
Sutcliffe, c Duckworth, b Macdonald	40	c Macdonald, b Sibbles	7
Oldroyd, c Taylor, b Macdonald	49		
Leyland, not out	211		
A. T. Barber, lbw, b Tyldesley (R.)	17		
Mitchell, c Macdonald, b Tyldesley (R.)	6		
Robinson, c Tyldesley (E.), b Hopwood	41		
Wood, b Hopwood	13		
Dennis, lbw, b Hopwood	0		
Rhodes, b Macdonald	13		
Bowes, not out	6		
Extras	12		
Total (for 9)	*417	Total (for 1)	11

*Innings declared

THE ROSES MATCHES 1919-1939
LANCASHIRE

First Innings

Watson, b Barber, b Leyland	36
Hallows, b Robinson	33
Tyldesley (E.), c Barber, b Robinson	0
Iddon, st Wood, b Rhodes	20
Hopwood, not out	107
Taylor, c Holmes, b Robinson	21
Eckersley, b Leyland	19
Sibbles, b Bowes	4
Duckworth, c Barber, b Leyland	13
Tyldesley (R.), c Sutcliffe, b Leyland	0
Macdonald, c Rhodes, b Bowes	34
Extras	18
	—
Total	305

BOWLING ANALYSIS

YORKSHIRE—First Innings

	O.	M.	R.	W.		O.	M.	R.	W.
Macdonald	37	6	109	3	Hopwood	30	4	64	3
Sibbles	37	4	106	1	Watson	6	1	22	0
Tyldesley (R.)	32	6	93	2	Iddon	5	2	11	0

Second Innings

	O.	M.	R.	W.		O.	M.	R.	W.
Macdonald	2	0	9	0	Sibbles	1·2	0	2	1

LANCASHIRE—First Innings

	O.	M.	R.	W.		O.	M.	R.	W.
Robinson	55	15	126	3	Rhodes	44	32	19	1
Bowes	32	10	59	2	Leyland	19	5	49	4
Dennis	19	5	34	0					

YORKSHIRE V LANCASHIRE   1930

August 2/4/5   Old Trafford

FIRST DAY

I N five hours, on an easy wicket and despite the most commonplace Yorkshire attack I have ever seen—an attack several times in the day troubled by a wet ball—Lancashire scored 218 for two. At lunch after one hundred minutes of dour cricket—'dour,' I believe, is the approved word for these occasions though I have a better one—Lancashire were 57 for the loss of Makepeace. Watson in an hour secreted eight runs exactly. Now all this statistical information might well seem to lay a solemn charge against the sportsmanship of Lancashire. But let us try to be charitable, and seek for extenuating causes. Perhaps our batsmen were playing according to some deep strategical purpose. Perhaps, before the match started the whole of the Lancashire eleven were addressed in the councils of the pavilion thuswise: 'Now boys, we want you today to curb a natural impetuosity, just for once. This is a solemn engagement, and much as we understand how hard it will be for you to deny yourselves a deep-rooted delight in breaking a cricket bat, nevertheless we appeal to you to make every effort (until Monday after lunch at any rate) NOT to get in the least violent or reckless while at the wicket.'

Or maybe the Yorkshire attack was not ordinary after all. And who knows for certain that the pitch was not quite unplayable for hours at a stretch? Perhaps the ball was jumping and shooting and spinning and swerving and stopping in the air, hovering like a hideous bird of prey before swooping down to the earth. Why, even when Oldroyd came on to bowl, with Lancashire's score 191 for two, his analysis after he had let five overs go circling out of his crafty right hand was: O5—M4—R1—W0. There's richness for you! Why haven't we heard before of Oldroyd as an England bowler; why are his subtle arts not known to the Selection Committee? A telegram ought to be sent to

297

Bradman: 'The game is up at last.' But this is irrelevance; moreover I am treating with flippancy a very austere occasion. (On Saturday a correspondent from Todmorden wrote to tell me that in his part of the world they often refuse Yorkshire pudding with their roast beef at this time of the year.) You cannot, of course, hope to keep high spirits altogether out of a Lancashire and Yorkshire match. The Lancashire batsmen even forgot themselves for a while on Saturday—and incidentally gave their absurd solemnity away. After lunch no fewer than sixty runs were made in an hour—safely made without a shadow of a risk. Again, after tea, thanks to some brilliant cutting by Iddon, runs flashed over the field for half an hour—flashed so stylishly that my mind was set thinking of the Canterbury festival miles away, a most delectable place and time of the season. (Think of it. Lancashire once on a time used to play Yorkshire on August Bank Holiday, and then the same week take part in the Canterbury Festival! More remarkable still, played there as brilliantly as Kent themselves, in the times when Marsham and Kenneth Hutchings and Tyldesley and Spooner loved to live dangerously at the wicket.)

It is a fair inference, from the two animated pieces of batsmanship accomplished by Lancashire on Saturday, that there was no serious reason, save an habitual lack of humour and imagination in these days, why Lancashire should not have scored before close of play at least 300. I decline to believe that Watson has so few strokes that in nearly three hours he can hit only three boundaries from mediocre bowling. And rather than believe that Oldroyd has the skill to deliver four consecutive maiden overs on an easy wicket—why, I'd rather believe that the public is foolish enough not to find out sooner or later that the Lancashire and Yorkshire match is an engagement to ignore, to stay away from—or to laugh out of existence. Yet it was a great match once; I say this for the benefit of the many small boys who were present on Saturday. Lancashire no doubt often went down in those days before the strong left arm of George Hirst, yet Spooner once made 200 in an afternoon, while the other men of Lancashire achieved something of immortality. Our modern players are not easily defeated, but their mulish ways will earn them little but mulish posterity. Again, though, I am wandering from the subject of the present match; the temptations to do so are many.

Hallows, at his own request, stood down from the Lancashire side. Makepeace went in first with Watson; Emmott Robinson bowled the first ball, then gathered in his two hands a load of sawdust and put it on to the moist earth and flattened it out with his own two cricket boots. Robinson flung himself at the wicket with all the familiar vehemence, as though to say 'If Ah can't get thi out, Ah'll mek thi a miserable man somehow'. Robinson caused the new ball to swerve at least a foot wide of the off; his was the only bowling I saw all day which obviously could not be hit safely at any time. Makepeace played with much of his old honest and intimate craftsmanship until he was caught by the stumper from a ball by Bowes which pitched on or near the wicket and rose sharply.

The action all day was broken by showers; they came suddenly, and sometimes they were gone before the cricketers had quite got into the pavilion. A stampede to cover before lunch was one of the quickest events of the morning. The damp grass was all in favour of the batsmen whose ease in defence was an eloquent commentary upon the general scarcity of scoring strokes.

After lunch Ernest Tyldesley cut Bowes square, a gorgeous hit which rattled against the rails even while Chester was making his own graceful if rhetorical signal of a boundary hit. (Besides, a boundary hit in a Lancashire and Yorkshire match is rhetorical.) Watson took warmth from Tyldesley and drove Rhodes magnificently to the on. Another great stroke—a cut by Watson—compelled a man in the crowd to cry out 'Beautiful!' in a frenzy of aesthetic emotion. I wondered when did this man last have occasion to use the word 'beautiful' in his daily speech? At a quarter past two Lancashire were 57 for one; at a quarter past three they were 111 for one. Watson reached 50 after he had been on view for two hours and forty minutes. At 113 Watson was caught at square leg from a long hop bowled by Leyland. Watson hit the ball hard, but not hard enough; it went straight to Bowes, who let it jump out of his hands, caught it again, fumbled it a second time, and at last gripped it firmly—the sort of catch which gives a fieldsman terrible shocks all in a fleeting second: 'Got it!—missed it!—no!—it's gone!—ah! thank God!'

Tyldesley, when obviously at the top of his form, stopped getting runs; he was half an hour moving from 44 to 47. The bowling did not reveal the slightest cause for Tyldesley's change of method and mood. Iddon began with a tentativeness dreadful to see. Then, after the tea interval, while the bowlers were entirely at a loss, gripping a greasy ball, he batted as finely as I have ever seen him bat. He hit two fours from one over by Leyland and in the next over from the same bowler he achieved a late cut of rare power and swiftness. In 25 minutes no fewer than 32 runs were scored—prodigious, though not unprecedented on these occasions, for as recently as Whitsuntide Yorkshire, having won the toss, played true cricket and, on the first day of the match, knocked Lancashire's bowling all over the field, not only for half an hour but for almost a whole day. Lancashire had only their own witnesses to blame that on Saturday they did not take a handsome revenge from the old enemy—and incidentally open out the way to victory outright in a game which, had it been tackled in a chivalrous spirit, might easily have given Old Trafford the match of the season and the county championship as well. Tyldesley in four hours and ten minutes arrived at his hundred; he made no mistake and too seldom ventured anywhere near the margin of error of his skill. All the same, it was a good innings.

The best thing of the day was Yorkshire's fielding; whenever it was challenged by anything like a strong stroke it was a delight for tired eyes to look upon—quick, eager, and pretty. On one occasion two men chased the same hit to the boundary edge at such a pace that the cap flew backwards from the head of one of them. It was as though, disappointed that no real cricket match was going on in the middle, they were relieving themselves by a foot race all to themselves. Perhaps, after all, it would be better to settle the whole difference between Lancashire and Yorkshire in some such way; or, if this would be too strenuous for every combatant— varying as they do in years and dignity—what about snakes

300

and ladders?

SECOND DAY

Lancashire suffered a great financial blow by the abandonment of Monday's play at Old Trafford. Any hope of a continuation was out of all question at a very early hour owing to the night's heavy rain.

THIRD DAY

Lancashire defeated Yorkshire on the first innings at Old Trafford yesterday after much interesting and keen cricket. In the morning we had from Lancashire a bout of batsmanship alive with swift and stylish strokes. Tyldesley was soon out, but Iddon played beautifully. The crowd very rightly argued that Lancashire 'can do it when they like.' The wicket was so dead that at the outset Rhodes bowled to Iddon without a slip. Iddon hit a long-hop to leg powerfully, and then in one over from Robinson he scored eleven handsome runs, a quick clean late-cut, a lovely cover drive, and a three to leg cleverly timed and placed from a slower ball.

Hopwood was out to Rhodes rather curiously; he ran for a leg-bye and was at the other end almost before Rhodes silently appealed for lbw as though he had been thinking it over. Iddon's dashing cricket was ended by a bad stroke which sent a return catch to Rhodes off a short ball. Then Taylor played one of the sweetest little innings seen in a Lancashire match for a long time; he leaned on his off-side strokes like the incomparable Woolley himself. Just before one o'clock Eckersley closed his innings, a declaration well in accord with the new spirit which all the morning had enlivened and refreshed us.

Yorkshire went in for a quarter of an hour before lunch, and Sutcliffe and Holmes seemed so comfortable that some of us asked whether, after the interval, Yorkshire would go for the 285 they needed, in four hours and a half, for the first-innings points. And after lunch Holmes and Sutcliffe looked ready to begin an attack on the Lancashire bowling any minute. Holmes was militant yet sure of his defences; he hit Macdonald savagely to leg for four. Sutcliffe drove

301

Hopwood through the covers with a most assured and polished stroke.

At half-past two Yorkshire were 32 for none, and I imagine Eckersley was thinking of giving Macdonald a rest, when Holmes made a mistake, probably the afternoon's turning point. He tried to drive to the on a ball from Macdonald which pitched well up to his bat. Somehow he missed it: he was late with his stroke and found himself bowled, to his apparent surprise. Two runs later a magnificent catch, by Richard Tyldesley at silly point, put an end to Sutcliffe's very promising innings. Sutcliffe exploited his own pretty forward push to a half-volley from Hopwood; the hit was low and clean. Tyldesley picked the ball up a foot from the ground. The crowd had scarcely got back the breath they lost in cheering Tyldesley when Leyland drove another half-volley from Hopwood straight to the bowler, who held the easy catch. In quick time Yorkshire had lost her three finest batsmen.

From this point onward Yorkshire were in the grip of heavy circumstances; they had no choice but to get their backs to the wall. To say the truth, Yorkshire fought with little of the old temper—until Emmott Robinson came in. Barber was caught in the leg trap from Macdonald's off-break, bowled skilfully round the wicket. Oldroyd did at least show fight, and had the misfortune to play a ball into his stumps. At three o'clock Yorkshire were 45 for five; now was it that Emmott was to be seen emerging from the pavilion with his pads on and—of course—with his bat in his right hand. He and Mitchell were very stubborn; little or no effort was made to get runs. A shower of rain possibly eased the wicket, though it was never really difficult at any time. Though Eckersley managed his bowling judiciously, Mitchell and Robinson seemed likely to settle down and take root. Robinson once astonished us by hitting recklessly at a ball from Macdonald; seemingly he had mistaken the howl of somebody in the crowd for the umpire's shout of 'No ball!' The Lancashire captain had to walk to the rails and ask for good behaviour. Robinson's indignation was excusable: was it not as though the allies of the old enemy were compelling him to hit boundaries under false pretences! At the tea interval Yorkshire were 69 for five; in an hour since the dismissal

302

of Holmes 37 had been scored for four wickets.

When the game was resumed Macdonald bowled fast-medium bumpers to a field well packed on the leg side. The plan was obvious enough, but it served Lancashire's purpose. And Macdonald did his work very well. Mitchell was caught from one of these rising balls when Yorkshire were 70. He was an obstacle to Lancashire for an hour and a quarter. Rhodes, the next man in, walked to the wicket acclaimed all the way by the crowd. We were watching him for the last time at Old Trafford. He did not stay long, for he played a bumper from Macdonald down into his stumps. Then he departed from our sight with the crowd still acclaiming his greatness. As he walked up the pavilion steps a thousand folk were saying, 'Never again will Old Trafford see him.' It was an incredible thought—Rhodes gone for ever from Lancashire and Yorkshire cricket—the eternal, legendary Rhodes! A page of history was turned over at Old Trafford yesterday, a page written not for an age but for all time.

No doubt Robinson surveyed the passing of Rhodes with no sentimental eye; it was his job now to play to the uttermost the part of the old soldier. He got down on his bat, he put the full blade of it to the ball whenever he was able. When he wasn't, he got his legs there, and on one occasion he chose to let a ball from Macdonald hit him hard on the body rather than risk a stroke to the leg trap. He scorned runs as though so many vain gewgaws. He saw Wood at the other end drive Richard Tyldesley to the off for four—and then talked to him in the middle of the pitch. Wood was missed at long-leg by Taylor, but he did not emulate Robinson's martyrdom; he played as though enjoying his strong free pulls, most of them fours from the moment his bat hit the ball. But Robinson remained in his element of 'orkardness' and stubbornness for nearly an hour and three-quarters. Then he actually got out to one of Macdonald's 'bumpers', hitting speculatively across and under the ball as it rose—a stroke designed primarily to save his skull. A man must live, of course, but Macdonald was not bowling really fast, and already had Robinson given us to understand that in the cause of Yorkshire he was ready to have his body rendered black and blue rather than fall victim to Macdonald. In estimating the length of Robinson's resistance at an hour and three-quarters I include, of course, his walk back to the pavilion.

Wood was gallant to the last, and before Tyldesley trapped him lbw he deservedly achieved the top score of an innings which for weakness of technique and resolution will, I trust, be speedily cast out of the mind of every Yorkshireman who saw it. Lancashire bowled and fielded splendidly, and made the most of the old enemy's quite unnatural lack of confidence. The day's play throughout saw Lancashire cricketers in a very happy and masterful vein. I am perpetually arguing in these columns that they are far better than they themselves seem to think. Macdonald proved that he is still, on his day, the most resourceful of fast bowlers, though this time his 'bumpers' were not his fastest. He shrewdly exploited a certain timidity and lack of mastery over the hook stroke.

SCORES

LANCASHIRE

First Innings

Makepeace, c Wood, b Bowes	14
Watson, c Bowes, b Leyland	50
Tyldesley (E.), b Bowes	107
Iddon, c & b Rhodes	70
Hopwood, lbw, b Rhodes	9
Taylor, not out	20
P. T. Eckersley, c Barber, b Rhodes	2
Extras	12
Total (for 6)	*284

*Innings declared

YORKSHIRE V LANCASHIRE 1930
YORKSHIRE

First Innings

Holmes, b Macdonald	18
Sutcliffe, c Tyldesley (R.), b Hopwood	15
Oldroyd, b Macdonald	4
Leyland, c & b Hopwood	2
A. T. Barber, c Tyldelsey (R.), b Macdonald	5
Mitchell, c Hopwood, b Macdonald	13
Robinson, c Sibbles, b Macdonald	11
Rhodes, b Macdonald	0
Wood, lbw, b Tyldesley (R.)	42
Macaulay, c Duckworth, b Macdonald	12
Bowes, not out	0
Extras	3
Total	125

BOWLING ANALYSIS

LANCASHIRE—First Innings

	O.	M.	R.	W.		O.	M.	R.	W.
Robinson	24	8	37	0	Rhodes	32.1	9	54	3
Bowes	34	6	80	2	Leyland	15	7	27	1
Macaulay	31	9	66	0	Oldroyd	7	4	8	0

YORKSHIRE—First Innings

	O.	M.	R.	W.		O.	M.	R.	W.
Macdonald	29	10	58	7	Tyldesley (R.)	16	8	32	1
Sibbles	5	4	8	0	Iddon	6	5	1	0
Hopwood	17	8	23	2	Watson	1	1	0	0

YORKSHIRE V LANCASHIRE 1931

May 23/25/26   Old Trafford

FIRST DAY

A SODDEN field prevented cricket at Old Trafford on Saturday until half-past three. Then Yorkshire went in to bat on a pitch bespattered hideously with sawdust, reminding us of a butcher's shop, with livers and plucks and lights somewhere about. I hate anything that spoils the green of a cricket field; I hate the mud which contaminates a cricket bat that has been used to flatten out some sinful spot on the wicket.

Sutcliffe and Holmes scored 53 in the olden style; they did not hurry, but behaved themselves like men who knew where they were and who was watching them. For a little more than an hour Sutcliffe and Holmes circumspectly put their bats to the ball, and a voice in the crowd was soon heard to howl the ancient howl—'Hit 'em!' I could not be sure why the runs came slowly—whether because of good bowling or, so to say, on principle. Sibbles sent down four maidens in succession. True, a boundary was hit by Holmes in the first over from Watson, who opened Lancashire's attack with Sibbles. But it was a ball which forcibly reminded us that Watson is a very reliable batsman. (Yet, once on a time, Watson gave proof of rare all-round talents; I can see now the ball with which he bowled Woolley at Dover three or four years ago; it pitched on Woolley's leg stump and knocked the off stump head-over-heels out of the ground.) Perhaps Watson was trying all the time he bowled on Saturday to repeat so grand a piece of pace and spin. (Such is life—we can never be certain from a mortal's poor fleshly deeds what his soul is aiming at.) Watson quickly passed out of the Lancashire attack, and Hopwood took his place. Richard Tyldesley came on in place of the persevering Sibbles, who is bowling better this year than for several seasons. Tyldesley wore a beautiful silk shirt, gorgeous to look at, inviting to the touch, and, let us trust, guaranteed unshrinkable. This, I take it, was a Lancashire

306

way of honouring not only the Lancashire and Yorkshire match but Whitsuntide, and West Houghton Sunday School, and the processions, and all the fine dressings-up that are achieved in the great annual ritual of our immortal if at present sadly harassed county.

Sutcliffe and Holmes played well in their contrasted ways—Sutcliffe all leaning attitudes, prettily self-conscious; Holmes with his military sharpness of movement; when he plays back and counters a difficult ball he is as incisively angular as a grenadier: you can almost catch the sound of accoutrements. A superb batsman Holmes, who always plays finely and then somehow gets out all of a sudden. Hopwood bowled him with a ball just a shade short of a length: Holmes played forward too soon: the ball turned and beat the bat and hit the wicket—not a huge break, not so wide as a church door, but it served.

Tyldesley bowled beautifully, despite the dead ground. Once or twice he might have got somebody out from edged strokes off his leg-break if the fieldsman at point had not been preposterously deep. Oldroyd did not enjoy Tyldesley at all until the rain came and rendered the ball too greasy to spin. Then the rate of scoring went indecorously ahead, and in the circumstances it was a good thing for Lancashire that rain drove everybody out of sight for the day just before half-past five. The drab afternoon contained one charming scene: that was when Old Trafford's ancient retainer came on the field with refreshments. He is a noble and handsome old man, white of hair, and belonging to an English period apparently gone for ever, a period in which it was possible for service to achieve more dignity than all our modern independence seems able to imagine. I never gaze upon Old Trafford's retainer without thinking of Jaikes in the old melodramas, who used to say. 'I know you are innocent, Master Wilfred, and until you come back we'll keep the old hall going. And let me help you, Master Wilfred; a lifetime's savings are at your disposal; they are no use to me, Master Wilfred, take them, and God bless you.'

Another incident in the brief day was Duckworth's chase from the wicket after a ball thumped well away to leg. It reminded me of the time when Strudwick was one of the country's quickest outfields. Paynter's running and picking up were a delight.

The rain has spoiled a good match; perhaps, with three full days for action, we might have seen Lancashire and Yorkshire anxious to get to grips, each team thirsting for points to the full, each eager to deal a knock-out blow. There may yet be fun, if the sun shines to-day. But if the rain persists, well, we'll all have to cultivate philosophy—like Mr. Agar.

SECOND DAY

Yesterday morning was full of clean winds which refreshed our faces and gave us a delicious sense that the summer's tan was beginning to make us almost handsome. The crowd did not fill the ground by any means, and the old-time hubbub and expectancy were not always in the air as they used to be when we were very young and when we went to Lancashire and Yorkshire matches early on Bank Holiday mornings on eager feet, hoping for the best but dreadfully afraid that George Hirst would do his worst and bowl Spooner and MacLaren out before we knew where we were.

The wicket at the outset, though not exactly difficult, enabled Richard Tyldesley to spin an occasional ball with some viciousness. Once or twice Oldroyd played at the going away ball with the light of speculation in his eyes. Any ball hereabout might well have proved his last: yet, such is life and cricket, he contrived to endure and exist. Hopwood's length prevented the making of runs, but he did not lend to the ball that hovering flight which is the true left-hander's means of challenging a batsman's thinking parts. Sutcliffe batted with an agreeable compound of science and sensibility; his strokes obeyed the first principles, yet he touched them with a bloom not to be imparted by the purely academic mind. He makes pretty flourishes—not necessary, maybe, for utilitarian ends, but for that very reason a sign that Sutcliffe, austere Yorkshireman though he be, none the less enjoys a private aestheticism of his own—the delectable, vain relish of the artist. Always does he give me the impression, as he achieves his various ornaments and preenings, and he sees himself in a sort of boudoir mirror of cricket. His batsmanship is all of a piece with his glossy black hair; an innings by Sutcliffe wears a parting down the middle and is fastidiously scented. Oldroyd made a complete contrast to Sutcliffe; Oldroyd is unmistakably Yorkshire. He hits to the on with a bat absolutely natural—as natural as Ilkley Moor baht 'at. Tyldesley beat him all over the place and Duckworth desperately tried to stump him. At first Oldroyd's efforts to hit were desperate rather than triumphant; he found the spin of Tyldesley taxing to his powers of ratiocination, and so he got his legs lumpishly in front. His two-eyed stance is squat, and even his finest strokes—and he can drive well—are entirely without culture's bloom. He bats with an accent; either Oldroyd is a popular edition of Emmott Robinson or Emmott Robinson is Oldroyd in an édition de luxe.

Richard Tyldesley had no luck, and Sibbles bowled in his place. Then Iddon was put on at Hopwood's end, and his first ball was about to bounce twice when Sutcliffe clouted it to leg. Lancashire's attack for the while had a nondescript look; Falstaff's ragged army would have bowled as well. The frequency of half-volleys and long-hops apparently went to the heads of Sutcliffe and Oldroyd; they began to shift themselves after scoring only 42 in the day's first hour. Sutcliffe was missed deep behind the bowler by Taylor; he drove loftily from Iddon and Taylor ran in but dropped the catch after getting his hands to the ball. Sutcliffe then was 64, and nine runs afterwards he pulled a stroke high to Eckersley at square leg-on, in front of the pavilion, but Eckersley misjudged the flight hopelessly and the ball passed over his head as he put up his hand, like a strap-hanger swaying in the Tube.

This mistake was morally rather than materially harmful; for Sutcliffe's innings came to an end almost as soon as the crowd had swallowed their chagrin at Lancashire's fallibility in the field. And—ironic justice!—it was a great catch that sent Sutcliffe away from the middle he so dearly loves and clings to; he drove—again recklessly—to deep long-on, where Hopwood caused great tumult and shouting by a graceful and dexterous catch, running yards sideways—the kind of catch we see on the picture covers of school tales. Sutcliffe's innings lasted two hours and twenty-five minutes; whenever the ball is turning he is a great resister. If I had to name a cricketer to play for my life by batting an hour on a doubtful wicket, Sutcliffe would be my choice. Of course, if Arthur Shrewsbury were alive I would not only trust him to save my life by staying in an hour against Parker and Grimmett on a 'sticky' pitch; I would even approach a life assurance company and take out an old-age endowment policy. It was hard to account for the recklessness with which Sutcliffe ended an innings which was described as 'wonderful' by one of the Lancashire players; perhaps he thought the pitch was becoming definitely bad.

At lunch Yorkshire were 164 for two; Lancashire ought to have taken more wickets. Tyldesley bowled with wretched luck, but the others could not turn the ball at an accurate length. Neither of Lancashire's left-handed bowlers gives the ball enough curve through the air. Parker almost certainly would have been deadly from the beginning of the day, for though the turf was not quick to the point of 'stickiness' it was always helpful to authentic spin.

There were alarums and excursions immediately after lunch—before we had settled into our seats and lighted our pipes. Sibbles yorked Oldroyd and then Leyland pulled a ball hard into Eckersley's hands at mid-on. Yorkshire were now 166 for four; Oldroyd for two and a half hours was very vigilant and practical. The spin whipped across unpleasantly when Greenwood and Mitchell defended Yorkshire's fifth wicket, but Lancashire's field remained defensively and not offensively set, with only one slip for Tyldesley's going-away ball. Greenwood achieved a glorious square cut, whereat Mitchell allowed himself to be extended full forward by Hopwood and stumped with Duckworth's swiftest flourish. Another exquisite cut, late off Tyldesley, announced the quality of Greenwood, who may well develop into one of our best amateur batsmen.

Emmott Robinson had scarcely entered the field of contention before rain drove everybody to shelter; it was a pity, for the shower was certain to ease the wicket just as the Lancashire attack was getting well on top. The weather proved a churlish spoil-sport, at the game's turning-point. There was an hour's interruption between half-past two and half-past three; then another rainstorm exasperatingly happened after twenty minutes of keen cricket, during which period Greenwood was leg before wicket to Tyldesley. Though the shower this time was slight, and the sun came forth straightway, the field was vacant of life for more than a quarter of an hour. Then the groundsman appeared and performed his celebrated fandango in the middle. Then followed the umpires, who looked at the pitch very dubiously, as though before venturing from shelter they had needed to send out a dove for a sign of grass land and subsiding waters. The waste of time was received by the crowd with a disappointing quiescence. Not until a quarter to five was play resumed: this second delay, following an insignificant little cloudburst, was hard to understand. Apparently a cricket crowd, even in days when the first class game depends on public support, has few inalienable rights; they had to wait, without any information about future proceedings, in fine weather, for three-quarters of an hour, for no apparent reason.

At a quarter to five the game condescended to continue, and I noticed that the bowlers did not use sawdust, not even after the ball had been driven along the grass to the outfield. It was of course a good thing for Lancashire that their attack had not to grapple with a wet ball. Emmott Robinson so far forgot where he was and the nature of the occasion as to permit himself to be stumped—a blot, at last, on an otherwise irreproachable career. The ball was now doing its work rapidly: obviously we could have had play half an hour sooner—but of course there was the tea interval to consider and deem inviolate. Wood and Macaulay scored 24 for the eighth Yorkshire wicket; Wood hit Richard Tyldesley to leg several times, with little room in which to achieve a hefty scooping stroke. Wood is a good workmanlike batsman. A brilliant catch by Ernest Tyldesley at cover got rid of Macaulay, and now Verity came out of the pavilion to the applause which would have been offered to Wilfred Rhodes had he been there in Verity's stead. Verity was quickly thrown out by a return of great alacrity by Iddon. Wood batted hard to the end; the innings was finished by a catch by Taylor at short third man from Bowes, who slashed at Hopwood's spin as though horrified at the very sight of it.

Taylor nearly dropped his chance, holding it only after a piece of juggling which probably caused his heart to appear momentarily in his mouth. The Lancashire bowling analysis paid a compliment to Sibbles, but Richard Tyldesley's figures only prove that figures are deceptive and fraudulent. Hopwood was persevering, but on yesterday's wicket left-handed spin should have been predominant in an attack, not merely accessory.

When the Lancashire innings began at 25 minutes to six, Emmott Robinson bowled the first over to render homage to the custom of the 'new ball.' At the other end of the wicket, though, Verity was put on without loss of time, and we could now see how a left-handed slow bowler's field is placed in accordance to the most ancient usage—two slips, a 'silly' mid-off, a cover, an extra cover, and a mid-off—the classic positions for slow 'going away' spin. Robinson bowled only two overs, one ball of which swerved in to Hallows, then turned away a foot. Robinson at the sight of this phenomenon of flight and break took off his cap and scratched his grey head. It was a sign of the wicket's susceptibility—and Macaulay came on for Robinson with an opportunist look in his eye. Exploiting the leg trap, he bowled round the wicket, and at once he caused Watson to make a 'Heaven help me' stab through the slips at a ball that went straight through. For half an hour Hallows and Watson played discreetly until Watson backed up for an impossible single, and found himself rightly sent back and run out. It was an inexplicable mishap, accountable only on the assumption that Watson wished to get Hallows away from the wicket attacked by Macaulay. Hallows and Watson had shown skill and policy by keeping themselves at the right ends of the pitch—Watson to counter the spin of Macaulay, Hallows to counter the spin of Verity. The pitch seemed a little quieter following the roller's pacific touch; at any rate neither Verity nor Macaulay turned the ball as keenly as Tyldesley had done earlier in the day. Another disaster of the first importance overwhelmed Lancashire at ten minutes past six; Ernest Tyldesley tried to push a full toss from Verity round to leg and, missing it strangely, was leg before wicket. Lancashire 22 for two—and Iddon was nearly caught off Verity the moment he arrived at the crease in the evening's soft sunlight. Verity has a beautiful action—supple, upright, and economic. He brings the ball from a height, and is quicker through the air than Rhodes (with whom he ought not to be compared; his style is different and his own). He can spin the ball well enough, and he has something of that 'extra' pace which made the incomparable Blythe more difficult to 'get at' than most slow bowlers. Verity announced his grand lineage—Peel cum Rhodes—with the ball that dismissed Iddon; it was after the eternal pattern of the slow left-hander's lovely and perilous spinner; it curved through the air, lured Iddon forward, then at the last fraction of the last second whipped away to find the bat's edge and fly thence to Wood's gloves. There is no counter in all the known arts of batsmanship for the perfectly pitched and spun ball of the left-handed bowler; it is one of the game's most artful and pretty tricks. At his best Verity can bowl this entrancing ball like Peel, like Rhodes, like Blythe, like Briggs, like Harry Dean—giving to the performance of it his own touch. He will some day make his length absolutely reliable; then we shall see a very masterful Verity. Lancashire are likely to spend a few hours on the rack this morning; yesterday they were not blessed by fortune. Before lunch Richard Tyldesley bowled well enough to take half a dozen wickets. And Ernest Tyldesley is the last man in the world to get out to an over-tossed ball.

THIRD DAY

I propose to waste little time over yesterday's play at Old Trafford; Yorkshire in the afternoon gave an exhibition which I imagine is without parallel in the annals of a great county. Yorkshire were unable to force Lancashire to follow on, but they went in again at a quarter to three, leading by 103 runs. No gesture of sportsmanship was made; Lyon and Fender might never have been born. Yorkshire not only declined to make a bid for victory; they did not even play a normal game on the fairly easy wicket. There was little enough time, true, for a finish now; still, some regard ought to have been shown to cricket's ordinary decencies. Yorkshire deliberately stonewalled, and in an hour and a half scored 28.

Sutcliffe was on view an hour and a quarter for eleven. I suggest that the Yorkshire committee might do worse than have an inquiry into the inexplicable behaviour of some of their players. If cricket were under the jurisdiction of a body similar to the Football Association, I wonder what would happen?

The play before lunch let us see a Yorkshire eleven so keen that the subsequent lapse from ambition and conscience was all the more incomprehensible. The wicket at the morning's outset was not perhaps so unpleasant as some of the Yorkshire bowlers would have liked; still the batsmen had to be on the look-out for the ball that sped through and kept low. Greenwood exploited all the possibilities of his spin bowlers. In forty minutes he tried nine changes, always trying to get the break turning away from the bat—for instance, Verity would be put on for a right-handed batsman, and taken off for the left-handers, who were usually tackled by Robinson and Macaulay with the off-spin backed up by a leg-trap. Hallows was in his strongest and most composed vein, watchful yet equable in temper and technique. Robinson bowled Paynter at five minutes to twelve; then Verity caused a ball to spin quite vehemently to Hopwood and got him caught at second slip. Taylor made a few stylish strokes but was out at 70, and Lancashire had then lost six wickets; there was the danger of a follow-on. Eckersley pulled Verity powerfully for four to long-on, then square to the boundary. Hallows also drove straight and handsomely. Just before lunch, when Yorkshire needed only to take one wicket, Robinson sent down to Duckworth an over so mild that I could not believe my eyes when I saw who was wheeling it up. Yorkshire seemingly gave up all hope of victory when Lancashire saved the follow-on. A magnificent one-handed catch by Mitchell, which dismissed Richard Tyldesley, was delightful and worthy of a better occasion. But the match's catch was the one-handed one of Hallows which wonderfully and mercifully took Holmes out of our sight.

Lancashire bowled very steadily when the Yorkshire farce took place; but no lover of the game could look on patiently. The Lancashire and Yorkshire match is becoming an eyesore and a nuisance; it is a pity we cannot somehow get rid of it.

Yet, once on a time, it was a great and chivalrous engagement. I feel sorry for the small boys present at Old Trafford yesterday afternoon; lucky those of us who knew and adored George Hirst, Reggie Spooner, Denton, MacLaren, and Lord Hawke. Yesterday afternoon's farce would have been impossible in the presence of Lord Hawke.

SCORES

YORKSHIRE

First Innings		Second Innings	
Holmes, b Hopwood	24	c Hallows, b Sibbles	4
Sutcliffe, c Hopwood, b Sibbles	75	b Tyldesley (R.)	11
Oldroyd, b Sibbles	55	not out	28
Leyland, c Eckersley, b Tyldesley (R.)	5	not out	27
Mitchell, st Duckworth, b Hopwood	1		
F. E. Greenwood, lbw, b Tyldesley (R.)	18		
Robinson, st Duckworth, b Tyldesley (R.)	4		
Wood, not out	32		
Macaulay, c Tyldesley (E.), b Sibbles	7		
Verity, run out	1		
Bowes, c Taylor, b Hopwood	0		
Extras	9	Extras	6
Total	231	Total (for 2)	76

LANCASHIRE

First Innings	
Watson, run out	9
Hallows, c Mitchell, b Verity	36
Tyldesley (E.), lbw, b Verity	0
Iddon, c Wood, b Verity	4
Paynter, b Robinson	12
Hopwood, c Mitchell, b Verity	10
Taylor, c Wood, b Robinson	4
P. T. Eckersley, c & b Robinson	18
Sibbles, c Wood, b Robinson	18
Tyldesley (R.), c Mitchell, b Verity	0
Duckworth, not out	7
Extras	10
Total	128

THE ROSES MATCHES 1919-1939
BOWLING ANALYSIS
YORKSHIRE—First Innings

	O.	M.	R.	W.		O.	M.	R.	W.
Sibbles	24	9	32	3	Tyldesley (R.)	40	7	92	3
Watson	6	2	17	0	Iddon	8	2	28	0
Hopwood	44	18	53	3					

Second Innings

	O.	M.	R.	W.		O.	M.	R.	W.
Sibbles	14	9	10	1	Taylor	1	0	2	0
Hopwood	23	14	12	0	Eckersley	1	1	0	0
Tyldesley (R.)	10	4	14	1	Iddon	7	3	8	0
Paynter	6	0	24	0					

LANCASHIRE—First Innings

	O.	M.	R.	W.		O.	M.	R.	W.
Robinson	24	13	29	4	Macaulay	23	10	35	0
Verity	28	9	54	5					

YORKSHIRE V LANCASHIRE 1931

August 1/3/4   Bramall Lane

FIRST DAY

LANCASHIRE suffered a trying day at Sheffield on Saturday, but there was the consolation of philosophy for them—it might have been worse, much worse. At five o'clock a great roar from a Bramall Lane crowd announced that Yorkshire's grand total had arrived at 300 for no wicket. At this moment I sat high in the air, in a press box only to be reached by climbing a staircase which is like some dizzy spiral in a dream of Piranesi—a staircase that 'winds about the axis of eternity.' Down below was the cockpit and the game; and Ernest Tyldesley, while fielding at deep long on, looked up and asked us humorously 'How many are out?'

Yes, indeed, it might have been worse. The wicket was a batsman's lap of luxury, comfortable in pace, with no ball, or hardly any, misbehaving a hair's breadth. Sutcliffe was at his soundest, and Holmes, after a doubtful beginning, was almost as solid and as much at ease. While the 300 went up and as the tumult and the shouting momentarily died down, I said to myself, 'A miracle will have to happen to put an end to this stand.'

And a miracle did happen, at twenty minutes past five, when Yorkshire were 323. Sutcliffe pulled a ball from Hopwood masterfully towards deep mid-on, a yard from the boundary. Paynter dashed forward with incredible alacrity, the ball fell far in front of him, so it seemed, and we got ready to applaud a gallant but vain effort. But Paynter by a convulsion of all his nerves and muscles hurled himself downwards and still farther forward; he snatched the ball an inch from the ground and then fell over and over, in a double somersault and yet somehow managed to keep grip on his prize.

The catch of the season; the catch of many seasons; the necessary miracle. Sutcliffe was 195 and ready to begin again

317

and to proceed inevitably to the day's end. And if he had stayed in Holmes might not have felt obliged to take risks, for while he and Sutcliffe remained together runs at the rate of seventy an hour could be scored without a ghost of hazard or any trouble whatever. All in all Lancashire emerged fortunately from a scalding day; the true tale of Yorkshire's mastery over the bowling would have been told by a close-of-day score of 400 for none.

No doubt Sutcliffe and Holmes each committed errors, especially at the morning's outset; Macdonald beat the bat of Sutcliffe with the last ball of his first over, missing the wicket by not many inches. And in Sibbles's first over Holmes helplessly hit a ball perilously near the hands of Iddon at mid on. Holmes for an hour seemed about to get out to any ball through failure to time his strokes. These miscalculations, though, must merely have mocked the Lancashire attack long before lunch was reached; they were like so many aggravating glimpses of a fallibility no bowler could seize upon, ironical proofs that, after all, Sutcliffe and Holmes were indeed human and not machines. Sutcliffe snicked a ball from Sibbles like lightning down in front of Paynter when his score was 118; Holmes gave a chance at the wicket just after he had made his hundred. Faint scratches on the thick walls of a partnership durable and as swollen as the Albert Hall! (Somehow Sutcliffe's cricket, so eternal and complacent and English middle class, reminds me of the Albert Hall; I'd love to see him bat in it—the place is big enough.)

The match lacked the old antagonism. Yorkshire, of course, are under no compulsion to pay more respect to Lancashire just now than to Derbyshire. The traditional smouldering fires were not there, not even the authentic sullenness. I am sorry to tell the sad news, but hardly ever did I hear an appeal for leg before wicket. Perhaps Macaulay and Emmott Robinson will this morning attend to the niceties.

Just before lunch Sutcliffe hit Macdonald for five fours in two overs; they do not indulge in such indecencies at Bank Holiday time even at Canterbury. The next thing, I fear, will be white tents and bunting at Bramall Lane. Change and decay all around I see; where is Harry Makepeace and his grim bat, and where are the endless maiden overs of Wilfred

Rhodes? Lancashire have a duty to perform in this engagement; the crowd must be reminded where they are and what they have come to see. A Lancashire and Yorkshire match without a single howl from some poor soul in agonies of tedium—such a match is a throw back to the days of the heathen and vandal.

Macdonald began with three slips, a third man, a mid-off, a cover, a deep leg, a mid-on and a deep mid-on. This placing of the field told us that the state of the pitch did not have the bowler's confidence. Sutcliffe, as I say, missed the last ball of Macdonald's first over; he played forward and the outswing beat him, or at any rate, it seemed to beat him. You can never be certain that Sutcliffe does not delay a stroke purposely to an outswinger; he can play marvellously late.

Holmes ought not to have been allowed to get through his opening half hour, a good ball was needed to take advantage of Holmes's temporary inability to use the middle of his bat. Sibbles worked hard without a single bit of luck. Macdonald, too, was steady to begin with; he sent down the best ball of the day, and perhaps not half a dozen people on the ground saw it. He bowled a quick break-back when Sutcliffe was 15; Sutcliffe missed the ball, which hit the pads protecting the stumps. Had the umpire been Mr. Lyttelton he would have instinctively put up the right forefinger.

Tyldesley came on for Macdonald after this fine ball had delighted the eye of the connoisseur. Holmes who had now batted for three-quarters of an hour without deserving one more than the eight runs he scraped in the time, pulled a dreadfully short ball from Tyldesley for four. Sutcliffe leaned on the half-volleys and let us admire his charming drives to the off; Holmes hit Tyldesley for another four and pulled a wretched long hop for three. Bad bowling enabled Holmes to recapture confidence. Sibbles bowled for seventy minutes hard and well. By now the stand was rooted in the earth. Macdonald came back in place of Tyldesley; and Sutcliffe hit the five fours I have already written about, brilliant strokes, vital with strength, contemptuous in their confidence and ease, drives and hooks. Occasionally Macdonald attempted to bump the ball but Sutcliffe has always enjoyed Macdonald's short stuff, even in the days when Macdonald was a great and beautiful bowler. At lunch Yorkshire were 123 for none; Sutcliffe 80, Holmes 38.

After lunch Macdonald sent a fine ball to Holmes, which flashed upwards past the batsman's wrists, even on the most comfortable wicket I have seen this year. Then Sibbles completely defeated, but could not bowl Sutcliffe, who was then 87. A great stroke off his pads, from Sibbles, told us that Holmes had discovered again his proper form, that quick-tempered military sort of batsmanship which makes a perfect contrast to the cool, veneered cricket of Sutcliffe. In an hour following the interval nearly 100 runs were hit to all parts of the field.

Sutcliffe played like a cricketer who would have smiled indulgently at you if you had reminded him that the game is full of uncertainties and that there are several ways whereby a batsman can occasionally get out. He drove almost negligently through the covers; he played the gently rising ball on the off side down to third man, running his own graceful run, how the bowlers must feel annoyed at it; and suddenly his general air of composed mastery would become aggressively dynamic at the sight of a long-hop on the leg stump, asking to be severely hooked.

Seldom have I seen batsmanship so certain of itself as Sutcliffe's was on Saturday; never did he let the easiness of his job blind him to the need to look out for an occasional good ball. Nothing can disturb Sutcliffe's temperament and his ability to play every ball on its merits. Time after time he delayed a stroke just in time to avoid hitting a slight leg spinner of Richard Tyldesley to the off-side field. And though Tyldesley on the whole bowled indifferently, he enjoyed a good period towards four o'clock, when he sent one ball which turned from leg to middle quickly, just as Sutcliffe was shaping for a push to the on. But Sutcliffe saw the break in time, and changed his stroke to half-cock, and thus got rid of it, though not too handsomely.

Sutcliffe made 100 out of 165 in two hours and a half. At half-past three bad light stopped play for ten minutes; when the match was continued the batting went on exactly where it had left off, both men playing more or less as they wished. No better batting has been witnessed in a Lancashire and

Yorkshire match for many years. Hopwood bowled to a leg trap, which lacked a man deep. It was juvenile strategy, because Hopwood merely directed the ball from over the wicket, without attempting a mask, to a place obviously outside the batsman's legs. Far better if he had emulated the wisdom of Rhodes, whenever a great stand occurred against him, on a good wicket—a well-placed off-side field and a good length from round the wicket. At tea Yorkshire were 280 for none, Sutcliffe 171 and Holmes 95. In an hour and three-quarters since lunch the Sheffield crowd had wallowed in 157 runs—91 made by Sutcliffe and 57 by Holmes.

Sutcliffe and Holmes easily broke the stand of 280 achieved in 1887 by Louis Hall and Lee against Lancashire at Bradford. But Holmes was definitely given a second innings when Yorkshire were 286; he snicked a vicious ball from Sibbles into Duckworth's gloves and it went through them swift to the earth in front of first slip—Iddon—who tried hard to retrieve Duckworth's mistake. In the same over, from Sibbles, Sutcliffe hit a ball terrifically hard to mid-on, who saved a four, or missed a catch, according to whether your point of view is broad or narrow. Sibbles deserved a wicket, so gallantly did he stick to a heart-breaking job, but not a thing came off for the poor lad. Sutcliffe drove Sibbles for four to the off, took off a glove, and drove the next ball to the on, again for four.

Intervention from the outside, from forces full of pity for Lancashire, came now at last. From one ball Holmes hit a better chance to Eckersley at mid-off; another boundary saved. From the next ball we saw Sutcliffe's pull and Paynter's catch. The first wicket stand of 323 lasted four hours and twenty-five minutes; Sutcliffe, when his score was 172, gave a distinct chance at the wicket, but it is not in my notes, and as the Judge in 'Pickwick' said . . .

Great cheering followed Sutcliffe home to the pavilion, and he raised his bat on high with a flourish which was more than an acknowledgment; it was a confirmation. He is in magnificent form this year. On Saturday he came to the wicket less to make a century than, in his own polite, polished and practical way, to keep an appointment with one, or rather to honour a century with his acquaintance. The best batsman in England today, and how well he seems to know it! The rest of the day's play needs no description. Holmes, hitting out, was caught at mid-off. The second wicket fell at 351, and Holmes batted nearly five hours. Not many of his strokes were remarkable enough to remain in the mind for long, but some of his drives and late cuts hinted of the clean, dapper technique which belongs to him in his best season.

Yorkshire rather spoiled the day in the last hour or so. A violent assault regardless of falling wickets might have scattered the weary Lancashire attack and sent the crowd home entirely hoarse and delirious. Leyland, quite out of form, could not hit accurately, and Mitchell played down the line of any good ball as though the match were just beginning. A run a minute, after 323 for one, was an unimaginative finish to an opulent day for Yorkshire. The Lancashire bowlers stuck very well to a rather hopeless task; but they were not good enough, either in length or flight, or tactics; they were beaten as much by the absurdly easy wicket as by the excellence of the batting.

SECOND DAY

A huge crowd roared at every run this morning while Yorkshire for 70 minutes forced the game. In this time 91 were made, and when Greenwood closed the innings the score stood vastly at 484 for seven. Richard Tyldesley did not bowl; the hard work was done with excellent spirit by Sibbles, who came in for wickets, and each time he took one he pulled out his handkerchief and blew his nose. Sibbles always blows his nose when he has got somebody out. Oldroyd hooked two short balls from Macdonald consecutively for four; other times other manners, as the French say.

The wicket was still ridiculously easy when the Lancashire innings began at five minutes to one, with the crowd simply ravenous for blood. These voracious instincts were immediately encouraged and aggravated for 90 minutes by Hallows, who did everything but get out. He stuck his pads in front of the stumps and trapped his bat down blindly to save himself from leg-before-wicket in the nick of time. Robinson stifled an appeal just as Hallows played the ball. Appeals ought never to be stifled in these matches; we are indeed

322

coming to something. After lunch a ball from Bowes kept low and astonished Hallows and probably Bowes himself, who at first could not achieve much more pace than Sibbles, hardly as much from the pitch. Hallows's innings seemed to hang on a terribly thin thread, but Hopwood's was the first wicket to fall at 42. Hopwood held out his bat with a fatal space between his arms and his body, and was caught by Wood from a ball that did not rise higher than its speed through the air advertised.

The Lancashire score was still 42 when Hallows pulled a half-volley from Robinson straight into the hands of Holmes at mid-on, who dropped an easy chance. The stroke was wretched, for the ball cried out to be driven to the off side. Bowes changed over to the football end (hideous habitation on a cricket field!), and his attack improved greatly in length and pace from the ground. Ernest Tyldesley, when his score was two, edged Bowes through the slips; for all he knew about it he was out. The Lancashire innings began by magically transforming the comfortable turf of the morning into a thing of hidden and evil vicissitude. A glorious out-swinger from Bowes beat Hallows at 16; he would have been caught behind the wicket but for a hair's breadth. Hallows began to suggest that his innings was charmed, that he had drunk some amazing potion rendering him impervious to mortal wounds. When a ball by Bowes kept low and Hallows missed it and was given out leg-before-wicket we simply witnessed an official interpretation of an error on Hallows's part which, for an hour and a half, had occurred and recurred until cricketers in the crowd with the sense of style were tired and sick of the sight of it. Hallows has for weeks been playing back at everything from a long-hop to a half-volley.

Bowes was now bowling with a keen alacrity that contradicted altogether his curiously lethargic run to the wicket. Twice in quick sequence he morally defeated Iddon. Lancashire were entirely on the defensive, driven there without a show of fight. For an hour and ten minutes Bowes bowled after lunch, and in each over he gave more trouble to the batsmen than Yorkshire had to endure at any moment of their thoroughly comfortable and prosperous innings. Bowes

323

was a different bowler the moment he changed ends. Verity came on in Bowes's place and tried to use a spot made by Sibbles. He bowled from over the wicket with five or six men on the on side and, of course, Lancashire tacitly agreed to this piece of spellbinding. In effect they said to Verity, 'Yes, heaven help us, there is a spot, as you suggest.' And they played back weakly with doubt. Most of the really profitable strokes were off the bat's edge.

The perfect Sheffield wicket, the despair of Lancashire's bowlers only a few hours before, had at half past three suffered an incredible transmogrification (no other word is expressive enough) into an incalculable mess of stickiness. The batting was about as feeble-hearted as any I have known. At the end of two hours' play Lancashire had made 87 for two, and we had seen only one true stroke, a drive by Hallows. Nothing but a change of temper could save Lancashire, and none was yet forthcoming. At 95 Verity bowled from the pavilion end with the left-hander's normal field. His first ball, quite straight and of ordinary length, caused Ernest Tyldesley to put out a speculative bat and lob a feminine return which Verity finely held as he fell over. Tyldesley could not have come to a worse end if he had aimed at the pavilion clock. Just in front of the tea interval Leyland bowled with Verity—two slow left-handers. A stranger coming into the ground now would have pardonably thought that the match was being played in hot sunshine baking a moist, unpleasant turf. And early this morning I was trying to think of any bowler of any period in cricket history who might have conquered the Sheffield wicket's docility. I could confidently suggest only Barnes at his best, Kortright, or Arthur Mailey.

As soon as Horrocks came in we heard the bat making a more confident sound; it was not the slow scoring some of us objected to between lunch and tea but the irresolute attitude of Lancashire's earlier players. Horrocks made his defensive strokes intelligently and coolly. He was excellent whenever the ball pitched on the leg stump. When Bowes bowled at him his main defect was palpable all over the field excepting, perhaps, to Bowes himself, who, despite a crowd of slip fielders and occasional encouragement from Horrocks, could not send the right ball along. Iddon, too, strengthened his game, and at last the Lancashire and Yorkshire match seemed like itself—the crowd at any rate played their old part well, for they howled and suffered nobly as the score remained still and the batsmen declined to get out. Horrocks stayed in nearly an hour, and then lost his wicket trying a huge pull from a short ball. The stroke told everybody plainly that Horrocks was making his first appearance in this severe engagement; no doubt the hitting of Sutcliffe and Holmes on Saturday misled him. Four runs after Horrocks got out Iddon played back at Verity's faster ball and departed caught at the wicket, after a useful innings which he obviously did not enjoy any more than the rest of us. In the same over Verity clean bowled Eckersley with another ball quicker than his customary pace. At the other end of the wicket Robinson was given permission to bowl slow balls, which were intended as off breaks; the bluff was gigantic and effective enough to make a cat laugh. No Lancashire batsman tried to drive Robinson through the enormous gap that separated deep square leg from long-on. I am quite prepared to hear from the Lancashire batsmen indeed that the Sheffield wicket began to crumble the moment Hallows and Hopwood looked at it at one o'clock on this warm, pleasant Bank Holiday. The simple explanation of Lancashire's supine cricket today is that the team at present is a poor one, and needs drastic rejuvenation in every technical department. And the sooner the work of making a new eleven is begun the better.

Paynter and Sibbles for a while stopped a collapse, but even Paynter curbed his natural temper and rare hitting powers. Almost in every over we saw an unlovely snick which caused a lover of cricket to hide his face in his hands; myself I tried to look as if I had been born in Laisterdyke or Mytholmroyd. Sibbles did at last go to the pitch of the ball and strike it soundly, not afraid that it would explode and blow him sky-high. He survived until Lancashire reached 161, and then was comprehensively bowled by Macaulay, who attacked with his own tireless zeal and animosity. The Yorkshire bowling had to answer no determined challenge; Lancashire's stroke-play was so lacking in faith and energy that we could not even admire Yorkshire's superb fielding;

it was given little to do, excepting Wood, who at one period was Lancashire's most prolific scorer. Leyland made a ball or two break from the spot at the pavilion end, but they were off-breaks to the batsmen and leg-breaks when they left Leyland's fingers—the reason for this curious bowling being that the said spot was tolerably mild and harmless. At any rate, it did not account for Lancashire's loss of four wickets at the other end.

But it is absurd to discuss the Sheffield wicket at all; Lancashire expected to make 400 on it at their own sweet time and pleasure. Their methods betrayed them, nothing else; the eye sees what the mind sees and Lancashire saw enough trouble in Yorkshire's moderately good bowlers to enable them to take the offensive and pitch whatever length they chose to pitch. The close-of-play score really flattered the afternoon's batting, which was weaker than any I could have imagined possible on the wicket. Paynter's innings was good enough—considering that for some fantastical reason he kept in abeyance his proper and natural strokes. But Duckworth held on and avoided disaster with an ease which rendered his air of very dour responsibility and ferocity quite superfluous. Lancashire have only themselves to blame for not coming out of the day's play with at least 250 runs for four wickets at most.

THIRD DAY

Time as well as the Lancashire batsmen was against Yorkshire when the game was continued on a quiet, pleasant morning disturbed only by the profane noises of somebody selling a football annual. It was urgently necessary for Yorkshire's chances that Duckworth and Richard Tyldesley or Macdonald should be bowled out promptly, and an attack made well before lunch on Lancashire's second innings.

Paynter's steady bat could not avail his side much if the other and weaker men were quickly settled. But Duckworth, Tyldesley, and Macdonald each put a very confident bat to the ball, and an hour passed by with no advance by Yorkshire excepting the capture of the wicket of Duckworth, who put an end to a valuable piece of obstinacy by a sudden and irrational effort to hit a boundary. Greenwood did not ask

Bowes to bowl for an hour, presumably wishing to keep his fast bowler fresh for the really serious work to come. When Bowes at last was obliged to take part in the attack Richard Tyldesley had helped Paynter to waste Yorkshire's time for half an hour, and straightway Bowes sent Tyldesley an outswinger which was glanced into the gloves of Wood. Macdonald for a quarter of an hour kept up his wicket with contemptuous languor; he made his strokes with time to spare, almost as though bored by the ease of the wicket and the ease of the bowling. It was ten minutes to one before Yorkshire took the last of the three Lancashire wickets left over from Monday. The comfortable way in which the Lancashire tail defended was pointed criticism of the wan efforts of the team's recognised batsmen; also they demonstrated the harmlessness of the wicket. Perhaps the wicket had managed to get up in the night and stretch itself. How astonishingly a wicket does change from minute to minute according to the testimony of batsmen who, of course, are never prejudiced one way or another.

Paynter, not out at the end, was always dependable, but he did not try to take charge of the game when the last Lancashire batsmen were in. Paynter opened the second innings with Hallows, and Leyland was one of Yorkshire's first bowlers, with Bowes. Leyland, with a new ball, instead of Robinson, made an inexplicable spectacle. Hallows survived until lunch, though obviously vulnerable. After the interval Leyland bowled him by inches and then caught a pushed return from a not very purposeful bat. Hallows can do nothing right just now.

Greenwood's tactics were interesting. He did not put on Bowes immediately after lunch, or Macaulay, but trusted to Leyland and Robinson, the latter exploiting very slow stuff. He changed Robinson for Verity, but not for long. Robinson came back and bowled slow again. The idea, no doubt, was to keep the potential spin turning against Paynter's left-handed bat. I say potential because actually there was little spin. And Paynter and Tyldesley batted with a confidence lacking entirely in the first innings. They did not worry about the runs, and rightly so, but now and again each player made a fine stroke, possibly for the crowd's sake; but if that was their charitable notion they were very much mistaken, for at every boundary hit the crowd more or less maintained a very stern silence.

Macaulay set a leg-trap suggesting a terrible wicket, and then sent up one or two quaint leg-breaks which absolutely contradicted the placing of his field. Verity also tried a leg-trap, and bowled temptingly from over the wicket. Whereat Paynter hit with violence round the corner and struck Sutcliffe terrifically hard on the leg. But Sutcliffe declined to be hurt. A few minutes afterwards Paynter hit another loose ball from Verity harder still, and Sutcliffe was again struck, this time on the arm. But again he declined to be hurt. The sympathetic fieldsmen gathered round, but Sutcliffe did not pander to them and lose his dignity. He walked away and stood in his own easy cross-legged attitude. Magnificent Sutcliffe, the Sir Willoughby Patterne of the cricket field! Paynter and E. Tyldesley batted without the slightest difficulty, their effortless methods causing us to wonder whether Monday afternoon was not a preposterous dream. The bowling was the same and the wicket the same; the difference was one of the mind. On Monday Lancashire created perils that had no objective existence. Paynter reached 50 in two hours: he had done splendid labour towards saving the game for Lancashire, and he showed rare resource by adapting his customary pugnacious driving powers to a situation which rendered boundary hits vain things. The crowd let out hoarse noises almost voluptuously, but as Tyldesley and Paynter were playing for a draw at the rate of fifty an hour it is possible that the crowd's impatience was not directed against slow runs but at the batsmen's refusal to get out.

At a quarter to four Lancashire were 100 for one wicket, and Mitchell and Oldroyd were bowling. The beautiful wicket had frustrated Yorkshire—that and a convenient return to sane thinking and clear sight in the Lancashire eleven. The leisureliness of Paynter's and Tyldesley's cricket, the perfect mastery of it, was a nice commentary on Lancashire's first innings, much more sardonic than anything written about it. At tea Tyldesley and Paynter were still not out, and Lancashire's total had reached 118 for one, after some two hours and a half of cricket which, apart from the obvious fallibility of Hallows, gave the Yorkshire attack no hope whatever. The stand of Paynter and Tyldesley seemed so certain and inevitable on the wicket that it would be easy to underrate the skill and judgment that performed it all. Paynter proved himself as good at pulling a match out of danger as on other occasions he is good at winning one.

Paynter was Yorkshire's bane for some six hours; he came to the wicket when failure of head and heart was losing Lancashire the match. He saw at once the truth about Yorkshire's bowling and was not to be deceived or disturbed. The Yorkshire attack did not fight hard as soon as they were found out by Paynter and Tyldesley; the bluff was blown. At twenty minutes to four Mitchell was asked to bowl—a precipitate throwing-up of the sponge. But I fancy the Yorkshire bowlers were prepared for long and fairly fruitless labour when they began their efforts yesterday. The Sheffield wicket is the despair of all bowlers—I am not sure, now, that Lancashire could not have run Yorkshire hard for first-innings points if the batsmen had not handicapped themselves by ridiculous self-doubt.

SCORES

YORKSHIRE

First Innings

Holmes, c Eckersley, b Macdonald	125
Sutcliffe, c Paynter, b Hopwood	195
Leyland, b Iddon	28
Mitchell, b Sibbles	58
F. E. Greenwood, c Duckworth, b Macdonald	22
Wood, c Macdonald, b Sibbles	12
Oldroyd, c Duckworth, b Paynter	17
Robinson, not out	5
Extras	22
	—
Total (for 7)	*484

*Innings declared

THE ROSES MATCHES 1919-1939
LANCASHIRE

First Innings		Second Innings	
Hallows, lbw, b Bowes	18	c & b Leyland	14
Hopwood, c Wood, b Bowes	20		
Tyldesley (E.), c & b Verity	22	c Holmes, b Verity	41
Iddon, c Wood, b Verity	30	not out	14
Horrocks, lbw, b Robinson	18		
Paynter, not out	45	not out	87
P. T. Eckersley, b Verity	0		
Sibbles, b Macaulay	14		
Duckworth, b Robinson	14		
Tyldesley (R.), c Wood, b Bowes	12		
Macdonald, b Verity	0		
Extras	28	Extras	9
Total	221	Total (for 2)	165

BOWLING ANALYSIS

YORKSHIRE—First Innings

	O.	M.	R.	W.		O.	M.	R.	W.
Macdonald	31	2	142	2	Hopwood	20	2	55	1
Sibbles	51	5	136	2	Paynter	10	3	34	1
Tyldesley (R.)	33	5	79	0	Iddon	7	2	16	1

LANCASHIRE—First Innings

	O.	M.	R.	W.		O.	M.	R.	W.
Bowes	36	16	45	3	Verity	25	7	57	4
Robinson	40	16	41	2	Leyland	4	1	14	0
Macaulay	35	18	36	1					

Second Innings

	O.	M.	R.	W.		O.	M.	R.	W.
Bowes	12	4	18	0	Mitchell	3	0	9	0
Leyland	24	5	49	1	Holmes	3	1	6	0
Verity	24	8	31	1	Greenwood	4	1	14	0
Macaulay	5	1	14	0	Oldroyd	7	2	7	0
Robinson	5	0	8	0					

YORKSHIRE V LANCASHIRE 1932

May 14/16/17 Bradford

FIRST DAY

THERE were strange and thrilling deeds at Bradford on Saturday; the old lance of chivalry was lifted up again at last. Paynter made 152 out of 209 in three hours and a half on a bowler's wicket. His hitting was severe and audacious.

At first the match acted in accordance with expectations and tradition. The pitch was so soft that we had to wait for play until a quarter to one. Then Lancashire scored only eleven runs in forty-five minutes. Watson's sense of the occasion was so acutely histrionic that he did not get a run for half an hour. During all this portentous play, voices in the crowd uttered the old tormented cry from the heart: ' 'It 'em! 'It 'em!' And I imagined the Yorkshire newspapers preparing the ancient familiar poster:

Slow Batting
by
Lancashire

We went to lunch resigned to a 'dour struggle.' Some of us, who knew that the wicket with the warm sunshine on it would soon become treacherous, gave Lancashire 120 all out at the most. Straightway after lunch Paynter stained the scutcheon of the match by hitting a six from Verity. The ball was really too short for a drive, but Paynter ran—actually ran—yards out of his ground, on feet so quick that you could not follow their twinkling movements. A few moments before Paynter achieved his sixer he had tried to hit Smailes for four to the on, against the off break (to a left-hander, of course, a leg-break), and only by luck did the consequent mishit skim over the heads of the slips. At the sight of such violent behaviour in a Lancashire and Yorkshire match there was only one thing to do—to take off one's spectacles and polish them.

Paynter proceeded to play the most original, the most

imaginative, the most courageous, and the most belligerent innings seen in a Lancashire and Yorkshire match since the war. And it was all done on a bowler's turf; between a quarter-past two and a quarter-past four the wicket was definitely deadly. Paynter's cricket had genius in the conception of his many terrific pulls to the on; skill alone cannot rise to five sixes in a Lancashire and Yorkshire match, with seventeen boundaries thrown in—all drastically smitten in three and a half hours, with the third fifty of the 152 made in less than half an hour. At one period Paynter drove and pulled thirty runs from three overs, including two sixes and four fours. His attack on Verity was prodigious. The slow left-handed bowling came in naturally to Paynter's favourite cross-bat pull and on-drive; poor Verity did not know where to pitch the ball—and Paynter did, and usually it was into the crowd or on to the top of the stands. Greenwood kept taking Verity off when Paynter was due for the bowling; the Yorkshire captain rightly expected Macaulay and Smailes to bother, with 'going-away spin,' the left-handed son of Nimshi and his furious driving. Paynter played up to his luck, for, to say the truth, he once or twice committed the gross error of a hit clean in the face of the angle of Macaulay's break.

But what does all this rationalistic talk amount to (if it is rational)? We are discussing a young cricketer's vision and pluck, not merely the cold principles of batsmanship. 'Grey, grey is all theory and green the golden tree of life.' Theory would have ruined Lancashire on Saturday; science could not possibly have found a point of vantage, an abstract position, to expound itself, on Saturday's impish, incalculable and thoroughly unscientific turf. Paynter conquered because he lifted the Lancashire innings out of the realms of reason, out of the reach of canny cause and effect; he plunged the whole afternoon into melodrama, where virtue is ever triumphant. Skill is only the machine: the driving force is spirit. Paynter could not have reached the heights of the heroic if his mind and heart had not, the moment he set foot on the field, urged him on. (Not often does a Lancashire and Yorkshire match inspire a sermon. There are no sermons in stonewallers.)

Paynter's innings was Johnny Tyldesley all over again,

alike in its strength and dancing feet, the quick eye and iron forearms, the mighty drives, the voracious leap to the half-volley, the vehemence of the pull from the short ball. And, what was more glorious still, it was alike to Johnny Tyldesley in its escapades, its contempt of the niggling canons, its accumulative fury, ending in wholesale pillage of all sorts and conditions of bowling—savage batsmanship, primitive in power, instinctive in execution, muscular yet flexible, merciless, contemptuous, with recurrent and, to the Yorkshire attack, exasperating moments of caution. Last year, at Sheffield, Paynter batted with a long-drawn-out obstinacy against Yorkshire, for hours and hours, helping to save a match half lost. After Saturday's red ruin Yorkshire will now be able to see Paynter 'in the round'—as a cricketer of uncommon quality, only needing a nicer mingling of aggression and horse-sense to take his place with the really great players of the day.

Watson and Paynter scored 67 for Lancashire's first wicket in ninety minutes. A pull from a full-toss by Verity, clean into square leg's hands, accounted for Watson. Ernest Tyldesley showed us a brilliant hook as soon as he came in: then he went on the defence, more or less capably, while Paynter ran amok. Paynter fell over himself while pulling Verity for four. Thrice in four balls from Smailes he drove to the boundary, and from the last ball of the same over he was nearly bowled trying for a six. It was almost impossible to drop the ball on a good length for Paynter; his eye was rapid and comprehensive; anything a shade short or over-tossed was lustfully massacred. And, as I say, all this gaudy play in a Lancashire and Yorkshire match! I imagined the confusion and scepticism in the offices of the Yorkshire newspapers. The old posters, of course, would not do; and in my mind's eye I saw in bold type a new poster:

Vulgar Batting
by
PAYNTER

Paynter and Ernest Tyldesley held the second Lancashire wicket eighty minutes while the score was taken from 67 to 138—Tyldesley's share twenty. When he had made 89,

Paynter hit tremendously to leg for four: Sutcliffe ducked his head in time, and only just in time. The next ball Paynter tried to repeat the stroke, but it was only a half hit. Sutcliffe missed the chance even though he got his hands well to it; no doubt he was apprehensive of another attempt on his life. At this period we expected a boundary hit as a matter of course whenever Paynter was tackling the bowlers. He seemed, indeed, to be intent on much more than fours or sixers; now and again, he was obviously trying to hit twelvers and eighteeners, if not twenty-fourers. Yet, nearly all the other Lancashire batsmen were more or less helpless all the time; few of them looked like staying. Of course, the difficulties of Verity's spin were harder for a right-handed batsman to solve than they were for Paynter.

Iddon was caught in the slips from a vicious going-away break. Hallows defended in his old cool way for a while; then he drove at a loose ball and sent a catch to the deep-field. Paynter reached his hundred, out of 149, in just under three hours; he henceforward put the Yorkshire attack completely to rout, until fancy saw them like a flying broken remnant. A long-handled drive from Verity soared to the top of the football stand; another six was a colossal pull, broad as the two counties of Lancashire and Yorkshire put together. An offdrive brilliant and beautiful in poise made a classical contrast. And the end of Paynter's innings was exactly right; he went down on the crest of the wave. He hit another six from Verity, and next ball a crashing four to leg; then next ball he was superbly stumped attempting to hit a faster one bowled protectively short and wide. He walked from the field a hero, who in years to come will join the legendary hosts of the greatest of all county matches. The Bradford crowd gave Paynter a good Yorkshire reception, all the heartier because at last he was safely out of the way.

Whereupon Yorkshire suffered the afternoon's least tolerable trial. It was bad enough for Paynter to have scored 152 on a wicket which Verity and Macaulay might well have ordered and paid for in advance. It must have been an insupportable experience for the Yorkshire attack now to find itself held up and taken liberties with by the boys Parkinson and Parkin. Believe it or believe it not, Parkinson hit a six, too. Perhaps it is as well, and only Christian charity, that Emmott Robinson was not there to see it. Parkinson made several pretty cuts, and on the whole showed an eager eye and a sensitive and agreeable technique.

Verity was hit for five sixes during the afternoon. His analysis of eight wickets for 107 was bad for the pitch. He can spin the ball keenly enough, but he lacks a plan in his control of length. Moreover, he seldom gets the batsman guessing while the ball is in the air. Macaulay did not have a fair share of fortune; none the less, an off-break bowler, helped by a pitch sticky for at least two hours, might have been expected to bowl out most left-handed batsmen as quickly as they came in. Paynter could scarcely have lasted half an hour had he not sent all ideas of consistency of length hurtling to the intense inane. There's nothing like letting the bowler understand firmly and at once that he really does not know how or where to bowl. I thought that Greenwood wasted heaps of runs by placing no long-leg fieldsman for Paynter; a third man is lost on him. But this is possibly to give information to the enemy, though it will come to them rather late in the day, after the damage has been done. I wonder what Wilfred Rhodes will think about it all when he reads the accounts this morning: A bowler's wicket.....Paynter 152.....five sixes.....seventeen boundaries.....the very moment his back is turned, so to say.

SECOND DAY

A sodden ground prevented cricket in the Lancashire and Yorkshire match until half-past two this afternoon. Then a splendid crowd cheered Sutcliffe and Holmes as they walked to the wicket. The very first ball of the day, an outswinging half-volley from Sibbles, got the wicket of Holmes, who chopped a catch to backward point. He came back to the pavilion in a silence that could be felt—broken only by the voice of one man, who announced to the world that he would be jiggered. Two consecutive maiden overs intensified the tragic moment, and Hopwood stuck up the immaculate Sutcliffe with two very nasty spinners. The crowd made apprehensive noises, and in the secret places of the heart prepared themselves for unmentionable horrors. Not for many years have I seen a Yorkshire eleven so severely worried by Lancashire as they were during this latest Bank Holiday. The wicket was not impossible yet, but the ball came from the earth at different paces and angles, and Sutcliffe and Mitchell many times smote it with passionate blows of the bat. Meanwhile the sun shone, hinting of wrath to come. Yorkshire, of course, deserved a sticky pitch, for Lancashire on Saturday had to put up with one.

For half an hour Sutcliffe and Mitchell defended austerely while the score staggered to the aggregate of eight, whereupon Mitchell was clean bowled playing forward to a pretty length ball by Sibbles. The second ball received by Leyland stood straight up and hit him on the hand: the pot was beginning to boil humorously. A glorious off-drive by Sutcliffe from one of Hopwood's own half-volleys provoked the Yorkshire roar, though there was as much relief as triumph in the sound of it. During all this palpitating crisis Sutcliffe seemed not at all perturbed: he played stylish strokes with the old, self-conscious momentary arrest of his pose, as though seeing himself and saying it was good. And at the end of each over he leaned nonchalantly on his bat, cross-legged (imagination saw him cross-gartered, too, like some Malvolio of the cricket field). A great player and deliciously aware of it himself.

Leyland and Sutcliffe held Yorkshire's third wicket for half an hour, and as they gradually added twenty runs the tension eased and the crowd began to look rather more like Whit Monday. Hopwood could not spin viciously: it appeared that Lancashire's chances again rested with Sibbles, who often caused the ball to rise awkwardly. It was from one of these jumping balls that Leyland fell to a catch at short-leg close in: he could not get away from it. Sutcliffe twice pulled short bowling from Hopwood to the edge of the field, the crowd trying loyally by lung power to increase the ball's momentum and transform sluggish threes into fours of prosperous velocity. It is possible that Eckersley was just wondering whether to take Hopwood off when Hopwood for the first time compelled his break to spit venomously. And the victim was Sutcliffe himself: he could not even exploit his masterful delayed stroke. The ball flew from his blade to

Sibbles in the slips. For 75 minutes Sutcliffe had, so to say, polished the obstinate rock of Yorkshire obstinacy, mingling defence and refined composure in proportion.

The pitch was now behaving quaintly, especially at the end to which Sibbles bowled—though it was not a bit more whimsical than on Saturday. Indeed, the conditions of play have so far in the match favoured both sides with an equal capriciousness. Another lively piece of spin by Hopwood accounted for Greenwood, who, like a man possessed entirely with agitation and trying to do many things at once, sent another slip catch. Hopwood's next ball, a dainty half-volley, clean bowled Smailes—Yorkshire 42 for six and signs of hysteria from a dear old lady in the crowd. The total was still 42 when Barber tried to drive Sibbles, only to be cleverly caught by Hallows, who held the ball after running with his back to the batsman at mid-on. Three wickets had fallen at this same inglorious total of 42. Most of the Yorkshire batsmen failed through poor footwork and excess of abstract science, just as all the Lancashire batsmen on Saturday, excepting the immortal Paynter, failed from the same cause, while the wicket was at its worst.

Yorkshire's pitiful innings of 46 contained not a single boundary hit, and the last six wickets were overwhelmed for eight runs. I heard the fact stated that the turf was better for bowlers than it was on Saturday, but from the evidence of my own eyes I maintain that the ball did its work at much the same pace. Yorkshire's misfortune was that they did not bat before lunch while the ground remained tolerably moist. The collapse proved the old story, which is that it is no use batsmen seeking to exploit academic strokes against spinning and jumping balls. The Yorkshire downfall, like that of most of the Lancashire batsmen, only served to demonstrate the common-sense methods on the wicket of Paynter. He was the real rationalist, because he solved his problems in a practical way by making it impossible for the Yorkshire bowlers to pitch a length. Moreover, he combined with his aggression the nicest judgment until he had the attack at his mercy.

Sibbles did not send down a single loose ball, and very cleverly did he ring the changes on his off-break and swinger. Magnificent fielding lent power to Sibbles and Hopwood.

Parkin nearly ran Sutcliffe out by an electrical throw-in. A new spirit has come to the Lancashire side—the dash and enterprise of youth and youth's splendid distrust of shibboleths. The reader will observe that in this account I have not tried very hard to adorn or decorate the day's story. The facts make their own purple periods. The simpler the narrative on these occasions the better.

Yorkshire's first innings lasted a few minutes under two hours, and Sibbles was hit for only 10 runs in that time, and he took seven wickets and deserved them all. Holmes and Sutcliffe again walked to the middle at five o'clock with responsibility plainly sitting upon the shoulders of both, yet even now Sutcliffe reclined on his bat elegantly while Sibbles prepared for the attack. Half an hour and more of bitter contention made the score-board announce to the downcast multitude that Yorkshire were actually 34 for none. Iddon bowled in the place of Hopwood, and at last Sibbles was given a resting period. Young Parkin, whose fielding all day had been swift and beautiful to see, bowled at Sibbles's end. His first ball got Holmes leg-before-wicket, and Duckworth's appeal was positively unchristian in its exultant altitude. At twenty minutes to six Sutcliffe hit a long hop from Parkin for four—this was Yorkshire's first boundary all day after some two hours and three-quarters of enchained and unhappy labour. Parkin then worried Sutcliffe with two clever off-breaks: either of them would have bowled a batsman less accomplished than Sutcliffe in the modern art of exploiting the second line of defence. And Sutcliffe nearly put up another break-back off Parkin to forward short leg: the boy is delightfully keen and needs nothing so much as experience. An ear-splitting, dogmatic, and unsuccessful appeal for leg-before-wicket by Duckworth awakened the irony of the crowd, which for too long had remained silent. And a sixer by Sutcliffe off Parkin caused quite a tornado of triumphant noises. Obviously it was a mightier sixer than any of Paynter's on Saturday, for the simple reason that it was hit by a Yorkshireman.

Sutcliffe reached a masterful 50 in rather beyond an hour; he thrives on adversity, he seldom wastes his qualities on prosaic, obscure, and insignificant occasions. With Sibbles out of action Lancashire's attack lost a deal of edge and accuracy. He bowled again at a quarter-past six, when Yorkshire were 75 for one, and straightway he forced Sutcliffe to half hit a jumping ball dangerously in front of short forward leg. At the sign of mortal error in Sutcliffe, Eckersley threw up his hands impulsively as though seeking visions of glory. For Sutcliffe, and only Sutcliffe, stands between Lancashire and a great victory, unless of course, the weather answers the prayers of innumerable Yorkshire boys tonight. These prayers, I trust, will be opposed tonight by equally patriotic Lancashire boys. The contending petitions will no doubt place Providence in a difficult position, but that cannot be helped. Victory in this match will come as new life to Lancashire cricket. To-day's achievement in itself tells eloquently enough of revolt from the ancient awe in the presence of Yorkshiremen.

THIRD DAY

Lancashire won a magnificent victory at Bradford yesterday by an innings and 50 runs: Yorkshire were all out at a quarter past one, and the small crowd departed severally in appropriate silence and meditation. The champion county deserved to lose; they found themselves outplayed at all points by a new-born Lancashire eleven—a side of eager cricketers all working together with a will and a relish. Old Trafford ought to be crowded this week for Kent and Surrey: not for many years have we had a Lancashire team so keen and ambitious. The skill may not be of the highest class in bowling; too much depends on Sibbles. But the spirit is there. On Monday the fielding flashed and darted over the field in a most invigorating way—and young Parkin was a Spring-heeled Jack of alacrity.

It cannot be said that Yorkshire yesterday put up a challenging fight. To say the truth, the batting was more deplorable on the whole than any I have seen in these great tussles. And much of the Lancashire attack contained spurious stuff. Hopwood got two wickets with full-tosses and another with a long-hop. Yorkshire urgently need a relay of sound batsmen to come in after the fall of the third wicket. On yesterday's showing David Hunter would be good enough to bat No. 5 in the Yorkshire team.

The wicket could not be trusted at the end to which Sibbles bowled with a sustained tenacity and sureness of length. At the other end there was little to contend with that is not normal to a Bradford pitch in rainy weather. Besides, if you are going to allow full-tosses to get you out, it is little use cursing the wicket. From the third ball of the day Sutcliffe drove Sibbles beautifully to the off for four; the last ball of the same over rang Yorkshire's death-knell. Sutcliffe was guilty of a rather careless stroke, for Sibbles attacked him on the leg stump, and instead of making his bat dead, Sutcliffe propelled the stroke too forcibly and sent a catch to forward short-leg—Ernest Tyldesley—who fell over and held the prize with transparent jubilation. Poor Sutcliffe realised his error even before the stroke was finished, and as his bat found contact with the ball he groaned out of a deep despair—realising he had blundered beyond all power of recovery. The first ball of the succeeding over, by Hopwood, settled the account of Mitchell most ingloriously. The ball swerved, but it was a full-toss, and Mitchell, trying to push to the on, inexplicably missed and was given out leg-before-wicket.

The Yorkshire score was only 91 when Barber let fly agriculturally at another full-toss from Hopwood and was bowled. The stroke brought to mind visions of windmills and rustic meadows. Leyland, stung to a death-or-glory desperation, pounced on a half-volley from Sibbles and drove a quite passionate four to the on. The he swept Hopwood to leg for three and shortly afterwards assaulted Sibbles for fourteen off three balls, a six magnificently straight and powerful, and two exquisitely placed drives. Hopwood was taken off in place of the alert and eager young Parkin. But Hopwood quickly came into action again—a lucky move, and not obviously rational seeing that he had not bowled well. For that matter, he bowled indifferently all the morning. Luck was with him, though, for after Greenwood had been brilliantly stumped by Duckworth playing out at a quick ball from Sibbles, Hopwood sent Leyland a very short ball which 'lifted' slightly just as Leyland's bat came across for a long-handled pull. He was really too far from the pitch of the long hop, using his arms overmuch, and he could not decrease the stroke's swing in time. He sent a catch to mid-on, where Eckersley jumped up alive with appetite and put the finishing touch to Yorkshire's funeral.

The victory was really achieved on Saturday by Paynter's glorious cricket, and, of course, Sibbles must be applauded for the way he jumped at the chance given him by the poorest Yorkshire batting side of recent years. I would like to dispel certain mistaken notions which have got abroad about Paynter's innings. It seems nowadays that if a county batsman hits a six he is regarded unsound. But is it sound science to allow the bowler to find dangerous places on an imperfect wicket; is it sound science to stand tight-footed and play tentatively at the ball as it begins to spin? What happened in this match, to the abstract scientists, those canny men who reduce batsmanship to a few inflexible canons based on what is possible on a hard wicket, where the straight bat can be trusted to play down the line of the ball? They were all reduced to helplessness; not one of them looked anything but vulnerable.

The fact I wish strongly to emphasise about Paynter's innings is that it was living science, distinct from the dead, barren theory of nearly all the others. He did not hit blindly—save once, when at the beginning of his innings he was indiscreet enough to try to hit against Macaulay's spin. For the most part Paynter's defensive play was as good as Sutcliffe's; on Saturday between half-past three and half-past four, when the wicket really was bad, he defended with the utmost regard for first principles, his head down, his feet near the line of the ball, his bat positive not negative, and his eye watchful. Never once did he edge a ball while playing defensively. No cricketer could possibly score 152 on a bad pitch by happy-go-lucky methods. Paynter has often proved that he knows how to maintain a truly scientific defence; at Sheffield last year he saved Lancashire from defeat by two long and entirely principled innings. The power and fury of his driving on Saturday were admirable in their discreet opportunism: he merely punished the loose bowling—having made it loose himself by swift resourceful footwork. But the thrilling rhetoric of his sixes and fours did not blind discern-

341

ing critics to the important fact that his innings as a whole was solidly founded on judgment, on a bat as straight—to the good ball—as any seen in the game. Heavens, has cricket come to this: that a batsman is suspected of heresy if he pulls a long hop out of the ground with a cross-bat? How on earth can you deal with a short ball with a *straight* bat? No doubt Paynter will never be a consistent run-getting machine. The country has more than enough of these robots. J. T. Tyldesley was never consistent. But when he did score a hundred he won a match. And that is what Paynter did on Saturday—and will continue to do so, many times and often, if he always listens to his natural impulses and turns a deaf ear to the unimaginative sophisticators of these days—dull purists who apparently never saw any batsmanship of the Tyldesley-David Denton epoch. At the present time there are few batsmen in the land I would sooner trust to win a match than Paynter—or to save a match, if it comes to that.

The rest of the match was pitiful anti-climax. Yorkshire's tail is long enough nowadays to wag the dog. Smailes was bowled by Parkin with an immense gap between his leg and bat. The less said about the other Yorkshire batsmen (a technical term) the better. Their efforts would have looked pretty on the village green. At the end the Lancashire fielding lost its glamour; Iddon missed a catch in the long field. Sibbles to the end was on top of his opposition; seldom has he bowled with a sharper edge. The wicket was definitely dangerous only in one spot at the pavilion end; Sibbles contrived to hit this spot at least once an over. His superb analysis came as the consequence of clever seam bowling; he did not spin the ball, but rather, he 'cut' it, trusting to his swing and the wicket to do the rest. Leyland's 43, scored in forty minutes with one six and five fours, was dashing cricket, hedged round by mortality. He has a hole in his bat, and the bowler who cannot find it in an hour must seem very like the hen that dashes itself against a hedgerow in the endeavour to get through a gap a yard at least wide.

YORKSHIRE V LANCASHIRE 1932
SCORES

LANCASHIRE
First Innings

Watson, c Holmes, b Verity	19
Paynter, st Wood, b Verity	152
Tyldesley (E.), lbw, b Verity	20
Iddon, c Sutcliffe, b Verity	2
Hallows, c Smailes, b Verity	0
Hopwood, c Mitchell, b Verity	2
Parkinson, c & b Bowes	39
Parkin, c Mitchell, b Verity	13
P. T. Eckersley, b Verity	5
Sibbles, not out	3
Duckworth, c Sutcliffe, b Bowes	2
Extras lb4, nb2	6
Total	263

YORKSHIRE

First Innings		Second Innings	
Holmes, c Tyldesley, b Sibbles	0	lbw, b Parkin	7
Sutcliffe, c Sibbles, b Hopwood	27	c Tyldesley, b Sibbles	61
Mitchell, b Sibbles	1	lbw, b Hopwood	13
Leyland, c Parkin, b Sibbles	6	c Eckersley, b Hopwood	43
Barber, c Hallows, b Sibbles	3	b Hopwood	2
F. E. Greenwood, c Watson, b Hopwood	3	st Duckworth, b Sibbles	9
Smailes, b Hopwood	0	b Parkin	7
Wood, lbw, b Sibbles	0	b Sibbles	11
Verity, not out	4	c Iddon, b Sibbles	8
Macaulay, c Watson, b Sibbles	0	not out	1
Bowes, c Watson, b Sibbles	0	c Watson, b Sibbles	0
Extras b2	2	Extras b1, lb4	5
Total	46	Total	167

BOWLING ANALYSIS
LANCASHIRE—First Innings

	O.	M.	R.	W.		O.	M.	R.	W.
Bowes	10	5	16	2	Verity	39	13	107	8
Smailes	13	4	30	0	Leyland	11	3	39	0
Macaulay	29	10	65	0					

YORKSHIRE—First Innings

	O.	M.	R.	W.		O.	M.	R.	W.
Sibbles	20	13	10	7	Hopwood	20	6	34	3

Second Innings

	O.	M.	R.	W.		O.	M.	R.	W.
Sibbles	27	8	58	5	Parkin	12	4	32	2
Hopwood	25	3	52	3	Parkinson	1	0	2	0
Iddon	10	2	18	0					

343

YORKSHIRE V LANCASHIRE 1932

July 30 August 1/2 Old Trafford

FIRST DAY

AS I approached the entrance of the ground at Old Trafford on Saturday, a few moments late, the place looked deserted; nobody was there, excepting a little boy who anxiously spelled out the notice which says that you pay your money at your own risk of the weather. Inside the ground a not very multitudinous crowd sat in silence; the occasion might well have been Lancashire v. Northamptonshire.

But perhaps the absence of noise was less a sign of lack of interest in the ancient feud than of sheer gloom in the hearts of Lancashire folk. For Lancashire's innings began dreadfully. Bowes made the new, shiny ball rear, and Watson, after ducking his head once or twice, without any sign of emotion whatever, put his bat up to another bumper and sent the simplest of chances to forward short-leg, who was Leyland, who probably held the catch saying: 'It's a shame to take the money.' A run later Hopwood was caught at the wicket from another of Bowes's rising balls; Lancashire were seven for two wickets—a state of things which years ago would have turned Old Trafford into a vast cauldron of seething, scandalised humanity. Not one exultant howl announced that anybody from Yorkshire on Saturday had come to watch the match; at one time they invaded us in hundreds, hordes from Kirkheaton, Laisterdyke, and other barbarous habitations.

The wicket was not difficult, and as soon as the new ball lost its propulsive powers Bowes dwindled considerably. Macaulay attacked with his own splendid show of temper, and after a few balls from the Manchester end he crossed over and tried his tricks from round the wicket. Verity was put on early; Leyland, too, swung his arm, and nobody dreamed of hitting his half-volleys. Macaulay apparently suffered from a strain, and he gave up bowling. Verity and Leyland sup-

344

ported the Yorkshire attack unchanged for a long while, and Ernest Tyldesley, with Iddon, experienced little difficulty in staving away the ruin which early on threatened to overwhelm Lancashire. Both defended easefully, and both seemed to be telling the Selection Committee that there is not much to choose between the spin of Verity and that of Leyland in point of dark craft and sinfully concealed obliquity. At lunch, after two hours' play, Lancashire were 64 for two—the usual 'dour' struggle, with the summer game turned into a penance.

After the interval Bowes bumped the ball again, and Ernest Tyldesley once had to get his head out of the way with dramatic swiftness, whereat a voice in the crowd became profane and said—but I would need Laurence Sterne's black marbled page to suggest what he did say. Still, his indignation did at least bring back to the game the authentic spirit—somebody obviously was taking the cricket to heart and suffering the proper miseries.

Lancashire's total reached 83 before the third wicket fell. Then Iddon was bowled by Bowes, who mixes his really quick ball cleverly. Iddon's valuable and dutiful innings of 32 lasted ten minutes short of two hours. Ernest Tyldesley batted with the skill and usage of years behind him, though he nearly played a ball from his pad to his wickets when his score was in the forties. Brilliant fielding deprived several of his strokes of their true value. He arrived at his fifty by means of a capital hook from Bowes; he had been Lancashire's hope and succour for two hours and twenty minutes.

Then Paynter woke up the gathering multitude by a fierce, rapid pull from Bowes to leg—a great stroke. It flashed through the encounter like the spark of a fire which for a long time has failed to get alight. Next over a pouncing slip catch by Mitchell accounted for Tyldesley. The pot was on the boil at last. Butterworth obstructed for ten minutes, then played a stroke forward from Bowes, who with unprecedented agility darted or gravitated to the earth and picked up the ball and threw it in and hit the stumps before Butterworth, so to say, knew where he was. Bowes really ought to give fair warning before indulging in such nerve-racking acts of fieldsmanship.

Half the Lancashire side were out for 105—a poor performance on a wicket which, but for an odd ball, did not lend to the bowlers particular assistance. Many balls, indeed, stopped quite still after falling on the ground—almost asking for a drastic blow from the bat. Paynter once again could not recapture the accuracy of stroke play which won him fame and prosperity in May; Verity bowled him leg stump, and the stroke he attempted was crooked as a railway signal on Sundays. Sibbles pulled his first ball, from Verity, into the hands of square-leg, who dropped the catch comically; the play lacked style rather terribly, and there was ironic laughter in the crowd. Verity bowled a capital length, but the turf seldom gave 'bite' to his break; the batting was crude in foot-work. The Yorkshire fielding, usually good, wavered again when Eckersley was missed from Bowes at short-leg; the game hereabout possessed a real Saturday-afternoon flavour in his batsmanship—the fours were missing, but all the in-security was there. Eckersley, trying a drive against Verity, was stumped by yards; the ball turned a foot and people said, 'Ah! A sticky wicket.' But it was only sticky in the sense defined by a famous Indian maharajah: 'A sticky wicket is one on which the ball sticks.'

Booth placed the occasion momentarily into its proper rural category by lifting Verity for four to the off; we usually have to wait for the 'tail-enders' nowadays to show us what a bat was made with a hump for—and if that sentence is ungrammatical blame the extraordinary excitement which has just seized me at the sight of a six at all during a weak innings by Lancashire. Another glorious hit into the pavilion by Booth stirred the crowd to the acclamation which in the olden times made a Lancashire and Yorkshire match epical. It was a beautiful stroke; an easeful pull square, clean over the rails. This was the way Verity would have been treated by Lancashire batsmen of J. T. Tyldesley's period; he would have got them out, of course, for he is a splendid bowler. But my!—how they would have lambasted him first on a wicket like Saturday's. And as a consequence of this punishment Verity would have been a better bowler still, because he would have found the need of strategy; he lacks, as it is, subtlety: he is not compelled to think by the modern batsman, who does not think himself, but mechanically

346

pushes out at the ball in front of his pads, over after over.

Yorkshire were handicapped by the absence of Macaulay, whose strain kept him out of the field after lunch; at four o'clock Mitchell also had to go into the pavilion limping. Dennis came out for Macaulay, and Mitchell, a brilliant fieldsman, had young Parkin for his deputy, and, of course, Parkin is almost as good in the field as Mitchell. This boy, I hope, will get another chance in the Lancashire eleven later on.

Thanks to Booth's bravery and energy, the Lancashire eighth wicket carried the score to 153; Booth was then bowled aiming at another six. He had a grand reception from the pavilion. If Booth, with little or no batting technique, was able to drive Verity, why couldn't the other and the accredited Lancashire batsmen drive him at all!

Duckworth joined Sibbles, wearing his England cap; what is wrong with the beautiful red rose of Lancashire in a match against Yorkshire? The crowd at this time of the day was fairly large, but the old vociferous humour did not announce itself; it was a quiet crowd on the whole, yet ready to applaud good play on both sides generously. Duckworth drove Verity for four to the on with a stroke of warlike power and appearance; his spirit, plus the technique of Ernest Tyldesley, would give us another J. T. Tyldesley. The closing part of Lancashire's innings, indeed, showed a grit which was woefully wanting at the beginning; even the stroke to deep-leg which got Duckworth caught was at any rate positive and not negative. Bowes again achieved an astonishing piece of fielding by throwing down the wicket of Hodgson from quite a distance wide of mid-on; he enjoyed a good day, though his short rising balls were absurdly flattered. The classical way of hooking a 'bumper' was to get the body rather to the offside, so that if the stroke missed its object the ball passed harmlessly by the batsman's left shoulder. On Saturday most batsmen stood still until the ball was 'on them': then they blindly scooped at it or ducked heads in sudden panic. Bowes cannot be called a fast bowler of pedigree so long as he relies so much on his short rising stuff; I would like to see Sutcliffe dealing with it.

Yorkshire's innings began at a quarter-past five; Sibbles's

347

first ball was hit for three to leg by Holmes. And from his third ball Sibbles missed a hard return, one-handed, from Sutcliffe. True the chance was not easy, but then, Sutcliffe must never be expected to hand an innings on a plate to a bowler—before he has scored or at any subsequent time. The crowd groaned at the spectacle of Sibbles giving Sutcliffe another innings; but Sibbles himself had the greatest cause of anybody for sorrow and chagrin. Personally, if I were to miss a catch from Sutcliffe before he scored I should fast and pray all the next day and probably wear a hair-shirt. Sutcliffe proceeded to force Sibbles twice to the off for fours by means of his own pretty 'leaning' drive. Modernist though he is and master of the second line of defence, Sutcliffe yet knows the advantage of playing to the off with his left side forward, and how beautifully he keeps his head down and 'over' the stroke! Holmes and Sutcliffe played with confidence; their bats made a purposeful sound, telling us that both men were getting set ball by ball. They, of course, declined to hurry themselves; they were like men building a stout wall brick by brick—and on the whole they were as interesting to look at. But the crowd stayed on; possibly it was a case similar to that of the man in Phil May's picture—'Anything in reason, but I will not go 'ome.'

Booth opened Lancashire's bowling with Sibbles, and Hodgson did not come on until the new ball had lost its polish. His first over contained four deliveries which shrieked to be cut, but the batsmen were masters of themselves and they did not cut. ('It's not a business stroke,' as a famous Yorkshireman once said, and his name was not J. T. Brown.) Sutcliffe cannot cut; he lets his body, and therefore his weight, fall away backwards towards square leg, as he tries the stroke.

At ten minutes past six, when Yorkshire were 43 after nearly an hour's hard work, Holmes was drawn forward by a pretty slow ball by Iddon, which turned enough to elude the bat and find the stumps. This advance of Lancashire at the end of the day made all the difference in the world to the positions of the two teams; with Sutcliffe and Holmes undefeated at close of play Yorkshire definitely would have been winning. In the next over bowled by Hodgson

Duckworth let out a terrific appeal for leg-before-wicket against Sutcliffe, and the crowd, or part of it, agreed with Duckworth and almost, but not quite, made as much noise as Duckworth himself.

At half-past six 227 runs had been scored in the day; Iddon bowled with admirable steadiness; his length has recently improved out of recognition.

SECOND DAY

There was no cricket until noon at Old Trafford yesterday, and it was marvellous that we saw any play all day. At breakfast the rain tumbled down, and, though the morning cleared, a huge cloud poised itself over the field even as the cricketers went into action. Had this cloud burst only for a minute a flood would have overwhelmed everybody ruinously.

The wicket at the outset was very soft; sawdust disfigured the earth. Lancashire proceeded to throw runs away by means of tactics as curious as any I can remember even in a cricket match. The position of the game at noon was this: Lancashire, having scored only 170, had to attack on a sodden turf, on which even a medium-paced bowler could not trust his foothold. The obvious policy for Lancashire was to keep the Yorkshire batsmen quiet by steady length bowling until such time as the pitch dried. Every run thrown away by Lancashire was bound to be inimical to them; later in the day there was the dreadful prospect of keen spin by Verity on a sticky wicket.

In these circumstances Eckersley put Hodgson on to bowl—the last man in England that any of us would expect to stand up on slippery grass. Poor Hodgson did his best, but he could not maintain control over the ball; he did very well to command an attitude of the body not definitely recumbent after each wheel of his arm. Hodgson was hit for more than 20 in six overs. But this was not Lancashire's only act of dubious policy; Iddon was taken off after a short spell—taken off immediately after he nearly got Sutcliffe caught at the wicket. Booth captured the wicket of Barber at 101, in his first over. But by this time Yorkshire were on top; they could not possibly have arranged the Lancashire attack more suitably for their purposes themselves. If Arthur Mold had been in the Lancashire eleven yesterday—let alone Hodgson—nobody would have looked for a moment to see him grappling with a slippery foothold.

When Leyland came in Iddon, of course, might have been a risky bowler to exploit; a left-handed batsman enjoys a left-handed bowler's break. Yet Butterworth was put on against Leyland, and a right-hander's leg-spin is easier for a left-handed batsman than any other spin in existence. I found it hard to watch all this waste of Lancashire's slender chances, all this questionable handling of the situation. Lancashire's luck was bad enough in having to bowl at all on the slow pitch: it was exasperating to see wrong ideas playing into Yorkshire's hands as well.

After lunch Hodgson bowled again—a succession of long-hops and full-tosses. He was lambasted for 21 in three overs. What cricket! Here was a problem for cricketers to revel in: while the turf remained easy the duty of the fielding side was to keep the runs down, to worry the batsmen by a persistently good length, to give nothing away, not the shadow of an easy run. And Lancashire served up all sorts of lengths, short stuff especially.

Sutcliffe played masterfully, and reached his century at his sweet will; Leyland too was at liberty to consider only his own inclinations. Just before lunch he drove a ball back to Sibbles terrifically, and Sibbles stopped it with his leg, and fell down in brief agony. Fortunately he was not crippled for life; he did not even need to leave the field. In less than three-quarters of an hour after lunch Sutcliffe and Leyland made 60 brilliant runs; they treated the bowling with a proper contempt. Sutcliffe opened out his style; a dashing drive over mid-off's head seemed to have a fine note of disdain. There was a lot of clever run-stealing too; Yorkshire were hereabouts taking revenge for the ignominy suffered at Bradford in May. They were given a grand start at the beginning of the day; at the chance of an inch, Yorkshiremen do not stop at an ell or a rod, pole, or perch. The big crowd was most sportsmanlike; big-hearted cheers greeted the splendid stroke play of Sutcliffe and Leyland; on no other ground in the land would a winning visiting team receive

350

applause so generous, certainly not in Kent. Possibly the Old Trafford multitude nowadays is glad to see good batting unconditionally, even at the expense of Lancashire bowlers in a Yorkshire match.

At last the incomparable Sutcliffe made a fatal mistake; he played too late and was leg-before-wicket to Sibbles, who missed him on Saturday before he had scored. The ball kept low. Sutcliffe's innings of 135 lasted three hours and three-quarters; and he and Leyland scored 141 for Yorkshire's third wicket in 105 minutes. When Sutcliffe returned from the wicket, trying to look modest, the pavilion rose at him—a great North Country gesture. Had he been a Lancashire cricketer he could not possibly have been greeted with warmer pride. Once again Sutcliffe proved his quality in a big match—though really he ought to have got a duck!

The crowd yesterday was more like the old vociferous gatherings; at one time of the afternoon, when Yorkshire were well on the high road to victory, a terrific howl suddenly came out of the packed seats. The match was then momentarily quiet, and the howl was not provoked by any particular incident: it was merely some man from Mytholmroyd giving vent to a satisfaction which had become too good to keep to himself. On Saturday no evidence could be found in the crowd that a single Yorkshire spectator was present; yesterday was different. When their county cricketers are winning Yorkshiremen appear as though out of the earth, quick and plentiful as mushrooms. I never see any of them away from home during a Yorkshire collapse; where do they hide, or how do they disguise themselves?

In the afternoon Eckersley could not take the field because of a strained shoulder. Mitchell pottered about exactly at the time of day when Verity must have been wanting to look at the wicket; and just after half-past three a clever catch on the on side, close in, caught Leyland, from Sibbles, who was now bowling well. Leyland's innings, full of his homely nature, lasted two hours and ten minutes; he hit fourteen fours. A ball or two later Sibbles clean bowled Sellers, and so half the Yorkshiremen were accounted for, with 265 scored. The pitch was playing quicker—all the more reason now had Lancashire to deplore the unsteadiness of their bowling earlier in the day, while the pitch was easy for batsmen. Iddon came on again and began to turn the ball—an ominous sight for Lancashiremen to see.

Some of us in our old-fashioned faith in the imagination of county captains expected Yorkshire either to declare at five o'clock or to follow the example of Sutcliffe and Leyland and force the pace so that Lancashire might be sent to the wicket for an uncomfortable hour or so at the afternoon's end. But the Yorkshire 'tail' played stupid nitwitted cricket; they would not try to get runs and would not get out. They merely bored us. Mitchell stonewalled endlessly—he really played the best cricket of the day for Lancashire; he stonewalled to the extent of 50 in two hours and twenty minutes. Macaulay, too, seemed to be batting for Lancashire. In one and the same day we have seen two shocking examples of bad tactics in the Lancashire and Yorkshire match, by the rival captains. Surely it was Yorkshire's sensible game to make the Lancashire batsmen face the music once again at half-past five at the latest. I sincerely hope Sussex can win the championship; as to Lancashire and Yorkshire, I am tired of their annual exhibition of 'dourness,' or—to give it the proper name—its solemn witless tedium. A plague on both your houses!

THIRD DAY

At lunch yesterday Lancashire seemed likely to save the match. The score was then 118 for one wicket, Ernest Tyldesley not out 54, Hopwood not out 40. The Old Trafford wicket was described by a Lancashire player as 'easy,' though now and again Verity found a spot. After lunch a dreadful collapse happened; five wickets fell in less than three-quarters of an hour for 25.

Lancashire were really 'let down' by Iddon and Paynter, two men who are supposed to be potential England cricketers. Both were guilty of irresolute behaviour at a crisis. Iddon stuck up his bat nervously at a rising ball which he could have avoided, given the wits. He sent a baby catch to forward short-leg. Paynter repeatedly walked across to the off side to balls from Bowes which missed his wicket by inches. 'He'll be bowled leg-stump in a minute,' said a friend who was sitting with me. And Paynter was bowled leg-stump. Had Paynter and Iddon endured for an hour between them Yorkshire could not easily have won; each of them displayed the skill and temperament of schoolboys. Booth, too, lost his wicket by stupid methods: he time after time moved backwards from Bowes, holding out a sinfully crooked bat.

It was left to Sibbles, Eckersley and Duckworth to show us how Lancashire might have defended to the day's end granted some solid support from Iddon and Paynter. Sibbles stayed in an hour and three-quarters, and was unbeaten at the finish—clear proof here of a fairly reliable pitch, for Sibbles is too slow in footwork to survive for long against a turning ball.

Shortly before three o'clock Lancashire were 143 for six; but only one more wicket was taken by Yorkshire in the next hour. Eckersley showed excellent obstinacy with Sibbles, and Duckworth struggled gamely for nearly half an hour. If the 'tail' could keep at bay the Yorkshiremen, why couldn't the batsmen responsible for the middle of the Lancashire innings set their teeth likewise? They might at at all events have spared us feebleness and incompetence.

Yorkshire really were lucky not to suffer the consequence of the shiftlessness which spoiled their batting late on Monday afternoon. A threatening raincloud came up the sky while Eckersley and Sibbles stonewalled at a quarter to four. If that cloud had burst Yorkshire would have had cause to curse themselves for not declaring at tea on Monday.

Watson was quickly accounted for when the match was continued on a cool morning. Then Ernest Tyldesley came forth and gave us the best that is in him, which means the best cricket possible for any living batsman to show to lovers of refined stroke-play. Two brilliant hooks in one over from Bowes let us understand he was seeing the ball. Meanwhile Hopwood played forward well and watched every trick of the Yorkshire bowlers. Now and again he took the liberty of driving a four to the off. The runs came almost at the rate of one a minute, which was an admirable tempo for a side fighting uphill. Verity was not put on until Lancashire were 67 for one; significantly enough, he attacked from over the wicket (cricketers will draw their own conclusions about the

353

state of the pitch). Verity occasionally spun the ball enough to make the difference between a thoroughly safe and unsafe stroke; and three slips crouched on the batsmen's doorstep holding out supplicatory hands. But Tyldesley and Hopwood for the most part looked at ease; the only criticism invited by their methods was that a drastic drive might have upset the length of Verity. It is strange that while modern batsmen are prepared to risk leg-before-wicket by getting in front they will not risk their wicket trying a hit. The one risk is quite as dangerous as the other, and, what is more, cannot obtain a boundary.

In Verity's first over after lunch a ball 'popped' ever so gently; Ernest Tyldesley played a 'dead bat' cleverly, but he could not kill his stroke altogether. He was beautifully caught at second slip by Mitchell who darted in and held his prize exultantly with one hand. Tyldesley's innings lasted nearly two hours; it was technically cultured and, better still, it was an innings of character. Tyldesley was out at 121, Iddon at 122, and Paynter at 124. No side in a losing position could very well hope to win through from such a breakdown. Butterworth hit one finely tempered four to the on before succumbing to Verity's spin. Hopwood was fifth out at 130, capitally caught one-handed by Bowes at mid-on. It was left to Sibbles, as I have said, to demonstrate how close the finish must have been if all his colleagues had placed faith in a straight bat and shown a cool and determined spirit. The .patience of Hopwood and the mastery of Tyldesley before lunch deserved a better end, or, rather, a better middle. Verity's bowling was always telling us how difficult he can be on a sticky pitch; yesterday, though, the wicket was one on which he ought not to have been given permission to dictate to the batsmen and exhibit a length of his own choosing. Yorkshire fielded keenly; Macaulay and Mitchell were constantly agile and hostile.

YORKSHIRE V LANCASHIRE 1932
SCORES

LANCASHIRE

First Innings		Second Innings	
Watson, c Leyland, b Bowes	1	c Wood, b Macaulay	16
Hopwood, c Wood, b Bowes	5	c Bowes, b Verity	44
Tyldesley, c Mitchell, b Verity	50	c Mitchell, b Verity	56
Iddon, b Bowes	32	c Leyland, b Bowes	1
Paynter, b Verity	12	b Bowes	0
H. R. W. Butterworth, run out	4	b Verity	12
P. T. Eckersley, st Wood, b Verity	7	lbw, b Macaulay	4
Sibbles, not out	20	not out	28
Booth, b Verity	26	b Bowes	5
Duckworth, c Barber, b Bowes	7	lbw, b Verity	6
Hodgson, run out	0	st Wood, b Verity	0
Extras b3, lb3	6	Extras b8, lb7	15
Total	170	Total	187

YORKSHIRE

First Innings

Holmes, b Iddon	18
Sutcliffe, lbw, b Sibbles	135
Barber, lbw, b Booth	17
Leyland, c Hopwood, b Sibbles	91
Mitchell, not out	56
A. B. Sellers, b Sibbles	0
Wood, b Hodgson	7
Verity, lbw, b Iddon	19
Rhodes, c Hodgson, b Butterworth	0
Macaulay, b Iddon	13
Extras b3, lb3	6
Total (for 9)	*362

*Innings declared

THE ROSES MATCHES 1919-1939
BOWLING ANALYSIS

LANCASHIRE—First Innings

	O.	M.	R.	W.		O.	M.	R.	W.
Bowes	38	8	57	4	Leyland	8	2	11	0
Macaulay	6	2	12	0	Rhodes	7	1	13	0
Verity	42	21	71	4					

Second Innings

	O.	M.	R.	W.		O.	M.	R.	W.
Bowes	34	10	59	3	Macaulay	31	9	54	2
Verity	34	18	35	5	Rhodes	8	0	24	0

YORKSHIRE—First Innings

	O.	M.	R.	W.		O.	M.	R.	W.
Sibbles	36	9	104	3	Hodgson	22	1	77	1
Booth	24	3	59	1	Butterworth	14	1	42	1
Iddon	36	5	60	3	Paynter	6	1	14	0

YORKSHIRE V LANCASHIRE 1933

June 3/5 Old Trafford

FIRST DAY

WHEN we arrived at Old Trafford on Saturday morning our ears were filled with the dulcet strains of broadcast music. Somebody at Old Trafford has been seized with the beautiful idea that even on a cricket field the modern age cannot live without the loudspeaker. This anonymous genius has probably not entirely realised some of the consequences which may occur from the innovation. We all know that music is supposed to soothe the savage breast. On the other hand, music has been known to excite man's worst passions. What if at a Lancashire and Yorkshire match some impressionable batsman should get inflamed by the wild whirring strains—and go mad and hit sixes before lunch. It is an awful thought; I trust it will be solemnly considered by the enterprising spirit who this year has made the first move towards 'brightening' Old Trafford. Perhaps, though, it is only a tentative step towards mightier reforms. In time, maybe, if only we are patient, there will be other attractions added to Old Trafford's loudspeakers—say a few side-shows with dancing, and a bearded lady, and other diversions. Then, gradually, the cricket can be got rid of altogether, to the approbation of all and sundry.

The music ceased when Lancashire took the field in lovely weather, the sky windy and fresh. An easy wicket was there for Sutcliffe and Holmes to bat upon; it was a good piece of fortune for Yorkshire to win the toss. Booth bowled the first over to Sutcliffe, and four balls swung away so far that Sutcliffe's protective withdrawals of his bat were only rhetorical. For half an hour both batsmen played confidently, and Hodgson tried in vain to make the ball rise. Holmes pulled a short length for four; the feeling began to get about that Sutcliffe and Holmes were ready to give us yet another of their own prosperous and durable stands. The downfall of Sutcliffe, at twelve o'clock exactly, was a bolt

357

from the blue; to the first ball of Booth's sixth over Sutcliffe played back; it was a glorious swinger which seemed to dip late from the middle to the off stump and whip back. Sutcliffe expressed mingled self-pity and astonishment as he heard the wicket rattle behind him; he should have played forward and died hereafter. He was unlucky to run so soon into such a ball. His abrupt departure, which was against his customary procedure at Old Trafford, took the life out of Yorkshire's cricket. For, though Mitchell came in with his cap's peak askew, it was as yet not definitely over his right ear. Not until he has belaboured an attack for two or three hours (for fifty runs or more) does Mitchell's cap achieve its proper angle of piratical swagger and menace. At half-past twelve, after an hour's play, Yorkshire had made only 41 runs; the occasion hereabout called for aid from the loud speakers—the 'Ride of the Valkyrie' or 'Softly Wakes My Heart'.

When Iddon bowled over the wicket, to a field with four men close in on the leg side, he was able to turn the ball considerably. He pitched a good length on to a mark made just outside the leg stump by Hodgson. This mark may well have some dire effect on the result of the game. Mitchell could make nothing at all of Iddon's spin; he stopped a half-volley with his pads and generally got himself into states of muscular and mental congestion. The batting was unbelievably crude; even Holmes had no strokes. In an hour and a half Yorkshire somehow scored 49; then Holmes, obviously goaded by his own dreariness, let fly suddenly with his bat clean across the spin of Iddon. The stroke was skied to the short-leg trap, where Booth held a catch after, no doubt, suffering at least one acute moment of apprehension.

When Leyland reached the wicket Iddon was taken off; slow left-handed bowlers nowadays do not care to bowl at left-handed batsmen. Mitchell achieved a fine on-drive, but a moment afterwards an even more dramatic event transpired. Leyland, trying to turn Parkinson to leg, was leg-before-wicket. Yorkshire 61 for three, and Iddon back to the attack for Mitchell and Barber. Eckersley handled his bowling cleverly.

After lunch Mitchell persisted with the use of his pads to

Iddon's spin; occasionally he stopped with them the sort of ball which David Denton used to hit yards over the rails at long-on. Iddon's accuracy was on the whole praiseworthy though, and at the other end of the pitch young Parkinson bowled ably, with pluck and judgment, though perhaps, after all, not a mountain of courage is needed to toss a leg-break well up the wicket to Mitchell. The cricket was commonplace and the crowd silent.

With every wish in the world to live in the present, I could not prevent my mind going back to Lancashire and Yorkshire matches of old, when the multitude at Old Trafford was lifted up and given visions to see by the gusty batting of Hirst and Denton against Brearley, by Johnny Tyldesley's aggressive forays on the bowling of Rhodes; by Spooner's style and brilliance against Hirst and his leg-trap. There are good cricketers today, I know—I have seen some of them at Lord's recently. But Old Trafford is unlucky; the place seems to take the enterprise out of batsmen's hearts. When did Old Trafford last see a really great piece of batsmanship, skilful and brave and beautiful, with the outfielders in vain chase and the crowd roaring home the ball to the boundary?

At a quarter to three Yorkshire were 95 after two and a quarter hours of play. Then Mitchell apparently hit a four—off a no-ball; the scoreboard placed four runs to Mitchell's credit. But it was a false alarm; the scoreboard altered the runs to four no-balls, which beat Duckworth and went to the leg-boundary very fine. Barber, who had apparently been at the wicket an hour, then drove Booth to the off for four, all run, a real stroke, a forward push. Next over, from Parkinson, Mitchell forced a ball to the on for three; the scoreboard whizzed dizzily and I nearly got vertigo watching the moving figures as they whirled round. But Mitchell's cap was not over his right ear yet; not yet had he really 'begun.' Hopwood was called up to bowl at 109; his first ball pitched half-way down the wicket or thereabouts, and Barber cut it vigorously straight to backward point for nothing. In an hour and a quarter after lunch not more than three good strokes were to be seen; many balls were stopped with the pads with no show of a stroke at all. Lancashire and Yorkshire matches in recent years have been notorious for dull batting, but this batting of Yorkshire was not only dull, it was ugly. When Mitchell was smothering the ball with his legs I felt a screen ought to have concealed him from the public gaze. Barber did at least look for loose balls and do his best to hit them.

At twenty minutes to four, after nearly three hours and a half's play, Yorkshire were 140 for three. At this moment Old Trafford's old retainer appeared on the field with drinks—a sight beautiful to see, the emblem of an ancient day that knew not radio, or world trade depression, or leg-theory, or Mitchell. (There was a Mitchell before in the Yorkshire eleven, ages past—but that is another story.) At five minutes to four Mitchell pulled a short ball from Parkinson for three; a virtue of this report (which I trust reflects faithfully the dullness of the afternoon) is that it gives the exact time when the best strokes occurred—one or two may have escaped my vigilance, but I do not think so. Barber reached fifty at the end of two hours; Mitchell arrived at his fifty after a sojourn of three hours and a quarter. Before the war the game's celebrated slow scorer was Quaife; people used to write passionate letters to the editor about him. Will some old cricketer find out how many times in his career Quaife batted more than three hours for fifty? Few, I suspect, very few. And Quaife, scoring or not, was always making pretty strokes and letting us see perfect footwork. Barber cut a short leg-break from Bennett with the spin for four, all run—this was the best stroke of the match so far. When the players left the field for tea at a quarter-past four Yorkshire were 174 for three after four hours' cricket.

Immediately following tea Barber, possessed by devils, attempted a big drive off Bennett; he skied the ball behind the bowler, and Eckersley held a clever catch. Barber and Mitchell scored one hundred and twenty for the fourth wicket in two hours and a half. It seemed longer than that. Just before five o'clock I noticed Mitchell's cap was still stuck with the peak over his right eye: it fitted him too tightly and cramped his style. Despite the hindrance, he drove Iddon to the off for a quite powerful four. Then Sellers waited for a leg-break from Parkinson, and cut it, as it turned, to the boundary. Booth returned to the attack with the new ball, and in his first over he beat Mitchell and missed the wicket by inches; Hodgson also bowled again. Sellers batted well, and forced a good ball from Booth to the on; Mitchell, too, became expensive; he is a fairly good batsman to the ball that does not spin. He reached his hundred in four hours and three-quarters; his second fifty was made in an hour and a half. But the fact about batsmen of Mitchell's type is that, whether they are making strokes or not, they are equally uninteresting to those of us who watch cricket for style and the personal touch.

At the end of play Yorkshire had pulled the game round entirely. But all afternoon the rate of scoring remained preposterously slow. And the crowd stayed on and endured the worst day's cricket I have ever seen. In the tea interval they bought the evening papers and read the old headlines, 'Grim struggle at Old Trafford,' and believed them. Nearly six hours' play on a good wicket in hot weather—and at the end 287 for five. Mitchell in five and a half hours 116. Only three real strokes all day, and not one which crashed to the boundary with a smack. Not the remotest possibility of a catch in the outfield. The crowd and the Lancashire fieldsmen watched it all with patience and fortitude.

SECOND DAY

Yesterday at Old Trafford Lancashire collapsed twice and were beaten by an innings and 156 runs. Yorkshire also collapsed in the earlier part of the morning. Twenty-four wickets fell between half-past eleven and six o'clock for 239 runs. The wicket crumbled inexplicably, and when Lancashire batted it was—to use the exaggeration of metaphor—a ploughed field. At the end of the match I walked on the field, with a thousand other people, and saw the pitch. It was even worse than I had suspected it to be all day. Never before on a county ground of any reputation have I seen a wicket so deplorably worn and knocked about.

A glorious day and a vast crowd—Old Trafford looked at its best yesterday morning, and an hour before the beginning of play Warwick Road was crowded with an eager hurrying multitude. Inside the ground the green of the turf refreshed the eyesight. The scene was ready for a sumptuous day of cricket in the heat. Even the music of the loud-speaker did not for a while sound out of place; the strains of Franz Lehar's lovely 'Vilia' song somehow mingled well with the sunny air.

Nearly fifteen thousand people watched the end of Yorkshire's innings, and saw five wickets collapse in an hour and a quarter for 54. Only Macaulay and Bowes made an attempt to hit the bowling of Iddon and Parkinson; Bowes indeed showed us the two handsomest drives of the whole innings. To the sober vision there was something ominous to Lancashire in this rapid overthrow of Yorkshire batsmen. It could be seen that Iddon and Parkinson both were able to spin the ball sharply—and this time Iddon bowled from the Manchester end and not on to the marks made on the pitch on Saturday by Hodgson. One ball from Parkinson pitched outside the leg stump and missed the off by a foot. Another ball from Iddon 'stood up' straight, after pitching a good length. Perhaps too much water went into the preparation of the wicket. It all boded ill for Lancashire.

When Bowes attacked at one o'clock the sense of atmosphere, known always at these great games of old, could be felt everywhere. There was a gasp as Bowes's fifth ball, a beauty, swung across the stumps, beat the bat, and missed the stumps by inches only. Then a great roar went into the sky as Watson drove Macaulay violently for four to the off, a startling stroke so soon in Lancashire's response to a heavy score. These cricketers beggar psychological analysis; on certain days they still stonewall for hours in circumstances which see their sides safe as houses. But devils of unreason will possess them suddenly in circumstances when the only policy should be momentary circumspection. Watson, after hitting his warlike four off Macaulay, tried a wild pull off the middle stump in the same over and sent the ball straight into square-leg's hands. Lover though I am of bold batsmanship, I am none the less a believer in the happy medium that can be found between persistent stonewalling to all bowling and reckless hitting indulged before the game's position asks for it. Yet it was hard not to be charmed with Watson's gesture; if the choice were thrust on me I would rather die with Watson (the Watson of yesterday) than live with the Mitchell of Saturday.

The Yorkshire attack was obviously on the kill, keen of edge and temper. Ernest Tyldesley gave a hard chance when he was one, to Macaulay in the slips; the ball swung late and came off the pitch viciously. Bowes bowled only three overs and then Verity came on, ten minutes before lunch, a strange move, seeing that the ball was still new, with Bowes bowling it dangerously. But it was a sign of the Yorkshiremen's views about the turf; Macaulay bowled round the wicket with four men holding out clutching hands in the leg trap. The Yorkshiremen were hostile, expecting a wicket every over. The Yorkshire attack, compared with Lancashire's, is as a blow on the head to a slow and hidden escape of gas. It is a direct attack, with Macaulay the great inspirer of antagonism. Give me eleven Macaulays and you can have the others, Bradman and all.

After lunch Bowes bowled again. Ernest Tyldesley hooked a 'bumper' off his face, a brilliant stroke, a brave stroke, a thrilling stroke, a beautiful stroke, the stroke of a man and a cricketer. It quickened the blood—a rising ball, a swift blow of the bat with Tyldesley's body suddenly galvanic, a cracking noise, and the ball at the on-boundary in a flash. The crowd roared—and roared again when in the same over Tyldesley glanced Bowes for four by means of his own exquisite leg-stroke, the body leaning over graciously. Hopwood, when he was 14, seemed to give a difficult chance at the wicket off Bowes—the game was magnificent now, every moment a crisis, skill against skill, spirit against spirit. Macaulay pounced down the wicket after his own bowling, and his eyes shot out fires of aggression.

Just after half-past two a shocking disaster occurred to Lancashire. Tyldesley was too late for a ball from Bowes which was tossed well up; Tyldesley's bat apparently hit his pad; it was a sad end to an innings of royal promise. Lancashire were 36 for two when Iddon came into the sunburnt field. His third ball, from Bowes, was cleverly held back; Bowes bowls a slow one admirably, with little change of his action. Iddon failed rather badly; to the first ball he received from Macaulay he made a half-drive, missed it, and was clean bowled amidst sounds of dismay. Then Paynter walked from the pavilion's shade and had the reception of a hero. And he needed to be one now—Lancashire 37 for three and Macaulay to tackle, a nasty bowler to a left-handed batsman at any time. Bowes set the outline of a 'body-line' field round Paynter's legs but he did not bump the ball, and Paynter drove an over-tossed length for four, and the crowd raved and rejoiced. A real cricket match, alive with hazards, vital with character.

Macaulay changed over to the Stretford end and Verity bowled from the Manchester end. Paynter was hopelessly beaten by Macaulay's spin, and drawn far out of his ground. But Wood missed the chance of stumping, which probably was not easy, for the ball turned a deal. Paynter then let his bat 'fly' at a spinner from Verity and skied a mis-hit to behind the wicket, far out of harm's way. Through all these shocks and vicissitudes Hopwood defended stoutly; in an hour and a quarter he made only 13. And nobody noticed his solid worthiness; he was like a tree standing safe and unhurt in a perilous thunderstorm. Paynter was uncomfortable, and a man in the crowd yelled out ' 'It 'em!' Perhaps it was Mitchell's brother. Macaulay hurled his body round in a contortion of frustration when the umpire disallowed an appeal for leg-before-wicket against Hopwood. But next over he appealed again as a rasping break-back hit Hopwood's pad, high up; this time Hopwood had to depart—Lancashire 61 for four. The first ball sent to Parkinson by Macaulay kicked wickedly; the next ball also got up and hit Parkinson in the small of the back. Macaulay appealed vociferously. Parkinson drove Macaulay superbly for four to the on, a gallant stroke in an hour of doom. Then he drove Verity as gallantly for four, also to the on. I have not known a finer afternoon's cricket for years. Paynter pulled a short ball from Macaulay for four, and Macaulay looked daggers. Parkinson again drove Verity for four, this time straight. A stand by Lancashire seemed to be blossoming, though Paynter was not himself. But doom was about to strike now.

Paynter was caught at backward point by Verity when Lancashire were 90; the ball came low from the bat, swift as a bird, and Verity merely bent down and picked the ball off his foot. Bennett tried to drive his first ball into the far distance;

he was bowled in the attempt. A marvellous slip catch accounted for Eckersley; he cut a ball late and Macaulay held it an inch from the ground as it was going away from him; he flung himself after the ball and caught it rolling over. An afternoon of cricket fit for the gods. Yorkshire magnificent!

Booth's first stroke went to Sutcliffe and he thought he was out; but Sutcliffe waved him back to the wicket. The ball had just hit the ground. Next ball Parkinson 'slogged' indiscreetly and was caught. Panic seemed to have got Lancashire well in grip. Four wickets down in six balls— Paynter, Bennett, Eckersley, and Parkinson. Duckworth was leg-before-wicket first ball; and thus did Macaulay achieve the hat-trick, with the fifth and sixth balls of one over and the first of the next. His victims were Paynter, Bennett, and Duckworth. Lancashire were all out at a quarter to four; the last five wickets fell for three runs.

Macaulay took four wickets in five balls. His opposition was frail indeed, but he himself created their weakness of resolution, not so much by skill as by his tremendous power of will. He bowled off-breaks with a cunning flight, but to skill he added superb fighting quality. Lancashire's wickets fell in this remarkable way:

1	2	3	4	5	6	7	8	9	10
5	36	37	57	90	90	91	92	92	93

Too soon in the day did Lancashire give up the pitch as 'impossible.' Watson's first stroke was desperate. Still, I for one do not complain to see a Lancashire collapse in which every effort is made to hit the loose ball.

When Lancashire followed on Watson and Hopwood scored 16 and then Watson was hit on the head by a rising ball from Bowes—a pure accident with no 'body-line' field set. The ball simply got up abruptly. Watson had to leave the field and could not bat again. A section of the crowd hooted Bowes, and probably some of the hooting was done by people who asked last winter why Woodfull and Bradman did not use their bats to Larwood. Ernest Tyldesley declined to bat while the hooting continued—a gentleman's action. If an English crowd, or part of one, is going to make a noise

because of an occasional accidental 'bumper,' what sort of
riot will happen when (that is, if) Larwood bowls persistent
'bumpers' to a leg field? Already it is clear that the Australian
protest was for the good of the game; we cannot have ill-
tempered disturbances on cricket grounds from crowds
which, being composed of human beings, are the same all
over the world. Bowes's 'bumper' yesterday was a thing not
of his own contriving. The attack objected to by the
Australians is a deliberate policy based on the *continuous*
exploitation of 'bumpers'.

Hopwood was caught at slip by Macaulay from a glorious
spinning-away ball of Verity; the wicket was now definitely a
'dry sticky' one. Lancashire were trapped on it, doomed to
certain death. Iddon was bowled first ball, driving straight
down the line, fast-footed, to spin that beat the bat easily.
The wicket was the worst I have ever seen at Old Trafford in
fine weather; it was as brown as a country lane.

Before tea Ernest Tyldesley and Parkinson were both out,
and then Lancashire were, at the second attempt, 48 for four.
It was a better score than any conceivable cricket team would
have made on the same pitch against Rhodes and Schofield
Haigh. There was much severe criticism passed in the crowd
upon Lancashire's batting, and, of course, it was bad. But
when it comes to vituperation against poor cricket I fancy
myself with any man in the world. And I will say this of
yesterday's play: Lancashire scored as many runs as I
expected them to score during the morning when I saw how
the wicket was behaving. The fact is that Lancashire's
batsmen at the moment, one or two excepted, do not possess
the technique which is needed on wickets which help a bowler
of skill to spin quickly. On yesterday's pitch J. T. Tyldesley
might have prevailed with his quick feet, or Makepeace with
his scientific use of the pads. Ordinary ability taught on the
smooth modern turf was bound to rapid destruction on a
wicket which was Macaulay's and Verity's opportunity.

Paynter played finely in his second innings; he hit a
colossal six off Verity. Hodgson also hit a six. But these were
luxuries of the voluptuous sort that the pagan Romans
indulged in when they knew their hour was at hand. The
match was all over at ten minutes to six. Yorkshire jumped to

their chances like champions. They are so obviously the champions of this season that they could afford to bat with the freedom of champions.

SCORES

YORKSHIRE

First Innings

Holmes, c Booth, b Iddon	22
Sutcliffe, b Booth	7
Mitchell, c Hodgson, b Parkinson	123
Leyland, lbw, b Parkinson	3
Barber, c Eckersley, b Bennett	62
A. B. Sellers, lbw, b Bennett	31
Verity, lbw, b Parkinson	27
Wood, b Iddon	6
Rhodes, b Iddon	3
Macaulay, b Iddon	5
Bowes, not out	13
Extras b11, lb23, nb5	39
Total	341

LANCASHIRE

First Innings		Second Innings	
Watson, c Leyland, b Macaulay	5	retired hurt	11
Hopwood, lbw, b Macaulay	13	c Macaulay, b Verity	12
Tyldesley, b Bowes	15	lbw, b Macaulay	13
Iddon, b Macaulay	1	b Verity	0
Paynter, c Verity, b Macaulay	17	not out	29
Parkinson, c Holmes, b Verity	24	b Macaulay	4
Bennett, b Macaulay	0	lbw, b Macaulay	2
Eckersley, c Macaulay, b Verity	0	b Verity	0
Booth, b Macaulay	1	c Sutcliffe, b Verity	0
Duckworth, lbw, b Macaulay	0	c Rhodes, b Macaulay	3
Hodgson, not out	1	c Sellers, b Macaulay	18
Extras b8, lb8	16		
Total	93	Total	92

THE ROSES MATCHES 1919-1939
BOWLING ANALYSIS

YORKSHIRE—First Innings

	O.	M.	R.	W.		O.	M.	R.	W.
Booth	34	9	48	1	Iddon	43	19	60	4
Hodgson	13	4	30	0	Hopwood	11	5	16	0
Parkinson	47	9	105	3	Bennett	12	0	43	2

LANCASHIRE—First Innings

	O.	M.	R.	W.		O.	M.	R.	W.
Bowes	10	3	22	1	Verity	11	2	27	2
Macaulay	19	10	28	7					

Second Innings

	O.	M.	R.	W.		O.	M.	R.	W.
Bowes	5	0	27	0	Verity	12	3	41	4
Rhodes	3	2	3	0	Macaulay	10	5	21	5

YORKSHIRE V LANCASHIRE 1933

August 5/7/8   Leeds

FIRST DAY

AT Leeds on Saturday the day was hot, with no air to refresh us. On an easy wicket Yorkshire stonewalled from half-past eleven until half-past six. At lunch, after two hours' play, Yorkshire were 64 for one wicket. Two and a quarter hours later Yorkshire—the same Yorkshire and in the same place and on the same Saturday of August 5, 1933—arrived at the aggregate of 166 for five. Then at six o'clock Wood achieved the only honest stroke of the day: a superb drive to the off. During the afternoon the crowd emitted sounds of torment; think of it, even a Yorkshire crowd dissatisfied with Yorkshire batsmen! And unreasonably so. ' 'It 'em, for Gawd's sake!' somebody howled. But what did the poor man imagine he was watching—a bif-bat match? O! the injustice of the mob; here were Yorkshire, heavily burdened with championship armour, sweating and struggling under the sun, baited and badgered by the notorious attack of Lancashire. Booth the modern Spofforth; Sibbles the reincarnation of Barnes; Parkinson more subtle than Mailey; Hopwood and Holroyd both as cunning as Rhodes and Johnny Briggs. And the Headingley crowd had the cruelty to call out to Mitchell and Verity ' 'It 'em!' Obviously these malcontents did not realise the hardships to which Mitchell and Verity were being exposed: Mitchell stayed in two hours ten minutes for 45; Verity stayed in nearly an hour and a half for 22. They both might have got the sunstroke. It is a heartless world and going to the dogs when a Yorkshire crowd, or part of it, can see the faintest wrong in a Yorkshire batsman.

Yorkshire most likely would have been all out an hour before close of play, and for a poor score, if Lancashire had held all the catches. Five or six were dropped. Holmes was missed, and Mitchell, when only 15, and Barber, when only 22, and Verity, and Rhodes. The culprits were Duckworth,

Booth, Hopwood (and/or Watson), and Holroyd. Parkinson bowled cleverly all day; true, he turned only a score of balls or so, but he twisted his hand over, and that was enough: the Yorkshiremen got their legs in front of the wickets and pushed out strokeless bats. Barber, whose innings of 81 lasted two hours and a half, looked at times a cricketer, and he made a few hits; Wood, too, used his shoulders. For the most part the Yorkshire champions seemed unable to lift up their bats more than a few inches from the ground. And sometimes their feet were apparently all mixed up with the wicket-keeper's. Some day a wicket-keeper will be struck on the pads, and in answer to a bowler's appeal one of our great modern batsmen will be given out leg-before.

No doubt the dreary, unlovely policy of Yorkshire will receive justification before Tuesday in the eyes of all those dreary and unlovely folk who go by results. Championship cricket is championship cricket, nowadays, and no laughing matter. I suggest the following examination for all young cricketers who at the present time have hopes that some day they will play in a Lancashire v Yorkshire match:—(1) Name; (2) County or Country of Origin (the latter question need not be answered by candidates in Lancashire; (3) Where and by whom did you have your strokes extracted? (4) Maker of candidate's pads; (5) Maker of Candidate's bat, if any; (6) have you ever, no matter how inadvertently, driven a ball, no matter of what length, in front of the wicket for four? (7) If so, why? (8) Give a brief statement of your idea of a cricket match; (9) have you ever read pernicious literature about the game by Nyren, E. V. Lucas, and Gilbert Jessop? Give, in a few words, your opinion of Hirst, Spooner, Denton, J. T. Tyldesley, and MacLaren, if you have ever heard of them.

Nearly twenty thousand people watched the agony. Booth and Sibbles bowled at the game's outset with the new ball. In a few overs they looked as though they needed another new ball, one each. Sutcliffe drove a full toss for four; then Parkinson came on, and at the first attempt he got Sutcliffe out leg-before-wicket by means of beautifully arched flight and an inch of spin. Thus did Parkinson save Lancashire a hundred runs; for Sutcliffe had looked to be in good mood. Holmes was sadly strokeless; he could push only a few yards away balls which a year or two ago he invariably pulled or drove for fours brilliantly. Mitchell bent down like a man convulsed in the pit of his stomach. When he was fifteen he hit a long-hop rashly to leg, where Booth missed an easy catch easily. Holroyd bowled inswingers; but nobody dreamed of driving them to long-on. After lunch Holmes fell to a slip catch, snicked from a hopeless stroke.

Leyland showed spirit for a while, until he drove at a ball from Booth and just touched it. Duckworth, though not in his best form, held a great catch, off the inside edge of the bat. Booth appealed once or twice for leg-before-wicket, but Morton, one of the shrewdest of our umpires, quashed the appeals. The crowd at the leg-side boundary were ironical at all appeals for leg-before-wicket—obviously they were against them on principle. Leg-before in a Lancashire and Yorkshire match—whoever heard of such a thing?

During the fourth-wicket stand of Mitchell and Barber, which added 26 in half an hour, the game woke up, and the occasion became almost animated. Mitchell was guilty of several fine strokes towards the covers: the sunshine blessed the scene: there was some cheering, and also there was the merry noise of men shouting their wares, match-cards, and football annuals, out of the corners of their mouths. Mitchell hit a four, and the bloom of life fell upon the hour. Such moments of vision come to us all everywhere, unexpectedly—when we see wind blowing over long grass; when we hear the sweet, sad melody in Tschaikovsky's "Romeo and Juliet" Overture; when we behold the Votive Church in Vienna covered with snow on a starlit night; when we read "Weep you no more, sad fountains"; when we see and hear Grock crash through the seat of his chair; when we look upon Adele Kern at the beginning of act 2 of "Rosenkavalier"; when we see blossom on a Cotswold orchard; and, of course, when we see a four driven on the off side in a Lancashire and Yorkshire match.

Mitchell's wicket, the fourth of the day to fall, was taken by the pertinacious Parkinson: Mitchell was leg-before-wicket, the end of all heroes in these mighty battles. Sellers for several overs could not find the ball; he was, for all he knew to the contrary, bowled four or five times in ten minutes. Lancashire enjoyed little luck; nothing was given to them. Hopwood bowled over the wicket, and at last dropped a ball into some uneven spot near the bowlers' footholds; he accounted for Sellers, who played a stroke once again into space and nothingness. Barber, given the courage, can drive splendidly; he reached his fifty in two hours; when he was 22 he ran out to a well-tossed ball from Parkinson which came off the pitch sharply. Duckworth at his best would have stumped him with time to spare.

A sensation occurred when Barber hit two successive balls for furious boundaries; the crowd gave the grand old roar which years ago was heard on Yorkshire cricket grounds unceasingly when Hirst and Denton cracked the superb fast bowling of Brearley all over the field. I have seen these two magnificent cricketers score nearly a hundred runs in an hour, with Yorkshire badly placed, on a broken wicket, against one of the most terrifying attacks Lancashire have boasted at any time. I have seen Spooner score 200 against Hirst, Rhodes, and Haigh in an afternoon; I have seen J. T. Tyldesley—but my mind is wandering.

Verity was missed in the slips when his score was ten; he helped Barber to carry or lift or haul or sustain the Yorkshire total from 164 for five to 214 for six, in eighty minutes. Barber was out to a real Duckworth catch off Sibbles, who came on at 200, and this time bowled capitally with the new ball. Then, as soon as Wood arrived, we saw the day's solitary great stroke, which I have already mentioned. Wood is good to watch; he really does make strokes. From the last ball of the day Duckworth caught and stumped Rhodes in one action; but as the moment his wicket-keeping is scarcely to be trusted, though, of course, genius will insist on breaking out. Eckersley made the most of his bowlers, who, no doubt, enjoyed the flattering reception given to them by the champion county.

The best thing of the day was the sight of George Hirst signing autographs for a crowd of adoring boys and girls. It is good to know that Hirst is not forgotten, that the present generation is keen to cherish his name. I spoke for a few moments to the greatest cricketer Yorkshire has ever possessed. He looked well and has recovered from his recent illness. Simply to come into contact with him was to feel again the greatness of cricket, all its old vitality, its character, spirit, humour, and bigness of conception.

SECOND DAY

Verity could not bowl to-day because of indisposition, and Holmes was away ill, too. Yet Yorkshire were strong enough for a while to drive Lancashire into a bitter corner. At lunch Lancashire were only 50 for the loss of Watson, Tyldesley, and Paynter. The crowd smacked its lips. Lancashire seemed ready to collapse and follow-on. A great and gallant stand between Hopwood and Hawkwood saved Lancashire and attained glory; by excellent cricket with strokes, real strokes, in it the score was taken from 50 for three to 202 runs in a little more than two hundred minutes. Both players had the pleasure of making hundreds against the ancient enemy. Hopwood has never exhibited a cleaner stroke technique. But we have come to expect every day a long innings from Hopwood; he is this season consistency itself. The honours of the match and the day must go generously to Hawkwood, who in his first ordeal in the face of Yorkshire, the champions, came in at a searching crisis and in three hours made a hundred runs almost faultlessly, free of a chance, and made them often with poise and elegance. His driving to the off gladdened the hearts of all lovers of cricket's handsomest stroke. He played his innings, too, hindered by a lame leg. Another page has at last been added to the book of Lancashire and Yorkshire matches which will be read in days to come proudly and enviously. 'Ah,' our grandchildren will say, 'the game is going to the dogs; there are no Hopwoods and Hawkwoods any more.' The Leeds wicket was all in the batsman's favour; brilliant fielding by Macaulay was really the cause of Lancashire's bad start. And, as thousands of Yorkshiremen will be telling us tomorrow, Yorkshire were indeed without Verity.

When the match went forward at half-past eleven Wood and Macaulay played the best cricket of the Yorkshire innings. A forcing stroke by Wood to the on boundary, made with strong wrists, provoked the authentic roar; the crowd to-day was alive and vocal most of the time, not like

Saturday's stupefied assemblage which watched the dreary action in silence, as though at the unveiling of the Cenotaph. Wood and Macaulay threatened a dangerous stand, so much so that it was a godsend to Lancashire when Sibbles at mid-wicket on the on side caught Wood beautifully with one hand, taking the ball an inch from the ground as it went away from him. Bowes, last man in, walked to the wicket slowly, wearing a thick sweater despite the humid atmosphere; he looked Arctic all over. He was not exposed for long to the blast of the Lancashire attack; he was run out, no doubt overwhelmed by his underwear. Yorkshire thus failed to achieve three hundred runs, but their total seemed to give general satisfaction to the multitude. One man stated publicly that he wagered a drink Lancashire would lose by an innings; then he went further and said, 'I'll bet two drinks.'

The Lancashire innings began at ten minutes past twelve, and when the Yorkshire team entered the field, bless my eyes and spectacles if I did not behold Emmott Robinson walking out and taking up a positon in the slips. He was acting as substitute for Verity, absent ill. Emmott Robinson in a Lancashire and Yorkshire match again—this was something like. I wondered if in his capacity as deputy fieldsman he would be allowed to appeal. Bowes bowled to four slips with the new ball, and in ten minutes he got a wicket. Watson slashed rather irrationally and too soon at an outswinger, and Macaulay at third slip held the mis-hit, and Robinson looked pleased as Punch, and Bowes expressed no question whatever. The crowd roared humorously when Hopwood dropped to the earth and avoided a bumper from Bowes, but they did not entirely approve a strong boundary hit by Hopwood off Sellers. Another four by Hopwood, a lovely straight drive off Sellers, was politely applauded and dismissed from the mind at once, for with Lancashire's total only 19 Ernest Tyldesley put his bat to another outswinger of Bowes, and again did Macaulay make a ghoulish catch. The sleepiness of Bowes's action belies his attack: he caused the ball to move in the air, as they say, and come from the pitch vitally and seek the bat's edge. He is not a fast bowler, but rather a fast-medium bowler with an occasional fast ball which may or may not bounce. He thrives on the modern batsman's inability to play pace of any sort.

At one o'clock Emmott Robinson decided that he had the right to appeal; he emitted one against Hopwood from his position at first slip to Macaulay, presumably for leg before wicket. It was the best appeal I have heard this year for passion and power. But Hardstaff, the umpire, regarded it not, and Robinson wore his old look of noble frustration. Paynter helped Hopwood temporarily to stop the Yorkshire advance; he seldom seemed happy, though, and Hopwood had, so to say, to bat for both ends of the wicket. He played with coolness and skill. Just before lunch Leyland was asked to bowl; he was given a wicket straightway. Paynter, intent upon not getting out, allowed Leyland to bowl him two full tosses with impunity, whereupon he played back to a ball well up to him and edged it to Macaulay in the slips. Macaulay, who had been stealing in nearer the bat all the over, swooped on the perishing stroke like a body-snatcher. Lancashire 50 for three; the bars did good business at lunch.

The ground was packed at a quarter past two; thousands of eyes were ready to watch another Lancashire holocaust, this time on a good wicket. Hawkwood, suffering from what Laurence Sterne would call a sciatica, was compelled to use Paynter as a runner. He was struck on the body by Bowes, but he ran into a ball which would have passed not far above the bails. Bowes is not formidable as soon as the seam and shine are gone, and today he did not intimidate by means of persistent bumpers. I fancy that J. T. Tyldesley could have cut and pulled Bowes for a violent hundred this afternoon without the slightest difficulty. And what he might have done with Leyland's slow stuff I rejoice to contemplate. Leyland, to be in the fashion, bowled over the wicket to a leg field; Hopwood drove two incipient full tosses for threes. The Yorkshire attack was tame enough hereabouts: only superb fielding made it appear hostile. Hopwood reached a splendid 50 out of a total of 82 in an hour and three-quarters. He then cut a rising ball square off his chest from Bowes, and Emmott Robinson, still at second slip, stood with folded arms and watched the ball go to the boundary with an inscrutable look on his face. Since last I saw him Robinson has had his hair cut and bought a fine new suit of flannels. But I imagine he suffered some private sorrow this afternoon to see about him so many Lancashire batsmen and the silly law preventing him all the time from bowling at them. Oh the things a Yorkshireman has to put up with!

Hawkwood defended pluckily and stopped a rare break-back from Macaulay, and received from Macaulay a glance of extreme friendliness for his pains. Hopwood and Hawkwood steadily improved Lancashire's situation: the hundred was reached without another disaster; the Yorkshire bowling had to be changed many times; the crowd grew restive; and a man announced that he was selling a particularly interesting football annual. A glorious cover drive by Hawkwood did not mend matters; disillusion crept over the multitude like a mist. Hawkwood drove Rhodes for another magnificent four through the covers; he batted nobly in spite of the pain his right leg was obviously giving him. He watched the ball and kept his head over it. Once he forgot where he was and attempted to smite a six, an indiscretion of extreme youth, no doubt. He reached his fifty in one hundred and five minutes, one of the most courageous innings played for Lancashire by a young cricketer for ages. He had the luck just to miss two consecutive balls from Bowes when he was 49; all in all though, his batting told of exceptional ability. His drives to the off were made with delightful ease and grace; he is not in style essentially an upright player, but whenever he received an overtossed ball on or near the off stump he lifted himself up and his stroke went through without an impediment, and it was a model of timing. And once he thrilled us with the beauty of a great pull; the boy is a cricketer and he must be encouraged.

By tea-time Hopwood and Hawkwood had put on 122 runs in two hours and a quarter, no mean progress considering the circumstances. Yorkshire were indeed unlucky not to have Verity bowling; moreover, Bowes appeared far from strong. After tea twenty runs were plundered from three nondescript overs by Leyland; Hawkwood developed his hook capitally. Twenty-eight runs raced over the grass in a quarter of an hour—21 of them made by Hawkwood. The two-hundredth run brought forth the new ball, and, sensibly, the batsmen held back their strokes momentarily, much to the impatience of the crowd, who, however, did not appear to like it when Hopwood hit a full toss from Rhodes to the edge of the field or when he smacked a Bowes bumper head high in front of point for four. People are so hard to please. Hopwood's hundred came after four hours and a quarter of nicely mingled defence and offence; Hawkwood's hundred was celebrated a few overs later; he got there with a confident off-drive. At ten minutes to six the Hopwood and Hawkwood stand had made 200 runs in 175 minutes, and the crowd were rightly thinking of going home, when Macaulay clean bowled Hawkwood with a ball of exquisite length. Hawkwood had the audacity to hit fifteen fours in his first Lancashire and Yorkshire match. A good day for Lancashire, and a splendid day for the return of Emmott Robinson.

THIRD DAY

The match was drawn at Headingley today, but Lancashire were no doubt satisfied to win five points. Throughout the game, save for the brief collapse before lunch on Monday, the team played keenly and well. It was good to see Lancashire compiling over four hundred runs despite the failure of Watson, Tyldesley, and Paynter, and also despite the absence of Iddon. Lancashire's batting is strong enough, but oh for another Macdonald, Parkin, or Richard Tyldesley.

Lancashire gave us a splendid piece of batting before lunch. The first-innings lead was obtained in two overs, and then, after Eckersley fell to Bowes at 315, Sibbles and Parkinson thumped the shorn Yorkshire attack all over the field and scored 79 in less than an hour. Sibbles began with one of the grandest drives I have seen this year: he stood up straight, swung his bat majestically at Bowes, and the speed of the stroke made the outfielders seem rooted to the earth. He enjoyed the stroke so intensely that he did it again; freer and finer driving could not well be wished for by anybody or from anybody. Parkinson made an exquisite cut off Macaulay, and sent the next ball through the covers for four; Macaulay was bowling round the wicket, and he gave Parkinson a good and a long look. Sibbles has never played a better innings for Lancashire. Rhodes and Macaulay were compelled to fall back on safety bowling, leg theory designed to keep the runs down. But Parkinson went his neat, busy way, making quick-witted strokes to the off and behind the wicket. Duckworth helped him to add 35 for the ninth wicket in twenty minutes, and when the Lancashire innings came to an end just before lunch we had seen 144 runs scored in less than two hours and by means of cricket that would have done honour to the beginning of any side's innings in England; there was no hint whatever while Sibbles and Parkinson batted that the county's bowlers were at the wicket. Yorkshire missed Verity indeed: the crowd lamented his absence audibly. But if a Yorkshire cricketer will get himself vaccinated on the eve of the most solemn and responsible match of the year, that, as they say, is his own look out. Parkinson was unbeaten for a vivacious 69; it was an innings full of life and ability.

Yorkshire went in again at a quarter past two, with all afternoon to get through, face to face with arrears of 135. The wicket was in beautiful condition; Macaulay said it would last another month, and he spoke with some authority. Holmes and Verity were not, of course, available as batsmen; therefore Lancashire needed only to take eight wickets in three hours and a half, not counting the extra half-hour. Sutcliffe and Barber were thoroughly at ease against Booth and Sibbles. The afternoon began to sleep in the sunshine. Hopwood came on and bowled over the wicket; at the other end Parkinson tried hard with spin and flight to shame the batsmen into a stroke. Nothing occurred for three-quarters of an hour; then Sutcliffe inexplicably missed a ball from Hopwood and was bowled. It was the error of a cricketer out of form. Mitchell and Barber proceeded to add eight in the next forty minutes; Hopwood pitched over after over on or just outside the leg stump. At one period his analysis was 15 overs, 12 maidens, four runs, one wicket. The tactics of the Lancashire bowling were shrewd hereabout; for of course if Yorkshire were to be beaten, runs had ruthlessly to be kept down. But the experiments of Parkinson prevented the Lancashire bowling from becoming merely negative; Hopwood and Parkinson both worked admirably to the only plan of campaign by which Lancashire possibly could have won in the time. The truth is that Lancashire today can boast not a single match-winning bowler.

There was a ripple of excitement when Barber reached out too far and was stumped at a quarter to four. Leyland though, came forth in reasonably good form, and a left-handed batsman was ideal as a means of upsetting the left-handed leg theory of Hopwood and the right-handed leg-breaks of Parkinson. Mitchell was in his element; the situation of his county rendered the idea of boundaries vain and godless; he reached the total of 38 in two hours. Lancashire have seen a lot of Mitchell's strong, if not classic, defences this year. Right to the end Lancashire worked hard to force a decision; honest industry could not possibly have done more. Leyland in the closing period showed the crowd several delightful strokes and put some necessary bloom upon Yorkshire's batting, which in this match has suggested eloquently that the champion county is only happy really when it is bowling and fielding.

SCORES

YORKSHIRE

First Innings		Second Innings	
Holmes, c Watson, b Sibbles	20		
Sutcliffe, lbw, b Parkinson	18	b Hopwood	19
Mitchell, lbw, b Parkinson	45	not out	48
Leyland, c Duckworth, b Booth	7	b Paynter	53
Barber, c Duckworth, b Sibbles	81	st Duckworth, b Parkinson	27
A. B. Sellers, b Hopwood	19		
Verity, st Duckworth, b Hopwood	22		
Wood, c Sibbles, b Booth	31		
Rhodes, st Duckworth, b Watson	16		
Macaulay, not out	13		
Bowes, run out	0		
Extras	24	Extras	6
Total	296	Total (for 3)	153

LANCASHIRE

First Innings

Hopwood, lbw, b Leyland	120
Watson, c Macaulay, b Bowes	2
Tyldesley, c Macaulay, b Bowes	1
Paynter, c Macaulay, b Leyland	14
Hawkwood, b Macaulay	113
Booth, b Bowes	6
Parkinson, not out	69
P. T. Eckersley, b Bowes	26
Sibbles, c Rhodes, b Barber	44
Duckworth, lbw, b Rhodes	16
Holroyd run out	0
Extras	20
Total	431

BOWLING ANALYSIS

YORKSHIRE—First Innings

	O.	M.	R.	W.		O.	M.	R.	W.
Sibbles	31	9	62	2	Parkinson	27	7	59	2
Booth	30	11	51	2	Watson	9	1	17	1
Holroyd	27	6	52	0	Hopwood	20	8	31	2

Second Innings

Sibbles	15	5	22	0	Hopwood	23	13	24	1
Booth	13	2	34	0	Holroyd	2	0	6	0
Parkinson	23	9	53	1	Paynter	4	1	8	1

LANCASHIRE—First Innings

	O.	M.	R.	W.		O.	M.	R.	W.
Bowes	43	8	109	4	Rhodes	36	10	89	1
Macaulay	42	17	83	1	Leyland	25	4	90	2
Sellers	10	1	29	0	Barber	5	0	11	1

YORKSHIRE V LANCASHIRE 1934

May 19/21/22 Bramall Lane

FIRST DAY

ON Saturday afternoon at Bramall Lane, in wintry blasts and under a gloomy sky, a six was hit by Mitchell in the presence of several witnesses. The cold was enough to drive any man out of his senses and to be fair to Mitchell, he hit the six off a no-ball. When this extraordinary incident occurred Yorkshire's score was more than one hundred for no wicket. I was watching the match with my back to the fire; the hospitality of the Committee of the Yorkshire C.C.C. is always vast and generous. On Saturday the terrors of the weather (and of the cricket) changed this hospitality into gracious succour and compassion; some of us would have died miserably but for the warmth of the pavilion's hearth. I have seen Lancashire and Yorkshire cricket matches man and boy for a lifetime in all sorts of conditions and circumstances; never before have I seen a six hit with my back to the fire.

Frankly, I was sorry that Mitchell so far forgot himself. It is really not an extenuation to say that the six was struck from a no-ball. For if we look closely into the matter, the fact emerges that a no-ball enforces and compels by artful suggestion the hitting of a six. A man of Mitchell's strength of will ought surely to be equal to any such insidious ways. A six on compulsion! Zounds, an' he were at the strappado or on all the racks of the world he would not hit a six on compulsion. Let him ask Emmott Robinson.

The Bramall Lane wicket was soft and easy all day—that is until rain came just before six o'clock and mercifully liberated everybody. A more harmless attack than Lancashire's could not well be imagined in a match possessing the traditions of Lancashire and Yorkshire cricket. Booth alone looked good enough for county company; during an hour's spell after lunch he caused the ball to come in to the bat with a rare velocity; good fortune would have granted

381

him three or four wickets. Parkinson tossed up a pretty flight, perfect for leg breaks. Unfortunately, he omitted to provide the requisite spin. The left-handed bowlers Iddon and Hopwood seemed ready to drop to the earth at any moment from sheer weakness; are there in all the Kingdom two bowling actions as unpromising and tentative as Iddon's and Hopwood's? They bowl as though treading on ice and about to slip and fall flat as soon as the arm comes over.

Remember the grand energy of Harry Dean's action, the surging run, the immense shoulder propulsion. Dean once told me that 'these young bowlers don't eat enough steaks' which he pronounced 'Sta-akes.' The smack of the soil is going out of Lancashire and Yorkshire cricket and instead we are beginning to get the flavour of half-education, city-life, the motor-bicycle and suede shoes. Will any 'modern' advocate argue that Saturday's play at Bramall Lane contained a pennyworth of the character which only the other year used to be put into Lancashire and Yorkshire matches by Robinson, Rhodes, Richard Tyldesley, Parkin, Makepeace?—not to go back to the legendary epoch of Hirst, Maclaren, Briggs, Peel, Brearley and the rest.

Sibbles bowled hard, without a single variation of length, direction, or flight. When he took the new ball at 200 two fours were driven from him; then in the same over he got Barber out leg-before-wicket. All of which sounds suspiciously as though Sibbles with a new ball achieved a straightness that would have seemed sinful heresy to Emmott Robinson. Taking one consideration with another, Lancashire did well to provide Yorkshire with no more than 293 runs in some 305 minutes, especially as at a quarter to four Yorkshire were 200 for one wicket.

The Lancashire attack after tea performed well enough the negative job of keeping the runs down; a crafty business no doubt, when at one end of the wicket you have Mitchell 'making merry,' as one Yorkshire newspaper so delightfully put it. I expected Leyland to open his shoulders after tea; his score was 22 at the interval, and in the fifty minutes that followed until the advent of rain, he could add merely another 15, at a period when it was Yorkshire's game to clinch by quick runs a solid prelude to the innings.

Booth's part in keeping Leyland quiet was substantial; he was the whole of the Lancashire attack; the others were supernumeraries, or—not to flatter them—supers. But the fielding maintained efficiency and good heart, despite an unaccountable failure of Duckworth to try to stump Mitchell when Mitchell was in the sixties. No, startled reader, Mitchell was not attempting yet another six; he played forward and missed a ball which rose sharply and 'went away' to the off; the chance was difficult, but Duckworth usually envisages miracles. Eckersley handled his shadowy bowling with all possible resource.

Sutcliffe and Mitchell scored 143 for Yorkshire's first wicket in two hours and forty minutes. In the second over of the morning, Sutcliffe was bowled by Booth, but it was a no-ball. Later in the day, Sutcliffe was caught from a 'skier' from a no-ball; it is a pity we cannot have a Lancashire and Yorkshire match played entirely with no-balls. Sutcliffe batted in his safest and most pleasant vein; I love to see him withdrawing his bat from an out-swinger. He lifts it up as though indignantly avoiding a stain on his character. Sutcliffe was rather careless to lose his wicket in the way he did; he pulled a ball round to square leg, where Sibbles held a good catch. Sutcliffe threw away a certain 150, to say the least.

Barber began with one or two strokes through the slips of the sort which are good if they are not bad and fatal. He then gave us an innings of 44 in less than an hour, during which abnormally vivacious interlude, 73 runs were noted and observed by the scorers. At half past three, Mitchell's total stood at 71; I say 'stood,' and I hold by it. An hour afterwards he was 98. He reached his hundred at the end of four hours and a quarter; then he made a magnificent drive from Sibbles. In the match at the Oval last September, between the Champion County and the Rest of England, Mitchell showed many fine hits; he is too easily suppressed by an occasion. Defence and nothing but defence will not go far towards beating Australia in four days. I cannot imagine that Mitchell's innings on Saturday, for all its cleverness, advanced his Test match chances. Leyland began well, like a batsman thoroughly in form. His inactivity after tea was

383

really a compliment to Booth.

The play was watched by the smallest crowd I have ever seen at these matches.

SECOND DAY

Play did not begin until after lunch today because of a wet turf. In brilliant sunshine that boded evil for Lancashire the game went on at a quarter-past two. The crowd sounded more like a Lancashire and Yorkshire match this time; the old Sheffield roar filled the air as soon as Leyland drove a four. Yorkshire added 53 in forty-five minutes and then declared. Sibbles achieved a remarkable return catch off a severe drive by Turner, and Leyland, in his efforts to force the pace, missed several balls which he would have placed easily for runs had he trusted to his usual scoring technique.

When Watson and Hopwood began the Lancashire innings Verity bowled with Bowes, new ball or no new ball. I admired the Yorkshire captain's indifference to the shibboleth of the day; Blythe and Rhodes always opened the attack on wickets softened by rain. But Verity could not spin the ball yet; the pitch played easily hereabout, and Bowes crossed over and Smailes was called up. I fancy Emmott Robinson would have advised a later declaration; it was his special gift to know to a minute at what time of day a piece of Yorkshire earth became patriotically helpful. Bowes gradually worked up his energy; his first over suggested that he had spent all Sunday on the sofa: if he did not bowl fast he once or twice adumbrated pace, and nearly got Watson caught at the wicket from an off-side ball which Watson, with a horizontal bat, tried to cut. It was an esoteric stroke in a Lancashire and Yorkshire match.

Bowes took a rest after half an hour's effort and Smailes endeavoured to fill the place of Macaulay by exploiting potential off-breaks from round the wicket. Moreover, Verity was put on again; in short, Sellers did all that he honestly could have done to persuade the batsmen that the wicket was suitable to all sorts and conditions of bowlers. If you have on your side a slow left-handed bowler, keep him at work for a long stretch at the outset of an innings if there has been rain: do not take him off and then change your mind

384

and call him back and generally give the enemy reason for thinking the wicket is not so bad after all. The turf, as I say, played comfortably enough for an hour, but if Wilfred Rhodes had been in action he would have done something to deceive us all to the view that the ball was perpetually spinning. Bowling changes do not always unsettle the minds of batsmen; sometimes they merely tell us that the attacking side's strategy is unsettled. Verity lacks subtlety of flight; if the turf is not definitely vicious he seldom seems hostile; he has not since he came into county cricket added much in the way of guile to his natural ability to turn the ball on a sensitive wicket.

Watson and Hopwood scored 36 in an hour; their leisureliness was apparently self-determined and the crowd began gently to barrack, not because Lancashire were not hitting fours but because Lancashire were not getting out. The crowd obtained satisfaction in the last over before tea. Sellers asked Verity once again to attack from the pavilion end, and Hopwood, who for a long time had been playing forward overmuch, played forward once too often and was caught ravenously at silly point; Verity for once in a while tried a slow ball. It was a stupid way to get out; still, Hopwood's push stroke had prevailed for seventy-five minutes and had killed valuable time for Yorkshire.

After tea Watson was nearly caught at first slip off Leyland; Ernest Tyldesley also was guilty of an excessive faith in the half-cock stroke; if Lancashire collapse now, said I to myself, they will betray themselves mainly because of speculative minds and strokes that begin close to the right knee and finish not far in front of it. As soon as an odd ball was seen to spin abruptly the footwork of Watson and Tyldesley was the picture of dubiety, and when Tyldesley was caught off the edge of his bat nobody had reason for surprise, least of all Tyldesley. At this time of day the hot sun was beginning to have some unchristian influence on the good Yorkshire earth aforesaid. Watson was bowled at 43 by Verity, but I will die in the belief that the ball came straight through with the bowler's arm. In the first half-hour after tea Lancashire lost two wickets and made two scoring strokes—at last the old Yorkshire bogey was to be seen sitting on Lancashire's chest, turnip and lantern and all.

Iddon and Paynter contrived to stay in momentarily while not only Verity but also Leyland pitched the ball wherever they chose or wherever the propulsive powers of their arms sent it. Leyland achieved an occasional long-hop and nobody essayed a clout out of the field. Iddon allowed Leyland to bluff him into a precipitate hit, woefully across a well-tossed ball, from the same Leyland who has obviously been hiding his bowling talents darkly for many a year. Lancashire were unlucky to find themselves batting on a wicket which, though by no means unpleasant, was of the kind which Blythe or Rhodes might have turned to advantage. But a batting breakdown against Leyland for next to no runs—this was indeed a strange sight to see.

Leyland bowled several excellent balls this afternoon: he bowled many loose ones too, and the Lancashire batsmen could not distinguish the good from the bad. Lancashire have lost the old technique against the turning ball and against the ball that pretends to turn. Gone the celebrated backplay of Makepeace with the bat held loosely by the left hand at the top of the handle: the dead bat which serves as a cushion for break. This afternoon we have seen Lancashire professionals pushing out with blind arm action: we have even seen vainglorious, fast-footed swings of the blade with the head flung backwards. We have seen neither the quick-footed, sticky-wicket technique of Johnny Tyldesley nor the canny pad play of Makepeace. We have certainly not seen a real sticky wicket or a Rhodes bowling on one. Still, Lancashire have good reason to deplore their luck: the turf was so docile for Yorkshire on Saturday.

Paynter defended cleverly enough: would he not have served his side better had he remembered his glorious innings on a bad wicket at Bradford a year or two ago? Can we believe that Leyland would have stood up to a vehement attack by the Paynter of that memorable and regrettably distant afternoon?

Lancashire have so far batted three hours. No side can stay in on a 'sticky' wicket for three hours and score less than a hundred runs in the time and *not* be all out. The paradox of the 'sticky' pitch is that either a batsman loses his wicket or he makes runs. This afternoon the ball turned slowly; that is my opinion, and the opinion of one or two experts who saw the game in 'the middle.' Lancashire's failure was largely the consequence of the half-hearted push-stroke. Yorkshire fielded with splendid opportunism; and Sellers made a great catch from a fine hit by Eckersley—one of the few honest hits of the Lancashire innings.

Lancashire made no attempt to change their methods as the wickets went down one by one. Nobody made the faintest effort to hit the terrible Leyland off his length—when, by accident or design, he found a length. No: everybody persisted with the push-stroke, hopefully feeling for the ball, the right foot pinned down to the ground. Lambs to the slaughter!—and how Bramall Lane revelled in the spectacle! But it is time the gods turned away from Yorkshire and spared a smile for our distressful county. Last Whit Monday Lancashire were trapped on a broken wicket at Manchester—and now the demon of demon bowlers, Maurice Leyland, at Bramall Lane, after the showers!

THIRD DAY

Yorkshire beat Lancashire here at 25 minutes to six by an innings and three runs, after a day of gallant fighting by Lancashire. The side did their best to regain the ground lost on the previous day, and in some ways it was a gallant failure. They struggled all day to beat the clock (and perhaps hoped for rain), but they failed because Bowes bowled well and because the opening batsmen and the tail-enders failed. Too great a strain was thrown on the middle batting.

When play started Lancashire had lost seven wickets for 93 runs, and the innings was polished off in a further 25 minutes. There was enthusiasm even in Bowes's bowling, and in five overs he took two wickets for two runs. Even Lancashire men felt that there was hope so long as Paynter was batting that the 104 runs would be scored to save the follow-on, but Bowes had Paynter caught in a rather obvious trap. Mixing bumpers with his good length bowling, Bowes tempted Paynter to go for a big hit, and with the batsman failing to get hold of the ball Davidson, at what professional cricketers call 'leg slip,' took a low catch with the air of a thoroughly good cricketer and a thoroughly good Yorkshireman. Duckworth would doubtless have stuck in a long time with the aid of his pads, but he had only one ball before Booth, having indulged in some hearty and not unsuccessful smacks, fell to Verity's second delivery. Verity, it will be seen, sent down 28 overs for only 25 runs and five wickets; yet there were people who saw the game from the best possible position willing to declare that not half a dozen balls during the Lancashire first innings were bowled with true left-handed spin and lift.

Lancashire were 235 behind, and soon after noon they went in again with only one task before them—to stay at the crease for five and a half hours. They could not win and their only hope was to wriggle out of a nasty corner with such credit as they could. Watson made some unfamiliar strokes when playing the bowling of Smailes, but it was Bowes who had him bowled, leg stump, by a swerving yorker. The first wicket went at 25, and the loss of such a batsman placed Lancashire in a struggling position from the start. Tyldesley played well, even if he used his pads to an unusual degree, and lunch-time came with no further disaster to Lancashire except that Hopwood had been out in the middle for seventy-five minutes and had scored only 13 out of 48.

The afternoon play was carried out in almost total silence except that a furious noise broke out whenever a wicket fell or when a catch was missed. The catch was important and will be dealt with later. Hopwood was out at 51, yorked by an uncommonly fast ball from Verity. Next man in was Iddon, who has not been an unqualified success in great matches. He began quite unlike the Iddon so familiar to Old Trafford crowds, striking the heroic note at once. Bowes, when Iddon came in, was bowling with that touch of spirit and 'bite' which one associates with, say, Macaulay. He at once bounced one to Iddon, and Iddon, using his bat like a baseball player, frightened the short-leg fieldsmen almost out of their lives, the ball crashing away in front of square-leg at a tremendous pace. Bowes and his ring of leg-side fieldsmen departed and Smailes came and went.

Iddon and Tyldesley scored at a reasonable pace, having regard to all the circumstances, but then came the dropped catch. Leyland came on for Smailes and his first ball Iddon drove back, hard it is true, but a not unreasonable catch to a Leyland. It was put on the floor, and the dropping of that catch meant not only a lot of hard work for Yorkshire but that we all had to miss tea.

Not long after the crowd had stopped talking about this catch, disaster came to Lancashire. Tyldesley, batting well and in his best form, lost his wicket in outrageously unlucky fashion. Verity was bowling no better than just steadily and he gave Tyldesley a ball which pitched inches outside the leg stump. Tyldesley followed it round, but the ball dropped in the 'rough stuff,' popped, and turned and went off the back of his bat into a pair of the safest hands in England at 'silly' backward point. Soon afterwards Verity came off after a spell of bowling lasting 85 minutes, during which he sent down fourteen overs, eight being maidens, for thirteen runs and two wickets. Paynter played an over from Leyland as though he would score a memorable century; there were two fours by splendid leg hits and another off the edge of his bat past first slip. But Paynter failed, dismissed in as near the same way as in the first innings as two incidents can be alike in cricket. Davidson was maybe standing a little fine, but again he darted forward and took the ball inches from the turf.

At 121 for four Lancashire were having decidedly the worst of it, but Iddon and Hawkwood made a great stand. The situation was like that in the Test match at Nottingham four years ago, when Bradman made a hundred. Those who were at Trent Bridge may remember that the game was held in the balance all day. Wickets fell but Australia kept level with their task, and only a substitute's catch won the match for England. It was a substitute this time that broke a partnership—Turner, deputy for the sick Macaulay. He had not taken a wicket this season until he had Iddon leg before at 176. Iddon played a good innings judged from every standpoint: he has certainly never played a 'shock' attack with greater skill or a better control of himself. He stood out against the Yorkshire attack for over two hours, and hit eight fours.

With all the batsmen of repute gone at half-past four, the

tea interval was claimed for play by the Yorkshire captain and the extra half-hour was talked about all round the ground. There was a brief stand, and then Parkinson was so clearly leg before that he was given 'out' from the press-box and the bar and tea-room and the ugly football stand before the umpire's finger went up. The new ball was claimed and Bowes and Leyland used it. Leyland has been a sinister figure—a sort of Lancashire 'public enemy No. 1' in this match. Hawkwood, who batted with style for nearly an hour, fell to the swerve of the new ball and the game was as good as over.

The stand for the last wicket was diverting. Duckworth made some astonishingly fine hits off Bowes, but refused to run lest the fast bowler should get at Booth. Booth hit Leyland for six with a magnificent straight drive and generally enjoyed himself. But Duckworth, after nursing the bowling for a quarter of an hour, skied an attempted drive and was caught behind the bowler, to the accompaniment of a howl of joy from 10,000 Yorkshiremen.

SCORES

YORKSHIRE

First Innings

Sutcliffe, c Sibbles, b Booth	73
Mitchell, c Watson, b Hopwood	121
Barber, lbw, b Sibbles	44
Leyland, not out	73
Davidson, b Sibbles	6
Turner, c & b Sibbles	5
A. B. Sellers, not out	6
Extras b5, lb10, nb3	18
	—
Total (for 5)	*346

*Innings declared

YORKSHIRE V LANCASHIRE 1934
LANCASHIRE

First Innings		Second Innings	
Watson, b Verity	22	b Bowes	15
Hopwood, c Sellers, b Verity	20	b Verity	14
Tyldesley, c Mitchell, b Leyland	1	c Mitchell, b Verity	27
Iddon, c & b Leyland	10	lbw, b Turner	62
Paynter, c Davidson, b Bowes	24	c Davidson, b Bowes	16
Hawkwood, lbw, b Leyland	4	b Bowes	38
Parkinson, c Mitchell, b Verity	3	lbw, b Verity	8
P. T. Eckersley, c Sellers, b Verity	0	lbw, b Leyland	4
Booth, st Wood, b Verity	10	c Leyland, b Bowes	0
Sibbles, b Bowes	15	not out	19
Duckworth, not out	0	c Turner, b Smailes	2
Extras b1, lb1	2	Extras b9, lb17, w1	27
Total	111	Total	232

BOWLING ANALYSIS

YORKSHIRE—First Innings

	O.	M.	R.	W.		O.	M.	R.	W.
Sibbles	38	10	106	3	Iddon	5	0	21	0
Booth	43	10	88	1	Parkinson	17	2	43	0
Hopwood	24	2	48	1	Watson	8	2	22	0

LANCASHIRE—First Innings

	O.	M.	R.	W.		O.	M.	R.	W.
Bowes	13	8	14	2	Smailes	11	5	15	0
Verity	28	17	25	5	Leyland	29	12	55	3

Second Innings

	O.	M.	R.	W.		O.	M.	R.	W.
Bowes	27	8	60	4	Turner	9	3	8	1
Smailes	17	4	35	1	Leyland	20	4	74	1
Verity	32	20	28	3					

YORKSHIRE V LANCASHIRE 1934

August 4/6/7   Old Trafford

FIRST DAY

ON Saturday Yorkshire batted a few minutes under six hours for 291 for six wickets. The play had little to do with cricket; the teams were like two timid boxers walking round one another afraid to come to grips. The Yorkshire batsmen on the whole declined to take a sportsman's risk; the Lancashire bowlers often seemed equally short of initiative. After lunch a ball from Hopwood spun and jumped; in the same over Barber hit a four, the ball going in the air on the on-side. The sight of this stroke should have delighted Hopwood's heart. 'That is what I want Barber to do,' he should have told himself. But Hopwood immediately set his field on the on-side—and bowled over the wicket. This was not the worst piece of cricket of a dismal day; but it was bad enough. The Lancashire and Yorkshire match is a dreary fraud, and nothing less.

The match had scarcely begun before Sutcliffe drove rashly at Pollard and sent the ball soaring over the head of mid-on, a dangerous stroke and, what is more, a stroke which made me blink with astonishment. I feared for a moment that I had mistaken my turning and come to the wrong match. At any rate, it was the kind of hit that is severely avoided in this engagement until the seven hundred and fifty goes up on Tuesday afternoon. Sutcliffe, I said to myself, has been reading pernicious literature by people who agitate for more light and more friskiness in Lancashire and Yorkshire matches. Sutcliffe actually hit a four at 11.45. But Sutcliffe remembered in good time where he was and the nature of the proceedings. Before his eyes was the chastening example of Mitchell. The first half-hour produced seventeen runs, Mitchell four of them.

Just after twelve o'clock Hopwood went on in place of Booth; he bowled from round the wicket, on a dead slow turf. Pollard worried Mitchell with his inswinger, which came from the ground at nicely diversified paces. Mitchell was still four at a quarter past twelve; he then hit a two off Pollard, a pretty forcing push in front of square-leg. Hopwood changed over to the Manchester end, and the sight-screen was moved to the accompaniment of vernacular cries of 'Whoa!' The morning was lit by brilliant sunshine; lovely shadows moved across the field. After an hour's play the score was 27, Mitchell six. The pomposity of it all was heavy and absurd; barracking began promptly at 12.35. There was a delirious scream when Mitchell glanced Booth for two; the hit was fielded swiftly and beautifully at long-on by Iddon, who threw in at the wickets and rattled them. At ten minutes to one, Mitchell's score moved uneasily in its sleep and went from eight to ten. His cap had by now tacked towards his right ear. He drove Parkinson with a shocking suddenness for four to the off, a splendid stroke. It is not yet known why he did it. He sent up Yorkshire's fifty after ninety minutes; he was himself forging ahead; his total had reached nineteen. Sutcliffe pulled Parkinson for four and, heavens! it was nearly a six.

At a quarter past one a ball from Hopwood 'popped.' I hoped fervently that after the luncheon interval the wicket would become really difficult and that we should see the tactics of Sutcliffe and Yorkshire properly paid out and castigated. A few minutes before the players departed to replenish their energies by the midday meal, Mitchell was twice nearly out—to Pollard and to Parkinson. The lunch score was 81 for none.

When the game was continued at a quarter past two in summer weather, the crowd was the smallest I have ever seen at a Lancashire and Yorkshire match on the first day, or for that matter at any match of importance. The people who stayed away were wise; you can fool the people for a time but not all the time. I suggest that at Whitsuntide and August Bank Holiday the match should be changed; we have seen enough of Lancashire v Yorkshire at the period of the county's holidays. A bigger crowd would come to see Lancashire v Kent or Glamorganshire. Not always has the holiday match at Old Trafford been Lancashire v Yorkshire; on the Whit Monday of 1902 Kent played at Old Trafford, and C. J. Burnup scored 200.

Shortly after lunch Sutcliffe left the field suffering from dizziness. Barber came in and hit a fierce four to the on, off Hopwood. Then Booth beat the bat of Mitchell, and seemed to rail against the unjust gods. Hopwood now bowled over the wicket, presumably to keep down the rate of scoring. 'Ah, but,' said an old member of the club to me on the pavilion, 'the Lancashire and Yorkshire match always was slow.' He should have known better; before the war this match was the greatest, the most heroic and dynamic in the land. I have seen Spooner smash the attack of Hirst, Rhodes and Haigh in an hour or two, with J. T. Tyldesley at the other end. I have seen Hirst and Denton crash boundary after boundary from Brearley at his best. I have seen K. G. Macleod save Lancashire from almost certain defeat by annihilating one of the best Yorkshire attacks of all times—a hundred in less than two hours, and sixes clean out of the Bramall Lane ground. I have seen a vast crowd at Old Trafford uplifted at August holiday-time, roaring the day long with inexpressible delight and pride in great deeds. Heaven knows I am not asking only for swashbuckling cricket. I have been thrilled and I have seen the crowd thrilled by the dour defensive play of Makepeace and Hallows pitted against an equally dour Rhodes and Emmott Robinson. My complaint against Saturday's play was that it lacked any point, any antagonism, any character at all. It was mere drift, mere slackness of mind.

Booth beat Mitchell once more, when he had accumulated 42 in two hours forty minutes. Yorkshire were then 107 for none, two-thirds of them got by defensive pushes of little skill and no beauty. The Lancashire attack for hours was merely industrious, quite without guile or sting. At three o'clock Mitchell was leg-before-wicket; in two hours three-quarters he had denied his true scoring strokes and made 45 out of 111. Mitchell at Lord's last week but one hit a glorious century, full of handsome drives. Why this nonsense of his every year at Old Trafford?—folly most foolish.

Yorkshire's second wicket should have fallen at 112; a fine ball from Hopwood drew Barber forward, but Duckworth fumbled the chance of stumping. (Of course, no wicket-keeper in a Lancashire and Yorkshire match expects an opportunity to stump anybody.) Leyland, who is incorrigible, drove a straight four as soon as he came in off Pollard; then he pulverised a no-ball. For the first time in the day we heard a bat making a noise. Barber, who is really a vital batsman, was kept quiet by Hopwood's over-the-wicket methods (bowlers can be as unenterprising as batsmen and as worthy of the barrackers' irony). Barber hit Hopwood for two fours the moment the length wavered. Another magnificent straight drive by Leyland shook the whole ground to life; eyes were rubbed, and by sheer habit some of us consulted our watches and looked for the morning cup of tea. Only 7,000 people had paid at the gates at three o'clock.

Iddon bowled over the wicket instead of Hopwood: his sixth ball stood up in a way that would have made Harry Dean's mouth water. The Lancashire left-handed bowling was, I thought, unimaginative not to exploit the pitch after lunch by trying to spin the ball from round the wicket. If Hopwood thought it worthwhile to bowl round the wicket at noon, surely round the wicket might have been tried three hours later on a sunny day? The Lancashire attack was often as timid in spirit as Yorkshire's batting. Iddon bowled Leyland at 149: the ball turned keenly. Iddon should have bowled round the wicket all the time; perhaps he cannot direct his attack that way now; bad habits (cultivated to perpetuate ca'canny) breed bad habits. Under A. C. MacLaren, Hopwood and Iddon would have been taught and encouraged to put their gifts of spin to offensive uses.

Barber was cleverly caught at the wicket off Booth almost before Leyland had taken off his pads. Sellers, in next, is a vastly improved batsman; he drove Booth twice for powerful boundaries to the off. Turner kept the match in the proper key—a flat key; he was one run at the end of three-quarters of an hour. The score at tea was 186 for three, after four 'mortal' hours.

When at length the 200 was reached and the new ball was used Duckworth stood back to Booth, and Sellers drove Booth for a boundary straight to the sight-screen. Sellers played the best innings of the day; he was always looking for runs and he ran between the wickets with a rare alacrity. He reached 50 in under two hours, which was extremely fast for the occasion. He was out to the first tame shot he made. Sutcliffe returned and completed his 50.

I departed from the scene at this point—one amongst many. On the railway station at Warwick Road a crowd stood waiting for the train in a depressed silence. They did not even curse the cricket; no spirit was left. A solitary voice expressed the sentiment of the whole day: 'And to think I paid three bob to see all that!' But he will not pay it again, and there will be thousands like him.

SECOND DAY

Not a ball could be bowled at Old Trafford yesterday in the match between Lancashire and Yorkshire. Such spectators as had paid for admission were given tickets available for any other match at Old Trafford this season.

THIRD DAY

There was a ripple of excitement at Old Trafford last evening. Lancashire lost the first-innings victory in the last over of the day, by eighteen runs. At tea the five points were in Lancashire's grip firmly; they were 192 for two wickets. Iddon not out 100. Iddon, his eye surely 'well-in,' proceeded to make another 42 in a few minutes under two hours. The change that came over his cricket seemed dictated less by the Yorkshire attack than by a mistaken policy.

One notable fact of the match is that after a day ruined by rain the best slow left-handed bowler in England was useless on the dead wicket. The root of all the present discontents about slow batting is the modern method of preparing wickets and keeping them covered in rainy weather. Before the war a left-handed bowler of half Verity's skill would have won a match outright at Old Trafford on a fine day that followed a wet day. The county committees are responsible for much of the dreary and barren play that afflicts us nowadays. We must get back to the reasonably 'natural' wicket.

The game was held back until noon by a damp pitch. Yorkshire declared at Saturday's score and the Lancashire innings began with a terrific fusillade of boundaries against

Bowes and Smailes, who dealt out a sequence of long-hops which would have provoked a deal of conversation between Rhodes and Emmott Robinson. Watson hit three of them, and then Hopwood hit two in an over as though for the delectation of Mitchell, whose fielding all day was a delight, whether he was getting a ball or not. In 23 minutes Lancashire scored 23 runs. Then Hopwood was out at 31. The indecorous pace was stopped by the advent of Macaulay, who for a period made his attack come from the dead pitch at a speed that allowed the batsmen no time for second thoughts. Macaulay, who bowls every ball with an idea behind it, immediately went round the wicket. He quickly found the edge of Iddon's bat and looked daggers. Macaulay is a cricketer of great character; his fine face tells you that.

After an hour's play Lancashire were 44; seven runs afterwards Macaulay hit the pads of Watson and his antagonistic appeal was supported by the umpire. Watson did not seem to enjoy the decision—but then lbw verdicts never were popular amongst batsmen. Ernest Tyldesley's first stroke was a fortuitous single off Bowes; the stroke set the key of one of the poorest innings Tyldesley has played for many days. Still, he kept up his wicket and left the situation to the control of Iddon, who began anonymously and, with lunch over, developed his game finely all round the wicket. At half-past one Lancashire were 62 for two; Yorkshire were now favourites for the vast prize of the first-innings points.

After the midday interval Bowes in vain tried to bump the ball on the ridiculously easy turf. He exploited a leg-trap of three fieldsmen, who held out supplicatory hands—also in vain. Batting seemed easy as shelling peas; Macaulay could not maintain keenness of speed from the wicket, which dried slowly and comfortably. An appeal by Wood for a catch at the wicket was unconvincing and delivered in a quite dreadful state of isolation. Ernest Tyldesley pulled Bowes for two and the 'trap' was disbanded without loss of time. Mitchell fell down flat to the earth trying to save runs at short-leg; he can fall quicker than any other fieldsman living; a diver does not leave his board with more speed and with more beautiful release of muscle. Iddon glanced Macaulay to leg exquisitely, and Lancashire's total reached 100 in just under two hours and a quarter.

Verity could not spin the ball and he was out of luck. When Iddon's score stood at 40 Yorkshire were guilty of a terrible mistake in the field; Verity persuaded Iddon to drive, and Barber, at long-off, dropped an easy catch. Verity looked philosophically at the disaster; it was a poor reward for intelligent bowling. Iddon paid thanks to the gods by hitting a four to the off in the same over; his cricket was blossoming hereabout; his bat was often lifted on high stylishly and belligerently. Iddon's straight drive is a sight worth seeing. Leyland bowled instead of Verity at 117; his first effort, a long-hop, made him smile, and also compelled him to go over the wicket—to keep the runs down at his end, so to say. Leyland is the happiest and most lovable cricketer in the world.

Ernest Tyldesley made only 28 in eighty minutes; he was uncertain in his stroke-play, and scarcely ever did he attempt a real hit. With so little at stake—the difference between three points and five—I should have thought Tyldesley in his ripe mastership would have jumped at an opportunity to enjoy himself.

The crowd revelled in Iddon's enterprise; they humorously barracked the slow, deliberate gait of Bowes as he walked to his bowling place. But it was friendly irony; Bowes has a winning way about him; he appeals to the schoolboys. Iddon drove a brilliant four off Leyland, and next ball smote a six by means of a huge pull. He proceeded to crash Smailes for two boundaries to the off in one over. The approach of his first hundred against Yorkshire did not disconcert him, and when, just before the tea interval, he reached it the rejoicings were general. The Yorkshire team joined in the tribute as they walked from the field; Sutcliffe delivered his applause like a man distributing largesse. Iddon got his hundred in two hours fifty minutes; the second half of it was magnificent; Iddon's second halves are always telling us that he is a splendid batsman, no relation to the hesitant individual who potters in the early part of the first half.

Immediately after tea Tyldesley was caught from a mis-hit on the on side; he and Iddon scored 142 in two hours twenty minutes; Tyldesley's share was 46, and if he hit two fours I missed one of them. A slump set in suddenly, just when the Lancashire innings seemed to be riding on a crest to the much-desired first-innings triumph. Paynter made a glorious straight drive off Bowes, who then got him caught in the slips from a stroke that advertised the swerving propensities of the new ball. Bowes at last received some tangible payment for an afternoon of capital bowling on a heartbreaking turf. At half-past three he had actually compelled a ball to bounce near Iddon's nose, a phenomenon which enabled us to understand that Iddon's favourite bowling is medium-paced.

Given the new ball at 200, Bowes again satisfied us that he is the best fast bowler in the country, apart from Larwood. Bowes accounted for Lister at 216, and the day was now as much Yorkshire's as Lancashire's. Iddon stopped a ball from Bowes wide to the off side by the simple but possibly painful device of putting his hindquarters to it. Iddon was compelled to check his tempo—though I doubt whether a batsman can do better than hit fours, whatever the game's position. Parkinson fell to a catch at the wicket at 238; Wood was in good form this time. At half-past five Lancashire had only four wickets in reserve and they still needed 54.

Booth was sent in next, presumably to hit. The gesture was sportsmanlike, but perhaps the wiser plan would have been to wait a little longer—until the ball had lost a little more of its 'newness.' A slogger needs an attack that is as straight as his bat is crooked. Bowes bowled Booth promptly. Lancashire 239 for seven. There was nothing for Iddon to do but take his courage in both hands. Iddon drove Bowes superbly for a straight four and Eckersley ran a sharp and political single to give Iddon the bowling again. Iddon drove Smailes terrifically, and Morton saved a certain four in the small of the back. A slash through the slips by Iddon stung Macaulay's hand abominably; it was not even a Press Box chance, and we never miss catches in the Press Box.

At six o'clock Lancashire wanted 34, with seven wickets down. Macaulay hit Eckersley on the pad; he did not appeal, but O! how he wished he could; he walked down the wicket almost as far as Eckersley and without the aid of the spoken word uttered volumes. Spirit and character again! Iddon, who is a cricketer of rare talent, lacked the commanding power of greatness; he could not take charge of the game at the psychological moment, though he always played well. Eckersley was leg-before-wicket at 259, time of day five minutes past six. Duckworth arrived, sticking out all over his anatomy with courage; he fell to a neat catch at square-leg off a stroke that probably sounded and felt good as he made it. But Duckworth should have been content to defend and leave the runs to Iddon.

Pollard put a straight bat to Macaulay and Smailes, while Iddon scored singles, not always judiciously. At 273, five minutes from close of play, Sellers daringly put on Leyland; only 19 were wanted—and Iddon allowed Leyland to bowl a maiden over, which delivered Pollard unto Bowes, who clinched the afternoon's business in the last over of the match. Iddon carried out his bat, and rather spoiled five hours of splendid skill by some lack of imagination at the finish.

SCORES

YORKSHIRE
First Innings

Sutcliffe, c Duckworth, b Watson	66
Mitchell, lbw, b Hopwood	46
Barber, c Duckworth, b Booth	25
Leyland, b Iddon	20
Turner, not out	48
A. B. Sellers, c Pollard, b Booth	54
Verity, c Duckworth, b Watson	8
Smailes, not out	1
Extras b10, lb12, w1	23
Total (for 6 dec)	291

YORKSHIRE V LANCASHIRE 1934
LANCASHIRE
First Innings

Watson, lbw, b Macaulay	21
Hopwood, c Sutcliffe, b Turner	12
Iddon, not out	142
Tyldesley, c Leyland, b Turner	46
Paynter, c Macaulay, b Bowes	7
W. H. Lister, c Macaulay, b Bowes	11
Parkinson, c Wood, b Smailes	5
Booth, b Bowes	0
P. T. Eckersley, c Wood, b Macaulay	4
Duckworth, c Verity, b Smailes	0
Pollard, b Bowes	2
Extras, b15, lb4, nb4	23
	—
Total	273

BOWLING ANALYSIS

YORKSHIRE—First Innings

	O.	M.	R.	W.		O.	M.	R.	W.
Booth	29	4	68	2	Parkinson	22	4	52	0
Pollard	23	3	56	0	Iddon	16	7	15	1
Hopwood	39	12	72	1	Watson	6	3	5	2

LANCASHIRE—First Innings

	O.	M.	R.	W.		O.	M.	R.	W.
Bowes	32	9	73	4	Macaulay	21	8	26	2
Smailes	24	2	57	2	Verity	11	2	25	0
Turner	21	5	45	2	Leyland	7	1	24	0

YORKSHIRE V LANCASHIRE 1935

June 8/10/11   Old Trafford

FIRST DAY

IN the Lancashire and Yorkshire game at Old Trafford, there was no play on Saturday.

SECOND DAY

A wet morning at Old Trafford suddenly turned fine, and play began at half-past eleven. The wicket had been covered; for a while it favoured the bouncing new ball, but on the whole it was easy and could be trusted.

The Yorkshire team took the field with the air of men meaning business; Macaulay examined the pitch with a quite passionate scrutiny. Bowes quickly got to work; he made the ball flash from the ground and find the shoulder of the bat; the last ball of his first over bowled Hawkwood, whose forward stroke seemed designed to cope at one and the same time with an inswinger and an outswinger, but not with the admirably straight ball that hit his stumps. Smailes, at the other end, sent an outswinger to Iddon that would have provoked Emmott Robinson to quiet irony, 'Keep 'em where they can reach 'em and don't waste t' new ball.' When Smailes did discover contact with the bat he struck the blade in the middle—once or twice to the surprise and relief of Hopwood. Bowes placed three men close to the leg stump, one of them—Mitchell, with his cap—almost on the wicket at forward mid-on; Yorkshire are great at the modern science of psychological suggestion. Every fieldsman does his best in dumb show to say to the batsman, 'It's no use struggling: everything's against you; the wicket is terrible, and you are only one against eleven of us, not counting the umpires.'

Iddon declined to play fair for Yorkshire; he drove Smailes for three, and then, against all the rules, he drove Bowes in front of the wicket. This was enough to cause Macaulay to take off his sweater and prepare to attack from the Stretford end; he wheeled his arm round violently, like Charlie Chaplin

402

preparing to throw a custard into somebody's face. His third ball was blocked by Iddon; Macaulay pounced on it and threatened to run Iddon out; Iddon was a foot behind the crease. Then Macaulay struck Iddon's thigh with an off-break and nobody appealed. I have always understood that in Lancashire and Yorkshire matches the appeal for leg before wicket was permissible to anything excepting concussion of the brain. Iddon cut Macaulay for one, a great stroke (good cricket cannot be measured always in runs); and in the same over Hopwood snicked a fine ball accidentally for three, and while he was running the look Macaulay gave him was rather wasted.

Apparently the pitch also was not playing fair for Yorkshire; it became docile. Bowes decided that Mitchell was too deep at his forward position on the wicket, so he brought him to somewhere just to the right of the line of the ball. Hopwood cut Bowes, and Macaulay fielded with a ghoulish brilliance and threw the ball in and narrowly missed striking Hopwood in the small of the back. The field of Bowes to Hopwood described a small intimate circle, quite a family circle, beginning with 'silly' point and ending with 'silly' mid-on. Hopwood scarcely had room to swing his bat, but of course he did not want to swing it. At the end of the first hour of the fray Yorkshire had captured only one wicket and Lancashire were 27. Bowes for an hour bowled magnificently, and was kept at bay only by sound and shrewd defensive batting by Hopwood and Iddon.

The first real appeal of the day occurred at twenty minutes to one; Macaulay began it terrifically when he crashed an off-break against Hopwood's legs. The appeal was dismissed with contumely by Woolley, the umpire. When Smailes bowled at Bowes's end Iddon drove the first boundary of the morning; every Yorkshireman on the field watched the stroke sadly all the way; the boundary might have been on the horizon.

Iddon played expert cricket, quick on his feet and supple; he was fortunate several times against Bowes with strokes that barely missed the out-swinger, but he deserved to prosper, for he showed fight. Hopwood, as usual, was a reliable wall; the mortar fell out of the bricks now and again, but the foundations seemed safe and of great age. Iddon looked a comfortable batsman at five minutes to one; he was then bowled by Smailes by a short-lengthed ball which was deceitfully quicker than anything Smailes had so far attempted. Iddon and Hopwood defended for an hour and a quarter, scoring fifty, mostly by afterthoughts, during which time Yorkshire tried earnestly to take a hundred wickets at least. At lunch Lancashire were 67 for two; custom may change in other places, but Bank Holiday at Old Trafford remains Bank Holiday.

Immediately after lunch Hopwood flicked an inswinger from Bowes to fine leg, where Smailes held a neat catch. It was not a case of vanity in Hopwood; the stroke was a reflex action. Smailes bowled some variable stuff, and Paynter pulled a long-hop with too much power, for three instead of six. The crowd was small and quiet; Toscanini and Beethoven would have given us a much more exciting slow movement. Farrimond came in and lost no time making one or two characteristic strokes to the on for nothing; Macaulay, standing in the slips, watched the strokes and folded his arms and plainly said '? ? ?'

A superb straight drive by Paynter off Smailes was the first noble blow of the afternoon; the ball left the bat faster than it came to it. Farrimond repeatedly placed his bat in the way of the ball, and when Macaulay bowled again Farrimond stole a single and helped Macaulay to retrieve the throw-in. Farrimond then performed his stroke off Macaulay—the scoop to leg—and I felt that Macaulay and the entire Yorkshire side were ready to gather round Farrimond and examine him in detail. But when Farrimond smote a 'bumper' from Bowes for four his originality could be seen from the distant outfield. He succumbed to Bowes (new rule); but not before he had employed his stroke in a fresh way, which sent the ball through the slips.

Washbrook, in at the fall of the fourth wicket at 98, was beaten before he had scored by Bowes and by Macaulay; the ball from Macaulay missed his wicket by an inch, and Macaulay made mystical signs and passes in the air. After two and three-quarter hours of visible motion Lancashire's total reached 100; the Yorkshire fielding was brilliant; Macaulay's alacrity to strokes from his own bowling was like a cat after a mouse. Washbrook wore a troubled tentative look; none the less, he pulled Verity for a grand six before he fell, in the same over, to a disgracefully clever catch; Washbrook merely stopped a ball which 'popped'; it bounced from the bat gently, and Sellers threw himself full stretch to the earth and held it. Bad light now stopped play; Lancashire were 107 for five.

Within fifteen minutes the umpires returned to the wicket, followed a minute afterwards by the players. Oldfield swept Verity to square leg for four—a valiant but cool hit. When Verity is not helped by the wicket we do not feel he is an aggressive bowler. Rhodes was always worrying the batsman, either off the ground or in the air. A rare quick ball of Bowes, lovely in length, with the pace skilfully disguised, got Oldfield caught at the wicket. Lancashire were 116 for six; and Paynter, after two hours' play, was 29; he improved on recent efforts considerably, but Lancashire needed runs, and he was set—in any case this is a two-day match, or isn't it? The scoring ceased when Parkinson joined Paynter; Lancashire's policy seemed to be, now that they had lost six wickets, to avoid defeat at all costs.

At tea Lancashire were 129 for six, after four hours' play. A few years ago we used to criticise Hallows because he only scored a hundred in four hours himself against Yorkshire! After tea Paynter hit two fours in quick succession and Parkinson got a three by permission of Verity, who mis-fielded a return. Paynter's valuable innings came to a dramatic end; a ball reared and shot from the shoulder of his bat high in the air; Verity jumped up and caught it one-handed. Paynter batted for two hours and a half; so well did he 'see' the bowling that he might have hit harder with safety. A quick ball defeated Parkinson's bat and he departed lbw after an innings of unusual discipline for him. I doubt if Lancashire would have made a smaller score than 153 on the good wicket had they played the Yorkshire attack on its merits.

Yorkshire began to bat at a quarter past five, and at once Sutcliffe commanded, or decreed, that the sight-screen be moved. Booth again bowled keenly with the new ball; he put

Hutton through a searching over. But Pollard and Iddon dealt the first retaliatory shock to Yorkshire and did much to counteract Lancashire's mistaken batsmanship; Sutcliffe edged an out-swinger and Iddon held a dexterous slip-catch. The Old Trafford pavilion gave Sutcliffe warm applause on his return; it was appreciation of a great Yorkshire and England player who has obligingly failed to get a hundred against Lancashire. Hutton defended with a style and steadiness that promised distinction to come, and, of course, Mitchell at Old Trafford is obstinacy itself. He forced a good-length ball from Booth off his pads to the on and four were run; it was the prettiest and easiest stroke of the day.

At six o'clock exactly Pollard bowled Hutton off his pads with a ball which was almost a shooter. And the game now flared up like a slow fire that has been struck by a violent and impatient poker. Mitchell was lbw, a ball from Booth deceived Leyland's forward push, and a great catch by Farrimond accounted for Sellers. All these disasters to Yorkshire occurred in a few minutes; the crowd woke up in the manner of heavy sleepers to the sound of an excited alarm clock. Booth and Pollard bowled heroically; if only Lancashire could bat with half the spirit of their bowling and fielding! There should be sport and agony at Old Trafford today.

THIRD DAY

The sixth and seventh Yorkshire wickets fell in the first minutes of yesterday morning; the news got around, and old gentlemen, a little late, broke into canters down Warwick Road with their watch-chains rattling on their waistcoats. Wood hit a ball from Pollard belligerently to square-leg, where Booth made a good catch. Yorkshire seemed in haste to win, for Verity also beat the air rhetorically and was caught by Farrimond—another wicket to Pollard, who at last had a lot of good work this summer recognised by fortune.

Smailes came next, looking big and not at all cast down by the situation—Yorkshire 58 for seven. He is a left-handed batsman, who has apparently not been told that to drive a half-volley in a Lancashire and Yorkshire match is not only dangerous but ill-mannered. He hurled his weight at an overtossed length from Booth, and the stroke was four all the way; he assaulted Pollard with the same unconstitutional violence. Booth made the mistake of pitching the ball too far up to the fast-footed Smailes.

Barber hit Booth with a swinging leg hit, and flicked a lovely four off his pads from Pollard. In a few minutes the atmosphere changed; crisis was ejected. There is nothing like a boundary blow or two for clearing the air. Booth put on his sweater at noon, and Parkinson went on in his place. His second ball kept low and struck Barber's pad, and everybody in the Lancashire side gave Barber out—but not the umpire. Barber played beautiful and quick-witted cricket. He crashed Pollard from his wrists to the off for four, and Yorkshire's total arrived unexpectedly at 102. Things were beginning to spoil Whitsuntide at Old Trafford after all.

At the pinch Smailes got himself caught at the wicket endeavouring to drive a rising ball out of the field. Barber took complete charge when Macaulay joined him; he drove Parkinson to the on boundary, and, on the whole, appeared dissatisfied that the hit had not gone for six. He attempted to make amends shortly afterwards, but inexplicably he produced from some dark corner of the Unconscious in him an ancestral mow or heave, which cost him his wicket. Thus he ruined a fine piece of batsmanship at a moment which saw the first-innings points almost in Yorkshire's grip; Macaulay obviously was ready to stay in all day with his nose-to-the-grass forward push.

At 115 for nine Bowes emerged from the pavilion; on his way to the wicket he probably realised that to every cricketer a day comes on which he plays the innings of his life. He looked at the bowling for a minute or two and proceeded to cut Parkinson by a masterful back stroke, with the spin, for four. Science and nothing less. The runs mounted up, and the crowd delivered expert advice to Lancashire. Macaulay gave a chance to Iddon in the slips off Pollard; it was dropped, to the sound of voices in distress. Four runs later, when Yorkshire were 139, Bowes, discarding Science for natural ability, mis-hit to mid-off, who also blundered. The fun ended in anticlimax; Booth struck Macaulay's pad and appealed, and while Macaulay was recovering his senses

Bowes galloped or charged down the wicket, anxious to get at the bowling again, only to be run out by yards. The morning's tension burst like a paper bag that has been blown up tight and suddenly thumped.

At one o'clock Lancashire batted again. Verity bowled swingers to three or four short-legs, a procedure which told us that Verity, for all his cleverness, does not belong to the Rhodes tradition. One or two balls almost shot, but the Lancashire batsmen thought the wicket was not more dependable than at any other period of the match.

After lunch Verity attempted spin and Macaulay attacked from round the wicket. The spell-binding had little effect on Hopwood and Hawkwood, though Hopwood was nearly caught and bowled by Verity and gave a chance to Wood off Verity. Verity was twice hit for fours by Hopwood from full tosses; Verity's 'flighted' balls sometimes deceive nobody but himself. He needs a 'sticky' wicket. Though Hawkwood was guilty of a bad stroke behind the stumps, he played well; a late cut by him lent a brief interest and splendour to the afternoon, which was drifting to nullity. The wind blew dust in the eyes and the day became a source of some misery. Rain descended fitfully when Lancashire were 80 for none. That was the end.

One of the best things in the match was Farrimond's wicket-keeping. The Yorkshire batting was a refreshing mixture of brilliance and insecurity. Somebody must write to Wilfred Rhodes about it.

YORKSHIRE V LANCASHIRE 1935
SCORES

LANCASHIRE

First Innings			Second Innings	
Hopwood, c Smailes, b Bowes	28		not out	31
Hawkwood, b Bowes	0		not out	39
Iddon, b Smailes	31			
Paynter, c Verity, b Macaulay	43			
Farrimond, lbw, b Bowes	13			
Washbrook, c Sellers, b Verity	7			
Oldfield, c Wood, b Bowes	8			
Parkinson, lbw, b Smailes	17			
P. T. Eckersley, not out	2			
Booth, lbw, b Macaulay	0			
Pollard, b Verity	4		Extras b9, lb1	10
Total	153		Total (for 0)	80

YORKSHIRE

First Innings	
Sutcliffe, c Iddon, b Pollard	4
Hutton, b Pollard	14
Mitchell, lbw, b Pollard	17
Leyland, c & b Booth	9
Barber, b Parkinson	41
A. B. Sellers, c Farrimond, b Booth	0
Wood, c Booth, b Pollard	5
Verity, c Farrimond, b Pollard	0
Smailes, c Farrimond, b Pollard	24
Macaulay, not out	8
Bowes, run out	17
Extras lb1	1
Total	140

THE ROSES MATCHES 1919-1939
BOWLING ANALYSIS

Lancashire—First Innings

	O.	M.	R.	W.		O.	M.	R.	W.
Bowes	30	11	53	4	Macaulay	18	4	37	2
Smailes	21	8	31	2	Verity	17	8	32	2

Second Innings

	O.	M.	R.	W.		O.	M.	R.	W.
Bowes	10	4	14	0	Verity	9	1	29	0
Smailes	5	1	9	0	Macaulay	8	2	18	0

Yorkshire—First Innings

	O.	M.	R.	W.		O.	M.	R.	W.
Booth	19	2	62	2	Parkinson	6	0	21	1
Pollard	24	7	56	6					

YORKSHIRE V LANCASHIRE 1935

August 3/5/6 Bradford

FIRST DAY

THERE was a sudden and shocking change in the fortunes of the game here today—and it happened at the end of the afternoon and nobody expected it. With a single fell swoop circumstances caught Lancashire by the neck; I cannot recall a more tragic reversal of a day's destinies. Up to teatime the match had been evenly fought; moreover, the cricket seldom suggested the great agony to come; it proceeded along industrious but anonymous ways; the crowd sat and looked on in a silence that was broken only now and then. The atmosphere and the wicket enabled the bowlers to swing the ball and make it jump from a good length. Lancashire attacked all day with determination; the accuracy and temper of the bowling of Phillipson and Pollard after lunch were admirable. Magnificent fielding compelled Yorkshire to toil and sweat for their runs. And Yorkshire's innings was brought to a violent end by Sibbles, who took three wickets for seven.

Now was it that strange forces entered the commonplace day. The light grew dim; and when Yorkshire took the field, followed by Hopwood and Watson, at half-past five we witnessed a ritual that expressed the Englishman's love of legality and proper procedure. Obviously the afternoon was now too dark for cricket. But one ball had to be bowled to satisfy the eternal fitness of things constitutional. Bowes bowled the ball; Hopwood appealed; and Umpire Woolley then walked solemnly across the ground to Umpire Oates. Presumably he said, 'They're appealing against the light. What of it?' And Oates no doubt replied: 'Well, perhaps it is a bit black, now that our attention has duly been drawn to it.' And everybody proceeded forthwith to grope their various ways back to the pavilion. A slight drizzle set in—and, so we said to ourselves, that was that for the day. The Lancashire players certainly gave the afternoon up as well and con-

411

vincingly over; no side likes to begin batting in the last hour even of a day of sunshine. The crowd began to go home; I myself got as far as the gate. Then, curiously and instinctively, I felt 'something happening' in the murky air; the light was no mere 'bad' one. It contained a bodeful gleam; it was not just absence of light, but visible darkness. I expected to hear the screech of the bird of ill-omen. I said to myself, 'I hope there's no more play, because if there is we'll see red ruin.'

The pall was lifted a little and the drizzle ceased. At a quarter to six the players went into action once more, looking unreal and insubstantial. The light was good only by the comparative test. Bowes seized his opportunities; I am certain he needed his spectacles; but everything else conspired with him and led him on—most of all the psychological unrest caused in the Lancashire side by the fact that they had, after all, to bat for half an hour.

The first ball of Bowes, as soon as the game began again, bowled Hopwood, who moved away from the wicket and played with a cross bat; apparently he heard the ball rather than saw it. Watson then hit a four off Rawlin, a fast medium bowler who runs as though travelling up the side of a hill. In the same over four byes occurred, whereat a man in the crowd clucked his lips and said testily: 'Would you believe it? Would you believe it?' Obviously he begrudged Lancashire eight runs; obviously he thought that Lancashire, in all fairness, should not be allowed *any* runs. Yorkshire's score of 31 the other day has palpably set up a new scale of values.

Watson pushed a ball from Bowes to the on side—and ran. The fieldsman chanced to be Mitchell, who threw down Paynter's wicket in one terrible and comprehensive aim. Then Watson flashed his bat at Bowes and was caught at cover brilliantly by Sellers; the stroke was of the dashing kind that Watson did not dream of making on Wednesday in the golden sunshine of Aigburth, on a perfect wicket, against Hampshire's perspiring attack. A slip catch of superb skill and beauty, taken with a sideways fall by Verity, accounted for Ernest Tyldesley, who barely snicked a magnificent outswinger of remarkable velocity from the earth. Lancashire were 15 for four, and the crowd sent forth ghoulish noises;

you could almost hear them licking their chops. Oldfield made one or two plucky hits, and Washbrook carried himself like a stout-hearted cricketer. These two young players rounded on the hunters and struggled with some defiance against the cruel net. But Washbrook got a fiendish ball that flew up at him and swung in; he was caught at the wicket amidst howls. In the closing ten minutes of the holocaust the style of Oldfield was touched with the pathos of burdened and doomed endeavour.

The Yorkshire crowd went home satisfied—but oh the misery of those who missed it by leaving the ground impatiently. What scenes and distress must have occurred in many a Yorkshire household on Saturday night when the wireless announced 'Lancashire 26 for five.' 'Why, they played again; well, I'll be ———. And it were all thy fault, mother, a worritin' about gettin' home in time for thi Aunt Alice, and she's not come yet, and I don't think she will now.'

The Yorkshire score of 225 was compiled in four hours and forty minutes. Considering the lively state of the wicket, it must be regarded as a formidable performance. Two missed catches betrayed Lancashire, and the irony is that the fielding was usually aggressive, swift, and sure. Leyland sent a sharp chance to Paynter at short-square-leg when he was ten; he went on to score a grand and pugnacious 58. Turner was missed in the slips by Ernest Tyldesley, and he went on to score a resolute and dour 57.

In two hours before lunch Yorkshire's main task was not to lose wickets. Mitchell played finely, and he was caught by a catch of the season in the deep field by Washbrook after what seemed suspiciously like an attempt to hit a six. Sutcliffe gave a poor account of himself; his innings of 28 lasted one hour and a half; he could not time his strokes, and he lacked the foundation-stone, or pedestal, of his own confidence and good opinion. He was run out by a wonderfully quick return by Oldfield and an incredibly rapid gathering of the ball by Duckworth, who, as far as I could see, swept off the bails with his head under his two arm-sockets. Sutcliffe could not believe he was really out, and for a moment he expressed by dumb-show his views. But the umpire is always the lord of all in the cricket field, whatever he may be in his own home when he gets back to it. At lunch Yorkshire were 75 for three.

Between a quarter-past two and three o'clock Phillipson and Pollard bowled so well that in a just universe they would have taken six wickets in the time. Wood touched a fulsome outswinger as he tried to drive, and Duckworth anticipated the consequences ruthlessly and took a catch at first slip. Duckworth was at his best all day—here, there, and everywhere, with as many arms as an Indian god. Leyland suffered some damaging blows on the arm; he left the field for iodine and plaster. While he was absent Sellers played defensively in front of his legs and sliced a catch to Watson in the slips. Leyland came back, to the joy of the multitude; he thumped Phillipson to the on-boundary at once and hit the next ball for a sumptuous boundary to the off. Pollard beat Leyland and registered despair; Turner defended with a straight bat. Yorkshire pulled the score round from 114 for five to 165 for six; Leyland's innings was a perfect mingling of sound defence and fierce attack; his drives and leg hits had rare precision and power. Duckworth caught Leyland from a fine glance; it was an outrageously dexterous catch; swift as a cat, and awful in its noise and pouncing opportunism.

Sibbles enjoyed a capital analysis; but the hostile work of Lancashire's attack was done by Phillipson and Pollard, supported by fielding which was so good and aggressive that it was shabbily rewarded by the ill-luck that caused the two highest scorers of the day to be dropped.

SECOND DAY

Magnificent bowling by Bowes ruined Lancashire's first innings entirely in three-quarters of an hour this morning, to the complete satisfaction of a vast and bloodthirsty crowd. The green wicket was a willing accomplice of his swerve and pace and bounce; he flashed the ball from the turf at vicious angles and the changes he worked on his outswinger and inswinger were demoralising. None but a great batsman could have hoped to contend against so terrible and beautiful an attack. The wonder is that he did not take three or four wickets every over.

Oldfield fell to a slip catch; he fluttered into the flame of an off-side ball like the moth into the candle. Eckersley showed fight and thrilled Lancastrians and outraged everybody else with a great hook for four off the aspiring Rawlin, who next ball bowled Eckersley with an imitation break-back. Rawlin also bowled Phillipson, but Bowes was Yorkshire's lightning and Rawlin merely a maker of stage thunder. Lancashire's last five wickets toppled almost as quickly as the first five had done on Saturday—so quickly indeed that a man near me could not blow up his air cushion; every time he filled his lungs and grew black in the face, a Lancashire batsman perished and all the poor patriot's wind escaped—and not only that but he could not even shout out his jubilation.

Shortly after half-past twelve Lancashire followed on, and at once Watson cut Bowes for four from the neighbourhood of the square-leg umpire. A Yorkshireman was heard to say as Watson's stroke reached the boundary, 'Well, anyhow, it will make the match interesting.' Thus did he philosophically support himself at the sight of Lancashire scoring any runs at all. Watson retreated again to Bowes, and his off stump escaped by an inch. Then Bowes bowled Hopwood with a grand ball; it swerved outwards late and the slip fielders made movements which anticipated a slip catch. But what happened was a sudden and shattering break-back which hit the top of the middle and off stumps. It was almost an honour and a privilege for a batsman to get such a ball.

Most of us expected a collapse of Lancashire yet again; Bowes was sending down unplayable swingers at will; he apparently had Watson at his mercy. Watson threw his bat at the attack of Bowes, only just keeping in touch with the handle; Watson was discreet even against the not exactly fast stuff of Rawlin, and was missed by Bowes at fifteen at mid-on; the ball dropped in front of Bowes, and the stroke spoke of much desperation. Watson obviously was prepared to hit fours or get out, but not prepared to play over the line of the ball. Sutcliffe missed him from a blind flick at another outswinger from Bowes—an easy chance. Watson was now sixteen, and I shall die in the belief that had the catch been held Lancashire would have lost before teatime. Paynter was out before lunch; the score was Lancashire 56 for two.

415

After the interval we saw some extraordinary cricket, not to say some incredible cricket. Bowes began again and Watson's mortality was exposed to the world; his innings hung on a broken string; his three stumps stood naked and lonely; the bowling played about the edge of his bat. He was a marked man. Ernest Tyldesley took him in charge, became his shield and protector. Watson was kept away from Bowes; singles were declined with contumely, so that Ernest Tyldesley could put his cool and masterful bat to Bowes. Tyldesley achieved an innings which saved the day for his county; he blunted Bowes's fierce spear; he defended with his body over the most hostile ball—and with what style and composure did he defend! His cricket moved us by its ease of technique and more than all by its serenity of mind.

Watson was militant enough against the other Yorkshire bowlers, who, to say the truth, were a poor lot. Watson was nearly caught at the wicket off Bowes at 41; escaping from the terror yet again, he pulled Turner twice for violent fours like a man of war. Ernest Tyldesley showed him and the rest of us how Bowes could be hooked majestically. Tyldesley lent authority to Lancashire's innings, and he fell in the effort to turn Fisher to leg for a single off the last ball of an over; his innings was easily the greatest of the day.

The moment that Bowes was temporarily tamed and out of action waiting for the new ball, Watson's innings cracked and boomed a heavy bombardment. His cricket rose from the dead; he cut and drove fiercely and relentlessly. Verity and Fisher were plunder for him; he batted with the hectic vigour of a man who knows he must take his chances before the bolt falls; he gorged on runs while Bowes was awaiting the new ball; he was like a condemned man gorging all the meats and stuffing in the world at one last banquet before the morning of execution. He was missed again at 87 in the slips off Verity; but he lambasted Verity unmercifully. And he hit Fisher for three fours off three consecutive balls. He actually reached his century in two and three-quarter hours, and struck and cut and pulled and snicked and hooked and drove nearly twenty fours. Oldfield and Washbrook played bravely while Watson staggered humanity; at tea Lancashire had not only saved the innings defeat; they were 44 ahead with six wickets in hand.

After tea Bowes came back with the new ball and Watson again dealt with him bat aslant and a long way from him. He perished at last, caught by Wood from an entirely helpless motion at nothing whatever. He was at the wicket, or contiguous to it, for three and a quarter hours and, angels and ministers of grace defend us, he hit twenty-five boundaries. Watson's hitting was for him unbelievably dazzling; the Military Cross is often won that way. The poor Yorkshire fielding missed him four times—at 15, 16, 41, and 87. To see Watson as a dramatic and powerful stroke player was to see a cricketer moved by circumstances out of his normal senses. The Yorkshire attack depended on Bowes utterly; the efforts of the others were the most harmless I have ever seen in a Yorkshire eleven. Verity obviously needs a rest; on any but a sticky wicket he is merely commonplace; today he could not even keep the runs down. Until he was worn out by strenuous labour Bowes was a great and penetrating bowler. He deserved a surer set of fieldsmen. Wood was no Duckworth and not even an Ames.

Bowes took his rests like the classical bowler who decided to go on at the other end; Pollard was missed off him in the slips straightway; seemingly there was not a real slip fieldsman in the vicinity. Washbrook cut and hooked Turner ferociously, but Yorkshire's bowling was ready for a hot bath and a feather bed. Washbrook was missed at backward point off Bowes when he was 37, and when the slips stopped the next ball the crowd roared ironically. Mitchell was compelled by a damaged hand to look upon his colleagues' exhibition of fingers and thumbs from a place far away at third man.

Yorkshire missed their way and threw opportunity to the wind scandalously. There is no excuse in a winning team for consistently bad catching. Wood, behind the wicket, was, from all visible signs, organised to the teeth to miss a chance. Yorkshire almost deserve to lose for their betrayal of the bowling of Bowes this morning and for an hour after lunch. Bowes and Ernest Tyldesley were the day's artists and true cricketers.

Rawlin caused a scene at five minutes past six by holding a hard return drive by Pollard, who played a valuable little in-

417

nings. Washbrook clove several streaky slip strokes, possibly to amuse the slips. And an appeal against an excellent light was presumably made for the amusement of the umpires. The best joke of the match, though, would occur if Lancashire won it. None but a good joke will beat Yorkshire's dropped catching.

THIRD DAY

Lancashire died with a fight today, but the wicket was easier for batsmen than at any other time of the match, in spite of some rough places at the pavilion end, on which Hopwood dropped the ball only to see it spin away prettily but harmlessly past the off stump.

At the morning's beginning Eckersley and Duckworth were out in the first two overs, Eckersley to a catch with one hand by Turner; it was so brilliant that Sutcliffe probably did not believe his eyes. Poor Sutcliffe suffered a bad match; he dropped another slip catch during a last wicket stand by Washbrook and Sibbles. This stand occurred when Lancashire were 313 for nine, only 141 ahead. A last wicket stand is provoking to the opposition at any time; in this morning's circumstances it was so funny that I wish every Lancashire reader of these notes could have been present at Bradford to shake with laughing at it all. Yorkshire sorely wanted a quick end to Lancashire's scandalously opulent second innings; the ancient foe were already too many runs to the good for the comfort of even broad-minded Yorkshire folk. And the rapid overthrow of Eckersley and Duckworth surely meant the end at last.

Sibbles declined to humour these patriotic views; he put the straightest of bats to the good balls and had the indecent temerity to turn a short one from Bowes to leg in style. Meanwhile Washbrook played a great game for Lancashire; he cut Bowes square with a fierce blow and performed the same stroke next over from Rawlin. Washbrook skied a no-ball to the on side, where, of course, the catch was missed. Sibbles actually went so far as to score a single off the last ball of an over by Rawlin, thus signifying to Bowes that he was anxious to get at him.

Washbrook drove a slow half-volley from Bowes for four,

whereat Bowes was reduced to the act of sending down several short bumpers. The sight of them and the inner meaning of them was enough to make the pavilion cat grin. The crowd's patience nearly dissolved into tears when Sutcliffe, at first slip, received a catch from Washbrook into his two hands and proceeded immediately to put it to the grass. Sutcliffe was apparently so certain he had caught the ball that he was about to walk towards the pavilion; he fortunately discovered his mistake in time and stayed where he was. Washbrook's score was 84 when this diverting incident happened. Sellers was obliged to change his attack; Verity relieved Rawlin, and the crowd cheered him for achieving a maiden—and it was not ironical applause at that. The last-wicket resistance might have persisted until many a Yorkshireman had turned redder in the face than usual; Washbrook ended it by unluckily treading on his wicket, making a good leg stroke.

Washbrook's innings today was as good as cricket well could be—strong, confident, cool, and vigorous with cuts and glances. He deserved his occasional luck; and Lancashire's 352, scored uphill after a sickening collapse, told a tale of splendid heart and no small skill.

At half past twelve Yorkshire began the task of getting 181 for victory. Sibbles and Phillipson were guilty of half-volleys in their endeavour to swing the ball; Sutcliffe made elegant pushes for twos and Mitchell drove a belligerent four to the on. In twenty minutes Yorkshire obtained 20, with ease, and Hopwood bowled instead of Sibbles, and Pollard went on for Phillipson. The runs ceased at once; Hopwood's length was a lesson to Verity in its nicely flighted curve. Pollard gave to his inswinger considerable vitality; what is more, he completely defeated Sutcliffe at 29. At lunch Yorkshire still needed 152 with nine wickets in reserve.

Eckersley continued his trust in Hopwood's accuracy and occasional spin. The alleged worn places possessed some psychological if little actual technical value. Mitchell and Barber for a period adopted attitudes of grave suspicion and put their bats to the ball like victors winning backwards so to say. Mitchell was at his best—safe, yet quick on the really bad ball. But when he was 39 and Yorkshire 69 he came terribly close to playing a ball from Pollard into his stumps. After that mischance the Lancashire attack's determination was all the more admirable because neither Mitchell nor Barber gave the faintest hint of fallibility for another hour. Eckersley changed bowler after bowler but to no perceptible end; runs came with a grim certainty.

At a quarter to four the game seemed won and lost—Yorkshire 135 for one. Suddenly Barber pulled Sibbles to deep long-leg with a swinging crack; Paynter ran in like the wind from the edge of the field and took a glorious catch at top speed a foot from the ground in front of him, and threw the ball triumphantly into the air the moment he gripped it. Barber hit five fours in an innings of solid common sense and scored 57 during the second-wicket partnership of 107 in two hours.

The tenacity of Lancashire was beyond praise; Yorkshire's innings had to begin again when Turner joined Mitchell, though only 46 were wanted now. Pollard and Sibbles gave nothing away and the fielding held a tight net. Turner went, leg-before-wicket to Sibbles, at 144; Sibbles was bowling round the wicket and causing the ball to nip a little. Few teams could have fought back against Yorkshire at Bradford as bravely as Lancashire in this match after a first innings of 53. Leyland's injured arm prevented him from coming in to bat in his proper place; Wood followed Turner, and for a while the atmosphere became tense again with possibilities. Yorkshire's great support and sure stay was Mitchell, and fortunately for them he was at his best and toughest. A grand cricketer who would be worth his place in any team for his fielding alone, his spirit, and the way he wears his cap.

Eckersley to the end made Yorkshire sweat for their honours; he tried Hopwood at the pavilion end, and Hopwood bowled a most canny maiden. Sibbles held up the proceedings, while he placed Washbrook to a fraction of an inch at third man. A few thumping blows by Wood settled the issue, and at half-past four we saw the finish of one of the most gallant and curious Lancashire and Yorkshire matches played for years. Both teams fought with spirit; let the good work go on until the dreary post-war affairs between these two great counties are forgotten.

YORKSHIRE

First Innings		Second Innings	
Sutcliffe, run out	28	lbw, b Pollard	13
Mitchell, c Washbrook, b Hopwood	35	not out	69
Barber, lbw, b Sibbles	1	c Paynter, b Sibbles	57
Leyland, c Duckworth, b Phillipson	58		
Wood, c Duckworth, b Phillipson	14	not out	33
Turner, c Watson, b Sibbles	57	lbw, b Sibbles	7
A. B. Sellers, c Watson, b Pollard	3		
Verity, c Phillipson, b Sibbles	0		
Fisher, c Duckworth, b Sibbles	12		
Rawlin, c Washbrook, b Sibbles	11		
Bowes, not out	0		
Extras	6	Extras	2
Total	225	Total (for 3)	181

LANCASHIRE

First Innings		Second Innings	
Watson, c Sellers, b Rawlin	7	c Wood, b Bowes	141
Hopwood, b Bowes	0	b Bowes	2
Paynter, run out	2	c Fisher, b Bowes	17
Tyldesley, c Verity, b Bowes	0	c Wood, b Fisher	28
Oldfield, c Verity, b Bowes	9	c sub, b Fisher	14
Washbrook, c Wood, b Bowes	5	hit wkt, b Bowes	85
Phillipson, b Rawlin	5	b Bowes	2
Pollard, b Bowes	4	c & b Rawlin	22
P. T. Eckersley, b Rawlin	11	c Turner, b Rawlin	12
Duckworth, not out	0	c Wood, b Bowes	0
Sibbles, c Wood, b Bowes	1	not out	12
Extras	9	Extras	17
Total	53	Total	352

THE ROSES MATCHES 1919-1939
BOWLING ANALYSIS

Yorkshire—First Innings

	O.	M.	R.	W.		O.	M.	R.	W.
Sibbles	26	7	56	5	Hopwood	12	4	16	1
Phillipson	23	6	72	2	Watson	10	1	17	0
Pollard	24	3	58	1					

Second Innings

Phillipson	11	1	41	0	Pollard	20	1	40	1
Sibbles	16	4	43	2	Watson	4	0	22	0
Hopwood	23	11	33	0					

Lancashire—First Innings

	O.	M.	R.	W.		O.	M.	R.	W.
Bowes	12	5	16	6	Rawlin	12	2	28	3

Second Innings

Bowes	36	9	83	6	Verity	26	7	58	0
Rawlin	24	2	89	2	Fisher	23	7	66	2
Turner	7	0	39	0					

YORKSHIRE V LANCASHIRE   1936

May 30 June 1/2   Leeds

FIRST DAY

THERE was no play at Leeds on Saturday in the match between Yorkshire and Lancashire. Heavy rain swept the field; the only way to escape from it was to bury ourselves in the underworld of the pavilion, where concrete floors made the feet cold; it was like being in the steerage of a not fashionable liner in an Atlantic storm.

Given fine weather today the cricket is likely to be amusing. Verity is in deadly form at the moment. And on the Lancashire side there is Hopwood, whose left-handed spin has been known to bite viciously into a baked wicket. It is the left-handed batsman's job to take care of slow left-handed bowlers. Paynter at Bradford once hit Verity all over the field on a bad wicket. Yorkshire will trust to Leyland who is also at his best this year. Lancashire have called on L. Warburton, the Central Lancashire League player; he appeared for the county in 1929 and scored 74 against Surrey at the Oval; 14 against Kent at Maidstone; and 19 against Warwickshire at Birmingham. He bowled, in these matches, 60 overs for 170 runs and two wickets. His presence in the Lancashire team today does not mean he is about to throw in his lot with first-class cricket. Ernest Tyldesley has come forward to take the place of the injured Oldfield. Tyldesley's experience and skill against the turning ball may well be severely tested in the next few hours. Verity has already taken 69 wickets for Yorkshire this season at the ridiculous figure of 8.63 each.

SECOND DAY

Rain has spoiled the game again today, interrupting the action—a term which I employ in a Pickwickian sense—from three o'clock until five minutes to six. Before the weather broke Yorkshire, on a fairly comfortable wicket, scored 105 in two and three-quarter hours. In that space of time Mitchell made 39. Yorkshire declined to adjust their batting to the needs of a two day match, though it was their good fortune to win the toss. No perceptible effort was indulged in by the batsmen to get runs at moderate speed according to a policy based on the notion (not fantastical) that later on the wicket might become friendly to Verity. A captain of imagination would not have scouted the idea of sending Leyland in with Sutcliffe, or at any rate of letting Mitchell know during the morning that if he, Mitchell, was feeling unusually static there were other men in the pavilion not wholly incapable of hitting mediocre bowling. But all this is probably heretical; instructions are not issued to county cricketers nowadays. And in any case a Yorkshire and Lancashire match is no laughing matter.

Sutcliffe at once attacked when the play was continued; Mitchell followed his example and was finely caught trying for a four by Lister, who fell forward at mid-off and held the ball as he stretched his length on the slimy earth. Sellers came in next, which was a warlike gesture of sorts late in the afternoon. A cricket captain obviously may give instructions to himself. But if Yorkshire had scored at the normal rate of one run a minute before the rain came they would not have needed to work up a frenzied and rather foolish tempo in the day's last half-hour.

Sellers was quickly given out leg-before by Hardstaff and Duckworth; then Smailes joined Sutcliffe, and not—for some dark reason—Leyland. Sutcliffe drove Warburton brilliantly to the off for four, and Warburton, who is not used to these matches, applauded. Yorkshire's belated endeavour to move the score along now was the only exciting phase in a disappointing day; that is why my account begins at the end. Warburton justified himself thoroughly; his pace is above medium; on a fast wicket his in-swinger and off spin and the occasional ball that goes away from the bat would keep the best players agile and perhaps apprehensive.

Sutcliffe again opened the Yorkshire innings, with Mitchell, which was a right and proper thing to see, for Sutcliffe's divinely appointed position in any batting order is No. 1. To see him come in after Hutton, Barber, and such like is as though we were to read in our history books about William the Conqueror (1066) coming after William Rufus and Stephen. Sutcliffe quickly made his presence known to the public; there was some disturbance in the crowd behind the bowler's arm, and Sutcliffe performed a comprehensive gesture which seemed intended to wave the whole pavilion into nothingness.

Warburton beat Mitchell with the second ball of the match; it was an inswinger, quick from the pitch, and it rose at an acute angle, colliding violently against some part of Mitchell's anatomy. Duckworth emitted a belligerent appeal, but the umpire, Hardstaff, dismissed it promptly, like a true cricketer of Nottinghamshire, where appeals are never thought of except when batsmen are clearly out and where appeals are so gently enunciated that umpires often are obliged to say to the bowlers and wicket-keepers and deep square-legs, 'Speak up, sir, if you please.' For a few overs Warburton was dangerous; he obtained vitality from the easy turf and he swung the ball inwards and, as I thought, occasionally caused a ball to break back after pitching.

Sutcliffe and Mitchell played, as I say, entirely defensive cricket and did not bestir themselves when the Lancashire attack dwindled as the ball lost seam and polish. Duckworth kept wicket beautifully, with less than his usual amount of rhetoric but with more certainty of touch than ever. At twelve o'clock the first boundary occurred, but it was the consequence of misfielding by Iddon, and I was astonished that the batsman did not protest. Pollard could achieve little or no pace from the turf, and though Sibbles forced Mitchell into a bad snick through the slips the Lancashire attack generally seemed short of hostility. Hopwood came on hoping to find the pitch ready for spin, but the fitful sunshine contained no warmth. Hopwood dropped a ball two or three inches short and Mitchell pulled it superbly for four by means of a late wrist and forearm action. This was the day's second four, and the time was five minutes to one. After a session of two hours the match was adjourned for lunch; Yorkshire were 74 for none, Sutcliffe 45 and Mitchell 29.

The turf was faster at a quarter past two and in consecutive overs Warburton and Pollard beat Mitchell and Sutcliffe. An on-drive by Mitchell off Pollard, only half hit, fell in front of Sibbles—it was scarcely a chance, to Sibbles. Sutcliffe reached fifty amid applause, which he acknowledged with motions of his bat which said, 'Yes, yes, I know, I know. We thank you, but really, really.'

The wicket now showed slight signs of life, and Warburton again nonplussed Mitchell. Warburton bowled admirably, but it was his misfortune to find Sutcliffe at his best and most sovereign; he played over the line of the ball and at each over's end he crossed his legs and reposed on his bat and surveyed the scene. Mitchell was not masterful; this time he scored slowly because he could not go faster, not on principle. Mitchell was barracked for not hitting fours, and when Warburton hit Mitchell on the pad nobody appealed. The famous match is degenerating.

Sutcliffe drove Pollard straight, and next ball hit him for four with a vivid hook. How like Sutcliffe to play his first great innings of the year in his county's greatest engagement; he is still the one and only Sutcliffe, who never wastes his powers on insignificant events. Today he looked England's No. 1 batsman in nearly all that he did or condescended to do. Personality came out of him and transformed dingy Leeds on a dull day into a throne-room and a state occasion. He was nearly bowled by the first ball he received from Warburton, which was the last of the day's first over, but afer that he batted as though unaware of the fact of human fallibility; whenever he was subsequently beaten, which was seldom, he appeared interested rather than surprised.

At three o'clock bad light stopped play, and shortly afterwards rain came in sheets out of the dark sky. The crowd then sought shelter, and some succeeded in finding it. They waited patiently for nearly three hours; there was some moaning and groaning towards the end. Thus was another Bank Holiday spent with Lancashire and Yorkshire on a cricket-field.

THIRD DAY

Rain put an end to the match this afternoon when Lancashire were in an unhappy but not, I think, in a really dangerous position. Yorkshire dallied for too long on Monday; they scarcely deserved to prosper after so much unimaginative batting. Sellers was obliged to continue the Yorkshire innings for an hour today—and it was at this period that the wicket was at its nastiest. Verity would have been able to attack Lancashire without waste of time and opportunity had Yorkshire scored runs at a normal pace on Monday's easy pitch.

Yorkshire declared at half-past twelve; the roller was applied, but Lancashire lost the wickets of Washbrook, Iddon, and Paynter, all to Verity for three runs. These batsmen seemed to be 'bluffed' out, as they say; the only ball to turn quickly was the one from which Iddon was caught at slip, and it pitched wide enough to be left safely alone. The Yorkshire fieldsmen surrounded the wicket, held out ravenous hands, and generally advertised to Lancashire the turf's viciousness and the futility of the struggle of mortal flesh in this world. When Lancashire's innings began they needed 76 to save the follow-on; five hours remained for cricket. Hopwood scored a single from Verity's first ball; the next was pitched up, almost a 'yorker,' and Washbrook struck over and across—his one serious fault at present; he will pull a forward stroke at the last second and allow his bat to become crooked to a length almost overtossed. From Verity's next ball Iddon threw his wicket away. And Paynter put his legs to the third ball of Verity's second over, attempting no stroke; he obstructed a straight one.

The crowd made the familiar Yorkshire noises; blood was savoured. But in a few moments Ernest Tyldesley relieved the tension for Lancashire; he played with a calm, impressive mastery; the ball appeared to hit the middle of his bat as though attracted to it by some sort of magnetism. Hopwood, too, was sound and vigilant, though once he popped a ball close to the clutching hands of Sellers at 'silly' mid-off. When Paynter came in Bowes was to be seen rubbing the new ball in the earth; Verity stood by watching him; probably he said, 'It's too kind of you, Bill—I couldn't do it myself; you'll want the seam yourself, perhaps.' Magnanimity, mutual and noble. What would Emmott Robinson have said had he been there to see, with his own eyes, the 'polish' on a new ball being rubbed away? Probably he would have objected on aesthetic grounds.

Verity took two wickets in his first over for one run; then Hopwood scored two to leg off Smailes, in a disapproving silence. The roar that announced Paynter's downfall had the authentic gloat in it; from the moment that Ernest Tyldesley began to play over the ball, with all his long experience and fine art, I felt disillusionment come over the field. A drive for four to the off by Tyldesley, from Smailes, was as easeful and handsome as anything witnessed in a fruitless match. It is absurd to think that Tyldesley's career has been interrupted; many cultured runs remain in his bat. Verity made the most of his chances; had the sun shone long enough he would no doubt have bowled deadly spin later on.

Sutcliffe deserved to reach his hundred, and a magnificent stroke in front of point suggested he was going to get it from the first overs of the morning. He succumbed to a pretty ball from Hopwood, which broke away sharply. Sutcliffe's innings lasted three hours and a half. Smailes tried in vain to drive Hopwood; he was caught at mid-on by Pollard. Hutton fell to Hopwood's spin first ball. Leyland and Turner, both left-handers, put Hopwood's clever spin in a quandary for a while, and Sibbles at the other end could not spin the necessary break-back. At last Hopwood tempted Turner to drive to the on, with the spin; Paynter achieved a dexterous deep field catch, taking the ball high up the chest. Warburton came on for Sibbles and bowled Wood immediately; then Verity was sent in, and as the innings was closed after he had played one or two balls it is to be assumed that he wanted to look at the pitch for himself before any reckless commitments were made. Duckworth was a great wicket-keeper throughout the match, and Hopwood's bowling was not inferior to Verity's though, of course, he enjoyed the wicket's most helpful moments.

YORKSHIRE V LANCASHIRE 1936
SCORES

YORKSHIRE

First Innings

Sutcliffe, c Duckworth, b Hopwood	89
Mitchell, c Lister, b Warburton	40
A. B. Sellers, lbw, b Warburton	0
Smailes, c Pollard, b Hopwood	10
Leyland, not out	21
Hutton, c Duckworth, b Hopwood	0
Turner, c Paynter, b Hopwood	4
Wood, b Warburton	5
Verity, not out	0
Extras b5, lb1	6
Total (for 7)	*175

*Innings declared

LANCASHIRE

First Innings

Washbrook, b Verity	0
Hopwood, not out	4
Iddon, c Sutcliffe, b Verity	0
Paynter, lbw, b Verity	0
E. Tyldesley, not out	12
Total (for 3)	16

BOWLING ANALYSIS

YORKSHIRE—First Innings

	O.	M.	R.	W.		O.	M.	R.	W.
Warburton	25	6	47	3	Hopwood	21	4	53	4
Pollard	18	3	37	0	Watson	6	1	5	0
Sibbles	19	4	27	0					

LANCASHIRE—First Innings

	O.	M.	R.	W.		O.	M.	R.	W.
Verity	6	4	2	3	Fisher	2	1	4	0
Smailes	4	0	10	0					

429

YORKSHIRE V LANCASHIRE 1936

August 1/3/4 Old Trafford

FIRST DAY

IT needed a determined detective to find evidence that a cricket match was going on at Old Trafford on Saturday, for now and again a skilful red-herring was thrown over the trail by the cunning culprits. It was necessary to look carefully and leave nothing to inference. Three sixes were hit during the afternoon, but they were most obvious feints, devised to put the sleuth on the wrong scent. For my part, follower that I am of the methods of Sherlock Holmes (and Lord Peter Wimsey), I prefer to run down the clue given by the discovery I made shortly towards three o'clock, of the presence on the ground of Fanny Walden. Obviously, my dear Watson, he would not have been near Old Trafford had the occasion been a potato-growing competition, or a railway journey from Colne to Exchange on a Saturday afternoon. There was, of course, the possibility that Walden had been left over from the Test match on the previous weekend—perhaps gathered up by mistake with all the wickets on Tuesday and put into a locker. Maybe he had escaped and was standing in the middle again to get some necessary air. But he was observed to be making the motions of an umpire pursuing his profession; moreover he was not alone in his activities; another umpire, more visible to normal eyesight, performed the familiar signs of the umpires' calling. Skelding wore white boots, and often he galumphed about the ground with complete disregard of the stately traditions of his union. Various individuals in white flannels confirmed the preliminary investigation. I admit, my dear Watson, that the scoreboard was seldom employed, but this was no ordinary cricket match—it was Lancashire playing Yorkshire. Hopwood may be said to have practically turned King's Evidence, and given the deception away altogether by making 31 runs in two hours and a half. Here was an unmistakable fingerprint. The most cunning ruse exploited was the way

430

that Old Trafford itself was disguised; the rambling roses on the rails of the ladies' pavilion were an artful dodge, but the subtlest planners of crime usually forget a detail of some sort, and the incriminating piles of sawdust discovered on the field completed a ruthless chain of proof. No doubt the police will get to work today and make a number of arrests.

While the affair is, so to say, sub judice, we must in this account of the proceedings be careful and try to state the facts as they appeared to the eye of the dispassionate student of cricket. On a slow easy pitch Lancashire batted four hours and a half for 190. Not half a dozen balls jumped viciously all day, and Verity was so little helped by the conditions that he could not get anybody out. Even Leyland's Oriental guiles counted for nothing. Washbrook was leg-before as soon as the Lancashire innings began; then rain stopped play—noticeably stopped it—for seventy minutes. In the last over before lunch Iddon was detected in the act of hitting a boundary, but he was bowled by a half volley before he could make a successful getaway. Lancashire reached the total of fifty in an hour and fifty minutes and both Hopwood and Paynter pushed out their bats at the ball in a stiff, blind manner which would have proved fatal if the ball had turned quickly. Hopwood, who this year is Lancashire's main prop, also succumbed in the way of heroes in Lancashire and Yorkshire matches—lbw. Paynter, after a suspicious examination of the occasion (he batted for hours as though with a dark lantern), suddenly hit a full toss from Leyland over the square-leg boundary. Later in the day he drove Smailes for another magnificent six; but the previous six had been committed apparently so many hours before that it could only be charged or indicted under a different count.

Lancashire's innings, I am afraid, will not be able to claim the lenient consideration of the First Offenders Act. The old school of Makepeace and Hallows was noisy and violent compared with Saturday's slow, silent, burrowers and moles of the earth. At tea after three and a half hours, Lancashire had scored 92—a piece of larceny so craftily concealed that the Yorkshire bowlers probably disbelieved the figures in the score-books and asked for a re-count. Paynter, having patiently picked the lock of the Yorkshire safe, suddenly helped himself greedily to the 'swag'; he showed his best skill, smote the ball with his broadest bat and accent, and hit two sixes and eight fours. To his credit he tried to force the game as soon as his team appeared to have recovered from a bad start; he lost his wicket gallantly, for after a quick-footed drive of rare power and style off Hutton he fell to a catch in the same over, aiming at another four. Paynter's innings of 92 lasted three and a quarter hours. Oldfield sternly disciplined his customary vivacity in the cause—he has recently been passing through a lean period. He has so far batted one hundred and thirty minutes for 28 not out.

From any view of cricket as sport, the day's play could not be taken seriously; the dreariness of the batting was absurd, coming as it did from a county which resides at the present time third from the bottom of the county championship table. If Lancashire are unable to win matches nowadays that is a phase in the club's history which most of us are ready to accept resignedly. But with the loss of the old grim efficiency and responsibilities, surely we have the right to expect some carefree play. Stonewalling that wins championships is presumably tolerable to many folk; stonewalling that does not win them will only keep the crowds away from Old Trafford. Lancashire cricket should realise that it has escaped from the old chains; nobody cares nowadays whether they are winning or losing. They are at liberty to enjoy themselves; and the crowds are ready to cheer gallant efforts towards freedom. There is a story in the forgotten pages of Artemus Ward. For twenty years a man had been in prison, in solitary confinement. One day he opened the window and got out. Why don't Lancashire open the window, too, and get out? Yorkshire fielded brilliantly; and I saw some promise in young Hutton's spin bowling; he was not at all upset by some vigorous hitting by Lister, who played the most aggressive innings of the day.

SECOND DAY

A cold, blustering wind blew over the field yesterday, and Fanny Walden often had to stand upon his tip-toes to put the bails back into their sockets on the high stumps. The wicket lent ample aid to the bowlers—it was made, as they say, for a

Parkin or a Macaulay; it was scarcely 'sticky' enough for slow left-handed spin. But at the day's beginning Verity was put on, after one over by Bowes. He and Smailes settled Lancashire's innings in half an hour; in the circumstances a total of 202 should have been useful enough.

As soon as Yorkshire began to bat a ball from Booth rose straight up and collided with Hutton's breastbone. Sutcliffe played another jumping ball skilfully down to the earth. None the less, he committed several snicks, and, though he made them look purposeful and of cool intent by means of his own decorative self-assurance, the evidence accumulated over by over that the pitch was no friend of batsmen. Hutton played with extraordinary judgment for a player of his slender years—here is England's No. 1 batsman of the near future; he is far better than Fagg already. He watched the bowling shrewdly and countered it with firm, scientific strokes. Sutcliffe was uneasy, for all his air of habitual mastery. Sibbles beat him when he was seven. He retaliated with a sudden and lofty drive to the sightscreen; I doubt if he wanted to make so violent a hit so early in the day. Another ball from Booth stood up after pitching a good length, and a moment afterwards Sutcliffe played forward, only to find himself caught at short leg from the nastiest of late 'jumpers.' Mitchell was nearly caught in Sibbles' leg-trap immediately; the batsmen could not trust the turf for a minute; if it was not spitting venom, the ball's rising angle varied without notice, and strokes needed to be played with a checked swing.

Hutton drove Sibbles for four beautifully, and Pollard bowled for Sibbles and Phillipson for Booth. Not until lunch was savoured in the wind did Hopwood get a chance, and his one over before the interval occurred in a slight shower of rain. After lunch Hopwood bowled straightway; unfortunately he could not spin to any fatal end. Hutton cut him superbly by moving back to a ball which dropped only a shade short. Mitchell stayed in an hour or thereabouts—minutes matter little to him. All his defensive powers were heightened by the holiday occasion; he takes guard uncommonly far behind the crease, a disciplinary measure, no doubt, against a natural and inborn tendency to get stumped.

He is a great character—no contemporary England team is complete without him.

Lancashire, for all the lack of spin in their attack, worked hard and well to force the old enemy into a corner. But for a blunder in the field they would have been winning at three o'clock. Sibbles went round the wicket to Leyland, and Leyland drove a ball straight to Hopwood at mid-off; Hopwood apparently was not expecting to catch anybody out this afternoon—he started late, got his hands to the ball too close to the ground, and easily missed the juicy chance. Leyland's score was eleven and Yorkshire's 89 for two. Eleven runs later Pollard bowled instead of Sibbles, and broke through the severe defences of Hutton with a lovely off-break or inswinger—Hutton, at any rate, played outside the ball. The young disciple of Sutcliffe announced the quality of his temperament and technique for two hours; at present he cultivates obstinacy as a first principle—he is only twenty years old, and has his reputation to make. But he possesses strokes and bowlers will feel them before long. It is a curious taste that prefers a Fagg to a Hutton in any class of cricket. The Australians are wiser: they catch them young.

Leyland swung his bat and used his shoulders, and terrific forearms. And the wicket seemed to grow easier. Lancashire apparently had missed an opportunity. But, at the pinch, luck gave our distressful county a huge smile; Leyland drove pugnaciously at Pollard; the hit was hard and the ball soared to long-on, where Iddon made a catch of perfect calculation. Leyland struck a little too soon; still, it was a healthy and hearty blow. Yorkshire 127 for four, and all the dangerous batsmen back in the pavilion. Obviously the pitch was not yet a reformed character, for Barber stopped Pollard above the diaphragm, and Duckworth rubbed his back, while Sellers came down the pitch and smote the offending Adam out of the earth passionately with his bat. On the whole the afternoon and the crowd were quiet; a diversion occurred at four o'clock when a collection was taken for Iddon's benefit; a sheet of canvas was carried round the field and people threw pennies into it. Some of the pennies missed the target; they were picked up with great dilligence, enthusiasm (and honesty) by a number of small boys. But contemporary crowds are not as humorous or as vocal as the crowds of old; they have their moods and points of view, no doubt— probably the reason of their apparent dullness is that the age we live in is, contrary to the general opinion, the most inhibited for centuries.

There was an amount of ugly pottering by Sellers and Barber; Sellers repeatedly missed Sibble's off-break as it turned away to leg; I wondered why Sibbles did not try, if only for luck, to bowl from round the wicket. At tea Yorkshire were 153 for four, after some three hours of batting. I could not help feeling that the Lancashire bowlers had failed to do themselves justice—153 for four is a good score on any wicket, and yesterday's wicket was, as I say, seldom trustworthy. The bowling seemingly depended on the batsmen's mortality; there was no positive hostile plan; good balls were to be seen from time to time, and on the whole the attack was steady. But a plan, a consistent and far-seeing strategy, could never be felt.

After tea Sellers was comprehensively bowled, and Paynter achieved a glorious catch at deep square-leg off a hit by Barber. Duckworth caught Turner rapaciously at 184, and now, with only three wickets in hand, Yorkshire wanted 19 to win the first-innings points. Verity and Wood settled the issue carefully in their nicely contrasted styles—Wood all humour and Yorkshire breadth; Verity a picture of correctitude, mathematical even during his slices through the slips, and capably of lordly reclinings on his bat while the field was changing over. Lancashire's score was passed at a quarter to six; the afternoon passed to a conventional end. Nothing in the day was more remarkable than the way the clouds above resisted temptation to burst; the match was equally austere in its self-restraint.

THIRD DAY

There was no cricket at Old Trafford yesterday until a quarter-past one. After lunch the wicket invited a spin bowler to enjoy himself, and in one over from Verity two balls jumped up viciously from a good length. But in the same over Hopwood hit two magnificent and warlike-boundaries—and Verity apparently lost confidence and length. He tried both ends of the pitch in vain; he seemed to bowl too fast. Bowes enlivened the moment by sending two short bouncers past the head of Washbrook. At this time of the afternoon Yorkshire obviously expected to win; the old hostile tricks were performed—the close, crouching field and, as the man in Tchekov says, all the rest of it. But Hopwood settled the issue, for Lancashire, by means of an innings as skilful and aggressive as any he has ever played. From the beginning he attacked; he hit Smailes and the new ball square; he turned Verity to leg more than once, and nothing is more annoying to a left-arm spin bowler than to be turned to leg. Washbrook also turned Verity to the leg boundary. In sixty-five minutes Hopwood reached 51, out of a total of 68. He made only one mis-hit, just before he got out, bowled by Leyland—I wonder what Rhodes would have said to find himself even temporarily deposed by Leyland on a 'turning' wicket. Hopwood's innings was the best of a dull match.

Washbrook improved considerably on recent form, but once again his pull betrayed him—and after another warning. He hit straight into Sutcliffe's hands, at mid-wicket; the chance was dropped. Washbrook, not to be frustrated, sent the succeeding ball into the same two hands, and this time they did not fumble. Hopwood was beaten at half-past three for 61, out of a total of 89. There was still a bare chance of a Yorkshire victory, for Iddon played badly and succumbed at five minutes to four; Lancashire now led by 72, and there was time for a collapse. Paynter again put his shrewdest bat to the ball; he seldom gave signs of fallibility. He watched the good break-backs of Smailes keenly, and he was as quick to see the loose stuff. Smailes was easily Yorkshire's best bowler, though after tea Bowes bestirred his limbs and, deep in a sweater's folds, took two wickets with unexpected swiftness. But Lancashire were too far ahead; Paynter held on until the proceedings had become entirely formal, and he lost his wicket only because a ball got up brutishly and defied science and eyesight. The dreary game perished in dreary weather; it did not deserve a better fate.

YORKSHIRE V LANCASHIRE 1936
SCORES

LANCASHIRE

First Innings		Second Innings	
Washbrook, lbw, b Smailes	3	c Sutcliffe, b Hutton	25
Hopwood, lbw, b Hutton	31	b Leyland	61
Iddon, b Smailes	9	lbw, b Smailes	14
Paynter, c Smailes, b Hutton	92	c Turner, b Smailes	37
Oldfield, c Verity, b Smailes	31	c Turner, b Bowes	11
W. H. L. Lister, st Wood, b Hutton	15	c Turner, b Bowes	0
Phillipson, c Sutcliffe, b Hutton	7	c Wood, b Bowes	7
Pollard, c Hutton, b Verity	0	c Hutton, b Smailes	1
Duckworth, c Sutcliffe, b Smailes	5	not out	0
Sibbles, not out	2	b Bowes	1
Booth, lbw, b Verity	0	b Smailes	7
Extras b2, lb3, w1, nb1	7	Extras b7, lb3	10
	—		—
Total	202	Total	174

YORKSHIRE

First Innings		Second Innings	
Sutcliffe, c Sibbles, b Booth	12	not out	2
Hutton, b Pollard	46	not out	7
Mitchell, c Duckworth, b Sibbles	19		
Leyland, c Iddon, b Pollard	38		
Barber, c Paynter, b Sibbles	33		
A. B. Sellers, b Booth	16		
Turner, c Duckworth, b Pollard	4		
Verity, c Phillipson, b Hopwood	25		
Wood, c Booth, b Sibbles	35		
Smailes, not out	3		
Extras b9, lb5, nb1	15	Extras b1	1
	—		—
Total (for 9)	246	Total (for 0)	10

THE ROSES MATCHES 1919-1939
BOWLING ANALYSIS

Lancashire—First Innings

	O.	M.	R.	W.		O.	M.	R.	W.
Bowes	14	6	9	0	Leyland	17	6	41	0
Verity	36	15	50	2	Hutton	15	4	49	4
Smailes	34	17	46	4					

Second Innings

	O.	M.	R.	W.		O.	M.	R.	W.
Bowes	15	6	17	4	Turner	2	0	9	0
Smailes	23	5	58	4	Leyland	6	2	8	1
Verity	15	3	47	0	Hutton	7	2	25	1

Yorkshire—First Innings

	O.	M.	R.	W.		O.	M.	R.	W.
Booth	23	4	44	2	Pollard	22	10	44	3
Sibbles	35	9	67	3	Hopwood	11	1	37	1
Phillipson	13	1	39	0					

Second Innings

	O.	M.	R.	W.		O.	M.	R.	W.
Paynter	1	0	2	0	Washbrook	1	0	3	0
Oldfield	1	1	0	0	Lister	1	0	4	0

YORKSHIRE V LANCASHIRE 1937

May 15/17/18 Old Trafford

FIRST DAY

A SMALL crowd at Old Trafford on Saturday saw Lancashire play small cricket. The batting was weak in spirit and skill. This match has lost character; the old masters may have been slow making their runs, but they were slow with a difference. The players today do not score quickly because they cannot; the men of the Makepeace-Hallows tradition did not score quickly because they would not. One of the richest comic sights in the land used to be Rhodes bowling with all his cunning, wide to the off side—bowling for hours to keep down runs against Makepeace, who would not have scored runs if they had been brought to him on a plate, so to say. On Saturday a ball actually hit a batsman's pad and nobody appealed. What is more, the bowler's name was Robinson. The Lancashire and Yorkshire match has obviously gone to the dogs; it has become refined. In the glorious years, if a ball were thrown to the wicket and it accidentally struck a batsman's pad between overs, why, there was, by honoured custom, an involuntary, if half-suppressed 'How's that?' from Emmott. Nobody glares down the wicket nowadays, as George Macaulay always did whenever an umpire said 'Not out.' I once saw Emmott Robinson reduced to helpless bewilderment after he had appealed at the last ball of an over, and appealed in vain. He scratched his head, could not understand so gross a miscarriage of justice. Then he ran to his wrong place in the field.

The cricketers are of small stature today; at any rate they are smaller in Lancashire, which is at present the poorest team that has ever taken the field for the county. None of us would object to a temporary fall from power if the spirit remained good. The crowd's complaint ('crowd' is a noun of multitude) on Saturday was not that Lancashire got out for a poor score, but that they got out miserably. The wicket was

439

not difficult until after lunch; even then the ball seldom stood up and spat. From the day's first over the Lancashire team gave themselves up to the slaughter. A brilliant catch on the leg side by Mitchell started the panic. Paynter was unlucky; his leg glance was good, but Mitchell, the greatest fielder in the world near the wicket, not excepting Fingleton, threw himself forward and saved a four and took a wicket at one and the same time. Hopwood was struggling an hour and a quarter for nineteen; Watson scratched a single in half an hour. Iddon showed a semblance of fight and was caught in his first attempt at a hit. Mitchell also caught Hopwood wonderfully; he was in his element amongst so many pushes and pokes.

The Yorkshiremen swarmed around the wickets; at times I felt that any moment a Lancashire batsman would swoon. In two hours before lunch only 51 runs were scored, and nobody could say where even these were made. Seldom was the bat lifted higher than the knee. But though these methods could not possibly lead anywhere, there was no general movement to change them until Lister came in. If Lancashire had taken courage, attacked the bowling right and left, they could scarcely have made less than 106; they would certainly have made a better impression. The team should be told that as it is not in their power to win many matches this year they might at least try to give us some cheerful entertainment. Saturday's exhibition was depressing to people who take cricket more seriously than nowadays I do. The pavilion resembled a funeral, and the cold grey skies seemed to be reflections of the dreary, futile innings.

Oldfield showed us a few pretty strokes, but they lacked strength, Washbrook was old and careworn for forty minutes while he scored two. It was ironical to watch Verity setting his field to save hypothetical fours. After lunch he was able to turn the ball abruptly from time to time; Smailes, too, could cause an off-break to gather velocity. Four byes, from a ball of Verity's which beat Oldfield, probably took the scorers by surprise and broke their pen-nibs. Washbrook was leg-before logically and inevitably; then a quick spinner from Verity found the edge of Oldfield's bat, and Smailes caught cleverly. Yorkshire's fielding was keen and triumphant.

440

Lister remembered that a bat has been known to hit a ball; he drove to the on for four, a real stroke, an assault on Verity. Verity bowled in his sweater for a while, no doubt aching for the sunshine of Sydney and Adelaide. Lister's innings came into the encircling gloom like the light of hope; alas! he was run out. He skied a ball to the off, nearly a chance, got one run from it and impulsively tried a second. Still it was a refreshing fault—eagerness to score. Sibbles and Duckworth were leg before in the same over; neither batsman did anything at all except get out. The innings, which seemed certain to fall below a hundred, was retrieved a little by some good hitting by Pollard and Booth; a stroke to leg by Pollard, off Smailes, was masterly. Booth, less concerned on the whole with the unities, hurled his bat around him; the last-wicket stand caused most of the other and accredited Lancashire batsmen to seem even more foolish at the end of the innings than they had looked while actually on view dangling pitifully before the Yorkshiremen, to be put out of their misery according to the Yorkshiremen's fancy and charity. It was good to see Verity getting wickets again: he had no luck on the hard Australian grounds against batsmen who understand footwork.

A remarkable change of atmosphere came over the afternoon when Yorkshire batted. Sutcliffe was charming, his true self, confident, skilful, and not heedless of his own arts. He moved quickly to the ball, and killed the spin. We saw again the old elegant leaning push to the off for four. To think that we left him behind and tried to begin an England innings in Australia with Fagg, or Worthington, or Verity! The dolours of the morning were forgotten at the sight of Sutcliffe standing cross-legged at the end of an over. Lovely also to see him, as of old, making his motion to warn a batsman against a second run—a wave of the hand as gentle and significant as Furtwängler obtaining a pianissimo. Here was the indefinable thing called personality; it is the beginning and end of cricket; the absence of it means death to the game. Hutton has something of Sutcliffe's method, but so far he is just a technician (who will shortly play for England). He played back to Sibbles and was bowled after he and Sutcliffe had scored 49. Sibbles bowled Sutcliffe as well, an important piece of work, for Sutcliffe looked ready to make, at his pleasure, his customary hundred against Lancashire.

Mitchell drove two superb fours in one over off Sibbles; this cricketer of character is often baffling. He can, according to some periodic law working in his innermost being, perform great strokes; then, for no apparent reason, he becomes dull and anonymous for hours. I once thought that an explanation of this strange case might be found in the way Mitchell wears his cap, and that his moods changed according to the position of the peak as it veered gradually towards the left or right ear. But I cannot get my data right or consistent on this point: for the time being, therefore, I must give Mitchell and his vagaries up; Leyland was steady, and at the afternoon's petrifying close Lancashire had received deserved chastisement.

SECOND DAY

There was corruption again as soon as the Lancashire and Yorkshire match began the second morning in the company of a crowd which this time constituted a quorum. Not less than seventy runs occurred during the first hour, and three wickets fell. Between half-past eleven and half-past one twelve boundaries were hit, with malice aforethought, and, what was worse, a six. The old order changeth. Speaking seriously (for all that is supposed to be funny), the cricket was excellent. Lancashire bowled so keenly and well that Yorkshire needed to bat at their cleverest. We saw a remarkable number of fine strokes, many of them by Mitchell, who seemed to want to score from every over. On the true pitch Yorkshire threatened a formidable total; the Lancashire attack must be praised for its persistence after a preliminary half-hour that gave it little cause for confidence. Suddenly a beautiful ball by Booth drew Leyland forward and bowled him. A few moments afterwards Barber was overthrown by Sibbles. These disasters to Yorkshire upset a man from Laisterdyke so much that when Sellers ventured a short run a warning cry of 'Whey!' was emitted—which I take it was Yorkshire for 'Whoa!' Sellers drove Iddon for the six aforementioned. In the effort of another short run Mitchell lost his cap and became, temporarily, a changed man. Though the batting looked good and aggressive, it did not suggest mastery. A pretty straight push by Mitchell, with his body inclining easefully over the ball, delighted the connoisseur. Sellers was caught at short leg in the over in which he smote his six; quick retribution was done to a blasphemous act.

Wood went through a few quaint motions against the new balls, but he was always busy. A maiden over by Pollard actually provoked applause; in the old days you no more dreamed of applauding a maiden over in a Lancashire and Yorkshire match, especially on Bank Holiday, than you dreamed of applauding the wickets or the sight-screens. Maiden overs were then the normal and basic condition of the engagement. Iddon beat Wood with a pretty spinner, and bowled ably on the whole. But he seems to keep a length only by severe and prolonged thinking, much as an actor with a bad memory remembers his part. Wood made a huge pull off Pollard; also he drove to the on in the same over, the image of his county, broad and humorous. The Yorkshire team never loses its nature, whether champions or not. And whenever Yorkshire are not the champions I feel that something has gone wrong with the order and rhythm of the cosmos of cricket.

Mitchell reverted to type and ceased perceptible action and shortly before one o'clock he played back too late to Booth and was bowled. His innings told of skill, experience, temperament, and a latent and almost heathen love of fine art. Booth used the new ball dangerously just now: he got Wood caught at the wicket from a stinging swinger. Smailes flung a loose bat about him for a while, making the handle appear abnormally long. At the wicket's other end Verity was stately, even disdainful. He made one drive of severely classic beauty before, almost at lunch, Smailes' stumps were rendered indecently disordered, not to say inchoate. Yorkshire were all out at half-past two, by which time the crowd had increased to 5,700—that is to say, those who had paid and, of course, nobody else counted on Bank Holiday.

The sunny morning thought better of it and gave way to a drab afternoon. The light was not beyond criticism when Hopwood and Paynter entered on Lancashire's arduous journey; none the less Paynter hit the first ball of the innings for three, and Hopwood obtained a four to leg off the second. It is to be hoped that Wilfred Rhodes does not hear of these strange doings until it is too late for him to squander money on an outraged telegram. The Lancashire batting had a hardier temper than on Saturday, and it was bad luck on Hopwood to find himself bowled round his legs. Still, as Bradman once said to me when I spoke of Worthington's bad luck at Melbourne: 'Well, maybe, but a batsman should not tread on his wicket.' Paynter struck two fours in one over from Robinson, and it is a mercy it was not Emmott Robinson; there would have been some murmuring. (Emmott, by the way, is now a county umpire. He will find it hard not to lead the appeals to himself for leg-before-wicket.) The crowd woke up when Iddon was nearly run out; the noise was authentic—indeed, the match now gained some atmosphere, for Lancashire were batting determinedly against vehement bowling and vehement fielding. Paynter, was admirable; his shrewd cricket deserved Rhodes's canniest length and Macaulay's nastiest looks. Verity beat him with a lovely break-back and gazed at the stumps like a mathematician working out a discrepancy somewhere. He then proceeded to bowl round the wicket. Verity's intellectual ways are a constant joy to witness; the beauty of his bowling has nothing to do with the wickets he takes, but is a thing in itself—to use an appropriate term. Probably he is annoyed if a batsman gets out to him from a ball not intended to take a wicket.

Iddon helped Paynter to lift the score to 75; the partnership last for an hour and a quarter, and I felt a want of resource in Yorkshire's attack. Iddon was bowled hitting sadly across a ball well up to him. Shortly before five o'clock the heavens darkened and rain descended and put an end to the festive day. In the departing crowd complaints were uttered against Lancashire's slow cricket. They were not justified this time, for Lancashire were saving, or trying to save, the match. A voice said, 'And we used to think that Hallows was dull.' Other times, other views; I admit that one straight drive by Hallows yesterday would have been finer than anything done by the contemporary Lancashire batsmen.

444

THIRD DAY

On a gloomy, dirty day Lancashire struggled hard to save themselves, but failed at the end, in spite of a long and skilful innings by Paynter and a dash of Watson at his freest. The game was delayed until a quarter past twelve; then the wicket was so dead that the Yorkshire attack seemed helpless. Both batsmen were at liberty to linger over their strokes. Verity pitched short balls to leg so frequently that I assumed he was doing it on purpose. He tried a few guiles from over the wicket before Sellers took him off for—bless us!—Leyland. Watson smote Leyland's full-toss soundly and drove Robinson twice for fours in an over. Leyland endeavoured to frustrate the sluggish earth by devices ballistic and other. At lunch Paynter and Watson were still not out and apparently thoroughly set for the afternoon.

For half an hour after lunch the batsmen were untroubled. Verity's thinking processes could be left in the encircling gloom and grime. Watson pulled Verity for a huge four. And now, perhaps, occurred the turning-point. Watson struck too soon at a full-toss from Verity; it was a ball which implored to be hit. Watson mistimed so badly that he was easily caught at mid-on. Watson deserved a less undignified end; he had played well for a hundred minutes. The Yorkshire attack tightened at once. It is not, by the way, a great attack; Verity is the only man of ideas, except of course, Leyland, whose bowling is so full of ideas that it becomes Oriental in its obliquity. Washbrook and Oldfield each failed again because each chose to push rather than to play a stroke. Hutton trapped them leg-before-wicket; he is no mean bowler; he spins from leg and flights the ball. Lister fell to a glorious catch at first slip by Robinson off one of the few balls which Verity caused to 'pop' all day. A moment afterwards there was a terrible mix-up, which ended in the running-out of Pollard. In the confusion—and the thick fog—it was hard exactly to say what happened. Paynter drove straight and the ball hit the opposite wicket. Pollard backed up, then ran, allowing Paynter to get in, while he fell on the earth, and somebody in the Yorkshire team yelled 'This end!' Everybody jumped about agitatedly, including the umpires. Lancashire were only seven ahead when the seventh wicket fell, and the time of day was twenty minutes to four.

But Lancashire would not perish yet, Sibbles stonewalled disdainfully. And Paynter proceeded with his obstinacy. He had to stop a number of severe break-backs from Smailes, difficult balls for a left-handed batsman. The wicket was at one end gaining some speed and viciousness. Paynter employed his pads to an inch whenever the ball encouraged the second line of defence. Seldom did he miss a loose ball with his bat. For nearly an hour the eighth wicket annoyed Yorkshire. The stand was the pluckier because it was inspired by the pathos of the lost cause. Paynter achieved the heroism of the doomed and afflicted; he was magnificent. Sibbles batted with the stately calm of the Elgin Marbles. Once, when Paynter was nearly stumped, a woman screamed in panic; probably she has a sister-in-law in Melbourne.

Sibbles's splendid innings succumbed to a smashing off-break. He was deservedly applauded as he groped his way back to the pavilion. And Paynter himself was bowled at this midnight hour; he, too, was beaten by an off-break—to him a most unpleasant leg-break. For more than five hours Paynter displayed the temperament and defence which was so badly needed in Australia at the middle of the English batting. This was the end of a match which none of us will wish to remember. As soon as it was over the weather brightened, like the rest of us.

YORKSHIRE V LANCASHIRE 1937
SCORES

LANCASHIRE

First Innings		Second Innings	
Paynter, c Mitchell, b Smailes	0	b Robinson	86
Hopwood, c Mitchell, b Robinson	19	b Verity	11
Iddon, c Barber, b Verity	25	b Smailes	16
Watson, c Mitchell, b Verity	1	c Leyland, b Verity	56
Washbrook, lbw, b Verity	2	lbw, b Hutton	4
Oldfield, c Smailes, b Verity	10	lbw, b Hutton	0
W. H. L. Lister, run out	14	c Robinson, b Verity	1
Pollard, c Mitchell, b Hargreaves	10	run out	0
Sibbles, lbw, b Verity	0	b Smailes	5
Duckworth, lbw, b Verity	0	not out	0
Booth, not out	12	c Mitchell, b Verity	0
Extras b10, lb3	13	Extras lb18	18
Total	106	Total	197

YORKSHIRE

First Innings		Second Innings	
Sutcliffe, b Sibbles	48	not out	20
Hutton, b Sibbles	13	not out	14
Mitchell, lbw, b Booth	77		
Leyland, b Booth	30		
Barber, b Sibbles	3		
A. B. Sellers, c Watson, b Iddon	17		
Wood, c Duckworth, b Booth	27		
Verity, b Pollard	9		
Smailes, b Pollard	18		
Robinson, c Watson, b Pollard	13		
Hargreaves, not out	1		
Extras b9, lb2, nb3	14	Extras b1	1
Total	270	Total (for 0)	35

THE ROSES MATCHES 1919-1939
BOWLING ANALYSIS

Lancashire—First Innings

	O.	M.	R.	W.		O.	M.	R.	W.
Smailes	26	9	44	1	Verity	34	15	32	6
Hargreaves	7	5	7	1	Robinson	13	7	10	1

Second Innings

	O.	M.	R.	W.		O.	M.	R.	W.
Smailes	34	12	56	2	Robinson	19	7	32	1
Hargreaves	9	3	7	0	Leyland	4	1	15	0
Verity	45	23	43	4	Hutton	12	5	26	2

Yorkshire—First Innings

	O.	M.	R.	W.		O.	M.	R.	W.
Booth	16	4	41	3	Iddon	15	1	47	1
Pollard	23	4	76	3	Watson	5	1	8	0
Sibbles	35	9	84	3					

Second Innings

	O.	M.	R.	W.		O.	M.	R.	W.
Booth	5	0	19	0	Hopwood	1	0	3	0
Pollard	4	2	12	0					

YORKSHIRE V LANCASHIRE 1937

July 31/August 2/3   Bramall Lane

FIRST DAY

THIS was a day of splendid cricket, worthy of the match in its greatest period. Lavish sunshine lighted the field and dispersed the vapours of Bramall Lane. A large crowd sweltered and saw skill and character in action. Sutcliffe lordly as ever, waving out of existence some human obstruction behind the bowler's arm. Once he left the wicket and walked across the ground to reprimand in person a movable object who wore a scarf and was hastening to his seat. We saw brilliant bowling after lunch by Pollard; we saw Mitchell at his dourest cap over the ear; we saw dashing fielding by Lancashire, by Washbrook and Oldfield especially, cricket at its keenest, most vehement, and humorous.

At the close of play, the score-board tried to persuade us that Lancashire were in a good positon. But the figures were deceptive. On Monday, I fear, Lancashire will need to struggle severely to hold their own. The Sheffield wicket is no longer a heaven for batsmen; the Yorkshire committee has rightly come to the decision that drawn matches are a handicap to a team which possesses championship ambition—and bowlers. The pitch has not been prepared overmuch; there is grass on it, and already a nasty spot has been discovered by Verity. One of the balls, to Paynter, just before half-past six broke enormously. The wicket does not promise to improve as it grows older. From the outset the Lancashire bowlers could make outswingers and inswingers come from the ground vivaciously. Yorkshire did well to lose only one wicket for 77 before lunch. Sutcliffe when only three gave a chance in the slips off Sibbles to Hopwood—it was not easy, and bear in mind that the awkwardness of any catch is a matter which must be considered in relation to a fieldsman's agility.

After lunch the Yorkshire innings was wrecked by Pollard

449

who whipped off the ground at a killing speed. In twelve overs he took five wickets, four of them clean bowled, the other leg before. I have seen no better attack this year from anybody. Sutcliffe calmly contemplated the encompassing ruin and went his way to a century. He was given the ovation of a monarch, and acknowledged it like a monarch. Wood thumped right and left with an amazing yet comical lack of science. Yorkshire after losing seven wickets for 165 reached 246.

When Lancashire batted Paynter and Washbrook were in at an unpleasant time, at the beginning of an innings, having to play in a fading if mellowing light. It was ominous that Sellers at once asked Verity to bowl, which Verity did, from over the wicket. He hit a spot and Washbrook repeatedly examined it, almost geologically. Fourth innings on the Sheffield wicket should no rain fall, will be untenable for somebody.

The morning began before we could say Jack or Emmott Robinson (there is by the way no Robinson appearing for Yorkshire in this engagement, not even the contemporary Yorkshire cricketer of that name—which he surely ought to change at once by deed-poll.) The first ball of Phillipson's second over flashed upward, swerved away late, and found the edge of Hutton's bat and went to Pollard at first slip. Pollard missed the catch with one hand, then caught it with the other. Now occurred the bad stroke by Sutcliffe, which provoked an awful gasp from the crowd. The Lancashire bowling did not for half an hour or so thoroughly explore the fallibility of the batsmen. Time after time Sutcliffe and Mitchell played late, without self-approval, at off-spinners of Sibbles' which lifted. Happily for them no fieldsman was placed close enough to the bat at short square leg. And magnificently though Lancashire fielded there seemed a gap on the off side through which Sutcliffe could perform his own graceful leaning push-drive.

After Hutton's downfall, which was a boon and a blessing to Lancashire, little came their way in the shape of luck. Mitchell just missed touching the second ball sent him by Phillipson, a hostile outswinger; and a ball in an unexpected hurry struck Sutcliffe's leg only a shade above the danger-line. Sutcliffe, though, expressed confidence all the time. He surveyed the scene at the end of every over cross-legged; there is nobody like him. Oh to think we left him behind last winter and took Fagg in his place!

The crowd generously applauded Oldfield's and Washbrook's agile and beautiful fielding. Both of them ran fast, picked up and threw in while spinning their young bodies round as though without bones or solid matter at all. They were thrilling to see.

Pollard came on at half-past twelve, but he was for a long time merely 'up and down.' Birtwell pitched his potential leg breaks accurately, and compelled Sutcliffe to reach forward more than once. Birtwell is promising beyond a doubt. He should use his slower and loftily flighted ball at least twice every three overs. Mitchell seldom tried to hit. Here is a strange man, a cricketer who once every year forgets custom and reveals himself a great and rational driver, a cold, scientific smasher of all bowlers. On Saturday he was content to push and prod and get into trouble.

After lunch Phillipson thwacked Mitchell's thigh and nearly knocked his cap off. Mitchell then drove hard, and beat Iddon's boots at cover. A short leg close up might have caught Sutcliffe easily when he was near fifty, off Sibbles—I do not think Sutcliffe could have played a different and deader stroke had the fieldsmen been there to warn him, for the ball jumped at the last second. Sutcliffe reached fifty with a really dangerous 'hoick' over the two short-legs which Sibbles at last employed; and three men chased the hit, racing each other passionately. A strong three off Phillipson was the first front-of-the-wicket stroke we saw from Mitchell, and he had been on view for two hours. But we were able to realise the value of Mitchell's innings as soon as he got out, and the wicket threw off its superficial air of being merely playful.

Seventy runs were scored in fifty minutes after lunch. Then suddenly Pollard crashed through Mitchell's defence leaving him, as they say, standing. Yorkshire 145 for two—and the crowd happy and willing to roar appreciation at the sight of a great ball rewarded. Here Sutcliffe 'foozled' a stroke against Birtwell.

A moment afterwards Pollard's speed thudded against

Barber's pads, and the umpire and Duckworth agreed he was lbw. Birtwell momentarily left the hot action, looking ill. But he returned and caught and bowled Yardley, who drove back too abruptly, deceived by flight. Birtwell tried a 'googly' at Barber's left-handed bat, a ruse which told of intelligence. At 159 Pollard knocked Turner's off stump aslant with a break-back which to a left-handed bat was no doubt a horror. And at 171 Sellers played on, beaten fairly and squarely by velocity from the pitch; he put back his own fallen bail, returned the ball to Pollard, and departed. Smailes was out promptly too—bowled by another ball from Pollard, perfect in length and off the pitch violently and into the stumps with a splatter. The crowd was rudely reduced to silence—or, at least, to taciturnity. Yorkshire 140 for one and 175 for seven.

Wood snicked his first ball from Pollard off the varnish of his off stump; he struck the next to the on for four vigorously and sightlessly. Sutcliffe at 90 jabbed Pollard by reflex action to the place which short square-leg should have covered, and in the same over Duckworth gave Sutcliffe out leg-before-wicket, but could not get anybody in authority to agree with his own unanimous appeal. Tumultuous cheers, three times three, announced that Sutcliffe had reached a hundred by means of a superb square drive. At tea Yorkshire were 221 for seven, Sutcliffe not out 100, Wood not out 28.

The first ball, when the game broke out again, was a half-volley from Phillipson. Wood lambasted it for four to the on, amidst tremendous approval. The second ball was also lambasted for three, and the crowd became black in the face with mingled heat and happiness. In the same over Wood was bowled while smiting the earth with his bat late enough to be in time for his second innings almost. Bowes came next, not Verity, and Sutcliffe let his bat swing to get runs before the end. He hit Sibbles square, like a lion, and drove to the on high and recklessly. Bowes defended once or twice and even went so far as to walk out of his ground and pat the wicket. Sutcliffe drove another boundary to the on off Phillipson before snicking him high to Duckworth, who held a great catch and gave Sutcliffe out ferociously as he held the ball. Sutcliffe for four hours and a half was himself enthroned.

Paynter and Washbrook stole runs at a terrific scamper

when they batted against Bowes and Smailes. But Bowes hit Paynter on the body, and Paynter chopped a ball from Smailes close to his stumps. Washbrook was more certain of touch than Paynter to begin with, but as soon as Verity came on the 'spot' exercised its influence. Washbrook played forward to Verity, missed a break which jumped—and Wood fumbled a chance of stumping, while Washbrook floundered a yard into the void. Paynter stiffened his defence, and began to meet the ball with his bat's middle. Washbrook, who had, half an hour before, made a magnificent hit to leg off Smailes, glanced Verity acutely to leg. But the 'spot' prevented a free forward stroke, either by actual influence on the spin or by influence on the batsmen's minds. Still, a few minutes from close of play all seemed to be going well for Lancashire. Paynter and Washbrook were more or less safely batting for Monday morning. When Hutton was put on to bowl, in place of Bowes, many onlookers wondered what Sellers was thinking about. He knew the nature of the wicket. Hutton bowled Washbrook beautifully with a 'googly' (bless us!) which dropped after a flight that was positively arch. Paynter has so far defended for an hour for fifteen; maybe the match depends on him on Monday, but he will not mind that.

SECOND DAY

Lancashire played well and tenaciously today on a wicket which behaved as it was expected to behave. The Yorkshire spin bowling could not take advantage of the worn places. So far so good; Lancashire's all-round ability will be rewarded by victory if there is justice in the world or in Yorkshire. The match has been a joy to see, and it deserves to achieve a finish and a death.

In Ethiopian heat, a crowd ready to explode with patriotism was given occasion to roar at the first ball bowled; Duckworth missed it with his bat and was leg before wicket to Bowes, who could scarcely have expected so early in the day to get anybody out, because Bowes needs time to set his limbs moving. The policy of Lancashire from the outset was 'Out, damned spot!' There was a rough place on the leg stump at the pavilion end of the pitch, in a nasty length. Verity at once began to explore or excavate, and after Iddon had hit him magnificently to leg for four he twice defeated and nearly bowled Iddon in the same over with spin that turned abruptly across and what is more, kicked alarmingly. Next over Verity attacked from round the wicket and used two slips and a silly point to Iddon and two short-legs and a silly mid-on to Paynter. These fieldsmen crouched low and held forth avaricious hands. Sellers was the point and the mid-on; he expressed war inveterate; also he expressed bluff and cajolery, for in Verity's third over he changed his position to short mid-on to Iddon. When he was not bowling Verity was sent to field at deep long-leg, which involved him in a long and stately walk. He did not persevere from round the wicket, but returned to his first position, which probably meant something intellectual or diabolical, or both or neither.

The crowd grew bigger and blacker and hotter every minute; on the huge mound there were the familiar Sheffield caps and shirt sleeves; the inhabitants of this mound at Sheffield are denizens rather than people when they gather in the mass; compared to the mound at Sheffield the hill of Sydney is a bank on which the wild thyme grows, a green and sylvan and peaceful spot.

Paynter caused hysteria when two spinners in succession from Verity were pushed within inches of the clutching hands; the spot was there sure enough and Lancashire's fate depended on whether Verity could or could not pitch the dangerous length. But there was occasionally trouble for the batsmen to contend with at the other end also; Bowes obtained rise for his swing and Paynter twice came terribly near to snicking fatally. None the less the batting of both Iddon and Paynter suggested determination to prevail at all costs over the hardships of the morning, psychological, strategical, or objectively real. Another great hit by Iddon to leg rather squarer off Verity told of watchfulness and opportunism. Again Verity spun at the right length and again Sellers swooped on to the wicket and snatched to an inch of a ghost of a chance; and again the crowd made the noise of hope deferred and cheated. Everybody apparently expected a wicket each over, Verity included; the hour's persistence of Paynter and Iddon was not in the bond and therefore reprehensible. Verity at last was moved from his country estate at long-leg and placed when not bowling nearer to the game's central position or metropolis. He spun viciously once more, and Iddon was nearly caught at silly point amidst horrible groans; a moment afterwards Paynter hit hard at Verity straight to Sellers at short mid-on, who could not hold the ball, which loyally bounced from mid-on to Verity himself, who gripped the catch to the sound of universal rejoicing. Paynter laboured severely and skilfully for more than an hour and a half.

Lancashire were 107 for three now, a moment of crisis with visible loads of responsibility on the backs of Iddon and Oldfield. Verity here turned a ball a foot at least, beating the bat and off stump after pitching on middle and leg. The solemn truth is that Verity missed a ripe chance. Whenever he, by accident or design, pitched the proper, sagacious length he was by help of the wicket deadly. But more often than not he bowled short of the length; it was possible even to cut him or to dab him through the slips for ones and twos, which is the modern equivalent of the cut. Wilfred Rhodes once said, 'They might have hit me for six sometimes, but they never cut me.'

When Oldfield came in Sellers surrounded him with a sticky-wicket trap, and Verity could not get Oldfield to play the stroke Sellers rightly angled after. Verity rested at the end of an hour and twenty minutes' abortive effort. Then Oldfield batted beautifully against the other Yorkshire bowlers; his wristwork was enchanting, and he passed Iddon's score with ease and fine art. At lunch the Lancashire score was fantastically 163 for three; it would have taken the appetite of Rhodes away totally; and Roy Kilner, master of over-the-wicket left-handed spin, would probably have refused a drink.

Oldfield reached fifty after not much more than an hour's supple, delicate play. The crowd became ironical at Iddon's masterful passivity, and so Iddon thumped a long-hop from Verity square for four, which gave the crowd further reason for noises significant of displeasure. More resonant was the sound which hailed at 176 the catching and bowling of Oldfield, who played too readily at a well-pitched ball;

Oldfield's innings was, after some vicissitudes against Verity, a cameo, an innings of bloom and pretty contours. Iddon was not out 39 when Oldfield left us; he had been batting now more than two hours, to the exasperation of all Yorkshiremen present. And in these matches it is necessary for the sake of the unities that somebody should, without fail, drive the crowds to misery. What are they doing at Bramall Lane on Bank Holidays if not for that? Iddon, as a fact, created one of the afternoon's blissful moments; he swept Verity again to square leg, a courageous stroke if not a discreet one, and he was caught; the roar of joy was a tribute to the ruthless calm of an admirable innings. And so at twenty minutes to three on a glorious afternoon the game was in the balance—Lancashire 182 for five.

At this precarious moment Hopwood committed blasphemy by smiting Turner to the on for four, a most violent crack, a piece of sheer invective and no less. Phillipson snicked Verity through the slips and Hopwood gave him the news that it was a four. Hopwood jumped out to Verity and drove him high to the on for three, a gallant hit at the sight of which the old brigade of Lancashire would have uttered profane words. Hopwood drove another dashing four and was caught at the wicket in the same over; the match was still in the scales; Lancashire 206 for six with Phillipson and Lister in and the crowd behind Yorkshire to a man—and a small boy whose appeals for leg before wicket told us that another bowler was getting himself ready for service in the cause of his wonderful county.

Sellers did not claim the new ball at 200 in spite of the position of affairs, Lancashire within reach of first-innings points. Sellers was, of course, in the right. I mention his disdain of the new ball as proof that the pitch was not insensitive to spin. Turner was able to compel late and tentative strokes; no further evidence need be called against the wicket's character. Lister drove Verity straight and with handsome poise, and the ball hit the screen with a majestic bang. Next over he drove Verity to the on boundary, another massive yet easeful hit. He pulled an off-break from Smailes so strongly that two fielders not far apart on the on boundary were rendered temporarily immobile. Phillipson after a long period of doggedness glanced Verity to leg for three, then Lister misdrove Verity to the off for four. A man in the crowd tendered advice now: 'Get that new ball and put Bill Bowes on,' with Bowes made to rhyme with cows, or rather, Cowes. The Yorkshire captain was sadly let down by his spin bowling and he had at last to put Bill Bowes on and demand the new ball, which as soon as Smailes hurled it down was struck twice by Lister in one over for boundaries as good as any cricketer could wish to make or to see; an off-drive was brilliant. Lister played splendid cricket; his bat was as sound and scientific for good balls as it was powerful and accurate, even serene, for half-volleys which craved to be driven. He was almost caught in the slips off Smailes when Lancashire needed, with four wickets in hand, five for the first-innings lead, and he hit another four to the off two balls later, making the scores even. Phillipson by a gentle push to the on sent Lancashire in front, an excellent performance which few Yorkshire bowlers were prepared to witness when they took the field this morning.

A superb on-drive off Bowes by Phillipson brought Lancashire beyond 250. Phillipson played cricket of commendable imperturbability.

Lister fell to a quick flashing one-handed catch from a cut at a wide ball; he was seventh out at 258 for an innings a captain always hopes and is expected to play, a brave and dashing and good-looking innings. A rapid failure of Pollard raised the steaming multitude's hopes once more, and once more they suffered frustration because Birtwell refused to get out immediately. He incurred barracking until he pulled Hutton to the leg boundary. And as Phillipson's innings gained ball by ball in composure and in its suggestion of a man at the wicket for some unspeakable time the crowd had every cause to give itself up to the silence of the aggrieved.

In the first over after tea Birtwell was bowled behind his legs and without his consent or knowledge, but even now the infamy was not ended; Phillipson cut Verity square for four, and was then barracked again because he would not miss straight balls. The crowd proceeded to incite Verity to body-line: 'Bowl at his yed,' urged a voice. But when Sibbles hit a three the crowd was dissatisfied just the same; it is hard to please people sometimes. A ponderous on-drive for four by Sibbles off Verity spoiled the afternoon entirely for thousands. Lancashire's last wicket not only enabled Phillipson to reach a valiant fifty but went on to the infuriating length of scoring 37, Sibbles driving with outrageous precision and brutality.

When Yorkshire batted again Sutcliffe and Hutton played with the utmost confidence until Iddon came on and did inestimable service to his side by bowling Sutcliffe with a prodigious break round Sutcliffe's leg spin off the spot. Sutcliffe did not realise he was out, but Duckworth and the umpire enlightened him politely and unambiguously.

THIRD DAY

Shortly after four o'clock today one of the finest of all Lancashire and Yorkshire matches was won and lost in the spirit of cricket. Lancashire's splendid all-round ability was rewarded, and Yorkshire shared the glory, for, from the first ball of the morning, Sellers decided to join issue to the death; his batsmen went for the runs vigorously and promptly, and then, after a dreadful collapse and after brilliant play by Washbrook had landed victory at his county's door, Yorkshire counter-attacked, and at the finish only the scoreboard could tell us which side was winning. Lancashire needed 91, and at half-past three they were 70 for none, cut and driven by Washbrook in swift and aggressive style. He got out to spin, and for another forty minutes Lancashire needed to struggle bitterly to score 21, almost in singles, while four more wickets were lost. At the day's outset Yorkshire believed that if they could set the enemy 150 the match after all would be theirs. I doubt if Lancashire could have gone beyond a hundred when Phillipson put us out of our misery with an off-drive to the boundary, the winning hit.

The pitch was shot through with irony. It was left to Iddon to show Yorkshire exactly where the evil spot on the pitch lay. Verity only discovered it after he came forth to bat: he was bewildered at once by a ball from Iddon which turned and kicked prodigiously. Verity learned the lesson and bowled beautifully in Lancashire's second innings on the length he should have found on Monday—though I think he made a mistake by bowling round the wicket. Iddon's use of the spot was astonishingly skilful; he achieved the bowling performance of his life—nine for 42 and after lunch, five for seven in 17 balls. It was all vastly humorous, a rare example of inducting a very celebrated grandmother in the art of sucking eggs.

This was Lancashire's first victory at Bramall Lane since 1899—during the reign of Queen Victoria, before, not the Great War, but the Boer War. From beginning to finish the engagement did honour to sport gallant and challenging, and, let us hope, killed for ever the dreary bore which since 1924 or thereabouts has masqueraded as the match that once saw MacLaren, Hirst, Tyldesley, Spooner, Denton, Haigh, and Brearley in heroic contention. The match which thrilled us these last few days will stand comparison with any of the illustrious past. Given the will—and a wicket of the right kind—cricket declines to be denied or put down or reduced to mathematics.

Mitchell sent Yorkshire's colours to the topmast, or wherever colours are sent to at the beginning of warlike action. He drove his first ball from Sibbles for a swaggering piratical four. To our horror, he was missed in the slips, an easy chance off Phillipson. Mitchell is one of the game's most dangerous batsmen whenever he determines to attack and scatter bowlers far and wide or perish in the attempt. In these moods his strokes have terror and grandeur; also they have rapid dexterity. He forced good-length balls from his body at a speed impossible to follow, even on the feet of Paynter, Washbrook, and Oldfield. Hutton joined the assault too, but he snicked once from Sibbles within inches of his off stump.

At noon Yorkshire were 65 for one, and it was now, at the height of Yorkshire's bombardment, that Lister sensibly and fearlessly exploited Iddon, who this year has often bowled with a frightening looseness. At first I thought Iddon was going to commit Verity's error of Monday—too much quickness and a short length. He was encouraged by Hutton, who struck across a spinning ball, almost a long-hop, a most culpable stroke which was easily caught on the off-side. Birtwell was put on at the end opposite to Iddon's, a luxury of slow bowling, surely. Mitchell drove him for a soaring six, and in the same over Barber pulled square for six and was caught at the wicket next ball. Lister tactfully took him off and kept one end tight while Iddon, who was Lancashire's only likely explorer or pioneer of spots, went on with his work. To his credit, he bowled little or no rubbish. Mitchell on the warpath could not hit him with safety. Yardley attempted to clear the leg boundary, and Paynter caught him at the second attempt.

Now began the agony. A ball from Iddon stood up and collided with Wood's chest. Wood a moment or two before had hauled Birtwell round to the on for four, a stroke which spoke the accent of Yorkshire. At five minutes past one Iddon dealt Yorkshire the severest blow of all; he bowled Mitchell with a ball well up to the bat; Mitchell tried to push safely to the on and missed. We could almost hear and feel his curses. Wood thwacked heavily and hit a ball on to his big toe and hopped about. Smailes unwisely endeavoured to play correct cricket; he is a hitter by nature and eyesight. In the last over before lunch he played forward for keeps; Iddon dashed yards across to the off side and scooped up a one-handed return catch of such ghoulish appetite that the crowd expressed unbelief and consternation. Yorkshire 149 for six, only 71 ahead. Even yet the patriots said Yorkshire would win.

From the first over after lunch, bowled by Pollard, ten runs were plundered desperately by Wood and Turner. And brilliant and rapacious stumping overwhelmed Turner—Duckworth at his quickest, most ruthless, and most screeching. Sellers drove a four off Iddon—and after that he received no more bowling, but was doomed to stand helpless and watch the awful suddenness of Yorkshire's doom. Iddon's spin reared up and Wood could do nothing but spoon a gentle catch to square-leg, a case of the enterprising burglar listening to the village brook a-gurgling. Bowes presumed to drive Iddon and was stumped by Duckworth in next to no time. Then Verity was trapped on the spot he could not himself root out until the match was lost. The crowd rendered unto Iddon warm and unsparing homage.

At a quarter to three Lancashire, or rather Washbrook, set about the ninety-one runs wanted for a win. He drove

Bowes's fifth ball straight for four and hit Smailes to the left of cover, a Bradman crack; and in the same over leaned forward, all confidence, and forced a three to the on. He was missed low down on the off side by Wood from a snick off an outswinger by Bowes. The crowd groaned mortification. Paynter also snicked luckily at Verity and was not in convincing form. Verity turned a ball a foot and Paynter was yards out of his ground, but Wood had not a chance, so savagely did the spin work. A brilliant cut by Washbrook, and a square drive, also by Washbrook, made Lancashire fifty in half an hour. Next Washbrook cut Turner straight from the shoulder, so to say; this was great batsmanship and no less. He was betrayed by the spot—Verity whipped across and upwards, and Washbrook had no choice but to send a catch.

Iddon was caught first ball in the slips, another instance of belated spin from Verity. At seventy-three the match suffered convulsion again; Oldfield, tense and grim, drove to mid-off and dashed for runs. The ball was fielded passionately by Sellers, who threw to Wood, who put down the wicket, his face going redder and redder, while Paynter was vainly running for his life. And Hopwood was leg before from a stroke difficult to classify—Lancashire 74 for four, and a minute or two afterwards 82 for five—Oldfield somehow skied behind the wicket and was caught by Smailes, racing from the slips.

Only nine were wanted with five wickets in hand when Lister became Phillipson's helpmate. I have never before known nine runs to count for so many and seem so far away. Ball after ball was sternly thrust away for nothings; the strain grew absurdly severe. Surely, we said, Lancashire cannot lose five wickets for less than nine—but we could not be sure. Lister was cool, and so was Phillipson. After all, more than two hours remained in which to score nine. Phillipson hinted of no stroke at all until, of a startling suddenness, he drove Turner for a splendid, even an extravagant, four to the off. This was the goal, the heart's desire. The populace greeted victors and vanquished alike. At Old Trafford tomorrow Lancashire must have a reception, not only a crowd but, as they say at Lord's, band if possible—and even the Lord Mayor and the chains.

By the way, during Yorkshire's collapse, I walked on the Mound and saw a Sheffield man deep in dejection. His wife was with him, and I heard her say, 'Well, you *would* come, wouldn't you?'

SCORES

YORKSHIRE

First Innings		Second Innings	
Sutcliffe, c Duckworth, b Phillipson	122	b Iddon	6
Hutton, c Pollard, b Phillipson	1	c Lister, b Iddon	38
Mitchell, b Pollard	71	b Iddon	46
Barber, lbw, (n.) b Pollard	0	c Duckworth, b Birtwell	23
N. W. D. Yardley, c & b Birtwell	3	c Paynter, b Iddon	1
Turner, b Pollard	6	st Duckworth, b Iddon	7
A. B. Sellers, b Pollard	3	not out	5
Smailes, b Pollard	1	c & b Iddon	11
Wood, b Phillipson	35	c Lister, b Iddon	29
Bowes, b Sibbles	0	st Duckworth, b Iddon	0
Verity, not out	0	c Birtwell, b Iddon	0
Extras b1, lb3	4	Extras lb2	2
Total	246	Total	168

LANCASHIRE

First Innings		Second Innings	
Paynter, c & b Verity	38	run out	22
Washbrook, b Hutton	32	c Turner, b Verity	44
Duckworth, lbw, b Bowes	2		
Iddon, c Hutton, b Verity	41	c Mitchell, b Verity	0
Oldfield, c & b Turner	51	c Smailes, b Turner	5
Hopwood, c Wood, b Turner	19	lbw, b Verity	0
Phillipson, not out	50	not out	13
W. H. L. Lister, c Mitchell, b Smailes	34	not out	3
Pollard, b Smailes	0		
A. J. Birtwell, b Turner	12		
Sibbles, c & b Smailes	23		
Extras b15, lb6, nb1	22	Extras b1, lb3	4
Total	324	Total (for 5)	91

462

YORKSHIRE V LANCASHIRE 1937
BOWLING ANALYSIS
YORKSHIRE—First Innings

	O.	M.	R.	W.		O.	M.	R.	W.
Phillipson	23	4	70	3	Birtwell	24	6	55	1
Sibbles	19	0	54	1	Iddon	5	2	4	0
Pollard	25	5	59	5					

Second Innings

	O.	M.	R.	W.		O.	M.	R.	W.
Phillipson	8	1	17	0	Birtwell	9	0	34	1
Sibbles	10	3	28	0	Iddon	18·5	3	42	9
Pollard	17	1	45	0					

LANCASHIRE—First Innings

	O.	M.	R.	W.		O.	M.	R.	W.
Bowes	24	8	47	1	Hutton	9	0	36	1
Smailes	23	4	63	3	Turner	19	4	35	3
Verity	47	11	121	2					

Second Innings

	O.	M.	R.	W.		O.	M.	R.	W.
Bowes	5	0	19	0	Verity	13	1	26	3
Smailes	3	0	22	0	Turner	7·2	1	20	1

YORKSHIRE V LANCASHIRE 1938

June 4/6/7 Bradford

FIRST DAY

LANCASHIRE today sadly blotted the reputation recently won for free and cheerful batting. Once again a Lancashire and Yorkshire match has been a public nuisance and a bore. I have seldom suffered tedium as dreadful as this. And on top of it all discomfort and shabbiness. the accommodation for the press at Bradford is inadequate, not to say inhumane; galley slaves were better off than the tortured souls who this afternoon have tried to make a truthful record of an event which ought really to be forgotten at once. If the good fairies granted me one wish I should ask for freedom to stay away from all Lancashire and Yorkshire cricket matches for the remainder of my days. I never expected to endure tribulation such as Saturday's—not at any rate in this world. The cricket caused aches of boredom; the environment in which it was played suited the stunted drabness of it. In a little short of six hours Lancashire made 232 against mediocre bowling. The pitch was comfortable enough, expecially after lunch. Hopwood's innings of 70, compiled in two hours, was a piece of levity in the general mortuary of the occasion. Nutter in two and a half hours scored 45. Farrimond committed the ugliest obstruction for an hour and eight runs. Whitsun in the North—stupid sport and a crowd silent and dejected. The Lancashire and Yorkshire match should be played in camera, with the players the only spectators. They deserve no better fate.

In the quiet of the morning Paynter and Place began the day's toil. Lister was fortunate to win the toss in unsettled weather on a slow and not difficult wicket. Wan sunshine appeared from somewhere, and the green trees outside the ground seemed to take courage and new heart, but on the whole gave us the impression that they were having a sort of Lancashire and Yorkshire struggle for existence all by themselves. The crowd, though small to begin with, was of the soil. 'You can have the Test matches,' said a man, suggesting that they were his property if he wanted them, 'but give me Yorkshire and Lankysheer.' Before the day was over he was sorry he had spoken. A Test match, of course, can be a polite and formal affair compared with the annual contention between Lancashire and Yorkshire—almost as polite and formal as Army manoeuvres compared with war. The crowd quickly had reason to suffer—and it is to suffer, I suppose, that crowds attend these matches. Place played forward to Smailes, who missed holding a trapped ball, which many spectators thought was a catch. Said the voice: 'If they're goin' to miss catches we might as well goa whoam,' and the suggestion was that even home would be preferable. Paynter nearly allowed Bowes to find the edge of his bat, but Bowes was not at his best, far from it. He seldom caused the swing to occur dangerously late. Place quickly consoled the gathering multitude; he sent a return catch to Turner, whom the eager, not to say bloodthirsty, Sellers asked to bowl instead of Smailes, after Lancashire had imperceptibly scored 19 in half an hour. Bowes suddenly took a wicket too—as though in his sleep. Paynter was an accessory after the act, for he pushed out his bat to a wide ball and edged a half-chance, which Verity seized in the slips by throwing himself to the earth and holding the catch with his right hand. Paynter could easily have let the ball pass harmlessly by—it was stupid of him to go after it merely to play a defensive push, nowhere in particular.

The loss of two wickets for twenty put the Lancashire innings into a palsy and green-sickness for the day. Smailes caused one or two balls to break back; Verity also was able to turn the ball mildly. Oldfield began confidently and drove once or twice to the off in style; then he suddenly became dubious, seeing strange phantasms of spin. The only vital thing in the match now was Yorkshire's superb fielding, which shot spears of antagonism at the wicket. From the position of silly mid-off Sellers cast the old evil eye of Yorkshire on Lancashire; if Lancashire had been playing, say, Leicestershire, the bowling would have received treatment on its merits. I thought that the ancient bogy had been laid but here it was again, white sheet, lantern, and turnip and all. Even Hutton was regarded as a mischievous bowler; Oldfield distrusted his simplest half-volleys, and was leg-before-wicket to one which emulated a googly as soon as it dropped on the ground. Instead of driving the ball for four, Oldfield made no stroke whatever; he put his bat over his shoulder and trusted fatally to his pads. In two hours before lunch Lancashire scored 67 for three and laid flattery with a trowel on the conscientious Yorkshire attack.

After lunch Hutton once more assisted Verity in the bluff—though Verity almost gave the game away by bowling over the wicket. Iddon, who in some ninety minutes had made 24 martyred runs, was nearly caught in the slips while groping out at Verity like an old lady looking under the bed. He was beaten shortly afterwards by a quick and good ball from Bowes which kept low. On the whole Bowes bowled in the manner of a slow-medium bowler subject to recurrent spasms of energy—the twitchings, so to say, of the somnambulist. A leg hit by Nutter at five minutes to three was the fourth warlike stroke of the innings so far. The batting was as apologetic as a poor relation; four byes from a full toss from Bowes were received gratefully, with a touch of the forelock and a 'Thank 'ee and God bless you.' A cut for four by Hopwood off Verity was in the circumstances bad manners and impertinence. But Hopwood played well in his own penny-saving money-box way. At the end of 165 minutes Lancashire had diligently saved up a hundred runs, for four wickets. A voice denoting somebody going red in the face shrieked, ' 'It 'em, for the love of God.' Still, when Nutter hit a half-volley of Smailes to the off for three nobody seemed to like it; the crowd had come to the match, as I say, to suffer.

At 112 Leyland deposed Verity in the Yorkshire succession of left-handed spinners—the Peel-Rhodes-Kilner dynasty. And Smailes tried slow off-breaks round the wicket to a leg-trap. Yorkshire explored every possibility, material and psychological. Nutter's innings gained temporarily in resolution, so much so that he stepped back and struck a short ball from Leyland to the off boundary, a really vehement hit. Nutter also hit Leyland square, another brilliant stroke—executed by means of a full-blooded swing of bat and body. He repeated the stroke in the same over, to the accompaniment of slight applause. At this point of the proceedings no great amount of observation was needed to find out that the attack was the poorest seen in a Yorkshire team in living memory. Can we imagine a single over by Hutton or Leyland tolerated in the Yorkshire teams of the past? The question is rhetorical—we cannot. None the less the amiable bowling continued to keep the Lancashire innings immobile and inhibited—between three o'clock and four o'clock Hopwood and Iddon added some forty runs. Bowes bowled slower and slower; the crowd sat around in a heap; the umpires sagged at the knees. I felt that nobody was trying to get runs and nobody trying to get wickets.

The roar which greeted the fall of Hopwood, caught at the wicket in the act of cutting (Heaven forgive him!), was not a roar of triumph but one of relief from durance vile. Lister hit a boundary and a three in an innings which, though of short duration, revived thousands of broken hearts. For a brief while Bowes and Smailes bowled as though with an object in life when the new ball was given to them at 200. Pollard played the best innings of the day, from the point of view of a cricket match. Strictly speaking, he was out of order. I cannot imagine why the later Lancashire batsmen did not hit out and try to send Yorkshire to the wicket at six o'clock. What, I wonder, was the idea behind Farrimond's innings? But perhaps I am out of order too, or, more likely, going off my head. What a day!

SECOND DAY

Lancashire have allowed Yorkshire to win on the first innings today in spite of the fact that shortly after lunch Yorkshire were 106 for six, with Hutton out and Sutcliffe out and Mitchell out and Leyland out. The bowling had been flattered on the comfortable wicket, though that is not said to deny its zest and occasional excellence. It was certainly a better attack than that of Yorkshire on Saturday, and in spite of their early disasters Yorkshire scored quicker than Lancashire scored on that same deplorable afternoon. Apart from the competitive interest there was not much in the cricket which rose above the commonplace. There was little character; the players could nearly all easily have been disguised Leicestershire men. Even Sutcliffe was scarcely to be recognised—like a renowned actor playing a super's part in a charity matinée.

In the day's closing period Lancashire lost more ground, for Place was caught at the wicket, feeling without conviction at a wide ball. Iddon was lucky to escape the consequences of a snick through the slips off Bowes, who this time caused the new ball to swing unpleasantly late away. Not without strained effort did Lancashire contrive not to lose another wicket in a searching half-hour.

The heavens frowned on the match this morning, and there was scarcely one touch of colour in the crowd. Noisy sellers of various wares made the occasion sound like the Caledonian Market. Verity was soon out; he stepped back and pulled a slightly short ball from Pollard round to leg and ran a single, only to be informed by several witnesses that he had trodden upon his wicket. This was bad luck for Verity, but really he ought never as a batsman to venture beyond his scope into realms of the esoteric. A severe hour now ensued, with Hutton and Mitchell suspicious and careful. Pollard bowled accurately, and one ball by him reduced Hutton to a perplexed immobility. But Phillipson again sadly fell below his form of last year. In an hour Mitchell and Hutton scored 40; their partnership suggested the laying down by hard labour (overtime on Bank Holidays) of a concrete pavement. Wilkinson came on to lend spin to Lancashire's more or less straight and much too honest attack; and after a few empirical overs he dealt Yorkshire two mortal wounds; he trapped Mitchell leg before wicket with a top spinner, and in the same over he removed Sutcliffe, who allowed a leg break, moreover a short leg break, to curl in and hit the stumps. I have never before seen Sutcliffe defeated as simply as this; he lost not only his wicket but temporarily his dignity, and, I thought, his eyesight.

A few moments after Sutcliffe's astonished withdrawal from the scene Nutter missed an easy return chance from Leyland amidst noises of agonised relief. Leyland was also befogged by a googly from Wilkinson and escaped being bowled by an inch when he let fly violently at Nutter.

Yorkshire hereabout seemed to suffer unexpected agitation. Hutton, though outwardly calm and old in the head, could not show us the strokes he is known or suspected to possess; a lofty on drive from Hutton was executed not entirely with his own consent, I fancied. Wilkinson bowled cleverly, causing in each over at least one question mark to occur in the batsman's mind: we could almost see the shape of it, phosphorescent in a darkening void. There was a pugnacious look about Leyland; he appeared ready to trust his good fortune. One of his on drives soared perilously near a fieldsman, but Leyland did not care and used all the strength of his arms, which are thick as hams. Pollard bowled him in the act of a stupendous drive. At lunch Yorkshire were 95 for four, and the crowd put up a good pretence of enjoyment and philosophy. Appetites were desperately large.

Worse events afflicted the packed thousands after the interval. Barber succumbed promptly to Pollard leg before wicket. Then the steadfast Hutton fell as suddenly as a tree in a storm; he played forward to Phillipson, and pace off the ground overwhelmed him. Yorkshire 104 for six. The silence of the multitude suggested a chess tournament with Alekhine playing Euwe. Hutton's innings of 44 lasted two and a quarter hours; I have yet to discover more than honest watchful utility in this young player; he has technical qualities, no doubt, but so far he has not in my presence revealed character, imagination, the power to take a bowler by the scruff of the neck. He commands strokes, no doubt; the question is when is he going to use them. Time is getting on.

The sun ventured to shine at a quarter to three, when Yorkshire were 120 for six. As Sellers and Turner sought to retrieve the scandalous day the quietude of the crowd was touching. The people of Yorkshire do not affect impartiality; they give themselves up without shame to the misery of a trying day for their cricketers. No note of angered criticism is heard; only lamentation and a certain bewilderment. There was no palpable reason why Yorkshire should have broken down so badly, for the wicket was easy, and apart from Wilkinson's spin the Lancashire attack, though accurate, contained no out-of-way problems. A googly from Wilkinson transformed Turner's body to a quaint condition of anatomical maladjustment; he nearly sent a slip catch and then extricated himself from his knot almost like a contortionist in the old music-hall. On the whole though, Sellers and Turner placed resolute bats to the ball; I felt the game slipping from Lancashire's grasp, and the crowd looked up and faced the situation with a renewed if rather a forced geniality. The two most imperturbable spectators present were Bobby Peel and G. P. Harrison, one of them the greatest of all slow left-handed bowlers, the other a fast bowler of the eighties who had the honour of receiving punishment from W. G. Grace. Peel is 81 years of age and Harrison is 76—hence no doubt their fortitude today.

At twenty minutes past three Sellers and Turner were still unbeaten and Yorkshire 152 for six: a voice took advantage of the easier positon to announce loudly and challengingly 'A'hm goin' for a drink': somebody had been practising self-denial quite long enough. Phillipson beat Turner with the best ball I have seen him bowl this year, but it missed the bails by an inch; Turner was then 30 and Yorkshire 160. I cannot believe that Phillipson will not shortly recapture his proper fire and energy. Iddon bowled at twenty minutes to four, but once again Lancashire failed to press an advantage home: it is a family failing, as Sir Thomas Beecham said when a famous singer told him that he was not letting his son enter the profession because of a lack of voice. Yorkshire as of old were fighting back while thousands of hearts beat again and men spoke to their wives, lighted pipes, and looked up. Sellers began to swing his bat; he hit and sliced ten in an over from Iddon; he reached 50 after eighty-five minutes of determined effort. Yorkshire reached 200 to the sound of the familiar roar, the first of the match. A moment later Sellers was leg before wicket to Phillipson and the new ball; he had done his share during a stand of 98 in a hundred minutes and grateful cheering hailed him home to the pavilion, which was a compressed mass of humanity of all ages, sexes, and denominations. I inadvertently disclosed my delight at the downfall of Sellers, then felt I was being eyed curiously from behind. Yorkshire's seventh wicket fell at 202; they needed 31 to gain the first-innings advantage.

470

In the tea interval an elated Yorkshire terrier rushed on the ground to look at the wicket, but he was promptly caught and sent back to his seat, from which he contented himself with open laughter at Lancashire's disappointment after they had threatened so much unpleasantness earlier in the afternoon. Also a number of spectators inspected the press through the windows of our box, behind which we probably looked like a number of vegetables in a hot-house. But that is where they were mistaken—the box was not hot.

After tea Smailes drove Phillipson brilliantly for four and was leg before wicket next ball or thereabouts. With two wickets to go Yorkshire needed 23; the crowd proceeded to work itself up and emitted admonitory howls because Lancashire appealed for another case of leg before wicket. What on earth is a Lancashire and Yorkshire match for if a man cannot appeal in one? Pollard stopped a leg-glance dexterously at short-leg; Lancashire's fielding was swift and sure all day. At the crisis Turner was joined in partnership by Wood, who looks so Yorkshire that you could tell at once he was a Yorkshireman if you met him accidentally in a crowd in Budapest, and better still, you would know as quickly that he was a Yorkshireman if you met him in a crowd in Bradford. Turner continued to play courageous cricket; he reached a most valuable fifty after two and a half hours' stern discipline for the cause. At ten minutes past five Yorkshire took the lead to roars so frenzied that it might have been the end of the match or even the end of the world.

Lancashire dwindled sadly; the bowling became merely persevering, so that Wood and Turner added for the ninth wicket no fewer than 63. Moreover they added them comfortably. The crowd was thus enabled to go home contented, the horrors of the afternoon gone like an unhappy vision. 'A great Yorkshire recovery,' they said, anticipating the newspapers. The phrase once broke my heart in my boyhood when Lord Hawke and Whitehead scored an unmentionable amount together after all the great players had fallen to Brearley. But I am wandering in my mind—Brearley, indeed, and MacLaren, and Tyldesley, and Spooner. They never existed, of course; a boy dreamed of them in school on lazy summer afternoons.

THIRD DAY

Yorkshire annihilated Lancashire today, and the match finished in warm sunshine at half-past four.

The collapse of Lancashire was one of the worst on record even in these panic-stricken matches. I watched Verity's bowling carefully with a good view; he was able occasionally to turn the ball, not quickly, from a place on or outside the off stump. The wicket was too good to enable him to spin from the leg or even from the middle stump. And no left-handed bowler can be said to be difficult if he is not spinning from the leg and middle. Lancashire got out because their minds were afflicted suddenly by the ancient bogy; Professor Freud, now in England, should be asked to treat the team. The players probably suffered much when young from Yorkshire pudding, or perhaps some of them had teeth taken out by dentists from Pudsey. More nerveless batting than Lancashire's today could scarcely be imagined. The irony was that in the first hour of the morning Paynter and Iddon played with a most affable air of comfort. Each hit a magnificent six—and a Lancashire batsman is feeling entirely at ease when he envisages a six against Yorkshire. Paynter was apparently so satisfied that the day was ambling to a certain draw that he ran out of his ground to a clever, quick ball from Verity, endeavouring to drive another six, and was stumped. The time of day was then twenty minutes to one, and for seventy minutes the occasion had been merely formal, with two batsmen doing their daily work against equally conscientious bowlers, everybody waiting for the clock to tick off the hours. At half-past twelve I inquired about an early train to Manchester; seldom have I known a match as obviously destined as this to drift to stalemate.

Even after Paynter departed, none of us saw a cloud on the horizon, though Oldfield shaped queerly at Verity. He was out driving at a half-volley and hitting at the point when the spin began. The ball flew from his bat's edge to the slips, and Oldfield did not know he was out until told officially. The fall of two wickets cramped Iddon, who, while Paynter was in with him, was at his best and most confident. He began to bend down over his bat and to grope. Hopwood also bent down. 'Heavens!' I thought, 'they are going to lose. They are

472

acting on the suggestions of Sellers.' For Sellers at once called in his fieldsmen. For an hour they had occupied more or less protective positions, to save runs. The pitch became deadly in the eyes and minds of Lancashire. There was certainly an odd dusty patch off the wicket at the end to which Verity bowled, and once or twice a ball from Smailes kept low. But a Peel and a Rhodes combined, aided by a wicket as sticky as Melbourne's, could not hope to sweep batsmen out of existence as swiftly as Lancashire were swept after lunch. In forty-five minutes six wickets fell for 18. Verity bowled six overs three balls for three maidens, nine runs, and four wickets. Hardly any Lancashire batsman was capable of a stroke now, save Pollard. Hardly any of them seemed capable of a stroke or of intending a stroke. There was no room for tears or for knocking at the breast. The crowd rolled up in thousands when the good news spread around Bradford. I was only amused and baffled. By the evidence of my eyes, and from my knowledge of cricket, I knew the fact—that on a tolerably good pitch the Lancashire batsmen were being bluffed out. Iddon played back to Hutton and was leg before wicket. Sellers dived from 'silly' mid-off and finely caught Nutter, who risked a forward push. Phillipson and Lister were leg before wicket in one over by Smailes; both balls kept low no doubt. But why continue the inquest? Hopwood blocked a half-volley and was bowled next ball by another half-volley. Farrimond got out to a stroke which was not only fatal but hideous. Iddon and Paynter probably looked upon the strange proceedings in bewilderment. Only a short time ago they had been marking time, with an occasional sixer for our delectation. I shall die in the belief that at half-past twelve Sellers had given the match up as a draw.

Sutcliffe began Yorkshire's easy task of scoring ninety-eight with all his old hauteur. He hooked and drove brilliantly. This was the first and only example of greatness in a poor match. There was the familiar aura about him. All his history came back as he played in the warm sunshine. He hit Nutter for fourteen in an over, two dazzling pulls and a crashing straight drive off a no-ball. Pollard bowled him with a great break-back which was a compliment to the old master.

Pollard attacked from the pavilion end, the end which should have been his on Monday, with the wind, but never was. He made Hutton and Mitchell fight hard; his bowling was by far the best seen in the three days. I could have understood Lancashire's collapse if the batsmen had been facing Pollard.

This was the worst defeat ever experienced by Lancashire against Yorkshire because if was inflicted by the poorest Yorkshire team, surely, that ever took the field. The match was lost—in spirit—before tea on Saturday. Nemesis, for once.

Yorkshire deserved cheers because of their rally from a dangerous position. They may not be technically a good side, but the old ability to hypnotise Lancashire is still theirs evidently. The artful persuasiveness of Verity probably made the pavilion cat laugh. I seemed to detect a glimmer of a smile on the face of Verity himself; he is a man of humour, and can relish a quiet chuckle. Poor Paynter, he little guessed that when he was stumped running after a six the match was lost. How should he have guessed? He and Iddon, by thoroughly happy and skilful play, had created the right atmosphere for their successors. The change that came over Iddon as soon as Paynter got out baffles my powers of psychological analysis. Freud must certainly be called in.

SCORES

LANCASHIRE

First Innings		Second Innings	
Place, c & b Turner	9	c Wood, b Bowes	0
Paynter, c Verity, b Bowes	10	st Wood, b Verity	32
Iddon, lbw, b Bowes	28	lbw, b Hutton	66
Oldfield, lbw, b Hutton	14	c Smailes, b Verity	1
Hopwood, c Wood, b Hutton	70	b Verity	24
Nutter, lbw, b Smailes	45	c Sellers, b Verity	0
W. H. L. Lister, b Verity	11	lbw, b Smailes	0
Phillipson, b Bowes	1	lbw, b Smailes	0
Farrimond, not out	8	c Sellers, b Verity	2
Pollard, st Wood, b Verity	20	c Turner, b Verity	7
Wilkinson, run out	1	not out	0
Extras b10, lb4, nb1	15	Extras lb5, w1	6
Total	232	Total	138

YORKSHIRE V LANCASHIRE 1938
YORKSHIRE

First Innings		Second Innings	
Verity, hit wkt. b Pollard	0		
Mitchell, lbw, b Wilkinson	26	not out	19
Hutton, b Phillipson	44	c Lister, b Iddon	33
Sutcliffe, b Wilkinson	0	b Pollard	29
Leyland, b Pollard	17	not out	11
Barber, lbw, b Pollard	5		
Turner, c Pollard, b Wilkinson	69		
A. B. Sellers, lbw, b Phillipson	50		
Smailes, lbw, b Phillipson	7		
Wood, c & b Nutter	35		
Bowes, not out	0		
Extras b2, lb10, nb8	20	Extras b4, nb2	6
Total	273	Total (for 2)	98

BOWLING ANALYSIS

Lancashire—First Innings

	O.	M.	R.	W.		O.	M.	R.	W.
Bowes	33	14	46	3	Hutton	17	2	40	2
Smailes	25	6	32	1	Leyland	6	3	14	0
Turner	9	2	24	1	Barber	1	0	4	0
Verity	31	9	57	2					

Second Innings

	O.	M.	R.	W.		O.	M.	R.	W.
Bowes	14	6	26	1	Hutton	3	0	4	1
Smailes	25	10	41	2	Leyland	3	0	12	0
Verity	24	11	49	6					

Yorkshire—First Innings

	O.	M.	R.	W.		O.	M.	R.	W.
Pollard	26	6	49	3	Wilkinson	27	7	61	3
Phillipson	24	6	54	3	Iddon	3	0	16	0
Nutter	24	4	73	1					

Second Innings

	O.	M.	R.	W.		O.	M.	R.	W.
Phillipson	3	0	13	0	Iddon	3	0	8	1
Pollard	9	2	21	1	Paynter	1	0	6	0
Nutter	1	0	14	0	Oldfield	1	0	6	0
Wilkinson	9	1	24	0					

475

YORKSHIRE V LANCASHIRE 1938

July 30 August 1/2 Old Trafford

FIRST DAY

LANCASHIRE again dropped a blot on the season's books by poor batting against Yorkshire on Saturday; there were all the old tremors, ditherings and loss of the use of the feet. The wicket enabled Yorkshire bowlers to turn the ball but for the most part the spin worked slowly until the day was advanced. I am not sure that it was not taking spin quicker when Sutcliffe and Gibb began a vital partnership than at any other time. Failing a comprehensive change in the affairs Lancashire are already a defeated team. Robinson bowled ably and Bowes also; they were encouraged to do their best by Lancashire, according to precedent.

One of Yorkshire's opening bowlers was Yardley, who does not give himself that honour when playing for his university. It seemed to me that, feeling a natural diffidence in this capacity, he took the precaution of disguising himself as Sutcliffe, but artfully complicated the illusion by not darkening his hair. Washbrook drove his first ball loftily to the vacant on-side field for four. Yorkshire of course exploited the usual close field; Sellers stood at short mid-on, under the batsman's nose crouching like a frog. Before the match began I saw an ambulance, and perhaps before long an ambulance will be regarded as much a part of the outfit of a cricket match as the sightscreen or the heavy roller. Washbrook cut Yardley for four and revealed a strange ignorance of the traditions of post-war Lancashire and Yorkshire matches; he appeared to be irreverently eager to hit boundaries before lunch. To the dismay of the hopeful onlookers, he suddenly fell to a catch at the wicket by Wood; he pushed his bat forward, top heavy of the body, at a ball from Bowes, and the late swing found the edge. Gibb, who is England's chosen wicket-keeper but not Yorkshire's, probably joined in the violent appeal that went up when Washbrook snicked; the vocal duties of a wicket-keeper can

476

be practised from most parts of the field, in fact, from every part of the field during a Lancashire and Yorkshire match.

Lancashire's first wicket fell at 17, by which time Verity had come on with intent to spin, or a persuasive suggestion of spin. But the sign of a wicket disagreeably dispositioned to batsmen occurred when a reasonable length ball from Bowes came up and thumped Iddon's gloves. Verity was unable at once either to achieve or imply spin so Robinson took his place (his name is an anachronism to these matches, and should be changed by deed-poll to Thompson). We shall one of these days have a man coming into the Yorkshire side calling himself George Hirst—part of the game, I suppose. Paynter pulled Bowes magnificently for four, off his breast-bone, a swift stroke which gave no chance to Leyland, who fielded at long-leg and contemplated the match from a perspective—like a longshoreman. At any moment I expected him to put his hand to his eyes. This hit by Paynter told us of an eagle vision, for the ball was only a shade short. Bowes at mid-off brilliantly fielded two strokes by Paynter in spite of giving us the painful idea of a man with a stone in his boot—under the big toe. He bowled admirably for an hour, then retired to his sweater, while Verity again practised his craftsmanship, now at the other end. After 65 minutes' play Lancashire were only 33; meanwhile the wicket was losing its deadness. Verity now began to give his slip fieldsmen the loveliest feelings of anticipation, and though Iddon drove Robinson for a lordly straight four there was a sense of hardship in Lancashire's innings, and when Paynter returned a ball to Verity hardship gave way to tribulation.

Oldfield's innings reminded me of the gallant efforts of a young animal with one foot caught in a trap. He pulled Robinson into the air to leg, dangerously near Sutcliffe, who, though yards away, succeeded in looking as though not in any way related to the stroke. Oldfield then struck desperately across Verity's spin and skied round the corner, where the ball safely fell on the dank earth. He drove a beautiful four to the off from Robinson, and with Iddon sound and composed, as he often has been, man and boy, these several years at holiday-time in Lancashire and Yorkshire, no further wicket went down before lunch.

After the interval Oldfield at once allowed himself to become bowled—by Robinson. Sixty-one for three. The sun mercifully declined to come out and a blustering wind swept the grass and travelled up Leyland's trousers. Verity drew Hopwood forward full stretch, and Hopwood missed spin by an inch, with his body infinitely extended. But Hopwood drove Robinson with a power which has been suspected in the family for years, and again Verity put him on a rack with a spinner, to which, of course, no footwork was employed. To stretch out at a going-away ball so that even if you reach it at the end you can exercise no control over the stroke—for countless years experience has demonstrated that this is a fatal way of playing a left-handed spin-bowler. Yet this way is preferred by most contemporary batsmen—preferred to the quick-footed movement which takes the bat over the ball at the crucial moment.

Iddon spoiled a valuable innings by groping half-cock: he was well caught in the leg-trap by Verity; he could not have fared less well had he banged away for death or glory. Why does a man prefer to be caught near the wicket rather than in the deep field? Nutter, in next, hit Verity to leg for four; there would have been some black looks if Wilfred Rhodes had seen the stroke. On a turning wicket any hit to leg from a left-handed slow bowler should go straight up like a burst water-main. Nutter also trusted his innings to a push stroke to an off-break, and he saw himself wonderfully well caught on the ground full stretch by Yardley, which made Lancashire five wickets for 86. And an off-break, as antique as a grand-father's clock, bowled Lister, who played forward, a stroke which a few years ago was considered obsolete in the Lancashire team ('Hey, lad, what's t' pads for?'). But the new rule has altered matters; Parkin's off-break would bring him a tremendous haul of wickets at the present day.

The ball was turning palpably at three o'clock, and Hopwood, though nearly stumped as he again elongated himself, and nearly caught in a labyrinth of slips, none the less batted like sticking-plaster, and amused the crowd when he turned Verity to leg slyly and artfully. Ten minutes afterwards he hit Verity once more to leg and sent Lancashire's score past the hundred. Hopwood played a fine game, and a period of resistance was achieved by Farrimond, who has cut down his margin of strokes to less than one. He was adjudged leg before, apparently without knowing anything about it. And when Verity rested at last Leyland was called in from the far distance, where he had been waiting for a catch, with the height of optimism, and he proceeded to bowl, first of all marking out his run aggressively. But he bowled for only two overs, then Verity came back and popped a ball to Pollard's shirt front. Pollard, for inscrutable reasons, decided to play seriously and anatomically; he groped out to Verity, and Mitchell, of all living Yorkshiremen, missed him in the slips. A small boy urged Pollard to 'Hit 'em!'—which was wisdom coming out of the mouths of babes and sucklings. Hopwood, with rapid eyesight, saw an off-break from Robinson that refused to break and he cut it for three, and next over he cut Verity for four—since when was the cut legalised, for the purpose of Lancashire and Yorkshire? The game is going to the dogs.

Hopwood's excellent and gallant innings ended in a very fierce attempt to drive Bowes in front of the wicket—further degeneracy. He has seldom played a more valuable and characteristic game; it was Hopwood from the primordial globule. And Pollard put vain science behind him and scutched (as they say) Verity for four to the on, and lifted him to the off, before sending a catch to Sutcliffe at long-on, which was judged to a nicety and caught with elegance. Lancashire's last man in, name of Rhodes—another anachronism—placed a ball gently into Bowes's hand, a return catch which Bowes could have taken in his sleep, and possibly did. Lancashire were all out at four o'clock.

Sutcliffe began his innings as only Sutcliffe can or ever will begin an innings. He picked a piece of dirt off the wicket as soon as he reached it, took guard, and wiped the bottom of his bat, then stopped Pollard in the middle of his run to the wicket—stopped him imperiously, like an officer in the constabulary pushing back an unlawful bus on point duty. A miserable spectator was waved out of all decent society; he had got in the line of Sutcliffe's vision. Sutcliffe and Mitchell scored eighteen together, and Mitchell survived the best over of the day, bowled by Pollard, with a terrific break-back in it, which Mitchell stopped late and violently. But it was Nutter who took Yorkshire's first wicket by a ball that rose in a temper and compelled the easiest catch. Sutcliffe edged Pollard through the slips and looked as though he had meant it; also he pulled Nutter square in the old swinging regal way—remember how, once on a time, on a Saturday evening, he hooked and pulled Macdonald! Wilkinson troubled his equanimity and almost trapped him leg-before-wicket; the crowd on the square-leg boundary gave him out in one voice, led by a small shrill boy.

There were further exciting sounds when Rhodes bowled a capital over to Gibb; one ball spat its spin upwards and might well have been contrived at the fingers of the one and only Rhodes—not forgetting even Cecil. Gibb did nothing for a long time except not lose his wicket—the turf seemed more unpleasant now than at any earlier part of the day. Lancashire, as usual against Yorkshire, bowled with all the force and character which should have been in their batting; at the end of a gruelling hour Yorkshire were only 39 for one; and Gibb then pulled a long-hop googly from Wilkinson to the on boundary.

Iddon bowled at 58, or prepared to bowl. The ridiculously narrow sightscreen had to be moved and Iddon had to try whether his arm would still come over. Then he marked out his run. And then the field required careful setting. The cosmic rhythm suffered interruption. And at last Iddon bowled his first ball—a wide. Gibb hit him for four to the on in the same over. The other balls were not bad, but with Rhodes spinning nicely at the other end two slow left-handers on together seemed a luxury. Nutter was probably resting because of sore shins; the few overs he had bowled an hour before were full of promise.

The scoring, according to the laws of the match, was imperceptible. Yorkshire were making sure. And so under a dreary sky the holiday crowd of the North took their pleasures with customary gloominess. Today there should be another opportunity for a display of public and patriotic affliction.

SECOND DAY

There was an extraordinary outburst of sunshine at Old Trafford yesterday which threatened to strike people down like flies; they were taken off their guard and sought refuge in dark glasses, while the women wore dresses so gay in colour that Old Trafford for once might have been indicted under some Act concerned with the welfare of public morality. People swarmed on the grass, that same grass which a week or so ago was covered with waters of tribulation, and wringing machines, and bags of sawdust which resembled drowned bodies. Quickly the crowd had reason to rejoice, for in Pollard's second over an inswinger smote the pads of Sutcliffe and he was out, leg before wicket, and obliged to leave the garish scene. It never appears right to me that Sutcliffe should ever have to submit to the orders of a common umpire. A clever spinner from Rhodes whipped across and nearly found the edge of Gibb's bat, but Gibb on the whole played ably, and was quick to pull a short length from Rhodes for four. Then a dash of forked-lightning fielding by Washbrook at short mid-on nearly ran out Barber; Washbrook swooped to the earth, picked up, twisted himself into a corkscrew, and threw in; he was vivid, quick as a monkey. Another spinner by Rhodes beat Gibb; Rhodes bowled well, but needed a little more nip off the turf. Though the wicket was easy, I felt that there were places on it from which any experienced exploiter of spin, especially off-spin at a good pace, might have given some slight trouble.

Gibb defended astutely, and in three-quarters of an hour added only sixteen to his score; but he proved his adhesive quality, and was always quick to hit an unmistakably short ball. In style he is as post-war as a petrol station. A sudden and beautiful 'googly' by Wilkinson overwhelmed him when a hundred by him seemed only a matter of time—of hours, maybe, but, anyhow, time. Leyland's first announcement of his arrival at the wicket was a mighty pull which went all agricultural at the last minute; the ball, from Wilkinson, snorted past the leg stump and Leyland, after he had realised where he was, ran for runs at headlong speed, happy and entirely without conscience. There was a lot of running about just now—Paynter saved fours on the edge of the multitude, and his pace was so breakneck that I cannot explain how he ever pulled himself up; he threatened to go careering over prone bodies and disappear from the premises. The Lancashire fielding prevented the faintest suggestion of slow play; nobody noticed that Barber did nothing for nearly an hour except worry, or as they say, worrit. Leyland twice drove a fine four to the off from Rhodes, who for an hour and twenty-five minutes pegged away and only failed by want of luck to take at least two wickets. It was five minutes to one before Nutter took part in the attack. When Pollard returned at 200, Barber drove the new ball consecutively for fours—and next over Leyland cut him late for four, the prettiest stroke in the world. He reached his fifty at lunch and then Yorkshire were 232 for three.

At a quarter-past two the crowd, nearly 30,000, and the ground made a grand sight; this was a glimpse into olden times, and for a moment I saw a vision of R. H. Spooner rippling the off side like wind playing on a field of poppies. An enormous amount of food was consumed during the interval, so that when the afternoon sun shone on the pavilion there was a certain amount of surreptitious and heavy sleep, which was startled into life when Barber missed a ball from Rhodes, well up to him, and departed, reluctantly, leg-before. Still, he had been long enough on view, almost like a permanent collection. Yardley, more fluent, came as a refreshment and change; his cricket meant something, even when he was only playing the ball. A flick of his wrists to the on, from a good-length ball by Pollard, obtained only two, and, of course, only a few handclaps greeted as clever and as handsome a stroke as you could wish to see. It is a materialistic world, even on Bank Holiday. The Lancashire bowling, if steady, had a certain defect; nobody made the ball 'move' away from the bat. Even Wilkinson's best ball was his googly, not his leg-break.

When Nutter came on for Pollard at the Manchester end Leyland struck his first ball straight for four and, having done so, stood entirely still and watched the perspective. In the same over he pulled to the on and drove to the off, both fours also. If Leyland is not good enough to play for England, who amongst living cricketers is? If he were an

Australian—a preposterous thought—he would certainly be playing for them. He is good enough for Yorkshire, isn't he? Very well then, argal and go to. When Yardley was 16 he missed pulling a short ball from Wilkinson, and was bowled within inches; Farrimond washed his hands of the matter and gave away four byes. A diversion set in on the popular side while a collection for Hopwood's benefit was taken in a sack. A number of small boys enjoyed the time of their lives chasing the pennies. They should have been turned upside down and shaken when the collection was finished.

Yardley was the fourth consecutive victim of leg-before, and now Sellers was given a resonant reception. Yorkshire were 285 for five. Leyland not out and not intending to get out, 81. Nutter, who disposed of Yardley, caused the ball to come off the pitch with more vivacity than any other Lancashire bowler; he even persuaded a ball here and there to 'run' away. Just before half past three Leyland reached his century, a rich piece of cricket, and the crowd roared and cheered as though they were his brothers and sisters and children and wives. It is curious how some cricketers can express their natures in every stroke, while others can only make the noise of a bat hitting a lump of leather. Sellers swept two fours to square leg, but he deals with spin-bowling so quaintly, moving to it like a crab, that I thought Wilkinson would get him out for the asking. But Wilkinson was not now at his best, his spin had little or no animosity. And so Sellers survived.

At 329 Iddon bowled for the first time during the day, and his first ball was thumped for four to the on by Leyland, who now was ready for fours on principle; his forearms seemed to me bigger and wider than ever—the umpire should have used the gauge on them. Sellers, at a quarter to four, without giving due and legal notice, hit a six off Iddon, a swinging clout to the on which sent two small boys somersaulting on the edge of the field. The best stroke in Sellers's useful innings was a quick pull from a short ball of Wilkinson; Sellers and Leyland scored at eighty an hour without hurry, and Sellers reached fifty in some seventy minutes. The Lancashire attack by this time had put ambition aside and were thoroughly philosophical. And the sun departed, no doubt thinking that that was sufficient for the day in Manchester—let's be reasonable in all things. Leyland was bowled, trying a stroke to leg, a minute before tea. Thirty thousand people stood up to hail him—and to recover the use of their spines. And a small child, who must have suffered a good deal, asked Sellers why he did not declare. Leyland and Sellers scored 108 for the sixth wicket, and Sellers made half of them, even though he has about one stroke to Leyland's half-dozen.

After tea, Wood made a few of his own lusty hits, including a most handsome drive to the off; it was as though he had suddenly put on his spats and talked with a B.B.C. accent. Nutter bowled him when Yorkshire were 300 ahead—and the crowd thoroughly tired of the sight of Yorkshire. They lifted up their spirits to applaud a calmly judged catch at deep long-off by Washbrook off a good hit by Robinson. But even now Sellers would not declare, but persisted with Yorkshire's innings to the bitter and unimaginative end. The crowd had the consolation of seeing Bowes walking to the wicket, which he did with humour and the most imperceptible movement in animate nature. After a waste of time Bowes sent a slip catch, and Lancashire's bowlers came home to rest at twenty minutes past five, Yorkshire 320 to the good.

Nutter's bowling analysis—27, 6, 68, 5—in an innings of 453 must go down amongst the best of the season by anybody and anywhere. In an age when batsmen receive all the glory, sometimes because they make 100 in four hours by waiting for long hops on a perfect wicket, let us honour a splendid performance by a young bowler.

Bowes pitched wide at the beginning of Lancashire's forlorn journey, a misuse of the new ball which would have driven Emmott Robinson mad. Washbrook hit him for six, a crashing and swinging leg-hit off a long hop. Next over Washbrook drove Yardley to the on for four. Verity bowled in Yardley's place, and his first ball, a rank full-toss, was sent away for four to leg by Paynter. A long-hop and a full-toss in successive overs by Yorkshiremen—we live in strange times. Against some sweet-tempered bowling, Lancashire avoided disaster until ten minutes from close of play. Washbrook then put his legs in front of a ball from Leyland. At the other end Gibb bowled, which was another curious occurrence in a day that seemed to hold the attention of the multitude to the end in spite of the return of a scowling sky and a wind that blew newspapers into the air. Perhaps Sellers may yet have reason to regret the time wasted after Leyland got out.

THIRD DAY

It will be merciful to draw a veil on the cricket yesterday. A heavy fall of rain in the small hours entirely destroyed the remote chance which Lancashire had of making a draw of the match. The ball turned at once, and that was enough. Lancashire's batsmen saw the awkward spin not only with the objective eye but also with the lurid eye of imagination. A few efforts at hitting were wistful; the batsmen did not go to the pitch of the ball, and even forgot the first principle, which insists that no stroke should be committed against the break. Iddon and Oldfield both perished to hits which they made at the request of the bowler, not because they themselves wished to make them. Magnificent catches near the wicket, and near the batsman's trousers pockets, settled Hopwood and Nutter; the ghoulish fieldsmen were Verity and Mitchell. Lister was bowled by an honest off-break, as in the first innings.

Paynter, as usual, struggled bitterly, and yet again proved his temperament. As I say, the pitch was Yorkshire's ally, but another of their allies, nearly as decisive, was the old Lancashire superstition about the essential satanism of all Yorkshiremen, who really are nice, cheerful, and hospitable folk. Take Bill Bowes and Maurice Leyland, for instance; Verity, I admit, has a lean antipathetic look about him; but really he is a charming man, who would never dream of exploiting anybody's shyness or want of Christian faith. Oh, no!

Paynter caused a forlorn cheer from the diminutive crowd when he cut a long-hop from Robinson for four, and then Mitchell actually missed Farrimond at second slip, and from the next ball Paynter nearly succumbed in the leg-trap; both of these mishaps occurred against Verity, who was now whipping across viciously. The wicket was beginning to spit out its venom—Lancashire were certainly unlucky to be trapped this way. But they lost on Saturday when the wicket was slow and easy. Paynter hit two fours off Robinson, who was promptly taken off, in spite of the obvious nastiness of his off-break. Bowes bowled instead, which meant that he was obliged to take off his sweater on a hot, humid morning. Farrimond prodded for a while, but a slip catch from Verity, if you trust to half-cock, is as inevitable as death at the end of a rope. During Farrimond's bewildered explorations a spectator remarked, 'He is not comfortable.' This profound statement was not challenged. Verity was at his best; his supple hand extracted the wickets with the delicacy of touch of the most affable dentist in the world. The match finished in gorgeous sunshine at half-past twelve.

Paynter was out to a vile ball, off his gloves, and few cricketers in the game today could have shown finer and more humorous determination. Of course, the better side won—no team are better in all the English counties than Yorkshire, and never have been. The crowd went home carrying their lunch-parcels. The day was ruined for them. But nobody with an ounce of cricket sense denied Yorkshire's superiority. I herewith make a suggestion, in all seriousness, to the Selection Committee. Play the Yorkshire team with or without Hammond and Paynter, in the Oval Test match. Perhaps it would be as well to omit Hammond, and even Paynter. The great thing would be to keep the Yorkshire team *as* a team.

For countless years Yorkshire have shown the proper balance and temper. They are as good, as we saw yesterday, as the Australians at exploiting a bluff. They possess the skill and the character. Would anybody in his senses prefer to see Hardstaff playing for England instead of Leyland, or Barnett instead of Mitchell? For the purposes of the Oval Test match, we need not consider the question of building up a team of young men. Then, granted that much, who would prefer Edrich or Fagg to Sutcliffe?

YORKSHIRE V LANCASHIRE 1938
SCORES

LANCASHIRE

First Innings		Second Innings	
Washbrook, c Wood, b Bowes	15	lbw, b Leyland	30
Paynter, c & b Verity	13	c Robinson, b Bowes	58
Iddon, c Verity, b Robinson	19	c Bowes, b Verity	14
Oldfield, b Robinson	17	c Sutcliffe, b Verity	1
Hopwood, c Leyland, b Bowes	45	c Verity, b Robinson	2
Nutter, c Yardley, b Robinson	6	c Mitchell, b Verity	0
W. R. L. Lister, b Robinson	2	b Robinson	1
Farrimond, lbw, b Robinson	4	c Mitchell, b Verity	2
Pollard, c Sutcliffe, b Verity	9	b Verity	2
Wilkinson, not out	0	not out	0
Rhodes, c & b Bowes	0	b Bowes	4
Extras lb3	3	Extras b5, lb1	6
Total	133	Total	120

YORKSHIRE

First Innings	
Sutcliffe, lbw, b Pollard	61
Mitchell, c Wilkinson, b Nutter	6
P. A. Gibb, lbw, b Wilkinson	78
Barber, lbw, b Rhodes	28
Leyland, b Nutter	135
N. W. D. Yardley, lbw, b Nutter	21
A. B. Sellers, not out	82
Wood, b Nutter	19
Robinson, c Washbrook, b Pollard	4
Verity, c Oldfield, b Nutter	6
Bowes, c Rhodes, b Pollard	1
Extras b6, lb4, nb1	12
Total	453

THE ROSES MATCHES 1919-1939
BOWLING ANALYSIS

Lancashire—First Innings

	O.	M.	R.	W.		O.	M.	R.	W.
Bowes	11	4	15	3	Robinson	26	8	57	5
Yardley	4	1	13	0	Leyland	2	2	0	0
Verity	26	12	45	2					

Second Innings

	O.	M.	R.	W.		O.	M.	R.	W.
Bowes	11	3	27	2	Robinson	15	5	36	2
Yardley	4	1	7	0	Leyland	3	0	12	1
Verity	20	8	21	5	Gibb	2	0	11	0

Yorkshire—First Innings

	O.	M.	R.	W.		O.	M.	R.	W.
Pollard	40	7	129	3	Rhodes	41	13	85	1
Nutter	27	6	68	5	Iddon	11	1	47	0
Wilkinson	32	4	112	1					

YORKSHIRE V LANCASHIRE   1939

May 27/29/30   Old Trafford

FIRST DAY

ON Saturday at Old Trafford Lancashire scored 300 in four and a half hours. They hit eighteen boundaries before lunch and twenty-one after. Nutter threw in a six. The match was against Yorkshire. At one point of this historic day Lancashire were 188 for eight. Then Pollard and Nutter laid about the Yorkshire bowling to the extent of 106 in seventy-five minutes. Lancashire threw away one or two wickets in the great cause of cheering us all up. But the policy of appeasement, as I feared, had no effect on Yorkshire. When they batted they grimly began to fortify their line; no risks were taken, and only 67 were scored in an hour and a quarter. On a perfect wicket they will today march ahead, unless severe measures are taken to resist. We must hope for the best; but I doubt if Lancashire's bowling will be good enough, unless Wilkinson strikes a deadly vein.

The match began on a cool morning with low drifting clouds hiding the sun, which broke through from time to time, making shadows so that the cricketers were followed about by bright light like characters in the ballet. (Bowes at mid-off, indeed, performed at least one pas de seul as he stopped a hit by Paynter). Bowes found the breeze and the atmosphere helpful to his own deadly skill with the new ball and caused much concern to Washbrook, who was lucky not to lose his wicket twice at least in the first half-hour. He snicked an involuntary four through the slips when he was six, and when he was 17 an outswinger skimmed from the edge of an entirely trustful bat and eluded the Yorkshire slips by inches. Bowes also thumped Washbrook's pads, and once there was a muffled appeal by somebody—muffled, I suppose, in accordance with the new non-aggression pact. Bowes was bowling too dangerously not to create trouble; but, such is life, that it was Paynter who became his victim, Paynter, who had just pulled Turner for four with a terrific display of

489

energy. A late swinger, rising from the pitch, forced Paynter to play on at ten minutes past twelve, when Lancashire were thirty-six.

Yardley bowled instead of Turner now, and Washbrook drove him straight and to the off, two vibrant fours in the over. Then Iddon looked at the Yorkshire attack carefully for a few moments, like a mouse inspecting rather sceptically the cheese in a mousetrap; he decided to drive Yardley, but a good stroke was fielded with ineffable grace by Bowes at mid-off. Next ball Iddon drove rather tamely to Yardley's right hand low down; the stroke was precipitate, and Yardley held a clever one-handed 'c and b.'

Lancashire were thus savouring the old trouble once more: 49 for two. But this time the batting was more than spirited enough. These quick advances of Yorkshire were the occasion of much unseemly rejoicing on the part of a number of Yorkshire folk present, disguised in macintoshes as Lancashire folk. Washbrook conquered uncertainty like a man; he drove Bowes for two on-boundaries in three balls, one a contumacious thump into the air—another sign of the times. At this point of the morning more fours happened than Emmott Robinson would have regarded as decent or even moral; Oldfield got one through the slips from an intended drive off Yardley, and in the same over flashed an off-boundary with his left leg across in such dashing style that I nearly warbled that ancient air 'When knights were bold.' Alas and lack-a-day. Washbrook was suddenly lbw as soon as Yardley changed over to give rest to Bowes, who had bowled many beautiful balls. In the comparatively brief space of time of seventy minutes Lancashire scored 73 for three. Washbrook 46. And, bless us, if Hopwood did not bring himself up to date by a four to leg off his second or third ball! The speed of the game made me think of the Scottish parson who in a season of drought offered up prayers for rain, and when floods occurred in the district offered up another prayer saying. 'But, O Lord, but be reasonable!' Another four by Hopwood through the slips brought his total to eleven in three or four minutes.

Oldfield, who opened with three charming leg glances, leaped at Robinson and crashed a drive at the covers, where a

490

four was saved by Mitchell, who threw himself on the earth in violent physical protest. Then Oldfield cut late for four, a hit so war-like that time seemed to turn on its tracks and we were back again at Old Trafford in the Johnny Tyldesley days. Lancashire reached a hundred for three in ninety minutes.

With a view to putting an end to this sort of loose behaviour, Professor Verity came on; Hopwood, without fair warning, ran at him (as they say in these parts) and 'scutched' him for four into the air to the vacant on side. Verity seemed to regard Hopwood reproachfully, as though saying: 'Leonard, I'm surprised at *you*. These modern young people I can understand, and perhaps forgive. They have been corrupted by the pernicious literature of that "Cricketer" person. But you, Leonard, have been brought up differently.'

At a quarter-past one another Lancashire wicket was lost. Oldfield tried a forward push off Yardley and was bowled by a pretty off-break. Lancashire 112 for four—before lunch at that. Hopwood was past praying for; he cut—I am prepared to swear it on 'Wisden,'—he deliberately cut Verity to the square boundary before Oldfield had taken off his pads, and then he jumped out to the last ball of the same over and 'clouted' it for another four. (I regret to have to use these low and common forms of speech, but the cricket left me with no alternative.) In the last over before lunch—bowled by Bowes, mark you—Nutter essayed a six to the on and sent the ball soaring straight up, high as Blackpool Tower. No fields-man could get near. I suggest that the next Lancashire and Yorkshire match be played on Ilkla Moor 'baht 'at. At lunch, after two hours of excellent fun, Lancashire were 130 for four. I suspect that the pavilion did not unanimously approve, though the common herd on the shilling side applauded without shame. Yardley, with three wickets to his credit, probably enjoyed his lunch as much as anybody.

After lunch there was a return to type and sweet reasonableness for a while; Hopwood and Nutter added only twelve in nearly half an hour, and the pavilion seemed happier now that they could feel they were amongst old friends. A straight drive for four by Nutter, off Yardley, was the only questionable proceeding in this period. Then another four to the on, also off Yardley, completed Hopwood's fifty in seventy-five minutes, whereat Verity bowled again, and Hopwood drove him far to the on boundary, swinging his bat like a heathen. Hopwood, I thought, played splendidly: but then I, too, am a heathen suckled in a creed overworn. Verity bowled him at 160, and half of Lancashire's wickets were disposed of by three o'clock.

Verity's first ball to Phillipson turned abruptly and hit a pad, and Verity stifled his appeal, no doubt almost cutting off his tongue. Hutton took part in the attack at 160. His first ball, a full toss, was driven back to him by Nutter, and the chance was missed to the mildly expressed relief of a thoroughly respectable and disinterested, not to say apathetic, crowd—excluding, of course, the aforesaid invading and barbarian Yorkshire folk. Two superb leg hits off Verity by Nutter in one over stirred as much applause as may be heard any afternoon on a lawn tennis court; in this same over Phillipson struck unscientifically across a half-volley and his wicket fell to a merely formal sign of public concern. There was a time when such cricket as Saturday's would have made the welkin ring at Old Trafford. Perhaps after all the crowd would have preferred stone-walling, with Lancashire 100 for one wicket at tea, and that one wicket leg before. Lister was immediately caught on the off side driving under a ball from Robinson, who bowled for Hutton; this disaster made Lancashire 183 for seven, and the sugar had now gone from the pill with a vengeance. In seventy minutes after lunch Lancashire scored only 54 for the loss of three wickets; the effort to clear their character and make amends for the morning's levity was not working well. Therefore Nutter, who played admirably, pulled Robinson's off-break round for a powerful square-leg four.

When Farrimond came in Sellers stood at silly-point and the familiar leg-trap appeared, crouching low as ever. This was old times back again (but not for long). Farrimond endeavoured to break the cordon and was caught at mid-off. Nutter, no doubt anticipating the end on the arrival of Pollard, thumped Robinson to the off for a four, pulled him twice to leg for fours, and cut him perfectly for one, all in five balls—an onslaught which sent Lancashire's total beyond

200, and also sent the leg-trap scampering. He reached his fifty by means of an extremely perilous snick between the wicket-keeper and first slip; still it counted for four. Then he drove Verity for six, to the off, a magnificent blow done with a sudden punch. There is no reason why Nutter should not develop into one of the best batsmen in the country; he has stroke and shrewd defence—both are needed, especially defence, even in Lancashire and Yorkshire matches of the new style. Pollard hit Verity to leg for four, a grand smack, then drove the new ball from Bowes straight for four, then snicked or bisected a good length off his middle stump for one. Another four through the slips off Bowes was one of the few strokes in Nutter's display that did not go from the middle of the bat. The ninth-wicket stand between Pollard and Nutter became the most profitable of the innings, and when the Lancashire total took on a more solid aspect the pavilion condescended to cheer up and show appreciation. They go by results on the pavilion at Old Trafford, and are immune from deeper and more spiritual influences. Lancashire's innings in spite of its waywardness, or rather because of it, was the most enjoyable I have seen them play in this match for many years.

Pollard declined to act as a sort of poor relation of Nutter; he gave proof of an income of his own, and if one or two of his strokes defied immediate analysis his cricket on the whole had an order and discretion most annoying to find in a number ten batsman, if you are a bowler on the other side. This ninth-wicket stand emerged from the stage of last-minute resistance; it ventured forth on its own account; it became independent and acquisitive. It changed the fortunes of the day, cheated Yorkshire at the pinch. Pollard reached a cool, if belligerent fifty, and it was not Pollard but Nutter who got out at 294. Nutter, I fancy, allowed a 'googly' from Hutton to bowl him. Once again Nutter failed to reach a hundred, but he will learn the knack before he is much older, and make a habit of it. Wilkinson followed the fashion and hit a straight four, which sent Lancashire's total to 300, and then Pollard, aiming at some object not located on the field of play or on the premises at all, was decisively bowled. The ovation given him demonstrated that the pavilion had wakened up at last.

There was significance in the fact that before the Yorkshire innings began the lightest of rollers was employed on the wicket; it was like a garden roller and could be pulled one-handed. I did not know that any such obsolete contrivance as this remained in the modern groundsman's armoury. The wicket was so good that it scarcely needed rolling.

Sutcliffe took the first over of Yorkshire's innings from Phillipson and scored a single to leg, and after completing the run put out his hand in the old admonitory way, commanding his partner not to try another run—yet. Yorkshire's attack, apart from Bowes, had looked ordinary, and on the easy wicket neither Phillipson nor Pollard could cause the batsmen to hasten over their strokes. Sutcliffe and Hutton did not depart from traditional usage; runs came sensibly, from strokes executed nose over the ball. Forty-one were scored in three-quarters of an hour, and by this time Wilkinson bowled. His first over called for close scrutiny; soon afterwards he spun one quickly, and Hutton played back late. We heard the ball strike pads; we saw a bail off. But Hutton stood there, obviously under the impression that the ball had rebounded from Farrimond. After a pause, in which a section of the crowd helpfully told the umpires what to do, Hutton was obliged to depart: he had apparently played on. Wilkinson's bowling was remarkably good; he compelled late strokes and anxious strokes. He nearly trapped Mitchell lbw straightway. There is nothing like spin and flight on such a turf as this. Towards the end of the day the sun shone, and brought out Sutcliffe's halo again. His batting wore an ominous appearance; a good ball will be needed today to prevent him from making a hundred.

SECOND DAY

Yorkshire ruthlessly went their way of conquest yesterday at Old Trafford. The opportunity presented by a flawless wicket was grasped with the iron hand. A Siegfried line was built by Sutcliffe and Mitchell; no risks were taken, no nonsense about throwing wickets away to make the crowd happy. In two hours before lunch Sutcliffe and Mitchell added 101; in two hours between lunch and tea they added another 161, and were still not out. Three wickets then fell in two overs, including Mitchell's and Sutcliffe's. Nature's law of compensation is merciful. But to watch Yorkshire (with Mitchell) for four hours at Old Trafford at Whitsun and no wickets—it needed a strong stomach.

The Lancashire attack, as I feared, proved more or less harmless. Wilkinson was disappointing; he is, I suspect, bowling a shade faster this year than last year, and as a consequence both his flight and his spin tend to suffer. Phillipson, Pollard, and Nutter toiled hard, but the more Lister rang the changes on their attack the more it remained the same honest-to-goodness but ineffectual thing. The large crowd had come into the sunshine with appetites stimulated by Saturday's cocktails. They were like prisoners who are given just a glimpse of blue sky and a free world; far better that Saturday's promise had never been made on a freer Lancashire and Yorkshire match! I can never understand why, during a long partnership on an easy pitch, somebody is not asked to bowl comic stuff, donkey-drops, or even grubs. Anything rather than the old routine up and down slavery hour after hour.

In the first over of the day, bowled by Phillipson, a ball—the only ball all day!—reared suddenly and struck Sutcliffe in or near the diaphragm. This was an act of deceit on the part of a wicket which was so beautiful that on Saturday Sellers had feared to spoil its complexion by using anything but the gentlest roller. The Lancashire players surrounded Sutcliffe to attend (such is the modern etiquette) to his bruise; but he waved them aside as though saying: 'It is all right. The Sutcliffes do not recognise pain.' But he was not for a while his own lordly self; he was unable to cope with two no-balls from Phillipson, and he missed hitting a long-hop from Wilkinson as severely as he intended.

Phillipson, with the new ball, obtained pace from the ground; it is a high compliment to say of a quick bowler that a batsman is unable to take liberties even with his no-balls. Mitchell drove a four off Wilkinson's first over, a stylish hit in front of point; I was not prepared, even in these degenerate days, to see Mitchell hitting boundaries at 25 minutes to twelve on a Whitsun Bank Holiday. He was wearing his cap with the peak as usual over his ear, which is his usual way of disguising himself as an aggressive fellow; but we have been misled too often in the past by that ruse; we know our Mitchell by now, and when he dug himself in and scored only 16 in an hour and ten minutes (including the aforesaid boundary) we knew who he really was and where we really were, at last.

Sutcliffe reached his fifty at ten minutes past twelve, then snicked another no-ball off his leg-stump, and frowned at the hiatus: 'We are not at our best this morning and we are not amused.' Wilkinson's length wavered considerably; Sutcliffe drove a full toss for four, or rather he leaned upon it, disdaining a show of vulgar acquisitiveness. 'We have not come to that yet. We have our family pride.' He was magnificent; he reclined on his bat and, as ever, surveyed the proceedings, cross-legged. Twenty years ago he played in his first Lancashire and Yorkshire match at Old Trafford, and he looks much the same as he did then, except for a hint of the spread of middle-age. He has rewritten pages of 'Wisden' and made them pages of 'Debretts.' Not since the days of the Hon. F. S. Jackson have these matches of the hoi polloi, these Lancashire and Yorkshire matches, known such an air of hauteur and privilege as Sutcliffe's; he is more royal than royalty.

When he was sixty-five he chopped a ball from Pollard off his stumps, and in the same over, a beautiful length beat him and nearly put an end to his innings. He was not disturbed; possibly he said, 'Well bowled.' A hint of ironic applause greeted a push for a single by Mitchell; the match was recovering dignity after Saturday's exhibition of bad taste. A capital over from Nutter troubled the poise of Sutcliffe further, but at the end of it he was to be seen examining his bat with the care of a connoisseur of fiddles examining a Strad.

At ten minutes to one the green light shone in Mitchell's mind and he hit two vigorous fours from an over by Nutter. Mitchell had in eighty minutes succeeded in scoring not more than twenty or so; next over he thrust his left leg across and drove Pollard for another four, a stroke of rare ease, power, and style. I like Mitchell; I like even his wilfulness—his 'nowtiness,' as they say in these parts. He is a character, a player who can hit like a mule and be as obstinate as a mule. He reached fifty today after his innings had lasted some two hours, and by this time the cap was more over the ear than ever. At lunch Yorkshire had reached 168 for one wicket—Sutcliffe 85, Mitchell 64—and resignation came over the crowd like a miasma. 'Why don't they hit out?' asked a disillusioned voice, meaning, of course, 'Why don't they get out?'

After the interval the crowd made a good sight. The sun shone from a blue sky; to sit in it was no doubt warm and pleasant. In the refrigerator of the press box we huddled in our overcoats, the sun never shines on the press box at Old Trafford. If these notes occasionally reveal gaps or lacunae, the explanation is that I have found it necessary to leave my post of observation to restore the circulation of the blood. Last year I took a hundred wickets for Lancashire by withdrawing my attention from the field of play; a wicket usually falls as soon as I turn my back. But yesterday I could no more break the Sutcliffe-Mitchell partnership than the Lancashire bowlers could, much as I lurked behind the pavilion and pretended to be absorbed in the tulips.

At half-past two Sutcliffe reached the century which I knew on Saturday he had an appointment with; even though he was not in his best form technically, obviously it was his pleasure and decree to score a century. That is usually enough for Sutcliffe; he does well in big matches by reason of some mysterious prerogative or divine right. 'We do not work for *our* centuries. We are not in Trade. We inherit them.'

Pollard and Phillipson seized the new ball at 200, with hope springing eternal. They caressed the shiny leather, pressed it to their loins, as though it contained the source of life. Sutcliffe promptly hooked Pollard as majestically as once, of old, he hooked Macdonald on a Saturday evening. The perfect wicket called for Macdonald's lithe strength, his power to bounce a batsman out of his senses. Poor Mac—was his shade present in yesterday's sunlight? It seems but recently that we looked on him, saw him running over the grass silently and gracefully, or saw him, dispossessed and indifferent, standing at mid-off.

When Yorkshire were 203 for one a slip chance was brilliantly held by Washbrook off Phillipson, sent by Mitchell; but there was a catch in it—or rather no catch—because the umpire had called a no-ball. Sheer waste and irony—in view of Lancashire's general inability to hold slip catches of any kind this year. 'Barracking' broke out with the old agony in it at three o'clock; the trouble, of course, was Mitchell, who has spoiled more than one Bank Holiday at Old Trafford in the past—I gave myself up to the worst when he hit that four at twenty-five minutes to twelve. A man in the crowd grew so agitated that he emerged from private to public speech. Apparently he was talking to himself, but passion magnified his utterance until it involved an audience. He apostrophised Mitchell—'this so-and-so Mitchell, 'e comes here every so-and-so year, so-and-so him, so-and-so poking about.' Then he directed his wrath on the sight-screens, and without justice made Mitchell responsible for them, without pointing out with sufficient clarity what the sightscreens had done. He was in that state in which all the miseries of life must be related to one cause that a man can get at. 'Every so-and-so year 'e comes here, this so-and-so Mitchell'—as though Mitchell came of his own personal intent and will, and not as a member of the Yorkshire team fulfilling an annual engagement. 'To 'ell with 'im, that's what I say.' He was terribly upset and would have been much happier at his work. The cup flowed over when Mitchell was clean bowled by Pollard. The angry man roared fiercely. But it was another no-ball. I have seldom seen a man so beside himself as this desperate man was now. He departed, was lost in the crowd. Probably he went home unappeasable. 'No—I won't want any food. Take it away. No—and I'm not goin' t' pictures either. That so-and-so Mitchell, every year he comes, so-and-so him.'

The deadly rhythm of the afternoon, the ruthless pendulum of the forward push, apparently got on Sutcliffe's mind; he drove Pollard straight, and hit Nutter so high that Oldfield lost his cap running after the ball and looking up at it until he risked a crick in the neck. In the same over Sutcliffe sent a drive crashing straight into the people sitting on the grass near the Stretford screen. The partnership at this point had made 200, and there seemed no way of ending or destroying it. A dazzling, indeed frenzied, attempt by Farrimond to stump Mitchell off Nutter awoke thousands of perishing hopes, but Mitchell got his foot back in time, and next ball he hit terrifically to the on, a stroke of almost sardonic rhetoric, to goad the crowd more and more.

Mitchell, completed his hundred after four hours or so's (or so-and-so's) of grim imperturbability, lighted by humour for those with eyes to see it. 'Put Paynter on,' somebody howled. 'Put 't roller on,' responded somebody else, not as much in purgatory. A colossal six by Mitchell off Wilkinson rubbed the wound of the afternoon with salt. A high, hard return by Sutcliffe, when he was 144 and Yorkshire 292, was stopped by Wilkinson and nearly caught—another sling and arrow. The crowd would have preferred a four that did not flatter or deceive. Again did Mitchell swing his shoulders to Wilkinson, and sent a six heaving over the on-side boundary, nearly dropping it crash into the collection canvas for Farrimond's benefit, and nearly interrupting (but not quite) the flow of Cecil Parker's eloquence.

During the tea interval a man attempted to introduce variety into the afternoon by announcing gifts for second-sight. He undertook to tell the crowd where and when their parents were born, and what days their birthdays fell on; he rose to his theme and ventured into cosmic matters. 'Give me a date,' he exhorted, 'any date in history. I'll tell you. Any event.' And a worn-out voice asked: 'When'll this ——— Mitchell get out?'

Mitchell got out in the first over after tea, caught at forward leg. The crowd was so stupefied that they did not roar. In the same over Yardley skied, trying a pull, and Nutter, the bowler, caught him. Next over Sutcliffe, aiming at the sightscreen, was bowled all over the wickets. This time the crowd expressed themselves to some tune or noise. Yorkshire 329 for one; Yorkshire 329 for four. 'A bit late in t' day,' said a voice; 'but it's better than nowt.' Sutcliffe and Mitchell held the second wicket for four and a half hours. Sutcliffe batted for nearly five and a half hours and was interesting all the time, whether below form or, towards the end, reminiscent of his best. Neither Sutcliffe nor Mitchell gave the Lancashire attack more than a glimpse of a mortal proneness to error.

The Lancashire bowlers stuck gamely to a disheartening job, but, as I say, a certain humorous relief might have helped. Sir John Squire once had to deal with two obstinate batsmen in a club match. He decided to bowl himself, and he cannot bowl, anyhow. But the two batsmen collided trying for a fifth run off Sir John's attack, and one of them had to be carried off the field. Sir John was extremely proud. 'I bowled for it,' he claimed. Barber and Turner, by methods strictly utilitarian, took Yorkshire's score to 393; Turner was caught from an edged stroke, and then Paynter nearly ran Sellers out from long-leg by an agile throw. Wilkinson bowled Barber with a 'googly' at 395.

Six wickets were down now and Yorkshire no more than 95 ahead, after all. But the Lancashire bowling was tiring or tired, and Wood is a grand hitter against all but the liveliest attack. He laid about him prodigiously and thumped four after four. He is so spaciously a Yorkshireman that he would be easily recognised at sight as a Yorkshireman if he were met in any bazaar of the Orient, or in the swamps at the source of the Amazon. He knocked Lancashire out flat, enjoyed himself, and, such is nature in him, communicated some of his enjoyment to the long-suffering crowd.

THIRD DAY

Lancashire collapsed badly at Old Trafford yesterday and were beaten at twenty minutes to four by an innings and 43 runs. The lunch score promised a fight, for Lancashire were then 124 for two, with Paynter and Oldfield in the high tide of a militant stand which began after Washbrook and Hopwood had fallen for 28. Bowes bowled his best, giving a remarkable exhibition of conserved energy. The pitch perhaps deteriorated a shade; at any rate, several balls kept abominably low. I am sorry that Lancashire lost; their spirit on Saturday deserved a better fate. One or two batsmen yesterday seemed undecided whether to attack or to defend; Paynter, Nutter, and Washbrook each got out aiming at or beyond the boundary. Lancashire supporters must not be too hard on the team; Yorkshire were easily the stronger combination, even if their attack, on the good wicket, depended heavily on Bowes. But something should be done at once to add variety to Lancashire's bowling and to strengthen the batting after the fall of the first or second wicket.

Sellers, of course, declared Yorkshire's innings closed straightway, and Lancashire began the task of saving the game at eleven o'clock on a delicious morning, with the gentle breeze mercifully blowing the smoke of Trafford Park the other way. The ground was more or less vacant after Monday's tumult, and would have been peaceful but for the continuous shouting of the hawkers selling, or trying to sell, chocolates, pastilles, and what not. They made the noise of the Caledonian Market. On a morning when the crowd is small, is it necessary that they should so raucously call attention to their wares? We can see them, we are not blind, and, let them be told, not deaf.

Bowes at once commanded respect by his clever and vital use of the new ball; but Lancashire's first wicket was lost impetuously. Washbrook hit a short ball from Turner square, freely, and in grand style. On most cricket fields the stroke would have been a fairly safe four. Hutton caught the excellent hit beautifully, in front of the pavilion, and Washbrook departed in sorrow. It was no doubt a careless way to get out at the beginning of a day in which Lancashire's main job was to give away nothing, to fight and defend every inch of ground. Hopwood was sent in next instead of Iddon, and this time he got down on his bat in the old way. Gone the jousting and tourney of Saturday; he was now armed for defence. Paynter, too, subjected every ball to close and suspicious scrutiny, yet from time to time he threatened to dislocate his shoulder blades in onslaughts on loose balls to leg. A superb maiden over by Bowes was applauded— presumably by Yorkshire folk who on Monday might have missed their trains home, after due celebration of the Mitchell-Sutcliffe non-aggression pact.

Hopwood for half an hour or so helped Paynter to hold the fort; then he tried to cut a ball which rose and swung viciously; it was, I think, a stroke forced on Hopwood by that extraordinary and last-second power which Bowes sometimes can impart to a ball on the best wicket. Hopwood's snick was caught gloriously by Verity, who flung himself backwards full-stretch in the slips, then got up calmly and assumed his usual mien of one who is present yet somehow not amongst us.

A spiteful ball from Bowes (whose spectacles belie him) doubled up Paynter for a while. In the same over another ball of Bowes's flashed from the pitch and struck Paynter on the hand. A section of the crowd shouted 'Tek 'im off,' but Paynter did not join in. Bowes bowled a fair length, and his attack on the perfect wicket was admirable. He alone could get life out of it. 'Tek 'im off,' said those folk whose memories were obviously so short that they had forgotten the great fast bowlers of yesteryear—Macdonald, for example. The way people work themselves up at Lancashire and Yorkshire matches is enough to make the pavilion cat laugh. (By the way, there is no pavilion cat at Old Trafford; cannot somebody oblige and lend one for the season, a Cheshire cat for preference, a neutral cat?)

Oldfield batted delightfully, and executed several thoroughly safe and brilliant late cuts. When Bowes was rested he was applauded for more than an hour's good work; Paynter bore the brunt of it, and stopped many a nasty ball, either with his bat or his wonderfully Lancastrian person, which apparently is made of sandbags, bolts and nuts, and pieces of old iron. Verity came on for Bowes, measuring his run with austere and mathematical exactitude; the umpires should be in a position to provide him with compass, spirit-level, chalk and a blackboard, and a cane to rap the knuckles of inattentive batsmen.

Oldfield's innings went from brilliance to brilliance, and he was discreet all the time. This was the Johnny Tyldesley touch, the Johnny Tyldesley way of saving a match; the good ball was respected, the bad one mercilessly chastised. He hit Robinson for three fours from consecutive balls, then was nearly caught on the off side off Robinson, but Yardley could only take the ball on the half-volley—another Johnny Tyldesley touch. Oldfield then jumped out to Robinson and made full tosses of two successive balls and crashed them to the on boundary; the next ball he glanced exquisitely for four to leg. He passed Paynter's score, reached fifty in quick time, and at lunch was not out 61, to Paynter's 54. Lancashire were, as I have said, 124 for two, and good digestion probably waited on appetite.

After lunch, Bowes bowled at the Manchester end, and Oldfield lay back and punched a slightly short ball straight for four; the next one kept low and beat him and ruined his wickets. Oldfield, third out at 131, played an innings which in the grave situation dressed responsibility in most attractive colours. Iddon came in at the crisis of the match to face an encouraged and refreshed quick and dangerous bowler, for the hostile attack of Bowes seemed to have little relation to his slow, painful way of walking and running; nature apparently tied Bowes together loosely with string, and at any minute he threatens to fall to bits, a leg here, an arm there, a boot somewhere else. Iddon smelt at a ball from Verity, like a man looking for an escape of gas, and was nearly caught at first slip.

Bowes thumped Paynter's body again, and Paynter, having rubbed the spot, came up again imperturbably; he is like one of those Aunt Sallys you hit on the head in a fair; it sways backwards, and then, just as you are holding out your hand for the coconut, comes up again, and you get nothing. Paynter was not to be moved for hours, or taken in by any of Verity's cajolery, or by the camouflaged battering-ram of Bowes. He batted according to his own science, feet mixed up, sometimes both off the ground; but bat always there, and his whole being, mind, body and guts saying: 'Get me out if tha can. Here's mi bat; there's t' wickets; and here's me.' Iddon tried the temperature of the waters with his big toe, then decided to plunge, and he drove Verity for four to the on, and looked a better man for it. He was caught at the wicket a moment later, off Bowes, from a ball that flashed up at a rare speed. Iddon hung out his bat, hoping for the best no doubt. Lancashire 143 for four—'That's torn it,' said a voice unfeelingly. And in the next over 'torn' the match indeed was; Paynter attempted to hook a ball on the rise, skied his stroke, and was easily caught at short square leg. His heroic and contumacious innings lasted three hours and ten minutes. Bowes tried Phillipson with a slow ball, using his spectacles intellectually; I imagine he got it from

Verity—chapter xxi, Book II. He is the most difficult bowler in England on a good wicket when he relies on a pace not above fast-medium.

Nutter audaciously pulled Bowes, and a magnificent hit he somehow made off a good if short ball; but he, like Washbrook, was caught at deep square leg. This disaster occurred at ten minutes past three; a moment afterwards Farrimond was bowled by a rank 'shooter.' For the rest apply to the scorers for full particulars. This was Yorkshire's third victory over Lancashire in three consecutive matches. Saturday's bright dawn flattered to deceive.

SCORES

LANCASHIRE

First Innings		Second Innings	
Washbrook, lbw, b Yardley	46	c Hutton, b Turner	1
Paynter, b Bowes	13	c Sellers, b Bowes	60
Iddon, c & b Yardley	1	c Wood, b Bowes	9
Oldfield, b Yardley	27	b Bowes	66
Hopwood, b Verity	54	c Verity, b Bowes	2
Nutter, b Hutton	85	c Hutton, b Bowes	6
Phillipson, b Verity	7	c Turner, b Verity	2
W. H. L. Lister, c Hutton, b Robinson	0	b Verity	3
Farrimond, c Barber, b Verity	1	lbw, b Bowes	8
Pollard, b Robinson	54	not out	9
Wilkinson, not out	4	c Wood, b Hutton	12
Extras b 1, lb 7	8	Extras b 6, lb 1	7
Total	300	Total	185

YORKSHIRE V LANCASHIRE 1939

YORKSHIRE

First Innings

Sutcliffe, b Phillipson	165
Hutton, b Wilkinson	13
Mitchell, c Phillipson, b Nutter	136
N. W. D. Yardley, b Nutter	0
Barber, b Wilkinson	34
Turner, c Pollard, b Nutter	29
A. B. Sellers, not out	53
Wood, b Wilkinson	65
Robinson, c Nutter, b Wilkinson	11
Verity, not out	0
Extras b 6, lb 11, nb 5	22
	—
Total (for 8)	*528

*Innings declared.

BOWLING ANALYSIS

LANCASHIRE—First Innings

	O.	M.	R.	W.		O.	M.	R.	W.
Bowes	22	4	75	1	Robinson	9	0	55	2
Turner	9	1	22	0	Verity	15	4	69	3
Yardley	15	3	52	3	Hutton	5	0	19	1

Second Innings

	O.	M.	R.	W.		O.	M.	R.	W.
Bowes	19	2	43	6	Robinson	8	0	37	0
Turner	7	5	12	1	Verity	17	4	37	2
Yardley	5	0	14	0	Hutton	4	0	35	1

YORKSHIRE—First Innings

	O.	M.	R.	W.		O.	M.	R.	W.
Phillipson	30	3	128	1	Wilkinson	36	2	168	4
Pollard	23	3	103	0	Iddon	6	0	19	0
Nutter	25	4	88	3					

YORKSHIRE V LANCASHIRE   1939

August 5/7/8   Leeds

FIRST DAY

THE day was generally cold and gloomy, but during the present summer we must not be pedantic, it is enough to say that the weather was fine for a while. On a slow wicket Lancashire with good fortune won the toss, then proceeded to make not a single run more than 54 for one wicket in two hours before lunch. Presumably the batsmen were waiting for the ball to do its work viciously before assailing it with violent methods.

It is hazardous to search the psychology or brain-centres of cricketers for light on their conduct; for instance, Paynter, though clearly resolved that on this occasion at any rate there was going to be no nonsense about boundaries or decadent cricket of the like, though this resolution was writ plain on his face and demeanour, none the less he did hit or commit four boundaries, then got out at one o'clock trying to cut a rising ball from Robinson which, of course, was going away from his bat. Paynter's stroke slashed wildly and he succumbed to a catch at the wicket. It was the kind of stroke a cricketer attempts after he has passed a century on a fast turf in dazzling sunshine. I imagine the stroke occurred without consent of Paynter's intellect; most likely the fell cause of it was some sudden spurt of atavistic blood, throw-back to primitive habits acquired long ago in cricket matches.

A man can never be sure of himself, heaven help us all. No matter how much we may seek to civilise our impulses the beast that is ancestral in us waits its chance and betrays us. Even years of Lancashire and Yorkshire matches have failed to evolve a truly well-bred batsman, the one that can stay in for hours and not hit a four of any sort. Washbrook actually performed one or two square cuts until the occasion dawned on him; he pulled himself together, and when, after lunch, Robinson bowled him, his innings had lasted two and a quarter hours for thirty.

Hopwood who, of course, is not unaccustomed to public appearances in these festival engagements, compiled eight in an hour ritualistically, then turned an off-break from Robinson round to short-leg's hands like a good, honest servitor doing what was expected of him at the right moment. Thus in 150 minutes Lancashire arrived at the total of 65 for three. What is more, the pitch was now taking Robinson's spin rather quickly. Everything had been done that could politely be done to lose the match already; the batting before the turf became at all active was, even for Lancashire against Yorkshire, too stately for words. But this is to take pompously an annual practice or custom which for a lifetime Lancashire have indulged in on Bank Holiday.

The smallest crowd yet witnessed at these matches sat in silence until the wickets began to fall; near the pavilion a poster blazened forth a clarion call, 'Wake up, Citizens of Leeds.' I cannot say whether the poster was erected before or after Lancashire had won the toss. At three o'clock Robinson was threatening to spin an off-break with something of Ted Wainwright's enormity. Verity came on too, and Sellers called up his bloodhounds. And it was now at this intimidatory moment that Oldfield flashed light colour and a flexible steel sort of skill into the parlous innings of his county; he waited prettily on bent knees for one of Robinson's off-breaks which did not break and cut late with a sprightly snap; he drove Robinson to the off by means of an anachronistic cover-drive as refreshing as the sight of distant green country on a modern motor road.

Iddon defended soberly and attended to the spots or blemishes on the pitch, but Oldfield pulled Robinson for another four, whereat Iddon emulated the stroke when Leyland bowled instead of Verity, who apparently could not work out in practice some eternal inner truth or principle, so he crossed over to the pavilion end, where it was darker. The sun, mercifully for Lancashire, withdrew a threat of appearing in the sky naked and unashamed. Iddon thumped Leyland for an off-boundary and sent the Lancashire score beyond a hundred at half-past three. Iddon pulled a long hop in the same over for another four; at last Lancashire were catching a glimpse of the fact that the Yorkshiremen are really kindly human beings who would not hurt a fly and love to chase a good stroke over the field, even a stroke of deceitful suddenness by a Lancashire man. Bowes set in pursuit of such a stroke struck to the on by Iddon; he got off the mark well with a strong, if high, knee-action, then seemed to think better of it; at any rate, he left it to the fielder covering him.

The sky clouded, and no doubt the wicket lost whatever of appetite the fleeting sunshine of three o'clock stimulated. Hutton was asked to bowl, and Leyland succeeded Verity at the pavilion end. Iddon, now playing serenely, drove Leyland straight for four; Leyland is a natural left-handed bowler who has not entirely given his mind to the job; his attack is potential of anything from spin and long hops to broad humour. Oldfield and Iddon added 68 inestimable runs. I thought during this period that Sellers gave Robinson too long a rest; no other bowler was able to obtain from the sluggish grass as much life as Robinson always could. As soon as he returned to the attack he spun an off-break which Iddon was obliged to hand on to Sellers in the leg-trap.

Then, when Lancashire were 133 for four, bad light stopped play; cold wind in the small of the back had put the present writer out of action some short time earlier in the proceedings. I visited a refreshment bar, underground near the bowels of the earth, a cellar or catacomb where, when I asked for a teaspoon for my cup of tea, a voice said, 'There it is—on t' string.' And there indeed it was; tied or secured to the premises.

Though the light and the temperature were not perceptibly alleviated the match went forward at half-past four; the north wind possessed teeth and used them unmercifully. Personally I prefer a wet summer. Oldfield defied the circumstances; from the charm and animation of his innings a momentary illusion of warmth and loveliness of scene was created. The innings was a mirage not in a hot desert but on a blasted heath. Oldfield drove Bowes for three to the off, running into the hit so quickly and instinctively that it was hard to say where footwork ended and actual stroke mechanism began. At the height and bloom of his game he was compelled to retire, seized by cramp in the left hand. Farrimond, the next man in, shovelled Robinson to square-leg for a single, a stroke more in keeping with the occasion than any of Oldfield's elegances, which, seen at Leeds on a day of this order, were like ortolans served with pork pies and pickled onions.

A chorus of voices barracked Farrimond, and when bad light and rain stopped play again the voices barracked not only Farrimond but everybody. The torment was in these voices; torment, indeed, is the life and soul of the party at any Lancashire and Yorkshire match. At twenty minutes to six the players ventured forth again, and at the end of the first over Sellers took the ball, which was wet, and spent the whole of the time his team occupied changing over in screwing it round and round in his hands to dry it; he looked as though he were winding it up.

Farrimond did not make many runs, but he obstructed the match usefully for half an hour, got in the way of Wood and a fair sight of the ball, and caused the crowd to suffer and groan. In other words, he contributed his share to the afternoon. He was out at 163, and Oldfield now came back, to the open disgust of a man in the shilling seats. Phillipson, like Farrimond, preferred obstructive methods; I thought he might with advantage to his side have tried to get runs while the ball was slippery. But, again like Farrimond, Phillipson had the satisfaction of knowing he had helped to spoil the holidays already for many folk.

SECOND DAY

Lancashire's long and slow innings received justification by results this afternoon: first-innings points in these matches are not to be despised. In days of old Lancashire batsmen have martyred themselves for as much. Lancashire conveniently arranged to get Yorkshire on a drying and unfriendly wicket, and superb fielding backed up some opportune bowling. But winning the toss in this match should have meant winning the match outright: at any rate, the risk of losing it should have been rendered negligible when Lancashire batted first on a dead, easy wicket. What is to come tomorrow is still unsure.

For an hour at the beginning of the day Yorkshire used all their arts of suggestion towards creating the illusion of a difficult wicket. After Saturday evening's rain the ground was heavy and lifeless for an hour or two, but Lancashire played the game—that is to say, they aided and abetted Sellers so that a stranger to these matches would have sworn that mischief lurked in every blade of grass and that Robinson and Verity were spinning the ball terribly.

It was Lancashire indeed, who really prompted Sellers to put forth the familiar spellbinder, for when Verity first went on shortly after half-past eleven Sellers set an open field with only one slip: everybody else stood fairly deep and Wood had nobody to talk to. But Oldfield and Phillipson on principle declined to go for runs while the pitch remained comfortable: Sellers therefore surrounded the batsmen, threatening suffocation. And Verity, by somehow causing two balls to jump sharply, clinched the situation, the general and good old-fashioned bluff.

When Yorkshire took the field Leyland did not accompany the others to the middle, but stood just within the playing premises at third man; he squared his shoulders, took in a quantity of air, and looked like an able-bodied seaman in his short-sleeved sweater. He experienced a busy half-hour; he seemed to pop up in different and distant parts of the field, port and starboard.

In an hour Lancashire added only 27, in spite of two threes from consecutive balls by Robinson, whose length more than once placed temptation before Oldfield and Phillipson shamefully. Verity tried over-the-wicket blandishments and after Lancashire reached 200 in six hours he received from the turf material confirmation of his inductions. He turned his break abruptly, and Phillipson, without knowing it, sent a catch to Mitchell in the slips, pure cause and effect. Lancashire now lost four wickets for 17, including that of Oldfield, whose innings was one of the most skilful he has ever given us. The style concealed the slow grimness of the purpose behind it: Oldfield batted four hours for his 77, and must have permitted many loose balls to pass unpunished according to plan, policy, or custom—I cannot say which.

Oldfield and Phillipson scored 37 together in eighty-five minutes while the wicket was at its easiest and while sawdust was liberally sprawled about to enable the bowlers to maintain some show of perpendicularity. This morning Verity bowled 15 eight-ball overs, eight maidens, for 13 runs and four wickets. I saw Bobby Peel watching the match, and I thought there was an expression of some slight perplexity in his face; maybe he has not yet brought himself up to date with the new rules of the Lancashire and Yorkshire match. There was a period when a team batting first on a slow wicket tried to score rapidly before the conditions became helpful to the bowler, but other times other manners, or, as Mr. Agate would say, autres temps, autres mœurs. I inferred that Lancashire were more concerned to keep Yorkshire off the slow wicket than to get runs themselves while they were on it.

When Yorkshire went in two overs before lunch the match really began for the crowd of more than twenty thousand: everybody woke up, spoke at once, and pandemonium yelped and howled when 14 runs were hit in these two overs and Mitchell edged a ball perilously over the slips and somebody gave Yorkshire a present of an overthrow! Something for nothing is grand business at Leeds on Bank Holiday.

After lunch Garlick bowled splendid and most unpleasant inswingers: to the horror of the multitude Hutton was seen to be in trouble. To universal amazement and sorrow, Garlick overwhelmed Hutton, beat his bat as he played back, and hit the stumps via pad or pads. Thus Yorkshire lost a great player with only 21 runs scored, and there was no Sutcliffe to reassure the people. Yorkshire without Sutcliffe on August Bank Holiday is the heavens without the sun, the throne-room without his Majesty, 'Hamlet' without the touch of Shakespeare—mere Holinshed.

The turf grew quicker: the batsmen needed to make haste and watch hard and well. The crowd's preliminary noises which had been anticipatory of familiar good things changed to a silence which stirred me to compassion. Bless us all, if Lancashire did not now look on top! A ball from Pollard rose up at Barber and Higson came forward and stood under Barber's nose at silly point, usurping Sellers's office or prerogative. I almost expected to see Sellers appearing on the balcony delivering a protest: 'I say, what's all this? We are Yorkshire, not you, Higson.'

Higson set a field as close and as aggressive as any ever seen even at Leeds. I was surprised that Mitchell, by sheer force of habit, did not fling down his bat and join the encircling Lancashire leg-trap. Garlick beat Barber and Mitchell with successive balls, and each time the non-striker was obliged to inform the striker (or struck) where the ball had gone. Garlick used the drying wicket beautifully: he was nearly unplayable about now and was countered only by skill and experience. Brocklebank came on for Pollard at thirty-seven, and, though he turned his leg-break viciously once, he dropped short of a length and Barber pulled him ferociously.

The Yorkshire temperature was lightening a little; then suddenly a remarkable catch disposed of Mitchell, who hit Garlick smack in the middle of the bat to short-leg, where Pollard made immense ground and held the ball left-handed to the stupefaction of thousands. Harangues and feuds broke out in the crowd, or rather they were aggravated: they were really in evidence all day. Garlick beat Leyland twice in the first over he swung at him away from his bat. The last ball of the same over struck Leyland's pads and Leyland could employ no definite stroke. It was nearly a case of immobile and impassive leg before wicket.

Garlick's luck was atrocious: in an hour after lunch he might easily have broken the back of the Yorkshire innings; his in-swinger whipped off the ground at a length difficult to cope with. A lovely leg-break confounded Leyland when he was four: Farrimond might have stumped him and thus given Brocklebank a distinguished first wicket in his first Lancashire and Yorkshire match. Though the clouds hid the sun the pitch increased in nastiness, and Leyland was missed at square-leg by Brocklebank off Garlick: this was a lamentable error and one's heart went out to the suffering fieldsman.

After an hour and a quarter's superlative bowling Garlick required a rest: by the iniquity of life he had taken two and not five wickets at least. Incredibly, Yorkshire arrived at a hundred and only two men out: then some poetic justice came the way of Lancashire, for Leyland was cleverly held at fine short-leg off Phillipson. Barber was 41 not out, and it was Barber who by strong and accurate play had weathered a dangerous sea for his county. He alone put a sure bat to the ball while his companions endured torments on the edge of precipices. Barber hit Brocklebank twice in an over for fours from short balls which were gifts of gold in the circumstances. Turner stopped a ball from Phillipson with his legs and lost the ball in his pads and gave his mind to releasing it by lawful methods: he might as well have used his hands, for the umpire was giving him out leg-before while his, Turner's, attention was wandering.

Yorkshire now were 110 for four, which was flattering to them and not fair: at the end of the wicket opposite to Barber life had hung on a thread. After tea Hopwood endeavoured to make good Lancashire's dire need of a left-handed slow bowler. The next wicket fell deservedly to Garlick, and his man was Barber, who drove precipitately at a ball which hung and was easily caught at long-on. For two hours Barber played natural-born Yorkshire cricket, vigilant yet aggressive.

Sellers met Barber on the way back to the pavilion where, by the way, a deputation of small, very small, boys waited for Barber. Sellers was clearly in a hurry to make sure of first-innings points before launching his attack on the match outright—Lebensraum so to say. Higson occupied silly mid-off for Sellers, and Sellers beckoned to him to come in a little closer, then pushed a ball from Hopwood within a yard of Higson.

Hopwood now and again hinted of the trouble which would have afflicted Yorkshire had Harry Dean been playing for Lancashire. A cross-bat heave ended Yardley's innings, which was another overdue wicket for Garlick. With six out for 134 Yorkshire seemed to be counting their chickens too soon. And here at five o'clock precisely Wood was caught at first slip incredibly by Pollard, who threw himself, all of himself, sideways and one-handed gripped a ball which flew off the top of the bat from a spinner by Hopwood. And Hopwood's next ball squatted and bowled Robinson.

Verity's opportunity to look personally into the nature of the pitch was excellent: he saw with a suitably inscrutable smile his captain bowled by Hopwood by another ball that did not rise an inch from the ground on pitching. Hopwood was enjoying a revival or renaissance as a bowler on a wicket fit to make Bobby Peel's old fingers itch again. The end of the Yorkshire innings consoled the crowd for the many frustrations of the afternoon. Bowes, who is adored in Yorkshire, played an innings of classic, not to say Attic, ease and grace. He hit Hopwood for a haughty six, and all the small boys went mad and crowed like cocks, because they regard Bowes as one of themselves: they believe that his pockets are stuffed with catapults and bull's-eyes. Bowes was not out 15 when Pollard knocked Verity's off-stump sideways, and over the field the small boys raced from the remotest parts to cheer the hero and see him so that they could tell all their small boy friends who were not there that they had seen him as near to me as you are.

Lancashire's second innings began tranquilly at a quarter to six, and, though Bowes was at once taken off for Verity, new ball despite, Paynter and Washbrook played like untroubled men until ten minutes from close of play a quicker low one by Verity entirely demolished Washbrook. Twenty-six thousand people enjoyed the cricket in their various ways, and there was no rain, not a drop.

THIRD DAY

As I feared yesterday, Lancashire lost this match. But there is no call for tears on their behalf. They went down with honour, beaten by superlative bowling by Robinson and by an innings of Hutton which will be talked of for as long as these famous matches are played. The winning hit was made from a missed and difficult chance: three minutes later the Headingley field was flooded. Had the catch been held there would have been no more play, and Yorkshire, one short of victory, would have been cheated.

I have seldom seen a day of grander cricket: let me as the rivers run over the field try to tell the story of it.

Five runs were scored from the morning's first over from Verity; then Robinson spun prodigiously at Hopwood and byes for easy singles were not taken, the policy being, of course, to keep Paynter away from off-breaks, which are always at their deadliest when whipping away from a left-handed batsman. In Robinson's second over the most vicious and most beautifully pitched off-break bowled Hopwood all the way; it drew him forward and came from the ground at a forked lightning angle that flashed the ball to the top of the stumps.

On this quicker pitch Robinson looked a terrifying bowler, but Paynter pulled him for four as soon as he received and saw a length which was the slightest short. Another delicious off-break bowled Oldfield at 42, and again Robinson's length lured the batsman headlong into a void dark and hopeless. An appeal against Iddon for leg-before off Robinson was dismissed by the umpire, Smith, but he was in a minority of one against ten thousand. In half an hour Paynter faced only one ball from Robinson, which meant that Verity was obliged to bowl at a stance which cancels out his spin considerably: this was good and shrewd North of England cricket sense.

Iddon picked out a half-volley from Robinson and drove a straight, handsome four, which was applauded by three Lancashire folk who were present. Overhead a black cloud threatened us: the scene was as bleak as the cricket: the huge stand seemed like a prison house, bare and stony: there are locks, bars, and bolts in it and places of subterranean mystery and remoteness. Cricket at Leeds is like cricket in a penal settlement.

After fifty minutes Paynter faced Robinson once more, and fell on the earth trying desperately to cope with off-spin: he was nearly stumped, but not quite. Iddon played bravely, calmly, and strongly and pulled Verity to the leg boundary with a majestical sweep of bat and body. At half-past twelve Lancashire had lost only two wickets in addition to that of Washbrook's, taken on Monday: this represented skilful defence against an attack, Robinson's especially, which might easily have run amok at once. Robinson at last trapped Paynter, sucked him out of his ground, and got him stumped: Paynter stretched so far that he had some difficulty in picking himself up; for two hours his innings obstructed the impatient Yorkshire attack and the even more impatient crowd.

Robinson in the same over entirely bemused Phillipson with spin, and now Lancashire were 75 for five, 129 ahead. Then Robinson sent almost a half-volley to Iddon, who struck hard for an on boundary, only, alas! to foozle his hit in a skein of spin and snick the ball into his stumps.

Robinson's next ball grazed Higson's wicket, and the next after that whizzed from the bat into the clutches of Verity in the slips. Robinson now was unplayable for all except the greatest masters of footwork. I have seen no more impossible, more devastating off-spin since Parkin's heyday. By the grace of God Verity was curiously unable to use the pitch: he had to be satisfied with run-saving accuracy.

The most perfect off-break conceivable bowled Farrimond at 77: in half an hour Lancashire lost five wickets for nine runs, all to Robinson. The ninth wicket added a precious fifteen, including a gigantic and gallant six by Garlick off Verity, who obtained his first reward of the morning when Bowes, with exemplary composure, caught Garlick at mid-on. Lancashire were all out before lunch for 92, which left Yorkshire with 147 to make for victory: today Robinson took eight wickets for 22. He seldom varied his superb off-break: if you have at your command a great technical trump why vary it indeed? Robinson often bowls a short length: he did so many times on Saturday, and Lancashire declined to help themselves. This morning Robinson's length seldom faltered: he was, as I say, technically as nearly unplayable as a bowler well can be.

Lancashire's collapse invited little or no censure: Robinson's spin accounted for it logically and beyond a peradventure. The only criticism permissible is that Paynter might have chanced his eye and arm a little more. And I cannot understand why nowadays Pollard is taking so pedantic a view of his batsmanship; a few fours all over the place, in the air, even over the heads of slips and wicket-keeper, would have served Lancashire better than the straight, conscientious blade which Pollard chose to show us. Is he contemplating opening some academy of batsmanship?

Yorkshire went in a few moments before lunch and scored five: lunch was consumed in an inferno of noise and impending catastrophe. At a quarter past two, under a sky like the roof of a cavern, Garlick attacked and soon he bowled Mitchell, who played back and much too late. He returned to the pavilion in a dense and depressing silence. An austere period occurred during which Hutton and Barber scarcely gave heart and cheerfulness to the crowd, and meanwhile the pall overhead passed funereally by. Twenty runs were picked out of a close, keen field in half an hour: Barber tried to cut Pollard now and was caught at the wicket. The stroke at such a moment of trial was reprehensible.

A four to the off by Hutton off Pollard came as an act of succour and liberation. Garlick bowled well again, causing his in-swinger to approximate to an off-break after pitching. Brilliant fielding by Washbrook flickered in the afternoon's dark like a will-o'-the-wisp. When Leyland batted he called for a runner: the light improved, revealing that Leyland's runner was Mitchell without cap, not carrying any weight so to say. Leyland limped and seemed restricted in the movement of his front leg; Garlick worried him technically and, I suspect, he was missed at the wicket.

Yorkshire reached 35 for two in sixty-five minutes, and Brocklebank came on for Pollard, and from his first ball Washbrook picked up an apparent four by Hutton, darting in gloriously at cover. Leyland hit Garlick to long-leg for four, and in the same over hit him again to square-leg high in the air and Brocklebank leaped up enormously, got a hand to the ball, knocked it up and nearly held it coming down: it would have been the greatest catch in living memory. Leyland was nine when this extraordinary occurrence electrified everybody. Mitchell ran his runs as deputy runner with rare alacrity: I almost expected to see a heading in a Yorkshire evening paper saying 'Bright batting by Mitchell.'

Higson took Brocklebank off after one or two overs and put Hopwood on; Garlick rested after ninety minutes' continuous and good work and Phillipson occupied his place. Higson controlled his attack thoughtfully, but there was no spin in it of Robinson's kind fit for the curious wicket, which was made for elaborate medium-paced off-breaks manipulated by strong wrists and fingers. Hutton took charge of the game magnificently, sparing Leyland as much responsibility as he possibly could. A swift turn to leg by Hutton defied pursuit even by Lancashire's eager and scudding field. Hutton attained his fifty out of about seventy, and Higson, who explored all his resources, brought on Iddon at 76 and recalled Garlick. Then the sun came forth dramatically. And in its radiant beams Garlick clean-bowled Leyland, whose cross-bat heave was suicide against a half-volley.

Leyland's innings lasted eighty minutes, during which he scored thirteen to Hutton's fifty. Next ball Turner was caught perfectly in the slips by Paynter, and the fat was in the fire at tea: Yorkshire 83 for four, 64 still urgently wanted, Hutton not out 59. After tea Yardley, when none, was badly missed at first slip by Garlick off Pollard; Yorkshire were 88 for four as this terrible mishap provoked general, if temporary, heart failure. It was a tragedy for Garlick, who had rendered his county inestimable service throughout the engagement.

A wonderful back-footed off-drive by Hutton for four off Garlick awoke the Yorkshire roar: he was playing the greatest innings of the match, cool, confident, sure. At 106 Yardley was fifth to go, 41 from the goal, and Sellers, with his chin sticking out, joined Hutton. The suspense was searching and trying, and hysteria threw a fit when Garlick beat Hutton and revived next ball at the sight of a classic square drive. Thirty-five needed. Five wickets to fall, at five o'clock. Higson handled his team wisely at this critical moment; he ordered the leg trap to fall back for Hutton to save the single and called it up for the encirclement of Sellers. And he entrusted the attack to Pollard and Garlick, who could be relied on not to give anything away and yet to bowl offensively. Higson made no fuss, no unnecessary movements; he was a captain following a plan based on a knowledge of what his resources contained and allowed him to do.

Hutton, who took five balls on an average out of every eight bowled throughout the innings, reached 91 out of 130, and here a frightful happening turned the ground into a welter of agitation: Sellers fell in mid-wicket trying with Hutton a sharp second run; the ball went to the wrong end, and Sellers escaped. Really the throw-in was to the right end, for Hutton was the man to run out if possible.

To make the climax unbearable rain began to threaten to cheat Yorkshire, now only fifteen from their heart's desire. Hutton, growing greater every minute, drove Garlick for four to the off, balanced and serene for all his opportunism: only eight wanted and the heavens ready to burst. Several boys screamed; their elders roared; caps went on high when Hutton got his century; umbrellas were opened desperately: a match and a crescendo in a thousand. And the crown and climax came with the winning hit, which Hutton sent soaring to cover, where Washbrook chased the ball and missed a cruelly hard chance. Had he caught it there would certainly have been no more play, for the clouds opened and let loose their torrents.

This one stroke by Hutton was the only uncontrolled one in his innings of three hours and a quarter, and, of course, he was making the last possible blow. No greater end than this could have crowned a great innings and a great match. The crowd hailed the day's hero, then fled. Lancashire came from the field noble in their frustration, with Pollard weary from hard and splendid effort and the captain, last of all, lost in the scurrying rabble.

SCORES

LANCASHIRE

First Innings		Second Innings	
Paynter, c Wood, b Robinson	23	st Wood, b Robinson	25
Washbrook, b Robinson	30	b Verity	12
Hopwood, c Verity, b Robinson	8	b Robinson	4
Oldfield, c Mitchell, b Verity	77	b Robinson	4
Iddon, c Turner, b Robinson	35	b Robinson	23
Phillipson, c Mitchell, b Verity	28	c Mitchell, b Robinson	0
Farrimond, c Wood, b Bowes	5	b Robinson	1
T. A. Higson, c Robinson, b Verity	0	c Verity, b Robinson	0
Pollard, b Robinson	0	not out	5
Garlick, not out	0	c Bowes, b Verity	11
J. M. Brocklebank, b Verity	4	lbw, b Robinson	0
Extras b1, lb 6	7	Extras lb 7	7
Total	217	Total	92

THE ROSES MATCHES 1919-1939
YORKSHIRE

First Innings		Second Innings	
Mitchell, c Pollard, b Garlick	27	b Garlick	4
Hutton, b Garlick	3	not out	105
Barber, c Phillipson, b Garlick	52	c Farrimond, b Pollard	6
Leyland, c Oldfield, b Phillipson	17	b Garlick	13
Turner, lbw, b Phillipson	4	c Paynter, b Garlick	0
N. W. D. Yardley, b Garlick	14	c Farrimond, b Pollard	8
A. B. Sellers, b Hopwood	10	not out	9
Wood, c Pollard, b Hopwood	4		
Robinson, b Hopwood	0		
Verity, b Pollard	2		
Bowes, not out	15		
Extras b 9, lb 5, nb 1	15	Extras lb 2	2
Total	163	Total (for 5)	147

BOWLING ANALYSIS

LANCASHIRE—First Innings

	O.	M.	R.	W.		O.	M.	R.	W.
Bowes	28	9	32	1	Verity	24	9	43	4
Turner	5	0	14	0	Leyland	9	3	27	0
Yardley	3	1	5	0	Hutton	3	0	9	0
Robinson	39	12	80	5					

Second Innings

	O.	M.	R.	W.		O.	M.	R.	W.
Bowes	2	0	4	0	Verity	20	8	46	2
Robinson	21	9	35	8					

YORKSHIRE—First Innings

	O.	M.	R.	W.		O.	M.	R.	W.
Phillipson	4	0	15	2	Brocklebank	6	0	31	0
Pollard	8	3	23	1	Hopwood	7	0	27	3
Garlick	20	5	52	4					

Second Innings

	O.	M.	R.	W.		O.	M.	R.	W.
Pollard	18	3	43	2	Hopwood	4	1	10	0
Garlick	23	5	66	3	Phillipson	2	0	11	0
Brocklebank	2	0	9	0	Iddon	1	0	6	0